THE LAW AND PRACTICE OF COMPANY MEETINGS

THE LAW AND PRACTICE OF COMPANY MEETINGS

Andrew C Hamer

icsa.
Publishing

Published by ICSA Information & Training Ltd
16 Park Crescent
London W1B 1AH

Designed and typeset by Paul Barrett Book Production, Cambridge
Printed in Great Britain by Hobbs the Printers Ltd, Totton, Hampshire

British Cataloguing in Publication Data
A catalogue record for this book is available from the British Library.

ISBN 9781860725821

Contents

Table of Cases

The following abbreviations are used throughout this Table of Cases:

App. Cas.	*Appeal Cases (Law Reports)*
BCC	*British Company Cases*
BCLC	*Butterworths Company Law Cases*
CA	*Court of Appeal* Ch. *Chancery (Law Reports)*
Ch. App.	*Chancery Appeals (Law Reports)*
Ch.D.	*Chancery Division (Law Reports)*
CPD	*Common Pleas Division (Law Reports)*
HLC	*English & Irish Appeals (House of Lords)*
H & M	*Hemming & Miller Law Reports*
KB	*Law Reports, King's Bench Division*
LJ	*Law Journal Reports*
LR	*Law Reports*
LT	*Law Times Reports*
LTJ	*Law Times Journal*
NSWLR	*New South Wales Law Reports*
PC	*Privy Council Appeals (Law Reports)*
QB	*Queen's Bench Reports*
QBD	*Queen's Bench Division*
SASR	*South Australian Law Reports*
SC	*Session Cases*
SJ	*Solicitors' Journal*
SLT	*Scottish Law Times*
TLR	*Times Law Reports*
WLR	*Weekly Law Reports* WN *Weekly Notes*

Table of Statutes

Table of Statutory Instruments

■ Other regulations

PART 1

Introduction

This book deals with meetings of companies incorporated under the UK Companies Acts. It is intended as a guide for those involved with the management and administration of companies. Accordingly, it does not cover meetings in insolvency.

Unless otherwise indicated:

■ all statutory references are to the relevant section number of the Companies Act 2006 as amended and in force on 1 January 2013 (e.g. 's. 308' refers to a section of the Companies Act 2006);

■ all references to 'the Act' or 'the 2006 Act' are to the Companies Act 2006;

■ all references to 'the 1985 Act' are to the Companies Act 1985;

■ all references to regulations of Table A (e.g. reg. 72) are to the 1985 Table A which is contained in the Companies (Table A–F) Regulations 1985 (as amended) (see **1.5**);

■ all references to model articles are to the model articles of association set out in the Companies (Model Articles) Regulations 2008 (SI 2008/3229);

■ where references are made to individual articles in the model articles, the following convention is used:

  – 'pcls' refers to an article in the model articles for a private company limited by shares (schedule 1 of the regulations),

  – 'clg' refers to an article in the model articles for a private company limited by guarantee (schedule 2 of the regulations),

  – 'plc' refers to an article in the model articles for a public limited company (schedule 3 of the regulations),

  – 'art' refers to an article which has the same number in all three versions of the model articles.

1

Law and practice

■ 1.1 Are meetings necessary?

The overriding purpose of the law of meetings is to ensure that those who are entitled to participate in the company's decision-making process are given a reasonable and fair opportunity to do so but also to ensure that decisions can be made by a majority of those who actually choose to participate.

A company is treated as a person in the eyes of the law and, as such, is able to do anything a natural legal person can do for the purposes of running a business, e.g. own property, enter into contracts, and sue and be sued in its own name. Despite being accorded this status, a company plainly does not have a mind of its own and cannot act without the intervention of human beings. Someone must act and make decisions on its behalf. Who may do so, and how, depends mainly on the Companies Act 2006 and a company's articles of association.

The Companies Act reserves certain matters to the members/shareholders but otherwise leaves matters of internal governance to be determined by the company in its own constitution (i.e. its articles of association). If the articles do not delegate the company's powers to anyone else, then those powers vest by default in its members. In practice, companies invariably adopt articles of association that delegate wide decision-making powers to the directors. They need not do so. However, it is normally easier to run a company if certain matters are delegated to the directors.

Articles of association invariably allow the directors to delegate their own powers to committees or individual executives. Where a power is delegated to an individual, it is obviously not necessary for that person to hold a meeting. However, where a power is vested in a body, it may be necessary to do so. That body could be the company in general meeting (i.e. the members or shareholders) or the board of directors acting under a power delegated to them by the articles.

Where a body (it does not matter which for now) has decision-making powers, you need a mechanism to determine the views of its members on proposals that are put to them. The members of a body will seldom agree on everything, unless there is only one member. Accordingly, it is sensible to allow decisions to be taken by a majority, but maybe to require a higher majority for certain types of important decisions. We could require the members to make decisions unanimously.

However, this would enable the minority to obstruct the will of the majority, which would seem to be unfair and could make it impossible for the company to reach any decisions. If we are going to allow decisions to be made by a majority, it would seem fair and sensible to give members of the body an opportunity to discuss any proposals before voting on them. This would allow members to question those making the proposal and give members who oppose the proposal an opportunity to persuade others to vote against it. In the past, the only practical way to ensure that all this happened was to require decisions to be taken at formal meetings. Generally speaking, this is still what the law requires, although there are lots of exceptions.

Public companies must still hold a meeting to obtain shareholder approval for certain things and must still hold annual general meetings.

However, members of private companies can take most decisions without holding meetings. This has been the case since 1989, when the Companies Act 1985 was amended to allow members of private companies to pass written resolutions. In order to do so under the 1985 Act, it was necessary for all the members to sign the resolution. In other words, they all had to agree to it. Where this was the case, it obviously did not make sense to require them to hold a meeting to debate the matter.

However, under the Companies Act 2006, members of private companies can now take decisions without holding a meeting even if they are not all of one mind. The 2006 Act written resolution procedure simply requires the requisite majority to consent to the proposal. In other words, the 2006 Act has all but dispensed with the idea that the minority in a private company must automatically be given an opportunity to air their views in an attempt to persuade others of the merits of their case. So, while meetings of the members are still necessary for public companies, they are not so for private companies.

Where a company's articles delegate powers to the directors, they must generally exercise those powers collectively in accordance with any decision-making procedures for directors specified in the company's articles. Articles nearly always make provision to enable the directors to make decisions by a majority at a properly constituted meeting of directors (known as a board meeting). If a company's articles do not do so, it is possible that the directors would have to make all decisions unanimously. The articles of both public and private companies also normally allow the directors to exercise their powers without holding a meeting, e.g. by written resolution or unanimous decision (see 6.2). In addition, articles usually authorise the directors to delegate their powers to committees of directors, individual executive directors and other employees and agents.

In practice, it may be possible to run a private company without holding formal meetings of either the members or the directors. This is not the case with public companies, which must still hold an annual general meeting of the members and will probably need to hold fairly regular board meetings. Private companies are not required to hold annual general meetings and, as we have already seen, their members can normally make decisions by written resolution. If directors take advantage of the procedures in most articles of association which allow them to pass written resolutions, then it is possible that a private company might never need to hold any meeting in the traditional sense.

■ 1.2 Holding proper meetings

To ensure that those entitled to participate in a company's decision-making process are given a reasonable and fair opportunity to do so, certain procedures must be followed at meetings. In short, meetings must be properly convened, properly constituted and properly held. They must be called, held and conducted in accordance with the articles, the Companies Acts and the general law of meetings. Although, the procedural requirements for general meetings (meetings of members) are more onerous than those for meetings of directors, the essential principles for both are as follows:

■ the meeting must be called by someone with authority to do so and in the correct manner;

■ notice of the meeting and the business to be transacted must be given in the correct manner to those entitled to receive it (generally speaking this will be those entitled to vote at the meeting);

■ a quorum must be present (i.e. the minimum number of persons necessary to transact business);

■ those entitled to attend and vote must be allowed to do so;

■ a chairman must be elected or appointed;

■ the business raised must be within the scope of the notice of meeting;

■ the meeting must be conducted properly, particularly in respect of voting; and

■ the decisions of the meeting should be recorded.

Failure to conduct a meeting in accordance with these principles, can render the proceedings liable to challenge. It is possible that nobody will challenge their validity. The worst-case scenario for a company is for someone to spot an irregularity but for nobody to be actually sure whether that irregularity would affect the validity of the proceedings. Rather than have this uncertainty hanging over its head, a company will often choose to hold another meeting to do things properly. Another option can be for the company itself to seek a court ruling on the validity of the proceedings.

■ 1.3 The law of meetings

One of the most difficult aspects of the law relating to company meetings is the complicated hierarchy of rules and procedures. Company meetings are governed by a combination of formal statutory rules, a company's own constitution (primarily its articles of association) and common law rules developed by the courts.

Publicly traded companies will also need to comply with additional rules. For example, companies listed on the London Stock Exchange must comply with the Listing Rules and the Disclosure and Transparency Rules. Although failure to comply with these rules will not necessarily directly affect the validity of a meeting or a particular transaction, the Financial Conduct Authority (FCA) may impose sanctions and penalties for non-compliance. Listed companies may also need to have regard to codes of practice, such as the UK Corporate Governance Code.

1.3.1 Statute

The main statutory rules relating to meetings are contained in the Companies Act 2006 ('the Act' or 'the 2006 Act'). Part 13 of the Companies Act 2006 sets out the main statutory rules governing meetings of members/shareholders and, in the case of private companies, members' written resolutions. The Act deliberately makes very little provision regarding meetings of directors and generally leaves such matters to be determined by a company's articles of association and, in default, the common law.

The provisions of Part 13 (Resolutions and Meetings) were brought into force on 1 October 2007, except for:

(a) s. 308 (manner in which notice to be given), s. 309 (publication of notice on website) and s. 333 (sending documents relating to meetings, etc in electronic form), which were all brought into force on 20 January 2007 together with the company communication provisions in ss. 1143–1148 and Schedules 4 and 5 to the Act; and

(b) ss. 327(2)(c) and 330(6)(c), which have not been commenced (and probably never will be).

The layout of Part 13 of the Act is summarised in **Annex A**. Various other sections of the Act specify the circumstances in which the approval of a company's members/shareholders is required and the type of resolution required. These sections are summarised in **Appendix 2** (Matters requiring members approval).

The expression 'the Companies Acts' includes:

- the Companies Act 2006;
- Part 2 of the Companies (Audit, Investigations and Community Enterprise) Act 2006;
- the provisions of the Companies Act 1985 that remain in force;
- the provisions of the Companies Consolidation (Consequential Provisions) Act 1985 that remain in force.

1.3.2 Statutory instruments

The Companies Act 2006 gives the 'Secretary of State' power to make regulations and issue orders on certain matters related to company law. The 'Secretary of State' is the minister in charge of the government department which has responsibility for company law. At present this is the Department for Business, Innovation and Skills (BIS). The relevant department was previously called the Department for Business, Enterprise and Regulatory Reform (BERR) and before that the Department of Trade and Industry (DTI).

Such regulations and orders are referred to collectively as 'statutory instruments' and each one has a unique SI number. They are often used to make detailed provision on matters governed by the Act. For example, the 2006 Act model articles are prescribed in the Companies (Model Articles) Regulations 2008 which were made under a power given by s. 19 of the Act. The unique SI number of these regulations is SI 2008/3229, which indicates that it was the 3,229th statutory instrument made in the year 2008 (not all SIs deal with matters of company law).

However, the Act also sometimes gives the Secretary of State power to issue regulations that actually amend the provisions of the Act.

1.3.3 Types of company

Several different types of company can be formed under the Companies Acts and each type can be subject to different statutory provisions. It is therefore essential to check whether the relevant statutory provisions or procedures are applicable to the type of company you are dealing with. The biggest differences in this regard arise between public and private companies. The rows in the table below show whether a company is public or private. The columns of the table also show other terminology used in the Acts to limit or define the scope of certain provisions. It should be noted that it is no longer possible to form a company limited by guarantee with a share capital (see s. 5).

	Limited company		Unlimited company
	Limited by shares	Limited by guarantee	
Public company	Public limited company (Plc)	–	–
Private company	Private company limited by shares (Ltd)	Private company limited by guarantee (Ltd)	Unlimited company (–)
	Private company limited by guarantee with a share capital (Ltd)		

1.3.4 Common law and precedent

The common law is the body of rules and principles developed by the courts to decide the competing merits of litigants in the absence of any legislative provision or other determining factor. Provisions contained in Acts of Parliament take precedence over any conflicting common law, although in some cases, legislation will specifically state that it is without prejudice to any common law rule. Throughout history, Parliament has frequently adopted legislation to codify existing common law rules, although it often takes the opportunity to modify them as well. A recent example of this was the codification in the Companies Act 2006, Part 10, of the common law rules regarding the duties of directors.

A company can exclude the operation of certain common law rules by making alternative provision in its articles of association.

Despite this relatively lowly position in the legal hierarchy, the common law is still of relevance in many areas relating to the law of meetings. For example, the Companies Act does not specify a minimum period of notice for board meetings, and neither do most articles. Accordingly, the common law rule applies, i.e. that the notice given must be reasonable in the circumstances. If the articles specified a minimum notice period of seven clear days, that rule would override the common law rule.

The courts are often called upon to rule on the interpretation and application of the Companies Acts and on the precise effect of provisions contained in a company's articles. Decisions in these cases provide precedents which are useful in clarifying the law. Most cases concerning company law are heard initially in the Chancery Division of the High Court. Appeals can be made to the Court of Appeal and, ultimately, to the Supreme Court (formerly known as the House of Lords). Generally speaking, decisions taken in higher courts are more influential and act as binding precedents for lower courts. Where the point at issue is the interpretation of EU law, the case may be referred to EU courts and tribunals.

Decisions of the courts which have a bearing on the law of meeting are referred to in this book by their case names and reference. The case reference is to the law report in which the case was reported. For example, *Byng v. London Life Association Ltd.* [1989] 1 All E.R. 560 refers to a case which was reported in the first volume of the All England Law Reports published in 1989 on page 560.

1.3.5 European law

A number of European Union Directives have had some influence on the law of meetings, e.g. the 12th Company Law Directive which requires Member States to allow private companies to be formed with only one member. However, because EU Directives must be applied by national legislation in each Member State, it is rarely necessary to refer to the original Directive. For example, the 12th Directive was initially implemented in the UK by the Companies (Single Member Private Limited Companies) Regulations 1992 which amended the Companies Act 1985, and is now reflected in the Companies Act 2006.

EU Regulations, on the other hand, are directly applicable in each Member State, and have been used to introduce the various European business vehicles, such as the European Public Company (SE), the European Co-operative (SCE) and the European Economic Interest Group (EEIG).

■ 1.4 Memorandum of association

UK companies have traditionally had two main constitutional documents – the memorandum of association and the articles of association. Under the Companies Act 2006, a memorandum of association must still be submitted to the Registrar of Companies before a company can be incorporated. However, its importance is much reduced because the only thing that it is allowed to contain is a subscribers' statement. For a company limited by shares, this statement will do no more than state the fact that each subscriber to the memorandum of association wishes to form a company under the Companies Act 2006 and agrees to become a member of the company. It does not even state how many shares each subscriber will take, as this information is provided in a separate document on incorporation.

Under previous Companies Acts, the memorandum was required to contain much more detailed information, including:

- the name of the company;
- whether the registered office of the company was to be situated in England and Wales, or in Scotland;
- the objects of the company, i.e. the purpose for which it was formed and the company's powers;
- the liability of the members, whether limited by shares, limited by guarantee or unlimited;
- whether it was a public or private company;
- in the case of a company limited by shares, the amount of share capital with which the company proposed to be registered and the division of the share capital into shares of a fixed amount, e.g. the share capital of the company is £100 divided into 100 shares of £1 each;
- in the case of a company limited by guarantee, the amount that each member guarantees to contribute in the event of insolvency.

Under previous Acts, the memorandum served as an application form during the incorporation process. It determined, among other things, what type of company the incorporators wished to be formed and, therefore, which provisions of the Act would apply to it. And, once the company was formed, the memorandum became one of its core constitutional documents, which was capable of amendment. Although the memorandum is still a bit like an application form under the Companies Act 2006, it is no longer capable of amendment. Everything which may need to be amended has been stripped out and is now either superfluous or to be found in the articles of association.

One of the important consequences of this change is that any provision (other than the subscribers' statement) in the memorandum of association of a company that was incorporated under a prior Companies Act is now deemed to form part of its articles of association (s. 28) and to be capable of modification in accordance with the procedures for amendment of the articles set out in ss. 21 and 22 of the

2006 Act. Companies formed on or after 1 October 2009 were incorporated under the Companies Act 2006. Companies formed before that date were incorporated under a previous Act (e.g. under the Companies Act 1985). Companies incorporated under a previous Act are sometimes referred to as 'existing companies' because they were already in existence on 1 October 2009.

Generally speaking, the memorandum provisions of existing companies will continue to have effect even though the Companies Act 2006 does not specifically require a company's articles to make provision in that regard. For example, the objects clause will still restrict the objects of the company, even though a company's articles are no longer required to include a statement of objects (s. 31).

■ 1.5 Articles of association

A company's articles of association ('articles') usually contain detailed provisions which govern the conduct of both general meetings and meetings of directors. A company must have articles prescribing regulations for the company (s. 18). A company may alter any of its articles by special resolution (s. 21), unless the article is an entrenched provision, in which case s. 22 applies.

A limited company need not submit articles of association with its application for registration. However, if it does not register its own articles, it will be deemed to have adopted the relevant set of model articles prescribed by the Secretary of State (s. 20). Unlimited companies must submit articles of association with their application for registration.

Even if articles are registered, the relevant model articles apply on formation to a limited company in so far as the registered articles do not exclude them (s. 20(1)). Listed companies usually adopt articles which exclude any relevant model articles in their entirety. Many private companies adopt what are known as 'short form' articles, which state that the company has adopted the model articles (or its predecessor, Table A) subject to a number of express exclusions, modifications or additions. In such circumstances, it is often helpful to produce a marked-up copy of the relevant model articles showing which provisions do and do not apply and any relevant modifications or additions. However, it should always be remembered that it is the 'short form' articles and not the new consolidated version that are registered at Companies House as the company's articles.

It is important to understand that the application of any model articles is frozen at the date of the company's incorporation. The model articles that apply to companies (if any) are the ones that were in force on the date of its incorporation. Accordingly, any subsequent statutory modification of those model articles has no effect on the company's constitution.

Articles must be contained in a single document and divided into paragraphs numbered consecutively (s. 18(3)).

1.5.1 Table A

Table A is the name that was given to the model articles prescribed for companies limited by shares under previous Companies Acts. Prior to 1 October 2009, a company limited by shares which did not register its own articles on incorporation was deemed to have adopted the version of Table A that was in force at that time as its articles of association. Indeed the provisions of the relevant Table A that were in force on the date of a company's incorporation are deemed to apply to that company in so far as its own articles do not exclude or modify them. This remains the case notwithstanding the fact that a different version of Table A may subsequently have been prescribed. Later versions of Table A (or the 2006 Act model articles) only apply to companies incorporated during the period that the relevant version was into force.

Different versions of Table A have been prescribed under each previous Companies Act. For example, a company incorporated under the Companies Act 1948 will be subject to the version prescribed in that Act. A company incorporated under the Companies Act 1985 will be subject to one of the versions of Table A prescribed for the purposes of that Act.

Several different versions of Table A were prescribed for the purposes of companies incorporated under the Companies Act 1985 in the Companies (Tables A to F) Regulations 1985 (SI 1985/805). The different versions were introduced by amendments made to those regulations.

The original version of Table A in those regulations applied from 1 July 1985 to 21 December 2000 inclusive. The original version of Table A in those regulations was amended on 22 December 2000 by the Companies Act 1985 (Electronic Communications) Order 2000 (SI 2000/3373) in order to facilitate the use of electronic communications. This amended version applied to companies incorporated between 22 December 2000 and 30 September 2007.

Before 1 October 2007, the same version of Table A was used for both public and private companies limited by shares. However, separate versions of the 1985 Table A were introduced for public and private companies incorporated on or after 1 October 2007. These changes were introduced to cater for the fact that, from that date, private companies were no longer required to hold annual general meetings. The new versions were introduced for companies limited by shares incorporated under the 1985 Act on or after 1 October 2007 by the Companies (Tables A to F) (Amendment) Regulations 2007 (SI 2007/2541) and the Companies (Tables A to F) (Amendment) (No. 2) Regulations 2007 (SI 2007/2826). However, they ceased to apply for companies incorporated on or after 1 October 2009 as that was the date from which companies began to be incorporated under the Companies Act 2006 and subject to the model articles prescribed under that Act.

The version of Table A reproduced at **Annex B2** is the version prescribed for private companies incorporated between 1 October 2007 and 30 September 2009. The annex also shows, by way of notes, the text of previous versions of the 1985 Table A. Any company that is subject to Table A that was incorporated prior to any of these amendments will need to refer to the notes. All references to 'Table A' or to regulations of Table A (e.g. reg. 34) in this book are to the 1985 Table A (as amended on 1 October 2007) unless otherwise indicated. **Annex B1** contains an index to the 1985 Table A.

For companies incorporated under the Companies Act 1948, the relevant version of Table A is the one contained in that Act ('the 1948 Table A'), which is specifically preserved by the Companies Consolidation (Consequential Provisions) Act 1985, s. 31(8). Part I of the 1948 Table A applies (subject to the savings set out in the Companies Act 1980, s. 88(4)) to private companies limited by shares and public companies limited by shares (Companies Act 1980, Schedule 3, para. 36(1)). However, Part II applies to private companies limited by shares only. The provisions of the 1948 Table A differ slightly in many important respects to those of the 1985 Table A and the 2006 Act model articles. These differences are highlighted where necessary throughout this book.

Some companies still exist which were formed under previous Companies Acts while previous versions of Table A were in force. However, they are now so few in number that it is not considered necessary to refer to the position under these versions.

All versions of Table A can be found on the Companies House website.

1.5.2 Relationship between Companies Acts and articles

Where articles refer to 'the Act', reference should be made to the article containing the definition of terms used (usually the first article) which will normally include the following or a similarly worded definition: 'the Act means the Companies Act 1985 including any statutory modification or re-enactment thereof for the time being in force.' For the present this means the Companies Act 1985 as amended.

In the case of the 1948 Table A, 'the Act' is defined as the Companies Act 1948. However, this and all references to section numbers in the 1948 Table A is deemed, by virtue of s. 17(2) of the Interpretation Act 1978, to refer to the Companies Act 2006 and its equivalent provisions.

The Companies Act 2006 includes a large number of provisions relating to company meetings. Generally speaking these requirements override any provisions contained in the articles of association and must therefore be followed. Articles are usually drafted to ensure that no conflicts exist at the time of drafting. However, conflicts can arise subsequently as a result of later amendments to company legislation or, indeed, as a result of amendments made to the articles in ignorance of the statutory requirements. The Companies Act 2006 made significant changes to company legislation, some of which could override provisions contained in the articles of a company incorporated before the Act came into force. Changes were also made, for example, to the Companies Act 1985 in 2000 to facilitate the use of electronic communications by companies and their members. These changes enable companies to take advantage of electronic communications, notwithstanding anything to the contrary contained in their articles. This was necessary because, at the time, most articles (including the version of the 1985 Table A that applied before the date of these changes) contained provisions which would otherwise have prevented the use of electronic communications. The relevant provisions of the Companies Act 1985 have now been superseded by the company communications provisions of the Companies Act 2006 and any company which amended its articles specifically to take account of the 1985 Act provisions may need to do so again to take account of these provisions. Strictly speaking, it is not necessary for any company to amend its articles to bring them into line with any new legislative requirements. However, failure to do so will often lead to confusion as to which rule applies and it is nearly always preferable to have articles which, if followed, ensure compliance with existing legislation.

The position is further complicated by the fact that some of the provisions of the Act only apply if the articles do not make alternative provision (e.g. s. 319 on who may chair a general meeting), while others invalidate the effect of articles not in accordance with certain minimum standards (e.g. s. 327 on the lodging of proxies). It is advisable to have amendments to the articles checked by a solicitor before they are made to ensure that they are consistent with the requirements of the Act.

■ 1.6 Contractual nature of a company's constitution

The provisions of a company's constitution bind the company and its members to the same extent as if there were covenants on the part of the company and of each member to observe those provisions (s. 33(1)). In addition, money payable by a member to the company under its constitution is a debt due from him to the company, and in England and Wales and Northern Ireland any such debt is of the nature of an ordinary contract debt (s. 33(2)).

Section 17 provides that unless the context otherwise requires, references in the Companies Acts to a company's constitution include the company's articles, and any resolutions and agreements to which Chapter 3 of Part 3 applies (i.e. resolutions and agreements which must be filed with the registrar – see **14.8**). A company's articles will also include any provisions of an old company's memorandum which are deemed to form part of its articles under s. 28.

This is known as the 'section 33 contract'. A company can enforce the contract against its members (*Hickman's case* [1915] 1 Ch. 881) and the members can enforce it against each other (*Rayfield v. Hands* [1960] Ch. 1). The members can also enforce the contract against the company, but only in limited circumstances (see **18.3**).

The section 33 contract differs in a number of ways from normal contracts. Provision is made in the Act for its terms to be altered by a special majority (see s. 21 on the amendments to the articles by special resolution). The consent of all the parties is required to vary normal contracts. And although the courts regard articles as commercial documents which should be construed so as to give them reasonable business efficacy (*Holmes v. Keyes* [1959] Ch. 199, 215, per Jenkins LJ), the Court of Appeal has held that terms cannot be implied into the articles in order to do so (*Bratton Seymour Service Co Ltd. v. Oxborough* [1992] B.C.L.C. 693).

■ 1.7 Corporate governance

Corporate governance is concerned, among other things, with ensuring that decisions are taken in an appropriate manner by appropriate people after due consideration of the relevant facts. Should a matter be approved by the members? Or is it an area that can be safely left within the remit of the board of directors? If not, should the non-executive directors have some special role? Should the board be able to delegate responsibility to an executive director or a committee of directors? Should members be informed about the decisions taken on their behalf by the directors? And, if so, what action should they be able to take if they are not happy with those decisions?

The answers to these questions will have practical implications for the decision-making structure adopted by companies. Codes of practice have emerged largely to fill the gaps left by the Companies Acts. The existence of these gaps is, for the most part, deliberate. UK company law does not tend to interfere in the internal management of companies, mainly in recognition of the fact that it is difficult to find a single solution to suit the needs of all companies. Codes of practice on corporate governance have become highly influential on corporate behaviour generally. They are, however, directed mainly towards listed companies, i.e. companies where the vast majority of members are not involved in the day-to-day management, where highly paid professional managers fulfil that role, and where the members behave on the whole as investors rather than owners and are almost totally reliant when making investment decisions on information published by the directors.

1.7.1 UK Corporate Governance Code

The most important code for the purposes of this book is the UK Corporate Governance Code. The Code includes recommendations on:

- role of the company secretary (see **1.8**);
- schedule of matters reserved to the board (see **3.12**);
- role of the chairman (see **4.7**);
- audit committees (see **5.13**);
- remuneration committees (see **5.14**);
- nomination committees (see **5.15**);
- constructive use of the AGM (see **10.8**); and
- retirement by rotation (see **25.14**).

References to the UK Corporate Governance Code in this book are to the version issued by the Financial Reporting Council on 30 September 2012, which came into force for financial periods commencing on or after 1 October 2012. The UK Code is targeted at companies with a premium listing of shares in the UK.

Compliance with Code is not mandatory for such companies. However, they are required under the Listing Rules to state in their annual report and accounts:

(a) how they have applied the main principles of the Code, in a manner that enables shareholders to evaluate how the principles have been applied (LR 9.8.6(5)); and

(b) whether or not they have complied throughout the accounting period with all relevant Code provisions, setting out the provisions, if any, they have not complied with, the period of non-compliance and the reasons for non-compliance (LR 9.8.6(6)).

The Code contains two types of principle – main and supporting. Strictly speaking, the Listing Rules only require listed companies to report on how they have applied the main principles. In practice, a company cannot really ignore the supporting principles when reporting on its application of the main principles as they expand upon the underlying purpose of those principles. The form and content of the statement on the application of the Code principles are not prescribed, the intention being that companies should have a free hand to explain their governance policies in the light of the principles, including any special circumstances applying to them that have led to a particular approach.

Comply or explain

In the second part of the statement, listed companies must confirm whether or not they have complied throughout the accounting period with the relevant Code provisions. A company that has not complied with the Code provisions, or complied with only some of the Code provisions or (in the case of provisions whose requirements are of a continuing nature) complied for only part of an accounting period, must specify the Code provisions with which it has not complied, and (where relevant) for what part of the period such non-compliance continued, and give reasons for any non-compliance.

It is recognised that departures may be justified in particular circumstances if good governance can be achieved by other means. A condition of doing so is that the reasons for the departure should be clearly explained to shareholders, who may wish to discuss the position with the company and whose voting intentions may be influenced as a result.

The 2012 edition of the Code clarifies what explanations for non-compliance are expected to cover:

> In providing an explanation, the company should aim to illustrate how its actual practices are consistent with the principle to which the particular provision relates, and contribute to good governance and promote delivery of business objectives. It should set out the background, provide a clear rationale for the action it is taking, and describe any mitigating actions taken to address any additional risk and maintain conformity with the relevant principle.

Where deviation from a particular provision is intended to be limited in time, the explanation should indicate when the company expects to conform with the provision.

1.7.2 Cadbury and Greenbury Reports

Listed companies in the UK have been required to report on their compliance with a corporate governance code since 1992. The first such code was published by a committee chaired by Sir Adrian Cadbury in the *Report of the Committee on the Financial Aspects of Corporate Governance* (Gee Publishing). That Code has been amended and renamed several times since 1992 but still forms the basis of the UK Corporate Governance Code. The Cadbury Committee's original report still contains some useful guidance on matters relevant to this book and is referred to simply as 'the Cadbury Report'.

The Cadbury Code required boards of directors to establish remuneration committees consisting of a majority of non-executive directors to make recommendations to the board on executive directors' salaries. However, the adoption of this recommendation did not put an end to public disquiet over the salaries paid to executive directors. Accordingly, in February 1995, the CBI formed a study group chaired by Sir Richard Greenbury 'to identify good practice in determining directors' remuneration and to prepare a code of such practice for use by UK plcs'. The study group (the 'Greenbury Committee') published its final report and a code of practice on 17 July 1995 (*Directors' Remuneration: Report of a Study Group Chaired by Sir Richard Greenbury*, Gee Publishing). The London Stock Exchange agreed to require UK listed companies to report on their compliance with the Greenbury code and to include in their annual reports a report on directors' remuneration disclosing, among other things:

- the company's policy on executive directors' remuneration;
- full details of each director's remuneration package, share options, incentive schemes, service contracts.

Most of the code provisions introduced following the Greenbury Report are still reflected in the UK Corporate Governance Code which, in any case, supersedes it.

■ 1.8 Company secretary

Every public company must appoint a company secretary (s. 271). Private companies are not required to have a secretary but may choose to do so (s. 270). The directors of a public company have a duty to appoint as secretary someone who is capable of carrying out the duties which the post entails (s. 273). This is normally satisfied by appointing a chartered secretary, lawyer or accountant, although the Act does not preclude the appointment of someone else who is appropriately qualified.

Although the Act does not specify the role of the company secretary, it often makes the secretary liable to criminal prosecution as an officer of the company in circumstances where the company has failed to comply with its obligations under the Act. The list of offences for which the secretary may be held liable under the Act corresponds fairly closely with what might be considered the company secretary's core duties. And, although the directors can also be held liable for all these offences (and more besides), they tend to delegate responsibility to the secretary for ensuring compliance with obligations for which the secretary shares liability. This is particularly true with regard to compliance with the statutory provisions on company meetings and minutes.

Accordingly, the company secretary will normally be responsible for the administration of general meetings, board meetings and other meetings of directors. However, the secretary has no inherent power to ensure compliance with the applicable rules and regulations. He does not even have a right to attend any of these meetings (unless entitled in some other capacity). The secretary will therefore be totally reliant on the fact that the directors follow his advice or on powers delegated by the directors to him.

The UK Corporate Governance Code states (at supporting principle B.5) that:

Under the direction of the chairman, the company secretary's responsibilities include ensuring good information flows within the board and its committees and between senior management and non-executive directors, as well as facilitating induction and assisting with professional development as required.

The company secretary should be responsible for advising the board through the chairman on all governance matters.

Code provision B.5.2 states:

All directors should have access to the advice and services of the company secretary, who is responsible to the board for ensuring that board procedures are complied with. Both the appointment and removal of the company secretary should be a matter for the board as a whole.

This recommendation has been included in the Code since its inception in 1992. In its report, the Cadbury Committee said:

The company secretary has a key role to play in ensuring that board procedures are both followed and regularly reviewed. The chairman and the board will look to the company secretary for guidance on what their responsibilities are under the rules and regulations to which they are subject and on how those responsibilities should be discharged. All directors should have access to the advice and services of the company secretary and should recognise that the chairman is entitled to the strong and positive support of the company secretary in ensuring the effective functioning of the board. It should be standard practice for the company secretary to administer, attend and prepare minutes of board meetings (Cadbury Report, para. 4.25).

2

Methods of communication

2.1 Summary

- The company communication provisions of the Companies Act 2006 specify the methods by which documents and information may be sent by or to a company. They generally make provision for a default of hard copy communications but allow the use of electronic and other methods, provided the recipient has agreed (or can be deemed to have agreed) (see **2.2**).
- Schedule 4 of the 2006 Act sets out the methods by which documents and information may be sent or supplied to a company by any person other than another company (see **2.4**).
- Schedule 5 of the 2006 Act sets out the methods by which documents and information may be sent or supplied by a company (e.g. to a member or debenture holder) and to communications from one company to another (see **2.5**).
- Special rules apply to communications with any joint holders and in the event of the death or bankruptcy of a shareholder (see **2.6**).
- Certain companies must allow electronic communications to be used in relation to proxy appointments and any company which provides an electronic address in certain documents relating to general meetings is deemed to have agreed that it can be used to communicate with the company for the purposes of that meeting (see **2.7**).
- Listed companies are allowed to use electronic communications for the purposes of communicating with investors (see **2.8**).
- A company may only use electronic communications to send documents and information to members if they have agreed to receive them in this manner. This normally requires a positive election on the part of the intended recipient. However, members can be deemed to have agreed to accept website communications in certain circumstances if they fail to reply to a consultation by the company. Website communications are also the default method of communication for listed companies with indirect investors nominated under s. 146 (see **2.9**).
- The version of Table A in force for companies incorporated between 22 December 2000 and 30 September 2007 makes provision for the use of electronic communications (see **2.10**) and refers to guidance issued by the ICSA on proof of service (see **2.12**).

■ Previous versions of Table A do not make provision for electronic communications and may even give the impression that everything must be done in paper form. Although the company communications provisions override anything to the contrary in a company's articles in certain respects, they do not do so in all respects. Although there is no need for a company to amend its articles in order to take advantage of electronic communications for statutory provisions, it is good practice to do so (see **2.11**).

■ The Institute of Chartered Secretaries and Administrators has issued guidance for companies on the use of electronic communications in relation to general meetings (see **2.12**). This guidance is important, not least because Table A refers to it in relation to proof of service of electronic communications (see **2.10**).

■ Electronic signatures are admissible as evidence in legal proceedings (see **2.13**).

■ 2.2 Company communications provisions

The provisions of the Companies Act 2006 that specify the permitted methods of communication both to and from companies are known as the 'company communications provisions'. The relevant provisions in Part 37 (ss. 1143 to 1148) and Schedules 4 and 5 of the Act came into force on 20 January 2007. They make hard copy the default method of communication, but allow electronic communications to be used where the intended recipient has agreed to accept communications in that manner.

The company communications provisions have effect 'for the purposes of any provision of the Companies Acts that authorises or requires documents or information to be sent or supplied by or to a company' (s. 1143(1)). However, their application in this regard is subject to any requirements imposed, or contrary provision made, by or under any enactment (s. 1143(2)) and, in relation to documents or information to be sent or supplied to the registrar, subject to the provisions of Part 35 (s. 1143(3)). For the purposes of subsection (2), a provision in any other enactment is not to be regarded as contrary to the company communications provisions by reason only of the fact that it expressly authorises a document or information to be sent or supplied in hard copy form, in electronic form or by means of a website (s. 1143(4)).

The company communications provisions do not apply to any documents or information required to be sent under other legislation or rules (e.g. the Listing Rules), unless those things can also be interpreted as being required or authorised under the Companies Acts. Even where something seems to be required or authorised by the Companies Acts, care needs to be taken to ensure that there is nothing in the other legislation or rules which overrides the company communications provisions. The requirements of the Stock Transfer Act 1963 are a good example of this. Section 770 of the 2006 Act prohibits a company from registering a transfer of shares without 'a proper instrument of transfer'. Instruments of transfer are therefore documents required to be sent to companies under the Companies Acts. However, s. 1 of the Stock Transfer Act 1963 prescribes the stock transfer form as the proper instrument of transfer for non-CREST transactions and requires such forms to be executed under hand. Accordingly, the company communications provisions do not apply in this regard.

Specific provision is, of course, often made in other legislation to enable documents or information to be sent electronically. This is certainly the case with regard to the additional matters that listed companies are required to send to investors under the Listing Rules and the Disclosure and Transparency Rules (see **2.8**).

Except where the Act specifically allows contrary provision to be made (e.g. in relation to deemed delivery), the company communications provisions are intended to override anything in a company's articles dealing with the methods of communication to be used in relation to documents or information required or authorised to be sent by or to a company under the Companies Acts. They do not override article provisions in relation to communications not required or authorised under the Companies Acts. For example, the company communications provisions would not apply in relation to any requirement in a company's articles requiring directors to resign by giving 'notice in writing' or any requirement to submit a letter of request to the company on transmission. The question as to whether electronic communications can be used for these purposes would need be determined in accordance with the company's articles and the general law. Articles sometimes require things to be done 'in writing'. Unless the term 'in writing' is expressly stated in the articles to include by electronic means, it is usually assumed to mean in paper form. The model articles define the term 'writing' as 'the representation or reproduction of words, symbols or other information in a visible form by any method or combination of methods, whether sent or supplied in electronic form or otherwise'.

If the articles do not specify the form in which a document or information must be sent by a member to the company and the relevant document or information is not required or authorised to be sent by that member under the Companies Acts, the company can generally choose whether to require it to be sent in hard copy or electronic form and whether to require the original or allow a copy to be sent.

2.2.1 Application to directors

Section 1148(3) clarifies that the company communications provisions apply to documents or information sent or supplied by or to the directors of the company acting on behalf of the company. This ensures that formal notices addressed to the directors (such as a demand for a requisitioned meeting) are brought within the ambit of the company communications provisions, together with communications made by directors on behalf of the company. It does not, however, necessarily extend the ambit of the company communications provisions to all communications between the company and its directors, unless those communications are required or authorised under the Companies Acts. On this basis, it is doubtful whether, for example, the company communication provisions are intended to apply to communications connected with board meetings because the Companies Acts do not particularly require or authorise companies to hold board meetings (except perhaps to approve the accounts). This subject is discussed in greater detail at **4.5.5**.

2.2.2 Documents sent to or by a company and from one company to another

Under the company communication provisions, different rules apply depending on whether documents or information are sent *to a company* or *by a company*. The different rules are set out in separate schedules to the Act:

- Schedule 4 sets out the rules for documents and information required or authorised to be sent *to a company* (e.g. by a member) (see **2.4**).
- Schedule 5 sets out the rules for documents and information required or authorised to be sent *by a company* (e.g. to a member or debenture holder) (see **2.5**).

Making separate provision in this manner, immediately raises the question as to which rules apply where something needs to be sent by one company to another. Section 1144(3) specifies that the rules in Sch. 5 apply in these circumstances. As a consequence, the rules in Sch. 5 apply not only where a company needs to communicate with a corporate shareholder or director, but also where that corporate shareholder or director needs to communicate with the company.

Somewhat surprisingly, the practical application of the rules in Schedule 5 to communications by a corporate shareholder or director with the company turn out to be exactly the same as the rules in Sch. 4 for communications by an individual. Accordingly, it is easier to understand the company communications provisions if you assume that:

(a) the rules in Sch. 4 apply to communications sent *to* a company by its shareholders, directors and debenture holders (whether they are individuals or companies);

(b) the rules in Sch. 5 apply to communications sent *by* a company to its shareholders, directors and debenture holders (whether they are individuals or companies).

2.2.3 Right to hard copy version

Section 1145 gives individual members or debenture holders the right to require that any document received electronically be sent without charge by the company in hard copy within 21 days of a request.

2.2.4 Interpretation provisions

Section 1148 of the 2006 Act defines various terms for the purposes of the company communications provisions. An 'address' includes a number or address used for the purposes of sending or receiving documents or information by electronic means. 'Company' includes any body corporate. 'Document' includes a summons, notice, order or other legal process and registers.

Section 1168 defines 'hard copy' and 'electronic form' as follows:

- Hard copy means 'on paper or similar form capable of being read'.
- Electronic form means by 'electronic means (for example, by e-mail or fax)' or 'by any other means while in an electronic form (for example, sending a disk by post)'.

Documents or information sent in electronic form must enable the recipient to retain a copy and read it with the naked eye (s. 1168(5) and (6)).

2.2.5 Authentication requirements

Section 1146 of the 2006 Act sets out the authentication requirements for documents sent to a company that the Companies Acts require to be authenticated (e.g. a meeting requisition). Hard copy documents are sufficiently authenticated if signed by the person sending or supplying them. Documents sent in electronic form are sufficiently authenticated:

(a) if the identity of the sender is confirmed in a manner specified by the company; or
(b) where no such manner is specified, the communication contains or is accompanied by a statement of the identity of the sender and the company has no reason to doubt the truth of that statement.

It follows from these rules that companies can specify the type of authentication required for any methods of electronic communication that they allow (e.g. by requiring shareholders to provide a unique shareholder reference number).

The above rules cannot be said to have clarified the position in relation to the use of fax for sending documents to a company. Doubt has previously been expressed as to the validity of signatures on faxed communications under the Companies Acts and it may still be advisable for companies to make specific provision in this regard in their articles and/or to inform shareholders of the relevant authentication requirements where communication by fax is allowed.

2.3 Deemed delivery

Section 1147 of the 2006 Act sets out when documents or information authorised or required by the Companies Acts to be sent by a company are deemed to have been delivered in the absence of contrary provisions in a company's articles or a relevant agreement or contract. The rules do not apply to any documents or information sent to a company, unless perhaps the other person sending the documents or information is another company.

Subject to any modification by a company's articles or a relevant agreement or contract, s. 1147 provides that documents and information:

(a) sent by post are deemed to be delivered 48 hours after they were posted provided the company can show that they were properly addressed, pre-paid and posted;
(b) sent in electronic form are deemed to have been received by the intended recipients 48 hours after they were sent provided the company can show they were properly addressed;
(c) sent or supplied via a website are deemed to have been received by the intended recipient when first made available on the website or, if later, when the recipient received (or is deemed to have received) notice of the fact that the material was available on the website.

In calculating the period of hours for the purposes of s. 1147, no account may be taken of any part of a day that is not a working day. A 'working day' is defined in s. 1173 of the 2006 Act for these purposes as a day that is not a Saturday or Sunday, Christmas Day, Good Friday, or any day which is a bank holiday in the part of the United Kingdom where the company is registered.

Section 1147 has effect subject to:

(a) in its application to documents or information sent or supplied by a company to its members, any contrary provision of the company's articles;
(b) in its application to documents or information sent or supplied by a company to its debenture holders, any contrary provision in the instrument constituting the debentures;
(c) in its application to documents or information sent or supplied by a company to a person otherwise in his capacity as a member or debenture holder, any contrary provision in an agreement between that person and the company (s. 1147(6)).

■ 2.4 Documents sent or supplied to a company

Schedule 4 of the 2006 Act sets out the methods by which documents and information may be sent or supplied to a company by any person other than another company. The methods include:

■ hard copy form by hand or by post (Sch. 4, Part 2, para. 2–4);
■ electronic form, provided that the company has agreed or can be deemed to have agreed (Sch. 4, Part 3, para. 5–7); and
■ any other form agreed by the company (Sch. 4, Part 4, para. 8).

Although company to company communications are governed by Schedule 5, the practical application of those rules to communications sent to a company by its corporate shareholders or debenture holders is essentially the same as the application of the rules in Schedule 4 for individuals.

2.4.1 Hard copy form

Under Sch. 4, paras. 2–4, hard copy documents and information may be sent or supplied to a company by hand or by post:

- to an address specified by the company for that purpose;
- to the company's registered office; or
- to an address to which any provision of the Companies Acts authorises the document or information to be sent or supplied.

Hard copy for these purposes means 'on paper or similar form capable of being read' (s. 1168). It is worth noticing in this regard that where the Act uses the expression 'in writing', it should no longer be assumed that this means in hard copy form.

The rules in Sch. 5, paras. 2–4, which would apply when a company, in its capacity as a corporate member, wishes to send hard copy communications to the company of which it is a member, are essentially the same as those in Sch. 4 for natural persons.

For the purposes of Schedules 4 and 5, a person posts a document by posting a pre-paid envelope containing the document or information (Sch. 4, para. 3(2) and Sch. 5, para. 3(2)). At first sight, this would seem to preclude the use of pre-paid cards. However, these would probably fall within the provisions on other agreed forms of communication in Sch. 4, para. 8, and Sch. 5, para. 15, particularly where the company has sent a reply-paid card for use by members. By sending such a card for their use, the company would undoubtedly be deemed to have agreed to accept communications from them in this manner.

2.4.2 Using electronic communications to send documents or information to a company

Part 3 of Sch. 4 covers the use of electronic communications by individuals for the purposes of sending documents or information to a company. Although Part 3 of Sch. 5 deals separately with the use of electronic communications between companies, its application is essentially the same in relation to communications by a corporate member or debenture holder with the company in which it holds shares or debentures.

Schedule 4, para. 6 provides that a document may only be sent or supplied to the company in electronic form if:

- the company has agreed (generally or specifically) to allow it to be sent in that manner; or
- it can be deemed to have so agreed by virtue of a provision in the Companies Acts (e.g. s. 333).

It is not necessary for the members to pass any resolution or for provision to be made in a company's articles to enable electronic communications to be used for this purpose. A company can signify its agreement to accept communications in electronic form in other ways and can be deemed to have done so in relation to a meeting if it includes an address capable of being used for that purpose in the notice or proxy forms sent to members (see **2.7**).

The document or information must be sent to an address specified by the company for this purpose, or deemed to have been so specified, e.g. by virtue of s. 333 (Sch. 4, para. 7(1)). However, where the document is sent or supplied in electronic form by hand or by post (e.g. by posting a CD-Rom), it must be delivered to an address that would be valid if it were in hard copy form (Sch. 4, para. 7(2)).

2.4.3 Using other methods for sending documents or information to a company

Schedule 4 provides that a document or information that is sent to a company by any other means is validly sent if it is sent in a form or manner that has been agreed by the company (Sch. 4, para. 8). Schedule 5 makes similar provision regarding the use of other methods of communication for the purposes of documents and information sent by corporate members or debenture holders (Sch. 5, para. 15).

As mentioned above, these provisions would almost certainly serve to authorise the use by members of reply-paid cards supplied to them by the company.

2.5 Communications by a company

Schedule 5 of the 2006 Act sets out the methods by which documents and information may be sent or supplied by a company to shareholders, debenture holders, directors and other persons. The available methods include:

- hard copy form by hand or by post (Sch. 5, Part 2, para. 2–4);
- electronic form, provided that the intended recipient has agreed or can be deemed to have agreed (Sch. 5, Part 3, para. 5–7);
- communications by means of a website (Sch. 5, Part 4, para. 8–14); and
- any other form agreed by the company (Sch. 4, Part 5, para. 15).

2.5.1 Hard copy form

Part 2 of Sch. 5 sets out the methods that may be used by a company for hard copy communications, including the methods of delivery and the addresses that can be used for these purposes. Hard copy is defined for these purposes as being 'on paper or similar form capable of being read' (s. 1168).

Hard copy documents or information must be either handed by the company to the intended recipient, or sent or supplied by hand or by post (Sch. 5, para.

3(1)). Posting is defined for these purposes as posting a pre-paid envelope containing the document or information. This definition would appear to prevent a company from using a postcard to send documents or information to its members or debenture holders without first obtaining their consent. As discussed above, it would not prevent the company from providing pre-paid cards for them to use to return information to the company.

The addresses that may be used by a company for communications in hard copy form include:

■ an address specified for the purpose by the intended recipient;
■ in the case of a company, its registered office;
■ in the case of a member of the company, the address shown in the register of members;
■ in the case of a director, the address shown in the register of directors; and
■ an address to which any provision of the Companies Acts authorises the document to be sent (Sch. 5, para. 4(1)).

There may sometimes be more than one address that a company can use to send hard copy communications to certain recipients. For example, a director may have provided the company with an address to be used for general communications purposes, but the company could still validly serve a document on that director by sending it to the service address recorded in the register of directors.

A company can use the intended recipient's last known address where it is unable to obtain an address specified by them for the purpose (Sch. 5, para. 4(2)).

2.5.2 Communications by a company in electronic form

Part 3 of Sch. 5 covers the use of electronic communications by a company. It states that a company can only send or supply a document or information in electronic form to a person who has agreed (generally or specifically) to receive it in that manner or to a company that is deemed under the Companies Acts to have so agreed (e.g. under s. 333 – see **2.7**) (Sch. 5, para. 6). The document or information may only be sent by electronic means to an address specified for the purpose by the intended recipient, or where the recipient is a company, deemed by a provision of the Companies Act to have been so specified (Sch. 5, para. 7(1)). But, where a document or information is sent in electronic form by hand or by post (e.g. by posting a CD-Rom), it must be either handed to the intended recipient or sent to an address that could be validly used for hard copy communications (Sch. 5, para. 7(2)).

2.5.3 Website communications by a company

Part 4 of Sch. 5 allows a company to send or supply a document or information by making it available on a website and notifying the intended recipient of the fact that it has done so. A document or information made available on a website for these purposes must be made available in a form, and by a means, that the company reasonably considers will enable the recipient to read it with the naked eye and retain a copy of it (Sch. 5, para. 12). The company must also notify the intended recipient that the document or information has been made available on the website, give the address of the website, the place on the website where it may be accessed and how to access the document or information (Sch. 5, para. 13).

The company must make the document available on the website throughout the period specified by any applicable provision of the Companies Acts or, if no such period is specified, for a period of 28 days commencing on the date that the notification is sent (Sch. 5, para. 14(1)). The document or information is taken to be 'sent' on the date the notification is sent, or if later, on the date that the document or information becomes available on the website (s. 1147). Any failure to make the document or information available throughout the relevant period can be disregarded if it is made available on the website for part of that period and the failure is wholly attributable to circumstances that it would not be reasonable to have expected the company to prevent or avoid (Sch. 5, para. 14(2)).

Website communications can only be used if the intended recipient:

■ has agreed (generally or specifically) to receive the document or information in that manner (Sch. 5, para. 9(a)); or
■ can be deemed to have so agreed by not responding to a consultation conducted in accordance with either Sch. 5, para. 10 (members and indirect investors) or Sch. 5, para. 11 (debenture holders) (Sch. 5, para. 9(b)).

A company that wishes to use website communications for Companies Act purposes need not have authority in its articles to do so, or pass an ordinary resolution of its members to that effect, unless it wishes to take advantage of the deemed consent provisions in Sch. 5. Unless it does one of these things, it must obtain the individual consent of the intended recipient to the use of website communications. This means that the intended recipient must have positively elected to receive website communications.

The deemed consent provisions in Sch. 5, para. 10 can only be used if the members have resolved that the company may send or supply documents or information to members of the company by making them available on a website (see **Precedent 2.8B**) or the articles contain provisions to that effect. If this authority is in place, then the company can conduct a consultation whereby members can be deemed to have agreed to opt for website communications if they fail to respond to a consultation for this purpose within 28 days. The consultation must be clear about the effect of a failure to respond and cannot be conducted more than once in any 12-month period (see **Precedent 2.8C**). This type of consultation can also be used to ascertain the wishes of a person nominated by a member to enjoy information rights under s. 146 or any person nominated by a member in accordance with the company's articles to enjoy or exercise any rights of the member.

Schedule 5, para. 11 provides a similar procedure for website communications with debenture holders, which allows the company to deem those debenture holders who do not respond to a consultation within 28 days to have elected to receive website communications. In this case, the relevant debenture holders must have passed a resolution allowing the company to use website communications or the relevant instrument creating the debenture must contain provision to that effect.

According to an *Implementation Briefing on Commencement Order No. 1* (see the BIS website), companies that were using website communications under the 1985 Act regime could continue to do so for the documents covered by the consent given under the 1985 Act without taking any further action. No resolution would be required to take advantage of the deemed consent consultation procedures if the company's articles already made provisions allowing it to send or supply documents or information to members by website. However, if the articles only covered certain documents, a new resolution would be required to provide general cover for other documents to be provided via the website communication method.

2.5.4 Other methods of communication by a company

Part 5 of Sch. 5 provides that a document or information that is sent or supplied otherwise than in hard copy, electronic form or via a website is validly sent if sent in a form or manner agreed by the intended recipient.

■ 2.6 Communications with joint shareholders and other special cases

2.6.1 Communications with joint holders

The rules in Sch. 5, para. 16 regarding communications with joint holders of shares or debentures apply subject to any contrary provision in a company's articles. They provide that anything to be agreed or specified by the holder must be agreed or specified by all the joint holders (Sch. 5, para. 16(2)) and that anything required to be sent or supplied to the holder may be sent or supplied to each of them or to the first-named holder in the relevant register (Sch. 5, para. 16(3)).

2.6.2 Communications with shareholders in the event of death or bankruptcy

Documents or information required or authorised to be sent to a member who has died or has been declared bankrupt may be sent to the persons claiming to be entitled to the shares in consequence of the death or bankruptcy either by name or by the title of representatives of the deceased, or trustee of the bankrupt, or by any like description (Sch. 5, para. 17). This rule also has effect subject to any contrary provision in a company's articles.

■ 2.7 Sending documents relating to meetings in electronic form

Section 333 of the 2006 Act provides that where a company has given an electronic address in a notice calling a general meeting (or a class meeting (see s. 335)), it is deemed to have agreed that any document or information relating to proceedings at that meeting may be sent by electronic means to that address (subject to any conditions or limitations specified in the notice).

Similarly, if a company includes an electronic address in an instrument of proxy or proxy invitation sent out by the company, it is deemed to have agreed that any document or information relating to proxies may be sent by electronic means to that address (subject to any conditions or limitations specified in the 'notice').

Documents relating to proxies for the purposes of s. 333 include proxy appointments, any documents necessary to show the validity of the appointment, and any notice of termination of the authority of the proxy (s. 333(3)).

'Electronic address' is defined for the purposes of s. 333 as including any address or number used for the purpose of sending or receiving documents or information by electronic means (s. 333(4)).

2.7.1 Traded company: duty to provide electronic address for receipt of proxies

A traded company (see **8.5.1**) must, when sending out an instrument of proxy for the purposes of a general meeting or issuing an invitation to appoint a proxy for those purposes, give an electronic address for the receipt of any document or information relating to proxies for the meeting (s. 333A(1)). In doing so, a traded company is deemed to have agreed that any document or information relating to proxies for the meeting may be sent by electronic means to that address (subject to any limitations specified by the company when giving the address) (s. 333A(2)).

Documents relating to proxies for the purposes of s. 333A include proxy appointments, any documents necessary to show the validity of the appointment, and any notice of termination of the authority of the proxy (s. 333A(3) and s. 333(3)).

'Electronic address' is defined for the purposes of s. 333A as including any address or number used for the purpose of sending or receiving documents or information by electronic means (s. 333A(3) and s. 333(4)).

■ 2.8 Electronic communications under the Listing Rules and Disclosure and Transparency Rules

The Listing Rules (LR) and the Disclosure and Transparency Rules (DTR) both require issuers whose shares or debt securities are traded on a regulated market in the UK to send certain additional information to holders of those securities.

LR 1.4.9G confirms that issuers can use electronic means to send documents required under the Listing Rules to security holders 'in accordance with DTR 6.1.8R'. DTR 6.1.7G also confirms that issuers can use electronic means to send information to shareholders or debt security holders. Accordingly, issuers must comply with DTR 6.18R in order to use electronic communications for the purposes of the Listing Rules and the Disclosure and Transparency Rules.

DTR 6.1.8(1) requires issuers to obtain the consent of the members in general meeting before using electronic communications for these purposes (the Companies Act 2006 only requires shareholder approval, as a body, if the company wants to take advantage of the deemed consent to website communications method of consultation).

Shareholder consent to the use of website communications obtained under the Companies Act 1985 regime could be carried over to the new regime (see Transitional Provision 12 in the DTR Sourcebook Transitional Provisions).

DTR 6.1.8(2) stipulates that the use of electronic means must not depend on the location of the seat of residence of the shareholders and other persons. As this rule is based on an EU Directive requirement, it is thought that it requires issuers who wish to use electronic communications to offer that option to all members or debt security holders based in the EEA.

DTR 6.1.8(3) requires identification arrangements to be put in place so that the shareholders, debt security holders, or other persons entitled to exercise or to direct the exercise of voting rights are effectively informed.

DTR 6.1.8(5) requires any apportionment of the costs entailed in conveying information by electronic means to be determined by the issuer in compliance with the principle of equal treatment set out in DTR 6.1.3R.

For issuers that are not subject to the company communications provisions in Sch. 5 of the 2006 Act, DTR 6.1.8(4) provides that shareholders, debt security holders and certain indirect investors must be:

(a) contacted in writing to request their consent for the use of electronic communications; if they do not object within a reasonable period of time, their consent can be considered to have been given; and

(b) able to request at any time in the future that information be conveyed in writing.

Schedule 5 of the Act also requires a company to obtain the individual consent of the intended recipient to the use of electronic communications. That consent must be given specifically (Sch. 5, para. 9(a)) except where the person fails to respond to a consultation regarding website communications conducted in accordance with the requirements of Sch. 5, para. 10 (in the case of members) or Sch. 5, para. 11 (in the case of debenture holders), in which case they may be deemed to have consented to receive communications from the company in that manner.

■ 2.9 Elections to receive electronic communications

A company must continue to send hard copies of any documents or information to any member, debt security holder or indirect investor who is entitled to receive them under the Companies Acts, unless that person has agreed that they may be sent electronically. The Act provides two options in this regard:

(a) a company may use electronic communications to send a full electronic version of the document to a person who has provided it with an address for that purpose (e.g. an e-mail address); and

(b) alternatively, a company may simply notify a person that the relevant documents have been published on a website together with details of how they may be accessed.

A company cannot use either of these methods without the agreement of the person concerned, although that agreement may be deemed in the case of website communications if a person fails to respond in time to a consultation conducted in accordance with either Sch. 5, para. 10 (members) or Sch. 5, para. 11 (debenture holders) of the 2006 Act.

Where consent is required to use non-hard copy communications, the Act does not require companies to obtain a person's written consent. Members could therefore be allowed to signify their consent in some other way, e.g. by registering on a website or sending an e-mail or, even, registering by telephone. Ideally, members should be required to authenticate their election in some way. If elections are made in writing, this can be done by signature or by any other accepted method of execution. If a company plans to allow members to make elections via e-mail, the web, telephone or fax, members could be required to authenticate their election by providing a PIN number allocated to them for this purpose.

There is nothing in the Act to prevent a person from electing to receive certain types of document one way and others in a different manner. A company need not, however, allow a person to make such an election. Indeed, a company need not provide members with any choice at all as to the available methods. It could, for example, decide to publish the documents on a website and only offer members the opportunity to receive notifications of the fact that the information has been so published and how to find it.

Listed companies will not only need to obtain the consent of members for the various statutory purposes but also in respect of documents which they are required to send pursuant to the Listing Rules and the Disclosure and Transparency Rules. The specimen forms of election at **Precedents 2.9A and 2.9C** have been adapted for this purpose. They also provide an example of the sort of explanation which may need to be given to members. Companies will need to draft their own guidance for members depending on the options being made available and the provisions of their own articles.

A consultation regarding the use of website communications, whereby those who not respond within 28 days can be deemed to have agreed to accept electronic communications, can only be conducted if the members have resolved that the company may send or supply documents or information by making them available on a website (see **Precedent 2.9B**) or the articles contain provisions to that effect. Under Sch. 5, para. 10 such a consultation with members or indirect investors must be clear about the effect of a failure to respond and cannot be conducted more than once in any 12-month period (see **Precedent 2.9C**).

Schedule 5, para. 11 provides a similar procedure for website communications with debenture holders, which allows the company to deem those debenture holders who do not respond to a consultation within 28 days to have elected to receive website communications. In this case, the relevant debenture holders must have passed a resolution allowing the company to use website communications or the relevant instrument creating the debenture must contain provision to that effect.

Companies will need to comply with applicable data protection rules and practices when collecting storing and using information provided by members, debenture holders or others for the purposes of electronic communications. Details of elections made by members and any electronic addresses provided by them should not be entered in any of the statutory registers in a manner which would require their disclosure to people inspecting the register. As the Act does not require these details to be entered in any statutory register, they are not covered by any of the applicable data protection exemptions for statutory registers. The form of election at **Precedent 2.9A** includes a specimen data protection statement.

2.9.1 Indirect investors

The default right given to indirect investors (see **8.7**) is for documents and information to be supplied by means of a website. If the nominated person is to receive hard copies of the documents, he must have asked the registered holder to nominate him to receive hard copy and must have supplied an address for this purpose. The nomination given to the company by the registered holder must then indicate that the investor wishes to receive hard copy communications and give the address supplied by that person. As an alternative, a person nominated to receive web-based communications only may directly revoke the implied agreement to receive web-based communications and thus become entitled to receive hard copy (see s. 147(6)). The fact that a person may be nominated to receive hard copy communications does not prevent the company from making use of the electronic communications provisions and seeking to obtain that person's agreement to the use of website communications (s. 147(4)).

▪ 2.10 Electronic communications under the 1985 Table A

None of the versions of Table A in use for companies incorporated prior to 22 December 2000 (including the original version of the 1985 Table A) made any provision for the use of electronic communications. Companies were not allowed to use electronic communications for Companies Acts purposes until 22 December 2000, when the 1985 Act was amended by the Companies Act 1985 (Electronic Communications) Order 2000. Table A was also amended by the 2000 Order to facilitate the use of electronic communications at the same time as these amendments to the 1985 Act were brought into force.

Accordingly, any company incorporated on or after 22 December 2000 that is subject to Table A will have articles that facilitate the use of electronic communications. **Annex B2** shows the 1985 Table A as amended by the 2000 Order, and by way of notes, the relevant provisions of Table A prior to their amendment. As mentioned previously, the original version did not make any provision for electronic communications and applied for companies limited by shares incorporated under the 1985 Act before 22 December 2000. This does not mean that they cannot make use of electronic communications for statutory purposes under the Companies Act 2006 (see **2.11**). Nor were they prevented from doing so under the Companies Act 1985.

However, the 1985 Act provided that where a company's articles made no provision for the use of electronic communications in relation to notices and proxies, the provisions of Table A (as amended by the 2000 Order) were deemed to apply. The 2006 Act does not do this. Instead it establishes a self-contained company communications regime that does not rely on a company's articles. Accordingly, the revisions to Table A made by the 2000 Order in this regard are no longer deemed to apply to companies incorporated before 22 December 2000. Under the 2006 Act, matters have to be determined on the basis that:

(a) the company communications provisions (where they apply) override anything to the contrary in a company's articles that appears to prevent the use of electronic communications;

(b) a company's articles will only override the company communications provisions where the 2006 Act specifically allows other provision to be made in that regard.

Companies incorporated after 22 December 2000 that adopted articles based on the revised version of the 1985 Table A should not face any particular problems in trying to reconcile them with the 2006 Act. One of the modifications made by the 2000 Order was to amend Table A, reg. 115 to provide that:

> Proof that notice contained in an electronic communication was sent in accordance with guidance issued by the Institute of Chartered Secretaries and Administrators shall be conclusive evidence that the notice was given.

The relevant guidance in this regard is ICSA's *Guidance on electronic communications with shareholders*. The guide is now in its second edition and can be found on the ICSA website (www.icsa.org.uk). Publication of the first edition of the ICSA guide was timed to coincide with changes made to the Companies

Act 1985 and Table A by the Companies Act 1985 (Electronic Communications) Order 2000. In the first edition of the ICSA guidance, the relevant recommendations were contained in Chapter 8. In the second edition, they can be found in paragraph B6. The wording from the second edition, published in February 2007, is reproduced at **Appendix 1**.

■ 2.11 Amending articles for electronic communications

Articles can sometimes give the impression that it is not possible for either the company or its members to use electronic communications. This is because they require various things to be done 'in writing' without defining what the term means. This is true of all versions of Table A in force prior to 22 October 2000. In the past, the term 'in writing' was used in articles and legislative provisions to indicate that a thing had to be done in hard copy form (e.g. paper form) rather than, say, orally. Accordingly, whenever the term 'in writing' is used, people like to see something that confirms that it can also be done 'electronically'.

The Companies Act 2006 provides confirmation that things that are required or authorised to be sent by or to a company can be sent electronically as long as the intended recipient has agreed to accept communications in that manner. Accordingly the Act overrides any possible obstacle caused by the meaning of the term 'in writing' in a company's articles, but only in relation to things that are required or authorised to be done under the Act. Most things that a company is required to do under its articles are also things that it is either required or authorised to do under the Act. However, several of the things that members are required to do under the articles are not specifically required under the Act or necessarily authorised to be done under it, except in the sense that the Act does not prohibit a company from requiring members to do these things. On the whole this does not matter because they are not normally the sort of things that companies would necessarily want members to be able to do electronically. For example, a company would not normally be willing to accept a scanned copy of a share certificate to be submitted with a share transfer.

If the articles do not specify the form in which a document or information must be sent by a member to the company and the relevant document or information is not required or authorised to be sent by that member under the Companies Acts, the company can generally choose whether to require it to be sent in hard copy or electronic form and whether to require the original or allow a copy to be sent.

Although the 2006 Act allows a company to take advantage of electronic communications without first amending its articles, it is probably preferable to do so. Despite the government's best efforts to eliminate any problems in this regard, a company may find it difficult to decide whether its own articles or the statutory provisions should be applied in certain circumstances. It is, in any case, best to avoid having articles that conflict with the Act if at all possible.

For companies with articles based on the original 1985 Table A, the best starting point may be to look at the amendments that were made to Table A by the Companies Act 1985 (Electronic Communications) Order 2000 (see **Annex B2**) and the approach adopted in the 2006 Act model articles for the relevant type of company (see **Annex C**). Schedule 1 of the 2000 Order sets out the changes that were made to Table A for these purposes, not all of which will necessarily be suitable any more for a company operating under the Companies Act 2006 regime.

A company may, of course, adopt article provisions which have a different effect from the model articles or Table A, and that modify some of the statutory defaults. Questions which should be considered when amending articles in these circumstances might include:

- Should the articles make specific provision to allow the use of website communications so as to allow a deemed consent-type consultation to be conducted without the approval of the members in general meeting?
- What provision should the articles make with regard to deemed delivery of notices (and documents) sent electronically? Should they, for example, be treated the same as a notice sent by post? Or should documents sent using electronic communications be deemed have been be served earlier? Should a notification of publication on a website be treated differently if sent by post or electronically?
- Should the articles require the company to send a paper copy of any notice or document where electronic transmission has failed or notify the member that a transmission has failed (if so, care would need to be taken not to prejudice any deemed service provisions)?
- Should the articles require the company to conduct a regular or periodic e-mail probe to check e-mail addresses held? The answer to this question will probably be no, although this would not stop a company from conducting a probe.
- Should the articles specify how electronic communications may be authenticated or executed? It is probably best to give the directors discretion in this regard. This question may not only be relevant with regard to proxy appointments.
- Should specific provision be made regarding what constitutes proof that an electronic communication has been sent? Table A refers to guidance issued by the ICSA in this regard. Neither the 2006 Act nor the model articles make any provision in this regard.
- In the case of a listed company, does any special provision need to be made for documents which the company must issue under the Listing Rules or the Disclosure and Transparency Rules?

■ 2.12 ICSA guidance on electronic communications with shareholders

The Institute of Chartered Secretaries and Administrators has published a guide to best practice on electronic communications with shareholders. The guide is now in its second edition and can be found on the ICSA website (www.icsa.org. uk). Publication of the first edition of the ICSA guide was timed to coincide with changes made to the Companies Act 1985 and Table A by the Companies Act 1985 (Electronic Communications) Order 2000. One of the modifications made to Table A by the Order was to amend reg. 115 to provide that proof that a notice contained in an electronic communication was sent in accordance with the ICSA guidance shall be conclusive evidence that the notice was given. The relevant recommendations (reproduced at **Appendix 1**) can be found at para. B6 of the second edition of the ICSA Guidance (or in substantially the same form in chapter 8 of the first edition).

The ICSA Guidance also includes best practice recommendations on:

A   Communication by means of a website
A1   Articles changes for companies
A2   Content and frequency of invitations to shareholders requesting agreement to website communications consultations with shareholders
A3   Responses to a deemed agreement to website invitation
A4   Notifications referring to material on the website
A5   Managing notifications of availability on the website without discouraging shareholder voting and participation
A6   Website management
A7   Period of availability of materials on the website
A8   Impact on printing requirements

B   Communications in electronic form
B1   Treating shareholders the same
B2   Ensuring in all communications in electronic form that the shareholder can 'retain a copy' of the document or information
B3   Impact on general meeting documentation
B4   Mix of hard copy and electronic communications
B5   Identification arrangements, record keeping and record dates
B6   Failed delivery or non-receipt of information
B7   Nominated persons under Part 9, Exercise of Members' Rights
B8   Deemed delivery

C   General
C1   Viruses
C2   Register of members
C3   Other electronic means

■ 2.13 Electronic signatures

Section 7 of the Electronic Communications Act 2000 ('the ECA 2000') makes provision for the admissibility in legal proceedings of:

■ an electronic signature incorporated into or logically associated with a particular electronic communication or particular electronic data; and
■ the certification by any person of such a signature.

An electronic signature (or any certification thereof) is admissible as evidence in relation to any of the following questions regarding the authenticity or integrity of a communication or data:

■ whether the communication or data comes from a particular person or other source;
■ whether it is accurately timed and dated;
■ whether it is intended to have legal effect;
■ whether there has been any tampering with, or other modification of, the communication or data (ECA 2000, s. 15(2)).

An electronic signature is defined in s. 7(2) of the ECA 2000 as:

so much of anything in electronic form as:
(a) is incorporated into or otherwise logically associated with any electronic communication or electronic data; and
(b) purports to be so incorporated or associated for the purpose of being used in establishing the authenticity of the communication or data, the integrity of the communication or data, or both.

This definition would allow a variety of methods to be used to apply an electronic signature. However, the security of the method used will have a bearing on the weight given to the evidence that is tendered in any legal proceedings. In order to ensure that an electronic signature is given at least the same (if not more) weight than a manual signature, it will be necessary to use the most modern cryptographic techniques. These involve the use of public and private keys to code and decode messages and algorithms which prevent the file which has been 'signed' from being tampered with.

Although it is possible to purchase commercially available software that will generate the public and private keys that must be used, most electronic signatures are purchased from commercial organisations that are able to certify for the benefit of third parties that the signature was purchased by the person that it purports to represent. The ECA 2000 provides that a person may certify an electronic signature by making a statement (whether before or after the making of the communication) confirming that the signature, a means of producing, communicating or verifying the signature, or a procedure applied to the signature, is (either alone or in combination with other factors) a valid means of establishing the authenticity of the communication or data, the integrity of the communication or data, or both (s. 7(3)).

A person could certify an electronic signature applied using an insecure method under this procedure. Difficulties may arise, however, where there is some dispute as to the validity of the electronic signature or as to whether the electronic signature was applied by or on behalf of the person it purports to represent. If the company is likely to need to rely on the validity of the electronic signature in legal proceedings, it is therefore preferable for it to insist that a secure method be used. This is certainly desirable with regard to the use of electronic signatures to sign the minutes.

2.13.1 Definition of electronic communications

An 'electronic communication' is defined in s. 15 of the Electronic Communications Act 2000 as:

> a communication transmitted (whether from one person to another, from one device to another or from a person to a device or vice versa):
> (a) by means of an electronic communications network; or
> (b) by other means but while in an electronic form.

The term electronic communication could therefore be said to embrace the following methods of communication:

- e-mail;
- internet delivery;
- telephone recordings and conversations;
- fax messages;
- text messages on mobile phones;
- radio and television signals; and
- documents provided on a floppy disk, CD-Rom or DVD-Rom or by any other way of transporting electronic media.

It should be noted that the definition of an electronic communication in the ECA 2000 does not have any particular relevance for the purposes of the company communications provisions of the Companies Act 2006, which adopt a slightly different phraseology with their own distinct definitions. It is questionable, therefore, whether it would be appropriate to use some of the above methods for Companies Acts purposes, particularly those which are of an ephemeral nature.

The admissibility of electronic signatures in legal proceedings may however be of significance in the following areas covered by this book:

- the retention of signed minutes in computerised form (see **26.9**);
- the authentication of proxy appointments made using electronic communications (see **16.11**); and
- the authentication of other electronic communications sent by or to the company (see **2.2.4**).

PART 2

Meetings of directors

Directors derive their powers from provisions that are usually contained in a company's articles of association. Generally speaking they must exercise those powers collectively at a board meeting. However, articles normally allow the directors to act by written resolution and to delegate their powers to some other body or person.

The procedures to be followed at meetings of directors are determined largely by a company's articles of association. The Companies Act 2006 interferes very little in this area. Where the articles are silent on any matter, the common law will apply. As most articles are modelled on the 1985 Table A or the 2006 Act model articles, these provide a convenient starting point for any study of this subject.

Articles usually provide that the proceedings of committees of directors are governed by the same rules as board meetings.

The courts will not necessarily invalidate a transaction merely because the directors failed to follow proper procedures, particularly where the directors could rectify that failing by holding a proper meeting. The courts will not, however, normally tolerate such failures where a director is interested in the transaction.

3

Directors

■ 3.1 Summary

- The Companies Act 2006 requires every private company to appoint at least one director and every public company to appoint at least two. Some of the practical procedures for the appointment (and removal) of directors are dealt with in **Chapter 25**.
- Articles usually give the directors power to manage the business of the company. However, the Act does not require this, nor does it confer any power on them to do so, either individually or as a body. Under the common law, a company's powers must be exercised by its members in general meeting unless its articles of association provide otherwise (see **3.2**).
- Although the distinction between executive and non-executive directors is not particularly important for Companies Act purposes, it is important for corporate governance purposes (see **3.3**).
- Several factors must be taken into account when determining whether the directors have power to act on behalf of the company (see **3.4**).
- The directors cannot exercise a delegated power which the company itself does not have. The company's own powers may be limited in this regard by a statement of objects set out in its constitution (see **3.5**).
- Most articles include what is known as a general management clause which gives the directors all the powers necessary to manage the company's business. The powers given to the directors under this type of clause may be limited by other provisions of the articles and will be subject to any provisions of the Act (see **3.6**).
- The articles are deemed to be a contract between the members and the company which governs the way the company is run. It follows that the only way the shareholders can interfere in matters delegated to the directors is to change that contract (i.e. to amend the articles by special resolution so as to restrict the directors' discretion) or to issue directions in accordance with procedures contained in the articles. Even then, such resolutions or directions will have not normally have any effect on the validity of any transaction previously entered into by the directors on behalf of the company (see **3.7**).

- Other articles may give the directors special powers which they would not otherwise have, e.g. the power to delegate and the power to fix the remuneration of directors (see **3.8**).
- If the directors are unable to act for any reason, their powers may by default revert to the members in general meeting (see **3.9**).
- Articles usually allow the directors to delegate 'any of their powers' to committees of the board and/or to executive directors. However, it has been held that this does not necessarily include special powers given to them by the articles, e.g. the power to pay the directors special remuneration (see **3.10**).
- Articles usually give the board specific power to appoint agents by power of attorney or otherwise (see **3.11**).
- The UK Corporate Governance Code requires directors of listed companies to produce a schedule of matters reserved for the decision of the board (see **3.12**).

■ 3.2 The board of directors

The Companies Act 2006 requires every public company to have at least two directors and every private company to have at least one (s. 154). A company can appoint another company as a director. However, at least one director in every UK company must be a natural person (s. 155(1)). An individual under the age of 16 cannot be appointed as a director (s. 157).

The directors usually undertake the day-to-day management of the company on behalf of the members. Although the Act does not specifically require this and does not directly confer any powers of management on the directors, it is drafted on the assumption that they will be responsible for the management of the company. Under common law, a company's powers must be exercised by its members in general meeting unless its memorandum or articles of association provide otherwise (*Mayor, Constables and Company of Merchants of the Staple of England v. Governor and Company of the Bank of England* (1887) 21 Q.B.D. 160).

It would not normally be practicable for a company's business to be managed on a day-to-day basis by the members, particularly if every matter requiring a decision had to be put to a general meeting called and held in accordance with the requirements of the Act. Even in an owner-managed business where there are relatively few members, it would normally be easier for them to manage the company as directors rather than as members. This is mainly because the formalities associated with board meetings are less onerous, but also because that is the way most companies are run and doing it in any other way would complicate matters unnecessarily and probably involve significant legal expenses.

In practice, the articles of most companies delegate wide powers of management to the directors. Generally speaking, these powers must be exercised by the board of directors collectively (i.e. at a board meeting). However, the articles may allow the directors to make decisions in other ways and invariably allow them to delegate their powers to some other individual or body.

In the UK, all directors are usually members of the same board and usually have one vote each. Under this unitary system, each director has an equal say in matters put to the board (although the chairman may sometimes have a casting vote). Articles usually allow the board to appoint one or more of the directors to some sort of executive office within the company (e.g. as managing director) and to delegate any of its powers to them. These executive directors are usually salaried and manage the business of the company on a day-to-day basis under delegated powers. Directors who are not executives are known as non-executive directors.

Boards rarely delegate all of their management powers to the executive directors and will normally retain responsibility for certain matters (such as the company's strategic direction). Where the board does delegate management powers to executives, it will be responsible for monitoring their performance and setting their pay, although in listed companies the latter role is often performed by a remuneration committee made up of non-executive directors.

On the continent, two-tier board systems are more common. The company is managed on a day-to-day basis by an executive board which is appointed by and accountable to a supervisory board. The supervisory board fulfils the monitoring role performed by non-executive directors in the UK and may include shareholder and employee representatives. The system is appealing to purists as it places the non-executives above the executives in the structural hierarchy. However, it is debatable whether these structural differences make it any easier for the part-time directors to perform their supervisory duties.

One of the main advantages of the unitary system is said to be that it enables the non-executive directors to contribute more effectively to the formulation of the company's strategy and to monitor the performance of the executives; its major disadvantage, that it is more difficult for the non-executive directors to be impartial and independent. The UK Corporate Governance Code is designed to address issues of this nature in the listed company environment.

■ 3.3 Types of director

3.3.1 Executive directors

An executive director is a director who holds some executive management position within the company. Under reg. 84 of Table A, the directors may appoint one or more of their number as managing director or to any other executive office (e.g. finance director) and determine the terms and remuneration of any such appointment. The model articles for private companies provide that directors may undertake any services for the company that the directors decide and are entitled to such remuneration as the directors determine. The appointment of executive directors and the terms of their appointments must therefore be approved by a resolution of the board (see **Precedent 3.3A**), unless the articles specifically allow another person or body to deal with these matters.

Salaried executive directors should be appointed under a formal service agreement which should state the title of the job to be performed, and make provision for matters such as notice and termination, the remuneration and other benefits associated with the appointment (including whether the remuneration payable is inclusive or exclusive of any director's fee which may be payable) and any restraints in the form of confidentiality undertakings and restrictive covenants in the event of leaving the service of the company. With regard to the duties to be performed it is normal for the service contract to include a more general provision stating that the director shall have such powers and duties as the board may determine from time to time (see **Precedent 3.3B**). This allows the board to modify authorisations generally without having to modify each executive director's contract.

Articles usually allow the board to delegate its powers to individual executive directors (e.g. reg. 72 of Table A, pcls 5, clg 5 and plc 5). The terms of any delegation should be approved by a resolution of the board (see **3.10**). In delegating its powers, the board may limit the executive's authority by imposing certain conditions. For example, the managing director may be given power to authorise capital expenditure up to a certain value with any expenditure above that amount requiring board approval. Limits on individual directors' authorities may also be reinforced by the adoption of a schedule of matters reserved to the board (see **3.12**).

A company's articles may require the executive directors to retire by rotation. Under Table A, executive directors are exempt from retirement by rotation but not from the requirement to retire at the first annual general meeting following their appointment (reg. 84). Under the model articles for public companies, executive directors are not exempt from either of these requirements (plc 21). The model articles for private companies do not make any provision whatsoever for retirement by rotation or otherwise. The UK Corporate Governance Code recommends that directors of listed companies should retire and offer themselves for re-election at least once every three years and that directors of FTSE 350 companies should do so annually (Code provision B.7.1).

3.3.2 Non-executive directors

Non-executive directors are directors who have not been appointed to any executive office within the company. The distinction between executive and non-executive directors will not always be clear cut, particularly where the status of the chairman is concerned. The UK Corporate Governance Code recommends as a principle that the board of a listed company should include a balance of executive and non-executive directors (and in particular independent non-executive directors) such that no individual or small group of individuals can dominate the board's decision taking (Code supporting principle B.1). It also states that at least half the board, excluding the chairman, should comprise non-executive directors determined by the board to be independent, although for a smaller company this requirement is replaced by a requirement for at least two independent non-executive directors (Code provision B.1.2). Non-executive directors considered by the board to be independent should be identified in the annual report and the board should state its reasons if it determines that a director is independent notwithstanding the existence of certain relationships or circumstances set out in the Code (Code provision B.1.1).

The main purpose of this disclosure obligation is to allow investors to make their own assessment as to the independence of the non-executive directors and, therefore to make their own judgement as to whether or not the company is complying with other recommendations in the Code (e.g. regarding the constitution of the audit, remuneration and nomination committees).

Whether or not they are independent, non-executive directors participate in the management of the company by attending board meetings and any committees of the board of which they are a member. Regulation 72 of Table A does not allow the board to delegate any of its powers to an individual non-executive director. However, the same result can be achieved by delegating to a board committee consisting of only one non-executive director. All three versions of the model articles allow the directors to delegate any of their powers to anyone they see fit (pcls, clg and plc 5).

Under Table A, fees paid to directors in their capacity as board members must be approved by an ordinary resolution of the members in general meeting (reg. 82). This applies to fees paid to executive and non-executive directors, although executive directors usually receive a salary instead of directors' fees and those salaries may be determined by the board without reference to the members (reg. 84). Regulation 82 is frequently modified to enable the board to fix the fees of non-executive directors without reference to the members or to enable them to do so subject to an aggregate cap approved by the members.

Under the model articles, the directors are given power to decide the salaries/fees paid to both executive and non-executive directors (pcls 19, clg 19, and plc 23).

All directors are usually entitled to be repaid any expenses they reasonably incur in connection with their duties (e.g. reg. 83 of Table A, pcls 20, clg 20 and plc 24).

3.3.3 Alternate directors

An alternate director is someone appointed by a director to participate in his absence at board meetings and who may also have power to participate in his stead in any other directors' decision-making processes provided for by the articles. The Act does not authorise a director to appoint an alternate or a proxy. Accordingly, a director may only appoint an alternate if the articles make specific provision to that effect (see further **4.11**).

3.3.4 *De facto and shadow directors*

De facto directors are people who act as directors and are held out to be directors by the company even though they have never actually been properly appointed as directors or have ceased to be directors. A company will normally be bound by the acts of any such director.

A shadow director is a person in accordance with whose instructions the directors of the company are accustomed to act. A person is not deemed to be a shadow director by reason only that the directors act on advice by him in a professional capacity (s. 250). Typically, a shadow director will tend to lurk in the shadows, sheltering behind others who, he claims, are the only directors of the company to the exclusion of himself.

De facto directors and shadow directors can both be disqualified under the Company Directors' Disqualification Act 1986 and may be liable for wrongful and fraudulent trading under the Insolvency Act 1986. Shadow directors are subject to some of the duties and penalties prescribed by the Companies Act 2006.

■ 3.4 Extent of the directors' powers

In order to decide whether a decision is within the directors' powers, the following issues need to be addressed:

- A transaction will not be within the powers of the directors if it is not within the powers of the company. See further **3.5** regarding the effect of any objects clause in this regard.
- Member/shareholder approval may be required under the Companies Acts (or under other applicable legislation, rule or code), or under the company's articles of association, or by virtue of a shareholders' agreement. See **Appendix 2** for examples of matters that require shareholder/member approval.
- If the articles give the directors power to manage the company and the decision concerns the management of the company, the directors may act under those powers unless:
  (a) some other provision in the articles restricts their powers in relation to the matter concerned (see **3.6**);
  (b) the members have given the directors a valid instruction which restricts their freedom to act (see **3.7**).
- If the decision does not concern the management of the company, the directors cannot act unless there is a special power in the articles which authorises them to do so (see **3.8**).
- If the decision relates to a matter which would otherwise constitute a breach of their fiduciary duties, the directors cannot act unless the articles allow them to do so (e.g. fix their own remuneration).

It is important to note that a company will normally be bound by transactions with third parties entered into by the directors on its behalf even though the directors may have exceeded their powers. It is equally important to note that the directors have a duty to act within their powers and can be sued by the company for any losses it suffers as a result of any breach of that duty.

■ 3.5 *Ultra vires* and the objects clause

A company's constitution may include an objects clause which limits or defines the purposes for which the company was formed. Historically, all companies were required to include an objects clause in their memorandum of association. Under the Companies Act 2006, company articles may still include a statement of objects but need not do so. If they do not, the company's objects are deemed to be unrestricted (s. 31(1)). The statement of objects can no longer be included in the memorandum of association and any objects clause in the memorandum of association of a company incorporated under a prior Act is now deemed to form part of its articles (s. 28).

Historically, the objects clause had the effect of limiting the powers of the company and rendering any acts of the company or its directors in excess of those powers unenforceable. In practice, companies often attempted to draft objects clauses that placed no restriction whatsoever on the company's objects or powers. However, a company could, if it chose to do so, try to limit the purposes for which it should be used. For example, if the clause stated that the object of the company was to build and operate a railway, the company and its directors would have no power to do anything else. Such a company could not provide banking services and any transaction by the company with a third party in connection with banking would therefore be *ultra vires* (i.e. beyond the company's powers) and invalid.

Historically, a third party was deemed to have notice of any such limitations, and be bound by them, by virtue of the fact that the constitutional documents containing the objects clause were filed and made available for inspection at Companies House. However, various statutory modifications have reduced the impact of the *ultra vires* rule in recent years.

These rules are now contained in ss. 39–42 of the 2006 Act. Section 39(1) provides that the validity of an act done by a company shall not be called into question on the ground of lack of capacity by reason of anything in its constitution. Section 40 provides that in favour of a person dealing with a company in good faith, the power of the directors to bind the company, or authorise others to do so, is deemed to be free of any limitation under the company's constitution.

Nevertheless, a member of the company may still bring proceedings to restrain an act which is beyond a company's capacity (s. 40(4)). In addition, it remains the duty of the directors to observe any limitations on their powers flowing from the company's constitution (s. 40(5)). Accordingly, the directors may still be held liable to compensate the company if it suffers a loss as a result of an *ultra vires* transaction approved by them. By participating in an *ultra vires* act, the directors are in breach of their duty to act within their powers under s. 171.

The directors effectively bear most of the risks of an *ultra vires* transaction. However, the court can relieve the directors of their liability if it is satisfied that they have acted honestly and reasonably and ought fairly to be excused (s. 1157). In addition, the members may ratify any act of the directors which was beyond the capacity of the company (s. 239).

■ 3.6 General management clause

Articles invariably contain a provision (known as the general management clause) which substantially reverses the common law rule that the company's powers must be exercised by the members in general meeting. Without such a clause it would be almost impossible for the directors to perform their normal managerial duties. It is even debateable whether they would have sufficient powers to perform their statutory duties under the Companies Act 2006.

Regulation 70 of Table A is typical of this type of provision, and provides:

70. Subject to the provisions of the Act, the memorandum and the articles and to any directions given by special resolution, the business of the company shall be managed by the directors who may exercise all the powers of the company. No alteration of the memorandum or articles and no such direction shall invalidate any prior act of the directors which would have been valid if that alteration had not been made or that direction had not been given. The powers given by this regulation shall not be limited by any special power given to the directors by the articles and a meeting of directors at which a quorum is present may exercise all powers exercisable by the directors.

It can be seen that reg. 70 gives the directors authority to exercise all the powers of the company which are not specifically excluded or reserved to the members by other provisions in the memorandum or articles or the Act. It also provides a special procedure under which the members in general meeting can give valid instructions to the directors (see **3.7**).

The model articles adopt a similar, but slightly different formula (pcls, clg and plc 3 and 4):

Directors' general authority

3. Subject to the articles, the directors are responsible for the management of the company's business, for which purpose they may exercise all the powers of the company.

Shareholders' reserve power

4(1). The shareholders may, by special resolution, direct the directors to take, or refrain from taking, specified action.

(2). No such special resolution invalidates anything which the directors have done before the passing of the resolution.

It has been held that a general management clause giving the directors all powers 'necessary in the management of the company' does not authorise them to present a winding up petition without the approval of the members because winding up is not connected with the management of the company (*Re Emmadart Ltd.* [1979] Ch. 540). Although, directors now have a statutory power to apply for a compulsory winding up under the Insolvency Act 1986, their powers may be subject to other limitations where this type of wording is adopted. Modern articles seek to avoid this problem by conferring powers on the directors without the condition that they be exercised in the management of the company. Regulation 70 of Table A uses the words '. . . the business of the company shall be managed by the directors who may exercise all the powers of the company'.

Under a general management clause it is usually safe to assume that the directors can do anything the company can do as long as they are not prevented from doing that thing by the Act or another provision in the articles (or a memorandum provision now deemed to form part of the articles). Thus in *Re Patent File Co.* (1870) L.R. 6 Ch. 83, Mellish L.J. said: 'The articles give to the directors the whole powers of the company, subject to the provisions [of the articles and] of the Companies Act . . . and I cannot find anything either in the Act or in the articles to prohibit their making a mortgage by deposit.' There are, of course, exceptions to this rule.

The directors may not do anything which would be a breach of their fiduciary duty to the company unless the articles give them specific powers in that regard (e.g. pay themselves a salary). In addition, they may not delegate their powers unless the articles so provide (see **3.10**).

3.6.1 Subject to the provisions of the Act

All powers conferred on the directors by the articles are subject to the provisions of the Companies Act 2006, whether or not this is stated in the articles. Thus, the directors cannot exercise any of the company's powers which are reserved to the members by the Act and must comply with the requirements of the Act when exercising their powers. For example, the directors cannot authorise loans above a certain amount to one of their number without the approval of the members. For further examples of transactions which require member approval, see **Appendix 2** which shows the type of resolution required for various types of business at general meetings.

The Act also requires the directors to have regard to the interests of various stakeholders (s. 172), and to comply with certain procedural requirements when exercising their powers, e.g. by notifying their interests in proposed transactions in accordance with s. 177.

3.6.2 Subject to the articles

The general management clause is normally expressed as being subject to other provisions in the articles of association or, in the case of older companies, in the memorandum of association (which will now be deemed to form part of the articles by virtue of s. 28). These may include provisions which:

- limit the capacity of the company and, therefore, the directors (e.g. an objects clause – see **3.5**);
- limit the powers of the directors (but not the members), e.g. a limit on directors' borrowing powers;

- reserve certain powers to the members, e.g. to approve the payment of dividend (although the articles may allow the directors to pay an interim dividend without reference to the members);
- determine the procedures which the directors must follow when exercising their powers, e.g. regulation of proceedings at meetings of directors;
- allow the directors to delegate their powers;
- relax the conditions members must satisfy in order to exercise certain statutory rights;
- provide additional procedures for removal of directors, e.g. by extraordinary resolution.

■ 3.7 Directions given by the members

Unless the articles contain some special provision allowing the members to give directions, the only way they can interfere in the exercise by the directors of their powers is to alter the articles in such a way that those powers revert back to the company in general meeting. In *Automatic Self-Cleansing Filter Syndicate Co. Ltd. v. Cunninghame* [1906] 2 Ch. 34, C.A., the members in general meeting passed an ordinary resolution (i.e. by a simple majority of those voting) instructing the directors to sell part of the business to another company on certain terms. The directors refused to carry out the sale and the Court of Appeal held that they were not bound to do so because the power to sell any of the company's property had been vested in them by the articles.

Most articles provide an alternative method for the members to give instructions to the directors. In *Automatic Self-Cleansing Filter* the directors' powers were 'subject to such regulations as may from time to time be made by extraordinary resolution' (a resolution that required a 75% majority of those voting). If the resolution to sell the business had been proposed and passed as an extraordinary resolution, the result would have been different. Whether or not such provision is made, the members may achieve the same result by proposing and passing a special resolution (which also requires a 75% majority) to amend the articles so that, for example, the powers revert back to the company in general meeting. Having done that, they need only pass an ordinary resolution (50% majority of those voting) to approve the proposed course of action.

In the case of the 1985 Table A (reg. 70) and the model articles (art. 4), the members may give the directors binding instructions by passing a special resolution. As the articles can be amended by special resolution, this does not place them in a significantly stronger position than if no such provision was made. The only real advantage is that it is not necessary for the resolution giving directions to be framed as an amendment of the articles. This allows the members to give directions in a specific instance without limiting the directors' powers generally. Although such a resolution would not, if passed, constitute an amendment to the articles, a copy of it would have to be filed at Companies House and attached to any copy of the articles issued after it had been passed.

The wording of reg. 80 of the 1948 Table A is more obscure and has caused a number of difficulties. It provides:

> 80. The business of the company shall be managed by the directors, who … may exercise all such powers of the company …, subject, nevertheless, to any of these regulations, to the provisions of the Act and to such regulations being not inconsistent with the aforesaid regulations or provisions, as may be prescribed by the company in general meeting …

The difficulty with this type of article is in deciding what the word 'regulations' means. In *Quin & Axtens v. Salmon* [1909] A.C. 442, it was held that it meant 'articles' throughout. If this interpretation is correct, the members may only interfere by changing the articles and the condition that such regulations must not be inconsistent with the articles becomes superfluous. In *Scott v. Scott* [1943] 1 All E.R. 582, it was held that the members in general meeting could not give the directors instructions to pay an interim dividend by ordinary resolution under an article similar to reg. 80 of the 1948 Table A. Lord Clauson pointed out (at p. 444) that if an ordinary resolution could be considered to be a regulation within the meaning of those words it would still be ineffective because it would be inconsistent with the existing articles.

Some companies have, in the past, adopted articles based on reg. 80 of the 1948 Act Table A, which allows the members to give directions by extraordinary resolution. If they also provide that such directions must not be 'inconsistent with the aforesaid regulations or provisions', such provisions may be of limited use to the members if the word regulations is taken to refer to the articles. It could be argued that any extraordinary resolution of the members which purports to fetter the discretion of the directors will be inconsistent with the articles. If so, the provision is almost superfluous because the only way the shareholders can avoid this is by amending the article which creates that inconsistency in the first place.

3.7.1 Prior acts of directors not invalidated

Most articles make some provision to ensure that prior acts of the directors are not invalidated by any subsequent direction by the members (see reg. 70 of Table A, and art 4(2) of the model articles). This type of provision ensures that the members cannot reverse a decision of the directors which has already been acted upon. Without it, third parties could never be sure that the company would be bound by the acts of its directors.

■ 3.8 Special powers

Articles usually give the directors a number of additional powers which they would not otherwise have under the general management clause because:

- they are not connected with the management of the company but with the relationship between the company and its members, e.g. the power to make calls (regs. 12 to 22 of Table A, and plc 54); or
- the exercise of such a power would otherwise be a breach of their fiduciary duties, e.g. the power to fix their own remuneration.

The articles may also include special provisions dealing with powers of management which the directors would ordinarily be assumed to have under the general management clause. It is normally presumed that the existence of a special power excludes the application of any power the directors may have under a general management clause in that regard. For example, the articles may include a provision giving the directors specific power to borrow money up to a stated limit for certain defined purposes. The directors would normally be deemed to have the power to borrow under the general management clause. However, as the powers under the general management clause are expressed as being subject to other articles, it is clear that their power to borrow will be restricted, at least for the purposes stated. What may not be clear, however, is whether the directors are still authorised under the general management clause to borrow for other purposes. This will depend on the exact wording of the articles, but where there is any doubt, it should be assumed that the article containing the special power on borrowing represents the final word in this regard and excludes any powers which might normally exist under the general management clause.

Modern articles often reverse this presumption by stating in the general management clause that the powers given shall not be limited by any special power given to the directors by any other article (see, e.g. reg. 70 of Table A). The purpose of these words is not to negate any restrictions contained in other articles but to preserve any powers the directors have under the general management clause which are not specifically excluded by other articles.

■ 3.9 Default powers of the members

Where the board of directors is unable or unwilling to conduct the company's business, the members in general meeting may be entitled, in default, to exercise powers given to the directors. For example, in *Barron v. Potter* [1914] 1 Ch. 895, the company's articles provided that the power to appoint directors was vested in the board and fixed the quorum for board meetings as two. One of the two directors appointed refused to attend meetings so that no business could be done. It was held that the power to appoint additional directors in these circumstances reverted to the company in general meeting as this was the only way to break the deadlock.

In *Foster v. Foster* [1916] 1 Ch. 532, the company's articles provided that the directors could not vote on any contract in which they were interested and that the quorum for board meetings was two. Two of the three directors of the company each wanted to be appointed as its salaried managing director. Although unable to vote on their own appointment, both were able to block the appointment of the other. It was held that the power to appoint a managing director reverted by default to the general meeting.

In *Barron v. Potter* and to a lesser extent in *Foster v. Foster*, the board's failure to act paralysed the company and the general meeting merely acted in order to break the deadlock. The courts will not, however, allow the members to usurp the board's powers where the directors are unable to agree on a business decision but are otherwise capable of managing the business. Thus in *Quin and Axtens Ltd. v. Salmon* [1909] A.C. 442, the company's articles provided that no decision regarding the acquisition or letting of certain properties would be valid if either of two named directors dissented. One of the named directors (Salmon) dissented on such a proposal. An extraordinary general meeting was then held at which the shareholders, by a simple majority, passed similar resolutions. The House of Lords ruled that the shareholders' resolutions were inconsistent with the articles which conferred general powers of management on the directors to the exclusion of the members.

■ 3.10 Delegation to committees and executive directors

Articles usually allow boards to delegate their powers. If no such provision is made, no such delegation is allowed.

The power to delegate to a committee cannot be used for an improper purpose, e.g. to exclude one or more of the directors from the forum where the board's decisions are taken (*Pullbrook v. Richmond Consolidated Mining Co.* (1878) 9 Ch.D. 610).

Regulation 72 of Table A is typical of the sort of provision one would expect to find on delegation in a company's articles. It provides:

> **72.** The directors may delegate any of their powers to any committee consisting of one or more directors. They may also delegate to any managing director or any director holding any other executive office such of their powers as they consider desirable to be exercised by him. Any such delegation may be made subject to any conditions the directors may impose, and either collaterally with or to the exclusion of their own powers and may be revoked or altered. Subject to any such conditions, the proceedings of a committee with two or more members shall be governed by the articles regulating the proceedings of directors so far as they are capable of applying.

The model articles probably provide a better and wider formula (pcls, clg and plc 5):

> 5(1) Subject to the articles, the directors may delegate any of the powers which are conferred on them under the articles—
> (a) to such person or committee;
> (b) by such means (including by power of attorney);

> (c) to such an extent;
> (d) in relation to such matters or territories; and
> (e) on such terms and conditions;
> as they think fit.
>
> (2) If the directors so specify, any such delegation may authorise further delegation of the directors' powers by any person to whom they are delegated.
>
> (3) The directors may revoke any delegation in whole or part, or alter its terms and conditions.

This formula improves on reg. 72 of Table A because it enables the directors to delegate their powers to anyone (not just to an executive director) and specifically allows for sub-delegation. It also combines in one provision the power given to the directors in reg. 71 of Table A to appoint agents, whether by power of attorney or otherwise.

3.10.1 Revocation and amendment of delegated authority

The board may at any time revoke a previous decision to delegate its powers (*Huth v. Clarke* (1890) 25 Q.B.D. 391). It follows that it must also be able to amend the extent of any delegation as it could achieve the same result by revoking the original powers and then delegating new powers. It is, of course, unnecessary to go through this convoluted procedure and a board resolution amending the delegated authority will suffice. Regulation 72 of Table A and art. 5 of the model articles specifically state that any delegation by the board may be revoked or altered. However, this will be the case unless the articles specify otherwise.

3.10.2 Exclusive authority

In *Huth v. Clarke* it was also held that the body which delegates the powers retains the authority to exercise them itself. Thus, unless the articles provide otherwise, the board retains collateral power to act even though it has delegated those powers to a committee or person. Regulation 72 of Table A states that the directors may delegate their powers either collaterally or to the exclusion of their own powers. However, it also provides that the directors may revoke any delegated powers. Accordingly, even if it has delegated to a committee to the exclusion of its own powers, it could revoke that authority and act itself. It is doubtful whether the courts would intervene even if the board failed to revoke the delegated authority before acting itself if it was clear that the board would have done so if it had known that this was necessary. In practice, therefore, in order to grant exclusive authority the articles must allow the directors to delegate their powers irrevocably.

3.10.3 Sub-delegation

Committees and executive directors cannot sub-delegate their powers unless authorised to do so by the board (*Cook v. Ward* (1877) 2 C.P.D. 255). This does not mean that a committee may not ask one or more of its members to make recommendations to a future meeting of the committee as long as the committee takes the final decision.

It is not particularly clear whether the articles need to make specific provision authorising sub-delegation. Listed companies began to make specific provision in this regard following the *Guinness* case (see below), presumably to clarify the position and to avoid any possibility of an adverse ruling. The model articles also make specific provision for sub-delegation, but only if the directors so specify.

Regulation 72 of Table A makes no specific provision for sub-delegation. However, companies have survived for hundreds of years without making specific provision in their articles in this regard. Although it is rare for board committees to sub-delegate, it is obvious that the managing director or chief executive of a large company must sub-delegate to other managers and employees of the company. Where no specific provision is made in the articles to allow sub-delegation, it is tempting to assume that it is something that the directors have power to determine as part of their general authority to delegate. Even if this is not the case, the apparent lack of sub-delegated authority may be of little consequence because of general agency principles, the indoor management rule and the possibility that the person exercising the powers may be deemed to be authorised to do so under articles such as reg. 71 of Table A. One of the circumstances in which these principles might not necessarily apply is where the act complained of involves a possible breach of directors' duties, as was the situation in the *Guinness* case.

3.10.4 Restrictions on power to delegate

Although articles usually state that the directors may delegate 'any of their powers', this may not include special powers given to the directors by the articles (e.g. the power to fix the remuneration of directors). This is a difficult area and the answer will depend on the construction of the articles in each case. What is beyond doubt is that the general power to delegate will, unless otherwise stated, cover the powers given to the directors under the general management clause.

In *Guinness plc v. Saunders* [1990] 1 All E.R. 652, the House of Lords held that an article giving the board of Guinness general power to delegate to committees did not authorise them to delegate a special power conferred by another article authorising the board to fix the special remuneration of a director serving on a committee. It reached this decision despite the fact 'the Board' was defined elsewhere in the articles as being: 'The Directors for the time being (or a quorum of such Directors assembled at a meeting of Directors duly convened) or any Committee authorised by the Board to act on its behalf.' Lord Templeman, who gave the main judgment, said: 'It cannot have been intended that any committee should be able to grant special remuneration to *any* director who serves on *any* committee.'

This decision arose from a dispute between Guinness plc and one of its former non-executive directors, Mr Ward, who had been paid £5.2m for services rendered to Guinness during its successful bid for Distillers. The payment had not been authorised by the board but by two out of the three members of the committee established by the board (of which Mr Ward was a member) with full power and authority to settle the terms of the offer, to approve any revisions of the offer and to authorise and approve, execute and do all such documents deeds, acts and things as they may consider necessary or desirable in connection with the making or implementation of the offer.

There can be no doubt that the House of Lords bent over backwards to ensure that Mr Ward accounted to Guinness for the money he had received and it may be that the effect of the judgment is only relevant to directors' remuneration. Directors are treated as fiduciaries under the common law and cannot claim remuneration unless the articles expressly provide for payment. The ability of the board to fix directors' remuneration is therefore dependent upon the existence of a special power contained in the articles. It seems from the *Guinness* case that this power cannot be delegated unless the articles make it absolutely clear that this is in fact intended.

However, it is possible that the *Guinness* case will have wider ramifications. Most articles include provisions giving the directors special powers in addition to the powers conferred by the general management clause; these special powers are expressed as being given to the directors collectively.

Following the decision in the *Guinness* case, some companies adopted articles along the following lines to clarify that the general power to delegate is not intended to be limited by anything in the articles which requires powers to be exercised by the board.

> The power to delegate contained in this Article shall be effective in relation to the powers, duties and discretions of the Board generally whether or not express reference is made in these Articles to powers, duties or discretions being exercised by the Board or by a committee authorised by the Board.

The model articles allow the directors to delegate 'any of the powers which are conferred on them under the articles' (art. 5). This would appear to allow them to delegate any special powers given to them under the articles.

■ 3.11 Appointment of other agents

Articles usually give the directors specific power to appoint other agents. This subject is dealt with in art. 5 of the model articles together with the general rules on delegation. However under Table A, it is dealt with separately by reg. 71:

> **71.** The directors may, by power of attorney or otherwise, appoint any person to be the agent of the company for such purposes and on such conditions as they determine, including authority for the agent to delegate all or any of his powers.

It is noteworthy that reg. 71 specifically states that the board may authorise an agent to delegate all or any of his powers.

■ 3.12 Schedule of matters reserved to the board

When boards delegate their powers they need to ensure that the proposed terms of delegation do not include matters upon which they would still expect to decide. Although this sounds obvious, it is not particularly easy to achieve. Executive directors normally need to be given wide powers for operational reasons, including the power to authorise company expenditure up to a relatively high amount. However, the board might want to have the final say on matters not in the ordinary course of business and capital expenditure above a much lower amount. Although it is possible to include these sort of exceptions in the terms of any delegated authority, it is also considered to be good practice for the board to adopt a schedule of matters reserved for its own decision, particularly where it has delegated different powers to a variety of executives and board committees.

Such a schedule will define the matters for which board approval is required. To this extent, it will define the residual role of the board, which can be a useful exercise in itself, particularly where the board includes non-executive directors. However, such a schedule can also be applied as an overriding exception or limit to the delegated authority of any individual or board committee. Indeed, it can also be applied as a limit to the authority of everyone else in the company, including those who derive their powers through a process of sub-delegation, typically through the chief executive. Obviously, the schedule needs to be made available internally for this to work properly.

Adopting a schedule of matters reserved for the board can make the process of delegation easier because it reduces the need to include detailed exceptions in the terms of any delegated authority. It makes it easier for everyone in the company to determine whether something needs board approval, and makes it easier for the board to modify the matters reserved for its own decision. Instead of modifying the delegated authority of each individual or committee, it merely has to modify the list of exceptions in the schedule.

Not surprisingly, the UK Corporate Governance Code recommends that boards of listed companies should adopt a formal schedule of matters specifically reserved to them for their collective decision (Code provision A.1.1). Although the Code does not require listed companies to publish the schedule, it requires them to include in the annual report a statement of how the board operates, which must include 'a high level statement of which types of decisions are to be taken by the board and which are to be delegated to management'.

The Cadbury Committee, upon whose initial recommendation the current code provision regarding matters reserved for the board was adopted, suggested that any such schedule should, as a minimum, cover:

- the acquisition and disposal of assets of the company or its subsidiaries that are material to the company;
- investments;
- capital projects;
- authority levels;
- treasury policies; and
- risk management policies (Cadbury Report, para. 4.24).

Naturally, listed companies will also need to bear in mind other aspects of the UK Corporate Governance Code when drafting such a schedule, including supporting principle A1 which states:

> The board's role is to provide entrepreneurial leadership of the company within a framework of prudent and effective controls which enables risk to be assessed and managed. The board should set the company's strategic aims, ensure that the necessary financial and human resources are in place for the company to meet its objectives and review management performance. The board should set the company's values and standards and ensure that its obligations to its shareholders and others are understood and met.

ICSA publishes an excellent guidance note on matters reserved for the board (*ICSA Guidance on Matters Reserved for the Board*, October 2007), which includes a model schedule intended to serve as a starting point for boards of directors wishing to adopt one.

3.12.1 Dealing with urgent business

The ICSA guidance recommends that in drawing up a schedule of matters reserved for the board, companies should also establish procedures for dealing with matters which need to be dealt with urgently between regular board meetings. It recommends that these procedures should balance the need for urgency with the overriding principle that each director should be given as much information as possible, the time to consider it properly and an opportunity to discuss the matter prior to the commitment of the company. This is an important discipline because boards rarely meet more than once a month and urgent matters can arise with alarming frequency. There is not much point in having a schedule of matters reserved to the board if the board is constantly being asked to ratify things that have already happened. If the board wants to have the last word on the matters included in the schedule, it may need to meet more frequently and be prepared to hold ad hoc meetings to deal with urgent matters. It will not always be necessary or appropriate to hold an emergency board meeting. This would usually be reserved for matters of the utmost importance, such as the launch by another company of a takeover bid. Other arrangements can be adopted to deal with less important (but no less urgent) matters. These procedures could include some sort of informal consultation process conducted by e-mail or telephone, or a written resolution procedure. If the matter is considered to be routine, and discussion is not thought to be necessary, one could question why it has been included as a matter reserved for the board in the first place, and whether it might not be better in the future to delegate such matters to a committee or individual.

The purpose of any informal consultation process will normally be to establish whether there is any substantial opposition to the proposal. Where this proves to be the case, it may be necessary to consider holding a formal board meeting. It is important to remember in this regard that, under most articles, any director can call a board meeting and that an informal consultation process will not normally constitute a valid board decision. In most cases, directors who oppose a proposal will not insist on a board meeting being held where it is clear that they are in the minority. However, they may take some convincing that they are in a minority, may genuinely believe that they can persuade the other directors of the merits of their case and may sometimes insist on a board meeting merely as a delaying tactic.

Generally speaking, it will be the chairman who is expected to decide, within any guidelines set by the board, what procedures should be followed in cases where an urgent decision is required, and what action to take where a proposal proves to be controversial.

When making urgent decisions, special care should be taken to ensure that the directors have made any necessary declarations of interest before the company enters into the relevant transaction or arrangement. It will not normally be possible for the directors to make any new declarations using the general notice procedure as there will not normally be another board meeting before the company enters into the transaction. Accordingly, directors will need to declare any new and relevant interests in accordance with the written notice procedures provided for in s. 184. The interests of the directors need to be borne in mind for the purposes of determining whether the board is capable of making a decision on the urgent business and whether there is, in fact, a valid majority in favour of the proposal.

If the method by which any urgent decision was reached does not constitute a valid decision-making process under the articles, the board should probably ratify the decision at its next meeting. If the decision was approved using a valid decision-making process, it should still be recorded, possibly by being noted in the minutes of the next board meeting, or if it was passed under some sort of written resolution procedure, in the usual manner adopted for such resolutions.

4

Board meetings

4.1 Summary

Most matters concerning proceedings at meetings of directors are determined by the articles and, in default, by reference to the common law. Although companies have considerable freedom to establish their own internal board procedures, most have historically adopted articles based on Table A. This is largely because its provisions have been tried and tested over many years and provide a solid foundation upon which new adaptations and procedures can be added. Although Table A will continue to be important for many companies, the focus in future will be on the new model articles prescribed for companies formed on or after 1 October 2009 under the Companies Act 2006. The following paragraphs focus on the provisions of the model articles and Table A and highlight areas where modifications are commonly made, particularly to Table A.

4.2 Collective exercise of powers

As a general rule, the directors must exercise their powers collectively, i.e. at a properly convened and constituted meeting of the board of directors, unless:

- the articles allow them to delegate their powers, e.g. to a committee (see **3.10**);
- the articles allow them to make decisions in some other way, e.g. by written resolution (see **6.2**);
- the directors all agree, in which case they may act informally (see **6.3**).

Where the directors are required to act collectively as a board, unanimity is not required. Under the common law, decisions may validly be made by a majority of the directors present at board meetings, provided that there are sufficient directors to form a quorum. Under the common law, a quorum exists where a majority of the directors are present at the meeting. Thus, if there are nine directors, five must be present to form a quorum. If five attend a meeting only three of them (i.e. one-third of the directors in total) need vote in favour of a proposal to bind the company. If seven attend, four must vote in favour, and so on. The common law principle that a majority of the directors present may bind the company is usually adopted in articles. However, articles usually specify a different quorum for meetings of directors and frequently allow the directors to alter that quorum (see **4.8**).

▪ 4.3 Who may call a meeting of directors?

Articles usually provide that any director may call a meeting of directors and that the secretary at the request of a director shall do so (e.g. pcls 9 and reg. 88 of Table A). Accordingly a director can normally call a meeting by giving due notice of it to the other directors or by authorising or instructing the secretary (if any) to give notice of it.

In practice, it is usual for boards of directors to fix the dates of meetings in advance so that the directors can plan their diaries. However, there may be occasions when an additional meeting is needed to deal with urgent business. Any additional meetings are usually called by the chairman and any director wishing to call a meeting would normally be expected to consult the chairman first. This ensures that the chairman is kept fully informed of the circumstances and may enable an alternative solution to be found, such as the use of a written resolution. If approached by a director, the secretary should seek to persuade the director to follow this course of action. Although the secretary cannot refuse to call a meeting if instructed to do so by a director, it is advisable to inform the chairman at the earliest opportunity of the situation if the director decides not to follow this advice.

▪ 4.4 Date, time and place

Generally, the directors can hold their meetings wherever they wish, including overseas. However, if the court is satisfied that a particular venue was chosen to ensure that certain directors are unable to attend, it may prevent the meeting from taking place or declare the proceedings invalid (*Martin v. Walker* (1918) 145 L.T.J. 377).

The person calling the meeting should specify the date, time and place at which it is to be held as this information must be given in the notice of the meeting. If a director instructs the company secretary to call a meeting, he or she may specify these matters or leave them to be settled by the secretary, perhaps after contacting the other directors to find the most suitable time and place.

Boards often meet at some regular date, time and place that most of the directors find convenient, e.g. on the second Thursday of each month at the company's registered office. They sometimes go so far as to include this in the board's internal procedures or standing orders. It would be very unusual for such a provision to find its way into a company's articles and almost certainly ill-advised.

▪ 4.5 Notice

The Act makes no provision with regard to notice of directors' meetings. Under the common law, reasonable notice of a meeting must be given to all the directors, although it may not always be necessary to give notice of the business. If proper notice is not given, the meeting and any business transacted at it is liable to be declared invalid. Although articles can modify the basic common law principles, they very rarely do so to any significant extent.

The courts are often reluctant to intervene in disputes regarding the adequacy of the notice given for meetings of directors, particularly where it is evident that a clear majority of the directors were in favour of the business conducted and that, if the meeting was declared invalid, they would simply go back to the office and make exactly the same decision again, albeit by following proper procedures. In addition, those who wish to complain about the adequacy of notice are expected to take prompt action otherwise the courts may rule that they are deemed to have acquiesced to the irregularity.

4.5.1 To whom notice must be given

As a general rule, notice must be given to all the directors. However, notice need not be given where:

- it can have no effect;
- all the directors agree to waive it; and
- the articles specifically provide that it need not be given.

With regard to the first heading, Lord Sterndale MR suggested in *Young v. Imperial Ladies Club Ltd*. [1920] 2 K.B. 523 (at p. 528) that notice may not be necessary if, for example, a director is so seriously ill that he would be unable to attend. It was held in that case that notice must be given to any director who would be able to travel back in time for the meeting. In the days before air travel, this would have excluded any director in the United States. However, the rule is unlikely to be of assistance today except in the most extreme circumstances.

Regulation 88 of Table A provides that a director who is absent from the United Kingdom is not entitled to receive notice of directors' meetings. The United Kingdom means England, Wales, Scotland or Northern Ireland. This rule is considered by many to be archaic in these days of modern communication and travel and is often modified, deleted or ignored, particularly where some of the directors live outside the UK. None of the model articles prescribed under the 2006 Act make similar provision.

Where articles make provision for the appointment of alternate directors, they usually make provision requiring notice of meetings to be given to any alternates in respect of any meeting which the person who appointed them would be entitled to attend (e.g. plc 26 and reg. 66 of Table A). Even if the articles make no such provision, alternate directors are probably entitled to receive notice of such meetings under common law principles.

Notice need not be given where the directors have agreed among themselves (or the articles prescribe) that meetings shall be held on a regular basis at a fixed time and place, e.g. on the first Thursday each month at 4 pm at the company's registered office. In such circumstances, notice would, however, need to be given for any meeting held at a different time or place.

4.5.2 Waiver of notice

Unless the articles provide otherwise, directors cannot waive in advance their right to receive notice of a meeting (*Re Portuguese Consolidated Copper Mines Ltd.* (1889) 42 Ch.D. 160). Table A makes no such provision and, subject to any other qualifications, notice must be given to all the directors even though some may have indicated in advance that they are unable or unwilling to attend. All three versions of the model articles make specific provision to allow directors to waive notice (pcls 9(4), clg 9(4) and plc 9(4)) by providing that:

> Notice of a directors' meeting need not be given to directors who waive their entitlement to notice of that meeting, by giving notice to that effect to the company not more than 7 days after the date on which the meeting is held. Where such notice is given after the meeting has been held, that does not affect the validity of the meeting, or of any business conducted at it.

Notice can be waived if all the directors are present and agree to hold a board meeting without notice. In *Smith v. Paringa Mines Ltd.* [1906] 2 Ch. 193, the two directors of a company met in the offices of one of them. The director who was the chairman proposed the appointment of a third director. Despite the objection of the other director to this appointment, the chairman declared the resolution carried by his casting vote. The appointment was held to be valid as they were both deemed to have agreed to treat their meeting as a board meeting. In *Barron v. Potter* [1914] 1 Ch. 895, a similar chance meeting between the directors of a company was held to be invalid as a board meeting as the director who proposed and purported to pass (by virtue of his casting vote) resolutions appointing new directors knew that the other director did not wish to attend any board meeting with him.

4.5.3 Length of notice

There is no strict rule as to the length of notice required for meetings of directors although there is an underlying assumption that it must be reasonable in the circumstances (*Browne v. La Trinidad* (1887) 37 Ch.D. 1). It is impossible to state conclusively the circumstances in which the notice given might be deemed unreasonable. It is fairly safe to assume that reasonable notice was given if none of the directors object or they all attend the meeting but, it does not necessarily follow that the notice given was unreasonable merely because a director objects. If a director does object to the notice given, the other directors should consider their position very carefully, taking into account all the other relevant factors. These might include:

(a) the length of notice usually given for similar meetings in that company; and
(b) the nature and urgency of the business to be transacted.

It goes without saying that the courts are more likely to intervene if it can be inferred that the purpose of calling the meeting at relatively short notice was to exclude a particular director from the decision-making process. A director should register his or her objection to the length of notice given immediately and should commence legal proceedings as soon as possible, otherwise the courts may refuse to intervene. In *Browne v. La Trinidad* the court accepted that the notice given to Mr Browne was unreasonable (less than ten minutes before the start of a board meeting at which it was decided to call an EGM to propose a resolution to remove him as a director). However, it refused to intervene, partly because he did not object at the time and only commenced proceedings shortly before the EGM was due to be held.

4.5.4 Content of notice

As a minimum, the notice must include the date, time and place of the meeting (see **Precedent 4.5**). It need not necessarily state the nature of the business to be transacted (*La Compagnie de Mayville v. Whitley* [1896] 1 Ch. 788). However, where notice of the business is given, it must not be deliberately misleading. In *Re Homer District Consolidated Gold Mines, ex parte Smith* (1888) 39 Ch.D. 546, a board meeting was called at very short notice and a resolution was passed to rescind a decision made at a meeting held only two weeks previously. The notice of the meeting was held to be invalid for a number of reasons, one of which was that it was misleading in so far as it did not mention this item of business.

In practice, detailed notice of the business of board meetings and board committees is usually given in the agenda papers circulated prior to the meeting (see **4.6**).

4.5.5 Form of notice

Articles often specify the manner in which notices required under the articles must be given. However, they usually state that these rules do not apply to meetings of directors. For example, reg. 111 of Table A (as amended on 20 December 2000) provides that notices may be given using electronic communications or, if that is not possible, in writing. However, it specifically states that these rules shall not apply to meetings of directors. For companies subject to the pre-December 2000 version of Table A, reg. 111 states that notices of directors' meetings 'need not be given in writing'. In both cases, the net result is that Table A does not actually specify the manner in which notices of meetings of directors should be served.

According to a case from 1887, in the absence of any specific provision in the articles, notice of a meeting of directors may be given either in writing or orally (*Browne v. La Trinidad* (1887) 37 Ch.D. 1). In 1887, the words 'in writing' meant in hard copy form. Today, one might expect the courts to adopt a more liberal approach which would admit the possibility of using electronic communications. However, common sense dictates that it will only be possible to rely on electronic communications where the director concerned has agreed to accept service in that manner.

The model articles prescribed under the 2006 Act basically follow the common sense approach that notice can be given using any method agreed by the director (see pcls 48, clg 34 and plc 79). They each provide:

(1) Subject to the articles, anything sent or supplied by or to the company under the articles may be sent or supplied in any way in which the Companies Act 2006 provides for documents or information which are authorised or required by any provision of that Act to be sent or supplied by or to the company.

(2) Subject to the articles, any notice or document to be sent or supplied to a director in connection with the taking of decisions by directors may also be sent or supplied by the means by which that director has asked to be sent or supplied with such notices or documents for the time being.

(3) A director may agree with the company that notices or documents sent to that director in a particular way are to be deemed to have been received within a specified time of their being sent, and for the specified time to be less than 48 hours.

In each case, sub-article (1) suggests that documents or information sent by or to the company *under the articles* can be sent in any manner provided for by the 2006 Act (i.e. under company communications provisions). This is useful because the company communications provisions of the Act only apply automatically to documents or information required or authorised to be sent under the Act. Without such an article they would not necessarily extend to documents or information required or authorised to be sent under the articles alone.

It is doubtful whether a notice of a directors' meetings is a document that is required or authorised to be sent by a company under the Act. There is no doubt whatsoever that such a notice is something that is required or authorised to be sent under the model articles (see pcls 9, clg 9 and plc 8). However, it is not necessarily something that is required or authorised to be sent by the company. The model articles provide that any director may call a directors' meeting by giving notice of the meeting to the other directors or by authorising the company secretary (if any) to give such notice. In other words, it is the director who wants to call the meeting who has to give notice of it. One could, of course, argue that the director who calls the meeting is acting on behalf of the company, and that the company communications provisions therefore apply to such notices by virtue of sub-article (1). If so, this would mean that notices of directors meetings can be sent in any form permitted by Sch. 5 of the Act, which sets out the rules for communications by a company. Under those rules, hard copy is the default method of communication. However, electronic, website and other methods of communication can be used if the intended recipient (i.e. a director) has agreed to accept service in that manner (see **2.5**).

The 2006 model articles do not appear to require notices of directors' meetings to be sent in accordance with the company communications provisions in

Sch. 5 of the Act. In all three versions of the model articles, sub-article (2) provides that any notice or document to be sent or supplied to a director in connection with the taking of decisions by directors *may also* be sent or supplied by the means by which that director has asked to be sent or supplied with such notices or documents for the time being. The words 'may also' in sub-article (2) seem to confirm that sub-article (1) is meant to apply to notices of directors' meetings, in which case it may seem somewhat superfluous to say that they can be sent in some other way because the company communications provisions allow documents or information to be sent by a company in any manner provided the recipient has agreed to accept service in that manner. However, sub-article (2) is not superfluous in so far as it relates to things that may, in practice, need to be sent to the directors in connection with a meeting (e.g. the agenda papers) that are not required to be sent *under the articles*. The model articles require notice of a directors' meeting to be given and state that the notice must notice must specify the date, time and place of the meeting and how the directors may participate in it. The model articles do not require notice of the business to be given or agenda papers to be sent out.

The use of the words 'director has asked' in sub-article (2) implies that a director must have agreed beforehand to the method of communication used. The fact that a director has asked the company to send notices and other documents in a particular way does not necessarily preclude the company from sending them in some other way, provided that the method it uses is effective under any applicable rules. For example, the fact that a director has asked for documents to be sent by e-mail would not necessarily preclude the company from providing them in hard copy form. The fact that a director has provided an address to which such hard copy documents should be sent would not necessarily preclude the company from sending them to the address recorded in the Register of Directors as his service address, if that was different. Under the company communications provisions, the address shown in the Register of Directors (i.e. the directors' service address) is the default address to be used for the service of hard copy communications on a director. The company can also use another address provided by the director for that purpose, but the company communications provisions do not seem to require it to do so (Sch. 5, para. 4(1)).

It is easy to imagine situations in which the court might, if asked, rule otherwise in this regard, particularly where the manner in which notice was given was deliberately chosen to ensure that the director did not, in practice, receive it in time. This could easily happen where a director has provided the company's registered office as his service address but has asked for notices and board agenda papers to be sent to his home address. Unless he regularly attends the registered office and opens his mail, he will not necessarily be aware of the fact that a notice has been sent to him via the registered office. Naturally, directors are meant to make arrangements to ensure that documents served on them at their service address are brought to their attention. If a director nominates the company's registered office as his service address, the assumption must presumably be that somebody from the company will do this. If nobody from the company bothers to do so, or somebody decides deliberately not to do so, in respect of a notice of meeting (which could be viewed as being sent by or on behalf of the company), it would seem to be unfair for the company to be able to claim that the notice had been validly served.

Following this line of reasoning, it would seem to be advisable for a company to use the method of communications that a director has asked it to use, and to notify him using that method if anything has been sent using a different method.

4.5.6 Deemed delivery

Section 1147 provides that documents and information sent by post or electronically are deemed to have been received after 48 hours. In calculating the period of hours for these purposes, no account may be taken of any part of a day that is not a working day (see **2.3**). However, the application of these default rules can be modified in relation to documents or information sent by a company to a person otherwise than in his capacity as a member or debenture holder, by any contrary provision in an agreement between the company and that person (s. 1147(6)(c)).

The deemed delivery rules in s. 1147 form part of the company communications provisions of the Act. Accordingly they only apply for the purposes of any provision of the Companies Acts which requires or authorises documents or information to be sent or supplied by a company (s. 1143). They do not apply to notices, agenda papers or documents sent to directors unless those things are required or authorised to be sent under the Companies Acts. Section 169 provides a good example of a notice that is required under the Act to be sent by a company to a director. It requires the company to notify a director of the fact that someone intends to propose a resolution at a general meeting to remove them as a director. The Act makes no provision whatsoever with regard to the notice that needs to be given for a meeting of directors. This is an area that is governed by a company's articles and the common law. Accordingly, the company communications provisions of the Act do not apply unless the articles say otherwise.

As we have already seen, all three versions of the model articles (see sub-article (1) of pcls 48, clg 34 and plc 79) do seem to apply the company communications provisions of the Act to anything that is required under the articles to be sent to a director, and that this does include notices of meetings (see pcls 9, clg 9 and plc 8), but not necessarily the agenda papers. Where the company communications provisions are deemed to apply (e.g. for documents such as notices), this means that the rules in s. 1147 regarding deemed delivery apply. As we have already seen, the application of the default rules in s. 1147 can be varied with the agreement of the director (see s. 1147(6)(c)). However, the model articles also provide (see sub-article (3) of pcls 48, clg 34 and plc 79) that a director may agree with the company that notices or documents sent to him in a particular way are to be deemed to have been received within a specified time of their being sent, and for the specified time to be less than 48 hours. This is consistent with the rules in s. 1147, but also enables the company to reach agreement regarding the delivery of documents that are not subject to the rules in s. 1147.

Any company whose articles make different provision from the statutory rules on deemed delivery in s. 1147 (e.g. by making provision for deemed service after 24 hours for documents sent by first class post) may no longer be able to apply those rules to documents required or authorised to be sent to directors under the Companies Acts because the default rules in s. 1147 (where they apply) can only be varied with the agreement of the director concerned. Such articles will still be effective in relation to any document or information that has to be sent to the directors under the articles if it is not required or authorised to be sent under the Act. Fortunately, this does not present a major problem for companies that are subject to the 1985 Table A, because it makes the same provision as the Act regarding deemed delivery by post and (for companies incorporated on or after 22 December 2000) for deemed delivery by electronic communications (see reg. 115 of Table A). For companies incorporated prior to 22 December 2000, Table A made no provision for electronic delivery, so the provisions of the Act apply in default.

4.5.7 Practical issues

It is common practice to schedule regular board and board committee meetings for the forthcoming year. This allows the directors to organise their diaries so that they are able to attend meetings. The schedule is normally appended to or included in the minutes of a board meeting. This satisfies the common law requirements as to notice provided that a copy is sent to each director and it shows the date, time and place of each meeting (see, however, the additional requirement in the model articles that the notice should specify how directors may participate in the meeting (if at all) without being present at the place where it is to take place). It is not strictly necessary to give every piece of information at the same time. However, each of the necessary components must be given within reasonable time before the meeting. It is also normal for a copy of the agenda for the meeting to be circulated to each director prior to the meeting. As this would normally specify the date, time and place of the meeting and any other necessary details, it will also serve as notice of the meeting provided that it is sent out early enough to comply with the requirement that notice must be reasonable in the circumstances.

For small companies with relatively few directors, it may not be necessary or possible to plan so far ahead. Meetings may simply be called on an ad hoc basis at relatively short notice. Even in large public companies it is sometimes necessary to hold additional board meetings to deal with matters which cannot wait until the next scheduled meeting. In such circumstances, it is a good practice for the chairman or the secretary to contact each director in order to explain the circumstances and to offer a range of possible dates for the meeting, making it clear that the one on which the most are able to attend will be chosen. Once this has been done, each director should be notified in the usual manner.

■ 4.6 The agenda

The agenda is an ordered list of the business to be transacted at a meeting. Although it is not strictly necessary to give notice of the business to be transacted at meetings of directors, it is normal for an agenda to be prepared and sent to each director prior to the meeting, together with any supporting papers that may be necessary to facilitate discussion of that business. If an agenda is sent to the directors prior to the meeting, it will constitute notice of the business and, as such, the rule that it must not be deliberately misleading will apply.

If the notice of meeting includes notice of the business to be transacted, that part of the notice can be referred to as the agenda (see **Precedents 4.6A–C**).

Items of business on the agenda are usually placed in the order that the business is to be taken at the meeting, although the board is not bound to take them in that order (*Re Cawley & Co.* (1889) 42 Ch.D. 209).

4.6.1 Any other business

In view of the fact that it is not necessary to give notice of the business to be transacted at board meetings, it would seem to be perfectly in order for business not included in the notice or the agenda to be raised under the heading 'any other business'. Two qualifications must be made to this principle. The first is that, in accordance with the ruling in *Homer*, the notice may be deemed to be invalid if the item is omitted so as to mislead members of the board that it will not be raised. The second is that it is unreasonable to expect the directors to make reasoned decisions if they are not given sufficient time to consider the merits of a proposal or the opportunity to consider any alternative proposals. Some chairmen refuse as a matter of principle to put matters raised under 'any other business' to a vote until the following meeting. In practice, however, it may sometimes be necessary to do so, e.g. where the matter is urgent and must be dealt with before the next meeting. This is unlikely to present a problem if the matter is uncontroversial and all the directors are happy for the business to be dealt with in this manner. It is obviously more risky if any of the directors object at the meeting or if the chairman is aware that the proposal is controversial and would probably have been opposed by directors who are not present. Allowing the business to be dealt with in these circumstances could be risky because the absent directors might seek to reverse the decision at the next meeting or via legal proceedings. Accordingly, the chairman should consider whether there might be a better way of dealing with the business. If the matter is urgent, this could include the possibility of holding another unscheduled board meeting or dealing with the business as a written resolution. If the matter is not urgent, it will nearly always be better to postpone any decision until the next scheduled meeting.

4.6.2 Practical issues with respect to the agenda

It is normal for the agenda to refer only briefly to the nature of the business to be transacted. For most items, the agenda will make some reference to supporting papers which contain the detailed proposals. If the business can be described accurately and briefly, the substance of the resolution to be put at the meeting may be included in the agenda. Even then, however, there may be some supporting papers and, if so, the agenda should include some reference to them. The overall objective when preparing the agenda should be to keep it as short as possible. This enables the directors to assess the business of the meeting at a glance.

Where supporting papers are required, they should be clearly identified, numbered and placed in the order in which they appear on the agenda. This task normally falls to the secretary, who should ensure that all reports and papers have been submitted and are listed in the proper form on the agenda.

The agenda and supporting papers should be sent in good time before the meeting so that the directors have sufficient time to read them. Many directors will not do this until the very last minute no matter when they receive the board papers. Nevertheless, they tend to forget this if the board papers are late and will not normally hesitate to complain. Most companies aim to get the agenda papers for board meetings out or in the hands of the directors about a week before the meeting, although the bottom line for company secretaries will often be to ensure that the papers arrive so that they are in the hands of the directors over the weekend prior to the meeting.

Many companies now send out the agenda and the agenda papers in electronic form (e.g. as a pdf file) or use software products like ICSA Software's *Boardpad*. It is not normally a good idea to rely on directors who prefer paper to print out and compile their own copy of the agenda papers from the electronic version. Whether a paper or electronic copy is produced, the agenda should be easy to navigate.

The UK Corporate Governance Code recommends as a principle that the board should be supplied in a timely manner with information in a form and of a quality appropriate to enable it to discharge its duties (Code principle B.5). The Code allocates primary responsibility for ensuring that this is done to the chairman and suggests that, although 'management' has an obligation to provide accurate, timely and clear information, directors should seek clarification or amplification where necessary (supporting principle B.5).

The company secretary will clearly have a major role to play in ensuring that this principle is applied in practice, and the Code recognises this by stating that the company secretary's responsibilities include ensuring good information flows within the board and its committees and between senior management and non-executive directors (supporting principle B.5).

The FRC's *Guidance on Board Effectiveness* recommends that the company secretary should ensure the presentation of high-quality information to the board and its committees. It suggests that non-executive directors should insist on receiving high-quality information sufficiently in advance so that there can be thorough consideration of the issues prior to, and informed debate and challenge at, board meetings. It defines high-quality information as that which is appropriate for making decisions on the issue at hand. And it suggests that the information should be accurate, clear, comprehensive, up to date and timely; contain a summary of the contents of any paper; and inform the director of what is expected of him on that issue.

4.7 Chairman

In theory, the duties of the chairman at a meeting of directors are largely the same as those of the chairman of a general meeting (see **Chapter 20**). However, meetings of directors are usually a lot less formal than general meetings. Decisions are often reached on a consensual basis and the chairman is less likely to be called upon to exercise formal control over the proceedings. At general meetings, the chairman does not usually owe his position to the members but to his office as chairman of the board. In contrast, the chairman of the board is invariably elected by the board members and can be removed by them. Unless the chairman is a majority shareholder, his position as the chairman of the board (and therefore chairman of the meeting) may therefore be more tenuous. Accordingly, at meetings of directors the chairman tends to act more as facilitator or arbiter, as opposed to an autocrat or judge.

4.7.1 Role and duties

The common law duties of the chairman, as expressed by Chitty J in *National Dwelling Society Ltd. v. Sykes* [1894] 3 Ch. 159, are also applicable to meetings of directors. It is therefore the duty of the chairman to ensure that:

(a) the meeting is properly conducted;
(b) all directors are given a fair opportunity to contribute to the deliberations;
(c) the sense of the meeting is properly ascertained and recorded; and
(d) order is preserved.

The chairman's authority is derived from the body which made the appointment. In other words, by electing a chairman, the directors are deemed to have conferred upon him all the powers necessary to fulfil the role. At general meetings, the chairman is deemed to have authority to rule on points of order and on other incidental questions that may arise during the meeting (*Re Indian Zoedone Co.* (1884) 26 Ch. D 70). This may also be the case at meetings of directors, although if challenged at the meeting, it may sometimes be prudent for the chairman to bend to the will of the majority, particularly where he owes his position to them. If called upon to make a ruling that may affect the outcome of a meeting of directors, the chairman plainly ought to try to make an impartial decision based on the facts. However, if he does not do so and his decision is challenged, there is no guarantee that the courts will intervene. The law takes a surprisingly pragmatic approach to procedural irregularities that occur in the decision-making process of directors. The courts invariably refuse to intervene where it is clear that if they did, the directors would merely make exactly the same decision again, albeit in accordance with proper procedures. It would be wrong to suggest that this means that a chairman who is, say, also a majority shareholder can ride completely roughshod over the views of the other directors. However, it probably does mean that the chairman can give due regard to the will of the majority. After all, if the chairman totally ignores this factor, it is likely that he is merely delaying the inevitable. In making his judgment, the chairman should consider whether or not any legal challenge to his decision would succeed.

Articles sometimes give the chairman power to determine certain matters himself. This is normally the case with regard to any question as to the right of a director to vote, where his ruling in relation to any director other than himself will normally be final and conclusive (see reg. 98 of Table A, pcls 14, clg 14 and plc 16). The chairman's role in this regard will be particularly important where the articles provide that a director who has a material interest in a transaction cannot vote on it. The chairman will often be called upon to decide whether a director's interest is material.

Articles also commonly give the chairman a casting vote at meetings of directors (see reg. 88 of Table A, pcls 13, clg 13 and plc 14). If they do not do so, he will not have a casting vote.

In the unlikely event that a meeting is disorderly, the chairman probably has inherent power to adjourn the meeting for the purposes of restoring order (*John v. Rees* [1969] 2 W.L.R. 1294). Otherwise the power to adjourn will rest with the meeting and the chairman should not adjourn or close the meeting without the consent of the meeting until all the business is transacted.

4.7.2 Governance role

Most articles allow any director to call a meeting. In practice, it will be the chairman who usually decides whether meetings are necessary and who settles the agenda. In doing so, he will take account of the views of other directors (particularly the chief executive) and the advice of the company secretary (particularly on formal items of business, but also on matters of governance).

The UK Corporate Governance Code makes a number of recommendations about the status of the chairman and his role within the corporate governance structure.

Principle A.2 of the Code states that there should be a clear division of responsibilities at the head of the company between the running of the board and the executive responsibility for the running of the company's business, and that no one individual should have unfettered powers of decision. The role of chairman and chief executive should not be exercised by the same individual (Code provision A.2.1).

According to the Code provision A.3, the chairman should be responsible:

(a) for leadership of the board and ensuring its effectiveness on all aspects of its role;
(b) for setting the board's agenda;
(c) for ensuring that adequate time is available for discussion of all items, in particular strategic issues;
(d) for promoting a culture of openness and debate by facilitating the effective contribution of non-executive directors in particular and ensuring constructive relations between executive and non-executive directors;
(e) for ensuring that the directors receive accurate, timely and clear information; and
(f) for ensuring effective communication with shareholders.

The *FRC's Guidance on Board Effectiveness* expands upon this by suggesting that the chairman's role includes:

(a) demonstrating ethical leadership;
(b) setting a board agenda which is primarily focused on strategy, performance, value creation and accountability, and ensuring that issues relevant to these areas are reserved for board decision;
(c) ensuring a timely flow of high-quality supporting information;
(d) making certain that the board determines the nature, and extent, of the significant risks the company is willing to embrace in the implementation of its strategy, and that there are no 'no go' areas which prevent directors from operating effective oversight in this area;
(e) regularly considering succession planning and the composition of the board;
(f) making certain that the board has effective decision-making processes and applies sufficient challenge to major proposals;
(g) ensuring the board's committees are properly structured with appropriate terms of reference;
(h) encouraging all board members to engage in board and committee meetings by drawing on their skills, experience, knowledge and, where appropriate, independence;
(i) fostering relationships founded on mutual respect and open communication – both in and outside the boardroom – between the non-executive directors and the executive team;
(j) developing productive working relationships with all executive directors, and the CEO in particular, providing support and advice while respecting executive responsibility;
(k) consulting the senior independent director on board matters in accordance with the Code;
(l) taking the lead on issues of director development, including through induction programmes for new directors and regular reviews with all directors;

(m) acting on the results of board evaluation;

(n) being aware of, and responding to, his or her own development needs, including people and other skills, especially when taking on the role for the first time; and

(o) ensuring effective communication with shareholders and other stakeholders and, in particular, that all directors are made aware of the views of those who provide the company's capital.

The FRC Guidance also points out that the chairman of each board committee should fulfil a leadership role similar to that of the chairman of the board, particularly in creating the conditions for overall committee and individual director effectiveness.

4.7.3 Appointment

Articles usually specify the method by which the chairman of the board of directors is to be appointed. For example, the model articles for private companies (pcls 12 and clg 12) provide:

12. Chairing of directors' meetings

(1) The directors may appoint a director to chair their meetings.

(2) The person so appointed for the time being is known as the chairman.

(3) The directors may terminate the chairman's appointment at any time.

(4) If the chairman is not participating in a directors' meeting within ten minutes of the time at which it was to start, the participating directors must appoint one of themselves to chair it.

The model articles for plcs make additional provision to allow the directors to appoint other directors as deputy or assistant chairmen to chair directors' meetings in the chairman's absence (plc 12). Regulation 91 of Table A makes similar provision in this regard.

The main objective of these provisions is to avoid the need to elect a chairman at each meeting of directors. A director appointed to the office of 'chairman' or 'chairman of the board of directors' has a right to chair any meeting of directors that he attends until removed from that office.

If, unusually, the articles make no provision with regard to the appointment of the chairman, the directors present at each meeting may elect one of their number to be the chairman of it.

If the office of chairman is unsalaried, a director is not deemed to have an interest in his or her appointment to that office and may therefore vote on a resolution to that effect (*Foster v. Foster* [1916] 1 Ch. 532). Where the office is salaried, a director will have a personal interest and may be prevented by the articles from voting on his or her own appointment. The same principles apply to any resolution to remove the chairman. A salaried chairman can therefore be removed more easily than an unsalaried chairman. Some articles specifically allow directors to be counted in the quorum at the meeting at which they are appointed to an office but not to vote, e.g. reg. 84(4) of the 1948 Act Table A.

The UK Corporate Governance Code recommends that, on appointment, the chairman should meet certain independence criteria and that the chief executive should not go on to be chairman of the same company (Code provision A.3.1). It also requires the chairman's other commitments to be disclosed to the board and included in the annual report (Code provision B.3.1).

4.7.4 Problems appointing a chairman

Under most articles, the person appointed as 'chairman' or 'chairman of the board of directors' is automatically entitled (until removed from office):

- to chair subsequent meetings of directors;
- to a casting vote at any meeting of directors which he chairs; and
- to chair general meetings of the company.

The ability of the chairman to exercise a casting vote at board meetings could easily tip the balance of power and it is not unusual for the directors to be unable to reach agreement on the appointment of a chairman for this reason. In these circumstances, the directors may prefer at each board meeting to elect one of their number as 'chairman of the meeting', leaving the office of 'chairman' or 'chairman of the board of directors' vacant, and the issue as to who is to chair general meetings to be determined on a case-by-case basis in accordance with the articles (see further **20.2**). Any person elected as the 'chairman of the meeting' would, however, still have a casting vote at a meeting of directors because articles usually confer that right on the 'chairman of the meeting' rather than on the 'chairman of the board of directors'.

Where the articles confer a casting vote on the chairman of the meeting in this manner, it is not uncommon for the directors to be unable to agree on the appointment of a chairman at all, particularly where there is an even number of directors who are equally divided in a power struggle. To avoid this problem, it may be advisable at the outset to remove the chairman's right to a casting vote by amending the articles.

In the event of complete deadlock, it may be possible for the directors to appoint someone as chairman of the meeting on the condition that they refrain from exercising the right to a casting vote, the assumption being that the person appointed will automatically be removed if he attempts to do so. It might, however, be safer to appoint no chairman at all or to invite someone who is not a director to chair or act as a facilitator at meetings.

4.7.5 No chairman

There would seem to be no logical reason why the board of directors should not be able to operate without a chairman. Most articles merely provide that the directors 'may' appoint one of their number to be chairman (e.g. reg. 91 of Table A, pcls 12, clg 12 and plc 12). This would seem to imply that they need not do so. The chairman is said to derive authority from the meeting. If no chairman is appointed, the meeting simply retains those powers itself. Matters which the chairman would normally be called upon to decide could be resolved by the meeting itself.

The board may also act without a chairman by way of written resolution in accordance with any provisions of the articles in that regard, or by a unanimous decision (preferably evidenced in writing) if the articles do not specifically provide for written resolutions.

4.7.6 Chairman not present

Articles commonly provide that if the chairman of the board is not present within a specified time after the scheduled start of the meeting, the directors may elect one of their number to chair the meeting. If the chairman of the board arrives after the directors have elected a person to chair the meeting, the person elected is under no obligation to vacate the chair, although it is normal practice to do so.

■ 4.8 Quorum

The quorum is the minimum number of directors who must be present and entitled to vote at a meeting of directors in order for it to transact business. A quorum must be present for each item of business considered and a director who is not entitled to vote (e.g. because he is interested in the transaction) cannot be counted in calculating whether a quorum exists for that item.

The quorum is normally fixed by the articles. If the articles are silent on the matter, the basic common law rule is that the quorum is a majority of the directors.

Articles normally give the directors limited powers to act where their number (i.e. the total number of directors in office and not merely the number present at the meeting) falls below the number fixed as the quorum.

4.8.1 Quorum fixed by or in accordance with the articles

■ Articles invariably specify the quorum for meetings of directors or a method of fixing one. For example, pcls 10, clg 10 and plc 10 all provide:

10 (1) At a directors' meeting, unless a quorum is participating, no proposal is to be voted on, except a proposal to call another meeting.

(2) The quorum for directors' meetings may be fixed from time to time by a decision of the directors, but it must never be less than two, and unless otherwise fixed, it is two.

Regulation 89 of Table A provides:

> **89.** The quorum for the transaction of business of the directors may be fixed by the directors and unless so fixed at any other number shall be two.

The articles may fix a quorum of one, and there is nothing to prevent the directors from doing so under articles such as reg. 89 of Table A (*Re Fireproof Doors Ltd.* [1916] 2 Ch. 142). Under the 2006 Act model articles, it is not possible for the directors to fix a quorum of less than two themselves, even if there is only one director. The reason why this is not allowed is because it not necessary. If there is only one director, the normal provisions of the model articles on directors' decision-making do not apply (see pcls 7, clg 7 and plc 7).

If the articles do not fix or provide for a method of fixing a quorum, the quorum for meetings of directors will be a majority of the directors currently holding office (*York Tramways Co. v. Willows* (1882) 8 Q.B.D. 685) or, where it can be shown that a standard practice has evolved over time, the number of directors who usually act in conducting the business of the company (*Re Tavistock Ironworks Co.* (1867) L.R. 4 Eq. 233). It goes without saying that where the articles make no provision, it is safer to assume that the quorum is a majority of the directors. It is worth noting in passing that if the articles do not specify the quorum, the number required to form a quorum under the common law (being a majority of the directors) automatically falls as the number of directors falls.

Where the articles do not specify a quorum but provide a method for fixing one, e.g. by a resolution of the directors, the quorum will be a majority of the directors until such time as alternative provision is made by that method (*York Tramways Co. v. Willows* (1882) 8 Q.B.D. 685). However, where the articles allow the directors to fix their own quorum and no resolution to that effect has ever been passed, the majority rule may be dispensed with if the court is satisfied that there was an understanding between all the directors which was followed (*Re Regent's Canal Iron Co.* [1867] W.N. 79). Again, it would always be safer to assume that the quorum is a majority of the directors unless the alternative quorum has been applied for a number of years.

4.8.2 Changing the quorum

Where the articles give the directors power to fix or alter the quorum, they may only exercise that power if they act in accordance with the existing rules and procedures governing their meetings, including the existing quorum requirements (*Re Portuguese Consolidated Copper Mines Ltd.* (1889) 42 Ch.D. 160). In other words, they cannot change the quorum unless there is a quorum under the existing rules. For an example of such a board resolution, see **Precedent 4.8A**.

If the articles allow the directors to fix or alter the quorum, they may do so by a written resolution as long as the articles allow them to act in this manner. It is doubtful whether such a resolution would be valid, however, if there were insufficient directors to form a quorum under the existing rules (*Hood Sailmakers Ltd. v. Axford* [1996] 4 All E.R. 830).

If the quorum is fixed by the articles and they make no separate provision for alteration, the quorum can only be changed by passing a special resolution at a general meeting to amend the relevant article.

4.8.3 Disinterested quorum

Under the common law a quorum must be present for each item of business at a meeting and only those entitled to vote may be counted in calculating whether a quorum exists (*Re Greymouth Point Elizabeth Railway and Coal Co. Ltd.* [1904] 1 Ch. 32). These principles apply to meetings of directors unless they are specifically excluded by the articles. Table A specifically provides that a director shall not be counted in the quorum in relation to a resolution on which he is not entitled to vote (reg. 95).

This rule can be of critical importance because articles frequently prohibit a director from voting at a meeting of directors on any matter in which he has a material interest (see for example, pcls 14, clg 14, plc 16 and reg. 94 of Table A). Where such restrictions operate, a quorum may, in fact, be present for some, but not all, items of business. Care should therefore be taken to check that a competent or disinterested quorum exists for each item of business.

The courts do not look favourably on techniques used by directors to avoid the operation of rules restricting their right to vote on matters in which they have an interest. Two such techniques were rejected in a case where a company's articles allowed directors to contract with the company but not to vote on any such contract. The quorum for board meetings had been fixed at three by the directors under powers given to them by the articles. At a meeting attended by four directors, a contract in which two of them were interested was passed by two separate resolutions. Each interested director voted only on the resolution concerning the other director. These resolutions were held to be invalid because there was in reality only one item of business. Treating it as two separate resolutions was merely a device to avoid the operation of the articles (this rule could prevent directors from voting on a number of separate resolutions to take out directors' and officers' insurance cover for each director where only one policy to cover them all is to be taken out). At a subsequent meeting attended by three directors, those present voted to reduce the quorum to two so as to allow a resolution to be passed issuing a debenture to one of the directors present. The resolution to alter the quorum was also held to be invalid because its sole purpose was to enable something to be done indirectly which could not be done directly (*Re North Eastern Insurance Co. Ltd.* [1919] 1 Ch. 198). In this case, the reason for altering the quorum was blatantly obvious. If it could be shown that the quorum was altered for other legitimate reasons, the resolutions at this second meeting may well have been valid.

Where articles prohibit a director from voting on any transaction in which he is interested, they usually specify some exceptions to that rule and make provision to allow the members in general meeting to suspend or relax the operation of the rules by ordinary resolution (see pcls 14, clg 14 and plc 16 and reg. 96 of Table A). If it is not possible for the directors to make a decision on a matter themselves, they should seek a dispensation from the members under these procedures and/ or consider proposing a suitable amendment to the articles in order to remove the obstacle (e.g. by widening the list of exceptions).

For small owner-managed companies, it is usually sensible to exclude or modify the relevant model articles so as to allow the directors to vote on any matter irrespective of any interest they may have in it (see **Precedent 4.8B**).

From a practical perspective, it is not necessary for a director who is unable to vote because of a material conflict to leave the meeting while the matter is being decided. A director can, of course, choose to do so. However, it is doubtful whether the other directors can force him to. It has been held that a director who is not entitled to vote at a board meeting cannot be excluded from the meeting (*Grimwade v. B.P.S. Syndicate Ltd.* (1915) 31 T.L.R 531). It may sometimes be in the interests of the conflicted director to leave the meeting in order to avoid coming into possession of confidential information that might place him in a difficult position. This sort of situation can arise with regard to proposals for management buyouts where it may also be thought necessary to withhold certain board papers from the conflicted directors.

4.8.4 Sole director

The default figure of two for the quorum at meetings of directors found in most articles would seem to be wholly inappropriate for a private company with only one director. Ideally, the articles should make alternative provision to cater for these circumstances. The model articles for private companies do so by disapplying the usual rules on directors' decision making where the company only has one director. In these circumstances the general rules do not apply and the director may take decisions without regard to any of the provisions of the articles relating to directors' decision making (pcls 7 and clg 7). This almost certainly represents the common law position for companies whose articles do not make specific provision in this regard. Nevertheless, a company with older articles may still prefer to make specific provision in its articles to clarify the position (either by following the format of the model articles mentioned above or **Precedent 4.8C**).

4.8.5 Practical issues when fixing a quorum

Generally speaking, it is preferable to fix a low quorum. Doing so facilitates the conduct of the board's business. If the quorum is too high, one or more of the directors may be able to obstruct the board by deliberately absenting themselves from meetings. A director cannot be forced to attend board meetings against his will. In *Barron v. Potter* [1914] 1 Ch. 895, the quorum was two and Barron, one of only two directors, refused to attend board meetings. Had he done so, Potter, the other director who was entitled to a casting vote as chairman, would have been able to appoint his own nominee as an additional director. Potter tried to hold a board meeting at a railway station and again at the company's offices at which he purported to propose and carry with his casting vote a resolution to appoint his nominee as an additional director. Barron made it clear that he refused to attend board meetings and it was held that he could not be forced to do so against his will. The appointment by Potter was therefore invalid.

In *Re Opera Photographic Ltd.* (1989) 5 B.C.C. 601, a director tried to prevent the board from convening a general meeting to remove him as a director by absenting himself from board meetings, thereby making it impossible to obtain a quorum at board meetings. The court ordered that a general meeting be called. In *Barron v. Potter*, it would have served no purpose for Potter to apply to the court for an order calling a general meeting. Barron had already requisitioned a general meeting to appoint new directors at which he would have been in the majority. Potter's only chance of success was therefore to entice Barron to attend a board meeting at which he had the casting vote.

Thus, although a director may be able to obstruct the business of the company by absenting himself from board meetings, the will of the majority will nearly always prevail as they will be in a position to remove him or to appoint additional directors unless the director has special class rights which enable him to veto appointments and removals.

It is, of course, sometimes desirable to establish a deadlocked company, e.g. where two members hold the same number of voting shares and are the only directors. In this case, it will be necessary to remove the chairman's casting vote at board and general meetings and fix a quorum of two at board meetings. If the directors fail to agree, it would serve no purpose applying to the court to call a general meeting as the balance of power would be the same.

The advantages of setting a relatively low figure as the quorum are plain. The other directors cannot call a meeting without giving reasonable notice. If the meeting is called to deal with routine or uncontroversial business, only sufficient directors to form a quorum need attend. However, whether all the directors attend or not, when an important or controversial item of business is considered, the will of the majority and not the minority will hold sway.

4.8.6 Number below quorum

Articles which allow the directors to act notwithstanding any vacancy in their number do not allow them to act where their number falls below that required to constitute a quorum. This issue is, however, normally addressed in modern articles. For example, Table A specifies that the minimum number of directors shall be two unless otherwise determined by ordinary resolution (reg. 64) and that the quorum for meetings of directors shall be two unless otherwise fixed by the directors (reg. 88). However, reg. 90 provides:

90. The continuing directors or a sole continuing director may act notwithstanding any vacancies in their number, but, if the number of directors is less than the number fixed as the quorum, the continuing directors or director may act only for the purpose of filling vacancies or of calling a general meeting.

Under this type of article the directors may act in the normal way where their number falls below the minimum prescribed by the articles as long as it is still sufficient to form a quorum. However, if the number remaining is not sufficient to form a quorum the directors may only act to appoint new directors and to call a general meeting.

The 2006 Act model articles for private companies make similar provision but say that the directors may only act if their number falls below the quorum in order to appoint further directors or to call a general meeting so as to enable the members to appoint further directors (pcls 11(3), clg 11(3)). The model articles for plcs also make similar provision but distinguish between the situation where there is only one director and where there is more than one (plc 11).

▪ 4.9 Voting

The rules on voting at directors' meetings are based on the common law but are subject to modification by the articles. Board meetings and board committees are usually conducted with less formality than shareholder meetings. Decisions are normally reached by consensus and matters are rarely put to a formal vote because it will normally be apparent without doing so which side would win.

When a resolution is put to a vote, each director will have one vote unless the articles provide otherwise. Questions are usually decided on a majority of votes cast for or against the resolution, although the articles may require a special majority for certain types of business. Most articles restrict the right to vote where a director has a personal interest in the matter under consideration. The chairman is commonly given a second or casting vote to be used in the event of a deadlock.

Table A provides:

88. . . . Questions arising at a meeting shall be decided by a majority of votes. In the case of an equality of votes, the chairman shall have a second or casting vote. A director who is also an alternate director shall be entitled in the absence of his appointor to a separate vote on behalf of his appointor in addition to his own vote.

The 2006 Act model articles do not really make direct provision as to voting at directors' meetings except to say that the general rule is that any decision of the directors must be either a majority decision at a meeting or a unanimous decision taken in accordance with article 8 (pcls 7 and clg 7) and to make provision for a chairman's casting vote (pcls 13 and clg 13). The model articles for plcs make more detailed provision as follows:

13 (1) Subject to the articles, a decision is taken at a directors' meeting by a majority of the votes of the participating directors.

(2) Subject to the articles, each director participating in a directors' meeting has one vote.

(3) Subject to the articles, if a director has an interest in an actual or proposed transaction or arrangement with the company—

(a) that director and that director's alternate may not vote on any proposal relating to it, but

(b) this does not preclude the alternate from voting in relation to that transaction or arrangement on behalf of another appointor who does not have such an interest.

4.9.1 Method of voting

Articles rarely specify the method of voting, e.g. reg. 88 of Table A simply states that questions shall be decided on a majority of votes. Voting is normally conducted by a show of hands or some other simple method of counting with each director having one vote. This method may not be satisfactory if any of the directors is entitled to more than one vote, e.g. a personal vote and one as an alternate for another director. A director who is present at the meeting and who has more than one vote has a right to have each of those votes counted and may have a right to demand a poll if they are not counted (see *R. v. Wimbledon Local Board* (1882) 8 Q.B.D. 459). The method of voting used should take account of the fact that some directors may have more votes than others. It is not necessary to follow the formal procedures used at company meetings. Voting papers could be used where it is difficult for the chairman to calculate the true number of votes for and against the resolution on a show of hands.

4.9.2 Chairman's casting vote

Unless the articles so provide, the chairman has no right to a casting vote (*Nell v. Longbottom* [1894] 1 Q.B. 767). Under most articles the person who acts as the chairman of a meeting of directors is given a casting vote (e.g. reg. 88 of Table A). The model articles under the 2006 Act also provide for a casting vote but provide that this does not apply if the chairman is not to be counted under the articles as participating in the decision-making process for quorum or voting purposes, e.g. because of a conflict of interest (pcls 13, clg 13 and plc 14). Although older articles may not make direct provision on this matter, it may be sensible to apply the same principle.

A casting vote may only be used where there has already been a vote and the number of votes for and against the resolution are exactly equal. It cannot be used where there is a majority in favour or against in order to manufacture a tie.

It is not necessary for the chairman to use any casting vote in the event of a tie. Indeed, it may be preferable not to do so if the chairman wishes to remain impartial. The chairman need not use the casting vote in the same way as his or her original vote on the resolution.

In exercising a casting vote the chairman can follow one of two guiding principles (which are quite capable of producing opposite results). The first, which is adopted by the Speaker of the House of Commons, is that the casting vote should be used to preserve the status quo. This may mean voting for or against the resolution depending on which way the resolution is worded. The second, which is perhaps more commonly applied, is that the chairman should use the casting vote in the best interests of the company. Clearly this second principle is more subjective than the first and depends on the chairman's view of what is in the interest of the company.

A casting vote may be exercised contingently. In *Bland v. Buchanan* [1901] 2 K.B. 75, the validity of a town councillor's vote was challenged during a meeting. The chairman realised that if the challenge proved to be well-founded, there would be a tied vote on a particular resolution. As he was not certain of the true position, he stated that if there was an equality of votes, he would use his casting vote in a particular way. The court commended the chairman's actions, stating that he had taken 'a very practical and business like view'.

4.9.3 Record of votes

It is not normal to record the number of votes cast for and against a proposal in the minutes of directors' meetings. However, directors have a right to have their opposition to a resolution recorded in the minutes whether or not a formal vote was put to the meeting. Their purpose in doing so will normally be to minimise their potential liabilities in respect of the decision. If the minutes record the fact that they opposed the decision, they are unlikely to share liability with the other directors if it turns out to be a bad decision.

4.9.4 Restrictions on voting

Articles frequently impose restrictions on the right to vote where a director has a personal interest in the subject of the resolution and provide that a director prohibited from voting shall not be counted in determining whether there is a quorum for that item of business (see regs. 94 and 95 of Table A, pcls 14, clg 14 and plc 16). However, provided that a quorum exists there is nothing to prevent the other directors from entering into a contract in which a director is interested.

In practice the restrictions on voting are themselves normally subject to a number of qualifications and articles usually provide a mechanism which allows the members to suspend or relax the restrictions contained in the articles (e.g. reg. 96 of Table A, pcls 14, clg 14 and plc 16).

Reg. 94 of Table A provides that a director shall not vote at a meeting of directors or a committee of directors on any resolution concerning a matter in which he has, directly or indirectly, an interest or duty which is material and which conflicts, or may conflict, with the interests of the company. However, it goes on to list a number of exceptions to this general rule. These exceptions cover the giving of guarantees, security or indemnities, subscribing for shares or other securities, underwriting an issue of securities, and pension scheme arrangements.

Reg. 94 also states that an interest of a person who is connected with a director shall be treated as an interest of the director. It also provides in relation to an alternate director that an interest of his appointor shall be treated as an interest of the alternate director without prejudice to any interest which the alternate director has otherwise. Thus an alternate director may not vote if either he or his appointor has a relevant interest.

In the 2006 Act model articles, most matters concerning conflicts of interest are dealt with in a single article (pcls 14, clg 14 and plc 16). However in the model articles for plcs, the position of alternate directors is dealt with in plc 13.

4.9.5 Practical issues on voting

It is difficult to frame many of the issues discussed at board meetings as formal resolutions and it can sometimes be counter-productive to do so. When the chairman feels that a consensus has been reached, he or she should attempt to summarise it. This gives the other directors an opportunity to object to that interpretation and is obviously helpful for the secretary in preparing the minutes. What often happens, however, is that the chairman ends the discussion by saying: 'I think we are all agreed on that subject and suggest we move on to the next item of business.' In such circumstances, if one were to go round the table asking each director what they thought had been agreed, each one would probably give a different answer. The other directors should not allow the chairman to get away with this, although it is often left to the secretary to ask the chairman to summarise what has been decided so that it can be properly recorded in the minutes.

■ 4.10 Participation in directors' meetings

Under the common law, it is necessary for a director to attend a meeting in person in order to participate in it and be counted in the quorum. In addition, there is no common law right for a director to appoint a proxy. Articles commonly vary these rules by allowing directors to appoint an alternate, who may then participate in meetings on their behalf if they are unable to do so themselves. In practice, it is often easier for a director who is unable to attend a meeting to participate via telephone or audio-visual links, and articles often make specific provision to allow this (see **4.10**). Where this is the case, there will not normally be any need for a director to appoint an alternate.

The 2006 Act model articles allow directors to participate in meetings using conference call technology. The model articles for public companies also allow directors to appoint an alternate, whereas the model articles for private companies do not. The usual provisions on alternate directors were omitted from the private company model articles as a simplification measure. Table A (1985) allows directors to appoint an alternate but does not specifically allow directors to participate in meetings by other means.

Methods of participation allowed under model articles and Table A

	In person	Conference calls	Alternate director
Model articles for a private company limited by shares	✓	✓	✗
Model articles for a private company limited by shares	✓	✓	✗
Model articles for a public company	✓	✓	✓
1985 Table A	✓	✗	✓
1948 Table A	✓	✗	✗

4.10.1 Conference calls

It is increasingly common for companies to enable directors to participate in board meetings and board committees by conference call and audio-visual links. The question as to whether participation in this manner is effective will depend, in part, on whether the company's articles of association make specific provision allowing directors to do so and, in the absence of any such provision, the relevant common law rules. Those common law rules were developed long before this type of technology became available, in an era where directors could only participate in meetings by gathering together in person at the time and place specified in the notice of meeting. Recent cases suggest that the courts are willing to adapt the old rules to reflect modern technological developments. However, for the avoidance of doubt, it is better to adopt articles which specifically authorise directors to participate in this manner and which avoid any of the potential pitfalls that could arise under the common law.

All three versions of the 2006 Act model articles make specific provision for participation by directors using conference call-type technology as follows:

10 (1) Subject to the articles, directors participate in a directors' meeting, or part of a directors' meeting, when—

(a) the meeting has been called and takes place in accordance with the articles, and

(b) they can each communicate to the others any information or opinions they have on any particular item of the business of the meeting.

(2) In determining whether directors are participating in a directors' meeting, it is irrelevant where any director is or how they communicate with each other.

(3) If all the directors participating in a meeting are not in the same place, they may decide that the meeting is to be treated as taking place wherever any of them is.

For a further example of an article which allows meetings to be conducted using conference call technology, see **Precedent 4.10**. Such articles need to clarify that directors who are in contact with the meeting by these other means may be counted in the quorum and may vote notwithstanding the fact that they are not personally present at the location where the meeting is taking place because there is a long-standing common law rule that would seem to suggest otherwise.

Table A makes no provision allowing directors to participate in meetings other than by attending in person or by appointing an alternate to vote on their behalf. Accordingly, for companies with articles similar to Table A there is a risk that participation in any other manner may not be effective. For example, there is a risk that the courts might decide that the board is incapable of acting where the number of directors physically present at the meeting is not sufficient to make a quorum, irrespective of the number participating by conference call. In addition, there is a slight risk that the courts might decide that even though there may be sufficient directors physically present to form a quorum, the votes of directors in communication by conference call or any other means should not be counted in determining the outcome of any vote.

In practice, the votes of directors in communication by other means will not always affect the outcome of any vote. In any case, there are a number of reasons to suppose that the courts would give effect to a decision carried on a formal vote by directors who were not physically present at the meeting. Logic suggests that in these circumstances the will of the majority should prevail no matter how it is expressed (i.e. whether in person or by telephone). It should also be noted that the courts are often reluctant to intervene in what they consider to be internal irregularities where it is obvious that the directors would merely make the same decision again (albeit by following proper procedures). Procedures adopted by the board may also be saved by the type of article which states that the directors may otherwise regulate their proceedings as they see fit.

In addition, the courts have already demonstrated a willingness to accept the fact that new technology may enable meetings to take place in different ways. In his leading judgment in the case of *Byng v. London Life Association Ltd.* [1989] 1 All E.R. 560, BrowneWilkinson VC stated (at 565):

> The rationale behind the requirement for meetings in the 1985 Act is that the members shall be able to attend in person so as to debate and vote on matters affecting the company. Until recently this could only be achieved by everyone being physically present in the same room face to face. Given modern technological advances, the same result can now be achieved without all the members coming face to face; without being physically in the same room they can be electronically in each other's presence so as to hear and be heard and

to see and be seen. The fact that such a meeting could not have been foreseen at the time the first statutory requirements for meetings were laid down, does not require us to hold that such a meeting is not within the meaning of the word 'meeting' in the 1985 Act.

The case concerned the validity of a general meeting held at a single venue at which overflow facilities were provided. The Court of Appeal accepted that such a meeting need not be held in one room as long as all the participants were in two-way audio and visual contact. Whether the court would apply the same exacting standards with regard to communications equipment for board meetings must be open to doubt, particularly in view of the fact that boards seem to be able to cope without being able to see each other.

It should also be noted that the Court of Appeal still seemed to consider it to be important that the meeting had a 'centre of gravity'. In his judgment in the *Byng* case, Mustill LJ said (at 572):

> I also accept that it possible to have a meeting, not all of whose members are present in the same room. It is unnecessary to consider the extreme case where none of the participants are face to face, but are linked by simultaneous audio-visual transmissions. This would require consideration of whether it is possible to convene a meeting which does not take place in any single location, and which consists only of the exchange of electronic impulses. No such problem arises here. If the arrangements had gone according to plan, and if the participants had first occupied Cinema 1 until it was full, and had then all found a place in the adjacent rooms by the time the business had commenced, and if they had been able to see hear and communicate with the other participants I would have seen no intellectual or practical objection to regarding this as a 'meeting'. Moreover, it would have been a meeting held at the place of which notice had been given, namely Cinema 1, since this was where the centre of gravity of the meeting was to be found.

Where no specific provision is made in a company's articles to allow for participation in directors' meetings by other means, the best solution is to amend the articles so that they do. However, failing that, it is suggested that the chances of any intervention by the court would be reduced by the inclusion in the notice of meeting a statement describing how participation in the meeting may be effected (e.g. either by personal attendance at a specified location or by being in contact with the people at that location via a communications facility). In addition, it might be worth examining the company's articles on alternate directors under which it may be possible for each director not physically present to appoint the chairman of the meeting to act as their alternate and to vote in accordance with their instructions during the meeting.

It should be noted that the principle of unanimous consent could also serve to validate decisions of directors not taken in accordance with the usual procedures required by the Act or the company's articles (see **6.3**).

4.10.2 Series of telephone calls

A decision made by a series of one-to-one telephone calls (or e-mail exchanges) will normally be valid under the principle of unanimous consent if all the directors agreed to that decision. However, this method of decision-making should not be relied upon to make decisions by a majority, unless the articles make specific provision in this regard.

The notion that a series of one-to-one telephone calls (or e-mail exchanges) should be treated as a meeting would stretch the common law concept of a meeting too far. The method does not allow a simultaneous transfer of views. There would be no meeting of minds at a particular point in time. Those who were contacted first may have changed their minds by the time the chairman has spoken to the last director. They might also have reached a different conclusion if they had heard the views of other directors. The same might be true of those who were contacted later in the series of calls if the chairman fails to explain adequately the views of the minority.

Some companies have adopted articles which specifically allow board decisions to be reached in this manner. On the whole though, such a method of decision-making is only suitable for issues which are simple or mere formalities. When using this type of decision-making process, special care will always need to be taken to ensure that directors have made any necessary declarations of interest. These would probably need to be made using the written notice procedure provided for in s. 184, rather than the general notice procedures in s. 185.

■ 4.11 Alternate directors

Directors who are also major shareholders will often wish to ensure that their views are represented at board meetings even though they are unable to attend or participate themselves. This is also the case in joint venture companies where each of the joint venture partners normally has the right to appoint a fixed number of directors and would normally want to ensure that they are fully represented at board meetings.

At common law there is no automatic right to vote by proxy. The Act confers a statutory right on the members to vote by proxy but does not make similar provision with regard to the directors. Thus a director who is unable to attend or participate in a meeting of directors will be unable to vote at that meeting unless the articles provide otherwise.

Table A and the 2006 Act model articles for plcs both provide a mechanism which allows directors to appoint another person to attend and vote in their stead at board and committee meetings. A person so appointed is known as an alternate director.

The 2006 Act model articles for private companies do not make any provision for the appointment of alternate directors. The relevant provisions were deliberately omitted in order to keep the private company model articles as simple as possible. The decision to do so was made easier because the model articles specifically allow directors to participate in meetings via conference calls. Accordingly, it was thought that they would be less likely to need to appoint alternates. This is almost certainly true. And in any case, it is relatively easy for a private company incorporated under the 2006 Act to make provision in its articles for alternate directors by adopting provisions similar to those in the plc model articles. These provide a much better model than Table A because the relevant provisions in the model articles are not so widely dispersed.

Both the model articles for plcs and Table A provide that alternate directors may be appointed and removed by notice to the company signed by the director making or revoking the appointment or in any other manner approved by the directors. However, both additionally require the board to approve any appointment of a person as an alternate director where the person nominated is not already a director of the company (reg. 65 of Table A, plc 25). Such approval is not required where another director is appointed. For examples of letters of appointment, see **Precedents 4.11 A–D**.

A person appointed as an alternate director is regarded as a director for Companies Act purposes. Accordingly, if the person appointed is not already a director of the company, the usual formalities for appointment of a new director should be followed (e.g. notification of appointment to the Registrar of Companies and entry in the register of directors).

A person who holds office only as an alternate director shall, if his appointor is not present, be counted in the quorum (reg. 89 of Table A, plc 26(3)). It should be noted in this regard that it is the alternate who is counted in the quorum rather than the person who appointed him. Thus, if two directors appoint the same alternate, that alternate can only be counted in the quorum once. If they had each appointed a different person, then both alternates could be counted in the quorum. The model articles for plcs clarify this by providing that an alternate cannot be counted as more than one director for the purposes of the quorum. Although this is not specifically stated in Table A, the same principle should be applied. It should also be noted that the relevant provision of Table A and the model articles only apply to a person who holds office only as an alternate director. In other words, if a director appoints another director as his alternate, that other director cannot be counted twice in the quorum. He will be counted in his own capacity as a director but not in his capacity as an alternate for any other director.

An alternate director can vote at a meeting of directors in the absence of his appointer (see reg. 66 of Table A and plc 26(1)). Both the model articles and Table A make special provision to clarify that where an existing director acts as an alternate director, any vote that he is entitled to cast as an alternate is in addition to any vote he is entitled to cast in his own right. The wording of the model articles for plcs in this regard clarify that such a director is entitled to an additional vote for each appointor (plc 15). The same can probably be assumed to be the case under reg. 66 of Table A, although on a literal reading it only appears to deal with the situation where a director has been appointed as an alternate for one other director. It should be noted that neither Table A or the model articles for plcs specifically deal with the situation where two or more directors appoint the same person as their alternate where that person is not a director. It is not entirely clear whether such a person would be entitled to one vote on behalf of each appointor. An alternate director may also sign a written resolution instead of his appointor (see reg. 93 of Table A and plc 26(3)).

Under Table A and the model articles for plcs, alternate directors are deemed to be directors, deemed responsible for their own acts and defaults and deemed not to be the agents of the person who appointed them (reg. 69 of Table A and plc 26(2)). Thus the chairman need not be concerned as to whether the alternate is voting in accordance with the instructions of his appointor.

The appointment of an alternate director will automatically cease on the occurrence of certain events (see regs. 67 and 68 of Table A and plc 27).

Under Table A, alternate directors have a right to receive notice of all meetings of directors and of all meetings of committees of directors of which his appointor is a member, to attend and vote at any such meeting at which the director appointing him is not personally present, and generally to perform all the functions of his appointor as a director in his absence (reg. 66). Under the model articles for plcs, alternate directors are given the same rights, in relation to any directors' meeting or directors' written resolution, as their appointor (plc 26(1)) but are also made subject to the same restrictions (plc 26(2)(c)). Those restrictions will include limitations on the right to vote where a conflict of interest arises under plc 16.

As alternate directors are deemed to be directors for the purposes of the articles (see reg. 69 of Table A and plc 26(2)), they will be subject to any rules in the articles which disqualify them from voting and/or being counted in the quorum where they themselves are interested in a transaction (see reg. 94 of Table A and plc 26(2)(a)). However, they will also be disqualified from voting where the director who appointed them is disqualified.

Table A states that 'in relation to an alternate director, an interest of his appointor shall be treated as an interest of the alternate director, without prejudice to any interest which the alternate director has otherwise' (Table A, reg. 94). Accordingly, under Table A, if a director is by virtue of any conflict of interest disqualified from voting and from being counted in the quorum, his alternate will be similarly disqualified. The model articles for public companies achieve the same result by providing that alternate directors are subject to the same restrictions as their appointors (see plc 26(2)(c)).

Table A provides that alternate directors are not entitled to receive any remuneration from the company for their services as an alternate director (reg. 66). The model articles for plcs make similar provision but clarify that the company can pay an alternate director out of the remuneration of his appointor if directed to do so by him in writing (plc 26(4)).

■ 4.12 Directors' interests in transactions or arrangements

Directors have a statutory duty to declare the nature and extent of any direct or indirect interest they may have in any:

(a) *proposed* transaction or arrangement with the company (s. 177); and
(b) *existing* transaction or arrangement with the company (s. 182).

At its most basic, a 'transaction or arrangement with the company' includes any contract between the company and a third party. A director could be interested in such a contract directly as the other contracting party, or indirectly because he is, for example, a shareholder of another company (or partner in a firm) which is a party to the contract. Strictly speaking, a director's duty of disclosure under these provisions also extends to other non-contractual arrangements that the company may enter into. Rather than try to define what these might be, it is safer to assume that directors must disclose their interest in anything that the company does unless that thing is covered by a statutory exception.

The requirement to disclose interests in *proposed* transactions or arrangements is, perhaps, easier to understand than the requirement to disclose interests in *existing* ones. It is obvious that the board of directors should be made aware of the fact that one of the directors has an interest in a *proposed* contract or arrangement before they decide whether or not the company should enter into it. If the director's interest is material, it should put them on alert as to whether the company is getting the best deal, particularly if the director concerned has been involved in negotiating the deal and appears to be promoting it.

It is also essential that directors make the necessary declarations if the company's articles prohibit a director who has such an interest from participating in any decision on that matter at a meeting of directors. The chairman and secretary of the meeting need to be able to work out who can vote, who can be counted in the quorum, and whether the meeting is able to make a decision on the proposal.

It is not necessarily as clear why the directors need to know about a director's interests in *existing* transactions or arrangements, i.e. those that the company has already entered into, possibly even before the director was appointed. The justification for this could partly be to ensure that the board does not inadvertently place a director in charge of managing an existing contractual relationship if he has a material interest in that contract. The board also needs to know whether a director might have an interest in promoting the continuation or renegotiation of an existing contract or arrangement.

A breach by a director of the duty of disclosure under s. 177 in relation to a *proposed* transaction or arrangement is not an criminal offence but gives rise to potential civil liability on the part of the director to account to the company for any profits he may have made from the transaction and potentially renders the contract voidable at the instance of the company (see below). A breach of the second duty under s. 182 regarding an *existing* transaction or arrangement is a criminal offence (s. 183), but does not give rise to the same civil remedies as the first. It may seem strange that a breach of the first duty relating to *proposed* transactions is not a criminal offence as well, particularly as this used to be the case under the equivalent provision of the 1985 Act (s. 317). However, it should be noted that under the 2006 Act any failure by a director to disclose an interest in a *proposed* transaction will, if the company enters into that transaction and the director's interest remains undisclosed, become a failure to disclose an interest in an *existing* transaction, which will then attract potential criminal penalties. However, no offence is committed if the company does not enter into the proposed contract or arrangement.

No declaration is required under either of the requirements of any interest of which the director is not aware or if the director is not aware of the transaction or arrangement in question – a director is treated as being aware of matters of which he ought reasonably to be aware. There is also no need to declare an interest:

(a) if it cannot reasonably be regarded as likely to give rise to a conflict of interest;
(b) if, or to the extent that, the other directors are already aware of it – for this purpose the other directors are treated as aware of anything of which they ought reasonably to be aware); or
(c) if, or to the extent that, it concerns terms of his service contract that have been or are to be considered by a meeting of the directors, or by a committee of the directors appointed for the purpose under the company's articles.

In the case of a *proposed* transaction or arrangement, a director is required to declare the nature and extent of his or her interest to the other directors before the company enters into the transaction or arrangement (s. 177).

In the case of an *existing* transaction or arrangement, a director is required to declare the nature and extent of his or her interest to the other directors as soon as is reasonably practicable (s. 182). However, the requirement to make a declaration interest in an *existing* transaction or arrangement under s. 182 does not apply if it has already been declared as an interest in a *proposed* transaction or arrangement under s. 177. Effectively, a declaration of interest in a *proposed* contract or arrangement carries forward as a declaration of interest in an *existing* contract or arrangement if the company enters into that contract or arrangement.

4.12.1 Methods of making a declaration
In the case of an interest in a *proposed* transaction or arrangement (s. 177), the declaration may (*but need not*) be made:

(a) at a meeting of the directors;
(b) by notice in writing to the directors in accordance with s. 184; or
(c) by general notice in accordance with s. 185.

In the case of an *existing* transaction or arrangement, the declaration *must* be made using one of three methods mentioned above.

If a declaration of interest proves to be, or becomes, inaccurate or incomplete, a further declaration must be made. Information regarding the extent of a director's interest is most likely to need updating. Directors may not always remember to do this, or realise that they have to. Accordingly it is good practice for the secretary to issue regular reminders and to ask directors to check whether the interests they have declared need to be updated. When doing so, care should be taken to ensure that the directors understand that they have an ongoing to duty to declare (and update) their interests, and that they should not do so only in response to a reminder.

General notice

The method that directors most commonly use to make a declaration of interest is to give general notice in accordance with s. 185. Under this method, the director gives notice to the other directors of the fact that he or she:

(a) has an interest (as a member, officer, employee or otherwise) in a specified body corporate or firm and is to be regarded as interested in any transaction or arrangement that may, after the date of the notice, be made with that body corporate or firm; or

(b) is connected with a specified person (other than a body corporate or firm) and is to be regarded as interested in any transaction or arrangement that may, after the date of the notice, be made with that person.

A general notice must state the nature and extent of the director's interest in the body corporate or firm or the nature of his connection with any specified person. It will not be effective unless it is given at a meeting of the directors, or the director concerned takes reasonable steps to secure that it is brought up and read at the next meeting of the directors after it is given. Subject to these conditions, a general notice is a sufficient declaration of interest in relation to the matters to which it relates. It is particularly important in this regard that the details regarding the nature and extent of a director's interests are kept up to date.

General notice need not be given in writing. It can, for example, be given orally at a board meeting. However, it is usual for directors to make such notifications in writing as they will often be quite detailed. Whether the notice is given in writing or orally, the fact that it has been given should be recorded in the minutes of the relevant board meeting at which it was given, brought up or read out. See **Precedents 4.12A and B** for a specimen form of disclosure of interests and the related board minute.

One obvious weakness with the general notice procedure is that a director may have made the declaration a long time ago. Although that declaration (if kept up to date) will ensure that he has complied with his statutory duties, the other directors may not necessarily remember what interests the director declared. Accordingly, when a transaction is raised at a board meeting, they may not necessarily remember that that the director has an interest in it unless he reminds them of that fact.

Although it is not necessary for statutory purposes for a director to remind the board of an interest that he has already declared, it will often be necessary for him to do so to enable the chairman of the meeting to decide whether the director can participate in the decision under any relevant article provisions.

Notice in writing

A director may also make a declaration by giving notice in writing in accordance with s. 184. Under this method, the director concerned must send the notice to the other directors either in hard copy form (by hand or by post) or, if the recipient has agreed to receive it in electronic form, in an agreed electronic form sent by agreed electronic means. The notice must disclose the nature and extent of the director's interest and, if it relates to a *proposed* transaction or arrangement, must be given before the company enters into the relevant transaction or arrangement. A declaration made by notice in writing is then deemed to form part of the proceedings at the next meeting of the directors after the notice is given, and must be minuted accordingly. It is good practice to raise the fact that such a declaration has been made at the meeting.

Declaration made at a meeting of directors

A director may make a declaration of interest for the purposes of ss. 177 and 182 at a 'meeting of directors'. Such a declaration would typically be made orally, although there is no reason why a director should not table a written declaration of interest at the meeting. The declaration would have to comply with all of the usual requirements, e.g. disclose the nature and extent of the director's interest and, for the purposes of a proposed transaction, be made before the company enters into that transaction. Subject to these conditions, a declaration of interest made at a meeting of directors will suffice even though some of the directors may have been absent from the meeting and may not therefore be aware that one was made. It is not necessary for the company to wait until the absent directors have been informed of the interest before entering into the transaction.

Declarations of interest made at a meeting of directors form part of the proceedings of that meeting and should therefore be minuted. If this is done properly and the minutes are circulated to the directors, those who were absent will be put on notice that a director declared an interest at the meeting. However, as mentioned above the validity of the declaration does not depend on this being done.

Declarations of interest at committee meetings

It should be noted that in a case decided under s. 317 of the 1985 Act, the Court of Appeal held that the requirement to make a declaration of interest at a 'meeting of directors' cannot be satisfied merely by making such a declaration at a board committee meeting (*Guinness plc v. Saunders* [1988] 2 All E.R. 940). In this case, a committee appointed to manage a takeover bid agreed to pay one of its members a success fee if the bid succeeded. It was assumed that the director concerned had made a declaration of interest to his fellow committee members about the fee arrangement. However, no attempt was made to inform the board of the committee's decision to enter into the arrangement with the director. The Court of Appeal ruled that the director had not properly declared his interest in the fee arrangement to the board and that the transaction was therefore voidable at the instance of the company. On appeal to the House of Lords, the case was decided on different grounds which did not depend on the meaning of the term 'a meeting of directors'. However, the Court of Appeal's ruling is still cited (rightly or wrongly) as authority for the proposition that a declaration of interest cannot be made for statutory purposes at a board committee meeting.

Even if it is assumed that the Court of Appeal's decision regarding what constitutes a meeting of directors for these purposes is correct, it does not necessarily mean that directors should not make declarations of interest at board committee meetings or that such declarations will always be invalid. Directors will still need to make declarations of interest at committee meetings so as to enable the chairman of the meeting to establish whether they are entitled under any relevant articles to participate in the decision and whether the meeting is quorate.

In connection with a *proposed* transaction or arrangement, s. 177 prescribes three methods that a director can use to make a declaration of interest. However, it specifically states that such a declaration 'need not be' made in one of those three ways. In other words, it admits the possibility of making a declaration in some other way.

In determining whether a declaration made in some other way is effective for the purposes of s. 177, the most important factor will presumably be whether it was (or can be deemed to have been) drawn to the attention of all the other directors before the company entered into the relevant transaction or arrangement. A declaration made by a director at a committee meeting in relation to a transaction that was considered at that meeting could, for example, be brought to the attention of the other directors before the transaction is entered into by circulating the minutes of that meeting which record that declaration of interest. If the director did this himself together with a covering note highlighting the fact that the minutes contain a declaration of interest by him, this would presumably constitute notice in writing for the purposes of s. 184. If the company secretary did this on behalf of the director, it is possible that it would still be construed as notice in writing. If not, it may still be effective as a declaration made in some other way.

Committee meetings obviously present a potential trap in this regard as it is clearly necessary for a director to ensure that a declaration of interest is properly made before the transaction is actually executed. In view of the decision of the Court of Appeal in the *Guinness* case, it is preferable for a director to make the necessary declaration in accordance with the written notice procedure. However, it is submitted that a declaration made at a committee meeting can be effective if it is drawn to the attention of the other directors of the company before the company enters into the transaction.

4.12.2 Interests of sole directors

A sole director of a company that is only required by law to have one director is not required to make any declarations of interest under either s. 177 or s. 182 because both sections require the declarations to be made to the other directors, of which there are none. This reverses the position under the equivalent provision of the 1985 Act (s. 317) in respect of which it had been held that a sole director of a private company must comply with the formalities by holding a meeting and making a declaration at that meeting (*Re Neptune (Vehicle Washing Equipment) Ltd*. [1995] 1 B.C.L.C. 352).

However, the 2006 Act makes special provision to cater for the situation where a company has only one director but should have at least two (i.e. a public company). Section 186 provides that where a declaration of interest in an existing transaction or arrangement under s. 182 is required of a sole director of a company that is required to have more than one director, the declaration must be recorded in writing, and the making of the declaration is deemed to form part of the proceedings at the next meeting of the directors after the notice is given, and should be minuted as such (s. 186). See also s. 231 (contract with sole member who is also a director: terms to be set out in writing or recorded in minutes).

The duty to declare interests in existing transactions or arrangements under s. 182 also applies to shadow directors but with certain adaptations as to the mechanism by which the relevant disclosures are required to be made (see s. 187).

4.12.3 Consequences of breach

The consequences of a breach of s. 177 in relation to proposed transaction or arrangement are the same as would apply if the corresponding common law rule or equitable principle applied (s. 178).

The basic common law position on directors' conflicts of interest is that they can only be ratified by the company in general meeting, unless the company's articles provided otherwise (*Aberdeen Rly. Co. v Blaikie Bros.* [1854] 1 Macq 461 and *North-West Transportation Co. Ltd. v. Beatty* (1887) 12 App. Cases 589).

As a result of these rulings it became standard practice for companies to adopt articles that allowed directors to be a party to or otherwise interested in transactions or arrangements without shareholder approval, provided that the director had disclosed the nature and extent of that interest. For example, reg. 85 of Table A provides:

> 85. Subject to the provisions of the Act, and provided that he has disclosed to the directors the nature and extent of any material interest of his, a director notwithstanding his office –
>
> (a) may be a party to, or otherwise interested in, any transaction or arrangement with the company or in which the company is otherwise interested...

Failure on the part of a director to comply with the relevant disclosure requirement in such an article rendered him liable to account to the company for any profit made and, subject to third party rights, rendered the contract voidable at the instance of the company (*Hely-Hutchinson v. Brayhead Ltd.* [1967] 3 All E.R. 98).

The 2006 Act model articles do not include a provision which specifically allows directors to be interested in company transactions. The reason why they do not do so is that the Act itself now authorises such conflicts provided that the director concerned has made any necessary declaration of interest in accordance with the requirements of the Act. Section 175 states that the general duty to avoid conflicts of interest, does not apply to a conflict of interest arising in relation to a transaction or arrangement with the company. In addition, s. 180(1) provides that in a case where s. 177 (duty to declare interest in proposed transaction or arrangement) is complied with, the transaction or arrangement is not liable to be set aside by virtue of any common law rule or equitable principle requiring the consent or approval of the members of the company. In other words, it is no longer necessary for a company's articles to authorise directors to have an interest in the company's transactions.

It is important to note, however, that a company is free to adopt articles that prohibit the directors from having any interest in a transaction or that require shareholders to approve certain types of transaction or that require the directors to adopt special procedures when approving certain types of transactions.

The general duties have effect subject to any rule of law enabling the company to give authority, specifically or generally, for anything to be done (or omitted) by the directors, or any of them, that would otherwise be a breach of duty, and where the company's articles contain provisions for dealing with conflicts of interest, are not infringed by anything done (or omitted) by the directors, or any of them, in accordance with those provisions (s. 180(4)). Otherwise, the general duties have effect (except as otherwise provided or the context otherwise requires) notwithstanding any enactment or rule of law (s. 180(5)).

This would seem to indicate that subject to the necessary disclosures being made, it is open to the directors to decide whether or not to enter into a transaction in which one or more of their number has an interest and, effectively, to authorise this type of breach of duty. It should be noted, however, that s. 180(1) is expressed as being subject to any contrary enactment (e.g. the specific member approval requirements set out in Part 10, Ch. 4 of the 2006 Act dealing with matters such as directors' loans and substantial property transactions), or any provision in the company's constitution imposing additional procedural requirements.

Articles commonly provide that a director who is interested in a transaction cannot vote or be counted in the quorum when that matter is being decided upon at a meeting of directors. Such articles commonly make provision for a number of exceptions to this rule and allow the members to disapply the normal rules by passing an ordinary resolution to allow a conflicted director to vote on a particular matter (see regs. 94 and 95 of Table A, pcls 14, clg 14 and plc 16).

Articles sometimes exclude a director who is interested in a transaction from voting without specifying whether that director can be counted for the purposes of calculating whether there is a quorum. It has been held that a director who cannot vote in such circumstances cannot be counted in the quorum unless the articles specify otherwise (*Re Greymouth Point Elizabeth Railway and Coal Co. Ltd.* [1904] 1 Ch. 32).

Somewhat surprisingly, there is no common law rule which prohibits a director from voting on a transaction in which he is interested at a meeting of directors. This is partly because, the common law position on conflicts was that they could only be authorised by a resolution of the members. Companies could, of course, modify this rule by making different provision in their articles and it became standard practice for them to do by adopting articles which allowed the non-conflicted members of the board to authorise such transactions, provided that the conflicted directors had made the necessary disclosures and did not participate in the decision.

The position under the 2006 Act would appear to be even stranger because, in the absence of any restrictions in the articles, mere disclosure by a director of an interest in a proposed transaction is all that is required. The law leaves it up to the members of the company to decide whether to impose any further restrictions on the directors in the company's articles. The default position under Table A and the model articles is, of course, that directors cannot vote on matters in which they have an interest (subject to certain exceptions). Accordingly, a company's members would need to have made an active decision at some point to dispense with these restrictions by adopting different articles. It has always been possible for a company to do this. Indeed, it is actually quite common for the articles of owner-managed companies to allow the directors to have an interest in a transaction and to vote on any such transaction notwithstanding the fact that they have an interest in it.

In the case of a proposed contract, the declaration must be made at the meeting of the directors at which the question of entering into the contract was first considered or, if the director was not at the date of that meeting interested in the proposed contract, at the next meeting of directors held after he became so interested. If a director becomes interested in an existing contract, the declaration must be made at the first meeting of directors after he becomes so interested.

■ 4.13 Adjournment

Articles rarely make specific provision with respect to adjournment of directors' meetings other than to state that the directors may adjourn. As a result, the common law rules on adjournment will normally apply and the power to adjourn will rest with the meeting (*National Dwelling Society Ltd. v. Sykes* [1894] 3 Ch. 159). It is not possible to adjourn a meeting that never actually started. A meeting cannot start unless there is a quorum. If a quorum is not obtained, the meeting cannot therefore be adjourned, unless the articles make some sort of provision for automatic adjournment in these circumstances. Although articles do this for shareholder meetings, they rarely make similar provision for meetings of directors. Accordingly, if a quorum is never obtained, a new meeting must be called.

If a quorum is present, the directors may adjourn. In practice, it is unusual for directors' meetings to be adjourned for more than a couple of hours, perhaps to allow lunch to be taken or further negotiations to take place before a final decision is made. Although there is strictly no need to give notice of an adjourned meeting (*Scadding v. Lorrant* (1851) 3 H.L.C. 418), it is normal practice to notify directors who were unable to attend the original meeting, if only to ensure that there is a quorum at the adjourned meeting. The quorum required at an adjourned meeting will be the same as for the original meeting.

■ 4.14 Standing orders and internal regulations

Boards frequently adopt standing orders or internal regulations which govern their own conduct and procedures. These will often seek to ensure that the directors comply with any relevant article provisions but also cover a range of matters not specifically governed by the articles, such as:

- length of notice for board meetings;
- location and frequency of meetings;
- requirements to give notice of business and circulate an agenda;
- procedures for the approval and circulation of the minutes of meetings; and
- schedule of matters reserved to the board.

Articles frequently include a provision which confirms that the directors may regulate their proceedings as they think fit, provided that they comply with any other relevant article provisions (e.g. reg. 88 of Table A). This is almost certainly the case whether or not the articles make specific provision in this regard. Although it is always better for the board to adopt written procedures, the courts will often take into account informal practices and procedures that may have been adopted over time.

Standing orders and internal regulations typically require thing to be done in a manner that would not necessarily be required under the articles or the common law. For example, they could specify a minimum period of notice for board meetings. They obviously cannot be used to override things that are required to be done under the articles, or not allowed to be done under the articles. It is possible that they could be used to override something that is required under the common law. However, as it would be impossible to predict with any certainty whether they would be effective in this regard, this is something that should be avoided.

Assuming that any regulations adopted by the directors are consistent with the articles and any common law requirements, the question arises as to whether the directors must comply with them and what the consequences would be if they do not do so. Much will depend on the way they are drafted. If they are framed as a code of best practice (in other words they are aspirational rather than mandatory), they are unlikely to be enforceable. If, however, they are drafted as regulations and clearly intended to be mandatory, it is arguable that the directors should comply with them. This does not necessarily mean that every decision taken by the board in breach of its own internal procedures will be invalid. It is obviously within the directors' powers to ratify a decision that has not been made in accordance with its own procedures. It would be up to a director to object to any breach of internal procedures. If nobody did object, it is likely that they would all be deemed to have acquiesced to the irregularity. However, if a director does object to an irregularity, then the chairman should probably seek to ensure that a majority of the directors are happy for the decision to be taken notwithstanding that irregularity. It may not be sufficient for the chairman to obtain the agreement of the directors who attend the meeting, unless a majority of the directors are actually present. Notwithstanding the fact that a quorum may be present, it would not make sense for a minority to override procedural rules adopted by the majority.

A director wishing to challenge the validity of a decision in legal proceedings on the basis of a breach of internal regulations would need to act quickly in order to avoid being deemed by the court to have acquiesced in the irregularity. The court would not intervene if the decision had already been ratified by the directors, and would be unlikely to declare any decision invalid where it is clear that a majority of the directors are in favour of it because any irregularities could be cured by the board going through the proper process (*Bentley-Stevens v. Jones* [1974] 1 W.L.R. 638).

Third parties are protected from any breach of internal procedures by the indoor management rule and ss. 39 and 40 of the Act (see **7.5**).

■ 4.15 Board effectiveness

The FRC's *Guidance on Board Effectiveness* suggests that well-informed and high-quality decision-making is a critical requirement for a board to be effective and that boards can minimise the risk of poor decisions by investing time in the design of their decision-making policies and processes, including the contribution of committees.

It recommends that good decision-making can be facilitated by:

(a) high-quality board documentation;
(b) obtaining expert opinions when necessary;
(c) allowing time for debate and challenge, especially for complex, contentious or business critical issues;
(d) achieving timely closure; and
(e) providing clarity on the actions required, and timescales and responsibilities.

It warns boards to be aware of factors which can limit effective decision making, such as:

(a) a dominant personality or group of directors on the board, which can inhibit contribution from other directors;
(b) insufficient attention to risk, and treating risk as a compliance issue rather than as part of the decision-making process, especially in cases where the level of risk involved in a project could endanger the stability and sustainability of the business itself;
(c) failure to recognise the value implications of running the business on the basis of self-interest and other poor ethical standards;
(d) a reluctance to involve non-executive directors, or of matters being brought to the board for sign-off rather than debate;
(e) complacent or intransigent attitudes;
(f) a weak organisational culture; or
(g) inadequate information or analysis.

On the basis that the judgment of even the most well-intentioned and experienced leaders can be distorted by factors such as conflicts of interest, emotional attachments and inappropriate reliance on previous experience and previous decisions, the FRC Guidance suggests that, for significant decisions, the board should consider:

(a) describing in board papers the process that has been used to arrive at and challenge the proposal prior to presenting it to the board, thereby allowing directors not involved in the project to assess the appropriateness of the process as a precursor to assessing the merits of the project itself; or
(b) where appropriate, putting in place additional safeguards to reduce the risk of distorted judgments by, for example, commissioning an independent report, seeking advice from an expert, introducing a devil's advocate to provide challenge, establishing a sole purpose sub-committee or convening additional meetings. Some chairmen favour separate discussions for important decisions; for example, concept, proposal for discussion, proposal for decision. This gives executive directors more opportunity to put the case at the earlier stages, and all directors the opportunity to share concerns or challenge assumptions well in advance of the point of decision.

It also suggests that boards can benefit from reviewing past decisions, particularly ones with poor outcomes. Such a review should not focus just on the merits of the decision itself but also on the decision-making process.

5

Committees of directors

■ 5.1 Summary

- Articles usually allow directors to delegate their powers to committees of directors. Where this is the case, the board can delegate certain duties to a committee and give it the necessary powers to make decisions so that they no longer need to be taken by the board. If the articles do not allow the directors to delegate their powers to committees, any decision of a committee would need to be ratified by the board. In practice, boards often establish committees to investigate things and make recommendations to the board. Such committees do not normally need to be given any powers. Where this is the case, it does not matter whether or not the directors are allowed to delegate their powers.
- Committees of directors should be established by a resolution of the board which should specify its membership and duties (see **5.2**).
- Only directors may be appointed as members unless the articles provide otherwise (see **5.2**).
- The directors may need to delegate some their powers to a committee to enable it carry out its duties (see **5.5**).
- Articles usually provide that the proceedings at committees of directors shall be governed by the regulations governing board meetings (see **5.6** to **5.11**) except where a committee of one director is appointed (see **5.12**).
- The UK Corporate Governance Code recommends that all listed companies should establish an audit committee (see **5.13**), a remuneration committee (see **5.14**) and a nomination committee (see **5.15**).

■ 5.2 Establishment of committees

Articles usually allow directors to delegate their powers to committees of directors. Where this is the case, the board can establish a committee to perform certain functions and authorise that committee to make decisions on its behalf. Directors can establish committees even if the articles do not allow them to delegate any of their powers to those committees. A committee could be established in these circumstances to make recommendations to the board on certain matters. This would not involve any delegation of powers as long as the board makes the final decision on those matters. In practice, boards often establish committees for this reason, even in companies where the board is able to delegate its powers.

It is important to understand the distinction between duties and powers in this context. The board can delegate certain duties to a committee without necessarily giving the committee any decision-making powers. However, committees established solely to make recommendations to the board sometimes need to be given certain ancillary powers (e.g. to enable them to conduct an investigation prior to making their recommendations).

One might imagine that a committee of the board can only be established by a formal decision of the board. This is, of course, the way that board committees ought to be constituted. However, the courts are sometimes willing to recognise the fact that a committee has been established even though the board never made a formal decision to establish one. Judges sometimes use this technique to regularise decisions made by individual directors or a small group of them where there has been no formal delegation by the board, particularly where the other directors have absented themselves from the decision-making process in full knowledge that the affairs of the company are being managed by a small group of directors. In these circumstances, the courts may simply deem the other directors to have agreed to the establishment of the committee in view of the fact they did nothing to prevent the affairs of the company from being managed in this way.

It would be wrong to suggest that a small group of directors can constitute themselves as a committee and exercise the company's powers without board approval. Such behaviour would probably constitute a breach of duty (at least initially), and render them liable to possible legal action. If the other directors allowed such behaviour to go unchecked for too long, the courts might conclude that the arrangements had been sanctioned by them. However, it would be dangerous to rely on this.

The proper way to establish a committee of the board is by a formal resolution of the board. Such a resolution will need to deal with the committee's:

- membership;
- duties;
- powers (including any limitations on those powers); and
- constitution.

It may be possible to deal with all these matters in one simple board resolution (see **Precedent 5.2A**). However, for standing committees it is normal to pass a resolution establishing the committee's terms of reference (including its delegated powers) and to deal with appointments separately.

■ 5.3 Which committees are board committees?

Before going any further, it is necessary to address what we mean when we refer to a board committee or a committee of directors. This may sound like a trite question. However, it is not necessarily easy to answer.

A company may have dozens of committees. Typically, only a few of them will be board committees. The rest will just be committees established by executives and other employees for management purposes. It is important to be able to recognise which committees are board committees because those committees have to be operated in accordance with the company's articles.

Although, it is good practice for any committee to keep minutes of its proceedings, it is much more important to do so for board committees. Articles often require minutes of board committee meetings to be kept. Even where they do not, it is likely that the directors are required to do so under the Act.

A committee will presumably be a committee of the board if it is established by the board and comprises of a subset of the board. Put another way, a committee will be a committee of directors if it is established by the board of directors and comprises of some, but not all, of the directors who serve on the board. We have already seen that boards can be deemed to have established a committee in certain circumstances. So it will not always be necessary for the committee to have been formally established, although it is inexcusable to rely on this as a method of establishing a committee.

The fact that the board appears to have formally established a committee may not make it a board committee? Say, for example, the board establishes an executive committee, which includes people who are not directors. Can such a committee be a committee of the board if it includes people who are not members of the board? Can it be a committee of directors if it includes people who are not directors? Can the board actually delegate its powers to such a committee? Has the board actually delegated any powers to that committee.

Articles often state that the directors may delegate their powers to a committee of directors (e.g. reg. 72 of Table A). Where this type of wording is used, it has to be assumed that the committee must be made up exclusively of directors, otherwise it would be committee of some people who are directors and some who are not. Recognising this as a potential difficulty, companies sometimes adopt articles which specifically allow the directors to delegate their powers to committees that are not made up exclusively of directors. Where this is the case, people who are not directors can be appointed as full voting members of the committee and participate in its decisions. No special provision needs to be made in the articles to appoint people who are not directors as non-voting members of a board committee.

The composition of the committee is particularly important where the board wishes to delegate any of its powers to the committee. The issue may not be relevant at all if the committee does not need to be given any delegate powers in order to perform its designated function (e.g. where the committee's sole function is to make recommendations to the board).

In practice, the executive committee may be nothing other than a sounding board for the chief executive, in which case it may not need to be given any delegated powers. It is normally the chief executive who makes the final decision on matters that come before the committee. Where this is the case, it is the chief executive who needs to be given delegated powers, not the committee. Indeed, in these circumstances, even though it may feel as though the executive committee has been established by the board, it is probably better to view it as a committee established by the chief executive for management purposes on the instructions of the board, rather than as a committee actually established by the board or a committee of the board. Indeed, it might have been easier to understand what was going on if we had called the committee the chief executive's committee from the start, which is something that many companies do.

If the articles do allow the directors to delegate their powers to a committee that is not made up exclusively of directors and the board does establish such a committee and authorises it to exercise certain delegated powers, one might naturally assume that the committee should be treated as a committee of the board and that any relevant article provisions regarding the operation of board committees will apply to that committee.

It is possible that this might be the case even though none of the members of the committee are actually directors. The idea that the board can appoint a committee of directors that does not include any directors may seem ludicrous. However, articles can sometimes be worded in such a way as to make the seemingly impossible possible.

It should be noted that the 2006 Act model articles allow the directors to delegate their powers to any person or committee. They do not specify that the committee must be a committee of directors (see pcls 5, clg 5 and plc 5). Indeed, the model articles specifically provide that committees to which the directors delegate any of their powers must follow procedures which are based as far as they are applicable on those provisions of the articles which govern the taking of decisions by directors. However, they also provide that the directors may make rules of procedure for all or any committees, which prevail over rules derived from the articles if they are not consistent with them (pcls 6, clg 6 and plc 6). Accordingly under the model articles, any committee to which the directors delegate any of their powers should be considered a committee of the board, even if it does not include any directors. It is important to note that this is only the case where the board has delegated any of its powers to that committee. However, this raises the question as to whether there needs to be some form of direct delegation by the board and whether the same principles can apply where there has been some sort of sub-delegation of powers to a committee. Say, for example, the board delegates wide powers to the chief executive and those powers include the power to sub-delegate. And say, for example, the chief executive delegates some of his or her duties to a committee and gives the committee power to make decisions. Surely such a committee would not be treated as a committee of the board for the purposes of model articles. If it was, every committee in the company that has decision-making powers would have to be treated as a committee of the board. It would seem to be sensible to limit the application of the articles to committees that derive their powers directly from the board.

In some cases, it might be better for a committee to be established under the direct authority of the board so that there is no doubt as to whether the articles are intended to apply to that committee. For example, it might be better to do this in order to establish a committee that is to act as a regional board or divisional board. It should not be forgotten that, under the model articles, the main board can establish constitutional rules for that committee which override the application of the articles.

Traditional articles like reg. 72 of Table A, also provide that the proceedings of a committee with two or more members shall be governed by the articles regulating the proceedings of directors so far as they are capable of applying. However, it is easier to identify the committees to which this rule applies under Table A if one assumes that reg. 72 only allows the directors to delegate their powers to a committee that actually is a committee of directors. Although Table A definitely does not allow the directors to delegate any of their powers to a committee that does not include any directors, it is possible to argue that it does allows the board to delegate to a committee that is not made up exclusively of directors. This is a fairly risky position to take. However, if one assumes it is the case, one also has to assume that the articles apply to any committees established by the board which include people who are not directors. Table A does not limit the application of the articles to committees with delegated powers.

Where any modifications are made to Table A to specifically allow people who are not directors to be appointed as members of a board committee, the application of the articles will clearly extend any committee that the board establishes.

■ 5.4 Committee membership

In most cases, it will be preferable to appoint named individuals as members of a board committee. This will certainly be the case for standing committees such as the audit and remuneration committees which are usually comprised wholly or mainly of non-executive directors. However, it is possible to appoint post-holders rather than named individuals. It may also be possible to establish a committee of 'any two directors' (or some other number), although this formula can cause some technical difficulties (see below).

5.4.1 Membership

Anyone appointed to serve on a committee will be a member of the committee. Each committee member will have a right to attend and vote at committee meetings and to participate in any other decision-making processes that it may adopt. The right to vote and participate may, of course, be subject to certain restrictions under the articles, e.g. where a director is interested in a matter that is being addressed by the committee. Although, it is possible to appoint non-voting members, it is not normally necessary to do so. A committee can invite anyone to attend its meetings and allow them to make proposals and participate in its discussions. It is possible to make provision in the committee's constitution to clarify that certain people who are not committee members have something akin to a right to attend. It is rarely advisable to actually go so far as to give non-members an inalienable right to attend. Instead it is better to provide that they have a right to do so unless invited by the committee to leave.

As mentioned in **5.3** above, the question as to whether members of board committees have to be directors depends on the construction of the articles. The underlying assumption would normally be that directors are the only people who may be appointed as full voting members of board committees. However, if the articles allow the directors to delegate their powers to committees which are not made up exclusively of directors, such committees still need to be treated as committees of the board.

The Listing Rules used to require directors to form the majority on board committees where the articles allowed co-opted members, and insisted that such committees act only where the majority of members present were directors. Although this rule was abolished in 1995, the articles of many listed companies still include such restrictions.

5.4.2 Committees of 'any two directors'

It is quite common for boards of directors to establish a committee of 'any two directors' or 'any three directors', etc (see **Precedent 5.4**). This method is most commonly used to allow directors to complete a transaction which the board has already authorised or to sign a document on behalf of the board. In such cases, it arguable whether it is necessary to establish a committee. It would be sufficient for the board to resolve, for example, that any two directors be authorised to sign a certain document on behalf of the board.

The 'any two directors' method is slightly less satisfactory where the committee is to be given discretionary powers. The technique was used by the board of Guinness during its takeover of Distillers in the 1980s to appoint a committee of any three directors:

> with full power and authority to settle the terms of the offer, to approve any revision of the offer which the committee might consider it desirable to make and [among other things] (vi) to authorise and approve, execute and do, or procure to be executed and done all documents, deeds, acts and things as they may consider necessary or desirable in connection with the making or implementation of the offer and/or the proposals referred to above and any revision thereof . . . (see *Guinness v. Saunders* [1990] 1 All E.R. 654).

Appointing such a committee could be viewed as appointing the whole board as a committee and fixing the quorum at the number of directors specified. In theory, all the directors are potential members of such a committee and are therefore entitled to receive notice of its meetings. If it is possible to appoint a committee of any two directors, it must also be acceptable to appoint a committee of 'any two' of a number of named directors. The end result is, of course, the same as if the board had appointed a committee of, say, four named directors and specified the quorum as two. If the articles prevent the board doing this by the normal method, it must be doubtful whether it can achieve the same result by using the 'any two directors' method. It is worthy of note on this score that the articles of Guinness gave the board specific power to fix the quorum of committees of the board.

It is also questionable what the position would be if, say, four directors attended a meeting of a committee of 'any two directors'. Could they all vote? And what would happen if two were in favour and two opposed to a proposal? Which (if any) of the directors would constitute the committee? In *Guinness v. Saunders*, Lord Templeman said, somewhat pointedly perhaps, that the three directors in that case 'constituted themselves as a committee'. Could three other directors have constituted themselves as a committee with the same powers?

In order to avoid these problems, some sort of control probably needs to be exercised on the calling of meetings of such a committee. Usually this will be the task of the person who prepares the documentation for the meeting. Indeed, it may be preferable to specify in the board resolution establishing such a committee that it may not meet unless the company secretary or some other specified person is present. These sort of safeguards may not be necessary where the committee is established to execute a document or perform some other mechanical process.

5.4.3 Committee of one

Articles often state that the directors may delegate their powers to a committee of one or more directors (e.g. reg. 72 of Table A). Even if they do not specifically refer to a committee of one, any power to delegate to a committee is deemed to include the power to delegate to a committee consisting of only one director, unless the articles specify otherwise (*Re Fireproof Doors Ltd.* [1916] 2 Ch. 142). This may be of relevance for companies with articles based on the 2006 Act model articles, none of which specifically state that a committee may consist of only one person.

■ 5.5 Powers and duties of committees

The extent of the powers delegated to a committee should be specified in the board resolution or the terms of reference approved by the board. To some extent, this will be apparent from the committee's duties or functions. However, it is safer to set out these powers explicitly. For example, if a committee is to be established to negotiate, agree and execute a contract for the purchase of a specified freehold property, it might be preferable to state explicitly that the committee has the power to appoint surveyors and solicitors and incur other costs which are necessary in the performance of its duties.

It may not be necessary to delegate any powers to a committee established solely to make recommendations to the board. Anybody may make recommendations to the board. Doing so is not something that requires any special powers.

However, committees established for this purpose may also benefit from having certain incidental powers (e.g. to retain external professional advisers) and it is preferable to specify these powers at the outset.

It is normal to draft more formal rules for standing committees in the form of terms of reference. A standing committee is one which is established permanently to perform certain duties on a regular basis. Terms of reference for such committees are usually adopted by a specific board resolution. Named individuals are then appointed as members of such committees by a separate resolution(s). See **Precedent 5.15** for specimen terms of reference of a nomination committee.

■ 5.6 Proceedings at committee meetings

The proceedings at committees of the board will be governed by the articles and in default by the common law of meetings. Articles usually provide that the proceedings at committee meetings shall be governed by the articles regulating the proceedings at board meetings so far as they are capable of applying. Regulation 72 of Table A adopts this style but only with respect to committees of two or more directors. The issues raised in connection with meetings of only one director are addressed in **5.12.**

The model articles adopt a similar formula but use a wording that removes much of the doubt as to the power of the directors to override the provisions of the articles (pcls, clg and plc 6).

5.6.1 Conditions imposed by the board

Regulation 72 of Table A provides that the board may impose conditions on the exercise by a committee of its delegated powers. The application to committees of the articles governing the proceedings at board meetings is made subject to any such conditions imposed by the directors. The word 'conditions' would seem to imply that the board may impose additional restrictions but may not relax the application of the articles. For example, the board could appoint the chairman of the committee and thereby limit the application of reg. 91 which would otherwise allow the committee to choose its own chairman. However, the board could not relax the application of reg. 95 which states that a director shall not be counted in the quorum present at a meeting in relation to a resolution on which he is not entitled to vote. To do so would be to remove an obstacle rather than impose an additional obstacle. It is acknowledged, however, that this interpretation of the meaning of the word 'conditions' can cause problems with regard to the quorum at committee meetings (see **5.8**).

Some articles use the word 'regulations' instead of 'conditions'. This might give the directors more latitude in disapplying the articles. It should be noted, however, that even this form of wording would not allow the directors to disapply an article which specifically states that it shall apply to committees of directors as well as the board, e.g. reg. 94 of Table A which sets out the circumstances in which a director cannot vote on a resolution.

The model articles allow the directors to make rules of procedure for all or any committees, which prevail over rules derived from the articles if they are not consistent with them (pcls, clg and plc 6(2)). Although this would appear to give the board extraordinary latitude to override restrictions contained in the articles, it is suggested that the courts would not take kindly to any hint that committees have been formed with rules that enable them to do things that the board would not be empowered to do itself (e.g. by purporting to disapply for the committee any rule preventing a conflicted director from voting). It is easy to imagine in this regard that the courts could interpret the words 'rules of procedure' very narrowly in certain circumstances, but particularly where there is an alleged breach of duty by a director.

■ 5.7 Appointment of committee chairman

Under the normal formula where the articles governing the proceedings of the board also apply to committees unless the board decides otherwise, any provisions regarding the appointment of a chairman of the board would also apply to a committee. Under most articles this would enable the committee members to appoint (and remove) one of their number as chairman of the committee (applying regs. 91 and 72 of Table A or arts. 12 and 6 of the model articles). Under both the model articles and Table A, the board may however nominate the chairman of the committee and in doing so can effectively override the committee's powers. A chairman appointed in this manner could not then be removed by the committee.

The chairman of any committee will have a casting vote if the articles confer a casting vote on the chairman of the board of directors, unless, of course, the board removes the casting vote as a condition on the exercise of the committee's powers.

Under some articles, the board may also appoint one or more deputy or vice chairmen to act in the chairman's absence. If the board fails to make provision in this regard with respect to a committee and the committee's quorum is such that meetings can still be held without the nominated chairman, the committee members present will have the power (e.g. in accordance with reg. 91 of Table A or art. 12 of the model articles) to appoint one of their number to chair meetings in the absence of the nominated chairman.

■ 5.8 Quorum requirements for committees

The common law rule is that a committee can only act if all its members are present. This rule can, of course, be modified by the articles. For example, the articles may give the board specific power to fix the quorum for board committees. Where this is the case, the common law rule will apply in default if the board fails to specify a quorum (*Re Liverpool Household Stores Association Limited* (1890)

59 L.J. Ch. 616). Even though this may be what the board intended, it is preferable to state the quorum in the resolution appointing the committee or the terms of reference approved by the board.

The 2006 Act model articles definitely allow the directors to set the quorum of any committee and any decision they make in this regard will definitely override the common law rule and any other quorum that may have been fixed under the articles for the board, that would otherwise apply in default (see pcls, clg and plc 6(2)).

Regulation 72 of Table A states that the proceedings of committees shall be governed by the articles regulating the proceedings of the board so far as they are capable of applying. The relevant provision of Table A dealing with the quorum at board meetings (reg. 89) is capable of applying to any committee with two or members. It provides that the quorum for the transaction of the business of the directors may be fixed by the directors and unless so fixed at any other number shall be two. As the board can fix a different quorum for its own meetings under reg. 89 of Table A, it can presumably also do so for any committee that it may establish.

Difficulties can arise however where a company's articles fix a much higher quorum for board meetings and do not allow the board to vary that figure. Say, for example, the articles provide for a fixed quorum of six for board meetings and do not allow the board to vary this themselves. Can the board establish a committee whose quorum is less than six? The answer to this question would appear to be quite simple. If the articles allow the board to establish a committee of less than six directors, the quorum for that committee must be less than six. Articles often specify that the board can delegate its powers to a committee of one or more directors (see reg. 72 of Table A). Where they say this, there would appear to be no question that board can establish a committee of less than six, even though the quorum for the board may be six. In these circumstances, the board quorum of six would not be capable of applying. Accordingly, the common law rule that the committee can only act if all its members are present would apply unless the board is allowed under the articles to fix a different quorum for the committee.

Where the common law rule applies, the directors can effectively reduce the committee's quorum by appointing less committee members. If they appoint five, all five have to participate in the committee's decisions. If they appoint four, all four must do so, and so on. If the board can vary the number of directors required to participate in the committee's decisions in this way, it would seem strange to say that they cannot appoint more committee members and specify that not all of them need to participate in the committee's decisions. However, it is submitted that this is what the position would be if the articles do not allow them to fix a different quorum for the committee.

It should be noted that delegation to a committee (or to an individual), by its very nature, can have the effect of allowing the directors to circumvent the usual quorum requirements for board meetings, particularly where the quorum for board meetings is set by the articles at a high figure. It is fairly obvious that the courts will not look kindly on any technique that the directors may use to circumvent the usual quorum requirements unless that technique is specifically allowed under the articles. In fact, the courts have, on occasion, refused to allow directors to do this even though it may appear to have been allowed under the articles (see below). The fact that they have done so helps to explain why the board cannot assume that it has the power to fix the quorum for any committee unless there is something in the articles which specifically allows them to do so. It is fairly obvious that where the quorum for board meetings is set by the articles at quite a high figure, the directors are more likely be tempted to try to establish a committee in order to circumvent their own quorum requirements. The courts are well aware of this, and are likely to interpret the provisions of the articles fairly strictly when assessing whether this is allowed.

Indeed, as mentioned above, the courts are sometimes to strike down something that appears to be allowed under the articles on the basis that the directors cannot delegate something to a committee merely to enable that committee to do something that the board was not capable of doing itself as a result of restrictions in the articles which prevented the directors from voting on or being counted in the quorum for matters in which they were interested. In this particular case, it was obvious that the only reason why the board had established a committee was to circumvent the normal rules. The court judged this to be an abuse by the directors of their powers.

5.8.1 Disinterested quorum

Articles usually provide that a director shall not be counted in the quorum present at a meeting in relation to a resolution on which he is not entitled to vote (e.g. reg. 95 of Table A, pcls 14, clg 14 and plc 16). This is merely a restatement of the common law rule and will always be the case unless the articles make specific provision to the contrary. Any article on this matter will also apply to meetings of a committee of directors by virtue of articles such as reg. 72 of Table A and art. 6(1) of the model articles. It is doubtful whether the directors can exclude the application of any such article by imposing a condition in accordance with reg. 72. It is also arguable that reg. 95 should be read in conjunction with reg. 94 which specifically states that it is applicable to committees of directors. It is hard to imagine any justifiable reason why the board would wish to disapply this sort of provision even if it was capable of doing so, as would seem to be the case under art. 6(2) of the model articles. As suggested above, there is a distinct danger that the courts would view any such proposal by the directors to be an abuse of their powers particularly where it could be construed as a device to enable them to do something as a committee that they would not be able to do as a board.

5.8.2 Quorum of one

The basic common law rule established in *Sharp v. Dawes* is that in order to hold a valid meeting there must be a meeting of minds, in other words, that there must be at least two people present who are entitled to attend and vote. However, even the common law recognises that a valid meeting can be held with only one person present where he or she is the only person entitled to attend and vote at meetings of that body, e.g. the sole holder of a class of shares (*East v. Bennet Bro. Ltd.* [1911] 1 Ch. 163).

In any case, the principle laid down in *Sharp v. Dawes* is a common law rule and, as such, is liable to modification by the articles. If the articles allow the directors to fix a quorum of one at board meetings and provide that the regulations governing board meetings shall also apply to committee meetings, it would seem that they may also fix a quorum of one for a committee of more than one director (*Re Fireproof Doors Ltd.* [1916] 2 Ch. 142). Regulation 89 of Table A allows the directors to fix a quorum of one for board meetings and therefore to do likewise for any committee.

5.8.3 Minimum number

Articles specifying the minimum number of directors are clearly not intended to apply to committees of the board and can be considered to be excluded by the words 'so far as they are capable of applying' in reg. 72 and similarly worded articles. The board may, however, specify as a condition in the board resolution establishing the committee the minimum number of members of that committee. If so, the committee will not be authorised to act if the number of members falls below that figure, say as a result of the death or resignation of committee members (*Re Liverpool Household Stores Association Limited* (1890) 59 L.J. Ch. 616). If the board resolution states that the committee shall consist of three members and then proceeds to name them, that would be equivalent to fixing a minimum number.

Regulation 90 of Table A provides that the continuing directors or sole continuing director may act notwithstanding any vacancies in their number. If reg. 90 applies to committees by virtue of reg. 72, it would appear that a committee may act notwithstanding any vacancies provided that there are sufficient members present to form a quorum. This would seem to defeat the object of setting a minimum in the first place. However, one might also say the same about the situation with regard to the board of directors.

■ 5.9 Voting

Articles usually prohibit the directors from voting on any matter in which they have an interest. Table A and the model articles both allow the directors to vote in certain limited circumstances where they are interested but otherwise imposes a general prohibition (reg. 94 of Table A, pcls 14, clg 14 and plc 16). Regulation 94 of Table A specifically states that these rules apply to any 'committee of directors' as well as the board. The relevant provisions of the model articles are not quite so explicit. Committees to which the directors delegate any of their powers must follow procedures which are based as far as they are applicable on those provisions of the articles which govern the taking of decisions by directors (pcls, clg and plc 6(1)). This presumably includes the article provisions on directors' conflicts. The model articles also refer to committees of directors in the provision giving the chairman power to decide whether or not a conflicted director may participate in the meeting (pcls 14(6), clg 14(6) and plc 16(5)).

Where non-directors are appointed as members of a board committee, it may be a good idea to clarify in the terms of reference their duties with regard to disclosure of interests and their right to vote on transactions in which they have an interest. Members of board committees who are not directors do not have a statutory duty to disclose such interests and articles on voting usually refer only to directors.

Articles sometimes provide that the majority of members present at a meeting must be directors where they allow non-directors to be appointed. This could also be included as a condition in the committee's terms of reference.

Under the common law, each member of the committee will have one vote. The articles may, however, make alternative provision with regard to board meetings and any such provisions may be adopted by default for committees by virtue of clauses like reg. 72 of Table A and art. 6 of the model articles. The most obvious example is where the articles provide for the appointment of alternate directors. If a director appoints another director as his or her alternate, the director so appointed will have two votes. Great care should, however, be taken where one or more directors have weighted voting rights in respect of the exercise by the board of certain powers and it is proposed to delegate those powers to a committee.

5.9.1 Disclosure of interests in transactions

It may not be sufficient for a director to declare an interest in a proposed transaction at a committee meeting for the purposes of s. 177. The declaration must be made to the other directors (s. 177(1)) before the company enters into the transaction or arrangement (s. 177(4)). The requirement to make the declaration to the other directors means to the other members of the board rather than just to those serving on the committee.

A declaration of interest made at a committee meeting that is subsequently brought to the attention of the other directors will probably suffice for the purposes of s. 177, provided that this happens before the transaction is entered into. This could be done in one of the ways permitted by s. 177(2), although it should be noted that subsection (2) does not specifically require the declaration to be made in one of those ways. A declaration of interest recorded in the minutes of a committee which are circulated to the entire board or laid at a board meeting may suffice for these purposes, although it may be preferable for the declaration to be made in one of the manners explicitly allowed (see **4.12**).

Where a committee has made a decision on a transaction or arrangement in which a director has declared an interest, it will be necessary to ensure that the company does not enter into that transaction or arrangement until the director has made the necessary declaration to the other directors. This will not be difficult where additional formalities are required. They can be delayed until the declaration has been properly made. However, there can be circumstances in which the committee's decision may create binding legal obligations on the part of the company, particularly where its decision relates to a proposal to enter into a contract with the director who declared the interest. In such circumstances it may be necessary to ensure that the committee's approval is made conditional on the necessary declaration having been made.

5.9.2 Alternate directors

There is no automatic right to appoint a proxy or an alternate at meetings of committees. The right to appoint an alternate depends entirely on the articles (see regs. 65 to 71 of Table A and plc 25 to 27). Table A deals explicitly with the position of alternates with regard to committees. To summarise, it provides that an alternate is entitled to receive notice of all meetings of committees of which his or her appointor is a member and to attend and vote at any such meeting in the absence of his or her appointor.

The model articles for public companies are rather less explicit in this regard but provide that alternates may act in relation to the taking of decisions by the directors in the absence of their appointor and, except where the articles specify otherwise, are deemed for all purposes to be directors (plc 25 and 26).

It is doubtful whether a person who is not a director but who is appointed as a member of a committee can appoint an alternate unless the articles specifically provide.

■ 5.10 Defects in appointment

Section 161 and articles based on it (e.g. reg. 92 of Table A) serve to validate the acts of committees where it is subsequently discovered that there is a defect in the appointment or qualification of directors who were members of it (see **7.2**).

■ 5.11 Directors' written resolutions

Articles on directors' written resolutions or unanimous decisions (see further **6.2**) often specifically extend this form of decision-making process to committees of the board. This is certainly the case with regard to reg. 93 of Table A, although not reg. 106 of the 1948 Table A or the model articles prescribed under the 2006 Act. However, in the case of the model articles, the written resolution procedures will almost certainly apply to committees by virtue of art. 6 which applies the articles governing the taking of decisions by directors to committees.

■ 5.12 Committee of one director

As a general rule, there must be at least two people present in order to hold a meeting (*Sharp v. Dawes* (1876) 2 Q.B.D. 26). Articles often specify that the board may delegate its powers to a committee of one. This is the case under reg. 72 of Table A, which does not provide any other way of delegating powers to a non-executive director. The 2006 Act model articles do not specify that the directors may delegate to a committee of only one director, but allow the directors to delegate their powers to any person they think fit (including a non-executive director) without having to establish a committee for that purpose. So, although it may be possible to establish a committee of one under the model articles, it is rather less likely that a company would want or need to do so. It is possible that the power to delegate to a committee will be deemed to include the power to delegate to a committee of one unless the articles provide otherwise (Re Fireproof Doors Ltd. [1916] 2 Ch. 142). However, it should be remembered that the courts do not like directors using techniques to enable a committee to do something that the board would not be allowed to do itself.

Most articles follow the formula that, in so far as they are capable of applying, the articles governing proceedings at board meetings shall apply to committees. Under the model articles, this rule applies to all committees to which the board has delegated its powers (art. 6(1)). Under reg. 72 of Table A, the rule only applies in relation to committees consisting of two or more directors. In other words, Table A makes no provision for the procedures to be followed at meetings of a committee of only one director.

Even if the articles do not follow Table A in this regard, the words 'so far as they are capable of applying' will exclude the application of many of the articles. However, any article which specifically states that it is applicable to committees of directors will still be relevant, e.g. Table A, reg. 93 (written resolutions) and reg. 94 (restrictions on voting).

Under the 2006 Act model articles, committees of one must follow procedures which are based as far as they are applicable on those provisions of the articles which govern the taking of decisions by directors (pcls, clg and plc 6(1)). However, it is worth noting that the model articles for private companies (but not those for plcs) also provide that the general rules about directors' decision-making do not apply if the company only has one director and no provision of the articles requires it to have more than one director (pcls 7 and clg 7). It is just about arguable that this article is capable of applying in the case of a committee of one to exclude the normal rules on directors' decision-making, although it is doubtful whether this is the intended effect or whether it would be safe to rely on it.

In theory, it will still be necessary for a director who is the sole member of a committee to hold meetings. In practice, it will not be necessary for him to give himself any notice and whenever he exercises his delegated powers he can be said to be holding a meeting. The principle of unanimous consent will rectify almost any procedural defect in this regard, although strenuous attempts should always be made to follow proper procedures where the director has a conflict of interest.

It is good practice for a director who is the sole member of a committee to keep a written record of his decisions. Probably the best way of doing this is for the director to act by written resolution (see **Precedent 5.12**) and for each resolution to be entered into a minute book kept for that purpose. Regulation 100 of Table A requires the directors to keep minutes of all proceedings at meetings of committees of directors. The model articles for private companies require the directors to a keep a record of every unanimous or majority decision taken by the directors (pcls 15, clg 15). The model articles for public companies require the company secretary to ensure that the company keeps a record, in writing, of all directors' written resolutions (plc 18).

■ 5.13 Audit committee

Listed companies are required by the UK Corporate Governance Code and the Disclosure and Transparency Rules to establish an audit committee to perform certain duties.

5.13.1 UK Corporate Governance Code

Principle C.3 of the UK Corporate Governance Code requires boards to establish formal and transparent arrangements for considering how they should apply financial reporting, risk management and internal control principles and for maintaining an appropriate relationship with the company's auditors. Code provision C.3.1 clarifies that this means establishing an audit committee.

The Code requires the audit committee to comprise of at least three or, in the case of smaller companies, two members, who should all be independent non-executive directors. At least one member of the audit committee should have recent and relevant financial experience (UK Corporate Governance Code, provision C.3.1).

Where a company has only a few independent non-executive directors, normally all of them will serve on the audit committee. If there are more independent non-executive directors than this, permitting selection from a larger group, three to five members is generally regarded as the optimum size for the committee.

5.13.2 Role of audit committee

The establishment of an audit committee is not intended to undermine the ultimate responsibility of the board for reviewing and approving the annual report and accounts and the half-yearly report. Rather, it is intended to ensure that the non-executive directors become actively involved in that process and have access to the resources necessary to enable them to make independent judgments. It also offers the auditors a direct link with the non-executive directors.

Code provision C.3.2 provides that the main role and responsibilities of the audit committee should be set out in written terms of reference and should include the following:

- to monitor the integrity of the financial statements of the company, and any formal announcements relating to the company's financial performance, reviewing significant financial reporting judgments contained in them;
- to review the company's internal financial controls and, unless expressly addressed by a separate board risk committee composed of independent directors, or by the board itself, to review the company's internal control and risk management systems;
- to monitor and review the effectiveness of the company's internal audit function;
- to make recommendations to the board, for it to put to the shareholders for their approval in general meeting, in relation to the appointment, reappointment and removal of the external auditor and to approve the remuneration and terms of engagement of the external auditor;
- to review and monitor the external auditor's independence and objectivity and the effectiveness of the audit process, taking into consideration relevant UK professional and regulatory requirements;
- to develop and implement policy on the engagement of the external auditor to supply non-audit services, taking into account relevant ethical guidance regarding the provision of non-audit services by the external audit firm, and to report to the board, identifying any matters in respect of which it considers that action or improvement is needed and making recommendations as to the steps to be taken;
- to report to the board on how it has discharged its responsibilities.

The Code also requires the audit committee:

- to review arrangements by which staff of the company may, in confidence, raise concerns about possible improprieties in matters of financial reporting or other matters. Its objective should be to ensure that arrangements are in place for the proportionate and independent investigation of such matters and for appropriate follow-up action (Code provision C.3.5);
- to monitor and review the effectiveness of the internal audit activities. Where there is no internal audit function, the audit committee should consider annually whether there is a need for one and make a recommendation to the board (Code provision C.3.6);
- to have primary responsibility for making recommendations on the appointment, reappointment and removal of the external auditors (Code provision C.3.7).

The terms of reference of the audit committee, including its role and the authority delegated to it by the board, should be made publicly available (Code provision C.3.3). ICSA publishes a Guidance Note *Terms of Reference – Audit Committee*.

5.13.3 Delegated powers

The primary purpose of the audit committee is not to exercise powers delegated by the board but to monitor and review matters connected with the financial statements and to make recommendations to the board arising from these activities. However, the committee may need to be given certain incidental powers to enable it to function effectively. These could include, for example, explicit powers of internal investigation and rights of access to any company information. In theory, this would enable the audit committee to cut through the usual chain of authority when conducting investigations. The committee will almost certainly need to be given power to retain independent professional advisers.

5.13.14 Statements in the annual report

The UK Corporate Governance Code requires the annual report of a listed company to contain a description of the composition and work of the audit committee and to include various statements relating to the committee's duties (Code provisions C.3.6 to C.3.8).

5.13.15 Disclosure and Transparency Rules/Audit Directive requirements

The UK Corporate Governance Code requirements on audit committees are also supplemented by certain mandatory requirements in the Disclosure and Transparency Rules (see DTR 7.1). These rules implement the requirements of the Audit Directive and, subject to certain exceptions, apply to issuers whose transferable securities are admitted to trading and which are required to appoint a statutory auditor (DTR 1B.1.2). The provisions of DTR 7.1 effectively replicate the provisions on audit committees in the UK Corporate Governance Code in that they require issuers to have a body which is responsible for performing the functions that an audit committee would typically carry out. At least one member of that body must be independent and at least one member must have competence in accounting and/or auditing (DTR 7.1.1), although the same member may satisfy both of these requirements (DTR 7.1.2).

The relevant body must, as a minimum (DTR 7.1.3):

■ monitor the financial reporting process;
■ monitor the effectiveness of the issuer's internal control, internal audit where applicable, and risk management systems;
■ monitor the statutory audit of the annual and consolidated accounts; and
■ review and monitor the independence of the statutory auditor, and in particular the provision of additional services to the issuer.

An issuer must base any proposal to appoint a statutory auditor on a recommendation made by the relevant body (DTR 7.1.4).

The issuer must make a statement disclosing which body carries out the above functions and how it is composed (DTR 7.1.5). This statement may be included in any statement the issuer is required to make under DTR 7.2 (Corporate governance statements) (DTR 7.1.6).

In the FCA's view, compliance with the provision on audit committees in the UK Corporate Governance Code will result in compliance with the requirements of DTR 7.1 on audit committees (DTR 7.1.7).

5.14 Remuneration committee

Articles invariably give the board of directors power to determine executive salaries and the members will normally have no direct say in the amount executives are paid. These arrangements are necessary because executive directors are usually employed under a service contract, the terms of which need to be settled before the executive joins the board. Members could be given a role in determining these salaries if the executive directors' contractual entitlements were made subject to the approval of the members in general meeting. However, any company which tried to impose such arrangements would probably find it impossible to recruit executives of desired calibre.

The usual procedure is therefore for the board to enter into a contract with the executive director on behalf of the company when it appoints him. If the director is subsequently dismissed (e.g. by the members at the next annual general meeting), he will be entitled to damages for breach of contract. The amount of damages will depend on the directors' remuneration but also on the period of notice the company is required to give under the contract.

5.14.1 UK Corporate Governance Code

The UK Corporate Governance Code requires listed companies to establish formal and transparent procedures for developing policy on executive remuneration and for fixing the remuneration packages of individual directors. It also provides that no director should be involved in deciding his or her own remuneration (Code principle D.2).

In practice, listed companies are expected to establish a remuneration committee to perform these functions. The committee should consist exclusively of independent non-executive directors and should comprise at least three or, in the case of smaller companies, two such directors (Code provision D.2.1). Smaller companies are defined for the purposes of the Code as those that were outside the FTSE 350 throughout the year immediately prior to the reporting year. The chairman and members of the committee should be identified in the annual report (Code provision A.1.2).

The company chairman may serve on the remuneration committee provided that he was considered independent on appointment as chairman (but should not also chair the committee) (Code provision D.2.1). The Code requires the remuneration committee to set the remuneration of the executive directors and the chairman (Code provision D.2.2), and also recommends as a general principle that no director should be involved in fixing his or her own remuneration (Code principle D.2). If the chairman serves on the committee, this does not necessarily present an insurmountable obstacle as the chairman could absent himself from discussions regarding his own remuneration or fees. It does, however, imply that the chairman should be treated as an executive for the purposes of remuneration even though he may be treated as a non-executive for other purposes. Remuneration committees are expected to consult the chairman and/or chief executive officer about their proposals relating to the remuneration of other executive directors (first supporting principle B.2). The use of the words 'other executive directors' in this supporting principle would seem to suggest again that the chairman should be treated as an executive.

5.14.2 Duties of the remuneration committee
The UK Corporate Governance Code requires the remuneration committee to be given delegated responsibility for setting the remuneration of all executive directors and the chairman, including pension rights and any compensation payments. The committee is also expected to recommend and monitor the level and structure of remuneration for senior management. The definition of 'senior management' for this purpose should be determined by the board but should normally include the first layer of management below board level (Code provision D.2.2).

The committee is required to make available its terms of reference, explaining its role and the authority delegated to it by the board (Code provision D.2.1). This can be done by making the document available on the company's website (see footnote 7 to the Code). For specimen terms of reference, see the ICSA Guidance Note *Terms of Reference – Remuneration Committee.*

5.14.3 Delegating powers to the committee: articles of association
The UK Corporate Governance Code envisages that the board will delegate authority to the remuneration committee to determine executive remuneration. This contrasts with the approach taken in the Cadbury Report (para. 4.42 of that report) that the remuneration committee should make recommendations to the board, with the board making the actual decision. Most listed companies' articles contain a general power enabling the board to delegate any of their powers to a committee of the board (following, for example, reg. 72 of Table A). However, as the delegation would involve questions of directors' fiduciary duties where directors' personal interests were involved, the case of *Guinness Plc v. Saunders* [1990] 1 All E.R. 652 (House of Lords) may be a cause for concern.

In the *Guinness* case it was held that a general provision in the articles allowing the board to delegate its powers to board committees did not extend to powers specifically given by the articles to 'the board' which the board would not otherwise have. Accordingly, in order to delegate the power to determine directors' remuneration to a committee of the board, it is essential that the articles allow the board to delegate not only its general powers but also any special powers, or specifically allow the board to delegate its power to fix directors' remuneration. If the articles do not allow such delegation, the decisions of the remuneration committee must be formally ratified by the board. Although this might constitute a technical breach of the UK Corporate Governance Code, it would not contravene the spirit if the board, as a matter of policy, adopted the recommendations of the remuneration committee without debate. This procedure would, however, raise questions as to whether the executive directors should vote on the recommendations of the remuneration committee. Clearly they should not do so with regard to their own remuneration, and it may, accordingly, be necessary to have a separate vote on the committee's proposals for each director.

■ 5.15 Nomination committee

All listed companies are required by the UK Corporate Governance Code to establish a nomination committee to lead the process for board appointments and make recommendations to the board (Code provision B.2.1).

A majority of members of the nomination committee should be independent non-executive directors. The committee should be chaired by the company chairman or an independent non-executive director (Code provision B.2.1). The chairman and members of the nomination committee should be identified in the annual report (Code provision A.1.2).

Although the UK Corporate Governance Code does not provide any specific guidance on the matter, nomination committees rarely consist of more than three directors. If an executive director (or possibly the chairman) is a member, this will be the minimum number required to comply with the requirement that the majority of members are independent non-executive directors. This may put pressure on companies to categorise the chairman as an independent non-executive even though he or she may not meet all the independence criteria in Code provision B.1.1.

5.15.1 Role of the committee

According to the UK Corporate Governance Code, the role of the committee is 'to lead the process for board appointments and make recommendations to the board'. The 2003 Combined Code included as an appendix a 'Summary of the Principal Duties of the Nomination Committee' taken from a report published by Sir Derek Higgs. Although this summary did not officially form part of the Code and is not reproduced in the 2008 version, it provides some guidance as to what 'leading the process for board appointments' might entail. It suggests that, in addition to identifying and nominating for the approval of the board any candidates to fill board vacancies, the committee's duties could include:

■ reviewing annually the time required from a non-executive director and making recommendations to the board regarding the reappointment of any non-executive director at the conclusion of their specified term of office;

- regularly reviewing the structure, size and composition (including the skills, knowledge and experience) of the board and making recommendations to the board with regard to any changes;
- keeping under review the leadership needs of the organisation, both executive and non-executive, with a view to ensuring the continued ability of the organisation to compete effectively in the marketplace;
- making recommendations to the board regarding plans for succession for both executive and non-executive directors; and
- making recommendations to the board concerning any matters relating to the continuation in office of any director at any time.

5.15.2 Terms of reference

The UK Corporate Governance Code requires the nomination committee to make available its terms of reference, which should explain its role and the authority delegated to it by the board (Code provision B.2.1). This requirement can be met by making the document available on the company's website (see footnote 7 to the Code).

Specimen terms of reference from the ICSA Guidance Note *Terms of Reference – Nomination Committee* can be found at **Precedent 5.15**.

A practical issue which will arise in operating a nomination committee is that the minutes/reports to the board of the committee will, for reasons of discretion, usually not include details of internal candidates considered in principle but rejected. The names of outside candidates under serious consideration by the committee (e.g. for non-executive directorship) would, again for reasons of discretion, no doubt be sounded out with the full board prior to the committee commencing discussions with the person concerned with a view to possibly making a recommendation for his or her appointment.

Appointment process

Prior to making any appointment, the UK Corporate Governance Code requires the nomination committee to evaluate the balance of skills, knowledge and experience on the board and, in the light of this evaluation, prepare a description of the role and capabilities required for that particular appointment (Code provision B.2.2). It is likely that the committee will be able to utilise the results of the annual performance evaluation process to perform this task. For the appointment of a new chairman, the Code also requires the committee to prepare a job specification which includes an assessment of the time commitment expected for the role (Code provision B.3.1).

Although the Code does not specifically require the use of external search consultants or open advertising, it requires a statement to be included in the annual report if neither were used when filling the post of chairman or recruiting a non-executive director (Code provision B.2.4).

Disclosure of commitments and terms of appointment

Other significant commitments of the chairman and any non-executive director should be disclosed to the board before appointment and, for the chairman only, included in the annual report. Changes to such commitments should also be reported to the board as they arise, and, in the case of the chairman, included in the next annual report (Code provisions B.3.1 and B.3.2).

The terms of appointment of non-executive directors should be made available for inspection by any person at the company's registered office during normal business hours and at the AGM (for 15 minutes prior to the meeting and during the meeting) (Code provision B.3.2). It should be noted that UK companies have to make executive directors' service contracts available for inspection by members under CA 2006, ss. 228 and 229.

Statement in annual report

A separate section of the annual report should describe the work of the nomination committee, including the process it has used in relation to board appointments. It should also include:

(a) a description of the board's policy on diversity, including gender, any measurable objectives that it has set for implementing the policy, and progress on achieving the objectives;

(b) where relevant, an explanation as to why neither an external search consultancy nor open advertising has been used in the appointment of a chairman or a non-executive director (Code provision B.2.4).

6

Directors' written resolutions and informal consent

6.1 Summary

- The Act allows members of a private company to act by written resolution but makes no equivalent provision with regard to directors. Articles commonly allow the board of directors and any committee of directors to make decisions by passing a written resolution. They normally require all the directors to sign the resolution in order to act in this way. However, they may make different provision (see **6.2**).
- A decision of the directors will not necessarily be invalid simply because they failed to approve the transaction at a meeting or in accordance with some other procedure provided for in the articles. The courts often apply the common law principle of unanimous consent where it is clear that all the directors approved the transaction or can be deemed to have acquiesced to the decision (see **6.3**).

6.2 Written resolutions

There is no equivalent for directors to the statutory procedure for written resolutions of the members (see **9.2**). The ability of the directors to act without holding formal meetings is therefore entirely dependent on the common law and the articles.

Most articles make specific provision enabling the directors to act by written resolution even though it is now firmly established that the directors may act outside formal board meetings if they all agree. This is partly because of the uncertainties in the common law but also because articles usually provide a slightly more relaxed regime.

See **Precedent 6.2A** for an example of a directors' written resolution.

6.2.1 Model articles for private companies

The model articles for private companies provide as a general rule that the directors must take decisions either by a majority at a meeting or as a unanimous decision in accordance with art. 8 (pcls and clg 7). This general rule does not apply, however, if the company only has one director and is not required by the articles to have more than one. In these circumstances, the sole director may make decisions without regard to any of the provisions of the articles relating to directors' decision making. Article 8 of the model articles for private companies provides:

Unanimous decisions

8 (1) A decision of the directors is taken in accordance with this article when all eligible directors indicate to each other by any means that they share a common view on a matter.

  (2) Such a decision may take the form of a resolution in writing, copies of which have been signed by each eligible director or to which each eligible director has otherwise indicated agreement in writing.

  (3) References in this article to eligible directors are to directors who would have been entitled to vote on the matter had it been proposed as a resolution at a directors' meeting.

  (4) A decision may not be taken in accordance with this article if the eligible directors would not have formed a quorum at such a meeting.

Article 8 allows the directors to signify their consent to a unanimous decision in a variety of ways. All that is required is that they must have indicated to each other in some way that they share a common view on the matter. This could, for example, be done at a face-to-face meeting, a series of face-to-face meetings, by a chain of e-mails or telephone conversations, or using the more traditional method of a written resolution. The article would seem to require the directors to share a common view and to have indicated that view to each other. Accordingly, unlike the common law principle of unanimous consent, it does not necessarily allow any of the directors to be deemed to have acquiesced in the decision. Neither, however, should the article necessarily be considered to exclude the common law principle of unanimous consent, which could still serve to validate decisions not made in accordance with the articles.

It should be noted however that, although it is not necessary under art. 8 for the directors to agree to a decision in writing, they are required to ensure that the company keeps a written record of every unanimous decision taken by them for at least ten years from the date of the decision (pcls and clg 15).

The record of the decision kept for these purposes need not be signed by all the eligible directors but probably ought to be authenticated by a director (preferably the chairman) or the company secretary (if the company has one). Nevertheless, it is almost certainly preferable for the copy of the decision retained for these purposes to be signed by all the eligible directors because this will then serve as evidence of their agreement.

Article 8 makes it clear that the unanimous decision-making procedure may not be used if the number of directors able to participate in the decision would not have been sufficient to form a quorum at a meeting of directors. Directors who would not have been entitled to vote on the matter had it been proposed as a resolution at a directors' meeting cannot be counted for these purposes. Effectively, directors who would not have been eligible to vote on the matter at a board meeting (e.g. because of a personal interest) are not required to consent to the decision and the fact that they may have purported to consent to it (or, perhaps even, to oppose it) is irrelevant for the purposes of determining whether the decision is valid.

It should be noted that 'in writing' is defined for the purposes of the model articles in article 1 (defined terms) as 'the representation or reproduction of words, symbols or other information in a visible form by any method or combination of methods, whether sent or supplied in electronic form or otherwise'. Accordingly, it is not necessary for the purposes of a written resolution under art. 8 for directors to sign a hard copy of the resolution under hand. Any method of signature, including some sort of electronic signature, would suffice for these purposes. Indeed, in the case of a written resolution sent to a director by e-mail, it is likely that an e-mailed reply clearly signifying consent would be satisfactory for these purposes, although it would obviously be preferable for evidential purposes if that e-mail was signed using a proper electronic signature (see **2.13**).

6.2.2 Model articles for public companies
The model articles for public companies also allow the directors to act without holding a meeting by the more traditional method of passing a written resolution (plc 7, 17 and 18). The plc model articles make far more detailed provision about who may propose a directors' written resolution and the procedures that must be followed in this regard.

Proposing directors' written resolutions

17. (1) Any director may propose a directors' written resolution.

(2) The company secretary must propose a directors' written resolution if a director so requests.

(3) A directors' written resolution is proposed by giving notice of the proposed resolution to the directors.

(4) Notice of a proposed directors' written resolution must indicate –
(a) the proposed resolution, and
(b) the time by which it is proposed that the directors should adopt it.

(5) Notice of a proposed directors' written resolution must be given in writing to each director.

(6) Any decision which a person giving notice of a proposed directors' written resolution takes regarding the process of adopting that resolution must be taken reasonably in good faith.

Adoption of directors' written resolutions

18. (1) A proposed directors' written resolution is adopted when all the directors who would have been entitled to vote on the resolution at a directors' meeting have signed one or more copies of it, provided that those directors would have formed a quorum at such a meeting.

(2) It is immaterial whether any director signs the resolution before or after the time by which the notice proposed that it should be adopted.

(3) Once a directors' written resolution has been adopted, it must be treated as if it had been a decision taken at a directors' meeting in accordance with the articles.

(4) The company secretary must ensure that the company keeps a record, in writing, of all directors' written resolutions for at least ten years from the date of their adoption.

The requirement in art. 17(4) that notice of a proposed directors' written resolution *must* indicate the time by which it is proposed that the directors should adopt it seems pernickety at best, when one considers that art. 18(2) specifically states that it is immaterial whether any director signs the resolution before or after the time by which the notice proposed that it should be adopted. Technically, this means that a written resolution that does not state a time by which it is proposed it should be adopted might be defective even though any such statement is largely superfluous. Hopefully, should this issue ever be raised in litigation, the courts will adopt a common sense approach and rule that the absence of any proposed deadline in the notice should be taken for the purposes of art. 17(4) to mean that there was no deadline.

It should be noted that 'in writing' is defined for the purposes of the model articles in art. 1 as 'the representation or reproduction of words, symbols or other information in a visible form by any method or combination of methods, whether sent or supplied in electronic form or otherwise'. Accordingly, notice of the resolution may be given in either hard copy or electronic form. In addition, the fact that directors are required by art. 18(1) to sign a copy of the resolution does not mean that this must be done by signature under hand on a hard copy version. Any method of signature, including some sort of electronic signature, would suffice for these purposes. Indeed, in the case of a written resolution sent to a director by e-mail, it is likely that an e-mailed reply clearly signifying consent would be satisfactory for these purposes, although it would obviously be preferable for evidential purposes if that e-mail was signed using a proper electronic signature (see **2.13**).

Under the model articles for public companies, an alternate director may sign a written resolution, but only if it is not signed or to be signed by that person's appointor (plc 26(3)). For these purposes, it is probably safe to say that the signature of an alternate can be ignored if the resolution is also signed by his appointor. An alternate is presumably entitled to receive notice of any proposed written resolution under plc 26(1) and will be subject to the same restrictions as his appointor regarding his participation in a decision made by written resolution (plc 26(2)(c)) as well as potentially being excluded from participating on his own account (plc 26(2)(a)).

6.2.3 Table A

Regulation 93 of Table A provides:

> 93. A resolution signed in writing by all the directors entitled to receive notice of a meeting of directors or of a committee of directors shall be as valid and effectual as if it had been passed at a meeting of directors or (as the case may be) a committee of directors duly convened and held and may consist of several documents in the like form each signed by one or more directors; but a resolution signed by an alternate director need not also be signed by his appointor and, if it is signed by a director who has appointed an alternate director, it need not be signed by the alternate in that capacity.

Under the common law, the unanimous agreement of the directors is required. Under reg. 93 the resolution need only be signed by the directors entitled to receive notice of a meeting of directors or of a committee of directors as the case may be.

Under Table A, the only occasion on which a director is not entitled to receive notice is when he or she is absent from the UK (reg. 88). Thus, in normal circumstances, the resolution must be signed by all the directors. If, however, one or more are outside the UK, then the requirement for unanimity no longer applies. This could give rise to some peculiar results. Say, for example, four out of seven directors travel abroad on a business trip, it would appear that the three directors who remain in the UK could pass a written resolution even though they are in the minority in terms of numbers. This is not particularly unusual because the same directors could convene a board meeting and pass the resolution in the usual manner. However, a more difficult question is whether the written resolution would still be valid where the quorum for board meetings was four.

The High Court was recently called upon to rule on a similar question under reg. 106 of the 1948 Table A, which is broadly the same as reg. 93 of the 1985 Table A. Carnwath J held that a directors' written resolution, passed in accordance with reg. 106 of the 1948 Table A, signed by only one director where the quorum for the transaction of business by the directors was two, was invalid, notwithstanding that the only other director was outside the United Kingdom and thus not entitled to notice of a meeting of directors (*Hood Sailmakers Ltd. v. Axford* [1996] 4 All E.R. 830). In reaching this decision, he relied on the fact that reg. 99 of the 1948 Table A refers to 'the quorum necessary for the transaction of the business' (as does reg. 88 of the 1985 Table A), and said that even though reg. 106 of the 1948 Table A indicates that a written resolution of the directors will be as valid and effectual as if it had been passed at a meeting of directors, the requirement for a quorum must be treated as a separate matter.

The absence of a director from the UK can also cause difficulties because neither version of Table A specifies the point at which the test of whether a director is entitled to receive notice should be applied. There would be no problem if the director was away on the day that all the directors in the UK signed the resolution. However, if the directors sign on different days, it is not clear whether a person who was absent for only part of the period between the first and last signatures should also sign. Say, for example, a company has four directors (A, B, C and D) who are each given a copy of a written resolution. A and B do not agree with the proposal and do not sign it. They leave the UK on business before C and D sign the resolution. If the critical point for the test is when the last director signs, then the resolution would be valid because A and B are absent from the UK and not therefore entitled to receive notice when C and D sign it.

Alternatively it could be argued that there is no single critical point, i.e. that a director who is present in the UK at some stage during the process must sign the resolution. The process could be deemed to start from the point the first director signed and finish at the point the last director signed. This would not make any difference in the above example but would if either C or D had signed a copy of the resolution before A and B left the UK. Finally, as the test is whether a director is entitled to receive notice, it could be argued that if a director actually receives a copy of a written resolution while in the UK and does not sign it, the resolution will not be valid without his or her signature. This is probably the safest assumption to make in this regard.

Where the articles make provision for the appointment of alternate directors and one or more of the directors have appointed an alternate, it would seem that their signature will also be necessary unless some sort of saving provision is included in the articles. This is because the word 'director' will be deemed to include alternates and because alternate directors are usually entitled to receive notice of all meetings of directors and committees of which their appointor is a member. Reg. 93 provides that a written resolution signed by an alternate director need not also be signed by his appointor and, if it is signed by a director who has appointed an alternate director, it need not be signed by the alternate in that capacity.

A director who is signing in his or her own capacity and as an alternate for another director should make this clear. If a director has appointed an alternate, the alternate's signature will be required where his or her appointor is not entitled to receive notice. However, reg. 93 would seem to suggest that the signature of the alternate might also be acceptable in other circumstances.

6.2.4 Director interested in contract

In *Re Charles Arkins and Co. Ltd.* [1929] S.A.S.R. 129, an Australian case based on an article which allowed decision by way of written resolution signed by all the directors currently in office, a written resolution was challenged on the basis that it had been signed by a director who was interested in the contract. Napier J rejected this argument and said: 'The signature to the resolution is not a vote . . . I can see no reason why I should qualify that article by implying something which is not expressed, namely, that the subject of the resolution must be one upon which all the directors are able to vote.' However, the decision in *Hood*

Sailmakers Ltd. v. Axford (see above) would seem to suggest that a written resolution will not be valid unless among the directors signing it there are sufficient to form a disinterested quorum.

6.2.5 Practical points on written resolutions

Most company secretaries prefer to obtain all the necessary signatures of the directors on the same day. If that is not possible, it is normally preferable to send out copies and obtain all the relevant signatures as quickly as possible. It is quite common for copies of the written resolution to be faxed or e-mailed to the directors and for the directors to be asked to fax back a signed copy or e-mail their consent to the company on the same day.

There is nothing to prevent the inclusion in articles of procedures to enable the directors to pass resolutions in writing where, for example, only three out of four directors or a certain percentage of them sign it (see example at **Precedent 6.2B**). Provision can also be made to allow directors to sign, approve or signify their agreement to written resolutions by methods other than a normal signature under hand on a hard copy version. The model articles achieve this by adopting a much wider definition of the term 'in writing' than might be traditionally applied.

6.2.6 Effective date and minutes

It must be presumed that a written resolution will not be effective until the last director required to sign it has done so.

It is not necessary to keep original signed copies of a director's written resolution, although it may be sensible to do so for evidential purposes. It is not particularly clear from s. 248 whether it is necessary to keep a record of written resolutions or unanimous decisions in the same way as is required with regard to minutes of meetings of directors. However, the model articles require companies to do so (pcls 15, clg 15 and plc 18(4)). The record kept for these purposes need not be the original signed copies (although they would be satisfactory). A record of the fact that a resolution had been passed or decision made in accordance with the relevant article would suffice for these purposes, although that record probably ought to be authenticated by a director (preferably the chairman) or the company secretary (if the company has one).

■ 6.3 Informal consent

Under the common law, if the directors unanimously agree on a particular course of action, there is no need for that decision to be taken at a formal meeting of directors. It is unwise to rely on this common law rule, particularly where the articles provide an alternative method of acting without holding a meeting, e.g. by passing a written resolution. It is always preferable to retain some evidence of the fact that all the directors agreed to act in a certain way. One of the dangers of relying on the principle of unanimous consent is that it might be difficult to prove that there was indeed unanimity, although this can sometimes be inferred from the fact that a director did not object within a reasonable time.

In *Re Bonneli's Telegraph Co.* (1871) L.R. 12 Eq. 246, the quorum for board meetings was three. Two out of the four directors signed a letter to C stating that they would secure the agreement of the other directors to C's appointment as agent in the sale of company's business on terms set out in the letter. The remaining two directors subsequently signed and sent a copy of that letter to C signifying their agreement to the appointment. Bacon V-C held that the directors had acted in a manner which was capable of binding the company. Unfortunately, in stating his reasons, he seemed to suggest that it was only necessary for three out of the four (i.e. a quorum) to agree, even though all the directors had agreed in the case before him. This reasoning runs counter to the generally accepted principle with regard to informal decisions of the members (see *Re Express Engineering Works Ltd.* [1920] 1 Ch. 466; *Re Duomatic Ltd.* [1969] 1 All E.R. 161). Indeed, for many years this flaw caused some commentators to question the application of the principle of unanimous informal consent to meetings of directors.

The issue has now been clarified by two recent cases. In *Charterhouse Investments Trust Ltd. v. Tempest Diesels Ltd.* [1986] B.C.L.C. 1, the board of TD Ltd. had not formally considered the disputed term in a contract for the sale of its business signed on its behalf by one of the directors. Hoffman J held that the term was binding because the other directors, by their actions and subsequent testimony, were clearly content to acquiesce in whatever lawful terms were agreed by that director.

In *Runciman v. Walter Runciman plc* [1992] B.C.L.C. 1084, variations in a director's service contract were not put to the board for formal approval. Following a takeover, the new owners of the company challenged the validity of those variations and, in particular, an increase in the period of notice from three to five years. In holding that they were valid, Simon Brown J said:

> The articles say nothing as to how or when the directors are to arrive at their determination. In my judgment, therefore, provided only and always that by the time the term relied upon is sought to be enforced all the other directors can be shown to have concurred in the agreement of that term, it can fairly and properly be said that they have indeed determined it as the article requires.

The *Runciman* case also highlights one of the factors which could easily defeat this type of informal decision-making, namely the requirement to be found in most articles for directors to disclose their interest in any contract approved by the board. Failure to do so will normally make the contract voidable at the instance of the company (in other words the company can decide whether to avoid the contract or to enforce it) (*Hely-Hutchinson v. Brayhead Ltd.* [1967] 3 All E.R. 98). In *Runciman*, Simon Brown J refused to apply this principle to the detriment of the director on the basis that it was a mere technical breach. In other cases, however, the courts might take a more stringent view (see **4.12**).

Although it is not clear from the reports of the two recent cases, it is highly likely that the articles of both companies also allowed the directors to act by written resolution. If so, it appears that the board may act by the unanimous consent of its directors without holding a formal meeting irrespective of the existence of specific provisions in the articles on written resolutions. In other words, the common law principles may still save certain decisions not taken in accordance with proper procedures even though the articles provide an alternative procedure that also depends on unanimity.

7

Failure by directors to comply with proper procedures

▪ 7.1 Summary

Although the directors have a duty to act in accordance with the provisions of the company's memorandum and articles of association in order to avoid personal liability, their failure to do so will not always invalidate the transaction, at least as far as innocent third parties are concerned. Protection against defects in the decision-making process is provided in statute, articles and the common law where, for example:

- the directors act beyond the company's powers (see **7.2**);
- the directors act beyond their powers (see **7.3**);
- there is a defect in the appointment or qualification of a director (see **7.4**);
- the directors fail to follow proper procedures (see **7.5**);
- under the principle of unanimous consent, where the directors fail to follow the proper formal procedures but can be shown to have all agreed informally to the proposed transaction (see **6.3**);
- the number of directors is less than the minimum prescribed by, or in accordance with, the articles (see **7.6**).

▪ 7.2 Acts beyond the company's capacity

The validity of an act done by a company cannot be called into question on the ground of lack of capacity by reason of anything contained in the company's constitution (e.g. the objects clause or statement of objects) (s. 39(1)). A member may still bring proceedings to restrain the doing of an act which is beyond the company's capacity; but no such proceedings shall lie in respect of an act to be done in fulfilment of a legal obligation arising from a previous act of the company (s. 40(4)).

It remains the duty of the directors to observe any limitations on their powers flowing from any limitation on the company's capacity (s. 171) and action by the directors which, but for s. 39(1), would be beyond the company's capacity may only be ratified by an ordinary resolution of the company passed in accordance with s. 239.

■ 7.3 Acts beyond the powers of the directors

In favour of a person dealing with a company in good faith, the power of the board of directors to bind the company, or authorise others to do so, is deemed by virtue of s. 40 to be free of any limitation under the company's constitution. Limitations under the company's constitution are deemed to include limitations deriving from a resolution of the company in general meeting or a meeting of any class of shareholders or from any shareholders' agreement (s. 40(3)). This section does not apply where a director is a party to the transaction (s. 41) (see below).

A person is not bound to make any enquiries as to the limitations on the powers of the board to bind the company or authorise others to do so, is presumed to have acted in good faith unless the contrary is proved and is not to be regarded as acting in bad faith by reason only of his knowing that an act is beyond the powers of the directors under the company's constitution (s. 40(2)).

A member may still bring proceedings to restrain the doing of an act which is beyond the powers of the directors provided that the act is not required to be done in fulfilment of a legal obligation arising from a previous act of the company (s. 40(4)).

The liability incurred by the directors, or any other person, by reason of the directors' exceeding their powers is also not affected (s. 40(5)). The company could therefore sue the directors itself. This is most likely to occur if a new board has been appointed or the company is in insolvency as the incumbent directors rarely initiate action against themselves. However, if the directors refuse to take action against themselves, the shareholders might be able to bring a derivative action on behalf of the company (see **18.4**).

Although it is possible for an act by the board of directors which is not beyond the powers of the company but which is beyond the board's powers to be ratified by an ordinary resolution of the company in general meeting after the event, it is not possible to authorise such acts in advance (*Irvine v. Union Bank of Australia* (1877) 2 App. Cas. 366 and *Grant v. UK Switchback Railways Co.* (1888) 40 Ch.D. 135).

7.3.1 Where a director is party to a transaction

Section 40 is qualified with respect to transactions to which directors or their associates are a party by s. 41. It provides that where the board of directors exceeds its powers under the company's constitution and one of the parties to the transaction with the company is a director of the company or its holding company or an associate of such a director, the transaction will be voidable at the instance of the company (s. 41(2)). This means that, assuming the transaction is still capable of being rescinded, the company can decide whether to treat it as void or to enforce its contractual rights. Whether or not the transaction is avoided, the director or his associate will be liable to account to the company for any gain which he has made directly or indirectly by the transaction and to indemnify the company for any loss or damage resulting from the transaction (s. 41(3)).

The transaction ceases to be voidable if:

- restitution of any money or other asset which was the subject of the transaction is no longer possible; or
- the company is indemnified for any loss or damage resulting from the transaction; or
- rights acquired in good faith for value and without actual notice of the directors' exceeding their powers by a person who is not a party to the transaction would be affected by the avoidance; or
- the transaction is affirmed by the company in general meeting, by ordinary or special resolution or otherwise as the case may require (s. 41(5)).

A person other than a director of the company is not liable if he shows that at the time the transaction was entered into he did not know that the directors were exceeding their powers (s. 41(5)). Section 41 does not affect the rights of an innocent party to a transaction and such parties may apply to the court for an order affirming, severing or setting aside the transaction (s. 41(6)).

■ 7.4 Defects in appointment or qualification of directors

7.4.1 CA 2006, section 161

Section 161 of the Companies Act 2006 serves to validate the acts of a person acting as a director notwithstanding that it is afterwards discovered:

(a) that there was a defect in his appointment;
(b) that he was disqualified from holding office;
(c) that he had ceased to hold office;
(d) that he was not entitled to vote on the matter in question.

This allows third parties to deal with the company through its directors without having to investigate whether they have been properly appointed. Articles usually contain similarly worded provisions, e.g. reg. 92 of Table A (see below).

Section 161 and such articles operate between the company and outsiders and between the company and its members (*Dawson v. African Consolidated Land & Trading Co* [1898] 1 Ch 6).

Anyone seeking to rely on such provisions must have acted in good faith. It is particularly important to note that the defect must have been discovered 'afterwards'. A person who merely has notice of the facts which give rise to the defect will not be prevented from relying on them unless they are also aware of the consequences of those facts (*Channel Collieries Trust Ltd. v. Dover, St Margaret's and Martin Hill Light Railway Co.* [1914] 2 Ch 506). The requirements of good faith will normally prevent a director from benefiting under such provisions. However, it has been held that a director who allotted himself shares in the knowledge that his appointment was invalid (i.e. in bad faith) could not subsequently avoid the allotment on the ground that it could not therefore be validated by a clause similar in terms to reg. 92 of Table A (*York Tramways v. Willows* (1882) 8 Q.B.D. 685).

Section 161 is wider in some respects than s. 285 of the Companies Act 1985, the provision it replaced, which only served to validate the acts of a director or manager notwithstanding any defect that may afterwards be discovered in his or her appointment or qualification. However, s. 161 does not seek to rectify any defect in the qualification of any director (see below) nor does it apply to managers. The removal of 'managers' from the ambit of the rule could possibly have an effect on the validity of acts done by people who are lawfully or otherwise fulfilling the role of a managing director even though not a member of the board, such as the salaried chief executive of a charity where the board is made up entirely of non-paid trustee-type directors. However, the validity of the acts of such managers will presumably depend rather more on their actual or apparent authority rather than on the validity of their appointment.

Section 285 was thought to apply only where there had been an appointment and not where there had been no appointment or reappointment at all. For example, it has been held that a provision similar to s. 285 in a company's articles did not validate the acts of a director who had vacated office at the end of the year in which he was due to retire by rotation owing to the fact that no annual general meeting had been held in that year at which he could be reappointed (*Morris v. Kanssen* [1946] A.C. 459). Such a defect would be rectified under articles similar to reg. 92 of Table A and under s. 161 of the 2006 Act.

Unlike s. 285 of the 1985 Act, s. 161 does not specifically state that it validates the acts of a director appointed with some defect as to qualification. Provisions similar to s. 285 have been held to validate acts where a director has been appointed without the necessary share qualification required by the articles (*Channel Collieries Trust Ltd. v. Dover, etc*) and where a director has becomes disqualified because ' . . . he ceases to hold the requisite number of shares or does some act or suffers something to happen which causes him to vacate his office ...' (Farwell J in *British Asbestos Co. v. Boyd* [1903] 2 Ch. 439). In the latter case, the director was appointed secretary and became disqualified by virtue of the articles which prohibited the person appointed as secretary from being a director.

Section 161 of the 2006 Act certainly covers cases where a director has ceased to hold office or become disqualified (which should not be interpreted only as having become disqualified from being a director because of a disqualification order) and probably still cover cases where there has been a failure to comply with something, like a share qualification, which is imposed by the articles as a condition precedent to a valid appointment as, in this case, the failure to comply could simply be viewed as the defect in the appointment. Such defects may still be validated by provisions in the articles, which rarely impose share qualifications in any case, but which often make provision for a period of grace in which the director may acquire the shares where they do.

7.4.2 Reg. 92 of Table A

Reg. 92 of Table A is very similar in its effect to s. 161 of the 2006 Act in that, unlike s. 285 of the 1985 Act and the relevant article in the *Morris v. Kanssen* case, it seeks to validate the acts of a director who has vacated office. It should also be noted that, like s. 161, it also seeks to validate the acts of a director who is not entitled to vote at any meeting of directors or any committee thereof. In fact, s. 161 can be viewed as a statutory codification of reg. 92, particularly as the model articles make no equivalent provision.

> **92.** All acts done by a meeting of directors, or of a committee of directors, or by a person acting as a director shall, notwithstanding that it be afterwards discovered that there was a defect in the appointment of any director or that any of them were disqualified from holding office, or had vacated office, or were not entitled to vote, be as valid as if every such person had been duly appointed and was qualified and had continued to be a director and had been entitled to vote.

■ 7.5 Indoor management rule

The 'indoor management rule' protects third parties dealing with the company from irregularities in the decision-making process, including acts of the board, board committees and individual directors. It can be applied in three different situations:

- where a director has no authority to act (*Re County Life Assurance Co. Ltd.* (1870) L.R. 5 Ch. App. 288);
- where the director would have had authority had certain conditions been satisfied (*Royal British Bank v. Turquand* (1856) 119 E.R. 886);
- where the director has authority to act but fails to follow the correct procedure (*Duck v. Tower Galvanising Co. Ltd.* [1901] 2 K.B. 314).

■ 7.6 Number of directors less than the prescribed minimum and quorum

Articles commonly require a company to have a minimum number of directors as well as specifying a quorum for meetings of directors. No such provision is made in any of the model articles. However, reg. 64 of Table A provides that, unless otherwise determined by ordinary resolution, the number of directors (other than alternate directors) shall not be less than two. It is not uncommon for a company's articles to set out a higher and more straightforward minimum requirement.

Such requirement can cause problems because, under the common law, if the articles prescribe a minimum number of directors and the actual number of directors falls below that minimum, the continuing directors cannot exercise any of their powers even though there are sufficient of them to form a quorum (*Re Alma Spinning Co.* (1880) 16 Ch.D. 681).

At first sight, this rule does not seem to present any problems for a company with Table A style articles because both the quorum and the minimum number of directors is two. However, it should not be forgotten that under reg. 64 of Table A the members may have imposed a higher minimum number by ordinary resolution.

In order to avoid any such difficulties where a minimum number of directors is imposed, it is normal for articles to include a clause allowing the continuing directors to act notwithstanding any such vacancy in their number. For example, reg. 90 of Table A provides:

90. The continuing directors or a sole continuing director may act notwithstanding any vacancies in their number, but, if the number of directors is less than the number fixed as the quorum, the continuing directors or director may act only for the purpose of filling vacancies or of calling a general meeting.

It has been held that, where a company's articles provided that the number of directors shall be not less than four, two directors shall constitute a quorum and that the continuing directors may act notwithstanding any vacancy in the board, an allotment of shares by only two directors following the resignation of two out of the original four was valid (*Re Scottish Petroleum Co.* (1883) 23 Ch.D. 413).

However, a similar article giving the continuing directors power to act notwithstanding any vacancy in their body was held not to operate where the minimum number of directors prescribed by the articles had never been reached (*Re Sly, Spink and Co.* [1911] 2 Ch. 430).

A question that begs to be asked is whether there is any point prescribing a minimum number of directors if the articles say that such a minimum can be ignored? The best answer that can be given is that the remaining directors may have a general duty to take steps to fill the vacancies so as to bring their number back to the prescribed minimum. In other words, they could not continue indefinitely to operate below the prescribed minimum. It may also be that if they fail to fill the vacancies, the members in general meeting may do so in default regardless of anything in the articles to the contrary (see **3.9**).

The articles of a company with four equal shareholders might require a minimum of four directors, the implication being that each of the members will be appointed as a director. The promoters or incorporators of a company may set a high figure to give the impression that the company is more respectable and that the executive directors will be monitored by an independent element on the board.

In reality, prescribing a minimum number of directors in the articles that is higher than the statutory minimum is likely to cause more problems than it is worth and it is notable that no minimum number is prescribed in any of the model articles.

7.6.1 Number of directors falls below quorum

Articles which allow the directors to act notwithstanding any vacancy in their number do not operate where the number of directors is less than that required to constitute a quorum unless specific provision is made. Modern articles usually give the continuing directors limited powers to act in these circumstances (see, for example, reg. 90 of Table A above). Because of the of the words 'falls below' in reg. 90, this type of article can only be relied upon if the minimum number of directors prescribed by the articles has at some time been reached.

Even if a company's articles make no provision for a minimum number of directors, they will normally give the directors limited powers to act where there are not sufficient to form a quorum. The powers given will normally be exclusively related to making further appointments to bring the number back up to the quorum. This is the case with the model articles for private companies which provide (pcls and clg 11(3)):

> 11 (3) If the total number of directors for the time being is less than the quorum required, the directors must not take any decision other than a decision –
> (a) to appoint further directors, or
> (b) to call a general meeting so as to enable the shareholders to appoint further directors.

The model articles for plcs make similar provision but provide for different rules depending on whether there is only one remaining director or more than one (plc 11). Some companies have adopted articles which go further by giving the continuing directors power to act where there is a matter which must be dealt with urgently.

PART 3
Members' decisions

8

Members' decisions

■ 8.1 Summary

- All shareholders are members. However not all members are shareholders, which is why we tend to use the word 'members' instead of 'shareholders' (see **8.2**).
- Members usually make decisions by passing resolutions in accordance with the requirements of the Act. However, that is not the only way (see **8.3**).
- Part 13 of the Companies Act 2006 sets out the methods by which members may pass resolutions (see **8.4**).
- Most meetings of the members or shareholders will be held as general meetings. The AGM is a type of general meeting. However, companies can be required to hold meetings that are not general meetings (e.g. meetings of a class of members) (see **8.6**).
- Shareholders in listed companies who hold shares on someone else's behalf can nominate the underlying investors as 'indirect investors'. Those people are then given certain information and voting rights that enable them to participate in the company's affairs (see **8.7**).
- The Act clarifies that the articles of association of any company may provide similar rights to underlying investors (see **8.8**).

■ 8.2 Members' decisions or shareholders' decisions?

This section of the book deals with members' decisions. When we say members, we mean members of the company, not members of the board or members of a committee. It might have been easier for most people to understand if we had said it was about shareholders' decisions. However, it is not just about shareholders' decisions.

Every company must have at least one member. In most cases, the only way to become a member is to become a shareholder. However, this is not true for every company. Companies limited by guarantee can have members who are not shareholders. In fact, you cannot form a guarantee company with a share capital anymore. So the vast majority of guarantee companies cannot have shareholders. They still have members though and those members still need to make decisions.

This section of the book is not just about how companies with shareholders may make decisions. It is also about how members of companies who are not shareholders may make decisions. That is why we said it was about members' decisions.

Indeed, that is the reason why, throughout this book, we often use the term 'member of the company' where the word 'shareholder' would seem to be more natural to most. We shouldn't really use the term 'shareholder' unless we are talking about a rule that only applies to companies that have shareholders. If we are talking about a rule that can also apply to companies that have members who are not shareholders, we really ought to use the term 'member'.

As far as companies with a share capital are concerned, it does not really matter which term we use. In such a company, the words 'member' and 'shareholder' can be used interchangeably. Everybody who is a shareholder in such a company is a member of it and it is not possible to become a member in any other way. So whenever we use the word 'member' it is always meant to include 'shareholders' unless we specify otherwise.

Obviously, it is important for us to use the right term when we are talking about a rule that only applies to companies who do not have shareholders. In this case, we need to say things like 'members of a company without a share capital' or 'members of a guarantee company'. We have tried to use the correct terminology in these cases and to clarify where different rules apply. However, we may have lapsed from this discipline occasionally. If so, we can only apologise.

8.2.1 Registered shareholder

If a company has a share capital, the only way to become a member of it will be to become a shareholder unless it is a guarantee company with a share capital formed before the prohibition on such companies came into force (see s. 5). When we say 'become a shareholder', we mean 'become the registered holder of those shares'. The registered holder is the person whose name is entered in the company's register of members as the holder of the shares. In companies that have shares, people often refer to the register of members as the share register. If a company has more than one class of shares, it will typically keep a separate share register for each class. Where this is the case, each of those registers combine to make up the register of members. This is why every person whose name is entered in any share register as the holder of any type of share automatically becomes a member of the company. The share registers are the company's register of members.

8.2.2 Nominee shareholders and underlying investors

It follows that, if somebody else holds shares on your behalf, you are not the registered shareholder and not a member of the company. It is the person who holds the shares on your behalf who is the member and the registered shareholder. People who hold shares through a nominee in this way often think of themselves as shareholders and may even refer to themselves as shareholders. However, they are not shareholders. And if they are not shareholders, they are not members either. They are nothing more than underlying investors. In most cases, a company can choose to ignore the fact that these indirect investors exist. In most cases, the company only has to deal with the person who is the registered shareholder. In most cases, underlying investors do not have any enforceable rights against the company. In most cases, the only rights they will have are those that arise under any agreement they have entered into with the person who is acting as their nominee. These rights are not enforceable against the company but against the nominee.

The reason why we keep saying 'in most cases' is that the Act provides a mechanism to enable underlying investors in listed companies to claim certain 'membership' rights through their nominee (see **8.7**). In addition, any company can choose to make provision in its articles to give underlying investors certain 'membership' rights (see **8.8**). We tend to refer to people who have such rights as 'indirect investors' in order to distinguish them from underlying investors who have no rights.

■ 8.3 Decision-making methods

Part 13 of the Companies Act 2006 sets out the main statutory rules governing the methods by which members of a company may make decisions. Members usually make decisions by passing resolutions. Part 13 sets out how they can pass those resolutions. Although the title of Part 13 is 'Resolutions and Meetings', it actually enables certain companies to pass resolutions without holding a meeting.

Part 13 begins (at s. 281) by saying that a resolution of the members of a private company (or of a class of members) *must* be passed either:

(a) as a written resolution in accordance with Part 13, Chapter 2 (see **9.2**), or
(b) at a meeting of the members.

However, for public companies, it states that a resolution of the members (or of a class of members) *must* be passed at a meeting of the members. In other words, a public company cannot take advantage of the statutory written resolution procedures in Part 13, Chapter 2.

Where resolutions are passed in accordance with Part 13, it is not necessary for all the members to participate in the decision or for them all to agree with it. The Act allows them to pass resolutions by a majority. The majority required will not always be the same. Certain matters have to be passed as a special resolution (which requires a 75% majority). However, unless stated otherwise, members can make decisions by ordinary resolution (i.e. by a simple majority).

Although the Act does not say so explicitly, it also recognises that members can also make unanimous decisions without following the usual formalities. The purpose of holding a meeting or circulating a written resolution is to discover whether the necessary majority are in favour of a proposal. Where it is clear that all the members agree, it is arguable that they should be able to dispense with these formalities. This is the underlying foundation of the common law principle of unanimous consent. This common law rule is preserved by s. 281(4). However, the principle can sometimes prove to have rocky foundations. The courts will not always apply it to rectify procedural irregularities, particularly where the members were not given the necessary information upon which to base their decision (see **9.5**). It is far safer therefore for a company to make decisions by passing formal resolutions in accordance with the requirements of the Act.

It should be noted in this regard that, although an informal decision is capable of having the same effect as a resolution, it is not treated under the Act as a resolution. That is why s. 281 does not say that a resolution can be passed as an informal decision. The best way to understand this is to say that all resolutions must be passed in accordance with the Act but that decisions do not necessarily have to be made by passing a resolution. One could argue that the Act is almost deliberately misleading in this regard. The government did consider making it more explicit in the Act that members can make decisions informally. However, it decided not to do so. The principle of unanimous consent is meant to be a closely guarded secret. On the whole, it is better if people who run companies don't know that it exists. On the whole, it is much safer for them to make decisions by passing resolutions in accordance with the Act. It is impossible to write a book about meetings without referring to the principle of unanimous consent. However, it gives the author no pleasure to think that, having explained it, readers might use it in preference to the procedures for passing resolutions under the Act. It is best to view the principle of unanimous consent as something that may get you out of a sticky situation when you have accidentally failed to do what was required in order to pass a resolution. Otherwise, it is best to forget that it exists. Unfortunately, this is not an easy thing to do. The principle just has too many memorable features. Of these, the most memorable is probably that it can apply in the absence of unanimity (see **9.5**)!

■ 8.4 Part 13 of the Companies Act 2006

Part 13 of the Companies Act 2006 is divided into Chapters as follows:

Chapter No.	Subject	Section Nos.
Chapter 1	General provisions about resolutions	281–287
Chapter 2	Written resolutions	288–300
Chapter 3	Resolutions at meetings	301–335
Chapter 4	Public Companies: Additional requirements for AGMs	336–340
Chapter 5	Additional requirements for quoted companies	341–354
Chapter 6	Records of resolutions and meetings	355–359
Chapter 7	Supplementary provisions	360–361

A more detailed version of this table showing the subject headings for each section can be found at **Annex A**.

Most of the provisions of Part 13 were brought into force on 1 October 2007, although s. 333 (sending documents relating to meetings etc in electronic form) was brought into force on 20 January 2007 together with the company communication provisions in ss. 1143 to 1148 and Schedules 4 and 5 of the Act. Part 9 of the Act (ss. 145 to 153) on indirect investor rights was also brought into force on 1 October 2007.

From 1 October 2007, separate versions of Table A for public and private companies came into force to cater for the fact that private companies were no longer required to hold annual general meetings from that date and to reflect the provisions of Part 13 of the Companies Act 2006 on resolutions and meetings that were commenced on that date. The amended versions of Table A only applied to companies incorporated between 1 October 2007 and 30 September 2009 and did not affect any company with articles already based on a previous version of Table A. The version of Table A applicable to private companies incorporated in that period is shown at **Annex B2**, together with notes showing the amendments made by the relevant regulations on 1 October 2007 and previous amendments made in December 2000.

From 1 October 2009, companies began to be incorporated under the Companies Act 2006 and new model articles prescribed for the purposes of the Act came into force. The three different versions for private companies limited by shares, private companies limited by guarantee and public companies can be found at **Annexes C2, C3** and **C4** respectively. **Annex C1** shows a comparative table of contents for the three different versions of the model articles.

■ 8.5 Traded and quoted companies

Various provisions on resolutions and meetings in Part 13 of the Act only apply to 'traded companies' or 'quoted companies'.

8.5.1 Traded companies

A 'traded company' is defined in s. 360C (for the purposes of Part 13 only) as 'a company any shares of which carry rights to vote at general meetings and are admitted to trading on a regulated market in an EEA State by or with the consent of the company'. This is similar to (but not exactly the same as) the definition of a 'traded company' used for the purposes of the annual return in Part 24 of the Act. The fact that a company is a 'traded company' for the purposes of the annual return, does not necessarily mean that it is a 'traded company' for the purposes of Part 13. The Part 13 definition requires the company's voting shares to be listed. For the purposes of Part 24, it does not matter whether the shares that are listed are voting shares.

The overwhelming majority of companies that fall within the definition of a traded company for the purposes of Part 13 will be public companies. However, it is also technically possible for a private company to be a traded company.

8.5.2 Quoted companies

Various provisions of the Act apply to quoted companies only. The term 'quoted company' was first introduced to define the type of company that must prepare a directors' remuneration report. However, it is now used for other purposes. The original definition in Part 15 of the Act (at s. 385) only applies for the purposes of Part 15. Accordingly, it has to be defined again if it is used for any other purpose. However, whenever it is used, the relevant definition always refers back to the original definition in s. 385 of Part 15. In other words, the same definition is used throughout the Act (see for example, the definition in Part 13, s. 361).

Section 385 of the Act defines a quoted company as a company whose equity share capital:

(a) has been included in the official list in accordance with the provisions of Part 6 of the FSMA 2000 (i.e. is officially listed in the UK);
(b) is officially listed in an EEA State; or
(c) is admitted to dealing on either the New York Stock Exchange or the exchange known as Nasdaq.

The 'official list' is maintained in the UK by the Financial Conduct Authority in accordance with s. 103(1) of the FSMA 2000. It should be noted that a UK company will be a 'quoted company' if any of its shares are listed. The shares need not be voting shares.

■ 8.6 Meetings of members

8.6.1 General meetings

Meeting of the members or shareholders of a company are usually referred to as 'general meetings'. However, it would be wrong to suggest that every meeting of members or shareholders will necessarily be a general meeting. A general meeting is a meeting of the members or shareholders who are entitled to make decisions on behalf of the company. This may not necessarily include all the members or all the shareholders. Some may not be entitled to vote. A general meeting is a meeting of the members who are entitled to vote. It is those members who collectively represent the mind of the company and who can make decisions on its behalf. Those decisions can be described as decisions of the company in general meeting.

The annual general meeting is a type of general meeting that certain companies (e.g. public companies) are required to hold. General meetings are sometimes referred to as company meetings or shareholder meetings.

A matter which requires the approval of the members in general meeting can be dealt with either at a general meeting called for that purpose or, if the company holds an annual general meeting, at an annual general meeting. Private companies are not normally required to hold annual general meetings unless their articles expressly require them to do so. Nevertheless, a private company will need to hold a general meeting to deal with business which needs member approval if it is not able to dispose of it by written resolution.

As public companies are required to hold an annual general meeting, they will only need to call other general meetings throughout the year to deal with business which cannot wait until the next annual general meeting. It is not necessary for a public company to lay its accounts, reappoint auditors or fix their remuneration at the annual general meeting. The Act simply requires accounts to be laid at a general meeting and for the auditors to be reappointed at that meeting. In other words, this can be done at any general meeting.

Some older articles of association refer to the annual general meeting as the 'ordinary meeting' and may use different terminology for general meetings. Older articles commonly provide that all general meetings other than the annual general meeting shall be called 'extraordinary general meetings' (e.g. the original version of reg. 36 of Table A). The Companies Act 2006 no longer makes that distinction and, as a consequence, neither do any of the model articles prescribed under the 2006 Act. The Act refers instead to general meetings and annual general meetings. Indeed, the distinction was eventually eliminated in the 1985 Table A by virtue of amendments made to coincide with the commencement of the provisions of the 2006 Act on general meetings. The convention used throughout this book is also not to refer to general meetings as extraordinary general meetings, unless the context requires otherwise. It should be remembered, however, that the term 'general meetings' can be used to refer to both general meetings and annual general meetings. The specific rules applicable to annual general meetings are covered in Chapter 10.

8.6.2 Class meetings

Many of the rules and procedures applicable to general meetings also apply to class meetings. A class meeting can be described as a meeting held to obtain the approval of a class of members or shareholders rather than the approval of all the members or shareholders who would be entitled to vote at a general meeting. If all the members of the company have exactly the same rights or they all hold exactly the same shares which confer exactly the same rights, the company will probably never need to hold a class meeting. However, if a company has members who have different rights (or different interests), it may occasionally need to hold a separate meeting to determine the views of those people. The main reason why a company would need to hold a class meeting is to obtain the approval of a particular class of members or shareholders to a proposal to change their rights. Any such proposal would need the approval of the members in general meeting and the separate approval of the members of that class.

Say for example a company had a class of non-voting shares that paid a fixed dividend each year. It would be unfair if the shareholders with voting shares were able to pass a resolution at a general meeting to reduce the dividend payable on the non-voting shares without the consent of the holders of those shares. The Act does not allow this. The non-voting shareholders would be required to approve the change. The rules governing class meetings and class rights are covered separately in Chapter 11.

One interesting thing about the above scenario is that it highlights the fact that a general meeting is in itself capable of being viewed as a class meeting. The non-voting shareholders would not be allowed to vote at the general meeting. In other words, there would be a class of members who are entitled to attend and vote at the meeting and a class who are not. In these circumstances, one could, of course, describe the general meeting as a meeting of the class of members who are entitled to attend and vote at general meetings. If that does not include all the members, then it must be a class meeting. In truth, it does not really matter one way or the other whether you view a general meeting as a class meeting. The important distinguishing feature of a general meeting is that it is a meeting of the members who represent the mind of the company and who can make decisions on its behalf. This is why we use phrases like 'the company in general meeting'. There are obviously some occasions where a decision of the company in general meeting on its own will not suffice, i.e. when we also need to obtain the separate approval of members of a specific class. It is best to view this as a requirement for the decision of the company in general meeting to be ratified by the members of the class that the decision affects. Where the members in general meeting make decisions that vary their own rights equally, it is plainly not necessary for them to hold a separate class meeting to ratify their own decision. Otherwise, we would be asking the same members to ratify a decision that they have already made at a general meeting.

8.6.3 Court meetings

The court can sometimes direct that a company must hold a meeting of members. This could be a general meeting or a class meeting. Generally speaking the court will order that the meeting be held in accordance with normal procedures. However, it can direct that different procedures be followed. If so, the meeting must be held in accordance with the directions of the court. This is, in reality, the only practical difference between court meetings and other meetings.

It should also be noted that in connection with a scheme of arrangement the court may sometimes direct that a separate meeting be held to obtain the approval of members with different interests even though they are notionally all members of the same class or hold shares of the same class.

8.6.4 Paper meetings

Companies often view the requirement to hold general meetings as an unnecessary administrative burden. Many prepare minutes of meetings which have not actually taken place. This practice is sometimes referred to as holding a 'paper meeting', a name which gives it a false aura of legality. In reality, a paper meeting is no better than no meeting at all. The fact that a set of minutes have been prepared recording that a meeting has been held and that certain decisions have been made does not make it true. Although minutes are evidence of the proceedings it would not take much to undermine their status as evidence. Where minutes are submitted as evidence in legal proceedings, somebody who is listed as being in attendance at the meeting is usually required to swear an affidavit that the meeting actually took place. If you are not prepared to perjure yourself in legal proceedings, you should not get involved in writing minutes of meetings that did not take place.

The fact that no meeting actually took place does not necessarily mean that all the decisions recorded in the minutes will be invalid. It is possible that that they will be capable of validation under the principle of unanimous consent (see **9.5**). Whether or not this is the case, the fact that you have had to admit that no meeting took place is not going to do much to improve your credibility as a witness. Indeed, anyone who participates in falsifying a company record in this way has probably committed an offence under s. 250 of the Companies Act 1985 (which, for the sake of clarity, has not been replaced by a provision of the 2006 Act and therefore remains in force).

Paper meetings are, therefore, something that should be avoided at all costs. In the case of a private company, if it is not possible to hold a meeting, it is better to make the decision by written resolution (see **9.2**). Even if you are relying on the principle of unanimous consent, it is pointless to lie about the fact that a meeting took place. It is far better to simply record the fact that the members have made the decision informally and even better from an evidential perspective to get them all to sign it to confirm that they have done so, or to get them signify their agreement in some other way that can be kept (e.g. e-mail). There is no need to mention any meeting that did not take place. There is no reason to lie.

8.6.5 Other meetings

Many of the common law principles that apply to general meetings will also apply to meetings of debenture holders and meetings in insolvency. These are not covered in this book as they are not governed by the Companies Acts. Meetings in insolvency are governed mainly by insolvency law. Meetings of debenture holders will be governed mainly by the debenture instrument or trust deed.

■ 8.7 Listed companies: rights of indirect investors

Sections 146–151 of the 2006 Act, which apply to companies whose shares are admitted to trading on a regulated market (such as the London Stock Exchange main listed market but not AIM), provide that shareholders (such as nominee companies) that hold shares on behalf of other persons may nominate them to receive certain information rights. The information rights concerned include the right to receive copies of all documents sent to shareholders generally (or to members of the relevant class of shares), including reports and accounts and any summary financial statements (see s. 146(3)).

The nomination(s) must be communicated to the company by the registered holder of the shares (and not, for example, by the investment manager who operates the nominee company concerned) and must relate to all (and not part only) of the information rights. The default right given by a nomination is for the documents to be supplied by means of a website – if the nominated person is to receive hard copies of the documents, he must have asked the registered holder to nominate him to receive hard copy (so a nominee company cannot make a 'blanket' nomination to receive hard copy for all its indirect investors; to be included in the nomination the indirect investor must have made a specific request for hard copy) and must have supplied an address for this purpose.

The nomination given to the company by the registered holder must then indicate that the person nominated wishes to receive hard copy communications and give the address supplied by that person. As an alternative, a person nominated to receive web-based communications only may directly revoke the implied agreement to receive web-based communications and thus become entitled to receive hard copy (see s. 147(6)). These provisions of the 2006 Act come into force on 1 October 2007 so as to enable nominations to be given and recorded (and if the company so wishes, acted on) but a company was not required to act on a nomination until 1 January 2008 (see SI 2007/2194, Sch. 3, para. 3).

The fact that a person may be nominated to receive hard copy communications does not prevent the company from making use of the electronic communications provisions and seeking to obtain from that person actual or deemed agreement to website based communications (s. 147(4)).

Information rights are enforceable by the registered member (and not by the nominated person) as if they were rights under the articles.

Where a copy of a notice of meeting is sent to a nominated person as part of the information rights this must be accompanied by a statement that:

(a) he may have a right under an agreement between him and the member by whom he was nominated to be appointed, or to have someone else appointed, as a proxy for the meeting; and
(b) if he has no such right or does not wish to exercise it, he may have a right under such an agreement to give instructions to the member as to the exercise of voting rights.

The copy notice may also not include the statement of member's rights in relation to appointment of proxy (prescribed by s. 325) or that statement must indicate that it does not apply to the nominated person (s. 149).

A nomination may be terminated by the registered member or the nominated person, and automatically ceases if the registered member or the nominated person dies or becomes bankrupt (or subject to a winding-up order). The company may also ask a nominated person if the nomination is to continue and if a reply is not received to that inquiry within 28 days the nomination is terminated; this will be a useful procedure to 'clean up' the nomination records periodically but such an inquiry may not be made of any particular nominated person more than once in any 12-month period (s. 148).

Should a member have nominated more persons than the number of shares he holds, the effect of all his nominations is suspended while that situation continues (s. 148(5)).

Issuers' registrars are seeking agreement with stock market participants for standardised formats for nominations. The ICSA Registrars Group has issued a suggested form for use for any nominations which may be made in paper form (see **Precedent 8.7**). The records of nominations kept by companies will not form part of the register of members.

Sections 152 and 153 make it easier for registered members to exercise rights in different ways to reflect the underlying holdings and allow indirect investors to participate in, for example, requests for resolutions at the AGM. Section 152 provides that a member can choose to split his holding and exercise rights attached to shares in different ways. This is to assist members who hold shares on behalf of more than one person, each of whom may want to exercise rights attaching to their shares in different ways (so, for example, it enables votes to be cast in different ways). If the member does not make it clear to the company in what way he is exercising his rights, the company can assume that all rights are being dealt with in the same way.

8.7.1 Indirect investors and the 100 shareholder test

Section 153 deals with provisions where the shareholder threshold required to trigger a right is 100 shareholders holding £100 each on average of paid-up capital. Indirect investors are enabled to count towards the total subject to certain conditions, intended to ensure that only genuine indirect investors are allowed to count towards the total, that the same shares cannot be used twice and that the indirect investor's contractual arrangements with the member allow the former to give voting instructions. Section 153 applies in relation to:

- section 314 (power to require circulation of statement) (see **13.15**);
- section 338 (public companies: power to require circulation of resolution for AGM) (see **10.4**);
- section 338A (traded companies: members' power to include matters in business dealt with at AGM) (see **10.5**);
- section 342 (power to require independent report on poll) (see **17.12**); and
- section 527 (power to require website publication of audit concerns) (see **25.4**).

It requires a listed company to act under any of those sections if it receives a request in relation to which the following conditions are met:

(a) it is made by at least 100 persons;
(b) it is authenticated by all the persons making it;
(c) in the case of any of those persons who is not a member of the company, it is accompanied by a statement –
  (i) of the full name and address of a person ('the member') who is a member of the company and holds shares on behalf of that person,
  (ii) that the member is holding those shares on behalf of that person in the course of a business,
  (iii) of the number of shares in the company that the member holds on behalf of that person,
  (iv) of the total amount paid up on those shares,
  (v) that those shares are not held on behalf of anyone else or, if they are, that the other person or persons are not among the other persons making the request,
  (vi) that some or all of those shares confer voting rights that are relevant for the purposes of making a request under the section in question, and
  (vii) that the person has the right to instruct the member how to exercise those rights;
(d) in the case of any of those persons who is a member of the company, it is accompanied by a statement –
  (i) that he holds shares otherwise than on behalf of another person, or
  (ii) that he holds shares on behalf of one or more other persons but those persons are not among the other persons making the request;
(e) it is accompanied by such evidence as the company may reasonably require of the matters mentioned in paragraph (c) and (d);
(f) the total amount of the sums paid up on –
  (i) shares held as mentioned in paragraph (c), and
  (ii) shares held as mentioned in paragraph (d), divided by the number of persons making the request, is not less than £100;
(g) the request complies with any other requirements of the section in question as to contents, timing and otherwise.

8.7.2 ICSA guidance on indirect investors

ICSA has published guidance on the rights of indirect investors (*Guidance Note: Indirect Investors – Information Rights and Voting*) which can be obtained from its website free of charge.

■ 8.8 Articles can make provision for indirect investors

Other provisions in Part 9 (which apply to all companies, not just to those traded on a regulated market) are designed to make it easier for investors to exercise their governance rights where they hold through a nominee. Section 145 removes any doubts as to the ability of a company to make provision in its articles for underlying beneficial owners to exercise membership rights. It provides that where a company makes provision, through its articles, to extend rights to those holding shares through intermediaries, the provision is legally effective in relation to a non-exhaustive list of various statutory requirements. The articles may specify that this entitlement can apply only to certain rights or to all rights, except the right to transfer the shares. Where a company makes relevant provision in its articles, all the references to 'member' in the Companies Acts' provisions (relative to the specified rights) should be read as if the reference to member was a reference to the person or persons nominated by the member. Non-members will not be given direct enforceable rights against the company. They may only enforce their rights through the member whose name is on the register and who has the right to enforce the articles. Companies appear to be taking a very cautious approach to the question of whether their articles should give rights to indirect investors as envisaged in this section.

9

Members' written resolutions and unanimous consent

9.1 Summary

The Act makes special provision to allow private companies to act by written resolution. Public companies are not allowed to pass resolutions using the statutory procedures (see **9.2**).

- The Act gives members of private companies the right to propose written resolutions themselves (see **9.3**).
- Articles may also appear to allow members to act by written resolution. In the case of a private company, the statutory procedures for passing written resolutions almost certainly take precedence over any procedures in the articles. It is not necessarily safe for a public company to assume that it can rely on any such written resolution procedures in its articles (see **9.4**).
- Under the common law principle of unanimous consent, it may not always be necessary to go through the usual process of holding a meeting and passing a formal resolution, if it can be shown that all the members who would have been entitled to vote agreed with the decision. Although this common law principle is often applied by the courts to rectify procedural failings, it is not always safe to rely on the fact that they will do so (see **9.5**).
- If the sole member of a company makes any informal decisions, he or she must provide the company with a written record of that decision (see **9.6**), which the company must then keep (see **26.6**).

9.2 Members' written resolutions

A private company may be able to avoid holding a general meeting (or a class meeting) by using the statutory procedures for written resolutions set out in Part 13, Chapter 2 of the Act (ss. 288 to 300).

A resolution agreed to by a private company as a written resolution in accordance with Part 13, Chapter 2 of the Act has effect as if it was passed by the company in general meeting (or a meeting of the relevant class of members) and any reference in any statute to a meeting at which a resolution is passed or to members voting in favour of a resolution shall be construed accordingly.

A provision of the articles of a private company is void in so far as it would have the effect that a resolution that is required by or otherwise provided for in an enactment could not be proposed and passed as a written resolution (s. 300). It should be noted that a written resolution is defined for these purposes as a resolution of a private company proposed and passed in accordance with Part 13, Chapter 2 of the Act.

9.2.1 Written resolution procedure

The 2006 Act makes it much easier for private companies to use written resolutions to conduct any business which requires member approval. Previously under the 1985 Act, in order to pass a resolution as a written resolution, all the members entitled to receive notice of meetings had to consent to the resolution in writing. The 2006 Act allows ordinary resolutions to be passed as written resolutions by members representing a simple majority of the total voting rights of eligible members and special resolutions by members representing a 75% majority of the voting rights of eligible members (ss. 282 and 283).

A private company wishing to take advantage of the written resolution procedures in Part 13, Chapter 2 of the 2006 Act must send a copy of the proposed written resolution to every member who would have been entitled to vote on the resolution on the date it is circulated.

A written resolution will lapse if it is not passed within the period of 28 days beginning with the circulation date or such other period specified for these purposes in the articles (s. 297(1)). The agreement of a member to a written resolution is ineffective if signified after the resolution has lapsed (s. 297(2)).

A member signifies his agreement to a written resolution when the company receives from him (or someone acting on his behalf) an authenticated document identifying the resolution to which it relates indicating his agreement to the resolution (s. 296(1)). The document must be sent to the company in hard copy form or electronic form (s. 296(2)). A member's agreement to a written resolution, once signified (i.e. received by the company in accordance with the above rules), may not be revoked (s. 296(3)).

9.2.2 Resolutions which may not be passed as written resolutions

Written resolutions may not be used to remove a director or auditor from office before the expiry of his period of office (s. 288(2)).

It may or may not be possible for a private company to hold an annual general meeting by written resolution. This was not possible under the Companies Act 1985 which actually required a meeting to be held, unless the company had dispensed with that requirement under the elective regime. Private companies are no longer required by the Companies Act 2006 to hold annual general meetings and they will only be required to do so if their articles expressly require an annual general meeting to be held. Depending on the construction of the articles, it may be possible to hold such a meeting and to transact any business by written resolution, although this may or may not be popular with the members. It is also debateable whether a private company required by its articles to lay its accounts before the members in general meeting could do this by written resolution. It would seem odd if this is the case, as the main purpose of laying accounts is not to approve them (this is done by the directors) but to make them an item of business at a meeting so as to enable them to be discussed at that meeting.

9.2.3 Date written resolution passed

A written resolution will be passed when the required majority of eligible members have signified their agreement to it (s. 296(4)).

9.2.4 Circulation of written resolutions proposed by the directors

Section 291 of the 2006 Act applies to the circulation of a written resolution proposed by the directors. The company must send or submit a copy of the resolution to every eligible member by:

(a) sending copies at the same time (so far as reasonably practicable) to each of them in hard copy form, electronic form or by means of a website;

(b) if it is possible to do so without undue delay, by submitting the same copy to each eligible member in turn (or different copies to each of a number of eligible members in turn); or

(c) by a combination of the above methods.

The copy of the resolution must be accompanied by a statement informing the member how to signify their agreement to the resolution and the date by which the resolution must be passed if it is not to lapse.

Failure to comply with s. 291 is an offence but does not affect the validity of the resolution if passed (s. 291(7)).

Special procedures apply to pass certain resolutions as written resolution. These adaptations generally require the same information to be circulated with the written resolution as would have been included in any notice had it been proposed at a general meeting. The relevant requirements are contained in the sections of the Act which impose the general requirements for that type of resolution, rather than in Part 13, Chapter 2. Examples of where special procedures are required include:

(a) a resolution approving a director's long-term service contract under s. 188;

(b) a resolution approving a director's loan, quasi loan or credit transaction under ss. 197, 198 or 201 respectively;

(c) a resolution to disapply pre-emption rights under s. 571;

(d) a resolution under s. 694 conferring authority to make an off-market purchase of the company's own shares (see s. 696);

(e) a resolution under s. 697 conferring authority to vary a contract for an off-market purchase of the company's own shares (see s. 699);

(f) a resolution under s. 700 releasing a company's rights under a contract for an off-market purchase of the company's own shares (see s. 699);

(g) a resolution giving approval under s. 716 for the redemption or purchase of company's own shares out of capital (see s. 718).

Sections 300A–300D (which were transitionally inserted by SI 2007/2194, art 6, Sch. 1, para. 13(4)) dealt with the special procedures where certain resolutions under the Companies Act 1985 were to be proposed (e.g. to disapply pre-emption rights under s. 95 of the 1985 Act). These sections were revoked by SI 2008/2860, art. 6(1)(c) with effect from 1 October 2009. The adaptations applied to:

(a) a resolution under s. 95(2) (1985) regarding disapplication of pre-emption rights (s. 300A);
(b) a resolution giving approval under s. 155(4) or (5) (1985) for financial assistance for purchase of a company's own shares or those of holding company (s. 300B);
(c) a resolution under s. 164(2) (1985) conferring authority to make an off-market purchase of the company's own shares (s. 300C(1)(a));
(d) a resolution under s. 164(7) (1985) conferring authority to vary a contract for an off-market purchase of the company's own shares (s. 300C(1)(b));
(e) a resolution under s. 164(3) (1985) varying, revoking or renewing any authority (s. 300C(1)(c));
(f) a resolution giving approval under s. 173(2) (1985) for the redemption or purchase of company's own shares out of capital (s. 300D).

9.2.5 Electronic communications

Where a company has given an electronic address in any document containing or accompanying a written resolution, it is deemed to have agreed that any document or information relating to that resolution may be sent by electronic means to that address subject to any conditions or limitations specified in the document (s. 298).

If a company sends a written resolution or a statement relating to a written resolution to a person by means of a website, the resolution or statement is not validly sent unless it is available on the website throughout the period beginning with the circulation date and ending on the date the resolution lapses under s. 297 (s. 299).

9.2.6 Form of written resolution

Although, the members may sign or authenticate separate documents, each document should accurately state the terms of the resolution. In practice, this means that the wording of the resolution on each document should be identical. It is preferable if the form of words which precede the substantive resolution make it clear that the resolution is being proposed as a written resolution under the statutory procedures (see **Precedent 9.2A** for a members resolution, **Precedent 9.22B** for a written resolution of a class of members).

9.2.7 Filing and recording of written resolutions

Written resolutions only need to be filed at Companies House if they have effect as a resolution which needs filing in itself (see **14.8**).

It should also be noted that it is not a requirement of the Act that the original signed copies of the resolution be filed at Companies House. All that needs to be filed is 'a copy' of the resolution certified by a director or the secretary (see **Precedent 14.8B**) for a specimen copy of a written resolution for filing at Companies House).

A company is required to keep a record of every written resolution (see **Precedent 9.2D**) and to make those records available for inspection and copying (see further **26.9** and **26.10**).

9.2.8 Copies to auditors

A private company's auditors (if any) will have a right to be sent all communications required to be circulated to the members under Part 13, Chapter 2 of the 2006 Act in relation to a written resolution (s. 502). This will include the proposed written resolution itself, any statement by the members and any additional documents required to be circulated with the resolution (see example letter at **Precedent 8.2C**). There is no suggestion in the 2006 Act that failure to send a copy of such communications to the auditors will invalidate the resolution. The relevant provision is merely expressed as a right given to the auditors rather than as a condition that must be complied with in order to pass a written resolution. Under the 1985 Act, failure to send a copy of a written resolution to the auditors was an offence. This is no longer the case under the 2006 Act.

■ 9.3 Members' power to propose written resolutions

The members of a private company may require the company to circulate a written resolution and to circulate with it a statement of not more than 1,000 words on the subject matter of the resolution.

A company is required to circulate the resolution and any accompanying statement once it has received requests to do so from members representing not less than 5% of the total voting rights of all members entitled to vote on the resolution or such lower percentage specified for this purpose by the articles (s. 292(4) & (5)). The requests may be made in hard copy or electronic form, must identify the resolution to which it relates together with any accompanying statement, and be authenticated by the person or persons making it (s. 292(6)).

If the members have deposited or tendered a sum to pay the expenses of circulating the resolution, the company must circulate it to all eligible members in accordance with the requirements of s. 293. Copies may be sent in hard copy or electronic form or by means of a website or, if it is possible to do so without undue delay, by submitting the same copy to each eligible member in turn, or a combination of these methods (s. 293(2)).

The resolution must be circulated to members not more than 21 days after the obligation under s. 292 arises (s. 293(3)) and be accompanied by guidance as to how to signify agreement to the resolution and the date by which it must be passed if it is not to lapse (s. 293(4)). Failure to comply with the circulation requirements in s. 293 is an offence but does not invalidate the written resolution concerned if it is passed.

The expenses of circulating a written resolution must be paid for by the members making the request unless the company resolves otherwise (s. 294(1)). Unless the company has previously so resolved, it is not bound to comply with a request unless the requisitionists deposit with it or tender a sum reasonably sufficient to meet the its expenses in doing so (s. 294(2)).

The company or any other person claiming to be aggrieved may apply to the court for an order preventing the circulation of a statement made in connection with a written resolution. The court may order the members who requested that the statement be circulated to pay the whole or part of the company's costs on such an application (s. 295).

■ 9.4 Written resolutions under powers in articles of association

9.4.1 Private companies

The articles of a private company may include a clause which appears to provide a different procedure for passing a written resolution of the members. For example reg. 53 of Table A states:

> **53.** A resolution in writing executed by or on behalf of each member who would have been entitled to vote upon it if it had been proposed at a general meeting at which he was present shall be as effectual as if it had been passed at a general meeting duly convened and held and may consist of several instruments in the like form executed by or on behalf of one or more members.

It should be noted that s. 281(1) of the Act states that a resolution of the members (or of a class of members) of a private company must be passed either:

(a) as a written resolution in accordance with Part 13, Chapter 2; or
(b) at a meeting of the members (to which the provisions of Part 13, Chapter 3 apply).

Accordingly, the statutory written resolution procedures for private companies should always be used in preference to any provisions of the articles.

9.4.2 Public companies

The articles of a public company could also include an article similar to reg. 53 of Table A. Public companies cannot pass written resolutions under the statutory procedures in Part 13, Chapter 2 of the Act. Section 380(2) of the Act states that a resolution of the members (or of a class of members) of a public company must be passed at a meeting of the members (to which the provisions of Part 13, Chapter 3 and, where relevant, Chapter 4 of the Act apply). Accordingly it is dangerous for a company to rely on any written resolution procedure in its articles. Such procedures might be valid under the common law principle of unanimous consent, if unanimity is in fact required under the relevant article procedure. However, it is not normally sensible for a public company to rely on such articles or the principle of unanimous consent. It should be noted that the 2006 Act model articles for public companies do not make any provision regarding members' written resolution, and that reg. 53 was dispensed with for public companies with effect from 1 October 2007.

■ 9.5 Unanimous consent rule

Under the common law principle of unanimous consent, the members may act informally without holding a meeting if they unanimously approve the transaction in some other manner, whether in writing or orally. In *Re Express Engineering Works Ltd.* [1920] 1 Ch. 466, five directors who were the only shareholders of the company, resolved at a board meeting to purchase some property from a syndicate in which they each had an interest. The company's articles disqualified directors from voting on any contract in which they were interested. The liquidator subsequently sought to have the transaction set aside on the basis that the directors were precluded from voting and that the members were only capable of acting at a properly constituted general meeting. The Court of Appeal held that although the meeting was referred to in the minutes as a board meeting, the unanimous informal consent of the five as the members of the company was capable of binding the company.

Provided all the members assent and the transaction is within the company's powers, the members may assent at different times (*Parker & Cooper v. Reading* [1926] Ch. 975).

In *Cane v. Jones* [1981] 1 All E.R. 533, it was held that an agreement signed by all the shareholders that the chairman should cease to be entitled to use his casting vote, had the same effect as a special resolution altering the articles to that effect, and it was immaterial that the statutory obligation to file such resolutions had not been complied with.

The fact that the informal consent of members must be unanimous was emphasised in *EBM Co. Ltd. v. Dominion Bank* [1937] 3 All E.R. 555. In this case, there were five shareholders, three of whom held over 99% of the shares. The other two shareholders had one share each. A resolution of the three major shareholders was held not to bind the company in relation to security given to a bank for a loan despite the fact that the other two holdings were insignificant.

9.5.1 Exceptions

Generally speaking, it is not a good idea to rely on the unanimous consent rule as a routine method of decision-making. It is, for example, infinitely preferable for a private company to act by written resolution in accordance with the statutory provisions (see **9.2**). The courts tend to apply the rule to rectify defects in the decision-making process in owner-managed companies that arise out of ignorance of the proper procedures. They also tend not to look too kindly on its deliberate use. For example, the courts will not apply the rule so as to enable the members to do something they would not have been able to do at a meeting (*Re New Cedos Engineering Co Ltd.* [1994] 1 B.C.L.C. 797).

In addition, they will not necessarily apply the rule where legislation requires certain formalities to be carried out in order for the resolution to be effective. The general approach of the courts in this regard appears to be that the rule will not apply where these formalities cannot be waived by the current members or where the formalities are designed to protect third parties. However, it is not always easy to predict how the courts will apply these general principles.

In *Re Duomatic Ltd.* [1969] 1 All E.R. 161, directors' salaries were paid without being authorised by a resolution of the shareholders as required by the articles. It was held that the agreement of the two directors who held all the voting shares amounted to an informal ratification of the payment of unauthorised salaries even though they had never constituted themselves as a shareholders' meeting. The fact that they had not informed or sought the agreement of the sole holder of the company's preference shares had no bearing because all that was required was the unanimous agreement of the members entitled to vote. However, the court came to a different conclusion in the same case in relation to a payment made to a director for loss of office because statute required particulars of the proposed payment to be disclosed to the members and no such disclosure had taken place with regard to the preference shareholder.

It has been held that the principle does not apply to approval of a contract for a purchase of shares under s. 164 of the 1985 Act (*R W Peak (Kings Lynn) Ltd* [1998] 1 B.C.L.C. 193) and doubt has been expressed whether the principle would apply in relation to a resolution to approve a substantial property transaction with a director (*Demite Ltd v Protec Health Ltd* [1998] B.C.C. 638). In *Re Barry Artist plc* [1985] B.C.L.C. 283, the court confirmed a reduction in capital which had been agreed informally by all the members with 'great reluctance' and warned that this procedure would not be accepted in future reductions.

By contrast, in *Atlas Wright (Europe) Ltd v Wright* [1999] 2 B.C.L.C. 301, the principle was applied to uphold approval of a service agreement under s. 319 of the 1985 Act. In *Re Torvale Group Ltd* [1999] 2 B.C.L.C. 605, it was applied to prevent a transaction from exceeding a limitation of directors' powers and being voidable under s. 322A of the 1985 Act.

■ 9.6 Decisions by a sole member

Where a company has only one member, it is of course, much more likely that that member will make informal decisions which rely on the principle of unanimous consent for their validity. Recognising that this will be the case, the Act provides that whenever a sole member takes any decision which could have been taken by the company in general meeting and that has effect as if it had been agreed at a general meeting, he shall (unless the decision is taken by way of written resolution) provide the company with a written record of that decision (s. 357) (see **Precedent 9.6**). A sole member who fails to comply with this requirement will be liable to a fine (s. 357(2) and (3)). However, failure to comply will not invalidate the decision of the sole member (s. 357(4)). The company must keep any record provided by a sole member in this regard for the same length of time as it would keep the minutes, had the decision been taken at a general meeting. Indeed, it would be normal for the records to be kept in much the same way as minutes and written resolutions (see **26.6**).

It is open to debate whether it is always advisable for the sole member of a company to rely on the principle of unanimous consent to validate informal decisions. As the Act requires a sole member to provide the company with a written record of any informal decisions, it would seem to be more sensible for them to make decisions by written resolution in accordance with the statutory procedures, and to obey all the conditions and limitations associated with those procedures (see **9.2**). If a thing cannot be done by written resolution under the statutory procedures, it is possible that it cannot be done informally.

Although the statutory written resolution procedures do not apply to public companies, the sole member of a public company would be well-advised to obey the same principles and limitations when making an informal decision that would apply if it was attempting to pass a written resolution under the statutory procedures. For example, it would not be sensible for the sole member of a public company to rely on an informal decision to remove a director as this cannot be done by written resolution of a private company.

10

Annual general meetings

■ 10.1 Summary

- A cross-referenced checklist for organising an annual general meeting be found in **Chapter 19** – Organising General Meetings.
- Private companies are not required to hold annual general meetings unless their articles expressly require one to be held or they fall within the definition of a traded company (see **10.2**).
- All public companies must hold an annual general meeting within six months of the end of their financial year. Special rules apply if a public company changes its accounting reference date (see **10.3**).
- Any company which is required by the Act to hold an AGM must also circulate any AGM resolutions proposed by members (see **10.4**).
- Traded companies are also required to circulate certain other types of business proposed by members (see **10.5**).
- Certain documents must be made available for inspection at the annual general meeting (see **10.6**).
- Public companies usually use the meeting to deal with business which must be put to a general meeting some time during the year, e.g. laying the accounts and reports before the members, reappointing auditors or any other business which requires shareholder approval (see **10.7**).
- Various bodies have made recommendations on how the AGM can be improved (see **10.8** and **10.9**).
- It is not easy for listed companies to make the AGM interesting as they have to guard against disclosing price sensitive or inside information (see **10.10**).
- As far as companies are concerned, an effective AGM is one where all the 'important' business is properly transacted and the will of the majority is allowed to prevail (see **10.11**).

■ 10.2 Annual general meetings – private companies

Until recently, all private companies were required to hold an annual general meeting every year. However, in 1989 the Companies Act 1985 was amended to allow private companies to dispense with holding annual general meetings and some of the associated formalities, such as the laying of the report and accounts and the annual appointment of auditors. In order to take advantage of these dispensations, a private company was required to pass a unanimous resolution of all its members, known as an elective resolution. In each case, the members could revoke such an election by passing an ordinary resolution to that effect. In addition, any member could require the company to hold an annual general meeting by giving notice to that effect before a certain deadline.

Subject to the exceptions noted below, private companies are no longer required to hold an annual general meeting. The underlying requirements of the Companies Act 1985 for private companies to hold an annual general meeting (s. 366, 1985 Act), to lay their accounts at a general meeting (s. 241, 1985 Act) and to reappoint auditors annually (s. 385, 1985 Act) were repealed on 1 October 2007.

The 2006 Act requires public companies to hold an annual general meeting but does not generally do so for most private companies. There are just two exceptions to this rule. The first is that a private company must continue to hold annual general meetings if any provision of its articles 'expressly' requires it to do so (see **10.2.1**). The second is that a private company which is also a traded company is required by the Act to hold annual general meetings (see **10.2.2**).

Members of private companies holding as little as 5% of the voting rights may requisition a general meeting (see **12.5**) and propose written resolutions (see **9.3**). These rights are clearly meant to act as a substitute for the right to propose resolutions at an annual general meeting.

10.2.1 Requirement to hold annual general meetings where articles expressly require

Any provision in a private company's memorandum or articles that 'expressly' requires the company to hold an annual general meeting will continue to have effect by virtue of the transitional provisions in para. 32 of Sch. 3 of the Third Companies Act 2006 Commencement Order (SI/2007/2194). The word 'expressly' must be stressed here and para. 32 confirms for the avoidance of doubt that provisions commonly found in company articles specifying that one or more directors are to retire at each annual general meeting are not to be treated as a provision 'expressly' requiring the company to hold an annual general meeting. This means that for most private companies, including those subject to the 1985 Table A, the requirement to hold an annual general meeting ceased after 1 October 2007. However, any company with articles similar to reg. 47 of the 1948 Act Table A (which states: 'The company shall in each year hold a general meeting as its annual general meeting in addition to any other meetings in that year ...') will have to continue holding annual general meetings until such time as they amend or delete the relevant article.

It should be noted that none of the provisions of the Act regarding annual general meetings will apply to any such meeting held by a private company unless it is directly required under the Act to hold annual general meetings because it is a traded company (see below). As a result, it may not even be clear whether there are any time limits for holding the meeting unless the articles so provide. It should be noted in this regard that older articles are more likely to adopt the formula of requiring a meeting to be held as the annual general meeting at least once every calendar year with not more than 15 months between meetings.

In the absence of any other provisions in its articles, a private company required by its articles to hold an annual general meeting will need to hold and call the meeting in accordance with the requirements of the Act on general meetings of private companies in Part 13, Chapter 3 of the 2006 Act. For example, under the Act the minimum notice period will be 14 clear days unless the articles provide otherwise. In addition, a private company that is required by its articles to hold annual general meetings may find that there is no business that needs to be transacted at that meeting. There is nothing in the Act that requires a private company to do anything at such a meeting (unless it is a traded company). Accordingly, everything will depend on the articles, which could, for example, require some of the directors to retire by rotation at each meeting or require the company to lay its accounts before the members at a general meeting or allow the members to propose AGM resolutions (members of private companies having no statutory rights in this regard).

This all suggests that a private company that wishes to continue holding annual general meetings may need to modify its articles to ensure that there is some purpose in doing so and that the meeting is called and held in the appropriate manner. Its articles could, for example, be modified to require the company to lay its accounts before the members, reappoint auditors annually at a general meeting, etc.

10.2.2 Private company which is also a traded company must hold AGMs

As mentioned above, a private company which is a traded company must also hold annual general meetings (s. 336(1A)). This requirement derives from amendments made to the Act by the Companies (Shareholders' Rights) Regulations 2009 (SI 2009/1632) in August 2009 for the purposes of implementing the EU Shareholders' Rights Directive. The Directive requires all traded companies to hold annual general meetings. A traded company is defined for these purposes as a company whose voting shares are traded on a regulated market with the consent of the company (see s. 360C). Most people would probably refer to these companies as 'listed companies'. However, it would only include a company whose voting shares are traded on the main market of the London Stock Exchange, which is a regulated market and not those traded on the Alternative Investment Market, which is not a regulated market.

Most listed companies are, of course, public companies. Private companies cannot make a public offer of their shares. Accordingly it is not normally possible to gain admission without converting into a public company if there is any sort of public offer involved. However, as long as there is no public offer, it would appear that the shares of a private company could technically be admitted to trading on a regulated market. Although this will rarely happen in practice (if ever), it explains why the requirement to hold an annual general meeting was extended by the Directive to private companies that are also traded.

Any private company incorporated in the UK that is also a traded company must hold an annual general meeting within nine months of its year-end (rather than the six-month time limit for public companies) in addition to any other meetings held during that period (s. 336(1A)). The minimum notice period for the meeting will be 21 clear days (s. 307A and s. 360). The notice must state that the meeting will be held as the annual general meeting (s. 337(1)), include the date time and place of the meeting (s. 311(1)), state the general nature of the business (s. 311(2)) and include the matters specified in s. 311(3) for inclusion in the notice by traded companies and the statement required by s. 337(3) regarding the rights of members under s. 338A to require the company to include a matter in the business to be dealt with at the meeting.

The company must also publish on a website before the meeting the matters specified in s. 311A (see **13.10**) and make facilities available to enable members to appoint proxies via a website and publish details of the address of that website (s. 333A) (see **16.10**).

The members of the company have a right to ask questions at the annual general meeting (and any other general meeting of the company) in accordance with s. 319A (see **21.8**) and to require the company to include matters (other than resolutions) in the business to be dealt with at the meeting (s. 338A) (see **10.5**). The results of any poll taken at a general meeting of a private company that is a traded company must be published on a website (s. 341(1A)) and, if the company is also a quoted company, the members will also have a right to require an independent report on any poll taken at a general meeting (s. 342) (see **17.12**).

Other than matters validly proposed by members, it is not clear from the Act what the business of the annual general meeting of a private company which is a traded company should be.

It should be noted that a number of the above requirements apply to any general meeting held by a private company that is a traded company and not just to the annual general meeting.

■ 10.3 Annual general meetings – public companies

Public companies are still required to hold an annual general meeting (s. 336). The meeting must be held within the six-month period beginning with the date following their accounting reference date/year-end (s. 336(1)). For example if a company's year-end is 31 December, its annual general meeting must be held by 30 June.

A private company that is a traded company must also hold an annual general meeting. However, the time limit in this case is nine months after the company's year-end (s. 336(1A)).

If a company fails to comply with the above requirements, an offence is committed by every officer in default for which the punishment is a fine (s. 336(3) and (4)).

However, a company that fails to comply following a change in its accounting reference date effected by shortening the previous accounting period is not treated as being in breach if it holds an annual general meeting within three months of the change (s. 336(2)).

A notice calling an annual general meeting of a public company (or a private company that is a traded company) must state that the meeting is an annual general meeting (s. 337(1)). The company must give at least 21 days' notice of the meeting (s. 307(2)). The notice required is clear days by virtue of s. 360. Shorter notice may be given of the annual general meeting of a public company which is not a traded company if all the members entitled to attend agree (s. 337(2)) (see **13.6**).

The requirement to hold an annual general meeting is not satisfied by holding a general meeting during the period in question, even if the business at that meeting is the same as that which would normally be dealt with at the annual general meeting. This is because s. 337 requires the notice of meeting to specify that the meeting will be held as the annual general meeting.

Members of public companies have a right to require the company to circulate resolutions for consideration at the annual general meeting (see **10.4**). This right is not extended to members of private companies that are traded companies. However, members of traded companies (whether public or private) have a right to require the company to include matters of business (other than resolutions) on the AGM agenda (see **10.5**).

Where a notice calling an annual general meeting of a traded company is given more than six weeks before the meeting, the notice must include:

- if the company is a public company, a statement of the right under s. 338 to require the company to give notice of a resolution to be moved at the meeting and a statement of the right under s. 338A to require the company to include a matter in the business to be dealt with at the meeting; and
- if the company is a private company, a statement of the right under s. 338A to require the company to include a matter (other than a resolution) in the business to be dealt with at the meeting (s. 337(3)).

10.3.1 AGM date following a change of ARD

Problems can arise with respect to the date of the annual general meeting when a company changes its accounting reference date and, in doing so, shortens its current financial year. The timing of the change may be such that the company finds itself automatically in breach of the normal requirement to hold an annual general meeting.

The Act provides that a company that fails to comply with the usual time limit for holding an annual general meeting following a change in its accounting reference date effected by shortening the previous accounting period is not treated as being in breach if it holds an annual general meeting within three months of the change (s. 336(2)).

10.3.2 Requirement to hold AGM following conversion

It can be difficult to decide whether it is necessary to hold an AGM following conversion of a company's status from public to private and vice versa, or whether an offence has been committed if one is not held. If a private company is re-registered as a public company and the period within which it must as a public company hold an AGM has not expired, it could (and probably should) hold an AGM within that period. However, if it converts after the time limit for holding an AGM has already expired, it is impossible for it to comply fully with the requirement to hold an AGM. If it is impossible to comply, it could be argued that it is not necessary to comply.

On the other hand if a public company has failed to hold an AGM within the period, it will already have committed an offence that presumably would not be extinguished by re-registering as a private company. However if it re-registers as a private company before the expiry of the period for a public company to hold an AGM, no offence would have been committed and the re-registered company would not (as a private company) be required to hold an AGM in that year, unless one of the usual exceptions for private companies applies.

■ 10.4 Circulation of members' AGM resolutions by a public company

Members of public companies have a statutory right under s. 338 to require the company to give notice of resolutions which the members intend to propose at annual general meetings. This right is not extended to the members of a private company even if the company is required to hold annual general meetings by the Act (because it is a traded company) or under its articles.

However, members of traded companies (whether public or private companies) have a statutory right to require the company to include in the business to be dealt with at the annual general meeting a matter (other than a proposed resolution) which may properly be included in the business (s. 338A) (see **10.5**).

In addition, members of all companies have a statutory right to have statements circulated by the company in connection with any business that is to be dealt with at any general meeting (ss. 314 to 316) (see **13.15**).

10.4.1 AGM notices of traded companies

If the AGM notice of a traded company (see **8.5.1**) is given more than six weeks before the meeting, it must (if the company is a public company) contain a statement regarding members' rights under s. 338 to require the company to give notice of a resolution to be moved at the meeting and (whether the company is public or private) contain a statement regarding members' rights under s. 338A to require the company to include a matter (other than a resolution) in the business to be dealt with at the meeting (s. 337(3)).

10.4.2 Conditions for valid requisition under s. 338

The members may not require the company to give notice of a resolution or other matter of business unless the resolution can be properly moved at the meeting or the matter of business can be properly included in the business of the meeting.

A resolution may properly be moved at an annual general meeting unless it would, if passed, be ineffective (whether by reason of inconsistency with any enactment or the company's constitution or otherwise), it is defamatory of any person, or it is frivolous or vexatious (s. 338(2)).

A company is required to give notice of a resolution under s. 338 once it has received requests to do so from:

(a) members representing not less than 5% of the total voting rights of all the members who have a right to vote on the resolution at the annual general meeting to which the requests relate (excluding any voting rights attached to shares held in treasury); or
(b) at least 100 members who have a right to vote on the resolution at the annual general meeting to which the requests relate and hold shares in the company on which there has been paid up an average sum, per member, of not less than £100 (s. 338(3)).

It should be noted that under (a) above, the validity of the demand must be determined by reference to the number of members who would have been entitled to vote if the meeting had been held on the date of the requisition. Thus, if preference dividends are in arrears on the date of the requisition and the company's articles give preference shareholders the right to vote in such circumstances, the requirements for a valid requisition will be more onerous.

In relation to (b) above, the number of shares which members must hold is calculated according to the nominal value of the shares. For example, if the nominal value is £1, each member must hold on average 100 fully paid shares. If the nominal value is 25p, each member must hold on average 400 shares.

It should be noted that any indirect investors in a company whose shares are admitted to trading on a regulated market are also able to participate in a request under s. 338 for the purposes of determining whether the 100 member test is satisfied (s. 153) (see **8.7.1**).

10.4.3 Time limit for making the request

A request under s. 338 must be must be received by the company at least six weeks before the meeting to which it relates, or if later, the time at which notice is given of that meeting (s. 338(4)). A company is not bound to comply with a demand made after the later of the above. In practice, the later of the two will normally be the time at which notice is given in view of the statutory requirement to give 21 clear days' notice of an annual general meeting, which normally works out at just over three weeks. It should be noted that notice will not be given until it is deemed to have been served and that due allowance will need to be made for the relevant service period. In practice, this means that a valid request can not only be made after the notices have been printed but can also be made for a short period after the notices have been sent out, that period being the applicable service period under the Act or the company's articles.

Although it will not normally be very relevant for the purposes of determining whether a request has been validly made, it should be noted that the requirements of s. 360 regarding clear days apply for the purposes of determining whether a request has been received six weeks before the meeting. In practice this means that the six-week time limit will not be satisfied unless the members submit their request to the company at least 42 clear days before the meeting (see **13.3**).

10.4.4 Form of the request

A request under s. 338 may be in hard copy or electronic form, must identify the resolution of which notice is to be given, and must be authenticated by the person or persons making it (see **Precedent 10.4A**). The usual rules set out in the company communications provisions of the 2006 Act determine the manner in which the request must be served on the company, whether it be in hard copy or electronic form (see **2.2**).

10.4.5 Company's duty

On receipt of a valid request, a company has a duty to give a copy of the resolution to each member of the company entitled to receive notice of the annual general meeting in the same manner as notice of the meeting, and at the same time as, or as soon as reasonably practical, after it gives notice of the meeting (s. 339(1)) (see **Precedent 10.4B**). The company need not, however, comply with the request of the members if they are liable to pay the company's expenses in complying the request under s. 340(2) and have not deposited or tendered a sum reasonably sufficient to do so (s. 339(2)).

Although the Act imposes the duty to circulate the requisitioned resolution on the company, it will fall to the directors to ensure compliance and it is noteworthy that it is the officers who are liable to a fine in default (s. 339(4)).

Notice of the resolution must be given to the members entitled to receive notice of the annual general meeting as determined by the Act and the company's articles of association. In addition, a copy should also be sent to:

(a) the directors (s. 310(1));

(b) any indirect investors (s. 146(3));

(c) the company's auditors who are entitled to receive all notices of, and other communications relating to, any general meeting which a member of the company is entitled to receive (s. 502(2)); and

(d) any other persons entitled to receive notices under the articles.

Members who are not entitled to have the notice sent to them but who are entitled to receive notice by some other means (e.g. holders of bearer shares who are entitled to be given notice by advertisement) must be given notice of the resolution in any manner permitted for giving such members notice of meetings.

Accidental failure to give notice of a requisitioned resolution to one or more members is disregarded for the purpose of determining whether notice of the resolution is duly given (s. 313). It should be noted that this provision applies to notice of a requisitioned resolution given under s. 339 notwithstanding anything in a company's articles.

The business which may be dealt with at an annual general meeting includes a resolution of which notice is given by the company in accordance with s. 339 (s. 339(3)).

It should be noted that, under s. 338, the members may only require a public company to give notice of a proposed resolution in respect of the annual general meeting. A public company is not required to include such a resolution in the notice of any other general meeting to be held before the next annual general meeting. If the members are not prepared to wait until the next annual general meeting, they should requisition a general meeting under s. 303, assuming that they are able to satisfy the conditions.

10.4.6 Cost of circulating a resolution

Under the 1985 Act, the right to requisition AGM resolutions was rarely exercised in practice, probably because the cost of exercising it fell upon the members themselves (unless the company in general meeting resolved otherwise). Under the 2006 Act, the company must bear the costs of circulating a resolution if a valid request is made before the end of the financial year preceding the meeting. However, if a valid request is made after the year-end, the resolution need not be circulated unless:

(a) the requisitionists have, within the time limits for making a valid requisition, 'deposited' or 'tendered' a sum reasonably sufficient to meet the company's expenses in circulating the resolution (s. 340(2)). The clear days rule in s. 360 applies for the purposes of determining whether they have done this within the six-week time limit, if that time limit applies (see **13.3**); or

(b) the company resolves otherwise (e.g. decides not to require the requisitionists to pay its costs).

It is obviously difficult for the requisitionists to make an accurate assessment of the company's costs and they may seek guidance from the company before depositing their request. If there is a dispute between the company and the requisitionists as to the sum required, the directors would be well-advised to give effect to the requisition as they could be liable to a fine for failing to comply with the requirements of s. 339 if the court takes the view that the sum deposited or tendered by the requisitionists was reasonably sufficient.

The cost of giving effect to a request should not be prohibitive if it is deposited in time for inclusion in the notice calling the annual general meeting. If the company has already printed the notice at the time of the deposit, it should attempt to minimise the cost of giving effect to the request by printing the resolution separately rather than, for example, having the original notice reprinted, particularly if that notice is embodied in the annual report and accounts. If a company does decide to reprint the notice, it does not necessarily follow that it may require the requisitionists to pay the whole of its costs in doing so.

In practice, the company (i.e. the directors or an authorised officer) may sometimes agree to give effect to a requisition without charge to the requisitionists. It is submitted that the requisitionists should still offer to pay any reasonable costs the directors may decide to impose in their original request to ensure that the directors have a duty to circulate the resolution (because the directors may not have a duty to circulate a resolution for which the members are potentially liable to pay the costs unless the members indicate that they are willing to bear those costs). It is also submitted that if the directors subsequently agree to waive the costs and proceed to circulate the resolution, that the company could not then require the requisitionists to pay the company's costs.

If the directors do not agree to waive the costs, the requisitionists can include in their request a resolution to be put to the annual general meeting that the company should bear the costs. If such a resolution is passed, the requistionists will not be liable to pay the company's costs under s. 340(2)(a). Requisitionists sometimes try to achieve this by embodying a proposal regarding costs in the requisitioned resolution. This has the advantage of ensuring that they will not be required to pay if the resolution is passed. However, it may be preferable from their point of view for the proposal to be drafted as a separate requisitioned resolution, particularly where their main proposal is one which requires a special majority. This is because the resolution regarding costs need only be passed as an ordinary resolution.

However, even if they do this, they must deposit or tender with the requisition a sum reasonably sufficient to meet the company's costs (on the basis that their resolution regarding costs may be defeated) unless the company has previously resolved that the expenses of circulating the resolution (or perhaps more likely, members' resolutions generally) should not be borne by the requisitionists.

The ICSA's *Guide to Best Practice for Annual General Meetings* recommends that unless the company agrees at the outset to absorb all the costs of circulation, members' resolutions should automatically be accompanied (in any notice) by another resolution giving shareholders the opportunity to decide whether the company or the requisitionists should bear the relevant costs. If the directors feel that any particular case does not justify the adoption of such a resolution, they should, however, be free to recommend a vote against it. The *Guide* also suggests that companies should consider including members' resolutions in the notice without charge.

■ 10.5 Traded companies: members' power to include other matters in AGM business

Members of traded companies (whether public or private companies) may require the company to include in the business to be dealt with at the annual general meeting a matter (other than a proposed resolution) which may properly be included in the business (s. 338A). For a definition of a traded company, see **8.5.1**.

This right presumably enables members to raise matters not already included on the agenda for the meeting (or not within the scope of the notice) without the need to frame the business as a resolution. For example, the members could require the directors to include an item enabling the discussion of the company's ethical policies at the meeting. Although the members of a traded company could probably raise this matter in the general question and answer session which occurs when the meeting considers the annual report (and may even have a right to do so under s. 319A), they would inevitably draw more attention to the issue by making it a formal agenda item, particularly if they also required the company to circulate a statement in connection with the business. It should also be noted that a requisition under s. 338A could be used in an attempt to ensure that the directors have an obligation to answer questions put to them at the meeting on the matter under s. 319A, which only applies in relation to business being dealt with at the meeting (see **20.8**).

Section 388A(2) provides that a matter may properly be included in the business at an annual general meeting unless it is defamatory of any person or it is frivolous or vexatious. The question as to whether a matter proposed by members is defamatory, frivolous or vexatious will be for the company to judge, at least initially. However, if a company wrongly refuses to include an item on these grounds, the members could take legal action to enforce their rights. It should also be noted that if the company fails to comply with a valid request, the directors and officers may be guilty of an offence (s. 340A(3)). Accordingly, the directors would need to be pretty sure of their grounds before refusing to comply with such a request. As no resolution needs to be proposed (or can be proposed) for the purposes of s. 338A, it seems likely that the courts would take a fairly stringent approach to any refusal to comply with a request.

It is assumed that members of a traded company could not add an item (other than a resolution) to the agenda under s. 338A and then seek to propose a resolution in connection with that business at the meeting on the basis that their resolution is within the scope of the notice.

10.5.1 Statement in AGM notice

If the AGM notice of a traded company is given more than six weeks before the meeting, it must contain a statement regarding members' rights under section 338A to require the company to include a matter (other than a resolution) in the business to be dealt with at the meeting (s. 337(3)). If the traded company is also a public company, it must also include a statement of members' rights to propose resolutions under s. 338.

10.5.2 Conditions for valid request

The conditions for a valid request under s. 338A are summarised below. It should be noted that they are almost identical to the conditions for proposing a resolution at the AGM of a public company under s. 338. Accordingly much of the discussion relating to a request under s. 338 (see **10.4**) will also be relevant to requests made under s. 338A.

A traded company is required to include a matter which may properly be included in the business to be dealt with once it has received requests that it do so from:

(a) members representing at least 5% of the total voting rights of all the members who have a right to vote at the meeting to which the requests relate; or

(b) at least 100 members who have a right to vote on the resolution at the annual general meeting to which the requests relate and hold shares in the company on which there has been paid up an average sum, per member, of at least £100 (s. 388A(3)).

Indirect investors may join in making such a request under s. 153 (see **8.7.1**).

A request under s. 388A may be made in hard copy or electronic form, must identify the matter to be included in the business, must be accompanied by a statement setting out the grounds for the request and must be authenticated by the person or persons making it (s. 388A(4)).

The request must be received by the company no later than six weeks before the meeting to which it relates, or, if later, the time at which notice is given of that meeting. In practice, the clear days rule in s. 360 applies for the purposes of calculating the six-week period. Accordingly it should therefore be interpreted as meaning 42 clear days before the meeting (see **13.3**).

10.5.3 Company's obligations

Section 340A(1) provides that a company that is required under section 338A to include any matter in the business to be dealt with at an annual general meeting must:

(a) give notice of it to each member of the company entitled to receive notice of the annual general meeting in the same manner as notice of the meeting and at the same time as, or as soon as reasonably practicable after, it gives notice of the meeting; and

(b) publish it on the same website as that on which the company published the information required by s. 311A.

However, the company's duty to circulate is subject to compliance by the requisitionists with any duty under s. 340B(2) to deposit or tender of sum in respect of expenses of circulation.

If a company fails to comply with a valid request, an offence is committed by every officer in default for which a fine may be imposed (s. 340A(3) and (4)).

10.5.4 Cost of circulation

Section 340B provides that the expenses of the company in complying with a request under s. 340A to circulate a matter (other than a resolution) need not be paid by the members who requested the inclusion of the matter in the business to be dealt with at the annual general meeting if requests sufficient to require the company to include the matter are received before the end of the financial year preceding the meeting.

Where this is not the case the expenses of the company in complying with the request must be paid by the members who requested the inclusion of the matter unless the company resolves otherwise. And unless the company has previously so resolved, it is not bound to comply with the request unless there is deposited with or tendered to it, not later than six weeks (i.e. 42 clear days) before the annual general meeting to which the requests relate, or if later, the time at which notice is given of that meeting, a sum reasonably sufficient to meet its expenses in complying with the request (s. 340B(2)).

■ 10.6 Documents to be displayed at the AGM

Companies used to be required to display a number of documents at the annual general meeting. Most of these requirements have now been abolished for one reason or another.

For example, companies used to be required to keep a register of directors' interests in shares or debentures of the company (s. 325, 1985 Act) and to make that register available for inspection at the annual general meeting (para. 29 of Sch. 13 of the 1985 Act). However, this requirement was abolished with effect from 6 April 2007 to coincide with the abolition of the requirement to keep the register.

The Companies Act 2006 still requires directors' service contracts to be made available for inspection, but not at the annual general meeting (s. 228). The Listing Rules used to require listed companies to make copies of directors' service contracts available for inspection at the annual general meeting for at least 15 minutes prior to and during the meeting. However, this requirement was abolished in 2005. The Listing Rules also used to require the notice convening the annual general meeting to contain a note informing members as to when and where directors' service contracts would be made available for inspection. This requirement was deleted in June 1996.

The UK Corporate Governance Code requires the terms and conditions of appointment of non-executive directors to be made available for inspection by any person at the company's registered office during normal business hours and at the AGM (for 15 minutes prior to the meeting and during the meeting).

In practice, the only other documents that are likely to have to be put on display anymore are those which the company has said it will display in the notice of the meeting, which could include, for example, copies of the articles where the company proposes to adopt an entirely new version.

■ 10.7 Business of the annual general meeting

There are only two things that the Act actually requires to be dealt with at the annual general meeting. Those two things are:

- resolutions proposed by shareholders (see **10.4**); and
- a resolution to allow a traded company to hold general meetings at 14 days' notice (see **25.16**).

The Act does not require anything else to be done at the annual general meeting, or prescribe that anything else can only be done at the annual general meeting. Nevertheless, it does still have a big influence on the type of business which is normally put before the meeting. This is partly because all public companies must at some stage after their year-end:

- lay their accounts before the members at a general meeting (s. 437);
- appoint or reappoint auditors at that meeting (s. 489(2));
- fix the auditors' remuneration at that meeting (s. 492); and
- if the company is a quoted company, put the directors' remuneration report prepared by the directors to members for approval at that meeting (s. 439).

The meeting at which all these matters have to be dealt with (i.e. the meeting at which accounts are laid) is referred to in s. 437 as the 'accounts meeting'. The accounts of a public company can be laid either at the annual general meeting or at a separate general meeting called for that purpose. If they are laid at the annual general meeting, that meeting will also be the 'accounts meeting'. If they are not, a separate general meeting will need to be held as the 'accounts meeting'.

Although the accounts need not be laid at the annual general meeting, it is plainly sensible to do so to avoid having to hold another general meeting. A company must still hold an annual general meeting even if it is not held as the accounts meeting. The fact that the deadline for holding annual general meetings and the normal deadline for filing the accounts of a public company are now the same makes it all the more likely that the company will be able use the annual general meeting as its accounts meeting.

If a company is required by law to hold a meeting of shareholders as its annual general meeting, it is also sensible to take the opportunity that the meeting presents to deal with other items of business that need shareholder approval. In addition, the company's articles may require certain matters to be dealt with at the annual general meeting (e.g. the re-election of directors retiring by rotation, etc).

All these factors combine to make the business of the annual general meeting fairly predictable and, in practice, the meeting will probably deal with some or all of the following items:

- laying of the accounts (see **25.2**);
- appointment of the auditors (see **25.5**) and fixing their remuneration (see **25.6**);
- in the case of a quoted company, the directors' remuneration report (see **25.3**);
- appointment of directors (see **25.13**);
- reappointment of directors retiring by rotation (see **25.14**);
- approval of any final dividend recommended by the board (see **25.12**);
- renewal by ordinary resolution of the directors' authority to allot shares in accordance with s. 551 (if required);
- special resolution to disapply pre-emption rights in accordance with s. 571 (if required);
- authority to buy-back own shares (if required);
- special resolutions to amend articles of association (if required);
- in the case of a traded company, a resolution to enable the company to give 14 days' notice of any general meeting held in the following year (s. 307A) (see **25.16**);
- other business required by the articles to be conducted at the annual general meeting;
- any other business which needs shareholder approval and which it is convenient to deal with at the meeting; and
- resolutions validly proposed by the members (see **10.4**).

10.7.1 No business to be transacted

If the accounts are not ready to be laid at the annual general meeting, the only business to be conducted could be the reappointment of directors retiring by rotation in accordance with the articles of association. If the articles make no such provision or none of the directors are subject to retirement by rotation, there may be no business to be transacted at the annual general meeting. Nevertheless, a meeting must still be held and notice of the meeting must be sent to members (indicating, if necessary, that no business is to be proposed by the directors).

Members may still have the right to propose resolutions and other agenda items themselves (see **10.4** and **10.5**). Even if they do not do so, some might still attend the meeting to seek an explanation as to why the accounts are not ready.

In practice, it may be difficult to obtain a quorum where there is no business to be transacted, in which case the meeting may never actually be properly held or never be properly completed because of the rules on adjournment in the company's articles in these circumstances (see **23.4**). Nevertheless, it is submitted that the directors will have done their duty under the Act and need not make any other attempt to hold the meeting unless it is necessary to enable appointments or reappointments of directors to take place in accordance with the articles.

■ 10.8 UK Code recommendations on constructive use of the AGM

Principle E.2 of the UK Corporate Governance Code recommends that companies should use the annual general meeting to communicate with investors and encourage their participation. Compliance with the Code provisions under this heading is unlikely to do much to help achieve this objective, although they are loosely connected.

The Combined Code used to recommend that companies and registrars should facilitate the attendance of major shareholders at the AGM. Somewhat strangely, this recommendation was included in the section of the Combined Code dealing with the obligations of institutional investors. It fell by the wayside when that section was replaced by the UK Stewardship Code.

10.8.1 AGM notice

The UK Corporate Governance Code recommends that companies should arrange for the notice of the AGM and related papers to be sent to shareholders at least 20 working days before the meeting (Code provision E.2.4). This recommendation is targeted principally at institutional investors and is intended to give them time to inform and consult beneficial holders and to submit proxies. The use of working days, rather than the usual clear days formula, ensures that additional notice is given if the notice period includes any public holidays. It is not totally clear whether the words 'sent to shareholders' should be interpreted as meaning posted to shareholders or received by shareholders, or whether the 20 working days is meant to be 20 clear working days. It is normally assumed that the recommendation requires the notice to be in shareholders' hands 20 clear working days before the meeting.

10.8.2 Directors to attend AGM

The UK Corporate Governance Code requires the chairman of the board to arrange for the chairmen of the audit, remuneration and nomination committees to be available to answer questions at the AGM and for all directors to attend

(Code provision E.2.3). The requirement for all directors to attend was introduced in 2003.

10.8.3 Proxies

The Code requires companies to record and count all proxy votes and, except where a poll is called, to announce at the meeting and on the company's website the level of proxies lodged on each resolution, and the number of votes for and against the resolution and the number of votes withheld, after it has been dealt with on a show of hands (Code provision E.2.2). Section 341 of the Act requires quoted companies to publish details of votes taken on a poll on a website (see **17.12**).

The Code also requires listed companies to provide a 'vote withheld' option on proxy appointment forms to enable shareholders to indicate if they have reservations on a resolution but do not wish to vote against. The proxy form and any announcements of voting should make it clear that a 'vote withheld' is not a vote in law and is not counted in the calculation of the proportion of the votes for and against the resolution (Code provision E.2.1).

10.8.4 Separate resolutions

Listed companies are required to propose a separate resolution at the AGM on each substantially separate issue, and should in particular propose a resolution at the AGM relating to the report and accounts (Code provision E.2).

10.8.5 Dialogue with institutional shareholders

The UK Corporate Governance Code states as a principle that listed companies should enter into a dialogue with shareholders based on the mutual understanding of objectives and that the board as a whole has responsibility for ensuring that a satisfactory dialogue takes place (Code principle E.1).

The Code recognises that most shareholder contact will be with the chief executive and finance director, but states that the chairman should ensure that all directors are made aware of their major shareholders' issues and concerns (Code supporting principle E.1).

The Code provisions suggest that:

(a) The chairman should ensure that the views of shareholders are communicated to the board as a whole and should discuss governance and strategy with major shareholders (Code provision E.1.1).
(b) Non-executive directors should be offered the opportunity to attend scheduled meetings with major shareholders and should expect to attend meetings if requested by major shareholders (Code provision E.1.1).
(c) The senior independent director should attend sufficient meetings with a range of major shareholders to listen to their views in order to help develop a balanced understanding of the issues and concerns of major shareholders (Code provision E.1.1).

(d) The board should state in the annual report the steps they have taken to ensure that the members of the board, and in particular the non-executive directors, develop an understanding of the views of major shareholders about the company, for example through direct face-to-face contact, analysts' or brokers' briefings and surveys of shareholder opinion (Code provision E.1.2).

The Higgs Report recommended that the company secretary should act as a conduit for contacts from major shareholders to non-executive directors (Higgs Report, para. 15.19).

10.8.6 Statement on dialogue in annual report

The board should state in the annual report the steps it has taken to ensure that members of the board, and in particular the non-executive directors, develop an understanding of the views of major shareholders about their company, for example through direct face-to-face contact, analysts or brokers briefings and surveys of shareholder opinion (Code provision E.1.2).

10.8.7 Institutional investors' obligations under the Stewardship Code

The UK Stewardship Code deals with the parallel obligations of institutional investors.

The Stewardship Code requires institutional investors to:

1. publicly disclose their policy on how they will discharge their stewardship responsibilities;
2. have a robust policy on managing conflicts of interest in relation to stewardship which should be publicly disclosed;
3. monitor their investee companies;
4. establish clear guidelines on when and how they will escalate their stewardship activities;
5. be willing to act collectively with other investors where appropriate;
6. have a clear policy on voting and disclosure of voting activity; and
7. report periodically on their stewardship and voting activities.

■ 10.9 ICSA's Guide to Best Practice for Annual General Meetings

In April 1996, the Department of Trade and Industry (now known as the Department for Business, Innovation and Skills (BIS)) issued a consultative document, *Shareholder Communications at the Annual General Meeting*, which asked whether shareholders should have a statutory right to have resolutions circulated free of charge and/or to ask questions at the AGM. The consultative document suggested that some of these issues could be dealt with by the development of best practice by companies. Accordingly, with the encouragement of the

BIS, the ICSA published a *Guide to Best Practice for Annual General Meetings* in September 1996. Several of the recommendations made in the ICSA Guide have been overtaken by subsequent events, including in the two areas covered by the original BIS consultation. Nevertheless, the ICSA Guide still contains some useful recommendations, which are summarised below.

The guide made 24 recommendations which listed companies in particular were encouraged to adopt. Where necessary, the recommendations have been annotated to indicate subsequent developments and parallel requirements. These annotations are shown in square brackets.

Shareholder communications

1. All companies should engage in an active policy of communication with all shareholders (not just institutional shareholders).
2. Companies should arrange for all correspondence from shareholders to receive a full reply from the company secretary, the chairman, another director, or another designated senior executive. If the enquiry concerns a particular product or plant, it may be appropriate for the response to come from the head of the business division or a particular factory.
3. Communications with members should be handled appropriately but sensitively in accordance with the company's shareholder communications policy.

AGM notice and venue

4. The AGM notice and accompanying documents should be circulated at least 20 working days (excluding weekends and bank holidays) in advance of the meeting [see also UK Corporate Governance Code provision E.2.4].
5. The venue for the AGM should be accessible by attendees who have disabilities and have facilities for those with poor hearing.
6. Companies should ensure that each item of special business included in the notice is accompanied by a full and detailed explanation.

Directors

7. Directors standing for re-election to the board should be named in the notice and form of proxy.
8. A brief description should be given of the directors standing for election or re-election, including their ages; their relevant experience (not merely a list of other directorships they hold); the dates that they were first appointed to the board; and details of any board committees to which they belong [this recommendation expands upon UK Corporate Governance Code provision B.7.1].
9. The articles of association of public companies should require all the directors to be subject to retirement by rotation [see also UK Corporate Governance Code provision B.7.1].
10. Wherever possible, all directors should attend the AGM, and be seated with the chairman, facing the shareholders [see also UK Corporate Governance Code provision E.2.3].

11. The chairman should not propose his own election or re-election or propose any resolution in which he has an interest.

AGM procedure

12. The resolution to receive or adopt the accounts should be separate from any resolution to approve the payment of the final dividend recommended by the directors. It is also best practice generally to deal with different items of business by way of separate resolutions [see also UK Corporate Governance Code provision E.2.1].
13. Boards should provide adequate time for shareholder questions at AGMs [see 21.8 regarding shareholders' right to ask questions].
14. When moving the adoption or receipt of the accounts, the chairman should allow shareholders to raise questions on any item concerning the company's past performance, its results and its intended future performance. However, the directors need not answer questions which are irrelevant to the company or its business or which could result in the release of commercially sensitive information. Nor should they disclose price-sensitive information unless it can be done in compliance with the Listing Rules and guidance regarding the release of price-sensitive information [see further **10.10** regarding the disclosure of price-sensitive (inside) information].
15. Before each resolution is put to the vote, the chairman should explain again its effect and purpose. If necessary, he should elaborate on the information previously provided in the explanatory circular which accompanied the notice of the meeting. He should also invite shareholders to speak.
16. Where concerns are raised by a shareholder at the AGM and the chairman undertakes to consider them, the shareholder should subsequently be sent a full report of the action taken.

Shareholder resolutions

17. Unless the company agrees at the outset to absorb all the costs of circulation, shareholder resolutions requisitioned under [the Act] should automatically be accompanied (in any notice) by another resolution giving shareholders the opportunity to decide whether the company or the requisitionists should bear the relevant costs. If the directors feel that any particular case does not justify the adoption of such a resolution, they should, however, be free to recommend a vote against it [see **10.4.6** regarding the rules for traded companies].

Polls and proxies

18. When announcing the decision on a poll, the total number of votes cast in favour of, and against, the resolution should be disclosed [a quoted company must now announce the results of any poll on a website in accordance with s. 341 (see **17.12**)].
19. If the chairman informs shareholders of the number of proxy votes he holds for and against a resolution during the meeting, he should clarify that those

numbers refer to the proxies lodged with the company (or its registrars) before the meeting and that some of those who lodged proxies may be present and, having heard the debate, could decide to vote differently [see UK Corporate Governance Code provision E.2.2].

20. All proxy forms should be worded to allow the proxy to vote or abstain on business which may come before the meeting which was not included in the notice, e.g. amendments and formal motions [see UK Corporate Governance Code provision E.2.2 and Listing Rule 9.3.6].

Enhancing the AGM

21. All companies should provide an updated trading statement at their AGM unless they have recently published a scheduled financial statement.

22. At least one of the executive directors of the company should make an oral report at the AGM, on those areas of the company's operations for which he or she has responsibility.

Disorder

23. All companies should establish procedures for dealing with disturbances at their AGMs.

Proxies' right to speak

24. All chairmen should seek the consent of the meeting to proxies speaking and participating in the debate. [This recommendation has been superseded by s. 324 of the Companies Act 2006, which enables all proxies to speak.]

These 24 best practice points are supplemented by several other suggestions and recommendations intended to stimulate discussion and further development by companies. For example, the *Guide* suggests that:

- Companies could announce the date of their next AGM much earlier (possibly at the preceding AGM or with the interim report).
- Companies should avoid holding their AGM on the same day as others in the same sector in order to facilitate the attendance of shareholders with holdings across a particular sector.
- When a particular issue has been raised by a shareholder, the chairman can assist the flow of the meeting by inviting other shareholders who wish to speak on the same subject to do so at that time.
- Companies should invite shareholders to submit questions in advance, but should not use this practice as a method of manipulating the AGM by requiring written notice of questions or to replace spontaneity at the AGM.
- If a valid demand for a poll is made, shareholders should be issued with poll cards immediately and asked to deposit them as they leave the meeting. This allows the meeting to continue with the minimum of disruption and enables shareholders who have to leave the meeting early to vote on the poll.

■ Although shareholders should be able to rely on the integrity of the company's registrars or auditors (properly supervised by and answerable to the company secretary, acting in that regard on behalf of the shareholders generally and not the directors) to act as scrutineers, one of the proposers of the poll could be invited to act as a joint scrutineer.

■ 10.10 Price sensitive (inside) information

The Disclosure and Transparency Rules impose a general obligation on the part of listed companies to notify a Regulatory Information Service as soon as possible of any inside information that directly concerns it as an issuer unless it is entitled to delay disclosure under the Disclosure and Transparency Rules (DTR 2.2.1). Inside information is defined for these purposes in s. 118C of the FSMA as information of a precise nature that:

(a) is not generally available;
(b) relates, directly or indirectly, to the issuer; and
(c) would, if generally available, be likely to have a significant effect on the price of its securities.

A company may delay disclosure of inside information under DTR 2.5.1 so as not to prejudice its legitimate interests provided that:

(a) such omission would not be likely to mislead the public;
(b) any person receiving the information owes the issuer a duty of confidentiality, regardless of whether that duty is based on law, regulations, articles or contract;
(c) the issuer is able to ensure the confidentiality of the information.

For the purposes of applying DTR 2.5.1, legitimate interests may, in particular, relate to negotiations where the outcome or normal pattern of the negotiations could be affected by public disclosure and decisions or contracts made by the management body that need the approval of another body of the issuer in order to become effective (DTR 2.5.3).

Where an issuer or its agent discloses inside information to any third party in the normal exercise of his employment, professional or duties, it must make complete and effective public disclosure via a Regulatory Information Service, simultaneously in the case of intentional disclosure and as soon as possible in the case of non-intentional disclosure, unless DTR 2.5.1 applies (DTR 2.5.6).

The Disclosure Rules include formal guidance on various aspects of a listed company's obligations of disclosure, including specific guidance on the meaning of inside information (see DTR 2.2.3 to DTR 2.2.10). The UKLA Knowledge Base also provides further guidance on 'Assessing and handling inside information' (see UKLA/TN/521.1).

In order to comply with these requirements, it is usual for listed companies to release a copy of the chairman's address via their regulatory information service immediately prior to the meeting, particularly where this includes updated trading information. However, this will not be necessary if the chairman merely recites information already published in the annual report. It may also be necessary to release the text of any presentations to be made by operational managers. As these presentations and the chairman's address will be prepared before the meeting, it will be possible to take advice from the company's advisers on the action which should be taken where there is any doubt, although most listed companies probably err on the side of disclosure these days.

The rules prohibiting the selective disclosure of price sensitive information also tend to inhibit the ability of directors to answer shareholders' questions at general meetings. Indeed, they are sometimes accused of emasculating one of the main purposes of the annual general meeting, i.e. to enable shareholders to hold the directors accountable for their stewardship of the company. This feeling may have arisen among shareholders because directors often cite these rules as the reason for not answering certain questions even though commercial confidentiality is probably the primary reason. The acid test in this regard is whether the directors would have answered the question if there were no rules on the release of price sensitive information. In most cases, the answer would probably be no.

Nevertheless, the Disclosure and Transparency Rules do impose limitations on listed companies which are predisposed towards answering shareholders' questions. And the main problem which the directors will face is trying to decide at the meeting whether the answer which they would like to give would constitute price sensitive/inside information.

Issuers must establish effective arrangements to deny access to inside information to persons other than those who require it for the exercise of their functions within the issuer (DTR 2.6.1). They must also have in place procedures that enable public disclosure to be made via a Regulatory Information Service as soon as possible in the event of a breach of confidentiality (DTR 2.6.2).

If in the course of a general meeting, previously unpublished price sensitive/inside information is inadvertently disclosed, it will of course be necessary for a listed company to make an announcement as soon as possible. It should also be noted that the results of resolutions taken at general meetings may in themselves be price sensitive information, particularly where a resolution has been defeated. A listed company must notify an RIS as soon as possible after a general meeting of all resolutions passed by the company (other than resolutions concerning ordinary business passed at an annual general meeting) (Listing Rule 9.6.18) and must send copies of all resolutions (other than those concerning ordinary business) to the FCA without delay after the relevant meeting (Listing Rules 9.6.2).

■ 10.11 Effectiveness of the AGM

The purpose of holding annual general meetings has been called into question on a number of occasions in recent years. This has already resulted in legislation to allow most private companies to dispense with holding annual general meetings completely. However, questions have even been raised with regard to the value of AGMs for listed companies. The Cadbury Committee observed that: 'If too many Annual General Meetings are at present an opportunity missed, this is because shareholders do not make the most of them and, in some cases, boards do not encourage them to do so' (*Cadbury Report*, para. 6.7).

Various bodies have made proposals to enhance the annual general meeting. The Hampel Committee made a number of recommendations which gave rise to the introduction of the constructive use of AGM requirements in the current UK Corporate Governance Code (see **10.8**). The Committee also made a number of non-Code recommendations for improving AGMs and communications with private investors:

■ Companies whose AGMs are well attended might consider adopting the practice of mounting a business presentation with a question-and-answer session at the AGM (Hampel Report, para. 5.13).

■ As well as allowing reasonable time for discussion at the AGM, the chairman should, if appropriate, also undertake to provide the questioner with a written answer to any significant question that cannot be answered on the spot (Hampel Report, para. 5.18).

■ So far as is practicable, private individuals should have access to the same information from companies as institutional shareholders (e.g. via the internet) (Hampel Report, para. 5.24).

■ Listed companies should prepare a resumé of the discussion at the AGM (but not a full and detailed record), together with voting figures on any poll, or a proxy count where no poll was called, and send this to shareholders on request (Hampel Report, para. 5.22) (see **19.7**).

Notwithstanding all these efforts, a committee established by the Government under the chairmanship of Paul Myners to examine ways of improving relationships between the City and industry reported that virtually all participants in its consultation exercise viewed the AGM as an expensive waste of time and money (*Myners Report, 'Developing a Winning Partnership'*, 1995).

Several factors have probably caused this antipathy towards the AGM to increase in recent years. Probably the most important of these is the increase in the proportion of shares held by institutional and overseas investors and the fact that they do not normally attend the meeting, preferring instead to vote by proxy. One of the consequences of this is that the views of private investors who attend the meeting are not as important as they once were.

In addition, single issue pressure groups often tend to dominate (and disrupt) the proceedings at listed company AGMs. This can make it difficult for other shareholders to raise legitimate questions and has undoubtedly caused some to decide not to attend.

Other reasons include the constraints imposed on listed companies regarding the release of price-sensitive information which limit the directors' ability to give meaningful answers to questions raised by shareholders at the meeting (see further **10.10**). Companies often complain about the standard of debate and questions raised by shareholders at the meeting. Directors complain that the only thing shareholders seem to be interested in is directors' pay.

For the moment, the weight of opinion still seems to be in favour of maintaining the annual general meeting for public companies. The main purpose of holding an annual general meeting, rather than conducting some sort of postal ballot, can be said to be:

- to give members an opportunity to question the directors face-to-face regarding their stewardship of the company, particularly in the context of the company's published accounts and, in the case of a quoted company, the directors' remuneration report; and
- to allow members to debate resolutions proposed by the directors or as members' resolutions before voting on them.

Company secretaries sometimes cite as evidence of the AGM's effectiveness the fact that, when taking decisions on certain policies and strategies, directors often consider whether they would feel comfortable justifying their proposed course of action at the AGM. The attendance of the press at listed company AGMs also means that directors are held accountable to a wider audience.

Although companies sometimes complain about the lack of participation at the AGM, their primary concern is almost certainly to transact the business of the meeting in compliance with all applicable legal requirements and to ensure that the will of the majority prevails. It is arguable that in order to achieve this, companies sometimes have to adopt measures that make the meeting more sterile and stage-managed. They often have to take measures to prevent dissident shareholders, who would have no chance of winning if a vote is taken, from achieving some sort of minor victory by disrupting the proceedings and thereby preventing a vote from being taken. Companies that have suffered at the hands of dissident shareholders can sometimes appear to focus more on quashing dissent rather than promoting debate and discussion. This is understandable to a certain extent because the dissident shareholder may only hold one or two shares each and may have purchased them, not as an investment, but with the sole aim of pursuing some sort of social or political campaign. The company will normally know from the proxy figures that the vast majority of investors do not support the dissident shareholders. The company's primary concern is to ensure that the will of the majority prevails, and if this means that the AGM becomes slightly more sterile in the process, then so be it.

For example, at the AGM of one listed company, the chairman refused to allow shareholders to ask questions unless they had been submitted in writing. At another, the chairman asked shareholders whether they had any comments to make on the resolutions at the start of the meeting and did not allow any further debate when he put the resolution to the meeting.

Listed companies do not like surprises and neither do their major shareholders who, for the most part, are institutional investors. Both parties have a vested interest in avoiding surprises and are becoming much more practised in the art of doing so. Institutional investors (and their representative bodies) issue guidance on most of the contentious issues that are likely to arise at the AGM, or insist on compliance with published codes such as the UK Corporate Governance Code. If a listed company wants to propose something different from the norm, it will tend to consult in advance with its major shareholders and their representative bodies to ensure that they are happy with the proposals. Indeed, such engagement is actively encouraged under the UK Corporate Governance and Stewardship Codes. Prior engagement normally helps companies to tailor their proposals to ensure that major shareholders do not vote against them.

Institutional investors are not only less likely to vote against the company's proposals, but increasingly likely to vote in favour. In the past, many institutional shareholders did not bother to vote unless they opposed a resolution. They are now much more likely to do so following a series of initiatives to encourage their participation, culminating in the Stewardship Code.

These factors combine to ensure that, if a listed company actually manages to conduct its annual general meeting properly, the outcome is practically assured. Companies can still be caught out occasionally, particularly on the thorny issue of directors' remuneration, as the 2011–12 'shareholder spring' attests. In that period, several high profile listed companies suffered defeats at the hands of shareholders on the resolution to approve the directors' remuneration report. The defeats reflected a change of public mood on the level of directors' remuneration following the banking crisis and the subsequent recession. To a certain extent investors also decided to give several companies a bloody nose to demonstrate that they were willing to do something about directors' pay and to divert attention from the fact that they had previously done very little about it.

Notwithstanding this mini-revolution, the outcome of most AGMs is for the most part pre-ordained before the meeting starts. This should not come as a great surprise. If the directors are doing a good job, are paying themselves a reasonable rate, and have consulted shareholders on their proposals there is no reason why anything controversial should happen at the AGM. There will not be much debate about the resolutions proposed by the directors and there will not be much reason for shareholders to grill them about their stewardship of the company. When things are going well, single issue shareholders will tend to dominate the proceedings. Indeed, the best way to improve the AGM when things are going well might be to try to persuade single issue shareholders to engage with the company in different ways. In the author's view, the AGM might be better if companies held some sort of separate 'stakeholder meeting' at which people were able to raise the sort of issues that often concern dissident shareholders.

It is fairly obvious that when things are not going so well the AGM might be very different affair. In these circumstances, the wrath of ordinary investors will probably far outweigh that of the single issue shareholders, who may feel like old friends to the directors in comparison.

The fact that public companies have to pass resolutions at a general meeting (usually the AGM) means that in certain circumstances the majority can be held hostage by the dissident minority. This could be prevented completely by allowing resolutions to be passed by a separate electronic/postal ballot. Companies could still be required to hold an annual general meeting at which shareholders could still debate the resolutions and hold the directors to account for their stewardship of the company. However, voting would not take place at the meeting. Shareholders could be allowed to tender their votes in writing or electronically before the meeting and for a short time after it. As the vote would not technically be taken at the meeting, the voting process would not be capable of being disrupted, and the will of the majority would always prevail. This would preserve the concept of the AGM but help solve some of the problems that sometimes cause it to be an unnecessarily sterile affair. Although technically, decisions would not be made at the meeting, they could not be made without holding a meeting.

11

Class meetings

■ 11.1 Summary

■ Not all members of a company will necessarily have the same rights. Where this is the case, the company has different classes of members. The rights of each class of members will be specified in the articles of association. This may occur in a company with a share capital (see **11.2**) and a company limited by guarantee (see **11.5**).

■ Class meetings are meetings of a specific class of members or the holders of a specific class of shares. A class meeting will typically be required where a company has more than one class of shares and proposes to vary the rights attached to a particular class or where the articles provide that a transaction requires the separate consent of a meeting of the holders of a certain class of shares.

■ Special procedures must be followed to vary the rights attached to different classes of shares. These procedures differ according to the manner in which those rights are conferred and whether the memorandum or articles make specific provision for variation of those rights (see **11.3**).

■ 11.2 Classes of shares

The articles of a company with a share capital will normally provide that it may divide its share capital into shares of more than one class (e.g. reg. 2 of Table A, pcls 22, plc 43). This means that the company can issue different types of shares which each give their holders different rights. Shares which give their holders the same rights are deemed to be shares of the same class. Holders of a different class of shares will usually have different rights regarding dividends, voting at general meetings, participation in capital and surplus assets on winding up, or some other matter.

For the purposes of the Companies Acts shares are of one class if the rights attached to them are in all respects uniform (s. 629(1)). For this purpose the rights attached to shares are not regarded as different from those attached to other shares by reason only that they do not carry the same rights to dividends in the 12 months immediately following their allotment (s. 629(2)).

Different classes of shares are usually given different designations (e.g. 'A' shares, 'B' shares, preference shares, etc) in order to distinguish them from other shares with different rights. However, this will not always be the case and shareholders holding shares of the same name may have different rights and constitute a separate class. This may arise as a result of a separate shareholders agreement under which the shareholders agree to modify the rights of the respective shareholders.

The rights attached to shares are usually specified in the articles. Any provision in this regard contained in the memorandum of a company incorporated before 1 October 2009 is now deemed to be a provision of its articles (s. 28). The rights attached to shares can also be governed to a certain extent by the terms of issue.

The holders of all classes of shares are members of the company. They are therefore entitled to receive notice of general meetings of the company and to attend and vote at such meetings unless those rights are withdrawn or restricted.

The most common classes of shares are:

- *Ordinary shares:* These are the shares which usually carry the right to vote at general meetings, to receive dividends and to participate in any surplus when the company is wound up. Where a company has only one class of shares, these will normally be called the ordinary shares, if they are called anything at all.

- *Preference shares:* These shares usually carry preferential dividend rights, usually a fixed percentage of their nominal value, which must be paid out of profits available for distribution before dividends are paid to the ordinary shareholders. These rights are often cumulative, which means that any dividends payable to the preference shareholders which are in arrears must be paid before the ordinary shareholders are paid a dividend. The articles usually give preference shareholders the right to vote at general meetings if their dividends are more than six months in arrears, but not otherwise. If the company is wound up, preference shareholders will usually have the right to have their capital returned before the ordinary shareholders but are not usually entitled to share in any surplus.

- *'A' and 'B' shares:* Companies tend to use the designations 'A' and 'B' shares where the rights of the holders are almost identical except for one thing. In some cases, the rights of the 'A' and 'B' shareholders may appear to be identical in every respect. This can happen where they have been established as a different class purely to enable a different dividend to be declared on each class. 'A' and 'B' shares are commonly found in joint venture companies where each partner will hold a separate class of shares which gives them the right to appoint one or more directors but which otherwise have the same rights. Having two categories of ordinary shares may also be used to give a minority shareholder (often the founder) certain entrenched rights, e.g. by giving him enhanced voting rights on any resolution to remove him as a director (see *Bushell v. Faith* [1970] A.C. 1099 which is discussed at **17.5**).

- *Non-voting shares:* These usually have the same rights as the ordinary shareholders to receive dividends, etc. However, they do not have the right to vote at general meetings.

■ 11.3 Variation of class rights of shareholders

The rights attached to different classes of shares may only be varied in accordance with s. 630 of the Act which provides safeguards to ensure that the interests of one class of shareholders are not prejudiced by another. The section applies to any variation of the rights attached to any class of shares in a company having a share capital. It does not apply to the variation of the rights of different classes of members of a company limited by guarantee (see **11.5**).

Section 630(2) provides that the rights attached to a class of a company's shares may only be varied:

(a) in accordance with any provision in the company's articles for the variation of those rights; or
(b) where the company's articles contain no such provision, if the holders of shares of that class consent to the variation in accordance with the requirements of that section.

The consent required for these purposes on the part of the holders of a class of a company's shares is:

(a) consent in writing from the holders of at least three-quarters in nominal value of the issued shares of that class (excluding any shares held as treasury shares); or
(b) a special resolution passed at a separate general meeting of the holders of that class sanctioning the variation (s. 630(4)).

It should be noted that the option to obtain consent in writing applies to both public and private companies and is not subject to the rules on written resolutions. A private company could, of course, also pass any special resolution as a written resolution.

Any amendment of a provision contained in a company's articles for the variation of the rights attached to a class of shares, or the insertion of any such provision into the articles, is itself to be treated as a variation of those rights (s. 630(5)). For the purposes of s. 630 and (except where the context otherwise requires) any provision in a company's articles for the variation of the rights attached to a class of shares, references to the variation of those rights include references to their abrogation (s. 630(6)).

The procedures for variation under the Companies Act 2006 are much simpler than the old procedures under Companies Act 1985 (s. 125), which differed according to the manner in which those rights are conferred and the existence in the memorandum or articles of provision for variation.

11.3.1 Special procedural requirements for a variation of class rights meeting

Subject to certain exceptions, s. 334 applies the provisions of Part 13, Chapter 3 (resolutions at meetings) with necessary modifications to any meeting of the holders of a class of shares (see further **11.4** regarding the general application of the Companies Act 2006 provisions on general meetings to class meetings). One of the exceptions provided for in s. 334(3) is that the provisions of s. 318 (quorum) and s. 321 (right to demand a poll) do not apply in relation to a class meeting held in connection with the variation of rights attached to a class of shares (but do apply in relation to a class meeting called for any other purpose).

Instead s. 334 provides that at a class meeting of a company with a share capital held to approve a variation of class rights:

- the quorum for a meeting other than an adjourned meeting, is two persons present holding at least one-third in nominal value of the issued shares of the class in question (excluding any shares of that class held as treasury shares) (s. 334(4)(a));
- the quorum for an adjourned meeting is one person present holding shares of the class in question (s. 334(4)(b));
- for the purposes of the above quorum requirements, where a person is present by proxy or proxies, he is treated as holding only the shares in respect of which those proxies are authorised to exercise voting rights (s. 334(5)); and
- any holder of shares of the class in question present may demand a poll (s. 334(6)).

For the purposes of s. 334, any amendment of a provision contained in a company's articles for the variation of the rights attached to a class of shares, or the insertion of any such provision into the articles, is itself to be treated as a variation of those rights, and references to the variation of rights attached to a class of shares include references to their abrogation (s. 334(7)).

The provisions of s. 334 with regard to the quorum can give rise to problems where the articles contain some other provision, e.g. where the articles provide for a quorum of ten at class meetings but make no provision as to the percentage of nominal value those members must hold. Read in isolation, the requirements of s. 334 on the quorum at a variation of class rights meeting appear very stark. Unlike s. 318 (quorum at general meetings), they are not expressed as being subject to the articles or as a minimum standard. This would seem to indicate that s. 334 takes precedence over anything in the articles where a variation of rights is concerned. However, some modern articles of listed companies provide that the quorum for a variation of rights shall be one or more persons, instead of two, representing at least one-third by nominal value. No doubt, such a provision was included in an attempt to reflect the fact that all the shares of a particular class may be held by a single person. It is slightly strange that the Act does not directly cater for this itself, although it does provide that the quorum at any adjourned meeting shall be one.

It has been held in relation to class meetings, that a single person may constitute a meeting where that person holds all the issued shares of a particular class (*East v. Bennett Bro. Ltd.* [1911] 1 Ch. 163).

A provision in a company's articles which purports to set a quorum of one at any variation of class rights meeting regardless of whether all the shares of a particular class are held by one person may fall foul of s. 334 if the shares are held more widely. The only thing that might save such a provision is if it can be viewed as forming part of the provisions in the articles for the variation of class rights under s. 630(2). Section 630(2) provides that rights attached to a class of shares may only be varied in accordance with the provisions in a company's articles for the variation of those rights or, where no such provision is made, if the holders consent to the variation in accordance with s. 630. If a company's articles set out a full alternative procedure for the variation of class rights, they may override s. 334, even though that procedure may involve the holding of a class meeting. If this is intended to be the case, it is by no means clear because s. 334 is not expressed as being subject to s. 630.

■ 11.4 Proceedings at class meetings

Subject to certain exceptions, the provisions on meetings in Part 13, Chapter 3 (ss. 301 to 335) apply with necessary modifications in relation to class meetings by virtue of s. 334 (for a company with a share capital) and s. 335 (for a company without a share capital).

However, the additional requirements relating to traded companies in ss. 311(3), 311A, 319A, 327(A1), 330(A1) and 333A are disapplied in relation to class meetings of a company with a share capital by s. 334(2).

Section 334(2A) clarifies that the notice requirements in s. 307(1) to (6) apply in relation to a meeting of holders of a class of shares in a traded company rather than s. 307A which deals with the notice requirements for general meetings of traded companies.

The following provisions are disapplied by s. 334(2) (companies with a share capital) and s. 335(2) (companies without a share capital) in relation to any class meeting:

- ss. 303 to 305 (members' power to require directors to call general meetings); and
- s. 306 (power of the court to order meetings).

In addition, s. 334(3) and s. 335(3) both disapply the following provisions but only in relation to a class meeting held in connection with a variation of rights (i.e. not in relation to a class meeting called for any other purpose):

- s. 318 (quorum); and
- s. 321 (right to demand a poll).

In both cases, for meetings held to consider a variation of class rights, ss. 334 and 335 substitute a modified quorum requirement and a different rule on the right to demand a poll. These modified requirements do not apply in the case of a class meeting not called for the purpose of a variation of class rights but may still apply in the case of a resolution proposed at such a meeting even though that particular resolution does not relate to a variation of rights. Sections 630 to 640 (variation of class rights) will obviously not apply to any resolution that does not concern a variation of class rights. Although it is rare for such resolutions to be proposed or for class meetings to be held where a variation of rights is not on the agenda, it is not impossible.

Many of the provisions of Part 13, Chapter 3 that are deemed to apply to class meetings (whether in relation to a variation of rights or otherwise) state that they are capable of modification by a company's articles. If a company establishes more than one class of share or more than one class of member and wishes the provisions regarding general meetings in its articles to apply to any class meetings that may be required, it ought perhaps to clarify in its articles that the relevant provisions apply (with suitable modification where necessary). It is likely that this will be the case anyway. However, it is best not to leave such matters to chance.

It may not be possible to override the specific rules on polls and the quorum that apply in relation to a class meeting held to consider a variation of rights by s. 334 (see **11.3.1**) and s. 335 (see **11.5.2**).

Table showing the provisions of Part 13, Chapter 3 that apply to class meetings by virtue of ss. 334 and 335

Section	Description	Companies *with* a share capital (s. 334)		Companies *without* a share capital (s. 335)	
		Variation of class rights meeting	*Any other class meeting*	*Variation of class rights meeting*	*Any other class meeting*
301	Resolutions at general meetings	Yes	Yes	Yes	Yes
302	Directors' power to call general meetings	Yes	Yes	Yes	Yes
303–305	Members' power to require directors to call general meetings	No (see s. 334(2))	No (see s. 334(2))	No (see s. 335(2))	No (see s. 335(2))

		Companies *with* a share capital (s. 334)		Companies *without* a share capital (s. 335)	
Section	Description	Variation of class rights meeting	Any other class meeting	Variation of class rights meeting	Any other class meeting
307	Notice required of general meetings	Yes	Yes	Yes	Yes
307A	Notice required of general meeting: certain meetings of traded companies	No (see s. 334(2A))	No (see s. 334(2A))	No (see note 1)	No (see note 1)
308	Manner in which notice to be given	Yes	Yes	Yes	Yes
309	Publication of notice of meeting on website	Yes	Yes	Yes	Yes
310	Persons entitled to receive notice	Yes	Yes	Yes	Yes
311	Contents of notice	Yes	Yes	Yes	Yes
311A	Traded companies: publication of information in advance of general meeting	No (see s. 334(2) (c))	No (see s. 334(2) (c))	No (see note 1)	No (see note 1)
312	Resolution requiring special notice	Yes	Yes	Yes	Yes
313	Accidental failure to give notice of resolution or meeting	Yes (except s. 311(3))	Yes (except s. 311(3))	Yes	Yes
314–317	Members' power to require circulation of statements	Yes	Yes	Yes	Yes
318	Quorum at meetings	No (see s. 334(3) to (5))	Yes	No (see s. 335(3) and (4))	Yes
319	Chairman of meeting	Yes	Yes	Yes	Yes
319A	Traded companies: questions at meetings	No (see s. 334(2) (c))	No (see s. 334(2) (c))	No (see note 1)	No (see note 1)

		Companies *with* a share capital (s. 334)		Companies *without* a share capital (s. 335)	
Section	Description	Variation of class rights meeting	Any other class meeting	Variation of class rights meeting	Any other class meeting
321	Right to demand a poll	No (see s. 334(3) and (6))	Yes	No (see s. 335(3) and (5))	Yes
322	Voting on a poll	Yes	Yes	Yes	Yes
322A	Voting on a poll: votes cast in advance	Yes	Yes	Yes	Yes
323	Representation of corporations at meetings	Yes	Yes	Yes	Yes
324	Rights to appoint proxies	Yes	Yes	Yes	Yes
324A	Obligation of proxy to vote in accordance with instructions	Yes	Yes	Yes	Yes
325	Notice of meeting to contain statement of rights	Yes	Yes	Yes	Yes
326	Company sponsored invitations	Yes	Yes	Yes	Yes
327	Notice required of appointment of proxy	Yes (except s. 327(A1))	Yes (except s. 327(A1))	Yes	Yes
328	Chairing meetings	Yes	Yes	Yes	Yes
329	Right of proxy to demand a poll	Yes	Yes	Yes	Yes
330	Notice required of termination of proxy's authority	Yes (except s. 330(A1))	Yes (except s. 330(A1))	Yes	Yes
331	Saving for more extensive rights conferred by articles	Yes	Yes	Yes	Yes

		Companies *with* a share capital (s. 334)		Companies *without* a share capital (s. 335)	
Section	Description	Variation of class rights meeting	Any other class meeting	Variation of class rights meeting	Any other class meeting
333	Sending documents relating to meetings etc in electronic form	Yes	Yes	Yes	Yes
333A	Traded company: duty to provide electronic address for receipt of proxies etc	No (see s. 334(2) (c))	No (see s. 334(2) (c))	No (see note 1)	No (see note 1)

Note 1: None of the provisions relating to traded companies can apply to a company without a share capital as a traded company must, by definition, have voting shares which are traded on a regulated market.

11.4.1 Notice

Section 307 (which is applied by s. 334 in relation to all class meetings) requires a company to give at least 14 days' notice of any class meeting to the holders of that class of shares (see **Precedent 11.4**). However, shorter notice may be given with the consent of members in accordance with s. 307(4) to (6).

The notice must be given in either hard copy or electronic form or by means of a website (s. 308). If it is published on a website, the company must also comply with s. 309.

Applying s. 310 with suitable modification, unless the articles make some other provision, notice of a class meeting must be served on every director and every holder of shares of that class and any person entitled to a share of that class in consequence of the death or bankruptcy of the holder if the company has been notified of that entitlement. Most articles do make other provision regarding the service of notices and will often restrict the right to receive notice (e.g. to the first named joint holder only).

The notice must state the date, time and place of the meeting (s. 311(1)) and, subject to anything to the contrary in the articles, the general nature of the business to be transacted. In practice, if a special resolution is to be proposed, the notice must also comply with the requirements of s. 283(6) regarding the inclusion of the text of the resolution and specifying that it is to be proposed as a special resolution.

Accidental failure to give notice to one or more persons of a class meeting or a resolution to be proposed at such a meeting will not automatically invalidate the proceedings or the resolution (s. 313).

Where a company has given an electronic address in any notice calling a class meeting or any instrument of proxy or instrument of proxy in relation to that meeting, it is deemed to have agreed that any document or information relating to that meeting or proxies in relation to that meeting may be sent by electronic means to the address (subject to any conditions or limitations specified in the notice) (s. 333).

11.4.2 Right to call a meeting

The holders of a class of shares have no statutory right to demand a class meeting (see s. 334(2)). However, there is no reason why a company's articles should not give them such a right.

11.4.3 Members' statements

The rules in ss. 314 to 317 allowing members to require the company to circulate a statement in connection with a proposed resolution or other business to be considered at the meeting will also apply to class meetings with suitable modification.

11.4.4 Appointment of chairman

Subject to the articles, any member or proxy elected by the members present at a class meeting may chair the meeting (ss. 319 and 328). In practice, most articles provide that the chairman of the board of directors or a director nominated by the board shall act as the chairman of any meeting and the class members will normally only be able to elect the chairman in default of these provisions.

11.4.5 Quorum

Section 318 applies to any class meeting that is not held for the purpose of considering a variation of class rights. If variation of class rights is to be considered at a class meeting, the quorum requirements will be as stated in s. 334(4) for companies with a share capital or s. 335(4) for companies without a share capital.

Where a class meeting is held for some other purpose, the rule in s. 318(1) will apply (with suitable modification) irrespective of anything contained in a company's articles. This rule provides that in the case of a private company limited by shares or by guarantee and only having one member, one qualifying person present at the meeting is a member. Whether this rule is capable of suitable modification for the purposes of class meetings is open to question.

The rule in s. 318(2), which provides for a quorum of two in any other case, is expressed as being subject to the provisions of a company's articles.

11.4.6 Resolutions

Section 281 provides that a resolution of a class of members of a private company must be passed either as a written resolution in accordance with Chapter 2 of Part 13 or at a meeting of the members (to which the provisions of Chapter 3 of Part 13 apply). A resolution of a class of members of a public company must be passed at a meeting of the members (to which the provisions of Chapter 3 and, where relevant, Chapter 4 of Part 13 apply).

Where a provision of the Companies Acts requires a resolution of a class of members and does not specify what kind of resolution is required, an ordinary resolution will suffice unless the company's articles require a higher majority (or unanimity) (s. 281(3)).

An ordinary resolution of a class of members is one that is passed in accordance with s. 282. A special resolution of a class of members is one that is passed in accordance with s. 283.

11.4.7 Written resolutions

A resolution of a class of members in a private company can be passed by written resolution or at a general meeting (s. 281(1)). A written resolution of a private company has effect as if passed (as the case may be) by the company in general meeting or by a meeting of a class of members of the company (s. 288(5)) (see **Precedent 9.2B**). The provisions of Part 13, Chapter 2 (written resolutions) will apply to any such written resolution (see **9.2**).

11.4.8 Voting

Subject to a company's articles, s. 284(1) provides that on a vote on a written resolution:

- in the case of a company having a share capital, every member has one vote in respect of each share or each £10 of stock held by him;
- in any other case, each member has one vote.

Subject to a company's articles, s. 284(2) provides that on a vote on a show of hands at a meeting:

- every member present in person has one vote;
- every proxy present who has been duly appointed by a member entitled to vote on the resolution has one vote.

Subject to a company's articles, s. 284(3) provides that on a vote on a poll taken at a meeting:

- in the case of a company having a share capital, every member has one vote in respect of each share or each £10 of stock held by him;
- in any other case, each member has one vote.

The other provisions of the Act on voting in ss. 284 to 287 also apply to class meetings. These provisions will apply to written resolutions of a class of members of a private company and class meetings, subject to any provisions in the articles. For example, articles usually contain provisions restricting the right to vote in certain circumstances (see **17.4**).

If variation of class rights is to be considered at a class meeting, the rules regarding the right to demand a poll will be as stated in s. 334(6) for companies with a share capital or s. 335(5) for companies without a share capital. For any other class meeting, s. 321 will apply and any provision of a company's articles will be void in so far as they do not comply with the minimum standards set out in that section.

11.4.9 Proxies and corporate representatives

Applying ss. 334 and 335, class members have a right to appoint a proxy under s. 324. The notice of any class meeting must contain a statement as to their rights to appoint a proxy (s. 325). If the company issues at its own expense invitations to members to appoint as a proxy a specified person or persons, the invitation must be issued to all the members of the class (s. 336). Any provision of a company's articles relating to the appointment of proxies will be void in so far as it would require any appointment or document to be received by the company or another person before the times set out in s. 327. The provisions of s. 330 on termination of a proxy's authority also apply.

A proxy may demand, or join in a demand, for a poll at a class meeting (s. 329). Nothing in ss. 324 to 330 (proxies) prevents a company's articles from conferring more extensive rights on members or proxies (s. 331).

A corporation may authorise one or more persons to act as its representative at a class meeting (s. 323).

11.4.10 Attendance

In *Carruth v. Imperial Chemical Industries Ltd.* [1937] A.C. 707, the directors convened an extraordinary general meeting of the company and two class meetings to approve a reduction of capital. The meetings were held on the same day and at the same venue. As one meeting finished, the next meeting was started and each meeting was attended by the holders of the other classes of shares. The resolution passed at one class meeting was challenged by a member of that class on the basis that people who were not members of that class were present at the meeting. The resolution was held to be valid and Lord Russell said:

> There are many matters relating to the conduct of a meeting which lie entirely in the hands of those persons who are present and constitute the meeting. Thus it rests with the meeting to decide whether notices, resolutions, minutes, accounts, and such like shall be read to the meeting or be taken as read; whether representatives of the Press, or any other persons not qualified to be summoned to the meeting, shall be permitted to be present, or if present, shall be permitted to remain; whether and when discussion shall be terminated and a vote taken; whether the meeting shall be adjourned. In all these matters, and they are only instances, the meeting decides, and if necessary a vote must be taken to ascertain the wishes of the majority. If no objection is taken by any constituent of the meeting, the meeting must be taken to be assenting to the course adopted.

11.4.11 Records of resolutions and minutes of meetings

Section 359 (records of resolutions and meetings of class of members) states that the provisions of Part 13, Chapter 6 (records of resolutions and meetings) apply, with necessary modifications, in relation to resolutions and meetings of holders of a class of shares, and in the case of a company without a share capital, a class of members, as they apply in relation to resolutions of members generally and to general meetings.

Accordingly the following provisions of the Act apply, with necessary modifications:

- s. 355 (records of resolutions and meetings etc);
- s. 356 (records as evidence of resolutions);
- s. 357 (records of decisions by sole member); and
- s. 358 (inspection of records of resolutions and meetings).

■ 11.5 Classes of members in guarantee companies

A company limited by guarantee may have different classes of members. Typically, the company's articles will allow the board of directors to establish different classes of member with different rights. An example might be a sports club which has full members, weekend members and junior members. Unless the articles provide for a method of variation, the class rights can only be varied in accordance with s. 631 (variation of class rights: companies without a share capital).

11.5.1 Variation of class rights: companies without a share capital

Section 631 deals with the variation of the rights of a class of members of a company where the company does not have a share capital. It provides that the rights of a class of members may only be varied:

(a) in accordance with provision in the company's articles for the variation of those rights; or
(b) where the company's articles contain no such provision, if the members of that class consent to the variation in accordance with s. 631.

Section 631(4) provides that the consent required for these purposes on the part of the members of a class is:

(a) consent in writing from at least three-quarters of the members of the class; or
(b) a special resolution passed at a separate general meeting of the members of that class sanctioning the variation.

It should be noted that the option to obtain consent in writing in (a) above applies to both public and private companies and is not subject to the rules on written resolutions. A private company could, of course, also use a written resolution to pass the necessary special resolution for the purposes of option (b), whereas a public company would have to hold a meeting.

Any amendment of a provision contained in a company's articles for the variation of the rights of a class of members, or the insertion of any such provision into the articles, is itself to be treated as a variation of those rights (s. 631(5)). For the purposes of s. 631, and (except where the context otherwise requires) any provision in a company's articles for the variation of the rights of a class of members, references to the variation of those rights include references to their abrogation (s. 631(6)).

11.5.2 Special procedures for variation of class rights meetings for companies without a share capital

Subject to certain exceptions, s. 335 applies the provisions of Part 13, Chapter 3 (resolutions at meetings) with necessary modifications to any meeting of the holders of a class of shares (see further **11.4** regarding the general application of the Companies Act 2006 provisions on general meetings to class meetings). One of the exceptions provided for in s. 335(3) is that the provisions of s. 318 (quorum) and s. 321 (right to demand a poll) do not apply in relation to a class meeting held in connection with the variation of rights attached to a class of shares (but do apply in relation to a class meeting called for any other purpose).

Instead s. 335 provides that for a variation of class rights meeting of a company without a share capital:

■ the quorum for a meeting other than an adjourned meeting, is two members of the class present (in person or by proxy) who together represent at least one-third of the voting rights of that class (s. 335(4)(a));
■ the quorum for an adjourned meeting is one member of the class present (in person or by proxy) (s. 335(4)(b));
■ any member of the class present (in person or by proxy) may demand a poll (s. 334(6)).

For the purposes of s. 335, any amendment of a provision contained in a company's articles for the variation of the rights attached to a class of shares, or the insertion of any such provision into the articles, is itself to be treated as a variation of those rights, and references to the variation of rights attached to a class of shares include references to their abrogation (s. 335(6)).

12

Calling general meetings

12.1 Summary

- Unless the time and place at which meetings are to be held each year is fixed, someone must be given the power to call meetings, i.e. to direct that a meeting will be held at a certain time and place to consider certain business. A general meeting must be convened (i.e. called) by a person or body with appropriate authority otherwise the meeting and any business transacted at it will be invalid.
- Articles traditionally give the board power to convene general meetings. However, the Companies Act also gives the directors authority to do so (see **12.2**).
- Articles usually provide alternative procedures for situations where the board of directors is unable or unwilling to exercise its powers (see **12.3**).
- The court also has power under the Act to direct that a general meeting be held (see **12.4**).
- Members who are able to satisfy certain requirements may require the directors to convene a general meeting to consider business proposed by them (see **12.5**).
- Member of private companies also have a right to propose written resolutions (see **9.3**).
- A resigning auditor has power to requisition a general meeting to consider the circumstances connected with his resignation (see **12.6**).

12.2 Meetings convened by the board of directors

Articles often give the board of directors power to convene general meetings (e.g. reg. 37 of Table A). However none of the model articles under the 2006 Act do so because the directors are now given that power by virtue of s. 302. The directors may exercise such powers whenever they think it appropriate in the interests of the company to do so (*Pergamon Press v. Maxwell* [1970] 1 W.L.R. 1167).

It has been held that, where the articles state that the directors may call general meetings, they must exercise that power collectively at a duly convened and constituted meeting of the board (*Browne v. La Trinidad* (1887) 37 Ch.D. 1.), although a decision taken by any other method provided for in a company's articles for collective decision-making by the directors (such as unanimous decisions and directors' written resolutions) will almost certainly suffice for these purposes. The case probably serves as a warning against the possibility of delegating the power to call general meetings. This is particularly dangerous if the power derives from the Act. This may even be the case for powers derived from the articles, even though the articles may also provide that the directors may delegate 'any of their powers'. This is because the courts could determine that the power to convene general meetings is a special power and not subject to the standard article on delegation. Modern articles sometimes seek to get round this type of restriction by specifying that the power to delegate shall also be effective in relation to any special powers. It would not normally be considered best practice for the directors to delegate responsibility for calling general meetings. Should it prove to be desirable to do so, great care should be taken to ensure that the power to delegate is applicable and, where there is any uncertainty, it is probably safest to assume that it is not.

A directors' resolution calling a general meeting should state the date, time and place of the meeting and its purpose (see **Precedents 12.2A and B**). A draft copy of the notice together with any additional documents which will accompany it should also be approved. The board should authorise someone (usually the secretary) to sign and issue the notice to all those entitled to receive it.

A further board meeting would be needed to approve the addition of any further item of business or to amend the substance of the notice.

12.2.1 Ratification of invalid notice

Notice of a general meeting given by any person without the sanction of the directors or other proper authority will be invalid (*Re Haycroft Gold Reduction Co.* [1900] 2 Ch. 230.). This is the case even if it was issued by the secretary in response to a valid requisition by the members under s. 368 (*Re State of Wyoming Syndicate* [1901] 2 Ch. 431). However, a meeting called without proper authority will be valid if it is ratified before the meeting by the body with authority to call the meeting. Thus, a notice issued by a director or the company secretary without the authority of the board, will be valid if it is subsequently ratified prior to the general meeting by the directors at a properly convened and constituted meeting of the board (*Hooper v. Kerr Stuart & Co.* (1900) 83 L.T. 729).

A general meeting convened by an irregularly constituted board (e.g. at an inquorate meeting) will be invalid. However, a defect in the appointment of any of the directors may be cured by s. 161 and any article in the form of reg. 92 of Table A which provides that all acts done by any meeting of directors, a committee of directors or by any person acting as a director, notwithstanding that it be afterwards discovered that there was some defect in the appointment of any such director or that they or any of them were disqualified, had vacated office, or were otherwise not entitled to vote, be valid as if every person had been duly appointed, was qualified to be a director and entitled to vote (*Transport Ltd. v. Schomberg* (1905) 21 T.L.R. 305) (see further **7.2**).

12.2.2 Practical procedures for convening annual general meeting

In practice, a proof of the annual general meeting notice is usually tabled at the board meeting held to approve the report and accounts and its contents are used to frame the appropriate board resolution convening the meeting. The board resolution should specify the date, time and place and the business to be transacted. The directors should also authorise the secretary to sign the notice and send copies to all persons entitled to receive it (i.e. the members and the auditors and anyone else specified in the articles) (see **Precedent 12.2B**).

As soon as the proof print of the report and accounts has been approved by the directors, the balance sheet, directors' report and auditors' report should be signed and dated by the appropriate people. A further copy should be prepared with the names of the signatories and the dates on which they signed inserted at the appropriate points. This copy can then be printed together with final copies of the notice and, if necessary, any circular or proxy cards.

The notice usually goes out under the name of the secretary who signs 'by order of the board'. It is usually dated for the day on which it is sent out and this date can be included in the proofs sent to the printers even though the notice may not yet have been physically signed. It is, however, also common for the notice to be signed and dated on the day it is approved by the board. Strictly speaking, of course, the date on the notice should be the date on which it was actually signed. Accordingly, if it is to show the date on which the notice is to be sent out, it should also be signed on that date.

If accounts are to be laid at the annual general meeting, copies of the report and accounts must be sent to members not less 21 days before the meeting. As members must be given 21 clear days' notice of the annual general meeting it is sensible to send both together. The notice of the meeting can be incorporated in the document containing the annual report and accounts.

▨ 12.3 Problems convening meetings

12.3.1 Number of directors below quorum

Articles often provide that where the number of directors falls below the number fixed as the quorum, the continuing directors may act for the purposes of calling a general meeting (e.g. reg. 90 of Table A). Reg. 90 also allows the continuing directors to exercise their powers under reg. 79 to appoint a director either to fill a casual vacancy or as an additional director. This type of article can only be invoked where the remaining directors would be unable to fulfil the quorum requirements even if they all attended a board meeting.

The model articles also allow the continuing directors to appoint further directors or to call a general meeting so as to enable the members to appoint further directors (pcls 11, clg 11, plc 11).

12.3.2 Not sufficient directors in UK

Regulation 37 of Table A provides that any director or any member(s) may call a general meeting if there are not sufficient directors in the United Kingdom to do so. Neither version of the model articles for private companies contains such a provision, although the model articles for public companies include a variation of it (see below).

Articles like reg. 37 of Table A are considered old-fashioned because they rely on absence from the United Kingdom, a factor which may not necessarily prevent the directors from calling a meeting in these days of modern communications. They are also of no assistance if there are sufficient directors in the United Kingdom but not sufficient of them are capable of acting, e.g. because of illness. The wording of Table A can be modified as follows to cover such circumstances:

> If at any time there are not within the United Kingdom sufficient directors *capable of acting to form a quorum*, any director or any two members of the company may convene a general meeting in the same manner as nearly as possible as that in which meetings may be convened by the board.

Without this type of modification, the members may sometimes need to requisition a general meeting under the statutory procedure and convene it themselves under those rules (see **12.5**) or, if this proves to be impossible, an application may need to be made to the court for an order calling a meeting under s. 306 (see **12.4**).

12.3.3 Model articles for public companies – director unwilling or unable to act

The model articles for public companies allow two or more members to call a general meeting (or instruct the company secretary to do so) for the purpose of appointing one or more directors if the company has fewer than two directors, and the director (if any) is unable or unwilling to appoint sufficient directors to make up a quorum or to call a general meeting to do so (plc 28).

This type of article is preferable to the formula used in reg. 37 of Table A as it does not rely on absence from the United Kingdom. However it only operates to allow the members to call general meetings for the purposes of appointing additional directors where the number of directors has fallen below two and only operates as a fallback to the powers given to any remaining director(s) to appoint sufficient directors or call a general meeting to do so (plc 11).

12.3.4 Private companies – death of all members and directors

Under the model articles for private companies, where, as a result of death, a private company has no members or directors, the personal representatives of the last member to die has the right, by notice in writing, to appoint a person to be director (pcls and clg 17(2)). Any director so appointed would then be able to exercise the statutory power to call general meetings.

12.3.5 Director refuses to attend board meetings

In small companies, it is not unusual for directors who are vehemently opposed to a particular proposal supported by the other directors to attempt to frustrate the will of the majority by refusing to attend board meetings. If their presence is necessary in order to form a quorum, this tactic will prevent the other directors getting their own way. Although it may not be the intention of the dissident director(s) to prevent the calling of a general meeting, this is often one of the side effects of such tactics. If they are not opposed to calling a meeting, and assuming the articles allow this, it might be possible to call the meeting by written resolution (see further **6.2**). A more dubious method might be to call a board meeting while the director(s) who refuse to attend are outside the United Kingdom and to call the general meeting under reg. 37 of Table A or its equivalent. Reasonable notice of such a board meeting would still need to be given and notice would need to be sent to the directors' usual address. The members could requisition a general meeting under s. 303 and, if the directors do not convene a meeting within 21 days, convene a meeting themselves in accordance with s. 305 (see **12.5**). If all else fails, an application may need to be made to the court under s. 306.

12.3.6 Directors refuse to call meeting

Where the directors refuse to call a general meeting, the members can requisition one under s. 303 and convene it themselves if the directors fail to do so within 21 days. Any director or member may apply to the court for an order in respect of a general meeting (see below).

■ 12.4 Powers of the court to call a general meeting

If for any reason it is impracticable to call a general meeting, or to conduct the meeting in the manner prescribed by the company's articles or the Act, the court may order a meeting of the company to be called, held and conducted in any manner it thinks fit (s. 306). The court may make such an order on the application of any member who would be entitled to vote at the meeting or any director. In doing so, the court may give such ancillary or consequential directions as it thinks fit (s. 306(3)), which may include a direction that one member present in person or by proxy be deemed to constitute a meeting (s. 306(4)). Any meeting called, held and conducted in accordance with an order of the court made under s. 306 is deemed for all purposes to be a meeting of the company duly called held and conducted (s. 306(5)).

These powers have been exercised where it was impracticable to hold a meeting with a quorum in accordance with the articles (*Re Edinburgh Workmen's Houses Improvement Co. Ltd.* 1934 S.L.T. 513) and where the directors, being minority shareholders, failed to call a general meeting (including an annual general meeting) thus preventing the majority shareholder from exercising his right to remove them (*Re El Sombrero Ltd.* [1958] Ch. 900 and *Re H. R. Paul & Son*

Ltd. (1973) 118 S. J. 166). The court has also used these powers to direct that a vote be taken by postal ballot because previous general meetings had been disrupted by protesters in such a violent manner that it was likely that most ordinary members would not attend any future meetings (*Re British Union for the Abolition of Vivisection* [1995] 2 B.C.L.C. 1).

The court may also convene a meeting under s. 896 where a compromise or arrangement is proposed between the company and its creditors.

■ 12.5 Members' requisition

The members of a company have a right to requisition a general meeting to be held at the company's expense. They must satisfy certain conditions, some of which vary according to the type of company. The normal procedure is for the members to submit their demand and, if the demand is valid, for the directors to call the meeting. However, if the directors fail to do so within a specified time, the requisitionists may call the meeting themselves and recover their expenses from the company.

Members of public companies (but not private companies) can also require the directors to include a resolution on the agenda of the annual general meeting (see **10.4**). Members of private companies (but not public companies) can propose written resolutions (see **9.3**).

12.5.1 Conditions for demand – percentages
The directors of a company are required by s. 303 to convene a general meeting of the company on receipt of a valid demand. A demand will not be valid unless it is made by:

(a) members representing at least 5% of such of the paid-up capital of the company as carries the right of voting at general meetings of the company (excluding any paid-up capital held as treasury shares); or
(b) in the case of a company not having a share capital (e.g. a company limited by guarantee), members who represent at least 5% of the total voting rights of all the members having a right to vote at general meetings.

It should be noted that these percentage requirements in the Act were amended by the Companies (Shareholders' Rights) Regulations 2009 (SI 2009/1632) with effect from August 2009 and that the Act previously required such demands to be supported by members holding at least 10% of the paid-up capital carrying voting rights or, in the case of a company without a share capital, at least 10% of the voting rights, although this was reduced in both cases to at least 5% for private companies in certain circumstances.

The reduction made by the regulations from 10% to 5% for public companies means that it is almost as easy for the members to requisition a general meeting as it is for them to propose resolutions at an annual general meeting, although the requirements for proposing an AGM resolution are still slightly less strict in that they provide for an addition test for making a valid demand (i.e. the 100 member test), which does not apply for requisitioning a general meeting.

In calculating whether a valid demand has been made by members of a company with a share capital, the critical factor is the amount of paid-up capital held by the members rather than the number of votes attached to those shares. Where all the shares are of equal value and carry the same number of votes, this calculation will be simple. However, care should be taken to ensure that shares which confer the right to vote in limited circumstances are included in the calculation if those circumstances operate at the time of the deposit. For example:

ABC plc has a share capital of 5,000 £1 ordinary shares and 2,000 £1 preference shares. The preference shareholders only have a right to vote if their dividends are in arrears. As long as the preference dividends are not in arrears, any ordinary shareholder(s) holding 250 or more shares can requisition a meeting. If the dividends are in arrears, a member(s) holding 350 or more shares (either ordinary shares, preference shares or a combination of the two) would be needed.

It should be noted that articles commonly remove the right to vote when any calls on a share are unpaid (e.g. reg. 57 of Table A and plc 41). It has also been held that the right to requisition a meeting requires paid-up share capital (*Re Bradford Investments plc* [1990] B.C.C. 740).

Articles cannot impose more stringent conditions than those established under s. 303. They may, however, provide a less stringent regime.

12.5.2 Conditions for demand – form of requisition

The requisition may be made in hard copy or electronic form and must be authenticated by the person or persons making it (s. 303(6)). If the request is made in hard copy form, it must be delivered to the company in accordance with the relevant company communications provisions. These would require it to be deposited at the registered office of the company. In addition it would need to be signed by the requisitionists (see **Precedent 12.5A**). In the case of joint holders, the requisition must be signed by each of them (*Patent Wood Keg Syndicate v. Pearse* [1906] W.N. 164). A requisition may consist of several requests in like form each signed by one or more requisitionists. This allows a master document to be prepared and for copies to be circulated to members for signature.

12.5.3 Conditions for demand – purpose of the meeting

The requisition must state the general nature of the business to be dealt with at the meeting and may include the text of a resolution that may properly be moved and is intended to be moved at the meeting (s. 303(4)).

According to s. 303(5), a resolution may properly be moved at a meeting unless:

(a) it would, if passed, be ineffective (whether by reason of inconsistency with any enactment or the company's constitution or otherwise);
(b) it is defamatory of any person; or
(c) it is frivolous or vexatious.

These rules can cause considerable difficulty for the requisitionists who may not have sufficient legal knowledge to be able to frame their request in a manner which is legally effective. It would appear from the above rules, that the directors would have an obligation to call a meeting as long as the request states the general nature of the business, even though none of the resolutions may be properly moved. However, even this might not be the case.

It has been held that the board cannot refuse to act on a requisition unless its objects cannot legally be carried into effect (*Isle of Wight Railway Co. v. Tahourdin* (1883) 25 Ch.D. 320). This case was decided under a previous regime under which the requistionists were required to state the 'objects' of the meeting. However, the word 'objects' is very similar to the existing requirement to state the general nature of the business (see **13.5**) and it can be assumed that if none of the business described in the statement of the 'general nature of the business' cannot be legally carried out, the directors will not be obliged to call a meeting and could, if necessary, apply to the court to prevent the requisitionists from doing so.

In *Rose v McGivern* [1998] 2 BCLC 593, the board of directors of the Royal Automobile Club refused to give effect to a requisition supported by more than one tenth of the members on three grounds:

(a) that the requisitionists had induced members to add their names to the requisition by giving misleading information in a letter;
(b) that the proposals in the requisition were invalid and would, if passed as resolutions be invalid; and
(c) even if other resolutions could be put to any meeting called pursuant to the requisition, they would be ineffective.

As the judge ruled that the requisitionists' letter was not misleading to any material degree he was not called upon to decide whether this could be a valid ground for refusing to call a requisitioned meeting. The company had argued that cases relating to misleading notices should also be applied in these circumstances. However, the judge noted that the circumstances of this case were different from those cited by the RAC and that different rules could therefore apply.

With regard to the second ground, the members' requisition stated that the meeting was being called to consider 'the Resolutions' set out in a letter circulated to shareholders seeking their support for the requisition. That letter stated:

At the EGM, resolutions will be put:
(a) to elect a new Board (Committee) of not more than ten members and which will not include the Executive Officers who will be concentrating on running the business of RACMS, and

(b) to authorise and instruct the new board (Committee) to proceed with the Scheme and report back to a further General Meeting at an early date.

Even if these 'resolutions' had been passed at a general meeting of the RAC, neither would, for obvious reasons, have had any legal effect. The company argued, therefore, that they were not obliged to call a meeting. The requisitionists argued that although expressed as resolutions, the requisition was merely intended to set out the purpose of the meeting and that the directors should have called the meeting and included in the notice a series of resolutions which they had subsequently submitted to the company to give effect to the requisition.

The judge accepted that the requisitionists could have submitted resolutions to give effect to their requisition if they had made it clear that what were stated as resolutions were merely their object or purpose in calling the meeting. However, he ruled that they were precluded from doing so because they had used the word 'Resolutions' in the body of the requisition.

He also held that, even if the additional resolutions submitted by the requisitionists had been valid on this count, the company would not have been bound to put them all to the meeting because the requisitionists had failed to get their timings right. The RAC's articles contained provisions requiring members wishing to propose a person as a director to give the company at least two months' notice. Although the requisitionists had submitted the required notices, in order for them to be effective, the directors would have had to have delayed calling the meeting. However, s. 368 of the 1985 Act required the directors to call a meeting forthwith on receipt of a valid requisition, i.e. immediately. If the directors had done so, the appointment resolutions would have been defective under the articles. Accordingly, the judge ruled that the directors would not have been obliged to include them in the notice.

There will be circumstances in which it is sufficient for the requisitionists to set out the general nature of the business. In normal circumstances that is all that will be required in order to give valid notice of business to be transacted at a general meeting. This is all that is required by s. 311(2), which applies subject to any provision of a company's articles. Most articles also only require notice of the general nature of the business to be given. However, they can contain exceptions which may serve to trip up the members, as was the case in the RAC case. Even though the requisitionists may not always need to include the text of a resolution in their request, they will need to prepare draft resolutions that can be moved at the meeting in order to put their objects into effect. As has been seen, it may sometimes be necessary for the requisitionists to submit those resolutions to the company before the notice is sent out. This will always be necessary if, for example, the business must be proposed as a special resolution. Such a resolution cannot validly be passed unless the notice of the meeting included the text of the resolution and specified the intention to propose it as a special resolution (s. 283(6)).

The directors have no obligation to help the requisitionists draft their requisition or any of the resolutions required to put it into effect, although one might venture to suggest that if the court felt that they had been deliberately obstructive, it might be more inclined to apply a more liberal interpretation of the law in favour of the requisitionists.

12.5.4 Directors must duly convene meeting

On receipt of a valid requisition, the directors must, within 21 days, convene a general meeting to be held on a date not more than 28 days after the date of the notice of the meeting (s. 304(1)). These requirements are intended to prevent the directors defeating the objects of the requisitionists by delaying the calling or holding of the meeting.

If the requests received by the company identify a resolution intended to be moved at the meeting, the notice of the meeting must include notice of the resolution (s. 304(2)). The business that may be dealt with at the meeting includes a resolution of which notice is given in accordance with s. 304 (s. 304(3)).

If a resolution is to be proposed as a special resolution, the directors are treated as not having duly called the meeting if they do not give the required notice of the resolution in accordance with s. 283.

If the directors do not properly comply with any of the above requirements, the requisitionists may convene the meeting.

When it convenes the meeting, the board may add other items to the agenda for the requisitioned meeting by giving notice in the normal manner. However, a member cannot raise any other matter at the meeting which was not specified in the requisition. For example, a member may not propose a resolution to remove a director at a requisitioned meeting where that was not one of the objects of the requisitionists (*Ball v. Metal Industries Ltd.* 1957 S.L.T. 124).

In practice, when convening a requisitioned meeting, the directors will probably want to send a circular with the notice to the members explaining the circumstances in which the meeting was being called and stating whether or not they support the proposals to be considered at the meeting. In most cases, the directors will probably oppose the proposals and may seek the support of the members to enable them to be defeated. The result would usually depend upon the measure of support given by proxy votes to each side.

If the directors proceed to call the meeting, the notice will be in the same form as for a general meeting convened by the directors in the usual way.

12.5.5 In default requisitionists may convene meeting

If, on receipt of a valid demand, the directors do not properly convene a meeting in accordance with the requirements of s. 304, the requisitionists (or any of them representing more than one half of their total voting rights) may themselves call a general meeting (s. 305(1)). The meeting must be called for a date not more than three months after the date on which the directors become subject to the requirement to call a meeting (s. 305(3)).

The meeting must be called in the same manner, as nearly as possible, as that in which meetings are required to be called by directors of the company (s. 305(4)) (see **Precedent 12.5B**). In order to do this, the requisitionists will need to obtain a list of members of the company and a copy of its articles of association, and ensure that they comply with any relevant article provisions together with any applicable rules of the Companies Act 2006.

Where the requests received by the company included the text of a resolution intended to be moved at the meeting, the notice of the meeting must include notice of the resolution (s. 305(2)). The business which may be dealt with at the meeting includes a resolution of which notice is given in accordance with this s. 305 (s. 305(5)).

Any reasonable expenses incurred by the members requesting the meeting by reason of the failure of the directors duly to call a meeting must be reimbursed by the company (s. 305(6)). Any sum so reimbursed shall be retained by the company out of any sums due or to become due from the company by way of fees or other remuneration in respect of the services of such of the directors as were in default (s. 305(7)).

■ 12.6 Requisition of a meeting by a resigning auditor

An auditor may resign his office by giving the company notice in writing to that effect together with a statement of circumstances (ss. 516 and 519). If the statement is of circumstances which the auditor believes should be brought to the attention of members, he may deposit at the same time a signed requisition calling on the directors of the company to convene an extraordinary general meeting for the purpose of receiving and considering his explanation of the circumstances of his resignation (s. 518(2)). The auditor also has a right to have a statement in writing of the circumstances connected with his resignation circulated to the members before any meeting convened on his requisition.

The directors must within 21 days from the date of the deposit of the requisition proceed to convene a meeting for a day not less than 28 days after the notice convening the meeting is given (s. 518(5)) and are liable to a fine in default. However, the auditor has no right to convene a meeting in default.

13

Notice of general meetings

13.1 Summary

- The Act makes detailed provision as to the length of notice that must be given to members of general meetings and the methods of giving notice.
- Public companies (and private companies that are traded companies) must give a minimum of 21 days' notice of annual general meetings. Other general meetings may be called with only 14 days' notice, unless the company is a traded company in which case the minimum notice period is 21 days but can be reduced to 14 days if the company complies with certain conditions (see **13.2**).
- Clear days' notice is required (see **13.3**).
- In order to calculate when notices must be sent, it is necessary to make allowance for the statutory notice period and the date on which the notice is deemed to be served (see **13.4** and **13.5**).
- Notice may be given in hard copy or electronic form or via a website (see **13.7**).
- The members may consent to receive shorter notice than the statutory minimum. The majority required differs according to the type of general meeting and the type of company (see **13.6**).
- In addition to the date, time and place, the notice must state the business of the meeting. The exact text or the entire substance of the resolution should be stated for certain types of resolution. However, it is normally sufficient to state the general nature of the business. Circulars and other documents sent with the notice can be used for this purpose and will be read in conjunction with it for the purposes of determining the validity of the notice (see **13.8** to **13.12**).
- All the members are entitled to receive notice of general meetings unless the articles provide otherwise. Other people also have a right to receive notice (see **13.13**).
- Special notice requirements exist for resolutions to remove a director or to remove or replace the auditors (see **13.14**).
- Members of public companies who satisfy certain qualifications have a statutory right to require the directors to give notice of resolutions which they wish to propose at an annual general meeting (see **10.4**). Members of traded companies also have a statutory right to require the company to include matters of business (other than resolutions) on the agenda for the annual general meeting (see **9.5**).

- Members of any company may require the directors to circulate a statement in connection with the business of any general meeting (see **13.15**).
- Accidental omission to give notice to a member will not normally invalidate the proceedings (see **13.16**).

13.2 Length of notice

Subject to the exception noted below in relation to traded companies, a general meeting of a private company (other than an adjourned meeting) must be called by notice of at least 14 days (s. 307(1)). This means clear days (s. 360) (see **13.3**).

Subject to the exception noted below in relation to traded companies, a general meeting of a public company (other than an adjourned meeting) must be called by notice:

- of at least 21 days in the case of an annual general meeting;
- of at least 14 days, in any other case (s. 307(2)).

The number of days in each case means clear days (s. 360).

Under the 1985 Act, general meetings sometimes had to be called with more than 14 clear days' notice because the Act required longer than 14 days' notice to be given of certain types of resolutions (e.g. 21 days' notice for special resolutions). The 2006 Act does not include any such requirements and, accordingly, the length of notice that is required to be given is dependent entirely upon the above rules and any additional requirements that may be contained in a company's articles.

A company's articles may specify a longer period of notice than the statutory minimum for any type of general meeting (s. 307(3)). However, unless the members consent to receive short notice in accordance with the statutory requirements (see **13.6**), meetings called with less than the notice required by the Act or the articles (if they specify a longer period of notice), will be invalid.

13.2.1 Notice requirements for general meetings of traded companies

Section 307A(1) provides that a general meeting of a traded company (see definition at **8.5.1**) must be called by notice of:

- at least 21 days in the case of an annual general meeting; and
- in any other case at least 14 days if two conditions are met, and at least 21 days if they are not.

The number of days in each case is clear days (s. 360) (see **13.3**).

The conditions for calling general meetings at 14 days' notice are:

- Condition A: that the company offers the facility for members to vote by electronic means accessible to all members who hold shares that carry rights to vote at general meetings. This condition is met if there is a facility, offered by the company and accessible to all such members, to appoint a proxy by means of a website; and

■ Condition B: that a special resolution reducing the period of notice to not less than 14 days has been passed at the immediately preceding annual general meeting, or at a general meeting held since that annual general meeting.

In the case of a newly incorporated company which has not yet held an annual general meeting, condition B is modified to require only that a special resolution reducing the period of notice to not less than 14 days has been passed (s. 307A(4)).

The articles of a traded company (see definition at **8.5.1**) may require a longer period of notice than that specified in subsection (1).

Where a general meeting is adjourned, the adjourned meeting may be called by shorter notice than required by subsection (1). But in the case of an adjournment for lack of a quorum, this exemption applies only if:

■ no business is to be dealt with at the adjourned meeting the general nature of which was not stated in the notice of the original meeting; and
■ the adjourned meeting is to be held at least 10 days after the original meeting.

The rules in s. 307A do not apply in relation to a general meeting of a traded company that is an opted-in company (as defined by s. 971(1)), where:

(a) the meeting is held to decide whether to take any action that might result in the frustration of a takeover bid for the company; or
(b) the meeting is held by virtue of s. 969 (power of offeror to require general meeting to be held).

13.2.2 UK Corporate Governance Code – AGM notice recommendation

The UK Corporate Governance Code recommends that listed companies should 'arrange for the notice of the AGM and related papers to be sent to shareholders at least 20 working days before the meeting' (Code provision E.2.4). The term 'working days' obviously intended to exclude weekends and bank holidays, which means that the notice is presumably required to be in the hands of shareholders at least four weeks before the meeting. The Code does not specify whether the expression 'working days' is intended to mean clear working days.

■ 13.3 Clear days

Section 360 provides that any reference in the following provisions to a period of notice, or to a period before a meeting by which a request must be received or sum deposited or tendered, is to clear days, i.e. a period of the specified length excluding the day of the meeting, and the day on which the notice is given, the request received or the sum deposited or tendered:

- s. 307(1) and (2) (notice required of general meeting);
- s. 307A(1), (4), (5) and (7)(b) (notice required of general meeting of traded company);
- s. 312(1) and (3) (resolution requiring special notice);
- s. 314(4)(d) (request to circulate members' statement);
- s. 316(2)(b) (expenses of circulating statement to be deposited or tendered before meeting);
- s. 337(3) (contents of notice of AGM of traded company);
- s. 338(4)(d)(i) (request to circulate member's resolution at AGM of public company);
- s. 338A(5) (request to include matter in the business to be dealt with at AGM of traded company);
- s. 340(2)(b)(i) (expenses of circulating statement to be deposited or tendered before meeting); and
- s. 340B(2)(b) (traded companies: duty to circulate members' matters for AGM).

This provision is not capable of modification by a company's articles in its application to the above provisions. However, a company's articles will often make the same provision and may extend the rule to other requirements in the articles (e.g. reg. 38 of Table A).

It has been decided in the English courts that unless the articles provide otherwise, the number of days' notice required under the Companies Act shall be interpreted as being clear days (*Re Hector Whaling Ltd.* [1936] Ch. 208). This is usually taken to mean that the day the notice is deemed to be served and the day of the meeting should not be counted. However, a more recent Scottish case has thrown this interpretation into doubt by ruling that, when calculating the period of notice required under the Companies Act the day of service must be excluded, but the day of the meeting may be counted (*Neil McLeod & Sons Ltd., Petitioners.* [1967] S.C. 16). Obviously, s. 360 clarifies that this is not the case with regard to the stated provisions.

In any case where it is not clear whether a notice requirement means clear days, it is always safer to assume that it does and, subject to any applicable provision of the articles, to apply the formula adopted in s. 360 rather than the one adopted by the Scottish courts in *Neil McLeod & Sons*.

◼ 13.4 Date of service

Under the clear days rule, a notice period cannot start running until the day after notice is given. Notice is not given until it has been served on all of the intended recipients (or can be deemed to have been served). The rules concerning deemed service or delivery in this regard are set out in s. 1147 of the company communications provisions of the 2006 Act. However, the rules set out in s. 1147 are capable of modification by a company's articles and frequently are modified.

Subject to any such modification by a company's articles, s. 1147 provides that:

■ notices sent by post which are properly addressed, pre-paid and posted are deemed to be delivered 48 hours after they were posted;
■ notices sent in electronic form that the company is able to show were properly addressed are deemed to have been received by the intended recipients 48 hours after they were sent; and
■ notices given via a website are deemed to have been received by the intended recipient when first made available on the website or, if later, when the recipient received (or is deemed to have received) notice of the fact that the material was available on the website.

In calculating the period of hours for the purposes of s. 1147, no account may be taken of any part of a day that is not a working day. A 'working day' is defined in s. 1173 of the 2006 Act for these purposes as a day that is not a Saturday or Sunday, Christmas Day, Good Friday, or any day which is a bank holiday in the part of the United Kingdom where the company is registered.

The model articles prescribed under the 2006 Act make no separate provision regarding deemed delivery. Accordingly, the provisions of s. 1147 apply by default. Table A provides that written notice sent by post shall be deemed to have been given 48 hours after the envelope containing it was posted (reg. 115 of Table A). As Table A makes no distinction between first and second class post, there is nothing to be gained from using first class post. However, articles sometimes clarify whether first or second class post should be used or make separate provision depending on which is used. For example the articles could provide that notices sent by first class post shall be deemed to have been served 24 hours after posting and those sent by second class, 48 hours after posting.

Subject to the articles, notices in hard copy form that are handed to the intended recipient or supplied by hand to their address can be assumed to be served immediately. Notices given by advertisement are deemed to have been served the day after the newspaper is published (*Sneath v. Valley Gold Ltd.* [1893] 1 Ch. 477) unless the articles provide otherwise.

13.4.1 Proof of service

The rules in s. 1147 regarding deemed delivery and service only apply where the company can show that notices sent by post were properly addressed, pre-paid and posted and that any notices sent in electronic form were properly addressed.

When notices are sent by post, there is, of course, a danger that some may be lost and not delivered. To avoid the possibility of a meeting being invalidated for this reason, articles sometimes provide that proof that an envelope containing a notice was properly addressed, stamped and posted shall be conclusive evidence that the notice was given (e.g. reg. 115 of Table A). When sending out written notices of meetings, it is advisable to obtain and retain a receipt (proof of posting) from the Post Office for this purpose. For companies with large shareholder registers, this may be impractical and an undertaking by the registrars that the proper procedures were followed will probably be sufficient.

Although it might be possible in theory to calculate the number of notices which should be sent out and to compare this with the number which were actually sent, it may be impossible in practice to discover the reason why the two figures do not reconcile. In *Re West Canadian Collieries Ltd.* [1962] Ch. 370, it was held that a failure to send notices to nine shareholders was accidental where the reason for the omission was that it had been forgotten that the plates for printing their addresses had been separated from the rest because earlier communications had been returned undelivered.

It has been held that articles similar to reg. 115 are effective only where there is uncertainty as to whether a document has been delivered and not where it is clear that it has not been delivered (*Re Thundercrest Ltd.* [1995] 1 B.C.L.C. 117). The notice in this case was given in connection with an offer of shares in accordance with ss. 89 and 90 of the 1985 Act. It was sent by recorded delivery (a method which requires the recipient to sign as acknowledgement of receipt). When it was returned to the company by the Post Office, it was therefore obvious that it had not been delivered. Judge Paul Baker said:

> The purpose of deeming provisions [such as reg. 115] in the case of management of companies is clear. In the case of uncertainty as to whether a document has been delivered, with large numbers of shareholders and so forth, there has to be some rule under which those in charge of the management can carry on the business without having to investigate every case where some shareholder comes along and says he has not got the document. The directors have to proceed and transact the company's business on the basis of the deeming provisions. But in my judgment, all that falls away when you find it is established without any possibility of challenge that the document has not been delivered.

Despite the best efforts of the judge to limit the application of this ruling, it is clear that it could cause problems if applied to notices of general meetings that are returned undelivered. This would not be a problem if the notice was actually delivered to the proper address but returned by the present occupiers. However, it could cause a problem where, say, the building has been demolished and it was not possible for the Post Office to deliver the letter at all. In practice, companies and registrars tend to ignore this problem, presumably on the basis that the case was either wrongly decided or that the same principles would not be applied to returned notices.

Regulation 115 of Table A (as amended) provides that proof that notice contained in an electronic communication was sent in accordance with guidance issued by the Institute of Chartered Secretaries and Administrators shall be conclusive evidence that the notice was given. The recommendations contained in Chapter 8 of the first edition of the ICSA guide were relevant for these purposes.

These recommendations are now reproduced in para. B6 of the 2007 version of the ICSA guidance, which is reproduced at **Appendix 1**).

Although none of the model articles under the 2006 Act make reference to the ICSA guide, it will still be of relevance to any company that is subject to the rules on deemed delivery in s. 1147, which require that the company is able to show that documents sent in electronic form were properly addressed.

Under the 1985 Act, the provisions of Table A (as amended by the Electronic Communications Order 2000) on electronic service of notices and notifications were deemed to apply to all companies unless their articles made separate provision in that regard (s. 369(4F), 1985 Act). This is no longer the case under the 2006 Act. Instead, the rules on deemed delivery in s. 1147 apply in the absence of any other provision in a company's articles.

13.4.2 Table A provisions on electronic service

Regulations 111 and 112 of Table A (as amended by the Electronic Communications Order 2000) provide that a company may give any notice to a member using electronic communications by sending it to an address for the time being notified for that purpose to the company. They also provide that an 'address', in relation to electronic communications, includes any number or address used for the purposes of such communications.

Regulation 112 provides that a member whose registered address is not within the United Kingdom and who gives to the company an address within the United Kingdom at which notices may be given to him, or an address to which notices may be sent by electronic communications, shall be entitled to have notices given to him at that address, but otherwise no such member shall be entitled to receive any notice from the company.

Regulation 115 of Table A (as amended) provides that a notice sent by electronic communications shall be deemed to have been given at the expiration of 48 hours after the time it was sent. Some companies have already adopted articles which provide for a shorter period in this regard. This is sensible, particularly where the articles already provide for a shorter period for notices sent through the post, but also because for certain types of electronic communications (but not all) service will in reality be effected if not instantaneously, then within a much shorter time frame.

As mentioned above, reg 115 of Table A (as amended) also provides that proof that notice contained in an electronic communication was sent in accordance with guidance issued by the Institute of Chartered Secretaries and Administrators shall be conclusive evidence that the notice was given.

■ 13.5 Practical issues on timing of notices

The date by which notices should be sent out needs to be calculated carefully in accordance with the above rules to ensure that proper notice is given. If the date of the meeting is already known it is necessary to work backwards from that date to establish the latest date by which the notices should be posted or served. The basic rules are that:

- the statutory period of notice commences the day after the notice has been served or is deemed to have been served on the member; and
- the meeting must be held after the last day of the period of notice required by statute or, if longer, by the articles.

To take an example, a public company which has adopted the model articles in full must post the notice of its annual general meeting at least 24 days before the date of the meeting. If the notices were posted on 1 April they would be deemed to have been served 48 hours later, i.e. on 3 April. The period of 21 days' notice would not commence until 4 April, the first clear day, and would expire on 24 April. The earliest date that the meeting could be held would therefore be on 25 April, the first clear day after the notice period has expired.

The same principles would apply to an extraordinary general meeting, and notices would have to be posted a minimum of 17 days before the date of the meeting.

Both the ICSA's *Guide to Best Practice for Annual General Meetings* and the UK Corporate Governance Code recommend that listed companies should circulate the notice of their annual general meetings at least 20 working days before the meeting, excluding weekends and bank holidays. This recommendation is intended to give nominees more time to obtain and submit proxy votes on behalf of underlying investors. Neither the ICSA guide nor the UK Code specifies whether this is intended to mean 20 clear working days. However, unless that interpretation is adopted, compliance with the recommendation makes only a slight difference to the date on which the notices must be sent out, unless there is a bank holiday within the period of notice.

■ 13.6 Consent to short notice

The members of a company may consent to receive less than the statutory minimum period of notice required under the Act. Different rules apply as to the majority that is required to consent to short notice depending on the type of meeting that is being held and the type of company that is proposing to hold it.

These concessions are useful where it is not possible to give the minimum period of notice required by s. 307(1) or (2) (or by the articles) and where an item of business needs to be expedited quickly. In practice, advantage of the concessions may be taken only by companies with a relatively small number of members.

Separate consent is no longer required to propose special resolutions because the Companies Act 2006 no longer imposes any requirements as to the period of notice that should be given for this type of resolution. However, it may not be possible to give less than 14 days' notice of resolution that is subject to the special notice rules (see **13.6.3**).

It is not necessary for consent to be given in writing. Consent could, for example, be given by a suitably authenticated electronic communication (see **13.6.4**).

13.6.1 Annual general meetings

An annual general meeting of a public company that is not a traded company may be called with less than 21 day's notice if all the members entitled to attend and vote give their consent (s. 337(2)). If accounts are to be laid at the annual general meeting of a public company, consent will probably also need to be given to accept the report and accounts less than 21 days before the meeting (see **Precedent 13.6A**). The consent of all the members of a public company is required to do this whether the accounts are to be laid at the annual general meeting or a general meeting (s. 424(3) and (4)).

The Act makes no provision to enable the annual general meeting of a traded companies (whether public or private) to be held at short notice. Section 337(2) only applies to public companies that are not traded companies.

13.6.2 General meetings

In the case of any other general meeting of a non-traded company, consent to short notice (see **Precedent 13.6B**) must be agreed to by a majority in number of the members having a right to attend and vote at the meeting, being a majority who:

- in the case of a private company, together hold not less than 90% of the share capital giving the right to attend and vote at the meeting (excluding any shares held in treasury);
- in the case of a public company, together hold not less than 95% of the share capital giving the right to attend and vote at the meeting (excluding any shares held in treasury); or
- in the case of a private company not having a share capital, together represent not less than 90% of the total voting rights (s. 307(5) and (6)).

It should be noted that the majority required is calculated by reference to the rights of all the members (excluding any treasury shares) and not simply by reference to the rights of those who actually attend the meeting. Where a majority of 95% is required, one member cannot form a majority in number and overrule the minority in this regard. However, a sole member would clearly be able to satisfy the requirements for both annual general meetings and extraordinary general meetings.

Section 307A, which sets out the notice requirements for general meetings of traded companies (whether public or private), makes no provision to enable meetings of such companies to be held at short notice.

13.6.3 Resolutions subject to the special notice rules

The Act makes no provision for consent to short notice of resolutions requiring special notice (e.g. a resolution to remove the auditors or a director). This is logical because the special notice requirements are intended to allow the auditors or the director concerned to prepare a statement for circulation to the members. It would appear that the requirement to give at least 14 days' notice of a resolution which requires special notice (see s. 312(3)) would prevent such a resolution from being proposed at a meeting called at shorter notice unless notice of the resolution had been given earlier than the notice of meeting, which would seem impracticable.

13.6.4 Practical points

In practice, consent to short notice will only be useful to companies with relatively few members, e.g. small private companies and subsidiaries. General meetings of traded companies cannot be called at short notice. It is not necessary for the members' consent to be given in writing. A resolution passed by the appropriate majority at the start of the meeting will suffice. Consent may be given in hard copy or electronic form in accordance with the usual rules under the company communications provisions. It is advisable to obtain the consent of members prior to the meeting. It may prove to be impossible to obtain the necessary majority at the meeting perhaps because some members do not attend or have not submitted proxies. Consent in writing is preferable as a method of proving compliance with the requirements of the Act. Where a meeting has been held at short notice, the minutes should record that fact, together with the fact that consent has been received by the requisite majority or, where applicable, all the members. Any form(s) of consent signed by the members could be entered in the minute book as proof for this purpose. Consents given in electronic form (e.g. by e-mail) could also be printed out and included, or referred to, in the minutes.

By consenting to short notice in accordance with the statutory provisions, the members do not consent to receive no notice at all. Some notice (however short) must be given prior to the meeting and that notice must be served in a manner allowed by the articles, unless all the members attend the meeting.

As a final point of detail, notice still needs to be given to any person entitled to receive it who is not entitled to vote at the meeting. This would include the auditors (if any) who have a statutory right to receive any notice of general meeting. Although the Act does not require the agreement of the auditors for a meeting to be held at short notice, it may be advisable to obtain from the auditors a letter of non-objection to the short notice. This may help to avoid any possibility of subsequent objection being taken to the proceedings of the meeting on procedural grounds; companies must send a copy of the notice of all general meetings to the auditors under s. 502 and, under that provision, the auditors have the right to attend all general meetings and to be heard on matters that concern them as auditors.

■ 13.7 Form and manner in which notice may be served

The company communications provisions of the 2006 Act (ss. 1143 to 1148 and Schedules 4 and 5) determine the form and manner in which notices of general meetings may be served (see **2.2**). In summary, these allow notice to be given:

- in hard copy form;
- in electronic form, provided the intended recipient has agreed to accept service in this manner;
- via a website, provided the intended recipient has agreed to accept service in this manner (or can be deemed to have agreed); or
- by any other means agreed to by the intended recipient.

Many of the company communications provisions set out in the Act override any contrary provisions in a company's articles, e.g. they override any provision in a company's articles which state that notice of general meetings must be given 'in writing', which in the absence of any definition in the articles is traditionally interpreted as meaning in hard copy form. This means that any company may serve notice in any manner allowed under the company communications provisions, provided it complies with any of the relevant conditions imposed by those provisions.

The company communications provisions of the Act provide a complete regime for the service of notices and other documents and information. Accordingly, the model articles make no further provision other than to extend the rules, subject to any other provision made in the articles, to 'anything sent or supplied by or to the company under the articles' (pcls 48, clg 34 and plc 79).

It should be noted that a company which has adopted articles based on the 1985 Table A (as amended on 22 December 2000 by the Electronic Communications Order 2000 (see **Annex B2**) and which complies with the requirements of regs. 111 to 116 (notices) of that version of Table A will also comply with the company communications provisions. This should come as no surprise because the company communications provisions can be viewed, to a certain extent, as a statutory codification of the relevant rules in Table A as amended by the 2000 Order.

Any company which still has articles based on an older version of Table A (or which has adopted its own bespoke articles) must, however, bear in mind the mandatory rules of the company communications provisions of the Act, when applying the rules in its articles on notices.

The company communications provisions have effect for the purposes of any provision of the Companies Acts that authorises or requires documents or information to be sent or supplied by or to a company (s. 1143(1)). A notice of general meeting is something that is required by the 2006 Act to be sent to certain people by the company (e.g. under s. 310 (members and directors), s. 146 (indirect investors) and s. 502 (auditors)). Accordingly, the company communications provisions have effect with regard to notices of general meetings sent by a company to any of those persons. They will also apply with regard to notices sent to any other person entitled to receive notice under the articles, if the articles extend the rules to notices sent to such persons.

The only provisions of the company communication provisions that are expressed as being subject to a company's articles are:

(a) s. 1147 (deemed delivery of documents and information) (see **13.4**);
(b para. 16 of Sch. 5 (documents and information to be supplied to joint holders of shares or debentures); and
(c) para. 17 of Sch. 5 (documents and information to be supplied in respect of a deceased or bankrupt shareholder).

It should be noted that, except in the two circumstances in (b) and (c) above, the company communications provisions do not determine to whom notice should be sent and that, even in this case, those provisions are expressed as being subject to the articles. However, other provisions of the Act do specify who is entitled to receive notice, although in the case of the members, s. 310 is capable of modification by the articles (see **13.13**).

Nevertheless, many of the company communications provisions can be viewed as being permissive in so far as they allow companies to send notices in certain ways, but do not necessarily require them to do so. For example, although a company can send notices by e-mail to members who have agreed to accept service in that manner, it is under no obligation to do so. It must, however, give notice in some manner and the default will be in hard copy form in accordance with the company communications provisions unless the intended recipient has agreed otherwise.

13.7.1 Written notice

If notice is given in writing, it must be given in the manner required for hard copy communications under the company communications provisions of the 2006 Act (see **2.2**). Accordingly written notice must be served either personally or by post. For these purposes a document or information is sent by post if it is sent in a pre-paid envelope containing the document or information to the person. Service by post includes ordinary and registered post and by recorded delivery (*Re Thundercrest Ltd.* [1995] 1 B.C.L.C. 117 and *TO Supplies (London) Ltd. v. Jerry Creighton Ltd.* [1951] 2 All E.R. 992).

The address which may be used for this purpose is one of the addresses specified in para. 4 of Sch. 5, which includes:

■ an address specified for this purpose by the intended recipient;
■ to a company at its registered office;
■ to a person in his capacity as a member of the company at his address as shown in the company's register of members;
■ to a person in his capacity as a director of the company at his address as shown in the company's register of directors; and
■ to an address to which any provision of the Companies Acts authorises the document or information to be supplied or sent.

Under Table A, members whose registered address is not within the United Kingdom are not entitled to receive notices unless they supply the company with an address (postal or electronic) in the United Kingdom for that purpose (reg. 112). Under articles similar to reg. 112, the company must maintain a separate record of the addresses supplied by overseas members for these purposes and their registered address should not be changed unless they specifically request that it be changed.

Articles sometimes allow notices to be served by advertisement. This is clearly necessary for companies which allow members to hold shares in bearer form. However, the ability to give notice by advertisement can also be useful in the event of a postal strike. It has been held that a provision in a company's articles (similar to reg. 115 of Table A) which stated that notices shall be deemed to have been served a certain period after posting did not apply where disruption to the postal service was such that placing the letters in a letter box could not reasonably be expected to result in delivery to members within that time (*Bradman v. Trinity Estates plc* [1989] B.C.L.C. 757). Public companies are increasingly taking power in their articles to give notice by advertisement in such circumstances. Such articles need to be carefully worded to ensure that they apply where there is only a partial disruption of the postal service. The Listing Rules used to require notices given by advertisement to be inserted in at least one national newspaper. However, this requirement was deleted in January 2000.

13.7.2 Giving notice electronically
Under the company communications provisions of the 2006 Act, a company can give notice of a general meeting via a website or by electronic communications (such as e-mail), notwithstanding any provision to the contrary in its articles, provided that person has agreed (or can be deemed to have agreed) to accept service in that manner (see **2.4** and **2.8**).

■ 13.8 Contents of notice

Notice of a general meeting must include:

- the name of the company (reg. 6(1) of the Companies (Trading Disclosures) Regulations 2008 (SI 2008/495);
- the type of meeting (e.g. whether the meeting is a general meeting or an annual general meeting in accordance with s. 337(1) or a class meeting) (see below);
- the time and date of the meeting (s. 311(1)(a));
- the place of the meeting (s. 311(1)(b));
- the general nature of the business to be dealt with at the meeting (s. 311(2)(a)) (in relation to a company other than a traded company, this requirement has effect subject to any provision of the company's articles (see **13.11**);
- the full text of any resolution to be proposed as a special resolution (s. 283(6)), extraordinary resolution (s. 378, 1985 Act), elective resolution (s. 379A, 1985 Act), or as an ordinary resolution for which special notice is required (s. 312(2));

- state on whose authority it is issued (e.g. the board, requisitioning members, court, etc.) and the name of the person who signed it on their behalf (e.g. the name of the secretary) (but see *Re Brick and Stone Company* [1878] W.N. 140);
- be dated; and
- include with reasonable prominence a statement of a member's right to appoint a proxy under s. 324 and any more extensive rights conferred by the company's articles to appoint more than one proxy (s. 325(1)).

At least one copy of the notice should be signed by or on behalf of the person or body under whose authority it is issued. In practice, it is normally signed and dated by the secretary or one of the directors above the words 'By order of the board'. The original signed copy should be retained by the company for evidential purposes. Copies of the notice sent to shareholders do not need to be signed but should include the name and position of the person who signed it on behalf of the board (see **Precedent 13.8**). It is helpful if the notice can be dated for the day on which it is to be posted or the advertisement is to be placed. However, this is not strictly necessary and will not always be possible in view of the fact that it should be dated for the day on which it is actually signed.

Although the Act and most articles only require the notice to specify 'annual general meetings' as such, it is plainly sensible to specify 'general meetings' as such. Although the Act no longer uses the term 'extraordinary general meeting', some articles still specify that any meeting other than the AGM shall be known as such. Where this is the case, it is sensible to describe the meeting in the notice as an 'extraordinary general meeting'. Where the articles do not make such provision, it is probably better to refer to the meeting as a 'general meeting', although the word 'meeting' would probably also suffice; the assumption being that it must be a general meeting if it is not specified as an annual general meeting. Plainly, the words used to describe a class meeting should attempt to define the class of members that will be meeting and should not be described as a general meeting.

A notice will be invalid if it states that the meeting will only be held in certain pre-determined circumstances (e.g. on the passing of a resolution by members of a different class), unless the articles specifically allow such notices to be given (*Alexander v. Simpson* (1889) 43 Ch.D. 139 and *Re North of England Steamship Co.* [1905] 2 Ch. 15). However, resolutions may be included in the business of a meeting which are contingent upon other events.

Notices may be required by the Act to be accompanied by certain statements (see **10.4**).

▨ 13.9 Additional content requirements for publicly traded companies

This paragraph sets out the additional content requirements for notices of meetings issued by companies that are publicly traded. Any company subject to these rules must also comply with the requirements set out above.

13.9.1 Additional requirements of the Act for traded companies

The Act imposes a number of additional requirements on traded companies. A traded company is defined for these purposes in s. 360C (see **8.5**).

Under s. 311(3), every notice of general meeting of a traded company must include:

(a) a statement giving details of the website on which the information required by s. 311A (traded companies: publication of information in advance of general meeting) is published (see **13.10**);

(b) a statement that the right to vote at the meeting is determined by reference to the register of members and of the time when that right is determined in accordance with s. 360B(2) (see **13.9.4**);

(c) a statement of the procedures with which members must comply in order to be able to attend and vote at the meeting (including the date by which they must comply);

(d) a statement giving details of any forms to be used for the appointment of a proxy;

(e) where the company offers the facility for members to vote in advance (see s. 322A) or by electronic means (see s. 360A), a statement of the procedure for doing so (including the date by which it must be done and details of any forms to be used);

(f) a statement of the right of members to ask questions in accordance with s. 319A (traded companies: questions at meetings).

Under s. 337(3), if the AGM notice of a traded company is given more than six weeks before the meeting, the notice must include a statement regarding members' rights under s. 338A to require the company to include a matter (other than a resolution) in the business to be dealt with at the meeting and, if the company is a public company, a statement of members' rights to propose resolutions under s. 338.

Any notice of meeting of a traded company must state the general nature of business of the meeting (s. 311(2)(a)).

13.9.2 Warnings for indirect investors

If a listed company is required under s. 146 to send a notice of meeting to an indirect investor (see **8.7**), the version of the notice sent to that person must state that they may have the right to be appointed as a proxy by the registered shareholder, and that they may be able to give voting instructions to the registered shareholder (who would then aggregate the votes and lodge them with the company) (s. 149(2)). The word 'may' has to be used as it is at the discretion of the registered shareholder whether to offer any of these voting facilities.

Furthermore, under s. 149(3) the standard proxy statement in any notice of general meeting, which tells the registered shareholder that he can appoint a proxy, must either:

(a) be omitted from the version sent to indirect investors; or

(b) contain the statement that it does not apply to them.

Sample wording which can be used where a single copy of the notice is produced can be found in the notes to the AGM notice in **Precedent 10.3**.

13.9.3 Note on possible audit concerns: quoted companies

Under s. 529, a quoted company (see definition at **8.5.2**) must, in any notice of a meeting which is to be held as the accounts meeting, draw attention to the possibility of a statement being placed on a website pursuant to a members' requests under s. 527, and the fact that members may make such a request free of charge, that a copy of any such statement will be forwarded to the company's auditors and that any published statement will form part of the business which may be dealt with at the meeting.

Members satisfying the requirements of s. 527 may require a quoted company to publish on a website a statement relating to the audit of the company's accounts which are to be laid before the next accounts meeting (including the auditor's report and the conduct of the audit) or, where applicable, any circumstances connected with an auditor of the company ceasing to hold office since the previous accounts meeting at which accounts were laid. Should a valid request for the publication of such a statement be received, the company must, within three working days of receipt, publish the statement on a website and forward a copy to its auditors. Any statement published on a website under these rules forms part of the business which may be dealt with at the next accounts meeting.

13.9.4 Companies with securities admitted to CREST

A company whose securities have been admitted to CREST, may specify in the notice a time by which a person must be entered on the relevant register of securities in order to have the right to attend and vote at the meeting (Uncertificated Securities Regulations 2001, reg. 41 (SI 2001/3755)). This time may not be more than 48 hours before the time fixed for the meeting, although in calculating this limit, no account need be taken of any part of a day that is not a working day. It should be noted that the effect of this rule is almost identical to s. 360B(2) of the Act (which applies to traded companies only). The only difference between the two provisions is that the former applies to a potentially wider range of companies (including AIM companies whose securities have been admitted to CREST).

Both provisions allow a snapshot of the register to be taken at a particular point prior to the meeting to be used for the purpose of verifying attendance and voting rights at the meeting. This is necessary because CREST operates on a real-time basis, which means that the dematerialised part of the register can alter right up to the meeting and during its course.

For a suitable form of wording for the note regarding the cut-off point, see the notes to the AGM notice in **Precedent 10.3**. This wording includes provisions concerning possible adjournment. This is necessary because the cut-off point for the original meeting would not necessarily apply on an adjournment – the cut-off point for the adjournment could not, under the Uncertificated Securities Regulations, be more than 48 hours before the time of the adjourned meeting.

The Uncertificated Securities Regulations also allow companies whose securities have been admitted to CREST to establish a record date for the purposes of determining entitlement to receive notice of a meeting. This date must be not more than 21 days before the date on which the notices are sent out (i.e. the actual date of posting – not just the date of signing shown on the notice).

In order to take advantage of this concession, the board of such a company should, when approving the notice of meeting, include in its resolution something along the following lines:

> For the purposes of regulation 41 of the Uncertificated Securities Regulations 2001 the members entitled to receive notice of [the annual general meeting for 20...] shall be those entered on the company's register of members at the close of business on ... 20...

No reference needs to be made in the notice itself to this aspect.

The company should agree the date to be stated in the resolution with its registrars (which should, of course, be the date at which the registrars will be preparing their label run for the meeting notice mailing).

To avoid possible legal disputes, it would be advisable for such a board resolution to be passed even if, as a courtesy, the company sends copies of the notice of meeting to persons who are only entered on the register during the notice period preceding the meeting.

13.9.5 Additional content requirements under the Listing Rules and the Disclosure and Transparency Rules

A notice of general meeting is a 'circular' for the purposes of the Listing Rules. Accordingly, it must comply with the requirements for circulars in Chapter 13 of the Listing Rules, including the basic requirements for all circulars and any specific requirements for notices, some of which depend on the business to be transacted (see **13.12**).

A listed company must provide information in the notice of any general meeting on the total number of shares and voting rights and the rights of holders to participate in meetings (DTR 6.1.12R). This is useful for anybody who is appointed as a proxy as it helps them to calculate whether or not they have a notifiable voting interest (3% or more) for the purposes of DTR 5. For an example of such a disclosure, see the notes to the AGM notice at **Precedent 10.3**.

The Listing Rules used to require listed companies to make directors' service contracts available for inspection at the AGM and to include a statement regarding their availability in the AGM notice. These requirements were abolished in June 1996. The UK Corporate Governance Code requires the terms and conditions of the appointment of non-executive directors to be made available for inspection at the AGM (Code provision B.3.2). However, it does not require any statement to be included in the notice in this regard.

■ 13.10 Information to be published on a website by a traded company before a general meeting

Section 311A requires a traded company (see definition at **8.5.1**) to publish the following information on a website before any general meeting:

- the matters set out in the notice of the meeting;
- the total numbers of shares in the company, and shares of each class, in respect of which members are entitled to exercise voting rights at the meeting; and
- the totals of the voting rights that members are entitled to exercise at the meeting in respect of the shares of each class.

The matters must be made available on the website throughout the period beginning with the first date on which notice of the meeting is given and ending with the conclusion of the meeting (s. 311A(2)). Members' statements, members' resolutions and members' matters of business received by the company after that date must be published as soon as reasonably practicable and be available on the website for the remainder of that period (s. 311A(3)). The number of shares and voting rights must be ascertained at the latest practicable time before the first date on which notice of the meeting is given (s. 311A(4)).

Failure to comply with the requirements of s. 311A regarding website publication is an offence, but it does not affect the validity of the meeting or of anything done at the meeting (s. 311A(5) to (7)).

■ 13.11 Notice of the business

Section 311(2) requires a company to state in any notice of a general meeting the general nature of any business to be transacted at that meeting, but allows this rule to be modified by a company's articles if the company is not a traded company. Most articles which make any provision in this regard also require notices to state the general nature of the business to be transacted (e.g. reg. 38 of Table A), although it is not uncommon to find articles that distinguish between 'ordinary business' and 'special business' in this regard (see **13.11.1**). The requirement for the notice to state the general nature of the business was not included in any previous Companies Acts. However, it could be said to represent what was the position under the common law. Accordingly, previous common law cases will still be highly influential in determining whether a company has complied with the requirement.

It should be noted that, under the common law, the adequacy of the notice regarding the explanation of the business is judged separately for each item of business. If no explanation and no notice of the business is included in a notice of meeting, it is possible that the whole of the notice could be declared invalid. However, the fact that the explanation for one item is found to be inadequate does not necessarily mean that the whole notice would be declared invalid or that the other items of business could not be properly transacted.

The requirement to state the general nature of the business should not be viewed simply as a requirement to state the text of the resolutions. It is not necessary to give the exact text of the resolutions to be proposed at a general meeting in the notice, unless specifically required by the Act (e.g. in relation to special resolutions and ordinary resolutions that require special notice). It is possible to state the general nature of the business without stating the exact text of the resolutions. Although it is normal to give the text of the resolutions in the notice, it is important to understand that this may not necessarily suffice for the purposes of the requirement to state the general nature of the business. Some sort of explanation of the business may also be required. Under the common law, the notice must give a 'fair and candid and reasonable explanation' of the purposes for which the meeting is called (*Kaye v. Croydon Tramways Co.* [1898] 1 Ch. 358).

Whether adequate notice of the business has been given will depend on the particular facts in each case. In *Normandy v. Ind, Coope & Co.* [1908] 1 Ch. 84, notice was given of a resolution to consider and, if thought fit, to approve a new set of articles to replace the existing articles. No indication of the content or effect of the new articles was given in the notice although it stated that copies were available for inspection at the company's office. It was held that the notice was defective because it did not properly inform the shareholders of the 'nature of the business'.

Notices are not construed with excessive strictness. The test the courts apply is what the notice would fairly convey to an ordinary person (*Henderson v. Bank of Australasia* (1890) 45 Ch.D. 330). In determining the validity of the notice the courts often apply the absent shareholder test. In *Tiessen v. Henderson* [1899] 1 Ch. 861, Kekewich J said (at p. 886):

> The question is merely whether each shareholder as and when he received notice of the meeting, in which I include the circular of the same date, had fair warning of what was to be submitted to the meeting. A shareholder may properly and prudently leave matters in which he takes no interest to the decision of the majority. But in that case he is content to be bound by the vote of the majority; because he knows the matter about which the majority are to vote at the meeting. If he does not know that, he has not a fair chance of determining in his own interest whether he ought to attend the meeting, make further inquiries, or leave others to determine the matter for him.

He added (at p. 870):

> The man I am protecting is not the dissentient, but the absent shareholder – the man who is absent because having reviewed and with more or less care

looked at this circular, he comes to the conclusion that on the whole he will not oppose the scheme, but leave it to the majority. I cannot tell whether he would have left it to the meeting to decide if he had known the real facts. He did not know the real facts; and, therefore, I think the resolution is not binding upon him.

There must be adequate disclosure of all material facts relevant to the question on which members will be asked to vote. In *Kaye v. Croydon Tramways Co.* [1898] 1 Ch. 358, a notice which failed to disclose the financial interest of the directors in a proposed reconstruction was held to be invalid. In *Baillie v. Oriental Telephone & Electric Co. Ltd.* [1915] 1 Ch. 503, notice of a resolution to sanction the remuneration of the directors in connection with services rendered to certain subsidiaries was held to be inadequate because it did not specify the amount of that remuneration. Many of the requirements of Chapter 13 of the Listing Rules regarding circulars are targeted towards ensuring that there is adequate disclosure of all material facts (see **13.12**). And to this extent the Listing Rules can be said to be a physical embodiment of the common law rules.

The common law recognises the concept of an explanatory circular. Indeed, it has been suggested that it is desirable to supplement the notice with an explanatory circular where the business is complex or important (*Young v. South African & Australian Exploration & Development Syndicate* [1896] 2 Ch. 268). Where a circular is sent with the notice, it will normally be read in conjunction with the notice in order to determine whether adequate notice of the business has been given (*Tiessen v. Henderson* [1899] 1 Ch. 861). The same is true of the directors' report (*Boschoek Proprietary Co. Ltd. v. Fuke* [1906] 1 Ch. 148) and presumably of any other document sent with the notice.

Business which has not been sufficiently notified or which is substantially different from that notified cannot be validly transacted (*Re Bridport Old Brewery Co.* (1867) 2 Ch.App. 19). However, amendments which are relevant to, and arise fairly out of, an item of business of which notice has been given may be proposed at the meeting (*Re Trench Tubeless Tyre Co.* [1900] 1 Ch. 408). For example, it has been held that a notice 'to elect directors' was sufficient for the meeting to elect directors up to the number permitted by the articles even though the notice only named one director (*Choppington Collieries Ltd. v. Johnson* [1944] 1 All E.R. 762). Amendments may not generally be made to the substance of resolutions proposed as special, extraordinary or resolutions requiring special notice (see further **24.4**).

The business actually carried out must substantially correspond to what was included in the notice. If notice is given of a single resolution which contains more than one proposal, it is not possible to adopt only part of it, because it is impossible for the court to know how many shareholders were satisfied with the arrangement as proposed and therefore abstained from attending the meeting (*Clinch v. Financial Corporation* (1898) L.R. 5 Eq. 450). Where notice was given of a meeting to consider resolutions for reconstruction and for winding up as incidental thereto and only a resolution to wind up was passed, it was held to be invalid as it resulted in a position fundamentally different from that contemplated by the notice (*Re Teede and Bishop* (1901) 70 L.J. Ch. 409). However, where the notice specified several separate resolutions and one of those was to wind up the company, that resolution was effective even though the other resolutions which were concerned with the sale of the undertaking and consequent reorganisation, were found to be ultra vires and therefore void (*Thomson v. Henderson's Transvaal Estates Co.* [1908] 1 Ch. 765). The difference between these two cases is that in the first the notice implied that a resolution to wind up would only be passed as part of a reconstruction. In the second, the notice of the resolution to wind up was capable of standing in its own right. It follows that if it is intended to make a resolution contingent on the passing of another resolution, this should be done either by combining the two proposals in one resolution or clearly stating in the notice that the resolution is (or resolutions are) contingent upon the passing of another resolution(s).

13.11.1 Ordinary and special business

Some companies still have articles which distinguish between ordinary and special business. These are usually based on reg. 52 of the 1948 Table A which defines special business as any business:

> that is transacted at an extraordinary general meeting, and also all that is transacted at an annual general meeting, with the exception of declaring a dividend, the consideration of the accounts, balance sheets, and the reports of the directors and auditors, and the election of directors in the place of those retiring and the appointment of, and the fixing of the remuneration, of the auditors.

Any resolution which is not special business will be ordinary business.

Reg. 50 of the 1948 Table A (see **Precedent 13.11**) provides that in the case of special business the notice shall specify 'the general nature of that business'. Thus it must give a 'fair and candid and reasonable explanation' of the business to be transacted and give all material information to enable it to be understood.

No such requirement exists with regard to ordinary business and the effect of such provisions is to enable a notice of annual general meetings to be given without setting out the nature of the ordinary business. The members are assumed to know that matters of ordinary business may be dealt with at the meeting by virtue of the articles.

In practice, most companies with such articles specify the nature of both ordinary and special business in any notices. Indeed, although articles may distinguish between ordinary and special business, they may still require the general nature of ordinary business to be specified in the notice. Whether or not this is the case, it would be impracticable for a listed company to do otherwise. This is because s. 311(2) specifies that a traded company must specify the general nature of the business in the notice. In addition, the form of proxy sent to members must allow them to instruct their proxy how to vote on all resolutions intended to be proposed at the meeting (Listing Rules, para. 13.28), and it would be confusing for members if resolutions were included on the proxy form but not in the notice.

■ 13.12 Listing rule requirements on circulars

Any circular that a company with a premium listing of equity shares sends to holders of its listed securities must comply with the requirements of Chapter 13 of the Listing Rules (LR 13). A circular is defined for the purposes of the Listing Rules in the Handbook Glossary as 'any document issued to holders of listed securities *including notices of meetings* but excluding prospectuses, listing particulars, annual reports and accounts, interim reports, proxy cards and dividend or interest vouchers'.

The requirement to send a circular arises most frequently in connection with matters that require shareholder approval, whether under the Act or the Listing Rules. Every notice of meeting sent to shareholders is a circular. As such, every notice of meeting must comply with the basic requirements for circulars in LR 13. One of those requirements is that the notice must be accompanied by an 'explanatory circular'. LR 13 sets out the minimum disclosures that should be made in the 'explanatory circular'.

The general purpose of the Listing Rules in this regard is to ensure that the purpose and effect of any business proposed at a meeting is properly explained and that shareholders are given all necessary background information. To a certain extent, the rules embody what a very strict judge might consider necessary for the purposes of giving proper notice of the business under the common law.

It should be noted that the Listing Rules require shareholders to approve certain transactions that would normally fall within the power of the directors (e.g. acquisitions and disposals classified as a Class 1 transaction and related-party transactions). LR 13 sets out in great detail the disclosures that must be made in any circular issued in connection with a Class 1 or related-party transaction. Any such circular must be approved by the UKLA before it is sent to shareholders. However, most other circulars issued in connection with general meetings do not need prior approval as long as they comply with content requirements of LR 13.

Ironically, the requirements of the Listing Rule requirements on circulars can be quite circular themselves when applied to notices of meetings. As the notice itself is treated as a circular, one could take the view that it must comply with all the requirements of Chapter 13 and include all the necessary explanations and disclosures. However, Listing Rule 13.8.8 specifically states that 'when holders of listed equity shares are sent a notice of meeting which includes any business, other than ordinary business at an annual general meeting, an explanatory circular must accompany the notice'. In other words, it says that the notice (which is a circular) must be accompanied by another circular.

The only sensible way of viewing the rules is to say that if the necessary explanations are not included in the notice, they must be included in the explanatory circular that accompanies it. In practice, companies usually produce a single document containing the formal notice of meeting and the necessary explanations. However, it is possible for the notice and explanatory circular to be contained in different documents. Where separate documents are produced, both will need to comply with the general requirements that apply to all circulars and the documents viewed as a whole will need to contain all the necessary disclosures and explanations. The Listing Rules specifically allow any explanation of the business of the AGM to be included in the directors' report. Very few companies choose to take advantage of this dispensation. Those that do also tend to include the AGM notice in the annual report.

In some cases, it is a practical necessity to produce two separate circulars, particularly where a meeting is being called to approve a Class 1 or related-party transaction. In these circumstances, there will normally be a circular calling the meeting and a separate Class 1 or related-party circular.

Most listed companies do not only deal with 'ordinary business' at their AGM. Accordingly, it will not normally be possible for them to take advantage of the exemption in LR 13.8.8 which states that it is not necessary to produce an explanatory circular in connection with an AGM at which only 'ordinary business' is to be proposed. In any case, it is questionable whether there is any advantage to be gained from claiming this exemption and difficult to define precisely when it applies in view of the fact that the Listing Rules no longer include a definition of 'ordinary business'. These factors combine to make the possibility of claiming exemption a matter of academic interest only, which is why we deal with it separately at **13.12.3**. On the whole it would make no difference to most listed companies if the exemption did not exist.

By their nature, most circulars have to be sent at the same time as the notice of meeting. However, a company can be required under the Listing Rules to prepare a supplementary circular. This is most likely to occur in relation to a class 1 transaction or a related-party transaction where the relevant circular has already been sent to shareholders but a material change occurs or a material new matter arises before the date of the meeting (see, e.g. LR 11.1.7C). Where a supplementary circular is required, it must be sent to shareholders no later than seven days prior to the date of the meeting at which any vote expressly required under the Listing Rules will be taken (LR 13.1.9 R). In order to comply with this requirement, it may be necessary to adjourn the meeting (LR 13.1.10 G).

Circulars may be sent to shareholders in hard copy or electronic form (LR 1.4.9). A copy of any circular issued by a listed company must be forwarded to the Document Viewing Facility (i.e. the National Storage Mechanism) at the same time as it is issued (LR 9.6.1) and an announcement must be made via an RIS of the fact that this has been done (LR 9.6.3).

13.12.1 Contents of circulars

All circulars (including any notice of meeting) issued by a listed company to holders of its listed securities must comply with the relevant content requirements of Chapter 13 of the Listing Rules (LR 13.1.3). The omission of any information must be authorised by the UKLA in advance (LR 13.1.7G).

Listing Rule 13.3.1 specifies the basic requirements for all circulars sent by a company to holders of its listed securities. All circulars must, for example, provide a clear and adequate explanation of their subject matter and, if voting or other action is required, contain all information necessary to allow the holders of the securities to make a properly informed decision.

If voting or other action is required, the circular must contain a heading drawing attention to the importance of the document and advising holders of securities who are in any doubt as to what action to take to consult an appropriate independent adviser. All circulars must also state that where all the securities have been sold or transferred by the addressee, the circular and any other relevant documents should be passed on to the person through whom the transfer was effected for transmission to the purchaser or transferee. These two elements are usually placed at the top of the front page of the circular.

Where voting is required, a circular must also contain a recommendation from the directors as to the voting action shareholders should take, indicating whether or not they think the proposal is in shareholders' best interests. This is usually included in an introductory statement/explanation by the chairman.

Information may be incorporated in a circular by reference to relevant information contained in an approved prospectus or listing particulars of the company or any other published document of that company which has been filed with the FCA (LR 13.1.3–6).

LR 13.8 specifies the information that must be included in any circular that relates to:

(a) a resolution giving authority to allot shares (LR 13.8.1);
(b) a resolution to disapply pre-emption rights (LR 13.8.2);
(c) a reduction of capital (LR 13.8.4);
(d) a capitalisation or bonus issue (LR 13.8.5);
(e) an election to receive a scrip dividend or participate in a dividend reinvestment plan (LR 13.8.6–7);
(f) a notice of meeting (LR 13.8.8–9);
(f) a resolution to amend the company's constitution (LR 13.8.10);
(g) a resolution to approve an employee share scheme or long term incentive plan (LR 13.8.11–14);
(h) a resolution to approve a discounted option arrangement (LR 13.8.15); and
(i) reminders of conversion rights (LR 13.8.16).

13.12.2 Approval of circulars

A circular or other document convening an AGM (i.e. the AGM notice and explanatory circular) need not be submitted to the UKLA for approval if only ordinary business is to be conducted at the AGM or, if any other matter referred to in LR 13.8 is also to be considered or proposed, provided that the circular or other document complies with the relevant provisions of LR 13.8 with regard to that other business (LR 13.8.8(3)). If any other business is to be dealt with at the AGM, the circular will normally need to be approved. One of the obvious problems that a company will face in deciding whether approval is required is the fact that the Listing Rules no longer define what is meant by 'ordinary business'. They used to include a definition. However, for some reason it was deleted in July 2005. The former definition certainly did not include every matter that would be considered to be routine at an AGM and was not particularly designed to. It covered resolutions to receive or approve the accounts, to declare a dividend, to reappoint directors, to appoint directors to replace those retiring and not offering themselves for re-election, to reappoint auditors and authorise the directors to fix their remuneration. There are many other matters of business that listed companies routinely put to members at the AGM that are not covered by the definition or the list of items in LR 13.8. For example, a resolution to approve the directors' remuneration report is not covered. In this particular instance, the UKLA has indicated in a letter to listed companies dated 29 January 2003, that for the purposes of the Listing Rules, the resolution to approve the directors' remuneration report will be regarded as a matter of a routine nature and that, accordingly, the notice/circular relating to such resolutions do not need to be submitted for approval prior to publication.

It should be noted that the above exemption only applies for the purposes of determining whether the AGM notice and circular needs to be approved. The question as to whether circulars issued in connection with a meeting other than the AGM need to be approved must be determined under the more general exemption provided for by LR 13.2.2. This states that a circular need not be approved if:

(a) it is of a type referred to in LR 13.8 (which includes a notice of meeting) or only relates to a change of name or is an information-only circular which does not relate to a shareholder vote, other than of a type referred to in LR 13.4.3R(3) in relation to a takeover offer which includes a working capital statement;

(b) it complies with the general requirements as to contents set out in LR 13.3 and any specific requirements contained in LR 13.8 for circulars of that type; and

(c) neither the circular nor the transaction, or matter to which it relates, has unusual features.

No other circular may be issued until it has been approved by the UKLA in final form (LR 13.2.1). The procedure for obtaining approval is set out in LR 13.2.4–9 and involves the submission by the company's sponsor of the circular to be approved together with any necessary declarations. Prior approval is, for example, always required for circulars issued in connection with Class 1 transactions and related-party transactions and resolutions seeking authority to purchase 25% or more of the company's equity shares. However, approval may also be required for circulars relating to other items of business. According to a UKLA Technical Note on approval of circulars (UKLA/TN/206.1):

> [I]t is for the issuer and its advisers to ascertain whether something is unusual and, if they are unable to conclude that no unusual features are present, the circular should be submitted for vetting. It is not the case, however, that any matter presented as an ordinary resolution at an AGM should be considered to be not unusual. It should be the substance of the resolution that determines whether it is unusual under LR 13.2.2R(3), and not simply its designation as an ordinary or special resolution.
>
> To illustrate, circulars relating to meetings requisitioned by shareholders should be considered as having unusual features whether the resolutions proposed are ordinary or special resolutions. Such circulars should be submitted to the UKLA for vetting and approval in advance of publication. Issuers are often required by law to send such circulars to shareholders within a short specified timeframe. Where this is the case we would encourage issuers or their advisers to contact us early on in the process and ensure that they allow sufficient time for the proposed circular to be vetted by the UKLA before it is published.

A listed company must send a circular to holders of its listed equity shares as soon as practicable after it has been approved (LR 13.2.10).

Where a circular relates to a proposed amendment to a company's constitution, the draft amendments must be sent to the UKLA and any regulated market on which the company's securities are issued no later than the date of calling the general meeting at which the amendments are to be proposed (DTR 6.1.2). The Listing Rules no longer require companies to submit a letter of compliance from their legal advisers confirming that the proposed amendments comply with the requirements of the Listing Rules.

13.12.3 Circumstances in which an explanatory circular is not required

Although Listing Rule 13.8.8 states that an AGM notice need not be accompanied by an explanatory circular if only 'ordinary business' is to be proposed at the meeting, it is almost impossible to state with any certainty the circumstances in which this dispensation might apply and questionable whether there is any real advantage to be gained from doing so. The Listing Rules used to include a definition of 'ordinary business'. However, for some reason the definition was deleted in July 2005. Nobody really knows why. However, the fact that it was makes it a lot more difficult to decide whether or not the dispensation applies. The articles of most listed companies used to distinguish between 'ordinary business' and 'special business' and used to provide that the AGM notice did not need to specify the nature of any ordinary business. The dispensation was originally included in the Listing Rules to reflect this. However, rather than rely on the definition of 'ordinary business' in a company's articles (which may not necessarily have been the same), the Listing Rules contained their own definition. As the Listing Rules no longer contain such a definition, it is difficult to know what definition to use. It is possible that companies are supposed to use the definition in their articles, even though one company's definition may not be the same as another's. It is possible that an unwritten rule is applied, which may be based on the definition that was deleted from the Listing Rules. If so, it may be worth knowing that under the former Listing Rule definition, ordinary business was limited to receiving or approving the accounts, the declaring of a dividend, reappointing directors, appointing directors to replace those retiring and not offering themselves for re-election, reappointing auditors and authorising the directors to fix their remuneration.

If that is what it still means, very few listed company AGMs will only deal with ordinary business, and if the AGM deals with anything else, an explanatory circular will be required.

However, for the sake of argument, let us assume that a listed company is proposing to hold an AGM at which only ordinary business is to be proposed. Would there be any real benefit in taking advantage of the dispensation?

Even, if the articles of a listed company still make provision for ordinary business, s. 311(2) of the Act now requires any notice of general meeting of a 'traded company' (which includes every UK company that is subject to Chapter 13 of the Listing Rules) to specify the general nature of any business to be transacted at the meeting and does not permit this rule to be modified by the articles. Accordingly, a UK company that is listed in the UK can no longer take advantage of any such provision in its articles, not that there was ever much advantage to be gained from doing so in any case. In some ways, this means that the reason for the dispensation in the Listing Rules no longer exists.

Even if an explanatory circular is not required, it should not be forgotten that the AGM notice in itself is a circular. So it would still be required to include all the usual elements that apply to all circulars were it not for the fact that LR 13.8.8(3) disapplies some of them. The rules that are disapplied by LR 13.8.8(3) in respect of an AGM notice where only ordinary business is proposed are as follows:

(a) the requirement for a circular to contain a heading drawing attention to the document's importance and advising security holders who are in any doubt as to what action to take to consult appropriate independent advisers (LR 13.3.1 R (4));

(b) the requirement for a circular to contain a recommendation from the board as to the voting action security holders should take for all resolutions proposed, indicating whether or not the proposal described in the circular is, in the board's opinion, in the best interests of security holders as a whole (LR 13.3.1 R (5)); and

(c) the requirement for a circular to state that if all the securities have been sold or transferred by the addressee the circular and any other relevant documents should be passed to the person through whom the sale or transfer was effected for transmission to the purchaser or transferee (LR 13.3.1 R (6)).

It should be noted that the following general requirements for circulars are not disapplied and would therefore still apply to the AGM notice:

(a) the requirement to provide a clear and adequate explanation of its subject matter giving due prominence to its essential characteristics, benefits and risks (LR 13.3.1 R);

(b) the requirement to state why the security holder is being asked to vote or, if no vote is required, why the circular is being sent (LR 13.3.1 R (2)); and

(c) if voting or other action is required, the requirement for the circular to contain all information necessary to allow the security holders to make a properly informed decision (LR 13.3.1 R (3)).

In other words, even though an explanatory circular is not required, it would seem that the AGM notice must still adequately explain the business. We appear to be going round in circles. The truth of the matter is that the nature of the ordinary business must be set out in the notice in accordance with the Act. Although, the Listing Rules do not impose any additional disclosure requirements regarding matters of ordinary business, they do require the business to be adequately explained. A resolution to reappoint a named director in the notice does not really need much additional explanation. However, if the notice merely said 'to reappoint directors retiring by rotation' (which might satisfy the requirement to state the general nature of the business), it would need further explanation because shareholders would not be able to work out which directors were retiring and offering themselves for re-election.

Where only ordinary business is to be proposed at the AGM, it would actually make more sense for the Listing Rules not to require any explanation of the business to be given, but for them to require the AGM notice to include the standard statements for investors. In other words, it would seem to make more sense if companies were required to do the things they are exempt from doing, and vice versa. In practice, as it currently stands, it would make very little difference if the ordinary business exemption for the AGM did not exist.

13.12.4 Class 1 and related-party transactions

A company with a premium listing will always need to issue an approved circular, and obtain shareholder approval for transactions that are categorised as a Class 1 transaction or a related-party transaction. The question as to whether a transaction falls within these categories is determined by the nature of the transaction and its size. The size of the transaction is determined by calculating four different ratios in accordance with the class tests set out in LR 10 Annex 1. All transactions carried out in the last 12 months that have not previously been approved by shareholders must be aggregated for the purposes of calculating the results of the class tests. The results of the tests determine how the transaction is classified and the actions that the company is required to take. Transactions can fall into the following categories:

(a) Class 1 transactions arise where any of the relevant percentages exceed 25%. If a transaction qualifies as a Class 1 transaction, a formal announcement and a circular must be issued and shareholder approval is required. If any of the percentages exceed 100%, the transaction will also be subject to the additional requirements for a reverse takeover set out in LR 5. The reverse takeover rules also apply where an acquisition gives rise to a substantial change of business or a change of control.

(b) Class 2 transactions arise where any of the relevant percentage ratios is 5% or more but each is less than 25%. In this case a formal announcement must be issued, but no circular or shareholder approval is normally required.

(c) Related-party transactions, broadly speaking, are transactions between a listed company or its subsidiaries and a related party or a transaction that may benefit a related party. Shareholder approval and a related party circular is required where any of the class tests give rise to a percentage ratio of 5% or more for such a transaction.

A circular under (a) or (c) above must comply with the relevant requirements of LR 13 for Class 1 circulars or related-party circular.

The 'Class 3' transaction category, which formerly arose where all the relevant percentages were under 5%, was abolished in October 2012. The Listing Rules used to require listed companies to announce certain details regarding such transactions via an RIS. Although that specific requirement has now been abolished, some such transactions may still need to be announced under the general disclosure requirements relating to inside information.

During takeovers and mergers numerous circulars will in practice be issued by both sides. The Takeover Code sets out the rules on the making of offers and the content of offer documents and replies thereto. Circulars issued by a listed company in connection with a takeover must comply with the requirements of the Listing Rules (see, in particular, LR 13.4.3 and the transaction rules in LR 10 and LR 11).

Although AIM companies are required to notify substantial transactions to the market through an RIS (AIM rules 12 and 13), shareholder approval is not required for any such transaction unless it involves a reverse takeover (AIM rule 14) or a fundamental change of business (AIM rule 15).

■ 13.13 Persons entitled to receive notice

Notice of a general meeting of a company must be sent to the following persons under the Act:

- every member of the company (s. 310(1)(a)), although this requirement is subject to any enactment and any provision of the company's articles (s. 310(2));
- every person who is entitled to a share in consequence of the death or bankruptcy of a member (s. 310(2)), although this requirement is subject to any enactment and any provision of the company's articles (s. 310(2));
- every director of the company (s. 310(1)(b), although this requirement is subject to any enactment and any provision of the company's articles (s. 310(2));
- the company's auditors, if any (s. 502(2));
- in the case of a company whose shares are traded of a regulated market, any indirect investors (s. 146).

Although the statutory requirement in s. 310 to give notice of general meetings to the directors is capable of modification by the articles, it is very rare for articles to do so. In fact, articles are more likely to specify that notice shall be given to the directors (e.g. reg. 38) because this was not formerly a statutory requirement under the 1985 Act.

Articles do frequently modify the statutory requirement to give notice of general meetings to every member. Where the articles are silent on the matter, notice must be given to every member of the company (s. 310(1)). This does not necessarily include each person who is a joint shareholder (see below). However, it would include members whose calls are either in arrears or who are resident abroad and the holders of all classes of shares whether or not they have a right to attend and vote. Articles usually modify or exclude the rights of these members to receive notice (see below).

Auditors have a statutory right to receive notices of meetings and any other communications relating to any general meeting which a member is entitled to receive (s. 502(2)). An auditor who has been removed under s. 510 retains the rights conferred by s. 502(2) in relation to any general meeting at which his term of office would otherwise have expired, or at which it is proposed to fill the vacancy caused by his removal. An auditor who has resigned from office under s. 516 also retains the rights conferred by s. 502(2) in relation to any general meeting requisitioned by him in connection with his resignation and any general meeting at which his term of office would otherwise have expired, or at which it is proposed to fill the vacancy caused by his resignation (s. 518(10)).

The right to receive notice is suspended for members who are enemies or who are situated in enemy territories. A meeting will be properly convened if no notice is served on such persons (*Re Anglo-International Bank* [1943] Ch. 233).

A listed company must provide information to shareholders on the place, time and agenda of meetings, the total number of shares and voting rights and the rights of holders to participate in meetings (DTR 6.1.12R).

13.13.1 Restrictions on right to receive notice

Articles often specify who is entitled to receive notice of general meetings. For example, reg. 38 of Table A provides that, subject to any restrictions imposed on shares, notice shall be given to all the members, all persons entitled to a share in consequence of the death or bankruptcy of a member, the directors, and the auditors. It should be noted that this includes nearly all of the person required to be given notice by the default statutory provisions. It should be noted that the model articles do not do so, presumably on the grounds that it would be superfluous to repeat the statutory obligations.

Other regulations in Table A (but not the model articles) specify the circumstances in which members are not entitled to receive notice. It should be noted that a person may have a right to receive notice but not a right to attend or vote at the meeting. A person may also have a right to attend and vote at a meeting but not to receive notice of it, e.g. a member whose registered address is outside the United Kingdom. The following restrictions on the right to receive notice of meetings are commonly found in articles:

■ *Joint shareholders*
Articles often provide that notice sent to the joint holder whose name stands first in the register of members in respect of the joint holding shall be sufficient notice to all the joint holders (e.g. reg. 112 of Table A). Companies often allow joint shareholders to split their holding, if it is capable of being split, so that two or more accounts are entered in the register of members each with a different name as the first named holder. By doing so, each joint holder whose name stands first in one of the accounts in the register is assured of receiving notice of any meeting.

If the articles make no provision as to joint shareholders, then para. 16 of Sch. 5 to the Act applies, which provides anything authorised or required to be sent or supplied to joint shareholders may be sent or supplied either to each of the joint holders, or to the holder whose name appears first in the register of members. This statutory provision is expressed as being subject to anything in a company's articles, although it would be unusual for articles to make any provision other than that made in reg. 112 of Table A.

■ *Death or bankruptcy of a shareholder*
The default position with regard to persons entitled to a share as a result of the death or bankruptcy is that they should be sent notices (s. 310(2)). This is reinforced by para. 17 of Sch. 5 to the Act, which provides that documents or information required or authorised to be sent or supplied to a member who has died or has been declared bankrupt may be sent or supplied to the persons claiming to be entitled to the shares in consequence of the death or bankruptcy by name, or by the title of representatives of the deceased, or trustee of the bankrupt, or by any like description, at the address in the United Kingdom supplied for the purpose by those so claiming. But until such an

address has been so supplied, a document or information may be sent or supplied in any manner in which it might have been sent or supplied if the death or bankruptcy had not occurred. Paragraph 17 is expressed as being subject to anything in the company's articles and includes definitions of bankruptcy for the purposes of the statutory rules.

Regulation 116 of Table A makes almost exactly the same provision as para. 17 of Sch. 5 to the Act. Indeed, para. 17 of Sch. 5 is clearly a statutory codification of reg. 116, which is the reason why no similar provision is made in the model articles prescribed under the 2006 Act as it would be superfluous to do so. The only difference between the two provisions is that Table A does not include any definition of bankruptcy for these purposes.

Persons entitled to a share in consequence of the death or bankruptcy of a shareholder are sometimes referred to as transmittees in articles. Articles normally provide that transmittees are bound by any prior notices served on the member (e.g. reg. 114 of Table A, pcls 29 and plc 68).

- *Address not within the UK*
  A member whose registered address is not within the United Kingdom may not be entitled to receive notices unless he has given the company an address within the United Kingdom at which notices may be served, e.g. reg. 112 of Table A. This type of article requires the company to keep a separate record of UK addresses notified by such persons as their address in the register of members will still be outside the United Kingdom (see *Parkstone Ltd. v. Gulf Guarantee Bank plc* [1990] B.C.L.C. 850 for a case on reg. 113 of the 1948 Table A).

- *Subsequent purchaser*
  A person who becomes entitled to have his name entered in the register of members as a member shall be bound by any notices given to the person from whom he derives his title, e.g. reg. 114 of Table A.

- *Calls unpaid*
  Articles commonly restrict the rights of members whose calls are in arrears to vote at a general meeting (e.g. reg. 57 of Table A and plc 41). Such members must still be given notice of that meeting unless the articles specify otherwise. Neither Table A nor the model articles for plcs make any provision in this regard.

- *Preference shareholders*
  It is common for companies with preference share capital to restrict the rights of preference shareholders to receive notice of, attend and vote at general meetings. However, neither Table A nor the model articles for plcs make any such provision and any company which intends to issue preference shares and which wishes to restrict these rights will need to make provision in its articles accordingly. Typically, the preference shareholders might be entitled under the articles to receive notice of any general meeting at which it is proposed to wind up the company or where a resolution is to be proposed that will affect the

rights and privileges of the preference shareholders. Where the right to receive dividends is cumulative, the preference shareholders will normally be entitled to receive notice of (and to attend and vote at) general meetings if those dividends are in arrears for a specified period (normally six months). Where preference dividends were payable each year out of profits earned in that year only, it was held that dividends were not in arrears for a particular year where there were no profits in that year. Accordingly, the preference shareholders had no right to receive notice (*Coulson v. Austin Motor Co.* (1927) 43 T.L.R. 493).

■ *Non-voting shares and other classes of share*

If a separate class of shares is established which gives the holders the right to vote at general meetings, there may be no need to make special provision as to notices as under the Act and most articles (e.g. reg. 38 of Table A) they would be entitled to receive notices of general meetings anyway. If any class of non-voting shares is established, it would be usual for the articles to exclude the right of the holders to receive notices. This would normally be done in one of the articles which establishes the rights of the holders of that type of share.

13.13.2 Record date

Companies whose securities have been admitted to CREST may set a record date for determining entitlement to receive notice of meetings. The date must not be more than 21 days before the date on which the notices are sent out (i.e. the actual date of posting and not necessarily the date of signing shown on the notice). If a company sets such a record date, only those members whose names have been entered on the relevant register of securities at the close of business on that date will be entitled to receive notice (Uncertificated Securities Regulations 1995, reg. 34 (see **Annex D**)). Boards may set a record date by including in their resolution to approve the notice something along the following lines (although no reference needs to be made in the notice itself to this resolution):

> For the purposes of regulation 34 of the Uncertificated Securities Regulations 1995, the members entitled to receive notice of [description of meeting] shall be those entered on the company's register of [members/other securities] at the close of business on [date].

■ 13.14 Special notice

Certain resolutions cannot validly be proposed at a general meeting unless special notice has been given in accordance with the requirements of s. 312. Special notice is required by the Act in relation to the following resolutions:

■ to remove a director by ordinary resolution before the expiration of his period of office or to appoint somebody instead of a director so removed at a meeting at which he is removed (s.168);

- to remove an auditor before the expiration of his term of office (ss. 510 and 511); and
- resolution at a general meeting of a company whose effect would be to appoint a person as auditor in place of a person (the 'outgoing auditor') whose term of office has ended, or is to end (s. 515).

Any such resolution will be invalid unless notice of the intention to propose it has been given to the company at least 28 clear days before the meeting at which it is to be proposed (see **Precedent 13.14A**). Subject to one exception, this is the case whether the resolution is to be proposed by a dissident member or to be included in the notice of a general meeting at the instigation of the board of directors. The exception to the rule is that, if after notice of the intention to propose the resolution has been given to the company, a meeting is called for a date 28 days or less after the notice has been given, the notice will be deemed to have been properly given, though not given within the time required (s. 312(4)). It should also be noted that, provided it is served at least 28 clear days before the meeting, special notice may be validly served on the company after the notice of meeting has been circulated. The 28-day notice period specified in s. 312(1) means clear days by virtue of the application of s. 360.

It can be implied from the words used in the Act that special notice must be given to the company by someone who would be entitled to propose the resolution at a general meeting. Plainly, this includes any member, but might also, at a stretch, include the person who will chair the general meeting (usually the chairman of the board of directors). However, if the resolution is to be proposed at the instigation of the board, it is infinitely preferable for a member (e.g. a director who is a member) to give the necessary notice to the company.

13.14.1 Company's obligations on receipt of special notice

On receipt of notice of the intention to propose one of the above resolutions, the company must comply with certain additional requirements which differ according to the subject of the resolution. For example, on receipt of special notice of the intention to propose a resolution to remove an auditor, the company must immediately send a copy of the notice to the auditor named in the resolution. The auditor concerned then has a right to have a statement circulated with the notice of the meeting (s. 511).

Where practicable, the company must give its members notice of any such resolution at the same time and in the same manner as it gives notice of the meeting. Where that is not practicable, the company must give its members notice at least 14 clear days before the meeting by advertisement in a newspaper having an appropriate circulation, or in any other manner allowed by the company's articles (s. 312(3) (see **Precedent 13.14B**)). The requirement to give 14 clear days' notice arises by virtue of the application of s. 360 to s. 312(3).

It would appear that the requirement to give at least 14 days' notice of a resolution which requires special notice would prevent such a resolution from being proposed at a meeting called at shorter notice unless notice of the resolution had been given earlier than the notice of meeting, which would seem impracticable.

There is nothing in s. 312 that requires a company to convene a meeting to consider a resolution for which special notice has been given. A public company will eventually need to hold an annual general meeting. However, a private company might never hold a meeting at which such a resolution could be proposed unless the member also gave notice under s. 303 requiring it to hold a general meeting for that purpose.

It has been held that a company is not obliged to include in the notice of the meeting a resolution submitted by a member, or to give members notice of it in any other manner, unless the member who submitted it has also satisfied the conditions of either s. 303 (members' power to require the directors to call a general meeting) or s. 338 (public companies: members power to require circulation of resolutions for AGM) (*Pedley v. Inland Waterways Association Ltd.* [1977] 1 All E.R. 209). Hoffman J ruled that the wording of the equivalent provision in the 1985 Act (s. 379(2)) was merely intended to confer on the members of a company the right to receive notice of any resolution of which special notice is required and has been duly given which is to form part of the agenda to be dealt with at the relevant meeting. Thus, a member who cannot comply with the usual conditions for requisitioning a meeting or an AGM resolution, cannot force the company to include the resolution in the notice of the meeting or to give notice of it in any other manner. A company may, of course, choose to include the resolution on the agenda even though the member has not satisfied these conditions and, if it does, it must allow the member to propose the resolution at the meeting.

The Act makes no provision for a penalty in the event of a failure by the company to give notice of the resolution in accordance with s. 312. It is not particularly clear whether a resolution subject to the special notice rules can be proposed if the company has not given notice of it to the members in accordance with s. 312. Section 312(4) rectifies any failure on the part of a member to give special notice of the intention to propose the resolution at least 28 clear days before the meeting where, after receiving the special notice from the member, the company calls a meeting for a date 28 clear days or less after it received the special notice. In other words, it prevents a company from manipulating the requirements of s. 312 to avoid any obligation it may otherwise have to give notice of the resolution. It should also be borne in mind that if such a resolution were to be requisitioned under s. 338 in relation to the annual general meeting of a public company, it would be an offence for the company to fail to give notice of it in accordance with the requirements of that section.

■ 13.15 Circulation of members' statements

The members of both public and private companies may require the company to circulate to its members a statement of not more than 1,000 words with respect to a matter referred to in a proposed resolution to be dealt with at a general meeting or any business to be dealt with at the meeting (s. 314). The statement could be made by members in connection with a meeting or resolution requisitioned by them or in connection with an item of business proposed by the directors.

The member or members making the request must represent at least 5% of the total voting rights of all the members who would be entitled to vote on the resolution at the AGM (excluding any rights attached to treasury shares). Alternatively, the requisition will also be valid if made by at least 100 members who would have the right to vote on the resolution and hold shares on which there has been paid up an average sum, per member, of at least £100.

The request may be made in hard copy or electronic form, must identify the statement to be circulated, must be authenticated by the person or persons making it (see **Precedent 13.15A**), and must be received by the company at least one week before the meeting to which it relates (s. 314(4)). The requirements of s. 360 regarding clear days' notice apply for the purposes of the request by members. In practice this means that a company need not comply with such a request unless it is received at least seven clear days before the meeting (see **13.3**).

On receipt of a valid request, the company must send a copy of the statement to every member entitled to receive notice of the meeting in the same manner and at the same time as, or as soon as reasonably practicable after, it gives notice of the meeting (s. 315(1)) (see **Precedent 13.15B**).

13.15.1 Cost of circulating a statement

A public company must bear the costs of circulating the statement if it relates to the company's AGM and is received before the end of the financial year preceding the meeting (s. 316(1)). In all other cases, a company need not circulate the statement unless the requisitionists deposit or tender within the time limit for making a valid request a sum reasonably sufficient to meet the company's expenses in circulating the statement (s. 316(2)). It should be noted that the requirements of s. 360 regarding clear days' notice also apply for the purposes of determining whether the members have deposited or tendered the necessary sum. In practice this means that they will need to do so at least seven clear days before the meeting (see **13.3**).

Although a requisition requiring a statement to be circulated can be deposited after the notice has been sent out, the cost of circulating it at this late stage will obviously be greater. Unless the directors agree to waive the costs of circulating a statement, the requisitionists will have no choice but to pay them. If the requisitioned statement is deposited at least six weeks before the meeting, the requisitionists could, however, also requisition a resolution proposing that the company bears its own costs in giving effect to the requisitioned statement.

It should be noted that as an alternative to requisitioning a statement under s. 314, any member may (on payment of the prescribed fee) demand a copy of the company's register of members and use the names and addresses of the members to circulate a statement to all or part of the members. This may well be cheaper if it is only necessary to target, say, shareholders holding more than 5% of the company's equity.

13.15.2 Abuse of rights under s. 314

If the court is satisfied that the rights conferred by s. 314 are being abused, it may on the application of the company or any other aggrieved person order that the company is not bound to circulate any such statement and that the requisitionists pay the whole or part of the company's costs (in Scotland, expenses) on such an application, even if they are not parties to the application (s. 317). In an Australian case on a similarly worded provision, it was held that the court had no power to order the deletion of the defamatory parts of a members' statement. It could only order that the whole statement should not be sent (*Re Harbour Lighterage Ltd.* (1968) 1 N.S.W.L.R. 438).

■ 13.16 Accidental failure to give proper notice

Unless all the members actually attend the meeting, the failure to give proper notice to any person entitled to receive it invalidates the meeting (*Smyth v. Darley* (1849) 2 H.L.C. 789). However, the Act provides that accidental failure to give notice of a general meeting or a resolution intended to be moved at a general meeting to one or more persons shall be disregarded for the purpose of establishing whether notice of the meeting or resolution (as the case may be) is duly given (s. 313(1)). Except in relation to notice given under s. 304 (notice of meetings required by members), s. 305 (notice of meetings called by members) and s. 339 (notice of resolutions at AGMs proposed by members), this rule is capable of modification by a company's articles.

On the whole articles do not particularly seek to modify this rule but may include provisions which have largely the same effect (e.g. reg. 39 of Table A). It has been held that such an article served to validate a meeting for which notice had not been given to several members because the address plates for those members had inadvertently been separated from the rest because their dividends had been returned uncashed (*Re West Canadian Collieries Ltd.* [1962] Ch. 370). However, a deliberate failure to send a notice to a member will not be validated even if the company had reason to believe that the notice would not reach the member at his registered address (*Musselwite v. C H Musselwite* [1962] Ch. 964). Once it is shown that some members were not given notice, the onus lies with those claiming that the meeting was valid to show that the omission was accidental (*POW Services Ltd. v. Clare* [1995] 2 B.C.L.C. 435).

Some companies have adopted articles which provide that a member shall not be entitled to receive notice if on the three most recent occasions on which they were sent documents by the company, they were returned undelivered, unless they have subsequently confirmed their address or notified a new address.

Articles commonly provide that a member present, either in person or by proxy, at any meeting of the company or of the holders of any class of shares shall be deemed to have received notice of the meeting and of the purposes for which it was called (e.g. reg. 113 of Table A). Even without such a provision, a member who was present and voted at a meeting of which irregular notice had been given may be deemed to have acquiesced in the irregularity (*Re British Sugar Refinery Co.* [1857] 26 L.J Ch. 369).

14

Resolutions

■ 14.1 Summary

- The type of resolution required to deal with an item of business is determined primarily by the Companies Act 2006 but can also depend on other factors. For each type of resolution, there are different requirements with regard to the majority required to pass it and there can be different notice requirements.
- An ordinary resolution is a resolution which can be passed by a simple majority of the votes (i.e. over 50%) (see **14.3**).
- A special resolution is a resolution which must be passed by a majority of at least 75%. The Act generally requires a special resolution where it is proposed to alter the rights of members or the constitution of the company (see **14.4**).
- An extraordinary resolution is also a resolution which must be passed by a majority of at least 75%. The 2006 Act does not make direct provision for, or require anything to be done by, extraordinary resolution. However, the provisions of the 1985 Act in this regard are preserved for the purposes of any requirements in a company's articles (see **14.5**).
- Elective resolutions were used under the Companies Act 1985 by private companies to dispense with various requirements connected with the holding of annual general meetings. All the members of the company had to vote in favour of the resolution (see **14.5**).
- Copies of certain resolutions must be filed at Companies House 15 days after they have been passed and be embodied in or annexed to every copy of the articles issued after the passing of the resolution (see **14.8**).
- A resolution will normally be passed on the date of the meeting (see **14.9**).

■ 14.2 Resolutions

Part 13, Chapter 1 of the Act sets out the general provisions about resolutions. Section 281 provides that a resolution of the members (or of a class of members) of:

(a) a private company must be passed:
    (i)   as a written resolution in accordance with the Companies Act 2006, Part 13, Chapter 2, or

(ii) at a meeting of the members (to which the provisions of the Companies Act 2006, Part 13, Chapter 3 apply) (s. 281(1)).

(b) a public company must be passed at a meeting of the members (to which the provisions of the Companies Act 2006, Part 13, Chapter 3 and, where relevant, Part 13, Chapter 4 of that Act apply).

Section 281(4) provides that nothing in Part 13 of the 2006 Act affects any enactment or rule of law as to:

- things done otherwise than by passing a resolution;
- circumstances in which a resolution is or is not treated as having been passed; or
- cases in which a person is precluded from alleging that a resolution has not been duly passed.

■ 14.3 Ordinary resolutions

As a general rule, unless the Companies Acts or a company's articles specify otherwise, all business at general meetings may be dealt with by ordinary resolution, although listed companies may also need to have regard to the requirements of FCA Rules and guidance issued by institutional investors. Where a provision of the Companies Acts requires a resolution of the company or of the members (or a class of members) and does not specify what type of resolution is required, an ordinary resolution will suffice unless the company's articles require a higher majority (or unanimity) (s. 281(3)). Anything that may be done by ordinary resolution may also be done by special resolution (s. 282(5)). However, a thing that is required to be done by special resolution cannot be done by ordinary resolution even if it is passed by the requisite majority of at least 75% because a special resolution must be proposed as a special resolution (see **13.4**).

An ordinary resolution is defined in s. 282 of the Act. In simple terms, it is a resolution of the members (or a class of members) which may be passed by a simple majority (s. 282(1)).

A written resolution is passed by a simple majority if it is passed by members representing a simple majority of the total voting rights of eligible members (s. 282(2)) (see **8.2** regarding the meaning of an eligible member for the purposes of a written resolution).

A resolution passed at a meeting on a show of hands is passed by a simple majority if it is passed by a simple majority of the votes cast by those entitled to vote (s. 282(3)) (see **16.6** regarding voting on a show of hands).

A resolution passed on a poll taken at a meeting is passed by a simple majority if it is passed by members representing a simple majority of the total voting rights of members who (being entitled to do so) vote in person or by proxy on the resolution (s. 282(4)).

It should be noted that an abstention or vote withheld on a resolution proposed at a meeting (whether on a show of hands or on a poll) is not considered to be a vote for these purposes. Accordingly, an ordinary resolution proposed at a general meeting will be passed if the number of votes cast in favour of the resolution exceeds the number against. However, failure to vote on a proposed written resolution has the same effect as voting against it.

Articles sometimes purport to give the chairman of the meeting a casting vote in addition to any other vote he may have if the outcome of a vote on either a show of hands or a poll is a tie (e.g. reg. 50 of the original version of Table A). The continuing validity of any such provision is open to some doubt (see **17.13**).

A copy of some, but not all, ordinary resolutions must be filed at Companies House. The table at **Appendix 2** shows the matters that require member or shareholder approval under the Act and other sources, what sort of resolution is required and whether the resolution has to be filed at Companies House.

■ 14.4 Special resolutions

A special resolution is defined in s. 283 as a resolution of the members (or of a class of members) of a company passed by a majority of not less than 75% (s. 283(1)).

A written resolution is passed by a majority of not less than 75% if it is passed by members representing not less than 75% of the total voting rights of eligible members (s. 283(2)) (see **8.2** regarding the meaning of an eligible member for the purposes of a written resolution).

Where a resolution of a private company is passed as a written resolution, the resolution is not a special resolution unless it stated that it was proposed as a special resolution, and if the resolution so stated, it may only be passed as a special resolution (s. 283(3)).

A resolution passed at a meeting on a show of hands is passed by a majority of not less than 75% if it is passed by not less than 75% of the votes cast by those entitled to vote.

A resolution passed on a poll taken at a meeting is passed by a majority of not less than 75% if it is passed by members representing not less than 75% of the total voting rights of the members who (being entitled to do so) vote in person or by proxy on the resolution (s. 283(5)).

Where a resolution is passed at a meeting:

(a) the resolution is not a special resolution unless the notice of the meeting included the text of the resolution and specified the intention to propose the resolution as a special resolution; and

(b) if the notice of the meeting so specified, the resolution may only be passed as a special resolution (s. 283(6)).

Under the Companies Act 1985, it was also necessary to give at least 21 days' notice of the intention to propose a resolution as a special resolution (s. 378(2), 1985 Act), although it was possible to give shorter notice with the consent of members holding not less than 95% of the voting rights. This is no longer a requirement under the 2006 Act. Accordingly, the period of notice given in respect of the resolution will be entirely dependent on the notice requirements for the meeting at which it is to be proposed.

The intention to propose a resolution as a special resolution should be clearly stated in the notice calling the meeting. The notice should also specify either the text or substance of the resolution (*Re Moorgate Mercantile Holdings Ltd*. [1980] 1 All E.R. 40) (see **24.4**).

A copy of every special resolution passed by a company must be filed at Companies House within 15 days of it being passed (ss. 29 and 30) (see **14.8**).

For a table showing items of business which must be passed by members as a special resolution, see **Appendix 2**.

■ 14.5 Extraordinary resolutions

The 2006 Act makes no specific provision for extraordinary resolutions. However, they are preserved by virtue of para. 23 of Sch. 3 to the Third Commencement Order (SI 2007/2194) (as amended by para. 2 of Sch. 5 to the Fifth Commencement Order (SI 2007/3495)). Subsection (1) of para. 23 provides that any reference to an extraordinary resolution in a company's memorandum or articles of association or any contractual provision continues to have effect and shall be construed in accordance with s. 378 of the Companies Act 1985 as if that section had not been repealed. Subsection (2) of para. 23 provides that Chapter 3 of Part 3 (resolutions affecting a company's constitution) of the 2006 Act applies to any such extraordinary resolution. Accordingly, a copy of any such extraordinary resolution must be filed at Companies House.

Companies which adopted articles based on the 1985 Table A before 1 October 2007 are likely to have at least one provision in their articles that requires something to be authorised by extraordinary resolution, unless they have subsequently amended their articles. Up until that point, reg. 117 of Table A required any distribution by a liquidator of surplus assets in kind to be authorised by an extraordinary resolution of the members. For companies incorporated with articles based on Table A on or after 1 October 2007, reg. 117 requires a special resolution.

Section 378 of the 1985 Act provides that a resolution is an extraordinary resolution when it has been passed by a majority of not less than 75% at a general meeting of which notice specifying the intention to propose the resolution as an extraordinary resolution has been duly given.

An extraordinary resolution will be invalid if the notice does not specify the intention to propose it as an extraordinary resolution (*MacConnell v. E Prill & Co Ltd*. [1916] 2 Ch. 57) and if it does not state the text or entire substance of the proposals to be submitted (*Re Moorgate Mercantile Holdings Ltd*. [1980] 1 All E.R. 40).

There are no specific requirements as to the period of notice which must be given for extraordinary resolutions. Accordingly, the period of notice required will be determined by the requirements for the type of meeting at which the resolution is to be proposed.

■ 14.6 Elective resolutions

The elective regime was introduced in 1989 to allow private companies to dispense with the AGM and a number of the associated formalities by passing elective resolutions to that effect. At the time, s. 366 of the Companies Act 1985 required private companies to hold AGMs. With the repeal on 1 October 2007 of this requirement for private companies and most of the associated formalities, most of the dispensations available under the elective regime were also repealed.

The only elective resolution still available to private companies after 1 October 2007 was an election under s. 80A of the 1985 Act to extend the period for which the members could authorise the directors to allot shares under s. 80 of the 1985 Act beyond the usual limit of five years. However, this power was also repealed on 1 October 2009, together with s. 379A of the 1985 Act, by the Eighth Commencement Order (SI 2008/2860).

Under the original elective regime, companies were permitted to:

(a) extend the period for which the members may authorise the directors to allot shares under s. 80 of the 1985 Act beyond the usual limit of five years (s. 80A of the 1985 Act); these two sections were repealed on 1 October 2009 but are subject to certain transitional provision in paras. 43 to 45 of Sch. 2 to Eighth Commencement Order (SI 2008/2860);

(b) dispense with the laying of accounts and reports before the company in general meeting (s. 252 and 253 of the 1985 Act); these two sections were repealed on 1 October 2007, together with the requirement in s. 241 of the 1985 Act to lay accounts in so far as it relates to private companies);

(c) dispense with holding of annual general meetings (s. 366A of the 1985 Act); this section was repealed on 1 October 2007) – para. 2(6) of Sch. 5 to the Fifth Commencement Order (SI 2007/3495) clarifies that a company is not to be treated as one whose articles expressly require it to hold an AGM if, immediately before 1 October 2007, there was in force an elective resolution to dispense with the AGM;

(d) reduce the percentage of shares required to be held by persons agreeing to an extraordinary general meeting being held (or to a resolution being passed as a special resolution) on short notice from 95% of the class down to not less than 90% (s. 369(4) and 378(3) of the 1985 Act); both sections were repealed on 1 October 2007) – if such a resolution was in force immediately before 1 October 2007 any provision of the articles specifying a different percentage may be disregarded unless the provision was adopted on or after that date (see para. 2 of Sch. 3 to the Sixth Commencement Order (SI 2008/674));

(e) the appointment of auditors annually (s. 386 of the 1985 Act); repealed for private companies with effect from 1 October).

The procedural requirements for passing an elective resolution were set out in s. 379A of the Companies Act 1985. This section was repealed by the Eighth Commencement Order with effect from 1 October 2009 and, accordingly, it is no longer possible to pass an elective resolution. Under the now repealed rules, elective resolutions had to be agreed to by all the members entitled to vote.

All elective resolutions could be revoked by an ordinary resolution and automatically ceased to have effect if the company was re-registered as a public company.

Elective resolutions and resolutions revoking such resolutions had to be filed with the registrar of companies (s. 380(4)(bb), 1985 Act). It is still possible that a private company may need to revoke an elective resolution if it is still in force. If this is done, it is suggested that the resolution be filed at Companies House.

14.7 Unanimous consent of members

The unanimous consent of members is required in order for a company to do for the following:

(a) to insert or amend entrenched provisions in a company's articles (s. 22);
(b) to re-register a private limited company as unlimited (s. 102);
(c) to re-register a public limited company as unlimited (s. 109); and
(d) to hold an annual general meeting of a public company at short notice (s. 337).

14.8 Filing of resolutions

The Act requires copies of certain resolutions to be filed with the registrar of companies at Companies House within 15 days of being passed (see **Precedent 14.8A to C**). The resolutions which must be filed include:

(a)   any special resolution (s. 29(1)(a));
(b)   any resolution or agreement agreed to by all the members that, if not so agreed, would not have been effective unless passed as a special resolution (s. 29(1)(b));
(c)   any resolution or agreement agreed to by all the members of a class of shareholders that, if not so agreed to, would not have been effective unless passed by some particular majority or otherwise in some particular manner (s. 29(1)(c));
(d)   any resolution or agreement that effectively binds all the members of a class of shareholders though not agreed to by all those members (s. 29(1)(d));.
(e)   any extraordinary resolution (s. 380(4)(b) of the 1985 Act), including any such resolution passed pursuant to a provision in a company's memorandum

and articles of association or any contractual provision (see para. 23 of Sch. 3 to the Third Commencement Order (SI 2007/2194) as amended by para. 2 of Sch. 5 to the Fifth Commencement Order (SI 2007/3495));

(f) an ordinary resolution under s. 551 giving the directors authority to allot shares (s. 551) – formerly s. 80 of the 1985 Act;

(g) an ordinary resolution under s. 601 authorising the transfer to a public company of a non-cash asset in initial period (s. 602);

(h) an ordinary resolution under s. 622 authorising the redenomination of a company's share capital (s. 622);

(i) a resolution conferring, varying, revoking or renewing authority under s. 701 (market purchase of a company's own shares) (s. 701(8)) – formerly s. 166 of the 1985 Act;

(j) a resolution of the members under para. 10 of Sch. 5 to the 2006 Act (company communication provisions: deemed agreement of members to use of website);

(k) any resolution for voluntary winding up passed under s. 84(1) of the Insolvency Act 1986;

(l) an ordinary resolution amending or revoking the authorised share capital clause in the memorandum of an existing company that is deemed to form part of its articles under s. 28 (para. 42 of Sch. 2 to the Eighth Commencement Order (SI 2008/2860));

(m) an ordinary resolution of an existing or transitional company that the directors should have the powers given by s. 550 of the Companies Act 2006 (power of directors to allot shares etc: private company with only one class of shares) (para. 43 of Sch. 2 to the Eighth Commencement Order (SI 2008/2860)).

The following directors' resolutions must also be filed at Companies House within 15 days of being passed:

(a) a resolution of the directors in compliance with a direction under s. 64 (change of name on Secretary of State's direction) – formerly s. 31(2) of the 1985 Act.

(b) a resolution of the directors of a public company under s. 664 to re-register as a private company to comply with section 662 – formerly s. 147(2) of the 1985 Act;

(c) a resolution passed by the directors of an old public company under s. 2(1) of the Companies Consolidation (Consequential Provisions) Act 1985 that a company should be re-registered as a public company;

(d) a resolution of the directors passed by virtue of reg. 16(2) of the Uncertificated Securities Regulations 2001 allowing title to the company's shares to be evidenced and transferred through CREST;

(e) a resolution of the directors passed by virtue of reg. 16(6) of the Uncertificated Securities Regulations 2001 preventing or reversing a resolution of the directors allowing title to the company's shares to be evidenced and transferred through CREST.

Where no authority is shown in the above lists, the requirement to file the resolution with the registrar can be found in the original section or paragraph which imposes the requirement for the resolution.

14.8.1 Documents to be incorporated in or accompany copies of articles issued by company

Section 36(1) provides that every copy of a company's articles issued by the company must be accompanied by:

(a) a copy of any resolution or agreement relating to the company to which Chapter 3 applies (resolutions and agreements affecting a company's constitution) (see above);
(b) where the company has been required to give notice to the registrar under section 34(2) (notice where company's constitution altered by enactment), a statement that the enactment in question alters the effect of the company's constitution;
(c) where the company's constitution is altered by a special enactment (see s. 34(4)), a copy of the enactment; and
(d) a copy of any order required to be sent to the registrar under s. 35(2)(a) (order of court or other authority altering company's constitution).

The articles do not need to be accompanied by a copy of a document or by a statement if:

(a) the effect of the resolution, agreement, enactment or order (as the case may be) on the company's constitution has been incorporated into the articles by amendment; or
(b) the resolution, agreement, enactment or order (as the case may be) is not for the time being in force (s. 36(2)).

If the company fails to comply with this section, an offence is committed by every officer of the company (including any liquidator) who is in default (s. 36(3) and (5)).

14.8.2 Resolutions and other constitutional documents to be provided to members

Section 32(1) provides that any member may request the company to send him the following documents:

(a) an up-to-date copy of the company's articles;
(b) a copy of any resolution or agreement relating to the company to which Chapter 3 applies (resolutions and agreements affecting a company's constitution) and that is for the time being in force;

(c) a copy of any document required to be sent to the registrar under –
   (i) s. 34(2) (notice where company's constitution altered by enactment); or
   (ii) s. 35(2)(a) (notice where order of court or other authority alters company's constitution);
(d) a copy of any court order under s. 899 (order sanctioning compromise or arrangement) or s. 900 (order facilitating reconstruction or amalgamation);
(e) a copy of any court order under s. 996 (protection of members against unfair prejudice: powers of the court) that alters the company's constitution;
(f) a copy of the company's current certificate of incorporation, and of any past certificates of incorporation;
(g) in the case of a company with a share capital, a current statement of capital;
(h) in the case of a company limited by guarantee, a copy of the statement of guarantee.

If a company fails to comply with such a request, an offence is committed by every officer of the company who is in default for which a fine may be levied (s. 32(3) and (4)). No time limit is imposed for satisfying such a request.

14.8.3 Listed company requirements on resolution
Listed companies must forward to the UKLA (via the National Storage Mechanism) a copy of any resolution passed by the company other than a resolution concerning the 'ordinary business' at an annual general meeting as soon as possible after the relevant meeting (LR 9.6.2). Listed companies must also notify an RIS as soon as possible after a general meeting of all resolutions passed by the company other than resolutions concerning ordinary business passed at the annual general meeting (LR 9.6.18). In practice, listed companies tend to file a copy of all resolutions and announce the results of all resolutions, including those that may only concern the 'ordinary business' because the Listing Rules do not define what is meant by the 'ordinary business'.

■ 14.9 Date a resolution is passed

The date of passing a resolution will be the date of the meeting or, if the resolution was passed at an adjourned meeting, the date of the adjourned meeting (s. 332). Where the business of a meeting is suspended for the purposes of calculating the results of poll conducted at the meeting, the date of the resolution will be the date of the meeting at which the poll was taken. Where the business of a meeting is suspended for the purposes of conducting a poll on a later date, the date of the resolution will be the date of the meeting at which the poll was taken or, if later, the result ascertained.

If a resolution is passed as a written resolution, it is passed on the date that it was agreed to by the last member required to agree to it in order to pass it.

15

Quorum

15.1 Summary

- The quorum is the minimum number of persons entitled to vote who must be present or represented at a meeting in order for it to transact any business. Articles usually specify the quorum for general meetings. In default, the Act provides that the quorum shall be two unless there is only one member, in which case it shall be one (s. 318).
- Corporate representatives are counted in calculating whether a quorum exists. Proxies must also be counted unless the articles provide otherwise. An individual may be counted more than once for the purposes of calculating whether a quorum exists where he or she represents more than one member (see **15.2**).
- However, a meeting cannot normally take place with only one person present (unless he is the only member or the proxy or representative of the only member) even if that person represents sufficient members to form a quorum or, indeed, represents all the other members (see **15.3**).
- Articles usually provide that a general meeting will be automatically adjourned if a quorum is not present within a specified period after the time appointed for the start of the meeting (see **15.4**).
- A quorum must be present throughout the meeting unless the articles provide otherwise (see **15.5**).
- The court may intervene where a member is abusing the quorum requirements to frustrate the will of the majority (see **15.6**).
- Articles may make provision for special quorum requirements in certain circumstances (see **15.7**).
- The Act provides that the quorum at meetings of single member companies shall be one member present in person or by proxy (see **15.8**).
- Special quorum requirements exist for class meetings held to consider a variation of the rights of class members (see **11.3**).

15.2 Who may be counted in the quorum

In the case of a company limited by shares or guarantee and having only one member, one qualifying person present at a general meeting is a quorum (s. 318(1)). For the purposes of s. 318 a 'qualifying person' means:

(a) an individual who is a member of the company;

(b) a person authorised under s. 323 to act as the representative of a corporate member in relation to the meeting; or

(c) a person appointed as proxy of a member in relation to the meeting.

Section 318 provides that, in any other case, subject to the provisions of the company's articles, two qualifying persons present at a meeting are a quorum, unless –

(a) each is a qualifying person only because he is authorised under s. 323 to act as the corporate representative of a corporate member in relation to the meeting and they are corporate representatives of the same member; or

(b) each is a qualifying person only because he is appointed as proxy of a member in relation to the meeting, and they are proxies of the same member.

Accordingly, it would appear that any member, corporate representative or proxy may be counted in the quorum unless a company's articles provide otherwise and that irrespective of anything in a company's articles the quorum at a general meeting of a company which is a private company limited by shares or by guarantee which has only one member shall be one person, who may be the member or a proxy or corporate representative of that member.

All three versions of model articles for companies incorporated under the 2006 Act make no separate provision or the quorum at general meetings and therefore rely totally on this statutory provision. Companies with older articles will usually find that they do make provision regarding the quorum at general meetings, which may or may not override the statutory rules. Clearly, articles cannot override the default statutory quorum rule for a private limited company with only one member. However, they may do so in other cases.

The old common law rule in this area was that to be counted in the quorum members had to be personally present, unless the articles provided otherwise. Corporate representatives were deemed to be members for these purposes and could always be counted (and still should be) unless they are not eligible to vote (*Re Kelantan Coco Nut Estates Ltd.* [1920] W.N. 274). However, members represented by a proxy could not be counted unless the articles allowed. Proxies could not be counted under articles like reg. 53 of 1948 Table A which states:

> 53. No business shall be transacted at any general meeting unless a quorum of members is present at the time when the meeting proceeds to business; save as herein otherwise provided *three members present in person shall be a quorum*.
>
> [The words in italics were substituted by the words 'two members present in person or by proxy shall be a quorum' by the Companies Act 1980, Sch. 3 and these words apply to any company registered on or after 22 December 1980.]

This type of provision would still act as exception to s. 318(2) so far as proxies are concerned.

In contrast, reg. 40 of the 1985 Table A explicitly allows members represented by proxy to be counted in the quorum. It provides:

> 40. No business shall be transacted at any meeting unless a quorum is present. Two persons entitled to vote upon the business to be transacted, each being a member or a proxy for a member or a duly authorised representative of a corporation, shall be a quorum.

It should be noted that reg. 40 of the 1985 Table A makes pretty much the same provision as s. 318(2) but does not specifically exclude proxies or corporate representatives representing the same member. However, it is recommended that where the articles allow members represented by proxy to be counted in calculating whether a quorum exists care should be taken to ensure that:

- proxies are not counted when the member who appointed them is also present; and
- a member represented by more than one proxy is only counted once.

15.2.1 Must the member be entitled to vote?

Under the common law, to be counted in the quorum, a person must first and foremost be eligible to vote (*Young v. South African & Australian Exploration & Development Syndicate* [1896] 2 Ch. 268; cf. *Re Greymouth Point Elizabeth Railway and Coal Co. Ltd.* [1904] 1 Ch. 32). A member may be ineligible to vote for a variety of reasons (see **17.4**). The most obvious is the fact that he may hold only non-voting shares. Another reason could be that there is a call outstanding on all of his shares and that he is prohibited from voting any of those shares under the articles (e.g. reg. 57 of Table A and plc 41). Restrictions on voting are normally applied to shares rather than to the holder. So a person may have a right to vote some but not all of his shares, in which case he may be counted in the quorum. However, this will not always be the case. For example, on a resolution under s. 239 to ratify a breach of conduct by a director, neither the votes of the director (if he is a member) nor any person connected with him may be counted. In this particular instance, the Act specifically provides that this does not prevent the director or the connected person from attending and participating in the meeting or from being counted in the quorum (s. 239(4)). However, the fact that the Act does so, demonstrates that the common law rule is still presumed to apply in other cases.

This means that unless contrary provision is made in the Act or a company's articles, a member who is not entitled to vote at all at the meeting probably cannot be counted in the quorum. And, if this is the case for the member, it must also be true for his proxy or corporate representative.

It should be noted that reg. 40 of the 1985 Table A does not allow anyone who is not entitled to vote to be counted for the purposes of the quorum. A question which may arise under articles like reg. 40 is whether exceptions like the one in s. 239 override the articles or vice versa. Can a director whose breach is being ratified and who is also a member be counted in the quorum or not? The answer to this question depends on whether or not the director is entitled to vote. The Act does not actually say that the director is not entitled to vote. What it actually says is that the directors' votes (as a member) in favour of a ratification resolution must be disregarded in determining whether the resolution is passed. So the director can actually vote and his votes will even be counted if he votes against the ratification of his own breach.

Similar provision is also made by the Act with regard to resolutions connected with an off-market purchase of own shares. For example, a resolution under s. 694 will not be effective if any member holding shares to which the resolution votes in favour of it and the resolution would not have been passed if he had not done so (s. 695). This does not mean that the member cannot vote; he can for example vote against the resolution and help to defeat it. Accordingly, it must be assumed that he can be counted in the quorum.

The biggest danger in this area would not seem to be any statutory restrictions on the right to vote but the possibility of restrictions in the articles, such as those that sometimes apply where calls are unpaid. It does not particularly make sense for such persons to be allowed to be counted in the quorum and they would definitely not be counted under Table A. Assuming that the common law rule still operates as an exception to s. 318, this would also be true under the model articles. It would be strange, for example, in the case of a public company which has adopted the model articles for public companies (which rely on s. 318 for the purposes of the quorum rules) and has proceeded to issue a separate class of non-voting shares if the holders of those non-voting shares could be counted for the purposes of determining whether there is a quorum at a general meeting of the company. The answer to this question does not presumably depend upon the company adopting a quorum article similar to reg. 40 of Table A, although it might be safer for the company to do so.

■ 15.3 More than one person

A quorum may exist even though the actual number of persons present is less than the number specified as the quorum by the articles. This is because a person may represent more than one member. For example, in *McLeod (Neil) & Sons, Petitioners*, 1967 S.C. 16, the quorum specified in the articles was three members personally present. It was held that a quorum was present at a meeting even though there were only two people present at a meeting where one of those members attended in his own capacity and as a trustee.

This rule is subject to the basic common law principle that for a meeting to take place there must be a coming together of at least two people. In *Sharp v. Dawes* [1876] 2 Q.B.D. 26, Mellish L.J. said: 'It is clear that, according to the ordinary use of the English language, a meeting could no more be constituted by one person than a meeting could have been constituted if no shareholder at all had attended.'

Thus, a meeting attended by only one member who held proxies for all the other members was held to be invalidly constituted (*Re Sanitary Carbon Co.* [1877] W.N. 233). Similarly, where a company's articles provided that two or more members present in person or by proxy shall be a quorum, one member present in his own capacity and in his capacity as the first named trustee for two trusts and as proxy for another member did not constitute a valid meeting (*Prain & Sons Ltd., Petitioners*, 1947 S.C. 325).

There are a number of important exceptions to the general rule that a meeting cannot take place without at least two persons.

A private limited company which has only one member may, notwithstanding any provision to the contrary in the articles, hold meetings with a quorum of one by virtue of s. 318(1).

The court may call or direct the calling of a general meeting and direct that one member present in person or by proxy shall be deemed to be a quorum (s. 306).

It has been held in relation to class meetings, that a single person may constitute a meeting where that person holds all the issued shares of a particular class (*East v. Bennett Bro. Ltd.* [1911] 1 Ch. 163). This principle does not apply where all the shares in a public company fall into the hands of a single member. In these circumstances the correct procedure would be for the member to transfer at least one share into the name of another person (normally a nominee) so that a meeting may be held. If this is not possible, an application should be made to the court under s. 306 for an order that a meeting may be held with a quorum of one.

■ 15.4 Failure to obtain a quorum

By its very nature any rule as to the quorum required at a meeting is one which requires a certain number of people to participate in a meeting in order for it to transact any business. Accordingly, as a general principle, a meeting obviously cannot transact any business if the quorum requirements are not satisfied. This may mean that the meeting can never start because a quorum is never obtained. It may also mean that there is a quorum for some items of business but not for others or that there was a quorum at the start of the meeting but that the quorum was not maintained. One of the first problems is what happens if there are not sufficient people to form a quorum at time appointed for the start of the meeting? How long do we have to wait to see whether a quorum is obtained? And what happens if it is not? Is the meeting automatically dissolved or can it be assumed to have been adjourned? These are questions that are normally, but not always, answered in a company's articles.

Articles normally provide for a general meeting to be adjourned (either automatically or by the chairman or the directors) if a quorum is not present at the appointed time of the meeting or within a short period thereafter. For example, the model articles provide that if the persons attending a general meeting within half an hour of the time at which the meeting was due to start do not constitute a quorum, *the chairman of the meeting must adjourn it* (pcls 41, clg 27 and plc 33). In doing so, the chairman must adjourn it to another date, time or place or to a date, time and place to be specified by the directors (see pcls 41(4), clg 27(4) and plc 33(4)). If the chairman appointed by the directors is not actually present, the members present may still elect a chairman even though there is not a quorum (see pcls 38, clg 24 and plc 30). The person elected may then decide whether to adjourn the meeting to another date, time and place or whether to allow the directors to do so. Under this regime, it is not particularly clear what happens if nobody turns up at all, or if the chairman fails to adjourn the meeting despite the blandishments of the model articles, or if nobody who turns up has power to adjourn the meeting because they were not appointed or elected as chairman of it. It is obviously best not to allow this to happen. However, if it does, it is possible that in any of these circumstances the meeting could be deemed to have been either dissolved or, perhaps, adjourned indefinitely to a date, time and place to be determined by the directors. It is not easy to say which although in either case it would be best to assume that notice of a new meeting will be required. If anybody actually turns up and purports to adjourn the meeting in the absence of the chairman, the courts could deem that person to have been elected as chairman even if they were not formally appointed or elected as such, particularly where they were the only one present, as would normally have to be the case for there to be a failure to obtain a quorum which is fixed at two.

Reg. 41 of the 1985 Table A provides that if a quorum is not present within half an hour from the time appointed for the meeting, the meeting shall stand adjourned to the same day in the next week at the same time and place or such time and place as the directors may determine. It can be seen that under Table A, a meeting will never be dissolved if nobody turns up. Instead it will simply be adjourned to the same time and place in the following week unless and until enough members turn up to start transacting the business or the directors decide that the meeting should be adjourned to another time and place. This leads one to wonder just how many company meetings are actually taking place every week without anyone knowing because they are constantly being adjourned from week to week under articles similar to Table A.

Under articles similar to the model articles and Table A, the quorum required for the transaction of business at the adjourned meeting will be the same as for the original meeting. However, it is not unusual for this rule to be modified so as to provide that if at the adjourned meeting a quorum is not present within a certain time, 'the members present shall be a quorum' (see example at **Precedent 23.4**). Thus the normal requirement of, say, eight members present in person or by proxy would be reduced to at least two. If the articles allow proxies to be included, it would seem that the words 'members present' would allow them to be included for this purpose. However, the principle in *Sharp v. Dawes* would probably prevent a meeting of one person being allowed in such circumstances even if that person held proxies for other members (see *Daimler Co. Ltd. v. Continental Tyre & Rubber Co (Great Britain) Ltd.* [1916] 2 A.C. 307).

It is also fairly common for articles to provide that a meeting convened on the requisition of members shall be dissolved if a quorum is not present within the allotted time (see example at **Precedent 15.4**). Where such provision is made, the directors would be well-advised to ensure that a quorum is present if they have taken the opportunity to propose resolutions at the meeting.

If it is impracticable or impossible to hold a meeting with a quorum in accordance with the articles, application can be made to the court under s. 306 for an order calling a meeting to be held with some other quorum (*Re Edinburgh Workmen's Houses Improvement Co. Ltd.* 1934 S. L.T. 513) (see **12.4**).

■ 15.5 Failure to maintain a quorum

For companies with articles similar to reg. 40 of the 1985 Act Table A, which provides that no business shall be transacted unless a quorum is present, a quorum must be present for each item of business throughout the meeting. This should be assumed to be the default position under the common law even in the absence of any direct provision in the articles. Although it is technically possible for a general meeting to be quorate for one item of business but not for another even though the same number of people are present from start to finish, articles tend to assume that it is fatal if a quorum should ever cease to exist and tend to invoke automatic adjournment rules if and when this happens at a general meeting.

For example, the model articles provide that 'if during a meeting a quorum ceases to be present, the chairman must adjourn it' (pcls 39, clg 27 and plc 33). Regulation 41 of the 1985 Table A provides that if during a meeting a quorum ceases to be present, the meeting shall stand adjourned to the same day in the next week at the same time and place or such time and place as the directors may determine.

Under both of these versions, it would appear that the meeting must be adjourned if a quorum ever ceases to exist because certain members cannot be counted in the quorum for a particular item of business. However, it is submitted that this is not the case. There would still be a quorum present at the meeting but simply not a quorum for that particular item of business. Accordingly, the meeting could proceed to transact the business for which it was quorate but would be unable to make a binding decision on the resolution for which it was not quorate.

Articles such as reg. 41 of Table A are designed to cater for the possibility that people may leave the meeting after it starts leaving it unable to transact any business. Strictly speaking, under reg. 41, a meeting will be adjourned automatically if sufficient members leave the meeting and the number remaining is not sufficient to form a quorum, even if those who have left actually return shortly thereafter. Where the number of members present is only just sufficient to form a quorum, the chairman should ask members not to leave the meeting without informing him that they are about to leave. This would allow him to propose a formal motion to adjourn the meeting to a time and place which is agreeable to the members before the member leaves and forces the meeting to be adjourned automatically.

In an attempt to avoid this problem altogether, articles sometimes provide that a quorum need only be present 'at the time when the meeting proceeds to business' (e.g. reg. 53 of 1948 Act Table A). If so, the meeting may continue to transact business even though the quorum is not subsequently maintained (*Re Hartley Baird* [1955] Ch. 143) provided that the number of persons present does not fall below two, in which case the *Sharp v. Dawes* principle applies (*Re London Flats Ltd.* [1969] 1 W.L.R. 711). This type of article also prevents a dissenting minority obstructing the transaction of business by absenting themselves from the meeting once they realise things are not going their way. It would obviously serve little purpose to have such an article unless the quorum is higher than two.

15.6 Abuse of quorum requirements

If a minority shareholder attempts to frustrate the will of the majority by refusing to attend a meeting and thereby preventing the formation of a quorum, the court may order the holding of a meeting under s. 306 (see further **12.4**) and direct that the quorum for that meeting shall be less than the number normally required (*Re El Sombrero Ltd.* [1958] Ch. 900 and *Re H. R. Paul & Son Ltd.* (1973) 118 S. J. 166). The court will only do so where the quorum is a fixed number of shareholders and the minority shareholder's ability to prevent the holding of meetings is merely a consequence of the number of shareholders there are at that time. It will not do so where the articles specifically provide that a meeting shall not be quorate without the presence of that shareholder (see below).

15.7 Special quorum requirements

The quorum requirements can be used to protect the interests of certain shareholders. The articles or a shareholders' agreement may provide that a quorum shall not exist unless a particular member or the holder of particular class of shares is present. These special requirements can be restricted to certain types of business, e.g. the appointment and removal of directors. Such provisions will usually be framed so that they attach special rights to a certain class of shares. The courts have held that where they apply to a named shareholder, that shareholder will be treated as having class rights which may not be modified unless the proper procedures for variation are followed. The Court of Appeal has also held that, where the articles or a shareholder agreement create class rights by requiring the presence of the holder of a certain class of share for meetings to be quorate, it would not be right for the court, on an application under s. 371 of the 1985 Act (the equivalent of the existing provision in s. 306 of the 2006 Act), to order that a meeting be held with some other quorum requirement (*Harman v. BML Group Ltd.* [1994] 1W.L.R. 893). Dillon LJ said: '. . . it is not right, in my view, to invoke s. 371 to override class rights attached to a class of shares which have been deliberately – in this case by the shareholders' agreement – imposed for the protection of the holders of those shares.'

An article which requires all the members entitled to vote to be present in person or by proxy in order to form a quorum (irrespective of the number of members there is at any particular time) may offer similar protection. However, such an article would not normally be advisable except for companies with very few members.

15.8 Single member companies

The Act provides that, notwithstanding anything to the contrary in the articles of a private company limited by shares or guarantee having only one member, one member present in person or represented by a proxy or corporate representative shall be a quorum at general meetings of the company (s. 318(1)).

16

Proxies and corporate representatives

■ 16.1 Summary

- The right to vote at general meetings enables members to influence or control the company. In order to maintain the balance of power, it is essential that members have the right to exercise their votes even though they are not able to attend the meeting in person.

- A company which is a member of another company clearly cannot attend and vote in person, and has the option of either appointing a proxy or corporate representative to do so on its behalf. Although not exactly the same, the rights of proxies and corporate representatives are very similar. The main difference is that the appointment of a corporate representative does not need to be notified in advance (see **16.2**).

- The Act prescribes the method of appointment, although articles may allow appointments to be made in other ways (see **16.3**).

- A corporate representative is entitled to exercise the same powers on behalf of the corporation as the corporation could exercise if it was an individual member of the company (see **16.4**).

- There used to be some debate as to whether a company may appoint more than one corporate representative. The 2006 Act has clarified that this is possible but did not initially make it any clearer what the effect of doing so might be. Accordingly companies adopted special procedures to deal with situations where a corporate shareholder had appointed multiple representatives. Amendments to the Act which came into force in August 2009 may make these procedures redundant (see **16.5**).

- The Act gives members a statutory right to appoint a proxy (see **16.6**). Proxies have certain rights that cannot be excluded by a company's articles. The articles may, however, extend those rights (see **16.7**).

- The notice of every general meeting must include a statement explaining to members their right to appoint a proxy (see **16.8**).

- The directors may send members proxy forms at the company's expense. However, they may not invite selected members to appoint a specific person as their proxy (see **16.9**).

- The methods which may be used to appoint proxies are governed by the Company Communications Provisions of the Act and a company's articles (see **16.10**).
- A company can allow members to make appointments electronically (see **16.11**).
- The default method of appointment is in writing (or hard copy form) (see **16.12**).
- Listed companies are required to send shareholders a proxy form which allows them to instruct their proxy how to vote. The proxy form must also allow members to instruct their proxy to withhold their vote on any resolution (see **16.13**).
- Articles usually require proxy forms to be delivered at least 48 hours before the time appointed for the meeting (see **16.14**).
- A proxy deposited in time for the original meeting will also be valid for any adjournment of that meeting. However, the articles may also allow proxies to be submitted between the original meeting and the adjourned meeting (see **16.15**).
- Articles also usually make special provision for the deposit of proxies in connection with a poll not taken at the meeting (see **16.16**).
- A member may revoke the appointment of a proxy. Articles normally require notice of revocation to be given to the company. However, a member may revoke the appointment of a proxy without giving notice by attending and voting in person at the meeting (see **16.17**).
- A member may change his or her voting instructions at any time before the vote is taken (see **16.18**).
- Articles usually make special provision with regard to the validity of proxies appointed by joint shareholders (see **16.19**) and proxies appointed by members who subsequently die or suffer from some mental disorder (see **16.17.1**).
- Proxies have a statutory obligation to vote in accordance with any voting instructions. However, a proxy cannot be forced to attend or vote on behalf of his or her appointer unless there is a contractual relationship between the parties or the proxy has a fiduciary duty to do so. The chairman has an obligation to vote in accordance with the instructions of members who have appointed him and to demand a poll where he holds proxy votes which would have changed the outcome of any vote on a show of hands (see **16.20**).
- The chairman is usually given authority under most articles to rule on the validity of proxy votes. Proxy forms may still be required as evidence in certain circumstances (see **16.21**).
- Some companies take special powers in their articles to destroy proxy forms a year after the meeting. Appointments made under those forms may still be valid unless some limit is placed on their period of validity (see **16.22**).

■ 16.2 Corporate representatives

A company which is a member of another company clearly cannot attend and vote in person at general meetings. In order to place them on the same footing as individual members, a corporation which is a member of another company is allowed to appoint one or more persons to act as its representative(s) at any meeting of the company (s. 323). This right is also extended to class meetings by virtue of ss. 334 and 335. A person so appointed by a company is usually known as a corporate representative.

The right to appoint a corporate representative is extended by s. 323 to any corporation that is a member of a UK company. For these purposes, a corporation includes any corporate body (whether or not a company within the meaning of the Companies Act 2006) which has separate legal personality. This includes overseas companies, but does not include a corporation sole or a partnership that, whether or not a legal person, is not regarded as a body corporate under the law by which it is governed (s. 1173).

■ 16.3 Appointment of corporate representatives

A corporation may appoint a person as its corporate representative by a resolution of its board of directors or other governing body (s. 323(1)). For these purposes the words 'other governing body' can include a liquidator (*Hillman v. Crystal Bowl Amusements and Others* [1973] 1 W.L.R. 162, C.A.).

As far as the Act and most articles are concerned, there is no requirement for a corporation to deposit a form of appointment prior to the meeting. The articles of listed companies normally specify that a corporate representative may be required by the company to produce evidence of his authority on admission or at any time during the meeting or in connection with the exercise of any right to vote on a poll (see **Precedent 16.3A**). Even though a company's articles may not make specific provision in this regard, a company can and should take steps to ensure that those who attend and vote are eligible to do so. For individual shareholders and creditors, proof of identity will be sufficient for these purposes. Clearly this will not be enough in the case of a corporate representative who must, in addition, be required to provide evidence of their authority, otherwise it would be possible for anyone to turn up off the street and claim to be a corporate representative.

Evidence of appointment should be produced by the representative on entering the meeting, unless it has previously been lodged. As it would appear that a resolution of the board of directors or other governing body is required, the evidence could be provided in the form of a certified copy of the relevant resolution. The resolution can be authenticated (certified) by any director, secretary or other authorised officer of the company. However, it is not uncommon for appointments to be made under seal. In these circumstances, it can probably be assumed that the appointment was properly authorised even though no evidence of a resolution of the directors has been provided (presumably on the basis that articles commonly require the board to authorise the use of the seal).

The appointment of a representative may relate to a specific meeting or, as is commonly the case, may be of more general application (see **Precedent 16.3B**).

ICSA's *Guidance on Proxies and Corporate Representatives at General Meetings* suggests that, in practice, registrars will accept a letter certifying the appointment provided it was an original, on the registered member's stationery and signed by an authorised signatory. It further suggests that, for the sake of clarity, such a letter would be expected to state the name of the registered shareholder as it appears on the share register. It should also give the designation (if any) of the shareholder's account, confirm the name of the appointee, state the date that the board resolution was passed and the number of shares to be voted if less than the total holding (see **Precedent 16.3C**).

16.3.1 Who may be appointed

A person appointed as a corporate representative need not be a member of the company. One might have thought, however, that the Act would require the person appointed to be an individual rather than another company, but this is not the case. The Act allows any 'person' to be appointed, which includes another company, although any such company will no more be able to attend meetings than the original corporate member. The fact that it does so may require a more liberal interpretation of the powers of a corporate representative because the only way a corporate representative that is a company could exercise the powers of the member would be if it was itself able to appoint individuals as representatives to act on its behalf, possibly as proxies or corporate representatives. If this is not the case, the appointment of another company as a corporate representative would be totally ineffective.

16.4 Rights of corporate representatives

Under s. 323(1), a corporate member may authorise a person to act as its corporate representative 'at any meeting of the company'. Where the corporate member authorises only one person as its corporate representative, that person is entitled to exercise the same powers on behalf of the corporate member as the corporate member could exercise if it were an individual member of the company (s. 323(2)). This is also generally the case where more than one representative is appointed, although the rule is subject to certain modifications (see **16.5**).

It should be noted that the powers that the corporate representative may exercise under the Act are not the general powers of the member but the powers that the member could exercise 'at any meeting of the company' if it were an individual member of the company.

There is no doubt whatsoever that these powers include the power to attend, speak, propose resolutions (including procedural resolutions and amendments to resolutions), chair the meeting, vote on a show of hands or on a poll and to join in a demand for a poll. These are all things that can be done at the meeting.

It has also been held that a corporate representative must be counted as a member for the purposes of calculating whether there is a quorum (*Re Kelantan Coco Nut Estates Ltd.* [1920] W.N. 274).

It is rather less clear whether a corporate representative can exercise powers that are incidental to the meeting, such as the right to appoint a proxy or, if the corporate representative appointed by the member is itself a company, appoint a corporate representative. The appointment of a proxy or corporate representative is normally something which a member must do before the meeting rather than 'at the meeting'.

This issue was addressed by ICSA as long ago as 1964 with regard to s. 139 of the Companies Act 1948, a provision equivalent to s. 323 of the 2006 Act. The advice given then in the Institute's journal, *The Chartered Secretary*, in December 1964 was that: 'A representative appointed under section 139 is not empowered, without express authority from the appointing corporation, to appoint a proxy to attend a meeting of the a company of which the corporation is a member.'

This may still be true on a literal reading of the 2006 Act. However, it is submitted that it would be dangerous for a company to treat any such appointment as void on these grounds alone as the words 'at any meeting of the company' in s. 323(1) could easily be interpreted by the courts to include things that are incidental to the meeting. Unless such an interpretation was applied, it would be impossible for a company appointed by a corporate member as its representative to exercise the member's rights at all. As a company, the representative would be unable to attend, vote or speak at the meeting itself. So the only way to give effect to the appointment would be to allow the representative to appoint a proxy or corporate representative.

In view of the uncertainty in this area, it would be preferable for the corporate member to confer express authority on its corporate representative in this regard. This is sometimes done by granting a power of attorney to the corporate representative. Unless something like this is done, the corporate representative may find it difficult to satisfy a request from the company holding the meeting for evidence of authority, particularly in relation to the appointment of a proxy, where articles tend to be more specific. If the corporate representative is unable to provide such evidence, the company could argue that the corporate member ought to take steps itself to appoint a proxy or a different corporate representative. Assuming that there is still time to do so, this could be viewed as a sensible course of action on the part of the company. If there is not, the company chairman might need to be asked to make a ruling on the validity of the appointment (and any votes cast under it).

■ 16.5 Multiple corporate representatives

The 2006 Act was drafted with the deliberate intention of enabling the appointment of multiple corporate representatives. This is something that was not thought possible under the Companies Act 1985. By allowing, multiple appointments, the 2006 Act ensures, for example, that a nominee company holding shares for a number of underlying investors can appoint a different person to represent each underlying holding if so desired. Unfortunately, the original provisions of the Act regarding the rights of multiple representatives caused considerable confusion and had to be amended.

16.5.1 Rights of multiple corporate representatives

This paragraph sets out the rights of multiple corporate representatives under the Act (as amended by the Companies (Shareholders' Rights) Regulations 2009 (SI 2009/1632) with effect from 1 August 2009. The original provisions of the Act and the procedures which companies and investors subsequently adopted to deal with the confusion caused by them (i.e. the appointment of a 'designated corporate representative') are explained in **16.5.2**.

A person authorised by a corporation is entitled to exercise (on behalf of the corporation) the same powers as the corporation could exercise if it were an individual member of the company (s. 323(2)). This rule generally applies where the corporation has appointed one or more representatives but is subject to the following modifications where more than one representative is appointed.

The first modification is that, on a vote taken on a show of hands, each authorised person has the same voting rights as the corporation would be entitled to (s. 323(3)). Thus, if the corporate member would have been entitled to vote on a show of hands, so will each its corporate representatives, with each one having the same number of votes as the corporate member (i.e. normally one each). If the corporate member would not have been entitled to vote on a show of hands, neither will any of its corporate representatives.

The second modification is that, in any case other than a vote on a show of hands, where more than one corporate representative for the same member purports to exercise a power under s. 323(2) in respect of the same shares, that power is treated as exercised if they purport to exercise it in the same way as each other but not if they purport to exercise the power in different ways to each other (s. 323(4)).

It is important to recognise that a power will only be treated as not exercised if the representatives exercise it in different ways over the same shares. If a corporate member appoints multiple representatives but each one represents a different block of shares, they may each validly exercise their powers in different ways. However, if any of them represent the same holding, and more than one of them attempts to exercise any of the members' powers, they must exercise those powers in the same way. It should be noted that in these circumstances it is not necessary for them to exercise the member's powers jointly. Any one of them may validly exercise the member's powers as long as the others do not attempt to exercise those powers in a different way.

16.5.2 Designated corporate representative

It should be noted that s. 323 was amended on 1 August 2009 by the Companies (Shareholders' Rights) Regulations 2009 (SI 2009/1632) and did not originally clarify that each representative has a vote on a show of hands or that any other powers which multiple corporate representatives purported to exercise in different ways would only be invalid if they were exercised over the same shares.

The original wording of s. 323 caused concern among institutional shareholders as it was thought that the possibility of multiple representatives' votes being treated as void could prevent the practice of treating designated accounts as separate shareholders for the purposes of voting and prevent different corporate representatives being appointed to represent a different part of a pooled account.

In order to avoid the uncertainties originally caused by s. 323(4), ICSA recommended in its *Guidance on Proxies and Corporate Representatives at General Meetings* that shareholders who wish to appoint multiple representatives should do so as proxies rather than corporate representatives. It noted that, under the 2006 Act, shareholders may appoint multiple proxies, each of whom may now speak and vote on a show of hands (as well as on a poll) at meetings and that the only advantage provided by the appointment of a corporate representative is that they may register at the meeting itself and do not need to be notified in advance.

However, the ICSA guidance also set out a process involving the appointment of a designated corporate representative (DCR), which it recommended should be used where it was necessary for multiple corporate representatives to be appointed (e.g. where the proxy deadline has been missed). This process is explained below. However, it should be noted that companies and investors may no longer feel it is necessary to follow these procedures following the amendments to the Act in 2009.

The method recommended by ICSA for dealing with multiple corporate representatives (referred to as the DCR method) involved one corporate representative acting as the designated corporate representative (DCR) on a poll. All of the other corporate representatives gave voting directions to the DCR by completing a voting directions card ('directions card') and only the DCR completed a poll card. When the DCR submitted his poll card, the voting directions of all of the other corporate representatives were given effect as votes cast (or withheld) by him on behalf of the underlying corporate member.

■ 16.6 Statutory right to appoint a proxy

A proxy is a person appointed by a member of a company, to attend, speak and vote on his behalf at a meeting of the company (including any adjournment thereof) but for no other purpose. Section 324(1) of the 2006 Act extends the right to appoint a proxy to all members (whether individuals or corporate members) of any type of company (including companies limited by guarantee). Sections 334 and 335 extend the right to appoint a proxy or proxies to class meetings.

Under the Companies Act 1985, only members of a company with a share capital were given a statutory right to appoint a proxy, although there was nothing in the Act to prevent the articles of a company limited by guarantee from giving members the right to do so, which they commonly did. However, the introduction of a statutory right to appoint a proxy on the part of members of guarantee companies may require those guarantee companies whose articles did not already confer that right to make provision in their articles regarding matters such as the method and timing of proxy appointments.

Under the Act, a member of a company limited by guarantee is only given the right to appoint one person as his proxy, whereas a member of a company with a share capital is given the right to appoint more than one, provided that each proxy is appointed to exercise the rights attached to different shares held by that member (s. 324(2)). It is not necessary in either case for a proxy to be a member of the company and a company's articles may not require a member to be appointed. The ability to appoint someone who is not a member is important as it ensures that a member can find someone who is willing to act. This would not necessarily be the case if the articles required only other members to be appointed.

The right of a member of a private company with a share capital to appoint more than one proxy represents a change to the position under the 1985 Act which only conferred on them a right to appoint a single proxy (s. 372(2)(b), 1985 Act). It should be noted, however, that the articles of private companies commonly allowed members to appoint more than one proxy (e.g. reg. 59 of Table A).

There is no common law right to vote by proxy (*Harben v. Phillips* (1883) 23 Ch.D. 14). The ability to do so is therefore governed entirely by the Act and by a company's articles.

The word 'proxy' is commonly used to describe the person appointed by a member, the form for the appointment sent to members and the votes held by a proxy (e.g. the chairman of the meeting). Only the first of these is strictly correct. A proxy is a person appointed by a member to attend and vote on his or her behalf. To avoid confusion, the instrument of appointment can be referred to as the 'proxy form' and votes cast by a proxy as 'proxy votes'.

■ 16.7 Rights of proxies

Proxies have a statutory right to attend, speak and vote on behalf of the members who appointed them (s. 324). The right to attend will, however, be subject to the usual rules on ejection in cases of severe disorder.

Under the 1985 Act, only a proxy appointed by a member of a private company was given the right to speak at the meeting. It made no such provision regarding proxies appointed by members of a public company. However, the articles of public companies sometimes gave proxies that right at the discretion of the chairman. Such articles have now been superseded by the 2006 Act, which gives the proxies of members of public companies a right to speak, although that right will be subject to all the usual limitations that would apply to a member.

Proxies must attend the meeting in person in order to vote unless provision is made in the articles to allow them to vote in advance (see s. 322A) (see **17.10**). Proxies appointed to attend and vote at the original meeting have a right to attend and vote at any adjournment of that meeting unless the articles provide otherwise (*Scadding v. Lorrant* (1851) 3 H.L.C. 418.), e.g. they require members to submit a new instrument of proxy for any adjourned meeting. It makes no difference in this regard whether the articles allow members to appoint proxies between the date of the original meeting and the adjourned meeting. In this case, instruments of proxy deposited for the original meeting and those deposited in accordance with the articles for the adjourned meeting will both be valid (see further **16.15**).

A proxy may be elected to be the chairman of a general meeting by a resolution of the company passed at the meeting (s. 328(1)). This rule is subject to any provision of the company's articles that states who may or who may not be chairman (s. 328(2)). See also *Re Bradford Investments plc* [1990] B.C.C. 740.

16.7.1 Right to vote on a show of hands

Historically, proxies were entitled to vote on a poll but not on a show of hands. The restriction on voting on a show of hands was normally imposed by a company's articles and not by anything in the Companies Acts. The default position under the 2006 Act is that proxies have a statutory right to vote on a show of hands but that this right is subject to any provision of the company's articles. Section 285(1) provides that on a vote on a resolution on a show of hands at a meeting, every proxy present who has been duly appointed by one or more members entitled to vote on the resolution has one vote. However, a person who has been appointed as a proxy for more than one member entitled to vote on the resolution and who has been instructed by one or more of those members to vote for the resolution and by one or more other of those members to vote against it, is allowed to vote on a show of hands both for and against the resolution (s. 285(2)). As noted above, however, these statutory rules are subject to anything to the contrary in a company's articles. In other words, a company's articles could exclude a proxy's right to vote on a show of hands. Most modern articles (including the model articles prescribed under the 2006 Act) do not do so. However, the position may not be totally clear under some older articles (see further **16.6**).

16.7.2 Proxies' rights on a poll

All proxies may demand or join in a demand for a poll (s. 329). On a poll, a member who is entitled to more than one vote need not use all his votes or cast all the votes he uses (whether in person or by proxy) in the same way (s. 322). There is nothing to prevent a person acting as the proxy for more than one member.

On a poll taken at a meeting of a company all or any of the voting rights of a member may be exercised by one or more duly appointed proxies (s. 285(3)). However, where a member appoints more than one proxy, this does not authorise the exercise by the proxies taken together of more extensive voting rights than could be exercised by the member in person (s. 285(4)). See further **16.16** regarding voting on a poll.

■ 16.8 Statement in the notice of the meeting

A statement must be included with reasonable prominence in the notice of every meeting of a company which informs the members of their statutory right to appoint a proxy (or proxies) under s. 324 and of any other more extensive rights conferred by the company's articles to appoint more than one proxy (s. 325). The statement is usually positioned at the end of the notice (see **Precedent 13.8**). The statement must either be omitted or modified in any version of the notice sent by a listed company to anyone nominated as an indirect investor (see **13.9.2**).

■ 16.9 Invitations to appoint a proxy

The Act does not require companies to send proxy forms to members, although listed companies are required to do so under the Listing Rules (see **16.13**). Notices of meetings convened by the court are normally required by the court to be accompanied by proxy forms. A company's articles could also require proxy forms to be circulated with the notice of any meeting, although this is very rare.

Any company may, however, issue proxy forms to members at the company's expense. Generally, any expenses incurred in good faith in the best interests of the company to secure votes in support of the directors' policy are payable out of the funds of the company. Thus, the directors may send proxy forms made out in their own names to shareholders accompanied by a stamped addressed envelope to encourage a greater response (*Peel v. London & North West Ry. Co.* [1907] 1 Ch. 5).

Invitations to appoint a person (e.g. the chairman) or one of a number of persons may only be issued at the company's expense if they are sent to all the members entitled to receive notice of the meeting (s. 326(1)). For the purposes of s. 326(1), an invitation will include any proxy form with the name of a person already inserted as the proxy or any document, circular or letter inviting members to appoint a particular person or persons as their proxy. An officer of the company who knowingly or wilfully permits the issue of invitations to selected members is liable to a fine. This does not prevent a company from issuing to a member at his request a form of appointment naming the proxy or a list of persons willing to act as proxy provided that form or list is freely available on request to all other members entitled to vote at the meeting (s. 326(2)).

It should be noted that s. 326 does not prevent anyone (including the directors) from soliciting proxies at their own expense.

16.9.1 Invitations by traded companies

A traded company (see definition at **8.5.1**) must provide an electronic address for the receipt of any document or information relating to proxies for a general meeting (s. 333A) and must do so either:

- by giving it when sending out an instrument of proxy for the purposes of the meeting or issuing an invitation to appoint a proxy for those purposes; or
- by ensuring that it is made available, throughout the period beginning with the first date on which notice of the meeting is given and ending with the conclusion of the meeting, on the website on which the information required by s. 311A(1) is made available.

■ 16.10 Appointment of a proxy

The relationship between a member and his proxy is one of principal and agent. In the normal course of events, an agent can be appointed either in writing or orally or by any other legal method, including the use of electronic communications. Although a person may validly appoint an agent without notifying anyone of the appointment, third parties usually demand to see evidence of the agent's authority to ensure that the principal will be bound by the acts of his purported agent. Companies usually require members to notify proxy appointments well in advance of the meeting so that they can check the validity of the appointment, but also so that they know in advance who must be admitted to the meeting and who may be excluded. If prior notification were not required, the company would have to try to check the validity of appointments at the meeting.

In the normal course of events, proxy forms provide evidence that any poll called at a meeting was properly conducted and that the votes cast by proxies on behalf of members were valid. They could, however, be used by someone seeking to challenge the result to show that some fraud had been committed (e.g. that their signature had been forged). Whether this would have any effect on the outcome of the meeting will depend partly on whether the company's articles give the chairman power to rule on the validity of votes cast at the meeting (see **16.21**). However, the courts would be unlikely to allow a company to rely on such an article where the company (or the chairman) was a party to the fraud.

16.10.1 Form and method of appointment

The Act does not generally dictate how proxies must be appointed except for traded companies, where s. 327(A1) specifies that appointments must be made 'in writing', which in the context of the Act means in hard copy or electronic form, as opposed to, say, orally. The Act does, however, impose certain restrictions on provisions which may be contained in a company's articles regarding how far in advance of the meeting any notice of appointment or revocation must be lodged with the company and does provide that, in certain circumstances, a company will be deemed to have agreed to accept electronic appointments.

Modern articles usually require appointments to be made in writing or electronically. Older articles may specify that appointments must be made in writing. Even where this is the case, a company may allow appointments to be made electronically by virtue of the company communications provisions and s. 333 of the 2006 Act which together have the effect of overriding any such barrier in the articles regarding electronic appointments where the directors have indicated in documents such as notices or proxy forms relating to the meeting that appointments may be made electronically. The company communications provisions apply to documents or information required or authorised to be sent or supplied by or to a company under the Companies Acts (see s. 1143). Members are entitled under the Act to appoint proxies, and companies are entitled under the Act to require evidence of appointment. Accordingly it is arguable that completed proxy forms are documents which are, at the very least, authorised under the Act to be sent to a company. If this is the case, Schs. 4 and 5 of the Act apply which allow documents or information to be sent or supplied to the company in electronic form if the company has agreed (generally or specifically) that it may be sent in that form (and has not revoked that agreement) or is deemed to have so agreed by virtue of a provision of the Companies Acts.

Section 333(1) provides that, where a company has given an electronic address in a notice calling a meeting, it is deemed to have agreed that any document or information relating to proceedings at the meeting may be sent by electronic means to that address (subject to any conditions or limitations specified in the notice).

In addition, s. 333(2) provides that, where a company has given an electronic address in an instrument of proxy sent out by the company or in an invitation to appoint a proxy issued by the company in relation to the meeting, it is deemed to have agreed that any document or information relating to proxies for that meeting may be sent by electronic means to that address (subject to any conditions or limitations specified in the notice). Section 333(3) clarifies that the documents relating to proxies that may be sent by electronic means in these circumstances include:

(a) the appointment of a proxy in relation to a meeting;
(b) any document necessary to show the validity of, or otherwise relating to, the appointment of a proxy; and
(c) notice of the termination of the authority of a proxy.

Section 333(4) clarifies that for the purposes of s. 333 'electronic address' means any address or number used for the purposes of sending or receiving documents or information by electronic means.

16.10.2 Traded companies must allow electronic appointments

If a traded company (see **8.5.1**) does not offer the facility to vote by electronic means to all members who hold shares that carry rights to vote at general meetings, it must give 21 days' notice of all meetings (s. 307A). This condition is met if there is a facility, offered by the company and accessible to all such members, to appoint a proxy by means of a website (s. 307A(2)).

A traded company is, in any case, required by s. 333A(1) to provide an electronic address for the receipt of any document or information relating to proxies for a general meeting and must do so either:

- by giving the address when sending out an instrument of proxy for the purposes of the meeting or issuing an invitation to appoint a proxy for those purposes; or
- by ensuring that it is made available, throughout the period beginning with the first date on which notice of the meeting is given and ending with the conclusion of the meeting, on the website on which the information required by s. 311A(1) is made available (s. 33A(2)).

In either case, the company is deemed to have agreed that any document or information relating to proxies for the meeting may be sent by electronic means to the address provided (subject to any limitations specified by the company when providing the address) (s. 333A(3)).

For the purposes of s. 333A, the terms 'documents relating to proxies' and 'electronic address' have the same meaning as they do for s. 333 (see above).

Subject to any limitations specified by the company, it would seem that compliance with s. 333A will almost certainly result in compliance with the condition in s. 307A regarding electronic proxy appointments which must be satisfied for a traded company to hold general meetings at less than 21 days' notice.

16.10.3 Other general rules regarding appointments

It is not necessary for a named person to be nominated as proxy as long as the person appointed is capable of being identified (*Bombay Burmah Trading Corporation Ltd. v. Dorabji Cursetji Shroff* [1905] A.C. 213). Members may, for example, nominate 'the chairman of the meeting' as their proxy.

Articles usually allow the appointment of a proxy to be executed on behalf of a member. In these circumstances, they normally require the authority under which the person executed the instrument of appointment (e.g. a power of attorney) or a copy of it to be deposited by the deadline for deposit of the instrument of proxy, e.g. reg. 62 of Table A. Articles sometimes give the directors power to dispense with this requirement.

A member may authorise (either in writing or orally) another person to complete the proxy form by filling in the name of the person entitled to vote (*Re Lancaster* (1877) 5 Ch.D. 911). A blank proxy form signed by a member given to a person in connection with a requisitioned meeting together with authority to fill it up was held to be valid for a later requisitioned meeting called for the same purpose after the original requisition had been withdrawn (*Sadgrove v. Bryden* [1907] 1 Ch. 318). The secretary has no authority to enter the date of the meeting in proxies returned without a date unless authorised by the member to do so, although that authority may be implied in some circumstances (*Ernest v. Loma Gold Mines* [1897] 1 Ch. 1).

■ 16.11 Electronic appointments

Unless a company is a traded company it need not allow members to make appointments using electronic communications. If it chooses not to do so, appointments must be made in accordance with its articles, which will normally by default require the appointment to be made in writing (which is normally taken to mean in hard copy form). The model articles provide that proxies may only validly be appointed by a notice in writing (pcls 45, clg 31 and plc 38). However, under the model articles, the words 'in writing' mean in hard copy or electronic form (see the definition in pcls, clg and plc 1).

A company could be forced unwittingly to accept electronic appointments if it includes an electronic address in the notice of meeting or any proxy form or proxy invitation sent to members, in which case it may very well be deemed to have agreed to allow members to use that address to make proxy electronic appointments using that address by virtue of s. 333. The biggest danger here would be to give an e-mail address in any document which could be deemed to form part of the notice (which could include almost any document sent out with the notice, including the report and accounts) without specifying that it may not be used to make proxy appointments.

16.11.1 Electronic appointments under the model articles

Under the model articles, the proxy notice (whether in hard copy or electronic form) must:

(a) state the name and address of the shareholder appointing the proxy;
(b) identify the person appointed to be that shareholder's proxy and the general meeting in relation to which that person is appointed;
(c) be signed by or on behalf of the shareholder appointing the proxy, or be authenticated in such manner as the directors may determine (see further **16.11.4**); and
(d) be delivered to the company in accordance with the articles and any instructions contained in the notice of the general meeting to which they relate (pcls 45(1), clg 31(1) and plc 38(1)).

Neither of the model articles for private companies impose any conditions as to the time for delivering proxy notices. Accordingly, it must be assumed that there is no time limit unless one can be imposed by the directors in the instructions contained in the notice.

The model articles for public companies do make provision requiring proxy notices to be submitted in advance (see **16.14**).

16.11.2 Situation where a company's articles make no provision for electronic proxy appointments

Although it is not necessary for a company to amend its articles before allowing members to make proxy appointments by e-mail or via a website (or any other electronic method), it is desirable to do (see **2.11** and below).

The articles of nearly every company incorporated before 22 December 2000 will, unless subsequently amended, probably require proxy appointments to be made in hard copy form. The Companies Act 1985 was amended with effect from that date by the Companies Act 1985 (Electronic Communications) Order 2000 to provide that, notwithstanding any provision to the contrary in a company's articles, the appointment of a proxy may be contained in an electronic communication sent to such address as may be notified by or on behalf of the company for that purpose (s. 372(2A), 1985 Act). In addition, a new provision was inserted (s. 372(2B), 1985 Act) which provided that, in so far as the articles of a company make no other provision in that behalf, the appointment of a proxy may be contained in an electronic communication in accordance with the provisions of Table A, as amended by the 2000 Order with effect from 22 December 2000. The amendments made to Table A by the 2000 Order were designed to facilitate the use of electronic communications generally, but specifically included modifications regarding the use of electronic communications for the purposes of proxy appointments (see **Annex B2**). Although these changes to Table A did not directly amend the articles of any existing company, they could be applied in relation to proxy appointments made electronically as if they had if the company decided to allow members to use electronic communications to appoint proxies and its articles make no alternative provision in this regard.

Although the Companies Act 2006, which has now replaced all of the relevant provisions of the 1985 Act, undoubtedly allows companies to permit members to appoint proxies by electronic means, it, does not make any similar provision regarding the deemed application of the amended Table A provisions or the equivalent provisions of the model articles. This means that a company whose articles require proxy appointments to be made in writing and which decides to allow electronic appointments or is deemed, by virtue of s. 333, to have so agreed, could find it difficult to decide how its articles apply in relation to electronic appointments, which they clearly never envisaged.

In practice, a company can probably ignore its articles for the most part as long as it sets out the rules that it wishes to apply in the notice of meeting. Section 333(1) provides that, where a company has given an electronic address in a notice calling a meeting, it is deemed to have agreed that any document or information relating to proceedings at the meeting may be sent by electronic means to that address (*subject to any conditions or limitations specified in the notice*). Section 333(2) provides that, where a company has given an electronic address in an instrument of proxy or in an invitation to appoint a proxy issued by the company in relation to the meeting, it is deemed to have agreed that any document or information relating to proxies for that meeting may be sent by electronic means to that address (*subject to any conditions or limitations specified in the notice*). The rules in articles regarding proxy appointments are nothing more than conditions. They set out how appointments must be made and notified to the company. Accordingly, a company whose articles do not specify the conditions for appointing proxies electronically can do so in the notice. It should be noted that it appears not to be sufficient to include these conditions on the proxy form or proxy invitations (unless they can be deemed to form part of the notice), although it would probably make sense to include them on those documents as well as the notice. One would expect that any such conditions ought to comply with the rules set out in s. 327 although, strictly speaking, this section only seems to apply to restrictions in the articles.

Generally speaking, if a company wishes to allow members to make proxy appointments using some form of electronic communications, it should notify them of the fact that this facility is being made available and specifically notify them of the address to be used for this purpose. In practice, this address will normally be the address of the company's website (or possibly an e-mail address). However, the definition of electronic communications is so wide that members could conceivably be allowed to use other methods of communication, including the telephone, mobile phone text messaging service or a fax message. An address in these cases would mean a telephone number.

Although the Act does not require companies to send proxy forms to members, it can be said to authorise them to do so. Accordingly, it can be assumed that the company communications provisions apply to proxy forms and that they may be sent to a member by electronic means or via a website provided that the member has agreed (or can be deemed to have agreed) in accordance with the normal rules (see **2.2**). Listed companies are required to make provision for electronic proxy appointments (see **16.13**).

In practice, most companies will probably only want to allow members to use methods of electronic communication which enable the company to ensure that the member uses its standard form of appointment and provides all the information necessary to ensure that the appointment is valid. Generally speaking, it has been found that the best way of achieving this is to provide some web-based method of appointment, although other workable methods could be devised.

16.11.3 Procedures for electronic appointments under Table A (as amended)

Regulation 62 of Table A (as amended by the 2000 Order) provides that the appointment of a proxy may be made by electronic communications, where an address has been specified for that purpose:

- in the notice convening the meeting; or
- in any instrument of proxy sent out by the company in relation to the meeting; or

■ in any invitation contained in an electronic communication to appoint a proxy issued by the company in relation to the meeting.

Under reg. 62 an appointment sent using electronic communications to any other address would not be valid and an appointment sent to the proper address would not be valid unless it was received not less than 48 hours before the time for holding the meeting or adjourned meeting at which the person named in the appointment proposes to vote.

In theory, reg. 62 also allows electronic communications to be used to send any authority under which the appointment is executed or a copy of such authority certified notarially or in some other way approved by the directors. Where the authority has been executed in writing, this would require some sort of electronic copy to be submitted. The directors will normally have discretion as to whether to accept this type of evidence or whether to demand it in hard copy form.

16.11.4 Authentication/execution

If a company intends to allow members to make electronic proxy appointments, it will need to devise a method of authentication. Where appointments are made in writing, they are authenticated by being executed, i.e. by the signature of an individual or the seal of a company. Although a company will often have no way of knowing whether the signatures on proxy forms are genuine, the existence of signed proxy forms enables this to be established after the event, should the need arise. They also provide the basis on which the chairman would make any ruling on the validity of votes tendered by proxy.

The company communications provisions of the 2006 Act provide that a document or information sent or supplied in electronic form is sufficiently authenticated:

■ if the identity of the sender is confirmed in a manner specified by the company; or
■ where no such manner has been specified by the company, if the communication contains or is accompanied by a statement of the identity of the sender and the company has no reason to doubt the truth of that statement (s. 1146(3)).

It should be noted that s. 1146(3) does not make reference to the manner of authentication specified in a company's articles but simply to the manner specified by the company. Accordingly, a company will presumably be bound to accept electronic appointments authenticated in the manner specified in any notice of meeting or proxy form or on a website provided by the company for the purpose of making proxy appointments even though that method of authentication may not appear to comply with any relevant article.

It should be noted however that where a document or information is sent or supplied by one person on behalf of another, s. 1146(3) does not override any provision of a company's articles under which the company may require reasonable evidence of the authority of the former to act on behalf of the latter (s. 1146(4)).

A company could, in theory, allow members to notify proxy appointments electronically without providing any authentication at all. In other words it could simply trust to luck that there will be no challenge as to the validity of any votes. Should there be a challenge, the chairman might find it difficult to rule on the validity of votes tendered by proxy in this manner, and his decision could conceivably be challenged in legal proceedings even where the articles provide that his ruling shall be conclusive in this regard. It is submitted therefore that members should be required to provide some sort of authentication when making electronic proxy appointments. It is notable in this regard that regs. 60 and 62 of Table A (as amended) still require appointments to be 'executed', which would seem to indicate that a substitute for manual signatures will be required where individuals make electronic appointments (see **Precedent 16.11** for an alternative form of words which may be used in this regard).

The closest equivalent to a manual signature for these purposes is the so-called electronic signature. Under the Electronic Communications Act 2000, electronic signatures are now admissible as evidence in legal proceedings (see **2.13**). An electronic signature may be applied to an electronic transmission using complex cryptographic techniques. These ensure that the document may only be unlocked by applying the public key of the person who encrypted it. If the document can be opened using the public key of the person who sent it, it must also have been encrypted using that person's private key. Using this type of electronic signature also ensures that the message cannot be tampered with before being opened by the recipient. Electronic signatures are in many ways more secure than manual signatures, unless the owner has allowed his private key to fall into the hands of some unauthorised person. However, they are, at present, only suitable for authenticating messages transmitted in a computerised form, whether as an e-mail or via the internet or otherwise. In addition, most people still do not have one. Accordingly, it is unlikely that many companies will be able to insist on this level of authentication if they wish to encourage members to use electronic communications.

Instead, most companies will probably require members to authenticate their appointment by confirming a unique identification number which the company or its registrars has allocated to them for these purposes, or which it may have already allocated for some other purpose. For example, most service registrars allocate a unique reference number to each shareholder which is often printed on share certificates and proxy forms. For reasons of security and practicality, it may be preferable to allocate a separate identification number for the purposes of electronic communications. Shareholders may, for example, want to change their number if they suspect that it has been compromised. However, unless shareholders are reminded what their number is each year, they are likely to forget it, and therefore be unable to use electronic communications. One way around this would be to enable shareholders to access their unique number via a website if they were able to provide answers to certain questions which were deemed sufficient to establish their identity.

Members could, of course, be allowed from the outset to allocate their own password or identification number. This would enable them to use the same code for their holdings in other companies. It is clear that the solution to these problems will always involve a trade off between security and usability. In practice most listed companies will probably rely on systems devised by their service registrars for these purposes. At the moment, it appears that service registrars are planning to use specially allocated PIN numbers for the purposes of authentication.

Although this method of authentication would come within the Electronic Communications Act 2000 definition of an electronic signature, it is clear that it would not be given the same weight as an electronic signature applied using modern cryptographic techniques in any legal proceedings. Generally speaking, this will not cause a problem in view of the provisions that are found in most articles regarding the validity of votes (see **17.14**).

16.11.5 Faxed proxies

A faxed proxy can just be viewed as an appointment in electronic form. If that is the case, its validity will depend mainly on whether the company agreed to accept appointments in that manner. One of the problems with using fax communications for the purposes of appointments is that the faxed copy may not provide very good evidence for the purposes of execution and authentication. However, it has been held that a proxy form delivered by fax is valid for the purposes of a creditors' meeting in relation to an individual voluntary arrangement to be entered into pursuant to the Insolvency Act 1986 (*Re a debtor* (No. 2021 of 1995) [1996] 1 B.C.L.C. 538). Although Laddie J. stressed that his ruling in this case did not apply to meetings held under the Companies Acts or, indeed, to other creditors' meetings held in accordance with the Insolvency Act 1986, the case may be of wider significance because it hinged on the question of whether the signature on a faxed proxy satisfied the requirements of rule 8.2(3) of the Insolvency Rules 1986 that 'a form of proxy shall be signed by the principal, or by some person authorised by him'. Laddie J. held that it did and, after examining the authorities, said:

> I have come to the conclusion that a proxy form is signed for the purposes of r 8.2(3) if it bears upon it some distinctive or personal marking which has been placed there by, or with the authority of, the creditor. When a creditor faxes a proxy form to the chairman of the creditors' meeting he transmits two things at the same time, the contents of the form and the signature applied to it. The receiving fax is in effect instructed by the transmitting creditor to reproduce his signature on the proxy form which is itself being created at the receiving

station. It follows that, in my view, the received fax is a proxy form signed by the principal or by someone authorised by him.

. . . From the chairman's point of view, there is nothing about a received fax which puts him in a worse position to detect forgeries than when he received through the post or by hand delivery a document signed by hand by a person whose signature he has never seen before or one signed by stamping. The reality is that fax transmission is likely to be a more reliable and certainly is a more speedy method of communication than post.

■ 16.12 Appointments in hard copy form

Where a company decides not to allow appointments of proxies to be made electronically, all appointments will probably need to be made in hard copy form. The articles of any company incorporated before 22 December 2000 will (unless subsequently amended) probably still require proxy appointments to be made in writing. Where the expression 'in writing' is used in articles without being defined, it is normally assumed that it means in hard copy form. Appointments will need to be made in hard copy form under the model articles where a company decides not to allow electronic appointments. Under the company communications provisions of the 2006 Act, it is not possible for a company to refuse to accept appointments solely on the basis that they are made in hard copy form. In other words, it is not possible to insist that all appointments to be made electronically.

Older articles sometimes require the instrument appointing a proxy to be attested (i.e. signed in the presence of a witness). An instrument of proxy which does not comply with such a requirement contained in the articles, will be invalid (*Harben v. Phillips* (1883) 23 Ch.D. 14) and a proxy cannot attest his or her own appointment in such circumstances (*Ex p. Cullen* [1891] 2 Q.B. 151).

16.12.1 Model articles

The model articles provide that proxies may only validly be appointed by a notice in writing, and refer to the instrument of appointment as a 'proxy notice' (pcls 45, clg 31 and plc 38). Under the model articles, the words 'in writing' mean in hard copy or electronic form (see the definition in pcls, clg and plc 1). The proxy notice must:

(a) state the name and address of the shareholder appointing the proxy;
(b) identify the person appointed to be that shareholder's proxy and the general meeting in relation to which that person is appointed;
(c) be signed by or on behalf of the shareholder appointing the proxy, or be authenticated in such manner as the directors may determine; and
(d) be delivered to the company in accordance with the articles and any instructions contained in the notice of the general meeting to which they relate (pcls 45(1), clg 31(1) and plc 38(1)).

The company may require proxy notices to be delivered in a particular form, and may specify different forms for different purposes (pcls 45(2), clg 31(2) and plc 38(2)).

Proxy notices may specify how the proxy appointed under them is to vote (or that the proxy is to abstain from voting) on one or more resolutions (pcls 45(3), clg 31(3) and plc 38(3)).

If a proxy notice is not executed by the person appointing the proxy, it must be accompanied by written evidence of the authority of the person who executed it to execute it on the appointor's behalf (pcls 46(4), clg 32(4) and plc 39(8)).

Section 1146 provides that a document or information sent or supplied by a person in hard copy form to a company is sufficiently authenticated if it is signed by the person sending or supplying it.

16.12.2 1985 Table A

Prior to 22 December 2000, reg. 60 provided that an instrument appointing a proxy shall be in writing executed by or on behalf of the appointor. It also specified the form of words which could be used to make the appointment. Although the amended version of reg. 60 still requires appointments to be executed by or on behalf of the appointor and specifies the form of words which may be used, it no longer requires appointments to be made in writing. Similar amendments have been made to reg. 61, which specifies the form of words which may be used by members to instruct their proxy how to vote.

In addition, reg. 62 of Table A (as amended) provides separate procedures for notifying the company of appointments made in writing and those made electronically. Where the appointment is made in writing, the instrument (proxy form) must be deposited at the office or such other place within the United Kingdom as is specified in the notice convening the meeting or in any instrument of proxy sent out by the company in relation to the meeting not less than 48 hours before the time for holding the meeting or adjourned meeting at which the person named in the instrument proposes to vote.

The provisions of Table A regarding the procedure for making appointments in writing are widely followed in most articles. Thus most articles require the proxy form to be executed by or on behalf of the appointor. In the case of an individual, this means signed. A corporation which is a member of a company may execute a proxy under its common seal or by signature in accordance with s. 44 (England, Wales and Northern Ireland) or s. 48 (Scotland). It is open to debate whether a company can refuse to accept a proxy executed under the hand of a duly authorised officer. Listed companies used to be required by the Listing Rules to allow companies to execute proxies in this manner. Although the requirement was deleted in January 2000, the articles of most listed companies still make specific provision allowing this. Where this method of execution is allowed, the articles will normally allow the directors to require the company to provide evidence of that person's authority (e.g. in the form of a certified board minute).

16.12.3 Form of proxy under Table A

Regulation 60 of Table A provides that appointments shall either be:

- in the same form as the specimen provided in that regulation (see below) or as close to it as circumstances allow;
- in any other form which is usual; or
- in any other form which the directors approve.

Under Table A, it can be assumed that proxy forms sent to members by the company have been approved by the directors for these purposes. Where proxy forms are not sent to members with the notice of the meeting, as will often be the case in private companies, members should use the specimen in the company's articles (if any) or, failing that, a form of words similar to the one set out in reg. 60 (which it would be difficult for the directors to assert is unusual). Whether any other form of words would be considered a 'usual form' may depend on the type of company and its previous practice in this regard.

The following form of proxy is prescribed by reg. 60:

XYZ Limited
Form of proxy
I/We, [name of member/names of joint holders], of [address/addresses], being a member/members of the above-named company, hereby appoint [name of proxy] of [address of proxy], or failing him, [name of alternate proxy, if any] of [address], as my/our proxy to vote in my/our name[s] and on my/our behalf at the annual/extraordinary general meeting of the company to be held on [date], and at any adjournment thereof.
Signature(s)   *[Date]*

Although this form of proxy appears to give the person appointed as proxy complete discretion as to how to vote, a member can issue separate voting instructions (see **16.20** for a discussion of a proxy's obligation to vote in accordance with instructions).

Reg. 61 of Table A prescribes the following form of proxy for use 'where it is desired to afford members an opportunity of instructing the proxy how he should vote':

PLC/Limited
I/We, [name of member/names of joint holders], of [address], being a member/members of the above-named company, hereby appoint [name of proxy] of [address of proxy], or failing him, [name of alternate proxy, if any] of [address], as my/our proxy to vote in my/our name[s] and on my/our behalf at the annual/extraordinary general meeting of the company to be held on [date], and at any adjournment thereof.
This form is to be used in respect of the resolutions mentioned below as follows:

Resolution No 1 *for *against
Resolution No 2 *for *against.
*Strike out whichever is not desired.
Unless otherwise instructed, the proxy may vote as he thinks fit or abstain from voting.
Signed this .... 19............ .

The words 'where it is desired to afford members an opportunity of instructing the proxy how he should vote' in reg. 61 seem to imply that the directors may, where it is not so desired, reject an appointment made in the form prescribed by that regulation (i.e. on a two-way proxy form). In fact, it is submitted that this form of appointment is now so common that it should be accepted under the heading 'or in any other form which is usual' in reg. 60.

■ 16.13 Additional rules regarding proxies for listed companies

The Disclosure and Transparency Rules (DTRs) require listed companies to issue a proxy form, on paper or, where applicable, by electronic means, to each person entitled to vote at a meeting of shareholders or a meeting of debt security holders (DTR 6.1.5(2) and 6.1.5(3)).

The proxy form must be made available either together with the notice concerning the meeting or after the announcement of the meeting (DTR 6.1.5(3)). Shareholders and debt security holders must not be prevented from exercising their rights by proxy, subject to the law of the country in which the issuer is incorporated (DTR 6.1.5(1)).

The proxy forms must make provision for 'at least three-way voting' – with provision for members to indicate which way their votes are to be cast on all resolutions other than those relating to the procedure of the meeting (Listing Rule 9.3.6). This rule requires listed companies to make provision for abstentions or a 'vote withheld' options on proxy forms in addition to the usual for and against options.

In addition, Listing Rule 9.3.6 requires proxy forms to state that if the form is returned without an indication as to how the proxy shall vote on any resolution, the proxy will exercise his discretion as to how he votes and as to whether or not he abstains from voting.

Listing Rule 9.3.6 also used to require proxy forms to state that a shareholder is entitled to appoint a proxy of his own choice (e.g. somebody other than a director named in the printed form) and should provide a space for the name of such a proxy. Although this requirement was deleted in August 2007, listed companies still comply with it.

If the resolutions to be proposed include the re-election of retiring directors and the number of retiring directors standing for re-election exceeds five, the proxy form may give shareholders the opportunity to vote for or against (or abstain from voting on) the re-election of the retiring directors as a whole but must also allow votes to be cast for or against (or for shareholders to abstain from voting on) the re-election of the retiring directors individually (LR 9.3.7).

Proxy forms which comply with the requirements of Chapter 13 of the Listing Rules and which have no unusual features (see, for example **Precedent 16.13**) do not need to be approved by the UK Listing Authority before they are despatched. However, two copies must be lodged with the FCA no later than the date on which they are despatched to holders of the relevant securities. It is difficult to say what might be considered an unusual feature on a proxy form.

16.13.1 Abstention boxes on proxy forms

As noted above, listed companies are required under the Listing Rules to provide for three-way voting on proxy forms. In addition, the UK Corporate Governance Code recommends that companies provide a 'vote withheld' option on proxy appointment forms to enable shareholders to indicate if they have reservations on a resolution but do not wish to vote against. Under the Code, the proxy form and any announcements of voting should make it clear that a 'vote withheld' is not a vote in law and is not counted in the calculation of the proportion of the votes for and against the resolution (Code provision E.2.1).

If members voting by proxy wish to abstain on a resolution, they must specifically instruct their proxy not to vote. In practice, where a traditional two-way proxy form is used, if a member marks a proxy card 'abstain', the company (or its registrar) should count this as an abstention. However, many shareholders do not know that this option is available or assume that not ticking 'for' or 'against' is an abstention.

Leaving the voting instructions on a two-way proxy form blank does not necessarily constitute an abstention because the standard wording on proxy forms provides:

I/We hereby authorise and instruct the proxy to vote on the resolutions to be proposed at such meeting as indicated in the boxes below. Unless otherwise directed, the proxy will vote or abstain from voting as he or she thinks fit.

This is the formula used in the two-way proxy form in Table A, so there is nothing unusual about it. Even if a shareholder gives voting instructions for some of the resolutions but not others, those for which he or she has given no instructions will be deemed to be a discretionary proxy.

■ 16.14 Time limit for deposit of proxies

A company may require proxy appointments (and any document relating to or necessary to show the validity of any such appointment) to be lodged or delivered by a specified time before the meeting. This is normally done to allow the validity of the instruments to be checked and the votes for and against the resolution to be counted before the meeting. If no such provision is made in the articles, the company must accept a vote tendered by proxy at the meeting even though the proxy is unable at the meeting to establish his authority (*Re English, Scottish & Australian Bank* [1893] 3 Ch. 385).

In the case of a traded company (see **8.5.1**), the appointment of a person as proxy must be notified to the company in writing and where such an appointment is made, the company may not require to be provided with anything else relating to the appointment other than reasonable evidence of the identity of the member and of the proxy, the member's instructions (if any) as to how the proxy is to vote, and where the proxy is appointed by a person acting on behalf of the member, the authority of that person to make the appointment (s. 327(A1)).

Section 327(2), which applies to all companies, provides that any provision of a company's articles will be void in so far as it would have the effect of requiring the appointment of a proxy or any document necessary to show the validity of, or otherwise relating to, the appointment of a proxy to be received by the company or another person earlier than:

(a) in the case of a meeting or adjourned meeting, 48 hours before the time for holding the meeting or adjourned meeting;
(b) in the case of a poll taken more than 48 hours after it was demanded, 24 hours before the time appointed for the taking of the poll.

Section 327(2)(c), which would in the case of a poll taken not more than 48 hours after it was demanded, make it illegal to require a proxy to be delivered before the time at which the poll was demanded, has not been commenced and, according to a government statement, will never be commenced.

In calculating the above periods, no account shall be taken of any part of a day that is not a working day (s. 327(3)). This means, for example, that a company's articles may require proxies to be delivered more than 48 hours before a meeting if the meeting takes place on a Monday or Tuesday, in which case some of the 48 hours would fall on non-working days.

The model articles for private companies do not impose any conditions as to the time for delivering proxy notices. Accordingly, it must be assumed that there is no time limit unless one can be imposed by the directors in the instructions contained in the notice. It is far from clear whether this is actually allowed and a person whose proxy vote was excluded on this basis might be able to challenge the validity of the proceedings.

The model articles for public companies do make provision requiring proxy notices to be submitted in advance. Any notice of a general meeting must specify the address or addresses ('proxy notification address') at which the company or its agents will receive proxy notices relating to that meeting, or any adjournment of it, delivered in hard copy or electronic form (plc 39(1)). A proxy notice must be delivered to a proxy notification address not less than 48 hours before the general meeting or adjourned meeting to which it relates (plc 39(3)). However, in the case of a poll not taken during the meeting but taken not more than 48 hours after it was demanded, the proxy notice must be delivered under the above rules or at the meeting at which the poll was demanded to the chairman, secretary or any director (plc 39(5)). In the case of a poll taken more than 48 hours after it is demanded, the notice must be delivered to a proxy notification address not less than 24 hours before the time appointed for the taking of the poll (plc 39(4)).

Most older articles require proxies to be deposited not less than 48 hours before the time for holding the meeting or adjourned meeting and make no provision for excluding hours which fall on non-working days (e.g. reg. 62 of Table A). In these circumstances, if a meeting is held on a Monday or a Tuesday, it will normally be necessary for someone to be present at the nominated office at the deadline to ensure that proxies delivered after that time are not accepted.

Proxy forms received after the time specified in the articles will not be valid for that meeting and should not be accepted under any circumstances.

16.14.1 Registrars Group guidance note on proxy voting

The ICSA's Registrars Group published a guidance note in March 2012 entitled *Practical Issues Around Voting at General Meetings*, which seeks to explain some of the practical processes used by company registrars to determine the voting rights of members and proxies and the validity of proxy voting instructions at general meetings. The main objective of the guidance is to ensure that investors are aware of what they need to do to ensure that their votes are counted. In this regard, it recommends that investors should:

(a) lodge their proxies and proxy instructions as early as possible before the deadline so as not only to maximise the chances of valid receipt and reconciliation but also to enable the company to enter into a dialogue with the investor should it choose to do so;

(b) make use of any proxy facilities provided through CREST to communicate with the company or, if that is not possible, any website facility provided by the company; and

(c) seek to avoid using more than one of the available methods for notifying proxy appointments and instructions in respect of the same holding.

The guidance also explains what registrars normally do when trying to reconcile invalid proxy voting instructions.

■ 16.15 Proxies at adjourned meetings

An instrument of proxy deposited prior to the original meeting will also be valid for any adjournment of that meeting, unless the articles provide otherwise (*Scadding v. Lorrant* (1851) 3 H.L.C. 418) (see **23.10**). Most articles provide that a proxy will be valid for any adjournment and also allow proxies to be submitted between the original meeting and the adjourned meeting, if there is sufficient time. For example, the model articles provide that unless a proxy notice indicates otherwise, it must be treated as appointing that person as a proxy in relation to any adjournment of the general meeting to which it relates as well as the meeting itself (pcls 45(4), clg 31(4) and plc 38(4)).

■ 16.16 Proxies on a poll

A proxy delivered after the time specified in the articles will not be valid on the suspension of business for the purposes of taking a poll (*Shaw v. Tati Concessions* [1913] 1 Ch. 292) unless the articles expressly allow proxies to be deposited at a specified time before the poll is taken (e.g. reg. 62 of Table A and plc 39). It should be noted in this regard that a poll directed to be taken on a later date is not treated as an adjournment but rather as a suspension of the proceedings, which is why separate provision needs to be made in articles of association in this regard. Reg. 62 provides that in the case of a poll taken more than 48 hours after it is demanded, proxies may be delivered *after the poll has been demanded* and not less than 24 hours before the time for the taking of the poll. On a strict interpretation of reg. 62, it would seem that a proxy deposited after the time allowed under the articles for the original meeting but before the poll was actually demanded would still not be valid for these purposes. The model articles for public companies only impose the condition that the proxy be delivered not less than 24 hours before the time for taking the poll (plc 39(4)). Accordingly, proxies submitted late for the original meeting will be valid on the poll.

Reg. 62 of Table A and art. 37(5) of the model articles for public companies both provide that in the case of a poll taken less than 48 hours after the meeting at which it was demanded, proxies may be delivered at the meeting at which the poll was demanded to the chairman or to the secretary or to any director. In this case, it would seem that all proxies delivered late for the original meeting would be invalid unless they were delivered at the meeting.

These provisions can cause problems for members who are represented at the original meeting by a proxy other than the chairman who is unable to attend the poll. The member would not be able to appoint a further proxy and would therefore have to attend the poll in person in order to vote. This problem can best be avoided by nominating the chairman of the meeting as proxy or as an alternate proxy by using the words 'or failing him, the chairman of the meeting'.

The model articles for private companies do not make any special provision for proxies on a poll because they require all polls to be taken immediately. It should also be noted, however, that they do not impose any time limits on the submission of proxies. Accordingly, a member could presumably deliver a proxy at any time before the meeting and, subject to any instructions contained in the notice of meeting, deliver that proxy at the meeting (see pcls 45(1) and clg 31(1)).

■ 16.17 Revocation of proxies

Section 330(A1) provides that in the case of a traded company (see **8.5.1**) the termination of the authority of a person to act as proxy must be notified to the company in writing. This provision was inserted by the Companies (Shareholders' Rights) Regulations 2009 (SI 2009/1632) in order to comply with an EU directive and may very well have a bearing on the application of the common law rules regarding revocation of proxies.

Section 330 also makes other provision regarding termination of a proxy's authority. These other rules apply to all companies (whether traded or otherwise).

Section 330(2) provides that the termination of the authority of a person to act as proxy does not affect whether he counts in deciding whether there is a quorum at a meeting, the validity of anything he does as chairman of a meeting, or the validity of a poll demanded by him at a meeting, unless the company receives notice of the termination before the commencement of the meeting.

Section 330(3) provides that the termination of the authority of a person to act as proxy does not affect the validity of a vote given by that person unless the company receives notice of the termination before the commencement of the meeting or adjourned meeting at which the vote is given or, in the case of a poll taken more than 48 hours after it is demanded, before the time appointed for taking the poll.

Section 330(4) provides that, if the company's articles require or permit members to give notice of termination to a person other than the company, the references above to the company receiving notice have effect as if they were or (as the case may be) included a reference to that person.

The above rules have effect subject to any provision of the company's articles which has the effect of requiring notice of termination to be received by the company or another person at a time earlier than that specified in those subsections (s. 330(5)). However, any provision of a company's articles is void in so far as it would have the effect of requiring notice of termination to be received by the company or another person earlier than:

- in the case of a meeting or adjourned meeting, 48 hours before the time for holding the meeting or adjourned meeting;
- in the case of a poll taken more than 48 hours after it was demanded, 24 hours before the time appointed for the taking of the poll (s. 330(6)).

In calculating the periods mentioned above, no account shall be taken of any part of a day that is not a working day (s. 330(7)). It should be noted that s. 330(6)(c), which would in the case of a poll taken not more than 48 hours after it was demanded, invalidate any provision in a company's articles which required notice of termination to be given before the time at which the poll was demanded, has not been commenced and is never likely to be.

Subject to the statutory rules on revocation for traded companies, it is arguable that the appointment of a proxy in relation to a share will automatically be revoked (terminated) on the registration of a transfer of that share. Revocation may also be automatic in certain other circumstances (see below). Revocation can also be effected by notifying the company that the appointment has been revoked or that the authority under which the instrument of proxy was signed has been revoked, e.g. the revocation of a power of attorney (*R. v. Wait* (1823) 11 Price 518). A proxy which is expressed as being irrevocable cannot be revoked.

Articles usually require notice of revocation to be given before the meeting or the time appointed for the taking of a poll. Under the model articles, a proxy appointment may be revoked by delivering to the company a notice in writing given by or on behalf of the person by whom or on whose behalf the proxy notice was given (pcls 46(2), clg 32(2) and plc 39(6)). In this case, 'in writing' means in hard copy or electronic form (pcls, clg and plc 1). However, notice of revocation can only be submitted in electronic form if the company has provided an address for that purpose (or can be deemed to have done so). Under the model articles for private companies, a notice revoking a proxy appointment only takes effect if it is delivered before the start of the meeting or adjourned meeting to which it relates (pcls 46(3), clg 32(3)). The model articles for public companies make the same provision but also provide that a notice revoking a proxy appointment will take effect, in the case of a poll not taken on the same day as the meeting or adjourned meeting, if it is delivered before the time appointed for taking the poll to which it relates (plc 39(6) and (7)).

Regulation 63 of Table A states:

> 63. A vote given or poll demanded by proxy or by the duly authorised representative of a corporation shall be valid notwithstanding the previous determination of the authority of the person voting or demanding a poll unless notice of the determination was received by the company at the office or at such other place at which the instrument of proxy was duly deposited before the commencement of the meeting or adjourned meeting at which the vote is given or the poll demanded or (in the case of a poll taken otherwise than on the same day as the meeting or adjourned meeting) the time appointed for taking the poll.

A proxy may vote on behalf of the member who appointed him even though that member attends the meeting. However, the proxy is impliedly revoked if the member votes in person (*Knight v. Bulkley* (1859) 5 Jur. (N.S) 817). This will be the case even where the articles require notice of revocation to be given to the company a specified period before the meeting (*Cousins v. International Brick Co. Ltd.* [1931] 2 Ch. 90, C.A.).

Under the model articles, a person who is entitled to attend, speak or vote (either on a show of hands or on a poll) at a general meeting remains so entitled in respect of that meeting or any adjournment of it, even though a valid proxy notice has been delivered to the company by or on behalf of that person (pcls 46(1), clg 32(1) and plc 39(2)).

The execution and deposit of a second or later instrument of proxy in respect of the same holding within the time allowed under the articles will act as a revocation of any previous appointment where members are entitled to appoint only one proxy (e.g. in the case of a company limited by guarantee). This may also be the case where the deadline for appointments has expired, which could result in the member not being represented at the meeting. Where more than one appointment is made within the period specified by the articles, the company should accept the last appointment to the exclusion of the first. Where it is not possible to determine when each proxy was executed, the company may need to resolve the matter in some other way, e.g. by assuming that the appointment last received was the last to be executed or that an electronic appointment received on the same day takes precedence over a hard copy appointment.

Where members are entitled to appoint more than one proxy, the deposit of a second instrument appointing a different person will not always be conclusive evidence of the intention to revoke the original appointment, except, perhaps, where the second appointment is accompanied by new voting instructions.

The ability to appoint more than one proxy allows nominee companies to appoint separate proxies to attend and vote on behalf of the various underlying holders. Several instruments of appointment, each representing different shares within the same registered holding, can be deposited. However, if the sum of the parts exceeds the whole, the company will obviously need to find some way of limiting the number of votes cast. It might inform the various proxy holders in the hope that they are able to come to an arrangement between themselves. If all the proxies attempt to vote, the company must scale down the votes of one or more of the proxies. One way of doing so might be to assume that the last proxy submitted had the effect of revoking (either in whole or in part) one or more of the previously submitted proxies on a first in first out basis.

16.17.1 Personal representatives

The death or insanity of a member automatically revokes any appointment by that person of a proxy unless the articles provide otherwise. Any transfer which occurs by operation of law could also potentially have this effect. Articles sometimes specifically provide that any proxy appointed by a member will still be valid in these circumstances unless the company receives notice of the event giving rise to revocation (e.g. the death of that member) (see **Precedent 16.17**). Even if the articles do not do so, it is difficult to see how the company (and the chairman of the meeting in particular) can do anything other than assume that all proxies are valid unless the company has been given satisfactory evidence to the contrary. The validity of votes tendered in these circumstances might fall to be decided by the chairman under (and his decision saved by) any provision on objections to the validity of votes (e.g. reg. 58 of Table A, pcls 43, clg 23 and plc 35) (see **16.21**).

A person who becomes entitled to a share in consequence of the death or bankruptcy of a member will not normally be entitled to attend or vote at any meeting of the company until he or she is registered as the holder of the share (e.g. reg. 31 of Table A, pcls 27(3) and plc 66(2)). It follows that such a person will not be entitled to appoint a proxy until registered as the holder. A proxy appointed by the deceased member will also no longer be valid, although in the absence of any provision in the articles, it is questionable what evidence the chairman ought to require. A rumour in this regard would presumably not be sufficient. If the shareholder died in front of the chairman's own eyes, it would be difficult for him to ignore that fact.

Regulation 56 of Table A deals with the position of a member in respect of whom an order has been made by the court on the ground of mental disorder. A receiver, curator bonis or other person authorised by the court in that regard may appoint a proxy provided that evidence of the authority of the person claiming the right to do so is deposited not less than 48 hours before the meeting at the same place as instruments of proxies must be deposited. No such provision is made in the model articles. However should a court order be received which deals with voting, it should be followed (see **17.4.8**).

■ 16.18 Change of voting instructions

Members may issue their proxy with voting instructions or change any voting instructions previously given to their proxy at any time before a vote is taken. This may cause particular problems for companies which issue two-way or three-way proxy forms inviting members to appoint the chairman of the meeting as their proxy. Unless the articles provide otherwise, the chairman should act on any change of instructions received in respect of those shares up to the time that the poll is taken.

It is common practice for chairmen to seek to deter members from demanding a poll by indicating at the meeting the number of proxies which they hold for and against the resolution, the implication being that the result is a foregone conclusion. In fact, the chairman can never be certain of the result of a poll until it is actually taken because his authority as a proxy may be revoked by a member voting in person at the meeting (unless perhaps it is a traded company, in which case under s. 330(A1) it appears that revocation may only be effected by notice in writing) and members may alter their instructions at any time prior to the taking of the poll.

■ 16.19 Joint shareholders

Section 286 provides that in the case of joint holders of shares of a company, only the vote of the senior holder who votes (and any proxies duly authorised by him) may be counted by the company. It also provides that for these purposes, the senior holder is determined by the order in which the names of the joint holders appear in the register of members. The model articles rely on this statutory provision. However, s. 286 is expressed as being subject to any provision of a company's articles. Accordingly, if a company's articles make any other provision, which would be unusual, they will override the statutory rules in this regard.

Most older articles include a provision which sets out the voting rights of joint shareholders. However, where they do, they normally make the same provision as s. 286. For example, reg. 55 of Table A states:

> In the case of joint holders the vote of the senior who tenders a vote, whether in person or by proxy, shall be accepted to the exclusion of the votes of the other joint holders; and the seniority shall be determined by the order in which the names of the holders stand in the register of members.

Under s. 286 and reg. 55 of Table A, if the joint holders of a share attend a meeting and vote in different ways on a resolution, only the vote of the most senior should be counted. If the senior does not vote, the vote (if any) of the next most senior should be counted.

Companies sometimes insist that proxy forms are signed by or on behalf of all the joint holders. It is, however, doubtful whether this practice is correct. Section 324 provides that any member of a company is entitled to appoint a proxy to exercise his right to attend, speak and vote. Each of the joint holders are members and each have a right to attend and speak and (if none of the more senior joint shareholders vote) to vote. It is arguable therefore that they should each be entitled to appoint a proxy. Under s. 286 and reg. 55 of Table A, the vote of a proxy appointed by the senior joint holder (or by the senior and any of the other joint holders) should be counted to the exclusion of any votes tendered by proxies appointed by any of the other joint holders. The vote of the senior tendered by proxy should also be counted to the exclusion of any vote tendered in person by any of the junior joint holders. The vote of a junior holder in these circumstances is not a revocation of the proxy of the senior. This will probably be so even where the proxy was appointed by all the joint holders.

■ 16.20 Proxies' obligations and discretions

16.20.1 Statutory obligation

Section 324A provides that a proxy must vote in accordance with any instructions given by the member by whom the proxy is appointed. The Act does not however specify what the consequences might be if the proxy does not do so.

A person who agrees to act as a proxy is considered to be the legally constituted agent of the member who makes the appointment (*Re English, Scottish & Australian Bank* [1893] 3 Ch. 385). However, the relationship of principal and agent 'can only be established by the consent of the principal and the agent' (per Lord Pearson in *Garnac Grain Co. Inc. v HMF Faure & Fairclough Ltd.* [1967] 2 All E.R. 353). Thus, a person appointed by a member as his proxy need not act in that capacity unless there is a binding contract between the parties or the proxy has a legal or equitable obligation to do so.

Where there is a contractual agreement to vote in a certain way, the court may enforce that contract by mandatory injunction (*Puddephatt v. Leith* [1916] Ch. 200). The member may also be entitled to damages for any loss he incurs as a result of his proxy failing to vote in accordance with instructions in breach of a contractual or fiduciary duty.

Where a proxy is appointed without consideration, a gratuitous agency will exist which gives rise to negative obligations on the part of the agent (e.g. not to vote contrary to the member's instructions, if any) but not positive obligations (e.g. to attend and vote). In *Oliver v. Dalgleish* [1963] 1 W.L.R. 1274, several members nominated the same person as their proxy but gave him different instructions as to how to vote on a series of resolutions. The proxy voted in favour of the resolutions without specifying how many votes he was casting. It was held that the chairman had acted improperly in rejecting all the proxy's votes. He should have accepted those for which the proxy had instructions to vote in favour of the resolutions. As the votes of those who had instructed the proxy to vote against the resolution would not have affected the outcome, the court did not rule on the proxy's obligation to vote. However, it was impliedly accepted that the proxy did not have an obligation to use them (see, however, below on the position of the chairman).

Not surprisingly, the courts have sought ways to ensure that proxy votes are given effect without tampering with the law of agency. The problem was first identified by Maugham J. in *Re Dorman Long & Co. Ltd.* [1934] Ch. 635 which arose after the court had made an order under a scheme of arrangement calling a meeting and requiring the directors of the company to issue two-way proxies to those entitled to attend and vote. Maugham J. held that as a result of the court's order the directors had a duty to use the proxy votes and the people who gave them were entitled to assume that they would be used. However, he doubted whether directors had a general duty to attend and vote in respect of proxies and he noted that it would be difficult to allow the proxies to have force if none of the directors named as proxy holders attended the meeting. He said:

> In a sense, in all these cases, the dice are loaded in favour of the views of the directors: . . . proxy forms are made out in favour of certain named directors and, although it is true that the word 'for' or 'against' may be inserted in the modern proxy form, the recipients of the circulars very often are in doubt as to whether the persons named as proxies are bound to put in votes by proxy with which they are not in agreement.

The statutory requirement on the part of a proxy to vote in accordance with any instructions given by the member who appointed him cannot generally be viewed as anything other than a requirement not to vote in a manner which is contrary to any instructions given by the member. It almost certainly does not give rise to a duty on the part of a named proxy to attend the meeting but could conceivably give rise to a duty to vote if in attendance and able to do so (on the basis that a failure to vote could have the effect of enabling other members to achieve a result that is different from the one desired by the member and could, therefore, be interpreted as being similar to voting in a manner which is contrary to the member's instructions). This interpretation would probably be more strictly applied where the person appointed as a proxy was a director or the chairman of the meeting. Any failure by such a person to vote in accordance with a member's instructions could render the proceedings liable to challenge if the outcome of the vote would have been different. However, it is far from clear whether this would be the case if the person who failed to vote was not under any fiduciary duty or not connected with the company.

It is exceedingly doubtful whether s. 234A imposes any duty on the company to ensure that proxies (other than those appointing the chairman of the meeting or a director) do not vote in a manner which is contrary to any instructions given by the member. In practice, even if the company has notice of the instructions given by the member to his proxy, it cannot be certain that the member has not issued revised instructions. Accordingly, it would seem to be dangerous for the company to refuse to accept proxy votes on these grounds.

16.20.2 Chairman's obligations

The position of the chairman of the meeting in relation to proxies is particularly important. Most two-way or three-way proxies name 'the chairman of the meeting' as the default proxy. Accordingly, the vast majority of shareholders appoint the chairman as their proxy. By doing so they at least ensure that their nominated proxy attends the meeting. They also secure the added benefit of appointing a person who has a duty to ascertain the sense of the meeting. In *Second Consolidated Trust Ltd. v. Ceylon Amalgamated Tea & Rubber Estates Ltd.* [1943] 2 All E.R. 567, the chairman of a public company failed to call a poll even though he had the power to do so under the company's articles and held sufficient two-way proxies to reverse a decision taken at a meeting on a show of hands. It was held that he had acted in breach of his duty to ascertain the sense of the meeting. Uthwatt J. said:

> It appears to me that the power to demand a poll is a power possessed by the chairman which is to be exercised or not to be exercised according to his decision whether it is necessary to exercise his power in order to ascertain the sense of the meeting upon the matter before them; in other words it is a power directed towards enabling him to carry on the meeting for the purpose for which it was convened. In addition to this duty to demand a poll or to exercise his power to demand a poll . . . he would be under a duty in law to exercise all the proxies which he held as chairman in accordance with the instructions they contained.

It would seem to be irrelevant for these purposes whether or not the chairman of the meeting is a director of the company. And, according to the judgment of

Uthwatt J., the duty to vote arises independently of the duty to demand a poll. It will therefore also apply where a poll is demanded by the members.

This above decision is now reinforced to a certain extent by s. 324A, which requires a proxy to vote in accordance with the member's instructions and may also impose additional duties on the chairman to exercise any votes given to him.

16.20.3 Proxies' discretion

Section 324A provides that a proxy must vote in accordance with any instructions given by the member. Accordingly, where a member issues voting instructions, the extent of the proxy's discretion will depend on the wording of those instructions and the form of appointment.

Under the model articles, proxy notices may specify how the proxy appointed under them is to vote (or that the proxy is to abstain from voting) on one or more resolutions (pcls 45(3), clg 31(3) and plc 38(3)).

Where a member uses a form of proxy similar to that contained in reg. 60 of Table A, the proxy has complete discretion as to how to vote on any resolution before the meeting. The form of proxy in reg. 61 allows members to instruct their proxy how to vote, and states that in the absence of any instructions the proxy may vote as he thinks fit or abstain from voting.

Where this form of words is used, this obviously means that the proxy may exercise his discretion on those resolutions of which the member has had notice but has not issued voting instructions. A more difficult question is whether the proxy can also vote on resolutions which come before the meeting of which the member has had no notice, such as amendments, proposals to adjourn, etc. In *Re Waxed Papers Ltd.* [1937] 2 All E.R. 481, a meeting was held to approve, with or without modifications, a proposed scheme of arrangement. Various members appointed the chairman of the meeting as their proxy with instructions to vote in favour of the proposed scheme 'either with or without modification as my proxy may approve'. The chairman cast those votes against an amendment which would have deferred consideration of the scheme until the accounts for the current year had been finalised. It was held that he had acted properly. On the wording of the instrument of appointment, the power conferred on the proxy was not limited to voting for or against the proposed scheme and was sufficiently wide to enable him to vote on any incidental matter which might arise before the main question.

In *Re Waxed Papers Ltd.* the chairman exercised his discretion in a manner which was consistent with the voting instructions he had been given. He would not have been able to carry out his instructions properly if he had allowed the amendment to be passed. In addition, it was not clear whether the members would have been in any better position had consideration of the proposed scheme been deferred. It is, however, relatively easy to envisage situations where it would be more advantageous for members if their proxy had not exercised his discretion in this way. Modern forms of proxy attempt to cater for this by using words such as:

I/We hereby authorise and instruct the proxy to vote on the resolutions to be proposed at such meeting as indicated in the boxes below. Unless otherwise directed, the proxy will vote or abstain from voting as he or she thinks fit. Should any resolutions, other than those specified, be proposed at the meeting, the proxy may vote thereon as he or she thinks fit.

Where this form of words is used, there can be no doubt that the proxy has complete discretion when voting on amendments, adjournments, etc. The model articles provide that unless a proxy notice indicates otherwise, it must be treated as allowing the person appointed under it as a proxy discretion as to how to vote on any *ancillary or procedural resolutions* put to the meeting, and appointing that person as a proxy in relation to any adjournment of the general meeting to which it relates as well as the meeting itself (pcls 45(4), clg 31(4) and plc 38(4)).

Whether, the proxy should follow any guiding principles in determining how to vote on such matters is a difficult question. The answer is probably no where there is no contractual or fiduciary relationship between the proxy and his appointor. However, where such a relationship exists the proxy presumably has a duty to act in the best interests of his appointor. It is arguable that the chairman of the meeting is in such a position, particularly where the company has issued proxy forms inviting members to appoint him as their proxy. The difficulties this can cause can be demonstrated by the chairman's options on a proposal to adjourn.

The approach taken by most chairmen on a proposal from the floor to adjourn is to assume that those members who have given instructions to vote in favour of the remaining resolutions proposed in the notice of meeting approve of the conduct of the business before the meeting at this time, and accordingly, would wish to vote against the proposal to adjourn. The chairman might also cast against the proposal those votes where he has been given discretion how to vote and abstain in relation to those members who have instructed him to vote against any of the remaining resolutions proposed in the notice of meeting. However, the chairman can hardly be expected to follow these guiding principles where he has proposed an adjournment to facilitate the conduct of the meeting. In such circumstances, he will normally assume that those who have instructed him to vote in favour of the resolutions would vote in favour of the adjournment. If the resolution is passed on a show of hands and would, in view of his discretionary votes be passed on a poll, it would appear that he would not be under any obligation to demand a poll.

Likewise, chairmen nearly always assume that those who have issued instructions to vote in favour of a resolution would wish to vote against any amendment to that resolution. This will normally be sufficient to defeat any amendment. However, they would probably not want to do so with regard to an amendment which was being proposed or supported by the board. Modern articles commonly require proposals to amend resolutions to be notified in advance of the meeting. This enables the chairman to take legal advice before the meeting on any proposed amendments and, almost certainly, serves to minimise the number of amendments proposed. In view of the fact that the vast majority of votes at meetings of listed companies are cast by proxy and the fact that a proxy has no real way of knowing how his appointor would have voted, this is perhaps a sensible precaution.

16.20.4 Limitation of liability in connection with proxies

It follows from the above discussion that a proxy has certain duties and could incur certain liabilities if he fails to perform those duties. Although these liabilities might be difficult for a shareholder to establish, some companies have adopted articles which seek to limit the liability of directors and others involved in the proxy process (see **Precedent 16.21**). Neither the model articles nor Table A make any such provision.

■ 16.21 Validity of proxies and their destruction

All decisions on the validity of proxies fall to the chairman to decide (*Re Indian Zoedone Co.* (1884) 26 Ch.D. 70). The chairman should not reject a properly executed proxy merely because he believes it has been obtained by misrepresentation (*Holmes v. Jackson* (1957) *The Times* 3 April) or because it contains a minor error, e.g. it describes the meeting as an annual general meeting instead of an extraordinary general meeting (*Oliver v. Dalgleish* [1963] 1 W.L.R. 1274).

However, in ruling on the validity of proxies, the chairman is effectively ruling on the validity of votes and is therefore protected by any article which provides that the chairman's ruling on any question of the validity of votes shall be final and conclusive (e.g. reg. 58 of Table A, pcls 43, clg 29 and plc 35). In *Wall v. London and Northern Assets Corporation (No. 2)* [1899] 1 Ch. 550, one of the two scrutineers raised objections to the validity of certain proxy votes on a poll. Despite the fact that his objections appeared to be well-founded and that the disputed votes would have affected the outcome of the meeting, the chairman ruled that they were valid and declared the resolution carried. The company's articles stated that every vote, whether given in person or by proxy, not disallowed at the meeting would be deemed valid for all purposes. North J held that the scrutineer (who was also a shareholder) could not object after the event unless it could be shown that there had been fraud.

■ 16.22 Maximum validity and destruction of proxies

Some companies have adopted articles which limit the period of validity of a proxy. This type of article tends to go hand in hand with articles which allow proxy appointments to be destroyed after a certain period, in which case it is sensible to limit their validity to that period. The example of such an article in **Precedent 16.22A** limits the validity of any proxy to 12 months. For an example of an article allowing proxy forms to be destroyed, see **Precedent 16.22B**. No such provision is made in both cases under either the model articles for private companies or Table A. However the model articles for public companies do allow proxy notices to be destroyed a year after the end of the meeting to which they relate (plc 82). Without an article such as the one in **Precedent 16.22A**, it can be seen that this could cause difficulties where a meeting has been adjourned indefinitely. Technically, such a meeting may never end until it is actually held and closed. Strictly speaking, therefore, proxies delivered for that meeting cannot be destroyed under that article unless they are deemed by some other provision to have expired. Unfortunately, under the model articles for public companies, no such provision is made.

Where no provision is made by the articles allowing for destruction of proxies, it is still the normal practice to destroy them after about a year. However, one of the benefits of having an article provision in this regard will be that it will also normally provide that it shall be conclusively presumed in favour of the company that any such document destroyed was valid. Even where no such provision is made, the chairman's decision as to the validity of proxy votes tendered at the meeting will be saved to a certain extent by the common law and articles on objections. In any case, the courts would normally expect any challenge that is capable of being founded on such matters to be brought fairly promptly. If a company is aware that such a challenge is being contemplated, it might be well-advised to retain the proxy forms as evidence irrespective of any provision on destruction in its articles, and should definitely do so if proceedings have already been commenced.

It should be noted that evidence submitted by a person of his authority to act on behalf of a member in connection with the appointment of a proxy (e.g. under a power of attorney) would not normally be destroyed if the authority was of a continuing nature.

17

Voting

17.1 Summary

- Every member of a company has a statutory right to vote unless the articles provide otherwise (see **17.2**).
- Membership is determined by the register of members (see **17.2.1**).
- Generally speaking, members are free to exercise their votes as they wish (see **17.3**).
- Articles usually specify the voting rights of members and the circumstances in which those rights are restricted or removed (see **17.4**).
- The articles may give some members enhanced voting rights in certain circumstances (see **17.5**).
- Members entitled to attend and vote at general meetings have a statutory right to appoint a proxy to attend and vote in their stead (see **16.6**). Corporate members have a statutory right to appoint a person as their representative to attend and vote at meetings (see **16.2**).
- Voting is usually conducted by a show of hands, at least initially (see **17.6**).
- The declaration by the chairman of the result of a vote on a show of hands is usually conclusive, unless a poll is demanded and held (see **17.7**).
- Voting on a show of hands does not reflect the fact that some members may be entitled to more votes than others by virtue of the number of shares they hold. In addition, it does not necessarily reflect the fact that a proxy may represent several different members. Accordingly, members and proxies are given a statutory right to demand a poll. The number of votes each member may cast on a poll, depends on the type of company and, if they hold shares, the number and type of shares that they hold (see **17.8**).
- The procedures for voting on a poll require careful planning (see **17.9**).
- A company's articles may contain provision enabling votes on a poll taken at a meeting to be cast in advance (see **17.10**).
- The results of a poll may not be known until after the meeting (see **17.11**).
- Quoted companies and traded companies must publish the results of any poll on a website. The members of a quoted company may also require the company to obtain an independent report on the conduct of a poll (see **17.12**).
- The articles may purport to give the chairman a casting vote (see **17.13**).

■ The chairman may be called upon to rule on the validity of votes tendered at the meeting. At common law, the validity of a resolution passed at a general meeting may be challenged if the result would have been different had certain votes not been wrongly counted or excluded. To avoid any uncertainty in this regard, articles usually provide that the chairman's ruling will be final or conclusive (see **17.14**).

■ 17.2 Right to vote

The default position under the Act is that every member of a company has the right to vote (s. 284). However, the section in which this is stated has effect subject to any provisions of a company's articles (s. 284(4)). Accordingly, the regime established in that section is only the starting point and is capable of modification by a company's articles.

Section 284 provides that on a vote on a resolution on a show of hands every member present in person has one vote and that, on a vote on a resolution taken on a poll at a meeting:

(a) every member of a company having a share capital shall have one vote for each share held (or, if the company's shares have been converted into stock, one vote for each £10 of stock held); and

(b) every member of a company limited by guarantee shall have one vote (s. 284).

The model articles prescribed under the 2006 Act rely on the default rules in s. 284 but include certain restrictions and variations. However, older articles often override s. 284 completely by setting out an alternative regime for the voting rights of members. This is usually done in an article which sets out the basic voting rights of members (e.g. reg. 54 of Table A) which are expressed as being subject to any other restrictions or enhancements set out in the articles (see **17.4**).

A members' right to vote may also be restricted in other ways or be disregarded for certain purposes, notwithstanding the provisions of the company's articles (see also **17.4**).

17.2.1 Membership

The register of members is evidence of membership for the purpose of voting (*Pender v. Lushington* (1877) 6 Ch.D. 70). The subscribers to the memorandum of association become members on incorporation and no entry on the register of members is required (*Nichol's Case* (1885) 29 Ch. D 421; see also s. 112(1)). Every other person who agrees to become a member, and whose name is entered in the register of members, is a member of the company (s. 112(2)).

The holders of preference shares or any other class of shares are members of the company for these purposes. However, their right to vote may be restricted by the articles of the company. The same principles apply with respect to guarantee companies where every class of member will have a right to vote unless the articles provide otherwise.

The default position is that it is the members in the register on the day of the meeting who have the right to vote. However, companies may sometimes be allowed to use a prior record date for the purposes of determining voting entitlements (see **17.4.3**).

17.2.2 Stock

The references to stock in s. 284 are to shares converted into stock. It is no longer possible under the Companies Act 2006 to convert shares into stock (s. 540(2)), although it is still possible to convert stock back into shares (s. 620). However, because there are still a few long-established companies that have stock instead of shares, s. 284 still makes reference to it. All listed companies used to have to convert their shares into stock to allow trading to take place on the London Stock Exchange. This was necessary because a company's shares had to be individually numbered, which would have made it virtually impossible to keep track of who owned each of those individually numbered shares, and to enter those numbers on share certificates, where the shares were publicly traded. Accordingly, companies used to convert their shares into stock, which did not have to be numbered and it was parcels of that stock that were traded on the markets rather than the shares. It has not been necessary for listed companies to do this for many years because all companies are allowed to decide not to have individually numbered shares as long as all the shares (or shares of the same class) have the same rights and are fully paid (s. 543).

17.2.3 Bearer shares

A bearer share is a share which is evidenced by a certificate which does not show the name of the holder and which can be transferred by the holder to another person by giving up possession. In the Act, these types of instrument are referred to as share warrants. Although a company will know who it issued the original share warrant to, it will for obvious reasons have no idea who currently retains possession of it or who is entitled exercise any of rights attached to the shares represented by the warrant. Accordingly, the register of members is normally amended to record the fact that a share warrant has been issued and to ensure that no person is named in the register as the holder of the shares specified in the warrant to ensure that they are not treated as members for the purposes of s. 112. The articles of companies that issue bearer shares will normally make special provision to enable the holders to exercise their rights. These normally involve depositing their certificates at a nominated bank or depositary before the meeting. The company will usually be required to publish notices of meetings by advertisement in national newspapers and explain the procedure which holders must follow in order to exercise their right to vote at the meeting. See **Precedent 17.2** for an example of an article dealing with bearer shares.

■ 17.3 Freedom to exercise voting rights

A member has a right to have any votes tendered accepted at a meeting of the company (*Pender v. Lushington* (1877) 6 Ch.D. 70) and a refusal to accept those votes may invalidate the resolution (see however, reg. 58 on the chairman's power to rule on the validity of votes). A member's vote is a property right which as a general rule can be exercised at that person's complete discretion. In casting their votes members are free to use their own judgment and act in their own interests even though those interests might conflict with the general interests of the company (*Carruth v. Imperial Chemical Industries Ltd.* [1937] A.C. 707).

A director who is also a member can exercise his votes against a resolution which the court has ordered the company to effect (*Northern Counties Securities Ltd. v. Jackson & Steeple Ltd.* [1974] 1 W.L.R. 1133). Walton J said:

> When a director votes as a director for or against any particular resolution in a directors' meeting he is voting as a person under a fiduciary duty to the company for the proposition that the company should take a certain course of action. When a shareholder is voting for or against a particular resolution he is voting as a person owing no fiduciary duty to the company and who is exercising his own right of property to vote as he thinks fit. The fact that the result of the voting at the meeting will bind the company cannot effect the position that in voting he is voting simply in exercise of his property rights.

A member may contract to vote in a certain way or at the direction of a third party, e.g. under a shareholders' agreement. The obligations under any such contract can be enforced by mandatory injunction provided that the contract is for consideration and the member continues to hold the shares (*Greenhalgh v. Mallard* [1943] 2 All E.R. 214). The company (unless it is a party to the contract) need only be concerned that the person tendering the vote is entitled to do so and not with the obligations of that person to vote in a certain way.

A member may vote in favour of a resolution in which he has a financial interest even if he is a director of the company (*North West Transportation Co. v. Beatty* (1887) 12 App. Cas. 589 and *East Pant-du United Lead Mining Co. Ltd. v. Merryweather* (1864) 2 M. & M. 254).

The rules are, of course, subject to certain exceptions, including:

(a) the requirements of the Act regarding resolutions to ratify a breach of conduct by a director and certain resolutions connected with the purchase by a company of its own shares or payment for a purchase or redemption out of capital (see **17.4.5**); and

(b) the common law requirement that members must exercise the power to alter the articles of association in good faith for the benefit of the company as a whole (see **18.5**).

■ 17.4 Restrictions on voting

The following paragraphs summarise the restrictions that can apply to the right of a member to vote. These restrictions may arise under a statutory provision or the company's articles, or by virtue of a court order. Companies have considerable discretion in determining who may vote and under what circumstances. The statutory rights of members as stated in s. 284 are capable of modification by a company's articles and frequently are modified, particularly where there is more than one class of share in issue. Restrictions on the right to vote can usually be found in articles which establish the rights of any class of members but may also be found in articles that deal with the transmission of shares, the non-payment of calls on shares and joint shareholders. Articles may impose other restrictions and it is important to examine the articles carefully in order to ascertain the true position.

17.4.1 General provisions on voting in a company's articles

A company's articles may contain a general provision on voting at general meetings which repeats or modifies the application of s. 284. No such provision is contained in any of the model articles prescribed under the 2006 Act. However, reg. 54 of Table A (as amended by SI 2007/2826 for companies incorporated on or after 1 October 2007) provides:

> **54.** Subject to any rights or restrictions attached to any shares, *on a show of hands every member who (being an individual) is present in person or by proxy or (being a corporation) present by a duly authorised representative or by proxy, unless the proxy (in either case) or the representative is himself a member entitled to vote, shall have one vote* and on a poll every member shall have one vote for every share of which he is the holder.

This article provision excludes the default statutory provision in s. 284 regarding votes for each £10 of stock held.

17.4.2 Members represented by proxy

A company's articles may restrict the right of a member who is represented by a proxy to vote on a show of hands. The default position under the Act is that proxies have a right to vote on a show of hands. However, this rule is capable of modification by a company's articles (see **13.6**). The version of reg. 54 of Table A reproduced above (i.e. as amended by SI 2007/2826 for companies incorporated under the 1985 Act between 1 October 2007 and 30 September 2009) allows proxies to vote on a show of hands but must be applied in accordance with statutory rights of proxies. However, the version of reg. 54 in force for companies incorporated under the 1985 Act before 1 October 2007 (which is reproduced below) purports not to give proxies the right to vote on a show of hands.

54. Subject to any rights or restrictions attached to any shares, *on a show of hands every member who (being an individual) is present in person or (being a corporation) present by a duly authorised representative, not being himself a member entitled to vote, shall have one vote* and on a poll every member shall have one vote for every share of which he is the holder.

Articles such as this override the provisions of the Act in so far as the rights of proxies to vote on a show of hands are concerned. Proxies have a statutory right to vote on a poll and to demand (or join in any demand) for a poll, and these rights cannot be excluded by the articles.

17.4.3 Record dates for traded companies and securities admitted to CREST

A company whose shares (or other securities) have been admitted to CREST may specify in the notice a time, not more than 48 hours before the time fixed for the meeting, by which a person must be entered on the relevant register of securities in order to have the right to attend and vote at that meeting (or meeting of the holders of those securities) (Uncertificated Securities Regulations, reg. 34 (see **Annex D**)).

Such a provision is necessary because CREST operates on a realtime basis and the dematerialised part of the register could be changing right up to (and even during) the meeting.

As reg. 34 uses the expression 'a time', it is probably safer to give a specific time in the notice rather than to use an expression like 'the close of business' (which could cause some uncertainty if the CREST system is operating unusual hours on that date). Where the meeting is to be held on a Monday or a Tuesday, the notice could specify, say, 11 pm on the Sunday preceding the meeting or a time early on Monday morning before any entries will have been made on the register. For a suggested form of wording, see **Precedent 10.3**.

In addition, the Act specifies that a traded company must determine the right to vote at a general meeting of the company by reference to the register of members as at a time (determined by the company) that is not more than 48 hours before the time for the holding of the meeting (s. 360B(2)). In calculating this period, no account is to be taken of any part of a day that is not a working day (s. 360B(3)).

A traded company is defined by s. 360C as a company which has shares that carry rights to vote at general meetings and are admitted to trading on a regulated market in an EEA State by or with the consent of the company. Most UK companies that fall within this definition will also be subject to the rule in the Uncertificated Securities Regulations by virtue of the fact that their shares will have been admitted to CREST. It should be noted that, for the moment, those regulations do not allow any part of a day that is not a working day to be excluded for the purposes of calculating the 48-hour time limit. However, the regulations may ultimately be amended to bring them into line with s. 360B, which was introduced to comply with an EU directive on shareholders' rights. It should also be noted that the regulations may apply to a wider range of companies than s. 360B. For example, they apply to AIM companies whose shares are admitted to CREST. Such companies are not traded companies for the purposes of s. 360B because AIM is not a regulated market.

Section 360B(1) provides that any provision of a traded company's articles is void in so far as it would have the effect of:

■ imposing a restriction on a right of a member to participate in and vote at a general meeting of the company unless the member's shares have (after having been acquired by the member and before the meeting) been deposited with, or transferred to, or registered in the name of another person; or
■ imposing a restriction on the right of a member to transfer shares in the company during the period of 48 hours before the time for the holding of a general meeting of the company if that right would not otherwise be subject to that restriction. In calculating this period, no account is to be taken of any part of a day that is not a working day (s. 360B(3)).

Section 360B(4) states that nothing in the above rules affects the operation of Part 22 of this Act (information about interests in a company's shares), Part 15 of the Companies Act 1985 (orders imposing restrictions on shares), or any provision in a company's articles or the model articles relating to the application of those Parts (s. 360B(4)).

17.4.4 Record dates generally

Companies whose shares are held in CREST do not need to make provision in their articles to enable a record date to be used for the purposes of determining the right to attend and vote at general meetings because they are allowed by law to do so. Companies that are not publicly traded do not normally need to use a record date for these purposes as they would not normally have any difficulty calculating voting and attendance rights on the basis of the register on the day of the meeting. In order to use a record date, it would be necessary for a company that was not a CREST participant to make some sort of provision in its articles.

Record dates can also be used for other purposes such as calculating dividend entitlements and the right to receive notices. In most cases, the record date will be set before the usual date for calculating entitlements. However, in the case of dividend entitlements, the record date used is usually later than the date of the meeting held to approve the dividend.

17.4.5 Special voting rules imposed by statute for certain resolutions

The Act sometimes requires the votes of certain members or the votes attached to certain shares to be disregarded in determining whether the requisite majority required to pass certain resolutions has been obtained. These restrictions apply in the following cases:

(a) an ordinary resolution of the company to ratify conduct by a director amounting to negligence, default, breach of duty or breach of trust in relation to the company (s. 239(2)), in which case the director's votes in favour are disregarded;

(b) any special resolution giving authority for off-market purchase of own shares (s. 694(2)), to vary a contract for off-market purchase (s. 697), or to release a company's rights under contract for off-market purchase (s. 700), in which case any votes attached to the shares which are the subject of the resolution are disregarded if they are cast in favour of the resolution; and

(c) a special resolution authorising a payment out of capital for the redemption or purchase of own shares (ss. 713 and 716), in which case any votes attached to the shares which are the subject of the resolution are disregarded if they are cast in favour of the resolution.

In each of the above cases, votes in favour of the resolution must be disregarded but votes against the resolution can be counted and could be used help to defeat the resolution. In the case of the resolutions regarding the purchase of owns shares, a member is allowed to use any other shares he holds (i.e. shares which are not the subject of the proposed buy-back) to vote either for or against the resolution. It should also be noted that the same restrictions apply where any of the above resolutions are passed as a written resolution.

17.4.6 Joint holders

Where members are allowed to hold shares jointly, the default position under the Act is that only the vote of the senior holder who votes (and any proxies duly authorised by him) may be counted by the company. Seniority for these purposes is determined by the order in which the names appear in the register of members (s. 286) (see **16.19**). Although this provision is capable of modification by a company's articles, it is very rare for a company's articles to do so. The model articles rely on the statutory provision in this regard and make no separate provision about the votes of joint shareholders. Table A makes exactly the same provision as s. 286 in this regard. Indeed, s. 286 can be viewed as a codification of reg. 55 of Table A.

Joint holders may be able to circumvent these restrictions by having their holdings split into two or more joint holdings, each having a different person registered as the senior joint holder (*Burns v. Siemens Brothers Dynamo Works Ltd.* [1919] 1 Ch. 225). By doing so, the joint holders gain an advantage with respect to voting on a show of hands and, in most cases, satisfying the requirements for demanding a poll.

17.4.7 Death and bankruptcy

Most articles restrict the right of a person who becomes entitled to a share in consequence of the death or bankruptcy of a member to attend and vote at any meeting of the company. Under the general law a personal representative is entitled to be registered as the holder of shares in the absence of any provisions to the contrary (*Scott v. Frank F Scott (London) Ltd.* [1940] Ch. 794). Articles usually provide that a personal representative or a trustee in bankruptcy may, upon providing satisfactory evidence of appointment, elect to become the holder of the share (by giving notice to that effect) or to have some other person registered as the holder (by executing an instrument of transfer). In addition they usually provide that personal representatives or trustees in bankruptcy shall not be entitled to attend or vote until they have been registered as the holders of the share (e.g. reg. 31 of Table A, pcls 27(3), and plc 66(2)).

If a company continues over a period of time to send notices of meetings and proxy forms to personal representatives or trustees in bankruptcy who have not elected to become the holders of the shares or to have them registered in the name of someone else, it is possible that the company may be estopped from denying their right to attend and vote because it has created a reasonable expectation on their part that they may attend and vote. It is questionable whether a company should stop sending notices of meetings and proxy forms in these circumstances, unless the articles allow. However, it would be sensible to include with any such documents a letter or note warning the representatives or trustees that they will not be entitled to vote without taking further action in accordance with the articles.

Normally the death of a member automatically revokes the appointment by that person of a proxy. However, articles sometimes provide that any proxy appointed by a member who subsequently dies will be valid unless the company receives notice in writing of the death of that member (see example at **Precedent 16.17**).

Personal representatives are entitled to determine the order in which their names appear on the register of members (*Re Saunders & Co Ltd.* [1908] 1 Ch. 415).

A bankrupt who remains registered as a member of the company is entitled to vote at general meetings but must vote in accordance with the directions of his trustee (*Morgan v. Gray* [1953] Ch. 83). It should be noted, however, that the company is not bound to ensure that those instructions have been followed.

17.4.8 Mental or physical incapacity

Articles sometimes make provision regarding voting by members who are suffering from some sort of mental incapacity. For example, reg. 56 of Table A provides that a member in respect of whom a mental health order has been made by any court having the jurisdiction (whether in the UK or elsewhere) may vote by his receiver, curator bonis or other person appointed by a court to act in a similar capacity. Evidence to the satisfaction of the directors of the authority of the person claiming to exercise the right to vote must be deposited at the registered office, or at such other place as is specified by the company for the deposit of proxies, not less than 48 hours before the meeting or adjourned meeting at which the right to vote is to be exercised and in default the right to vote shall not be exercisable.

No specific provision in this regard is included in any of the model articles prescribed under the 2006 Act, although they do require any proxy form not executed by the person appointing the proxy (in this case the incapacitated member), to be accompanied by evidence of the authority of the person who executed it (pcls 46(4), clg 32(4) and plc 39(8)).

In England and Wales, orders of the type envisaged by reg. 58 of Table A will be made by the Court of Protection under the Mental Capacity Act 2005. The Court of Protection may make orders appointing a 'deputy' (formerly termed a 'receiver') to deal with the income or property of a person who, in the judgment of the court, lacks capacity. Such orders may authorise the deputy (or deputies) to receive all income of the person and give such other directions as are appropriate at the time. Orders will vary in their terms, and particular care should be taken to ensure that all acts by the deputy in connection with the shareholding are within his powers as expressed in the order appointing him. The order received in the first instance may, for example, relate only to income from the shareholding, leaving other aspects to be dealt with in subsequent orders or directions.

All orders will bear the official seal of the Court. The administrative aspects of Court of Protection orders are dealt with by the Public Guardianship Office. The equivalent Scottish document is known as an appointment of guardian.

If a Court of Protection order is received for registration, the existence of the order, together with the name and address of the deputy (or deputies) and the date of registration should be entered in the register of members. Future communications to the shareholder should be addressed to the deputy, who should be described as 'deputy (appointed by the Court of Protection) for ....
......'. However, the account of the shareholder in the register of members should remain in the same position, as legally the person lacking capacity is still the registered shareholder.

A Court of Protection order will continue in force until the death of the shareholder concerned (unless the order is earlier revoked and the deputy is discharged by the Court). On the death of the shareholder the order will lapse and the powers of the deputy terminate, whereupon the company may then take the usual action in relation to a deceased shareholder on proof of death.

It should be noted that the Mental Capacity Act 2005, which came into force on 1 October 2007 and applies only in England and Wales, enables individuals to grant a lasting power of attorney, which will continue in force even if they should lose their capacity. Such powers do not become effective until they have been registered with the Public Guardian. The prescribed form for lasting powers of attorney, and the procedure for registration, is set out in the Lasting Powers of Attorney, Enduring Powers of Attorney and Public Guardian Regulations 2007 (SI 2007/1253).

Enduring powers of attorney created before 1 October 2007 under the Enduring Powers of Attorney Act 1985 and not revoked are still valid (subject to certain conditions) but, if the donor of the power has become mentally incapable, must be registered with the Public Guardian before they can be used. See Schedule 4 of the Mental Capacity Act 2005 for the detailed provisions governing such enduring powers.

17.4.9 Calls unpaid

Articles commonly restrict the voting rights of members in respect of shares on which calls or other sums presently payable have not been paid. The scope of the restrictions which can be imposed vary and care should be taken to ensure that the power to disenfranchise is properly exercised. The model articles for private companies limited by shares do not make any such provision, presumably because all shares are meant to be issued fully paid (pcls 21). Where the articles do include such a restriction, they will normally provide that no voting rights attached to a share may be exercised unless all amounts payable to the company in respect of that share have been paid (e.g. reg. 57 of Table A and plc 41). However, reg. 65 of the 1948 Table A provides that no *member* shall be entitled to vote at any general meeting unless *all* calls or other sums presently payable by him in respect of shares have been paid. In other words, a member will be disqualified from voting even if a call on only one of his shares remains unpaid. Modern articles often impose similar restrictions but give the directors the option not to enforce them (see example at **Precedent 17.4A**).

It has been held that where shares in a public company are allotted for consideration other than cash without an independent valuation, the effect of s. 103(6) is to create an immediate liability which, together with an article similar to reg. 65 of the 1948 Table A, has the effect of disenfranchising the allottees (*Re Bradford Investments plc* [1990] B.C.C. 740).

17.4.10 Failure to respond to s. 793 inquiry

Public companies often take power in their articles to disenfranchise shares held by a member who has not replied to a notice served under s. 793 of the 2006 Act inquiring as to any beneficial interests in shares (see example at **Precedent 17.4B**). The Listing Rules require that where such power is taken in the articles of a listed company, the sanction may not take effect earlier than 14 days after the service of the s. 793 notice. In addition, any sanctions imposed must cease after not more than seven days after:

(a) receipt by the issuer of notice that the shareholding has been sold to an unconnected third party through a RIE or an overseas exchange or by the acceptance of a takeover offer; or

(b) due compliance, to the satisfaction of the issuer, with the notice under s. 793 (Listing Rule 9.3.9).

A company can apply to the court for an order imposing certain restrictions on shares (including the removal of voting rights) where a person has failed to give the information required following service of a s. 793 notice (s. 794).

17.4.11 Investigations into ownership and interests by the Secretary of State

The Secretary of State in carrying out an investigation under s. 442 of the 1985 Act (power to investigate company ownership) or s. 444 of the 1985 Act (power to obtain information as those interested in shares) may impose voting restrictions on those shares (s. 445 of the 1985 Act).

17.4.12 Non-voting or restricted voting shares

Articles usually provide that the company may issue more than one class of shares with such rights and restrictions as may be determined by ordinary resolution or by the directors. Shares will be of a different class if they give their holders different rights from other shares. The rights of the holders will typically be set out in the resolution creating the class or set out in the articles of association. A company may issue non-voting shares or shares with restricted voting rights. Preference shares are an example of a class of shares with restricted voting rights (see below).

17.4.13 Preference shares

Preference shares are perhaps the most common class of shares issued in addition to the ordinary shares. They usually have priority over the ordinary shares with respect to the payment of dividends and repayment of capital on winding up. The holders are usually entitled to a fixed rate of dividend and are not normally entitled to vote unless those dividends are in arrears by more than six months.

■ 17.5 Enhanced voting rights

The articles may give members enhanced voting rights in certain circumstances. The most common example is as a protection for a founder member against removal as a director of a private limited company (see **Precedent 17.5**). The method employed in **Precedent 17.5** does not create a different class of shares – any member who is a director will be entitled to more votes per share on a resolution to remove him as a director or to amend the article conferring those rights. Normally, the number of extra votes will be sufficient to defeat the other members. If the membership of the company subsequently changes, it may be necessary to amend this type of article to preserve that position. This sort of protection against removal was held to be valid in *Bushell v. Faith* [1970] A.C. 1099 (see **25.15**).

If it is intended to give some but not all members protection against removal as a director, it is necessary to give those members a different class of shares with different voting rights.

■ 17.6 Voting on a show of hands

Under the common law, voting is conducted on a show of hands at a meeting unless there are regulations or enactments to the contrary (*R. v. Rector of*

Birmingham (1837) 1 Ad. & El. 254). The Act is drafted on the assumption that voting will proceed first by some means other than a poll and the articles of most companies adopt the common law practice. There is, however, no statutory requirement to do so and a company's articles could provide, for example, that voting shall be conducted by a poll on all substantive resolutions. In the US, voting at general meetings of listed corporations must be conducted in this way and many UK listed companies now adopt this practice.

However, the articles of most companies provide that a resolution put to the vote at a general meeting shall be decided on a show of hands unless a poll is duly demanded (e.g. reg. 46 of Table A, pcls 42, clg 28 and plc 34).

Under the common law, each member present has one vote on a show of hands regardless of any other factors such as the number of shares held (*Re Horbury Bridge Coal, Iron & Waggon Co.* (1879) 11 Ch.D. 109) or the fact that he may be attending in more than one capacity (*Ernest v. Loma Gold Mines* [1897] 1 Ch. 1).

Section 284(2) of the Act provides that on a vote on a resolution on a show of hands at a meeting, each member present in person has one vote. However, s. 284(4) states that this rule is capable of modification by the articles (s. 284(4)) (see further below). In the case of joint shareholders, only the vote of the senior holder who votes (and any proxies duly authorised by him) may be counted by the company unless the articles provide otherwise. For these purposes, the senior holder is determined by the order in which the names of the joint holders appear in the register of members, unless the articles provide otherwise (s. 286).

The default rule of one vote for each member present in person in s. 284(2) also applies in relation to a single corporate representative appointed by a corporate member by virtue of the fact that such a representative is deemed under s. 323 to have the same rights as a member who is an individual. However, if a corporate member appoints multiple representatives, each representative has the same voting rights as the corporation would be entitled to on a show of hands (s. 323(3)). It should be noted that the statutory rules regarding corporate representatives are not capable of modification by the articles except to the extent that the articles may exclude or enhance the voting rights of the member (and therefore the corporate representative). Accordingly, under the above formula, any modification made by a company's articles to the default one member-one vote rule would also apply to both single and multiple corporate representatives.

Section 285 of the Act also gives proxies a statutory right to vote on a show of hands. However, the relevant provisions are expressed as being subject to anything in a company's articles and may therefore be modified or excluded. Section 285(1) provides that, on a vote on a resolution on a show of hands at a meeting every proxy present who has been duly appointed by one or more members entitled to vote on the resolution has one vote. This means that, subject to the articles, if a member who is entitled to vote appoints multiple proxies, each proxy for that member has a right to one vote on a show of hands. Under s. 285(1), a person who has been appointed as the proxy of more than one member entitled to vote on the resolution would have only one vote if instructed by all those members to vote in the same way. However, s. 285(2) provides that if the proxy has been instructed by one or more of those members to vote for the resolution and by one or more other of those members to vote against it, he shall have one vote for and one vote against the resolution on a show of hands. This rule may or may not apply where a proxy has been instructed to vote one way by certain members and is inclined to vote the opposite way on behalf of other members who have given him discretion as to how to vote.

It should be noted that all three versions of the model articles prescribed under the 2006 Act rely totally on the statutory default provisions with respect to voting on a show of hands. However, older articles may make separate provision. Where they do so, they will usually provide something along the lines that 'subject to any rights or restrictions attached to any shares, on a show of hands every member who (being an individual) is present in person or (being a corporation) present by a duly authorised representative, not being himself a member entitled to vote, shall have one vote'. It should be noted that s. 323 modifies this rule so far as multiple corporate representatives of the same member are concerned, who are each given a right to vote on a show of hands by that section where the member who appointed them has a right to vote. Articles on voting on a show of hands may or may not allow proxies to vote on a show of hands. Older articles are often silent on the matter. Total silence on matters of voting will mean that the default statutory rules apply. However, in the example quoted above, it is arguable that the failure to mention proxies in the list of those entitled to vote on a show of hands means that the articles override the statutory rules.

The position with regard to proxies under Table A depends on the version that was in force when the company was incorporated. The position for a company incorporated under the 1985 Act prior to 1 October 2007 that is subject to reg. 54 of Table A is that proxies are not entitled to vote on a show of hands. However, for a company incorporated under the 1985 Act between 1 October 2007 and 30 September 2009 that is subject to reg. 54 of the later version of Table A, the position is that proxies are entitled to vote on a show of hands.

It can be seen from the above rules that voting on a show of hands does not necessarily proceed strictly on the basis of one-member-one vote (a member who appoints multiple proxies or corporate representatives may secure the right to more than one vote). Neither can it be said to proceed strictly on the basis that each person present who is entitled to vote gets only one vote (although this is closer to the truth it is not always true because a proxy representing more than one member may be able to vote both for and against the resolution). These anomalies do not really matter because voting on a show of hands is not intended to be a perfect democratic process. In a company with a share capital each of the members may hold different numbers of shares or have different voting rights which are not taken into account on a show of hands. It is, of course, possible that the result of a vote would be different if these factors were taken into account and it is for this reason that members are given the right to demand a poll, a method of voting that ensures that they are taken into account.

Nevertheless, voting on a show of hands is clearly a much quicker method of voting and is ideally suited to situations where resolutions are passed without any opposition. Even where a vote is not unanimous, it could be viewed as an advantage to be able to assume that those who oppose it do not have sufficient votes to defeat the resolution on a poll, although the disadvantage here is that it may be very difficult for anybody other than the chairman to know whether the outcome would be different on a poll and therefore whether it is worth demanding one.

17.6.1 UK Corporate Governance Code

The UK Corporate Governance Code recommends that listed companies should count all proxy votes before the meeting and, should for each resolution, after a vote on a show of hands has been taken, ensure that the following information is given at the meeting:

(a) the number of shares in respect of which proxy appointments have been validly made;
(b) the number of votes for the resolution;
(c) the number of votes against the resolution; and
(d) the number of shares in respect of which the vote was directed to be withheld (Code provision E.2.2).

The purpose of this requirement is presumably to ensure that the members present have as much information as possible to enable them to decide whether or not it is worth demanding a poll. In practice, many listed companies make this information available to members at the beginning of the meeting on a printed schedule. This is obviously far more useful to members attending than an announcement by the chairman after the vote has been taken or a brief glimpse of the details given using some means of projection, although one or both of these methods can be used.

■ 17.7 Declaration by chairman of result on a show of hands

On a vote on a resolution at a meeting on a show of hands, a declaration by the chairman that the resolution has or has not been passed, or passed with a particular majority, is conclusive evidence of that fact without proof of the number or proportion of the votes recorded in favour of or against the resolution (s. 320(1)). An entry in respect of such a declaration in minutes of the meeting recorded in accordance with s. 355 is also conclusive evidence of that fact without such proof (s. 320(2)). Section 320 does not have effect if a poll is demanded in respect of the resolution (and the demand is not subsequently withdrawn).

Articles sometimes duplicate the effect of s. 320 (e.g. reg. 47 of Table A). However, the statutory provision cannot be overridden by a company's articles.

A declaration actually made by the chairman in good faith will, under s. 320 and articles similar to reg. 47, be conclusive and will prevent the question being reopened in legal proceedings. This is so even where there is evidence that the chairman's declaration was wrong, unless there is evidence of fraud or manifest error.

At a meeting where there had been confusion as to whether a special resolution and a resolution to adjourn had been carried it was held that the declaration of the chairman (as recorded in the minutes) precluded any inquiry into the number of shareholders who voted for or against the resolutions and, in the absence of fraud, was conclusive (*Arnot v. United African Lands* [1901] 1 Ch. 518). Similarly on a petition for a compulsory winding up the court refused to consider the question whether an extraordinary resolution had been carried by the requisite majority (*Re Hadleigh Castle Gold Mines* [1900] 2 Ch. 419).

A special resolution to reduce a company's capital was confirmed by the court despite the fact that there was evidence that it was carried by the votes of members not qualified to vote. However, no poll was demanded and it was held that the declaration of the chairman could not be reviewed (*Graham's Morocco Co. Ltd. Petitioners*, 1932 S.C. 269).

The court will, however, intervene where there has been a manifest error. Where a chairman declared the result of a vote on a show of hands to be six in favour and 23 against but went on to declare: 'but there are 200 voting by proxy and I declare the resolution carried as required by Act of Parliament', the court was prepared to intervene (*Re Caratal (New) Mines* [1902] 2 Ch. 498). Buckley J. said:

> I am asked to affirm a proposition that if a chairman makes a declaration and in it actually gives the numbers of votes for and against the resolution, which he is bound to recognise, and adds that there are proxies (which in law he cannot regard), and then declares the result is that the statutory majority has been obtained, although the numbers stated by him show that it has not been obtained, the declaration is conclusive. In my judgment that proposition cannot be supported.

■ 17.8 Voting on a poll

A poll is a vote conducted by voting papers (or some equivalent electronic method) rather than by a show of hands. The voting rights of members on a poll will be determined by the articles and, in default, by the Act. Generally speaking, for a company with a share capital, members will be entitled to one vote for each share held, although members holding certain shares may have no votes and others may have enhanced voting rights. This normally means that members with larger holdings of ordinary shares will have a greater say in the result than they would on a show of hands. In addition, a show of hands does not necessarily reflect the fact that a person may actually be voting as the proxy or representative of more than one member.

In the case of a company without a share capital (e.g. a guarantee company), the members will normally have no more votes on a poll than they do on a show of hands. However, the outcome of a vote on a show of hands may still be different to the outcome of a vote taken on a poll because some of the people able to vote on a show of hands may be acting as the proxy or representative of several members. This is not reflected when they vote on a show of hands but is when a vote is taken on a poll.

Irrespective of anything contained in a company's articles, votes may be tendered on a poll either by the member in person, by a corporate representative or by a proxy.

On a poll, all or any of the voting rights of a member may be exercised by one or more duly appointed proxies (s. 285(3)). However, where a member appoints more than one proxy, this does not authorise the exercise by the proxies taken together of more extensive voting rights than could be exercised by the member in person (s. 285(4)).

A corporate representative is entitled to exercise (on behalf of the corporation) the same powers at a meeting as the corporation could exercise if it were an individual member of the company (s. 323(2)) and is therefore authorised to vote on a poll on its behalf. See, however, **15.5** regarding the rules regarding multiple corporate representatives.

On a poll taken at a meeting of the company or a meeting of any class of members, a member entitled to more than one vote need not, if he votes, use all his votes or cast all the votes he uses in the same way (s. 322).

Articles sometimes purport to give the chairman of the meeting a casting vote in addition to any other vote he may have if the outcome of a vote on either a show of hands or a poll is a tie (e.g. reg. 50 of the original version of Table A). The continuing validity of any such provision is open to some doubt (see **17.13**).

A member not present at the meeting at which a poll is demanded may vote on a poll taken at a later time or date (*R. v. Wimbledon Local Board* (1882) Q.B.D. 459).

■ 17.9 Poll procedures

Under the common law, where the method of voting used at a meeting is a show of hands, any person who is entitled to vote at a meeting may demand a poll (*R. v. Wimbledon Local Board* (1882) Q.B.D. 459). This common rule applies to company meetings unless the articles provide otherwise. In practice, articles frequently modify the conditions which a person must satisfy in order to make a valid demand for a poll. In a large company with many thousands of shares, it would be ludicrous for one member holding only one share to be allowed to demand a poll without the support of other members. It would not be fair if the conditions made it almost impossible for the members to demand a poll. To ensure that this does not happen, the Act provides certain safeguards regarding the conditions for making a valid demand (see below) and, perhaps more importantly, states that a provision in a company's articles will be void in so far as it excludes the right to demand a poll on any question other than a resolution to elect the chairman of the meeting or to adjourn the meeting (s. 321(1)). The model articles and Table A allow a poll to be demanded on both the election of the chairman and a resolution to adjourn. However, Table A and the model articles for public companies require any poll demanded on these questions to be taken immediately (reg. 51 of Table A and plc 37(4)). The model articles for private companies require all polls to be taken immediately (pcls 44(4), clg 30(4)).

17.9.1 Valid demand

A poll may be demanded either on or before the declaration of the result of a show of hands by any person or persons entitled under the articles to do so. This will usually include the chairman, members (whether represented in person or by proxy or a corporate representative) satisfying certain conditions and, in some cases, the directors.

Under s. 321(2), a provision contained in a company's articles will be void in so far as it would have the effect of making ineffective a demand for a poll:

(a) by not less than five members having the right to vote on the resolution; or

(b) by a member or members representing not less than 10% of the total voting rights of all the members having the right to vote on the resolution (excluding any voting rights attached to any shares in the company held as treasury shares); or

(c) by a member or members holding shares in the company conferring a right to vote on the resolution, being shares on which an aggregate sum has been paid up equal to not less than 10% of the total sum paid up on all the shares conferring that right (excluding shares in the company conferring a right to vote on the resolution which are held as treasury shares).

If an article is deemed to be void under s. 321(2), the common law right to demand a poll will apply whereby one member may make a valid demand (*R. v. Wimbledon Local Board* (1882) Q.B.D. 459).

A proxy has the right to demand or join in the demand for a poll (s. 329). In applying the provisions of s. 321(2) (requirements for effective demand), s. 329(2) provides that a demand by a proxy counts:

(a) for the purposes of the 'not less than five members' test, as a demand by the member;

(b) for the purposes of the '10% of voting rights test', as a demand by a member representing the voting rights that the proxy is authorised to exercise;

(c) for the purposes of the '10% of paid up share capital conferring the right to vote' test, as a demand by a member holding the shares to which those rights are attached.

It is questionable whether two or more proxies appointed by the same member can defeat any provision regarding the specific number of members who must join in a demand for a poll. Section 329(2) only applies for the purposes of determining whether the provisions in a company's articles are valid. It suggests that demands by proxies for the same member do not need to be treated as demands by different members but as demands by the same member. However, the answer will depend on the precise wording of a company's articles.

Articles often relax the conditions for a valid demand. For example, reg. 46 of Table A enables a valid demand to be made by two (rather than five) members having the right to vote at the meeting. It has been held that where the articles state that 'members' holding a certain percentage of shares may demand a poll, a single member holding that percentage may demand a poll (*Siemens Bros & Co. v. Burns* [1918] 2 Ch. 324). In this case the company's articles stated in the definitions section (usually the first article) that words in the singular should be taken to include the plural and vice versa. Most articles track the wording of s. 321 to avoid any problem in this regard.

In the absence of any provision to the contrary in the articles, joint holders should be counted as a single member for the purposes of demanding a poll (*Cory v. Reindeer Steamship Co.* (1915) 31 T.L.R. 530). Under reg. 46 of Table A only members entitled to vote may join in a demand for a poll. As only the senior of the joint holders present in person or by proxy may vote, only he may join in the demand for a poll.

The chairman has no right to direct that a poll be taken unless it is duly demanded or he is given that power by the articles (*Campbell v. Maund* (1836) 5 Ad. & E. 865). Articles usually give the chairman the power to demand a poll (e.g. reg. 46 of Table A, pcls 44(2), clg 30(2) and plc 36(2)). The chairman of the meeting will, however, usually be entitled to demand or join in a demand for a poll in his capacity as a proxy. Where the chairman has the power to call a poll, he must exercise that power if it is necessary to ascertain the true sense of the meeting. For example, where the chairman has been instructed by proxies to vote in a certain way and those votes, if cast, would produce a different result from the one on the vote on a show of hands, he has a duty to demand a poll (*Second Consolidated Trust Ltd. v. Ceylon Amalgamated Tea & Rubber Estates Ltd.* [1943] 2 All E.R. 567) (see **15.20**).

17.9.2 Special rules

The Act provides that different rules shall apply when deciding whether a valid demand has been made in certain circumstances. These rules override any provision of a company's articles. For example, at a class meeting held to consider a variation of rights, any member of that class, whether present in person or by proxy, may demand a poll (s. 334(6) (meetings relating to class of shareholders) and s. 335(5) (class meetings of companies without a share capital)).

In addition, any member, whether present in person or by proxy, may demand a poll in the following circumstances:

(a) on any special resolution under s. 694 giving authority for an off-market purchase of own shares (s. 695(4)(b)), under s. 697 to vary a contract for an off-market purchase (s. 698(4)(b)), or under s. 700 to release a company's rights under a contract for an off-market purchase (s. 700(5));

(b) on a special resolution under s. 716 approving a payment out of capital for the purchase or redemption of the company's own shares (s. 717(4)(b)).

17.9.3 Withdrawal of demand

Articles usually provide that a demand for a poll may, before the poll is taken, be withdrawn but only with the consent of the chairman (e.g. reg. 48 of Table A, pcls 44(3), clg (3) and plc 36(3)). Regulation 48 of Table A goes on to say that a demand so withdrawn shall not be taken to have invalidated the result of a show of hands declared before the demand was made. The purpose of this provision in Table A (which is not repeated in any of the model articles) is to clarify that it is not necessary to take another vote on a show of hands. Under the common law, the result of a show of hands ceases to have any effect once a valid demand for a poll has been made (*R. v. Cooper* (1870) L.R. 5 Q.B. 457). Unless provision is made in the articles similar to Table A, it is arguable that it would be dangerous for the chairman to assume that the previous vote on a show of hands was still valid and safer for him not to consent to the withdrawal of the demand and to proceed with the poll. Another possibility is that if a valid demand for a poll is withdrawn, the chairman could call for another vote on a show of hands to be taken. However, it would be slightly disturbing if the outcome of this second show of hands was different to the first. If that were to happen, it would suggest that a poll probably would have been the most desirable option and the chairman might reasonably be expected to call one himself at this juncture if he has the power to do so.

If the chairman does decide to take any previous vote on a show of hands as the result of the vote on that resolution, it is suggested that he should make a declaration to that effect and if he has not already done so, declare the resolution carried or not carried, as the case may be. In view of the statutory provisions regarding any such declaration by the chairman, this would be conclusive evidence that the resolution has or has not been passed, or passed with a particular majority, without proof of the number or proportion of the votes recorded in favour of or against the resolution (s. 320(1)). This provision does not have effect if a poll is demanded in respect of the resolution (and the demand is not subsequently withdrawn) (s. 320(3)). However, it must still be assumed to apply where a demand for a poll has been made but subsequently withdrawn. Accordingly, the effect of any such declaration could presumably prevent the operation of the common law rule in *R. v. Cooper*.

If a poll demanded before a vote on a show of hands is subsequently withdrawn, it is plainly necessary to put the resolution to a vote by a show of hands. The model articles do not bother making any provision in this regard. However reg. 51 of Table A provides that, if a poll is demanded before the declaration of the result of a show of hands and the demand is duly withdrawn, the meeting shall continue as if the demand had not been made.

17.9.4 Conduct of poll

Articles usually specify the manner in which the poll is to be conducted or who may determine the manner in which it is to be conducted. The model articles for private companies require all polls to be taken immediately in such manner as the chairman of the meeting directs (pcls 44(4), clg 30(4)). Neither the model articles for public companies nor Table A require polls to be taken immediately, except on a resolution to adjourn or to appoint a chairman of the meeting (reg. 51 of Table A and plc 37(4)). They both provide that any other poll shall be taken as the chairman directs within 30 days and that he may appoint scrutineers (who need not be members) and that the result of the poll shall be deemed to be the resolution of the meeting at which the poll was demanded (regs. 49 and 51 of Table A and plc 37).

A poll cannot be taken on a number of resolutions together. In other words, the members must be given an opportunity to vote for or against each resolution separately (*Patent Wood Keg Syndicate v. Pearse* [1909] W.N. 164). See, however, *Re R. E. Jones Ltd.* (1933) 50 T.L.R. 31 where the members agreed to this procedure being used. This does not mean that separate voting papers must be used for each resolution as long as the voting papers allow members to vote for some resolutions and against others (see **Precedents 17.9A to C**).

Where the articles allow the chairman to determine the method of taking the poll but also require the personal attendance of the voter or the proxy appointed, the chairman has no right to direct that the poll be taken by voting papers to be returned by members through the post (*McMillan v. Le Roi Mining Co. Ltd.* [1906] 1 Ch. 331).

Unless the articles specify the length of time for which the poll is to continue, the chairman should not close it as long as votes are still being tendered (*R. v. St Pancras Local Board* (1839) 11 Ad. & El. 356). Where the articles provide that a poll shall be taken 'in such manner as the chairman may direct' the chairman may direct that it be taken immediately (*Re Chillington Iron Co.* (1885) 29 Ch.D. 159). However, where the articles provided for a poll to be taken at a time and place to be fixed by the directors within seven days of the meeting, it was held that the chairman could not direct that a poll be taken immediately (*Re British Flax Producers Co. Ltd.* (1889) 60 L.T. 215).

Regulation 51 of Table A avoids these problems by providing that a poll shall be taken either forthwith or at such time and place as the chairman directs as

long as this is not more than 30 days after the poll is demanded. The model articles for public companies simply provide that a poll must be taken when, where
and in such manner as the chairman directs but must be taken within 30 days of
being demanded (plc 37).

Where articles require a poll to be taken forthwith (or immediately) this means
as soon as practicable (*Jackson v. Hamlyn* [1953] Ch. 577).

Table A and the model articles for public companies both provide that a
demand for a poll shall not prevent the continuance of a meeting for the transaction of any business other than the question on which the poll was demanded
(reg. 51 of Table A and plc 37(6)).

17.9.5 Notice of a poll

A poll taken at a later date is deemed to be a continuance of the original meeting.
The original meeting is deemed to have been suspended rather than adjourned
and it is not necessary to give any notice unless the articles so require (*Shaw v. Tati
Concessions Ltd.* [1913] 1 Ch. 292). Articles often contain provisions which specify
when notice of a poll must be given. Plainly, this is not necessary for the model
articles for private companies, which require all polls to be taken immediately.
However, Table A and the model articles for public companies both provide that no
notice need be given of a poll not taken forthwith if the time and place at which it
is to be taken is announced at the meeting at which it is demanded, but that in any
other case at least seven clear days' notice specifying the time and place at which the
poll is to be taken must be given to all the members (including those who did not
attend the meeting) (reg. 52 of Table A and plc 37(7) and (8)). If the chairman does
not announce the date and time of the poll at the meeting, it follows that it cannot
be held for about eight or nine days and then only if proper notice has been given.

17.9.6 Procedure on a poll

The procedure for conducting a poll will obviously depend in part on any specific
provision made in that regard by a company's articles. Accordingly, the following
outline is only provided as a guide and should be read in conjunction with any
article provisions governing voting by shareholders on a poll.

Action before the meeting

- A summary should be produced of the total proxy votes given in favour of
  the chairman for each resolution indicating the number of votes he has been
  instructed to cast for or against the resolution, any votes withheld and the
  number of votes where the chairman has been given discretion as to how to
  vote.
- A summary should also be produced of any proxies given in favour of other
  persons together with any voting instructions (if any).
- In the case of a listed company, it will be necessary to amalgamate the two
  summaries in order to prepare a schedule of votes tendered by proxy for the

purposes of the disclosures required to be made at the meeting in accordance with the recommendations of the UK Corporate Governance Code (see **10.8.3**).

■ Appoint the people who will conduct any poll which is taken and/or act as scrutineers (usually employees of the company or its solicitors, registrars or auditors) and arrange for their attendance.

■ In the case of a quoted company, monitor whether a valid demand for independent report on a poll has been made and take action accordingly (see **17.12**).

■ Prepare voting papers (see **Precedents 17.9A to C**).

■ Draft script for chairman (see **Appendix 3**).

■ Ascertain the conditions under which a valid demand may be made and brief chairman accordingly.

■ Brief staff and scrutineers and liaise with any independent assessor.

■ Obtain an up-to-date list of members entitled to vote (or if class meeting, members of that class) and annotate which, if any, are not entitled to vote owing to some special restriction (see **17.4**) and which, if any, are entitled to any enhanced voting rights (see **17.5**).

When a poll is demanded

■ If appropriate, the chairman may suggest the demand be withdrawn in view of proxy position.

■ If not withdrawn, take the names of those making the demand and check against the register of members whether they satisfy the conditions for a valid demand.

■ If the demand is not valid or it is withdrawn, the chairman should rule accordingly and proceed with the business:
  - if the demand was made before a vote was taken on a show of hands, the chairman may invite members to vote on the resolution in that manner and declare the result accordingly or decide to continue to proceed with the poll; or
  - if the demand was made after the chairman had declared the result of the vote on a show of hands, the chairman may decide to continue to proceed with the poll or to proceed with the business (see, however, **17.9.3**).

If demand valid

■ The chairman should advise the meeting of the validity of the demand.

■ The chairman should announce when the poll will be held. Depending on the articles and the nature of the business, this may be:
  - immediately;
  - at the conclusion of meeting; or
  - at a later date.

■ If the poll is to be held later (i.e. not immediately), the chairman should proceed to the next item of business.

Holding a poll

- The chairman should explain the procedure for the taking of the poll (see chairman's script at **Appendix 3**).
- Voting papers should be issued to all those entitled to vote (see **Precedents 17.9A and B**).
- The chairman should complete voting forms in respect of proxy votes held by him (see **Precedent 17.9C**).
- Completed voting papers should be collected.
- Each voting paper should be checked for completeness.
- Where the votes are given by proxy:
  - check that person voting has been validly appointed as a proxy; and
  - that proxy has followed member's instruction, if any (see **16.20**).
- Any voting paper not on the face of it valid should be referred to the scrutineers (if any). In cases of doubt the chairman should be asked to make a ruling (see **17.14**).
- Verify holdings against the register of members (or the list of entitlements to vote prepared before the meeting).
- Eliminate votes given by proxy (including those given to the chairman in that capacity) where the member voted in person on the poll.
- If a member has appointed more than one proxy, ensure that the total number of votes cast does not exceed that member's holding. Refer any problems to the chairman.
- Count the votes for and against.
- Prepare a summary of the votes cast for and against in person and by proxy, votes withheld, abstentions and spoilt votes.
- Scrutineers to sign summary and certify the result of the poll.
- Report the result to the chairman.

Declaration of result of poll

- At the meeting
  - if the poll was directed to be taken at a later time, the meeting should be resumed at the appointed time and the result declared; or
  - if the poll was taken immediately, the chairman to announce result when other business completed.
- If the resolution is passed, a copy of it may need to be filed at Companies House and, in the case of listed companies, with the UK Listing Authority (see **14.8**).

■ 17.10 Voting on a poll: votes cast in advance

A company's articles may contain provision to the effect that on a vote on a resolution on a poll taken at a meeting, the votes may include votes cast in advance (s. 322A(1)). This provision was introduced by the Companies (Shareholders'

Rights) Regulations 2009 (SI 2009/1632) to comply with a requirement of the Shareholders' Rights Directive. The ability to vote in advance on a poll is already provided by the system which enables members to appoint the chairman of the meeting as their proxy and to instruct him how to vote. Accordingly, it is not clear what advantage would be gained by a company or its members from a separate system allowing votes on a poll to be cast in advance.

If such a system for voting in advance is provided for in a company's articles, it must comply with certain conditions. The condition in s. 322A(2) only applies to companies that are traded companies (see definition at **8.5.1**). It provides that any article relating to voting in advance at a general meeting may be made subject only to such requirements and restrictions as are necessary to ensure the identification of the person voting, and that are proportionate to the achievement of that objective. However, it also clarifies that nothing in this rule affects any power of a company to require reasonable evidence of the entitlement of any person who is not a member to vote. A traded company for these purposes is defined in s. 380C as a company any shares of which carry rights to vote at general meetings and are admitted to trading on a regulated market in an EEA state by or with the consent of the company.

The condition in s. 322A(3) applies to any company which makes provision in its articles for voting in advance. It provides that any provision of a company's articles is void in so far as it would have the effect of requiring any document casting a vote in advance to be received by the company or another person earlier than:

- in the case of a poll taken more than 48 hours after it was demanded, 24 hours before the time appointed for the taking of the poll; and
- in the case of any other poll, 48 hours before the time for holding the meeting or adjourned meeting.

In calculating the above periods, no account may be taken of any part of a day that is not a working day (s. 322A(4)).

■ 17.11 Results of a poll

The date of a resolution passed on a poll is the date the result of the poll is ascertained (*Holmes v. Keyes* [1959] Ch. 199). Articles may seem to override this rule by providing that the result of the poll shall be the decision of the meeting in respect of the resolution on which the poll was demanded (e.g. reg. 49 of Table A and plc 37(3)). However, all this type of article provision probably does is enable a meeting to be closed pending the outcome of the poll. It is feasible that a company's articles could provide that the date of a resolution passed on a poll is deemed to be the date on which the poll was taken or the date on which voting on the poll closed. However, this is not normally considered necessary because the company will normally seek to ensure that the results of the poll are determined on the day it is taken or on the day that voting on it was closed.

Probably the least satisfactory aspect of voting on a poll rather than a show of hands is the fact that the result of the poll is rarely known until after the meeting. This often means that the members who attended the meeting will have no idea whether the resolution has been passed or defeated, let alone how many votes were cast for or against it. The only exception would appear to be where the articles require a poll to be taken immediately. In some cases, e.g. on a poll on a resolution to adjourn or to appoint a chairman of the meeting, the requirement that the poll be taken immediately implies that the result must also be determined before the meeting can progress. However, there is no reason why this should be the case for any other poll taken under the model articles for private companies, which require all polls to be taken immediately. In practice, unless there is a good reason why the business of the meeting should be suspended until the outcome of the vote on the poll is determined, it is suggested that once the poll has been taken, the meeting may proceed to the next item of business and the results of the poll can be declared as and when they become available.

There is no requirement to notify members of the results of the poll. This is the case even with regard to the members who demanded it. This is not to say that the company should refuse to reveal the results of the poll. The result must be recorded in the minutes and any member may request a copy of the minutes (see **26.10**). In addition, if the resolution is one which must be filed at Companies House, the fact that it has been passed will become a matter of public record (see **14.8**).

Quoted companies are required to publish the results of any poll on a website (see **17.12**). Listed companies must announce the results of resolutions passed at any meeting of the company and file copies of any such resolutions with the UK Listing Authority (see **14.8.3**).

There is no reason why a company should not notify the results of a poll to the members who demanded it. However, a publicly traded company should bear in mind that the result may be price-sensitive information and it may therefore need to be announced before the members are notified. Some companies advertise the results of the poll in a newspaper.

A company may, if it so desires, inform the members how particular votes were cast. It has been held that this is not confidential information and that the company has a right to the information if the poll is conducted by independent scrutineers (*Haarhaus & Co GmbH v. Law Debenture Trust Corp. plc* [1988] B.C.L.C. 640).

■ 17.12 Website publication of poll results and independent reports on a poll

17.12.1 Quoted companies – website publication
Quoted companies (see definition at **8.5.2**) are required to disclose on a website the results of any poll taken at a general meeting, specifying the number of votes cast for and against (s. 341).

The information required to be made available under s. 341 must be made available on a website maintained by or on behalf of the company as soon as reasonably practicable and be kept available for two years after publication (s. 353).

17.12.2 Traded company website publication requirements
Under s. 341(1A) a traded company (see definition at **8.5.1**) must publish the following information on its website in relation to a poll taken at a general meeting:

(a) the date of the meeting;
(b) the text of the resolution or, as the case may be, a description of the subject matter of the poll;
(c) the number of votes validly cast;
(d) the proportion of the company's issued share capital (determined at the time at which the right to vote is determined under s. 360B(2)) represented by those votes;
(e) the number of votes cast in favour;
(f) the number of votes cast against; and
(g) the number of abstentions (if counted).

The company must comply with this requirement by the end of the 16-day period beginning with the day of the meeting, or, or if later, the end of the first working day following the day on which the result of the poll is declared (s. 341(1B)).

The information must be made available on a website maintained by or on behalf of the company and be kept available for two years after publication in accordance with s. 353.

17.12.3 Independent report on a poll
Members of quoted companies (see definition at **8.5.2**) are given a right to require an independent scrutiny of any polled vote, with the scrutineer's report having to be disclosed on the company's website (ss. 342–354). The directors are required to obtain an independent report if they receive requests to do so from members representing 5% of the total voting rights or at least 100 members holding on average £100's worth of share capital each. A request may be made in hard copy or electronic form, must identify the poll or polls to which it relates and must be received by the company not later than one week after the date on which the poll is taken.

On receipt of a valid request, a company must appoint an independent assessor to prepare a report who meets the requirements of s. 344 as to independence and has no other role in relation to any poll on which he is to report (e.g. collecting and counting votes) (s. 343). These rules will prevent a company from appointing its registrar as the independent assessor.

In his report, the independent assessor is required to state:

(a) whether the procedures adopted in connection with the poll or polls were adequate;

(b) whether the votes cast were fairly and accurately recorded;

(c) whether the validity of members' appointments of proxies was fairly assessed;

(d) whether the notice of meeting complied with s. 325; and

(e) whether there was any breach of s. 326 (company-sponsored invitations to appoint a proxy).

Sections 348 and 349 give the independent assessor a right to attend the meeting and a right of access to relevant information.

Where an independent assessor has been appointed to report on a poll, the company must make the following information available on a website (s. 351):

(a) the fact of his appointment and his identity;

(b) the text of any resolutions or a description of the subject matter of the poll(s) to which his appointment relates; and

(c) a copy of his report.

The information required to be made available under s. 351 must be made available on a website maintained by or on behalf of the company as soon as reasonably practicable and be kept available for two years after publication (s. 353).

■ 17.13 Chairman's casting vote

Articles may purport to give the chairman a casting vote. None of the model articles do so as it is thought that the chairman's casting vote is incompatible with the provisions on voting and resolutions in the 2006 Act.

Table A originally contained a provision giving the chairman a casting vote (reg. 50). However this was deleted for companies incorporated under the Companies Act 1985 between 1 October 2007 and 30 September 2009 inclusive.

Regulation 50 will still apply to any company incorporated before 1 October 2007 that is subject to Table A, assuming that its application has not been excluded. As mentioned previously, it is thought that the chairman's casting vote conflicts with certain provisions of the 2006 Act. The provisions in question are ss. 281 and 282 of the Act. Section 281(3) provides that where a provision of the Companies Acts requires a resolution of a company, or of the members (or a class of members) of a company, and does not specify what kind of resolution is required, what is required is an ordinary resolution unless the company's articles require a higher majority (or unanimity). The Companies Acts have never previously included a provision to this effect, although this has always been assumed to be the position. Neither has any previous version of the Companies Act ever attempted to define what actually constitutes an ordinary resolution, and it is the fact that the 2006 Act does so in s. 282 which potentially causes problems with regard to the chairman's casting vote. Previously the question as to what constitutes an ordinary resolution (or a resolution of the company) would have been determined by a combination of the common law and a company's articles.

The common law rule is the members of a body may ordinarily make decisions at a meeting by a resolution passed by a simple majority. As this is a common law rule, it was subject to variation by a company's articles. So any resolution passed by virtue of the chairman's casting vote would still be valid.

Statutory provisions such as s. 282 override any common law rule and article provisions unless specific provision is made to preserve their operation. Section 282 makes no such provision, although a saving was subsequently introduced by the Third Commencement Order which has the effect of preserving the operation of certain articles giving the chairman a casting vote. The reason why the saving was introduced is explained below. The effect of the saving and subsequent modifications that have been made to it are explained in **17.13.1**.

Section 282(1) provides that an ordinary resolution of the members (or of a class of members) of a company means a resolution that is passed by a simple majority. Section 282(2) and (3) originally provided that:

(2) a resolution passed at a meeting on a show of hands is passed by a simple majority if it is passed by a simple majority of [(a) the members who, being entitled to do so, vote in person on the resolution, and (b) the persons who vote on the resolution as duly appointed proxies of members entitled to vote on it]; and

(3) a resolution passed on a poll taken at a meeting is passed by a simple majority if it is passed by members representing a simple majority of the total voting rights of members who (being entitled to do so) vote in person, by proxy on the resolution.

Note: The words in square brackets above were substituted with the words '[the votes cast by those entitled to vote]' by SI 2009/1632.

It can be seen that the original wording of s. 282 only allowed the votes of members (and, by virtue of ss. 285 and 323 respectively, the votes of members represented by proxy or corporate representative) to be counted in determining whether a resolution is passed as an ordinary resolution. It should be noted, however, that s. 282(2) was subsequently amended by SI 2009/1632 to provide that an ordinary resolution passed on a show of hands is passed if it is passed 'by a simple majority of the votes cast by those entitled to vote'. It is submitted that a casting vote given to the chairman under the articles could be an entitlement to vote for these purposes and that under s. 282 (as amended) any such provision giving the chairman a casting vote could therefore be effective on a show of hands. The amendments did not, however, change the position with regard to the chairman's casting vote on a poll which may still be ineffective unless the saving described in **17.13.1** applies because s. 282(3) still refers to votes cast by members (whether in person, by proxy or in advance). It should be noted in this regard that ss. 281 and 282 may only apply in relation to resolutions required under the Companies Acts to be passed as an ordinary resolution. Even if one assumes that the chairman's casting vote is not effective on a poll taken on such a resolution, it may still be effective in relation to resolutions that are not required under the Companies Acts but which are, for example, required under a company's articles or under the common law.

It could be argued that the (probably unintended) consequences of the amendments made to s. 282 are rather unsatisfactory as it is more appropriate for the chairman to have a casting vote after a poll has been taken than after a vote on a show of hands, unless the chairman is sure that the outcome of any poll would be exactly the same as the vote on a show of hands. Where the chairman is not sure that the outcome would be the same, the proper course of action would presumably be for him to call a poll, assuming he has power to do so, although it could be argued that the chairman could sometimes exercise his casting vote to ensure that the will of the majority prevails (or what he believes would have been the will of the majority if a poll had been taken).

17.13.1 Saving for companies incorporated before 1 October 2007

The validity of articles giving the chairman a casting vote may be preserved in the case of companies that were incorporated before 1 October 2007 and whose articles included such a provision immediately before that date. Paragraph 23A of Sch. 3 to the Third Commencement Order (SI 2007/2194) includes a saving (which was inserted by Sch. 5, para. 2(5) of the Fifth Companies Act 2006 Commencement Order (SI 2007/3495)) designed to ensure that articles giving the chairman a casting vote still have effect and which allows companies that have removed such a provision since 1 October 2007 to revert to it should they wish to do so. It should be noted that this saving does not apply to a company that is a traded company by virtue of an amendment (shown in square brackets below) made to para. 23A by the Companies (Shareholders' Rights) Regulations 2009 (SI 2009/1632).

> 23A. (1) This paragraph applies where, immediately before 1st October 2007, the articles of a company provided that in the event of equality of votes on an ordinary resolution, whether on a show of hands or on a poll, the chairman should have a casting vote in addition to any other vote that the chairman might have.
>
> (2) If that provision has not been removed by a subsequent alteration of the articles, it continues to have effect notwithstanding sections 281(3) and 282.
>
> (3) If that provision has been removed by a subsequent alteration of the articles, the company may at any time restore that provision, which shall have effect notwithstanding sections 281(3) and 282.
>
> [(4) Nothing in this paragraph applies in relation to a traded company (as defined by section 360C of the Companies Act 2006).]

17.13.2 Operation of the chairman's casting vote

Where a company's articles provide for the chairman to have a casting vote and that article is still effective (see above), they will normally make provision similar to reg. 50 of the original version of the 1985 Table, which states:

> 50. In the case of an equality of votes, whether on a show of hands or on a poll, the chairman shall be entitled to a casting vote in addition to any other vote he may have.

The circumstances in which it is reasonable for the chairman to use his or her casting vote on a show of hands are fairly limited. It is submitted that in most cases, in order to ascertain the true sense of the meeting, the chairman should exercise his power to demand a poll rather than use the casting vote, particularly where he holds proxies on behalf of the members. A casting vote cannot be used to manufacture a tie.

The chairman should use his casting vote in the best interests of the company. This is, of course, a vague duty and it is unlikely that the chairman will be entirely impartial. In Parliament, the Speaker normally uses his or her casting vote to maintain the status quo. This would normally entail voting against the resolution as most resolutions seek to change the status quo. However, in these circumstances it is not necessary for the chairman to do anything because the resolution would not be passed if the number of votes cast both for and against it were the same.

The existence of a chairman's casting vote could in certain circumstances be intended to ensure that one group of shareholders is able to hold sway over another. For example, a company may have been established with two groups of shareholders each holding an equal number of shares but with one group holding 'A ordinary shares' and the other 'B ordinary shares'. The 'A ordinary shareholders' may have been given the right to appoint three directors and the 'B ordinary shareholders' the right to appoint only two directors. This would mean that the 'A ordinary shareholders' would be able to determine who is appointed chairman of the board of directors and, therefore, who will chair general meetings and get the casting vote. In other words, the whole structure of the company's shares is designed to ensure that one group of shareholders actually has more control than the other. In these circumstances, one might reasonably expect the chairman to exercise his casting vote in the interests of his own group of shareholders.

The courts have endorsed the use by the chairman of a 'conditional' casting vote where the validity of some votes had been in doubt and it was not clear whether or not the vote was tied (see **17.14**).

■ 17.14 Objections to qualification of voter

Articles usually provide that objections to the qualification of any voter must be raised at the meeting at which the vote objected to is tendered and that every vote not disallowed at the meeting shall be valid. Objections made in due time are normally required to be referred to the chairman whose decision shall be final and conclusive (e.g. reg. 58 of Table A, pcls 43, clg 29 and plc 35). Section 287 states that nothing in Part 13, Chapter 1 of the Act affects any provision of a company's articles requiring an objection to a person's entitlement to vote on a resolution to be made in accordance with the articles and for the determination of any such objection to be final and conclusive, or the grounds on which such a determination may be questioned in legal proceedings. Accordingly, such article provisions must still be assumed to be binding and votes not disallowed cannot be challenged afterwards unless the chairman is guilty of fraud or some other misconduct (*Wall v. London and Northern Assets Corporation* [1898] 2 Ch. 469).

In *Re Bradford Investments plc* [1990] B.C.C. 740, such an article was held not to operate with regard to rulings made by a person who was not a member, proxy or corporate representative but who had presided over the election of a chairman of the meeting.

Articles may also make separate provision regarding counting errors (see example at **Precedent 17.14**).

18

Shareholder remedies

18.1 Summary

- Certain breaches of the statutory requirements relating to general meetings may make the meeting, or some of the business transacted at it, liable to challenge (see **18.2**).
- Shareholders can enforce their rights as members under the articles against the company and against other members. However, the court may refuse to intervene where the breach is deemed to be a mere internal irregularity which could be cured by the majority simply by following the correct procedure (see **18.3**).
- The proper plaintiff in the case of wrongs done to the company is the company itself. The courts will only allow shareholders to bring actions on behalf of the company against the wrongdoers in very limited circumstances. As a general rule the will of the majority is allowed to prevail (see **18.4**).
- Although a company may alter its articles, the alterations must not discriminate unfairly against the minority (see **18.5**).
- Shareholders may apply to the court for relief from conduct which is unfairly prejudicial. The court's remedy in most cases of unfair prejudice will be to order the majority shareholders to purchase the shares of the minority (see **18.6**).
- A member may also apply to the court to have the company wound up on just and equitable grounds under s. 122(1)(g) of the Insolvency Act 1986. The court may grant such an order even though the company has been run in accordance with the Act and the company's constitution (see **18.7**).
- The remedies outlined above tend to be used as a last resort. The Act provides various other means by which shareholders may be able to reconcile their problems (see **18.8**).

18.2 Breach of statutory requirements

Meetings held and decisions made in breach of any statutory requirements are liable to be declared invalid. For example, a resolution which the Act requires to be passed as a special resolution will be invalid if it is only passed as an ordinary resolution. A general meeting called at less than the statutory minimum period of notice is liable to be declared invalid, unless the members have consented to shorter notice.

It might be thought that any such breach of a statutory requirement would automatically render a decision taken at a general meeting invalid. However, this will not necessarily always be the case where:

(a) the relevant statutory provision can be modified by a company's articles and the company complied with any relevant modification of that provision contained in its articles;

(b) the relevant statutory provision specifically provides that failure to comply shall not invalidate a decision (e.g. where a sole member fails to provide a written record of a decision which has effect as if taken at a general meeting); and

(c) the courts decide otherwise under a common law rule such as the principle of unanimous consent.

A breach of a statutory requirement may not be noticed until long after the general meeting took place or the decision was made, or may never be noticed at all. Even if the breach is noticed, it may be that there is nobody concerned enough to challenge the validity of the proceedings or the decision. However, a person who has sufficient interest could challenge the validity of a decision in an attempt to prevent it from being implemented or taking effect. Generally speaking this sort of action needs to be taken fairly promptly and the longer a person waits, the less inclined the courts become to intervene, particularly where intervention may prejudice the interests of innocent third parties. One of the ways the courts can avoid having to do so is by applying the principle of unanimous consent and by deeming the members to have acquiesced in an irregularity by failing to take action soon enough.

However, the courts are sometimes prepared to intervene long after the event. For example, the courts are routinely prepared to intervene long after the event if there has been a breach of any of the procedural requirements for obtaining approval for an off-market contract for the purchase of own shares. The court will often declare such a resolution invalid, order the member whose shares were purportedly purchased to repay any money they received and order that their name be restored to the register. The court will not normally have any qualms in doing so, particularly when a company is being wound up as insolvent because the beneficiaries of such an order would be the creditors.

Although it may not always be possible to predict conclusively whether a breach of a statutory requirement will invalidate a meeting or a decision, it can be said to render the meeting or the decision liable to challenge. This uncertainty is dangerous from the perspective of the company, its directors and, in some cases, the members. The occurrence of a breach can give rise to potential civil liabilities on the part of some or all of them. A company and its directors would not normally want this kind of uncertainty hanging over them and would normally want to take steps to rectify the breach once it becomes known. In cases of doubt the company might even seek a court declaration that the decision-making process was valid. The danger of leaving the matter unsettled is that there might be someone out there who one day has sufficient incentive to take action. Very often, that will be the company itself (after a new board has been appointed) or, where the company has become insolvent, the liquidator.

■ 18.3 Section 33 contract

The provisions of a company's constitution bind the company and its members to the same extent as if there were covenants on the part of the company and of each member to observe those provisions (s. 33). This provision creates a contract (the 'section 33 contract') between the company and its members, the terms of which are contained in the company's constitution.

Section 17 provides that unless the context otherwise requires, references in the Companies Acts to a company's constitution include the company's articles, and any resolutions and agreements to which Chapter 3 of Part 3 applies (i.e. resolutions and agreements which must be filed with the registrar). A company's articles will include any provisions of an old company's memorandum which are deemed to form part of its articles under s. 28.

The s. 33 contract differs in a number of ways from normal contracts. Provision is made in the Act for its terms to be altered by a special majority (see s. 21). The consent of all the parties is required to vary normal contracts. And although the courts regard articles as commercial documents which should be construed so as to give them reasonable business efficacy (*Holmes v. Keyes* [1959] Ch. 199, 215, per Jenkins LJ), the Court of Appeal has held that terms cannot be implied into the articles in order to do so (*Bratton Seymour Service Co Ltd. v. Oxborough* [1992] B.C.L.C. 693).

A company can enforce the s. 33 contract against its members (*Hickman's case* [1915] 1 Ch. 881) and the members can enforce it against each other (*Rayfield v. Hands* [1960] Ch. 1). The members can also enforce the contract against the company, but only in limited circumstances.

It has been held on a number of occasions that members may only enforce provisions in the articles which confer rights on them in their capacity as members. For example, it has been held that a member cannot enforce a provision in the articles that he should be the company's solicitor (*Eley v. Positive Government Security Life Assurance Co Ltd.* (1976) 1 Ex. D. 88) but can enforce his right to vote under the articles (*Pender v. Lushington* (1877) 6 Ch.D. 70). The application of this rule in cases involving shareholder directors is less certain. In *Browne v. La Trinidad* (1887) 37 Ch.D. 1, the Court of Appeal refused to enforce a provision in the company's articles that a member should be a director and should not be removed from office. However, in *Quinn & Axtens Ltd. v. Salmon* [1909] A.C. 442, the court upheld a provision in the articles giving a director a right to veto certain board resolutions.

The second major exception for shareholders is that they may not be able to bring personal actions for breaches which the courts consider to be mere internal irregularities. As a general rule the courts impose this restriction where it is clear that even if the action is allowed, the majority will still get its own way by following the correct procedures. For example, in *MacDougall v. Gardiner* (1875) 1 Ch.D. 13, the court refused to declare an adjournment passed on a show of hands invalid simply because the chairman had improperly refused to allow a minority shareholder to demand a poll. Where, however, it is clear that the breach affected the outcome of the meeting, the courts will allow an action to proceed, e.g. where the chairman improperly excluded some votes cast by a proxy in favour of a resolution which would have been passed had they been accepted (*Oliver v. Dalgleish* [1963] 1 W.L.R. 1274).

■ 18.4 Derivative actions

The courts have applied a longstanding rule which limits the ability of shareholders to bring actions on behalf of the company (derivative actions) for wrongs done to the company. This rule has been known as the 'rule in *Foss v. Harbottle*' because it was first firmly established in case of that name in 1843. The rule is founded on two important principles. The first is that where a wrong is done to a company, only the company can take action against the wrongdoers and not individual members (the proper plaintiff principle). The second is that the will of the majority of the members should generally be allowed to prevail in the running of the company's business. Thus in *Foss v. Harbottle* (1843) 2 Hare 461 the court refused to intervene in a case brought by minority shareholders who alleged that the directors had misapplied the company's property, because the acts complained of were capable of being confirmed by the members and there was nothing to prevent the company from obtaining redress in its corporate capacity.

This rule in *Foss v. Harbottle* is subject to certain important exceptions. These were set out by the Court of Appeal in *Edwards v. Halliwell* [1950] 2 All E.R. 1064 and restated in *Prudential Assurance Co Ltd. v. Newman Industries (No. 2)* [1982] Ch. 204 as follows:

(1) The proper plaintiff in an action in respect of a wrong alleged to be done to a corporation is, *prima facie*, the corporation.

(2) Where the alleged wrong is a transaction which might be made binding on the corporation and on all its members by a simple majority of the members, no individual member of the corporation is allowed to maintain an action in respect of that matter because, if the majority confirms the transaction, [the question is at an end]; or if the majority challenges the transaction, there is no valid reason why the company should not sue.

(3) There is no room for the operation of the rule if the alleged wrong is ultra vires the corporation, because the majority of members cannot confirm the transaction.

(4) There is also no room for the operation of the rule if the transaction complained of could be validly done or sanctioned only by a special resolution or the like, because a simple majority cannot confirm a transaction which requires the concurrence of a greater majority.

(5) There is an exception to the rule where what has been done amounts to fraud and the wrongdoers are themselves in control of the company.

18.4.1 *Ultra vires* transactions

The exception to the rule in *Foss v. Harbottle* that the majority cannot confirm an act which is *ultra vires* the company (i.e. beyond the capacity of the company as prescribed by the objects clause in the memorandum) is now qualified by s. 239 which provides a procedure which enables the members to ratify acts of the directors (including those which are beyond the powers of the company) by ordinary resolution, albeit one where any votes in favour of ratification cast by a director (as a member of the company) or any connected persons are disregarded.

It should also be noted that s. 40(4) specifically preserves a shareholder's right to bring a personal action against the company to restrain it from committing an *ultra vires* act.

Section 239 does not, however, allow a company to ratify transactions which are *ultra vires* because they are illegal (e.g. in breach of a statutory requirement) and a shareholder will be able to bring a derivative action against the wrongdoers on behalf of the company in these circumstances (*Smith v. Croft (No. 2)* [1988] Ch. 114).

18.4.2 Special resolution procedures

Members can bring actions to restrain breaches of special majority procedures (whether they are contained in the Act or the memorandum or articles) and to prevent the company from acting on resolutions passed as a result of such breaches. In *Edwards v. Halliwell* [1950] 2 All E.R. 1064, the Court of Appeal declared a decision by a trade union to increase its membership fees invalid because a requirement in its constitution that a two-thirds majority of the members should agree had not been observed.

18.4.3 Statutory derivative claims

Derivative actions used to be allowed by virtue of an equitable concession by the Court of Chancery which made an exception to the general rule that the proper plaintiff in an action seeking redress for a wrong done to the company is the company itself.

The Companies Act 2006 introduced a statutory procedure for derivative claims (and in Scotland, derivative proceedings) which largely replaces those aspects of the rule in *Foss v. Harbottle* that apply to such claims or proceedings. Under s. 260 a member may bring proceedings in respect of a cause of action on behalf of a company seeking relief on behalf of the company. Such claims can be brought only in relation to a cause of action arising from an actual or proposed act or omission involving negligence, default, breach of duty or breach of trust by a director, former director or shadow director of a company.

The procedure for making an application in s. 261 requires an initial petition to be made to the court for permission to proceed with the case. Section 262 enables a member to apply for permission to continue a claim brought originally by the company as a derivate claim where the company has failed to prosecute the claim diligently or the manner in which it has commenced the claim amounts to an abuse of the process of the court.

Section 263 sets out the grounds on which the court must decide whether permission to proceed with a derivative action should be given. Permission or leave must be refused if the court is satisfied:

(a) that a person acting in accordance with s. 172 (duty to promote the success of the company) would not seek to continue the claim; or
(b) where the cause of action arises from an act or omission that is yet to occur, that the act or omission has been authorised by the company; or
(c) where the cause of action arises from an act or omission that has already occurred, that the act or omission was authorised by the company before it occurred, or has been ratified by the company since it occurred.

In considering whether to give permission (or leave) the court must also take into account, in particular:

(a) whether the member is acting in good faith in seeking to continue the claim;
(b) the importance that a person acting in accordance with s. 172 (duty to promote the success of the company) would attach to continuing it;
(c) where the cause of action results from an act or omission that is yet to occur, whether the act or omission could be, and in the circumstances would be likely to be authorised by the company before it occurs, or ratified by the company after it occurs;
(d) where the cause of action arises from an act or omission that has already occurred, whether the act or omission could be, and in the circumstances would be likely to be, ratified by the company;
(e) whether the company has decided not to pursue the claim;
(f) whether the act or omission in respect of which the claim is brought gives rise to a cause of action that the member could pursue in his own right rather than on behalf of the company.

The requirement to take into account whether the member is acting in good faith in seeking to continue the claim reflects the common law rule that a member may be prevented from pursuing a derivative action where there is evidence of '. . . behaviour by the minority shareholder, which, in the eyes of equity, would render it unjust to allow a claim brought by the company at his insistence to succeed' (*Nurcumbe v. Nurcombe* [1985] 1 W.L.R. 370, 378, per Browne-Wilkinson LJ).

In addition, in considering whether to give permission (or leave) the court shall have particular regard to any evidence before it as to the views of members of the company who have no personal interest, direct or indirect, in the matter (s. 263(4)). This provision is designed to reflect a ruling in *Smith v. Croft (No. 2)* [1988] Ch. 114, in which Knox J held that a shareholder could not bring a derivative action if an 'independent organ' did not want it to proceed. In this case, the wrongdoer controlled about 66% of the voting rights at general meetings and the plaintiffs about 14%. Another shareholder who was judged by Knox J to be independent held about 19% and opposed the action being brought. The plaintiff and this independent shareholder were deemed to constitute an independent organ and Knox J dismissed the action on the basis that this independent organ did not want it to proceed.

18.4.4 Fraud on the minority

Derivative actions were designed by the courts to enable members to bring an action on behalf of the company where the wrongdoers have committed a 'fraud on the minority' and control the company. The word 'fraud' in this context embraced a wider equitable meaning than deceit and in reality could be considered to be a wrong done to the company rather than to the minority. Lord Davey defined fraud in *Burland v. Earle* [1902] A.C. 83 as embracing all cases where the wrongdoers 'are endeavouring, directly or indirectly, to appropriate to themselves money, property or advantages which belong to the company or in which the other shareholders are entitled to participate'. It should be noted that this definition did not embrace situations where the wrongdoers did not benefit. Neither did it cover negligence on the part of the directors. In *Pavlides v. Jensen* [1956] Ch. 565, it was held that a shareholder could not sue the directors for negligently selling a mine at a gross undervalue under the fraud on the minority exception to the rule in *Foss v. Harbottle*. In these circumstances, it was thought that the proper course would be for the company to sue the directors and, if the directors sought to prevent it from doing so for their own benefit, this would probably constitute a fraud on the minority.

The statutory procedure probably enables a wider range of derivative claims to be brought on behalf of the company. However, at heart, their main purpose is probably still to provide redress where there has been a fraud on the minority.

In order to bring a derivative claim under the statutory procedure it is probably no longer necessary to prove that that the alleged wrongdoers control the company. This was relatively simple to prove where they owned a majority of shares conferring voting rights and it was not necessary in such circumstances to demonstrate that the wrongdoers have refused to institute proceedings (*Mason v. Harris* (1879) 11 Ch.D. 97). However, it was rather more difficult in the case of listed companies notwithstanding the fact that it had been held to be sufficient to demonstrate that the wrongdoers secured with their votes the passing of a resolution that the company would not institute proceedings, even if they did not own a majority of the voting shares (*Cook v. Deeks* [1916] 1 A.C. 554). In *Prudential Assurance Co. Ltd. v Newman Industries (No. 2)* [1982] Ch. 204 it was observed as a dictum that control 'embraces a wide spectrum extending from an overall absolute majority of votes at one end to a majority of votes at the other made up of those likely to be cast by the delinquent himself plus those voting with him as a result of influence or apathy'.

■ 18.5 Alteration of articles

The Act allows a company to alter its articles by special resolution (s. 21), subject to any entrenched provisions (see s. 22). However, this power of amendment must be exercised by the members in good faith for the benefit of the company as a whole (*Allen v. Gold Reefs of West Africa Ltd.* [1900] 1 Ch. 656). In *Greenhalgh v. Ardene Cinemas Ltd.* [1951] Ch. 286, Evershed MR said [at p. 291]:

> Certain principles, I think, can be safely stated as emerging from the authorities. In the first place, I think it is now plain that 'bona fide for the benefit of the company as a whole' means not two things but one thing. It means that the shareholder must proceed upon what, in his honest opinion, is for the benefit of the company as a whole. The second thing is that the phrase 'the company as a whole' does not . . . mean the company as a commercial entity, distinct from the corporators: it means the corporators as a general body. That is to say, the case may be taken of an individual hypothetical member and it may be asked whether what is proposed is, in the honest opinion of those who voted in its favour, for that person's benefit. I think that the matter can, in practice, be more accurately and precisely stated by looking at the converse and saying that a special resolution of this kind would be liable to be impeached if the effect of it were to discriminate between the majority shareholders and the minority shareholders.

If the shareholders have acted honestly in what they believe to be the best interests of the company, the court is unlikely to interfere unless there are no reasonable grounds upon which such a decision could be reached (*Shuttleworth v. Cox Bros. & Co.* [1927] 2 K.B. 9).

Thus an alteration which gave rights of expropriation at a fair value with respect to the shares of any member who was in business as a competitor was held to be valid even though such a member existed at the time of the alteration (*Sidebottom v. Kershaw, Leese & Co.* [1920] 1 Ch. 154 (C.A.)). However, an alteration which enabled the majority to require any member (other than a named member) to transfer his shares was held to be invalid (*Dafen Tinplate Co. Ltd. v. Llanelly Steel Co.* (1917) Ltd. [1920] 2 Ch. 124).

An alteration giving the company a lien over fully-paid shares for other debts of the holder was held to be valid because it was capable of applying to all fully paid shares, even though at the time the change only adversely affected the position of those who sought to challenge it (*Allen v. Gold Reefs of West Africa Ltd.* [1900] 1 Ch. 656).

It should be noted that even though minority shareholders might not succeed under this heading, they could be entitled to relief under the unfair prejudice procedures set out below.

■ 18.6 Unfairly prejudicial conduct

A member may petition the court for relief from unfairly prejudicial conduct under s. 994. This statutory remedy has removed many of the obstacles which prevented minority shareholders from seeking relief under the common law. Any member may petition the court and there is no need to satisfy the requirements of the rule in *Foss v. Harbottle*. Relief under s. 994 is not restricted to minority shareholders although the court will not grant a majority shareholder a remedy if he can easily rid himself of the prejudice by using his majority shareholding (*Re Baltic Real Estate (No. 2)* [1993] B.C.L.C. 246).

Where the court is satisfied that a petition is well founded, it may make any order it thinks fit for giving relief in respect of the matters complained of (s. 996). The order may, for example:

- regulate the conduct of the company's affairs in the future;
- require the company to refrain from doing or continuing an act complained of;
- require the company to do an act which the petitioner has complained it has omitted to do;
- authorise civil proceedings to be brought in the name of and on behalf of the company by such person or persons and on such terms as the court may direct;
- require the company not to make any, or any specified, alterations to its articles without leave of the court; and
- provide for the purchase of the shares of any members of the company by other members or by the company itself and in the case of a purchase by the company itself, the reduction of the company's capital accordingly.

The court may grant a petitioner relief under s. 994 where the company's affairs are being (or have been) conducted in a manner which is unfairly prejudicial to the interests of its members generally or some of the members (including at least the petitioner), or where any actual or proposed act or omission of the company (including an act or omission on its behalf) is or would be so prejudicial (s. 994(1)). According to a study undertaken on behalf of the Law Commission for its Consultation Paper No. 142 'Shareholder Remedies', the conduct which most petitioners (over 67%) complain of in cases brought under this heading is exclusion from the management of the company. It also reported that nearly 70% of petitioners seek an order for the purchase of their shares.

For an example of a case on exclusion from the company's management, see *Re Saul D Harrison & Sons plc* [1995] 1 B.C.L.C. 14, where the court held that the petitioner had a legitimate expectation of being able to participate in the management of the company and that his exclusion could therefore be unfairly prejudicial to his interests.

Relief has been given where a member who held 60% of a company's shares voted to allot himself new shares to increase his holding to 96% and reduce the holding of a minority shareholder from 40 to 4% (*Re D R Chemicals* (1989) 5 B.C.C. 39). In this case the majority shareholder was ordered to purchase the minority shareholder's 40% holding at a price to be fixed by independent valuation.

Cases have also been brought successfully where there has been a deliberate diversion of the company's business by those in control to another business owned by them, e.g. *Re London School of Electronics Ltd.* [1986] Ch. 211.

In *Re a Company (No. 002612 of 1984)* (1986) 2 B.C.C. 99, it was held that a director's remuneration of over £350,000 over a 14-month period was plainly in excess of anything he had earned and was therefore unfairly prejudicial to the petitioner's interests. Excessive remuneration is often linked to the non-payment of dividends. However, the non-payment of dividends could in itself be unfairly prejudicial even though it affects all shareholders equally.

The courts are reluctant to grant relief for mismanagement (*Re Elingdata Ltd.* [1991] B.C.L.C. 959). However, in *Re Macro (Ipswich) Ltd.* [1994] 2 B.C.L.C. 354, Arden J granted relief for specific acts of mismanagement which had been repeated over many years and which the respondent had failed to prevent or rectify. A failure to provide information about how the company is being run to a person who has a right to be consulted on major decisions could constitute unfairly prejudicial conduct (*Re R A Noble* [1983] B.C.L.C. 273).

The Secretary of State may also petition the court for an order if it appears to him that a company's affairs are being or have been conducted in a manner which is unfairly prejudicial to the interests of its members or some of its members (s. 995).

■ 18.7 Just and equitable winding up

Shareholders may in certain circumstances petition the court under s. 122(1)(g) of the Insolvency Act 1986 for an order that the company be wound up on just and equitable grounds. Indeed, this is often pleaded in the alternative to a petition under the unfair prejudice procedures. The House of Lords has held that a member may petition for a winding up on just and equitable grounds if he can show any circumstances affecting him in his relations with the company or with the other shareholders for which winding up is a just and equitable solution (*Ebrahimi v. Westbourne Galleries Ltd.* [1973] A.C. 360). In that case, the plaintiff and a Mr Nazar formed a private company in 1958 to carry on a business, which they had previously done as equal partners, and were appointed the company's first directors. Shortly afterwards, N's son also became a director and between them N and his son controlled the majority of votes at general meetings. All the company's profits were distributed as directors' remuneration and no dividends were ever paid. At a general meeting in 1969, Mr Ebrahimi was removed as a director by N and his son in accordance with the statutory procedures. Mr Ebrahimi petitioned the court to wind up the company on just and equitable grounds and this was allowed even though N and his son had acted in strict accordance with the Act and the company's articles. Lord Wiberforce explained the meaning of 'just and equitable' by saying:

> The words are a recognition of the fact that a limited company is more than a mere legal entity, with a personality in law of its own: that there is room in company law for recognition of the fact that behind it, or amongst it, there are individuals, with rights, expectations and obligations inter se which are not necessarily submerged in the company structure . . . The just and equitable provision does not . . . entitle one party to disregard the obligations he assumes by entering a company, nor the court to dispense him from it. It does, as equity always does, enable the court to subject the exercise of legal rights to equitable considerations; considerations, that is, of a personal character arising between one individual and another, which may make it unjust, or inequitable, to insist on legal rights, or to exercise them in a particular way.

The courts have also wound up companies under this heading where:

■ it was no longer possible to achieve the purpose for which the company was formed (see *Re Eastern Telegraph Co. Ltd.* [1974] 2 All E.R.104);
■ the company was promoted fraudulently (*Re Thomas Edward Brinsmead & Sons* [1897] 1 Ch. 406, C.A.); and
■ the company was formed for an illegal purpose (*Re The International Securities Corporation Ltd.* (1908) 24 T.L.R. 837).

■ 18.8 Other remedies

The remedies outlined above tend to be used as a last resort. The Act provides various other means by which shareholders may be able to reconcile their problems. For example:

■ The Secretary of State has wide powers to appoint inspectors to investigate matters, which may have been drawn to his attention by a member (ss. 431 and 442 of the 1985 Act). He may as a result of these investigations apply for a winding up order under the Insolvency Act 1986 or petition for an order under the unfair prejudice rules in Part 30 of the Companies Act 2006.
■ Shareholders representing a certain percentage of the total voting rights may require the directors to convene a general meeting and, if the directors fail to do so, may convene it themselves (ss. 303 to 305) (see **12.5**).
■ If for any reason it is impracticable to call a meeting of a company, or to conduct the meeting in the manner prescribed by the articles or the Act, any

member may apply to the court for an order calling a meeting (s. 306) (see **12.4**).

- Members of any company may require the directors to circulate a statement in connection with any business to be proposed at a general meeting (ss. 314 to 317) (see **13.15**);
- Members of a public company may require the company to give notice of AGM resolutions they intend to propose (s. 338) (see **10.4**).
- Resolutions varying class rights may be challenged by members holding not less than 15% of that class who did not vote in favour of the change (ss. 633 and 644).
- Members may by ordinary resolution remove a director before the expiry of his term of office (s. 168) (see **25.15**).
- Application may be made to the court for an order that the company's register of members be rectified (s. 125).
- Members have various rights of inspection of company registers and the right to copies of them on payment of a fee.
- A company must send members copies of its accounts which must be prepared in accordance with the requirements of the Part 15 of the Act.
- A company's accounts must be audited unless it is exempt as a small company or as a dormant company. However, even where the company is exempt, members holding just 10% of the shares or voting rights may require an audit (s. 476).

PART 4
Running general meetings

This section deals with the organisation of general meetings and draws together practical and legal issues that may arise when the meeting is held. It also includes specific guidance on common items of business.

19

Organising general meetings

■ 19.1 Summary

- This chapter deals with some of the more practical aspects of organising an annual general meeting, although many of the issues raised will also be relevant to other meetings. It includes a checklist for organising annual general meetings which has been cross-referenced to the relevant paragraphs and chapters in this book (see **19.2**).
- Setting a date and choosing a venue for the meeting are both important tasks. The directors may determine where the meeting will be held, provided that the location is not chosen with the deliberate intention of excluding certain members (see **19.3**).
- The venue should be large enough to accommodate all the members wishing to attend. If not, the meeting will have to be adjourned. The secretary will therefore need to estimate the attendance and be prepared to advise the chairman on the action to take in the event that the room is too small (see **19.4**).
- If members are forced to sit in an uncomfortable environment, they tend to become irritable. Naturally, this is the last thing the chairman and the directors need. Attention to 'hygiene factors' is therefore important. However, shareholders may also complain if the venue is too extravagant, particularly if profits and dividends are down. The final decision will almost always be a compromise between cost, quality, size and availability (see **19.5**).
- Companies are making greater use of websites for the purposes of general meetings. In some cases the provision of website facilities is voluntary. For example, some larger companies now use their website to provide webcasts of the annual general meeting (see **19.6**).
- In other cases the use of websites is obligatory (see **19.7**).
- We also examine in this section, the possibility of holding fully electronic meetings (see **19.8**).

■ 19.2 Cross-referenced checklist for annual general meeting

Date of meeting
- Calculate last date on which AGM must be held (see **10.2** and **19.3**).
- Choose a suitable date or range of possible dates before the last date.

- Consult chairman and other relevant personnel.
- Fix date and inform relevant company personnel and external advisers, e.g. registrars, auditors, solicitor, broker, PR consultants, etc.
- If a suitable opportunity arrives, inform the members.

Venue
- Estimate likely attendance (see **19.4**).
- Determine other requirements, e.g. location, cost, etc (see **19.5**).
- Select and visit potential venues.
- Assess general suitability of each venue (see **19.3** to **19.5**).
- Assess suitability for security purposes (see **22.3**).
- Provisionally book preferred venue.
- Consult chairman (and any other directors who wish to be consulted).
- If they approve, book venue and obtain confirmation of booking.
- Agree and sign contract.
- Obtain map of venue location and travel instructions.

Other arrangements
- Make arrangements for
  - catering (if required);
  - security and stewards (see **22.2** and **22.3**);
  - audio-visual equipment (if required);
  - voting equipment (if required);
  - printing of signs for AGM;
  - stage design (if required); and
  - display stands (if required).

Planning the AGM mailing
- Calculate last date notice must be sent out bearing in mind
  - notice requirements (see **13.2**);
  - requirement for clear days' notice (see **13.2**);
  - date notice deemed given if sent by post or electronically (see **13.7.1**);
  - application of UK Corporate Governance Code recommendation (see **13.2.2**).
- Set date for posting of notice and accounts (preferably before last date).
- If not possible within time limit, consider trying to obtain consent to short notice (see **13.6**), otherwise change date of AGM.
- Set dates for:
  - final draft of notice;
  - finalisation of accounts and audit;
  - board meeting to approve accounts and convene AGM (see *note 1*);
  - printing of notice, proxies, circulars, accounts and other documents to go with AGM mailing (inform printers);

- printing of address labels (if by registrar, inform registrar stating where they are to be sent).

Drafting the notice, etc

- Prepare rough outline of business to be transacted at the AGM (see **10.7** and **Chapter 24**).
- If listed, check whether the notice and any accompanying circular will need to be approved by the UKLA before it is sent out (see **13.12.2**).
- Check whether special notice is required for any resolution (see **13.14**).
- Check type of resolution required for each item of business to be proposed (see **Chapter 14** and **Appendix 2**).
- Calculate which (if any) of the directors must retire by rotation (see **25.14**).
- Confirm that auditors are willing to be reappointed (see **25.5**).
- Check whether directors' authority to allot needs to be renewed (see **25.17**).
- Include any valid resolutions or statements submitted by members (see **10.4**).
- Draft the AGM notice and circular (see **13.8** and **Precedent 10.3**).
- If a traded company, make preparations for publication of notice and other statements on website (see **19.7**).
- Draft proxy cards and prepare website facilities for proxy appointments (if required) (see **Chapter 16**).
- Draft attendance card (if required) (see **22.2**).
- Draft invitation to members to submit questions in advance (if required) (see **21.7**).

Board meeting to convene AGM and approve results and dividends

- Prepare and send out notice of board meeting including resolutions:
  - to approve report and accounts;
  - to authorise signing of accounts and reports;
  - to recommend a dividend;
  - to convene the annual general meeting and approve business (see **12.2**);
  - to authorise secretary to sign and send out notices, etc;
  - to recommend the appointment of any directors (if articles require) (see **25.13**);
  - to approve the release of any preliminary announcement or results announcement (listed plc only);
  - to nominate director to act as chairman of the general meeting in the absence of the chairman of the board (see **20.2**).
- Immediately before meeting check again for any valid members' resolutions and include in papers put to the board (see **10.4**).
- Hold board meeting and pass resolutions.
- If problems convening meeting, see **12.3**.

Immediately after the board meeting

- Release any preliminary announcement (listed plc only).
- Balance sheet signed by a director.
- Directors' report signed by a director or secretary.
- Auditors' report signed by auditors.
- Notice signed and dated by secretary (see **13.7**).
- Calculate required number of copies of:
  - annual report (including extra copies);
  - notice, circular and proxy cards.
- Final proofs of report and accounts, proxy cards, notice, etc sent to printers with instructions as to numbers required.

Sending out the notice

- Send report and accounts, notice, etc. to persons entitled to receive them (see **25.2**).
- File annual report at Companies House.
- Send report and accounts to others on mailing list kept for that purpose.
- If a traded company, publish notice and other statements on website (see **19.7**).
- Make available any website facilities for making proxy appointments.

Miscellaneous matters

- Make arrangements to enable the payment of the dividend (if subsequently approved).
- Calculate cut off time for valid proxies (see **16.14**) and, if necessary, inform registrars.
- Monitor proxies received.
- If necessary, contact major shareholders to encourage submission of proxies.
- At appropriate time on cut off date for proxies prepare:
  - schedule of proxies appointed for the use of staff on the registration desk;
  - schedule of voting instructions for the chairman where the member has appointed chairman as proxy.
- Print voting cards and poll cards (if required).

Preparations immediately before AGM

- Arrange for proposers and seconders of resolutions (as required).
- Finalise chairman's agenda/script (see **Appendix 3**).
- Prepare AGM briefing document (see **Appendix 4**).
- If members were invited to submit questions in advance, prepare answers.
- Brief chairman.
- Rehearse questions and answers.
- Allocate following duties to staff and brief accordingly (see **Appendix 4**):

- registration (see **22.2**);
- poll (see **17.9**);
- roving microphone;
- stewards and security (see **22.2**).

■ Rehearse AGM.

■ Confirm final arrangements with venue, security staff, registrars, etc.

■ Make arrangements for the release of an announcement if it is intended to reveal price-sensitive information at the meeting (listed plc only) (see **10.10**).

Day of the annual general meeting

■ Things to take to the meeting:
- directors' service contracts/non-executive directors' terms of appointment (see **10.6**);
- spare copies of report and accounts and notice;
- chairman's agenda/script (plus copies for other directors who are to propose resolutions);
- questions and answers script;
- memorandum and articles of association (indexed);
- consolidated version of Companies Act 2006 (as amended);
- a textbook on the law and procedures of meetings;
- summary of proxies received;
- original proxy forms and summary sheets;
- register of members (usually supplied by registrar);
- attendance sheets for members, proxies and corporate representatives, and guests (see **21.3**);
- notepads, pens and pencils;
- name plates for top table and name badges;
- reserved seats signs;
- voting cards;
- calculator with printed roll for counting votes on a poll;
- telephone numbers of crucial participants.

■ Final briefing of staff.

■ Check that quorum present (see **Chapter 15**).

■ Open meeting and conduct business (see chairman's scripts at **Appendix 3**).

■ Record proceedings (see **26.14.3**).

After the meeting

■ Prepare minutes for signature by chairman (see **Chapter 26**).

■ Take actions required as a result of resolutions passed.

■ Authorise payment of dividend.

■ File any necessary copies of resolutions at Companies House (see **14.8**).

■ Announce results of resolutions and send copies of resolutions sent to UK Listing Authority (listed plc only) (see **14.8**).

- Publish the results of any poll on a website (quoted companies only) (see **17.12**).
- Publish results of any independent report on a poll on a website (see **17.12.3**).
- Respond to shareholder questions raised at meeting (see **21.7**).
- Review the organisation of the AGM.
- Book venue for next AGM.

19.3 Date and location of meeting

Generally speaking, it is preferable to hold general meetings in the country of incorporation. However, the directors may determine the place at which the meeting shall be held and, in the absence of fraud, their decision cannot be challenged (*Martin v. Walker* (1918) 145 L.T.J. 377). The directors must therefore exercise their power to select the place of the meeting in the best interests of the company. If they call a meeting to be held at a time and place which clearly restricts the ability of a significant proportion of the members to attend, their decision is liable to challenge (*Cannon v. Trask* (1875) L.R. 20 Eq. 669).

These rules would not prevent a UK-registered company holding a meeting outside the UK if, for example, the majority of its shareholders were resident in the country in which the meeting was to be held or that country was the most convenient for the members as a whole. Some companies hold their meetings in multiple locations at the same time, which may not necessarily be in the same country.

19.3.1 Choosing a date for the annual general meeting

Before choosing a date for the annual general meeting, it is necessary to calculate the last date on which the meeting must be held. For public companies required to hold an annual general meeting under the Act, this is now a very simple process as the meeting must now be held within six months of the year-end (or nine months in the case of a private company that is a traded company). Any date during that period may be chosen and it does not matter how long there is between each annual general meeting or whether by selecting a certain date no annual general meeting will be held in any particular calendar year. Although the meeting is still called the annual general meeting, it is not necessary for a meeting to be held annually.

Under the Companies Act 1985, companies were required to hold an annual general meeting in each calendar year with not more than 15 months being allowed to elapse between the date of one annual general meeting and the next. Newly registered companies were required to hold their first annual general meeting within 18 months of incorporation and, as long as they complied with this requirement, were not required to hold an annual general meeting in the year of incorporation or the following year (s. 366, 1985 Act).

Under the 2006 Act, a company may not be required to hold an annual general meeting in a particular year, perhaps because its year-end falls in the second half of the year or because it has extended the accounting period by changing its accounting reference date. For example, a public company with a 30 September year-end could choose to hold its annual general meeting for the financial year ending 30 September 2010 in December 2010, but choose to hold its next annual general meeting in January 2012.

A company incorporated under an earlier Act may find that its articles follow the traditional model by requiring an annual general meeting to be held once every calendar year. A company required by the 2006 Act to hold an annual general meeting must comply with the timing requirements of the Act in order to avoid committing an offence. However, it should also seek to comply with the requirements of the articles, particularly where a proportion of the directors are required to retire by rotation at each annual general meeting because failure to hold a meeting in any particular year could cause complications in this regard. In the long term it might be better for such a company to delete the AGM timing requirements from its articles or to bring them in line with the Act. On the other hand, there is no particular reason why a private company that wishes to continue holding annual general meetings, despite not being required to do so by the Act, should not continue to do so in accordance with the old timing model.

It obviously makes sense for a public company to aim for an AGM date which allows the report and accounts to be laid before the meeting and it may be advisable to delay the meeting in order to do so (if that is possible in view of the above requirements). Public companies must lay their accounts before the members in general meeting no later than the end of the period for filing them with the registrar of companies. This period is normally six months after the year-end (ss. 437 and 442). However, this will not always be the case. For example, the company may apply to the Secretary of State for a filing extension, and the filing deadline may be different for the company's first accounts or if it subsequently changes its accounting reference date (see below).

The existence of other companies within the group that are required to hold an annual general meeting may influence the choice of date. It may be desirable to hold the annual general meetings of these companies on the same day, particularly if the membership of each company is similar.

Listed companies will often seek to avoid holding their annual general meeting on the same date as other companies in the same sector. Other factors which may determine the date chosen might include the availability of the chairman and other directors, the availability of a suitable venue and the availability of the auditors, registrars and other advisers. In order to ensure that all these factors can be co-ordinated, it may be necessary to begin planning the annual general meeting a long way in advance. Many listed companies book the venue of the annual general meeting up to two years in advance.

Finally, it should not be forgotten that 21 clear days' notice of the annual general meeting must be given unless the consent of all the members to shorter notice can be obtained. Traded companies are not allowed to hold a meeting at less than 21 days' notice (see **13.6**). If the accounts which are to be laid at the meeting are sent out less than 21 days before the meeting, separate consent will also be required (s. 424(4)) (see **25.2**).

19.4 Estimating attendance

Ideally, the venue for a general meeting should be capable of accommodating all the members. For companies with few members, this is relatively easy to arrange. However, for companies with thousands of shareholders, this is impractical. Instead, the company secretary must try to predict the number of members and guests likely to attend. The starting point for this exercise for an annual general meeting will normally be to examine attendance levels in previous years. If the number of shareholders has increased or decreased significantly, appropriate adjustments should be made.

If the company's results are not as good as expected or the company has been the subject of adverse press comment, the proportion of members attending will probably be higher than normal. Numbers will also increase where food and drink or company products are offered for the first time (numbers might not fall quite so dramatically when any such perks are withdrawn – shareholders may attend to complain about the change of policy!). An interesting or unusual venue may also attract more shareholders as may a change of venue to a location which is more accessible.

Whatever figure is finally arrived at, most company secretaries tend to add a little extra for contingency purposes. Preparations for the meeting are usually made a long way in advance and it is sensible to assume that something may subsequently happen which brings shareholders out of the woodwork.

Some companies conduct surveys of a sample of their members in order to estimate the likely attendance. Others ask shareholders to return a reply-paid card if they intend to attend. Such methods usually produce a forecast which is higher than the actual attendance on the day. To this extent, they can be a useful guide to the absolute maximum attendance, particularly for a newly listed company or one which has recently undergone a major change in its shareholder base, e.g. following a takeover or merger. One company which asked all its members to return a card indicating whether they would attend, found that the responses tallied almost exactly with the actual attendance. However, on analysing the responses, it found that this was because the number of shareholders who said they would attend but did not turn up was practically the same as the number who did not respond but attended on the day.

Having determined the maximum number of members for whom accommodation will be provided, additional provision should be made for guests, the press and employees.

19.4.1 Room size

If the estimate of the maximum attendance differs greatly from the normal attendance, the prime consideration may be flexibility. A large room capable of being partitioned off may be preferable to separate overspill rooms which need to be connected by audio-visual links to the main meeting room. Such links are expensive to establish and can be unreliable (see **4.10** and **23.6** for discussion as to their legality where no provision is made in the articles). Such arrangements are provided for under the model articles (see pcls 37, clg 23 and plc 29). For an alternative article dealing with overflow arrangements for general meetings, see **Precedent 19.4**. For an example of a chairman's script dealing with a situation where it is impossible to accommodate all the members, see **Appendix 3**.

It is usual for the board of directors to be seated with the chairman, facing the shareholders. Indeed, this is one of the best practice points in ICSA's *Guide to Best Practice for Annual General Meetings*. The company secretary will usually be seated on the top table or platform next to the chairman. Some companies also invite the audit partner and the company's solicitor to sit on the top table. Some venues have built in stage areas and platforms. However, the seating capacity of the room may depend on the size of the platform required. It is becoming increasingly common for each director to have a screen which is used to display either the running order or information compiled by researchers which may be helpful for the directors when answering questions from shareholders. The chairman may make use of an autocue facility.

■ 19.5 Other factors influencing the choice of venue

Several other factors will influence the choice of venue and some of these are considered below. It can be useful to produce a checklist of the company's main requirements in order to compare the suitability of the various venues considered. An example of such a checklist can be found at Table 19.1 below.

19.5.1 Availability
The meeting room(s) should be booked to allow for the possibility that the meeting may take longer than usual. Nothing is likely to annoy shareholders more than for discussion to be cut short because the room has to be vacated. Indeed, the chairman may find it necessary to adjourn the meeting in such circumstances which could be both costly and embarrassing. Adequate time must also be allowed to set up the room before the meeting and for taking down any stage designs and displays after the meeting. This may mean booking the room for the day before the meeting and for a few hours after the meeting is due to close.

19.5.2 Terms of licence
The terms and conditions of the venue (e.g. dress codes, security checks, etc) should be checked to ensure that they are not inconsistent with the company's legal obligations to admit all shareholders (see **22.2**). Problems can also arise if it is not possible for the company to restrict public access to the meeting venue.

19.5.3 Location

Is the venue easily accessible by road and public transport? Is it in a pleasant and safe area? Does it have access for the disabled? The ICSA's *Guide to Best Practice for Annual General Meetings* recommends that the venue for the AGM should be accessible by attendees who have disabilities, and have facilities for those with poor hearing.

19.5.4 Noise levels

Is the room relatively sound proof? The most common problem with hotel conference rooms is that they are situated next to the kitchen and catering staff are rarely responsive to requests to keep the noise down. Partitioned rooms should be avoided unless you can afford to reserve the whole suite as it is inevitable that the adjoining section(s) will be hired by people whose activities involve making a great deal of noise. Although the partitions themselves are normally soundproof, the connecting doors frequently are not. Also check whether the owners intend to do any building, decorating or repairs around the date of the meeting. The venue may look wonderful when you book it. Things could be very different on the day. If possible, obtain a written undertaking that no such work will be carried out on the day.

19.5.5 Lighting, heating and air conditioning

Can the lights, heating and air conditioning be adjusted easily and are they sufficient? In many venues access to these controls is restricted. If so, will a member of staff be available to make the necessary adjustments?

19.5.6 Layout

Other questions regarding the layout of the venue which may need to be resolved include:

■ What seating arrangement can be provided comfortably (e.g. theatre, classroom, or boardroom styles)?
■ Can areas be cordoned off for different classes of members or non-members?
■ Are the seating arrangements comfortable?
■ Will everyone be able to see the top table?
■ Do the facilities enable adequate security arrangements to be put in place?

19.5.7 Registration and help desks

In addition to the main meeting room, the venue will need to have a suitable area for registration. Ideally, it should not be possible for members to gain entry to the meeting room without passing through the registration area. If there is more than one entrance to the venue, the registration area might need to be located immediately outside the entrance to the meeting room. The size of the registration area will depend on the number of members and guests that are expected to attend. It may need to be large enough to accommodate several registration desks and the company's registrars may need power points if they plan to access the register of members using computer equipment.

Many companies provide shareholder help desks to deal with members' enquiries about dividends and other issues relating to their shareholdings. Retail and consumer companies often establish separate help desks to deal with enquiries which are customer related. By doing so, members are less likely to raise these issues at the meeting and the chairman is able to refer a member who asks such a question to the relevant help desk. If these facilities are to be provided, they will need to be situated in a prominent position, perhaps in the foyer.

19.5.8 Security

Space may be needed for security checks to be carried out prior to registration to prevent members bringing into the meeting any objects which could be used to disrupt the meeting, e.g. banners, missiles, whistles, klaxons, etc (see further **22.2** and **22.3**).

19.5.9 Sound system and recordings

Sound equipment may be necessary for the top table and for taking questions from the floor. It should be remembered that the acoustics in an empty room are far better than when it is full of people. If the meeting room is large, it will almost certainly be necessary to provide some means of amplification for shareholders who wish to ask questions during the meeting. This can be done using roving microphones. However, the modern trend is to provide one or more fixed microphones from which shareholders must put questions. If microphones are not provided, the chairman should be briefed to repeat or summarise the questions put from the floor before answering them.

It is often beneficial to record the proceedings (including questions from the floor) so that a transcript can be made. The company may also wish to make arrangements for the proceedings to be videotaped, possibly for transmission as a webcast or on a late night TV slot which shareholders who were unable to attend can record and watch at their leisure.

19.5.10 Refreshments

Where refreshments are provided, they are normally served in a separate room so that the catering staff do not disrupt the meeting. Exhibitions of company products or its history could also be placed in this area or in the main meeting room.

19.5.11 Directors' room

The availability of a meeting or preparation room for the directors and an office for the meeting organisers should also be considered.

19.5.12 Staff

Are the staff friendly and helpful? Do they have sufficient staff to cater for your needs? Will a manager be on hand throughout the meeting to handle any problems?

19.5.13 Toilets and cloakroom facilities

The standard of both the ladies and the gents toilets should be checked. It may also be necessary to provide facilities for members to leave their coats and baggage, particularly if certain items are not allowed to be taken into the meeting.

19.5.14 Other facilities

The availability of telephone, internet, fax and photocopying facilities may be important to the organisers and to members attending.

19.6 Webcasts

Larger listed companies tend to make their AGM available on a live video webcast (normally via the company's website). This obviously enables a much wider audience to view the proceedings, but does not allow them to participate. Where the proceedings are being recorded, but particularly where they are being filmed, it is usual to warn shareholders in advance in the AGM circular and at the start of the meeting.

Some companies also make an edited version of the live video webcast (possibly including the chairman's statement, other presentations made by operational managers and the general question and answer session) available shortly after the meeting on their website.

Companies that do not feel that the expense of video webcast can be justified, sometimes make a sound recording available on their website. As many companies record the proceedings for their own purposes, this does not require much extra effort.

Unfortunately, as with a great deal of the documentation made available on the company's website, access to these facilities may need to be made subject to restrictions for overseas investors.

19.7 Use of websites

Companies are required or authorised to use websites for a variety of purposes connected with general meetings. Indeed, for those who use communications via website as their default method of communicating with shareholders, the content and design of the company's website has become a very important issue.

Websites are required or authorised to be used for the following purposes.

19.7.1 Traded companies

Traded companies (see definition at **8.5.1**) are required under s. 311A to publish the following information on their websites throughout the period beginning with the first date on which notice of the meeting is given and ending with the conclusion of the meeting and to include in the notice a statement giving details of the website on which the information is published (s. 311(3)):

- the matters set out in the notice of the meeting;
- the total numbers of shares in the company (and shares of each class) in respect of which members are entitled to exercise voting rights at the meeting, ascertained at the latest practicable time before the first date on which notice of the meeting is given; and
- the totals of the voting rights that members are entitled to exercise at the meeting in respect of the shares of each class.

A traded company must also ensure that any members' statements regarding audit concerns (under s. 527), members' resolutions (under s. 388) and members' matters of business (under s. 388A) received by the company after the first date on which notice of the meeting is given are made available on a website. This information must be made available as soon as reasonably practicable. It should be noted in this regard that any such statements, resolutions and matters of business received before that date will also be published on the website as they will be expected to form part of the notice of meeting.

The above information must be made available on a website that is maintained by or on behalf of the company and identifies the company (s. 311A(2)). Access to the information on the website, and the ability to obtain a hard copy of the information from the website, must not be conditional on payment of a fee or otherwise restricted (s. 311A(3)). The information must be made available on the website throughout the period of two years beginning with the date on which it is first made available in accordance with s. 311A (s. 311A(4)). Failure to do so does not affect the validity of the meeting or of anything done at the meeting (s. 311A(7)), but is an offence (s. 311A(8)) for which any officer in default may be fined (s. 311A(9)). However, any failure to make information available throughout the two-year period is disregarded if the information is made available on the website for part of that period and the failure is wholly attributable to circumstances that it would not be reasonable to have expected the company to prevent or avoid (s. 311A(5)).

Quoted companies and traded companies are required to publish the results of any poll on their website. Quoted companies are also required to publish any independent report on a poll on their website (see **17.12**).

Quoted companies may be required by members satisfying the requirements of s. 527 to publish on a website a statement by them relating to the audit of the company's accounts which are to be laid before the next accounts meeting (including the auditor's report and the conduct of the audit) or, where applicable, any circumstances connected with an auditor of the company ceasing to hold office since the previous accounts meeting at which accounts were laid (see **25.4**).

Traded companies (see definition at **8.5.1**) are not required to answer questions at general meetings if the answer has already been given on the company's website in the form of an answer to a question (s. 319A). This means that listed companies will need to create a specific Q&A section on their websites to which shareholders who ask questions at the meeting may be referred if necessary.

A traded company must give an electronic address that can be used by members for the purposes of appointing proxies either on the website maintained for the purposes of s. 311A or in every instrument of proxy sent out by the company for the purposes of a general meeting of the company, and every invitation to appoint a proxy issued by the company for the purposes of such a meeting (s. 333A(1)). This address must for all practical purposes be a website address where it is possible for members to appoint proxies. This service is normally provided by a company's registrars and it is likely that the address provided will link directly to them, although it could direct the members to the company's website first. If a traded company does not offer the facility to vote by electronic means to all members who hold shares that carry rights to vote at general meetings, it must give 21 days' notice of all meetings (s. 307A).

Just about the only thing that is not required to be published on a traded company's website is the minutes of the meeting. The results of any poll must be published on the website but not any vote on a show of hands. Listed companies are required to announce the fact that certain resolutions have been passed under the Listing Rules (see **14.8.3**). This announcement is normally made available somewhere on the company's website. However, it is not always easy to find and it might be easier for shareholders if the page on the company's website dealing with the annual general meeting for that year contained a link to the announcement. There is no particular reason why the minutes of the meeting should not be made available on the website as well, although companies tend not to do this.

The Hampel Committee recommended that listed companies should prepare a resumé of the discussion at the AGM and make it available to shareholders on request (Hampel Report, para. 5.22). Generally speaking it is safe to say that companies have not embraced this recommendation with any great enthusiasm, although some do provide edited highlights by way of a webcast. Few seem to consider that shareholders would be particularly interested in accessing a resumé of the discussion. Most of the discussion at meetings takes the form of questions and answers. It is inevitable that question and answers posed by shareholders will be given greater prominence on the websites of listed companies in view of the requirements of s. 319A regarding shareholder questions at general meetings. Listed companies will almost certainly need to create a specific Q&A section on their websites to which shareholders who ask questions at the meeting may be referred if necessary.

■ 19.8 Electronic meetings

Section 322A(1) provides that a company's articles may contain provision to the effect that on a vote on a resolution on a poll taken at a meeting, the votes may include votes cast in advance. Section 322A(3) allows a company to impose the same maximum time limits on voting in advance as are allowed for appointing proxies. However, it does not require those time limits to be imposed.

It is possible that, in the future, systems for voting in advance could be devised which enable shareholders to vote right up until the time of the meeting (and possibly up until the time the poll on any resolution is closed), and that this could facilitate true electronic meetings. In the author's view, it might be better for public companies to try to devise voting procedures that enable the voting process to be divorced from the meeting itself (see **10.11**).

Section 360A specifically provides that nothing in Part 13 (meetings and resolutions) of the Companies Act 2006 shall be taken to preclude the holding and conducting of a meeting in such a way that persons who are not present together at the same place may by electronic means attend and speak and vote at it. This provision was inserted for the purposes of compliance with the EU Shareholders' Rights Directive.

Section 360A(2) provides that, in the case of a traded company (see definition at **8.5.1**), the use of electronic means for the purpose of enabling members to participate in a general meeting may be made subject only to such requirements and restrictions as are necessary to ensure the identification of those taking part and the security of the electronic communication, and that are proportionate to the achievement of those objectives. It is assumed that this provision is intended to prevent some shareholders from being excluded from participating in a meeting by electronic means on any other grounds right from the start, rather than to prevent the chairman of the meeting imposing rules of conduct that could, for example, curtail their right to participate in some respects and which could ultimately result in their expulsion.

If electronic meetings are to become a reality in the near future, it will probably be necessary to adopt a more modern approach regarding the right to speak. Modern articles nearly always interpret this as requiring a person to be heard by others participating in the meeting. However, there would seem to be no reason why a person should not be allowed to choose to exercise his right to speak by some other method (e.g. via a bulletin board or other online facility) which is then made available and drawn to the attention of other participants. One of the problems for large companies which could have thousands of shareholders wishing to participate in a meeting held in this manner, would be to manage, co-ordinate and control these online contributions. It should be noted, however, that the right to speak does not necessarily always guarantee that all shareholders who wish to do so will be afforded that opportunity. Accordingly, there would appear to be no reason why any online contributions should not be moderated, subject to the application of the rules regarding shareholders' questions.

It is arguable that, irrespective of s. 360A, there is nothing in the Act to prevent a company from holding electronic meetings. However, it is also undeniable that it would be extremely expensive and difficult to do so for a company with a large number of shareholders, and that modifications would need to be made to the company's articles, e.g. to cater for this method of participation for the purposes of voting, speaking, attendance and quorum requirements and to prevent the proceedings from being invalidated by any failure of communications. In practice, it might be easier for a company with relatively few shareholders to run electronic meetings, although it is doubtful whether such companies would want to invest the time and money required to do so.

Companies could allow shareholders to participate to a limited extent in general meetings by providing a system similar to a bulletin board specifically designed for the meeting without actually treating them as present at the meeting or affording them any right to vote or speak at the meeting. Shareholders could be required to log in using a password and could be invited to submit questions and comments via this facility in advance and, possibly, during the meeting. The chairman, with the assistance of a moderator, could choose whether to read out contributions made and questions asked via the bulletin board. It is suggested that many shareholders would feel more comfortable making contributions in this manner than having to stand up and make a speech at the meeting. Implementing such a system on a concessionary and voluntary basis might provide a useful testing bed for a possible move towards full electronic participation.

20

Chairman

■ 20.1 Summary

- In view of the importance of the role, it is common for the articles to determine who should chair general meetings rather than allow the members to elect the chairman at each meeting. However, members have a residual right to elect the chairman if none of those designated to do so are willing or able (see **20.2**).

- The members may remove a chairman appointed by them but may not have any power to do so where the appointment is determined by the articles (see **20.3**).

- The chairman has a duty to ensure that the meeting is properly conducted (see **20.5**), that all shades of opinion are given a fair hearing (see **20.6**), and that the sense of the meeting is properly ascertained and recorded (see **20.7**).

- It is also the chairman's duty to maintain order (see **22.4**).

- The chairman is given a wide variety of powers to enable these duties to be performed (see **20.8**).

- See also **Chapter 24** on amendments, **Chapter 23** on adjournment and other procedural motions.

- Where a meeting is being held at more than one location, it will be necessary to appoint somebody to manage the proceedings at each of those locations. These people are sometimes referred to as 'subsidiary chairmen'. It is advantageous if they can be given powers similar to that of the chairman (see **20.9**).

- It is usual for the company secretary to prepare a script for the chairman (see **20.10** and **Appendix 3** for various examples of a chairman's script).

■ 20.2 Appointment of chairman

A general meeting cannot proceed without a chairman for legal and practical reasons. There must be someone to put motions to the meeting, declare the results of voting, and rule on points of order.

The Act includes two provisions regarding the appointment of a chairman, both of which are expressed as being subject to any provision of a company's articles:

(a) a member may be elected to be the chairman of a general meeting by a resolution of the company passed at the meeting (s. 319); and

(b) a proxy may be elected to be the chairman of a general meeting by a resolution of the company passed at the meeting (s. 328).

A corporate representative would also be entitled to act as the chairman of a general meeting under this default statutory regime on the basis that any such representative is entitled to exercise the same powers on behalf of the corporation as the corporation could exercise if it were an individual member of the company (s. 323(2)).

Articles usually provide an alternative regime for the appointment of the chairman. They normally provide for general meetings to be chaired by the person (if any) who has been appointed as chairman of the board of directors, but also make provision for another person to be appointed if the chairman of the board is not present or is unwilling to act (e.g. regs. 42 and 43 of Table A, pcls 39, clg 25 and plc 31). In the following example taken from the model articles for private companies limited by shares, references to 'the chairman' are to 'the chairman of the board':

> **39.**— (1) If the directors have appointed a chairman, the chairman shall chair general meetings if present and willing to do so.
>
> (2) If the directors have not appointed a chairman, or if the chairman is unwilling to chair the meeting or is not present within ten minutes of the time at which a meeting was due to start—
>
> (a) the directors present, or
>
> (b) (if no directors are present), the meeting, must appoint a director or shareholder to chair the meeting, and the appointment of the chairman of the meeting must be the first business of the meeting.
>
> (3) The person chairing a meeting in accordance with this article is referred to as 'the chairman of the meeting'.

It can be seen that articles normally allow the directors to decide who will chair general meetings and it is unusual for anyone other than a director to be chosen by them to do so. The only occasion on which the members would normally get to elect a chairman is where there are no directors present or willing to act. Where no director is willing to chair the meeting, articles often require a 'member' or 'shareholder' to be appointed or elected to act as chairman. It is somewhat surprising that the model articles prescribed under the 2006 Act use this formula in view of the default provision in s. 328 which states that a proxy may do so, subject to anything in the company's articles on the matter. The words 'member' or 'shareholder' in the model articles would appear to exclude the possibility that a proxy may be appointed. However, it is submitted that this is not necessarily the case. It has been held that the word member (or shareholder) must include a proxy where the articles say that proxies can be counted in calculating whether there is a quorum and only proxies are present (*Re Bradford Investments plc* [1990] B.C.C. 740). There is no particular reason to suppose that a proxy could not also chair the meeting if duly elected to do so even if there were members present. In the same case, it was held that a person who is neither a member, corporate representative or a proxy may take the chair at the start of the meeting to preside over the election of a chairman. However, the court held that the rulings of such a person (who in this case was largely self-appointed) were liable to challenge in the courts irrespective of anything contained in the articles, e.g. on the validity of any votes tendered in the election process.

Any objection to the appointment of a chairman at a meeting should be made immediately as any irregularity in the nomination may be cured by the acquiescence of those present (*Booth v. Arnold* [1985] 1 Q.B. 571).

■ 20.3 Removal of the chairman

A chairman elected by the meeting, e.g. when no director is present or willing to act in that capacity, may be removed by the meeting (*Cornwall v. Woods* (1846) 4 notes of Cases 555). This is normally done by a motion of no confidence in the chair. If such a resolution is proposed, the chairman should step down until the result of the vote is determined.

It is doubtful whether a person who holds office as the chairman by virtue of the articles and his or her position in the company (e.g. as the chairman of the board or as a director) can be removed by the members. If the chairman did relinquish the chair under pressure from the members, the selection of a replacement would be determined by the articles, and the members would only have power to appoint their own chairman if there was no other person specified by the articles as a potential candidate who was willing or able to act as chairman.

■ 20.4 Chairman's duties

In common law, the person appointed as the chairman of the meeting is deemed to have been given authority by the meeting to regulate its proceedings. As this is a form of delegated authority, the chairman must still act in accordance with the wishes of the majority at the meeting, unless exercising a power conferred by statute or the company's articles of association, or one which the courts have ruled can be exercised by the chairman without reference to the members (e.g. the power to adjourn to restore order).

The chairman has an overriding duty to act in good faith in the best interests of the company and is responsible for:

■ the proper conduct of the meeting (see **20.5**);
■ the preservation of order (see **22.4**);

- ensuring that all shades of opinion are given a fair hearing (see **20.6**); and
- ensuring that the sense of the meeting is properly ascertained and recorded (see **20.7**).

■ 20.5 Proper conduct of the meeting

The chairman must ensure that the meeting is conducted in accordance with the requirements of the Act, the company's articles of association and any applicable common law rules, and will normally be guided in this respect by the company secretary.

The chairman should not open the meeting before the time specified in the notice and should, as far as possible, ensure that the meeting starts on time and that all the business on the agenda is transacted. The start of the meeting can be delayed in certain circumstances. The most obvious is where there is no quorum, in which case the meeting cannot proceed to business in any case. The chairman can also legitimately delay the meeting to allow members who arrived on time to register and gain admittance (see Chairman's Scripts at **Appendix 3**). As a rule of thumb, it is not advisable to delay the meeting for any longer than about ten to fifteen minutes. Problems which take longer than this to sort out should be dealt with by proposing an adjournment immediately after opening the meeting (see **Chapter 23**).

The chairman may rule on any question raised from the floor relating to the conduct of the meeting (*Re Indian Zoedone Co.* (1884) 26 Ch.D. 70). If his decision is challenged, the matter should be put to the meeting and decided by the majority of those present (*Wandsworth and Putney Gas Light Co. v. Wright* (1870) 22 L.T. 404). It is relatively unusual for matters to get to this stage because either the chairman or the objectors will often give way if they sense that the mood of the meeting is against them. Any formal vote on such matters would normally be decided on a show of hands by a simple majority. If that vote went against the chairman, he could consider calling a poll, assuming he has power to do so under the articles.

If the chairman conducts the meeting in a certain way or makes a ruling that is not challenged at the meeting, the members present may be deemed to have acquiesced or consented to that conduct. In *Carruth v. Imperial Chemical Industries Ltd.* [1937] A.C. 707, the directors convened an extraordinary general meeting of the company and two meetings of different classes of shares to be held on the same day and at the same venue to approve a reduction of capital. As one meeting finished, the next meeting was started and each meeting was attended by each of the different classes of member. The resolution of one class of members was challenged on the ground that people who were not members of that class were present at the meeting. The resolution was held to be valid and Lord Russell said:

There are many matters relating to the conduct of a meeting which lie entirely in the hands of those persons who are present and constitute the meeting. Thus it rests with the meeting to decide whether notices, resolutions, minutes, accounts, and such like shall be read to the meeting or be taken as read; whether representatives of the press, or any other persons not qualified to be summoned to the meeting, shall be permitted to be present, or if present, shall be permitted to remain; whether and when discussion shall be terminated and a vote taken; whether the meeting shall be adjourned. In all these matters, and they are only instances, the meeting decides, and if necessary a vote must be taken to ascertain the wishes of the majority. If no objection is taken by any constituent of the meeting, the meeting must be taken to be assenting to the course adopted.

It should be noted that certain procedural matters have to be dealt with by a formal resolution and that it is preferable to deal with procedural matters that may be critical to the outcome of the meeting as a formal resolution. This topic is discussed further in **Chapter 23** in relation to procedural motions and adjournments (see, in particular, **23.2**), and **Chapter 24** in relation to amendments.

The chairman cannot close the meeting until all the business has been dealt with. In *National Dwelling Society Ltd. v. Sykes*, the chairman wrongly refused to accept an amendment to a resolution to receive the report and accounts and closed the meeting before all the business had been transacted. The members elected another chairman to transact the unfinished business and adjourned the meeting. It was held that the chairman had acted outside his powers by closing the meeting without its consent before the business had been completed and that the meeting could go on with the business for which it had been convened and appoint another chairman to conduct that business.

■ 20.6 Ensuring that all shades of opinion are given a fair hearing

The chairman should seek to ensure that all members who hold different views on a resolution before the meeting are given a fair hearing. To do otherwise would defeat one of the objects of holding the meeting. In particular, the chairman should not curtail the debate unless the minority has had a reasonable opportunity to put its views (*Wall v. London & Northern Assets Corporation Ltd.* [1898] 2 Ch. 469).

The amount of time that should be made available for debate will vary depending on the nature of the business and the number of people wishing to speak on it. This does not mean that the discussion should be allowed to go on forever. Shortly before closing the debate, the chairman should ask members to refrain from speaking unless they have a different point to make. Although it is not an easy thing to do without causing offence, the chairman should at this point cut short any speaker who is repeating a point made earlier in the debate in order to ensure that those with different views are given a fair hearing. When the chairman considers that a full range of views have been expressed, he may seek to curtail discussion and put the resolution to a vote. If any member objects, the chairman could seek the consent of the meeting by proposing a formal 'closure motion', i.e. that the question before the meeting be now put to the vote (see **23.14** and, for an example of a chairman's script, **Appendix 3**). However, the chairman may be justified in putting the resolution to the vote without obtaining the consent of the meeting if the minority have been given a fair hearing and/ or the members present are filibustering (trying to prevent the completion of the business of the meeting). This is only sensible if the chairman is confident that he has the support of the majority or that the resolution would be carried (or defeated, as the case may be) on a poll, if one was called.

See further **21.5** to **21.8** regarding members' right to speak and to ask questions.

■ 20.7 Ascertaining and recording the sense of the meeting

In *National Dwelling Society Ltd. v. Sykes* [1894] 3 Ch. 159, it was held that the chairman has a duty to ensure that 'the sense of the meeting is properly ascertained with regard to any question which is properly before the meeting'. In doing so the chairman should put resolutions to a vote, ensure that the votes are properly counted and declare the results of that vote.

In order to prevent issues regarding the precise number of votes cast for and against the resolution being reopened after the meeting, s. 320 provides that that a declaration by the chairman of the result of a show of hands is conclusive evidence that the resolution has or has not been passed, or passed with a particular majority, without proof of the number or proportion of the votes recorded in favour of or against the resolution (s. 320(1)). In addition, an entry in the minutes of a general meeting in respect of a declaration by the chairman as to the result of a show of hands is conclusive evidence of that fact without such proof (s. 320(2)).

The court has refused to intervene in several cases where questions have been raised as to the validity of the chairman's declaration and have confirmed that the word 'conclusive' means exactly that (see *Arnot v. United African Lands* [1901] 1 Ch. 518; *Re Hadleigh Castle Gold Mines* [1900] 2 Ch. 419; and *Graham's Morocco Co. Ltd., Petitioners*, 1932 S.C. 269). However, the court has intervened in a case where the chairman put a resolution and declared the result in the following fashion: 'Those in favour . . . 6. Those against . . . 23 but there are 200 voting by proxy and I declare the resolution carried as required by Act of Parliament.' Buckley J. refused to hold that the chairman's declaration was conclusive as it was clear from his declaration that he had acted on a mistaken principle (*Re Caratal (New) Mines Ltd.* [1902] 2 Ch. 498).

Every company is required to produce and keep minutes of all proceedings of general meetings. The directors can be fined for any default by the company of the provisions of the Act relating to the maintenance of minutes. The chairman can be said to have a special duty in this regard in so far as minutes signed by the chairman of the meeting are evidence of the proceedings (see **Chapter 26**).

■ 20.8 Chairman's powers

The chairman is given the following powers under statute and the general law:

(a) to make a conclusive declaration of the result of any vote taken on a show of hands (see **20.7**);
(b) to make rulings on the conduct of the proceedings (see **20.5**);
(c) to adjourn the meeting for the purpose of restoring order (see **22.4**);
(d) to adjourn the meeting to facilitate its conduct or to conduct a poll (see **23.6**); and
(e) to order the ejection of members who are disrupting the proceedings (see **22.4.2**)).

In addition, a company's articles of association may give the chairman power to:

(a) call a poll (see **17.9**);
(b) rule conclusively on the validity of any votes tendered at the meeting (see **17.14**);
(c) rule conclusively on the validity of proposed amendments (see **24.4**); and
(d) make security arrangements for general meetings (see **22.2**).

The articles may also purport to give the chairman a casting vote in the event of a tie. Such a power cannot be exercised in relation to a meeting of a traded company (see definition at **8.5.1**) and may not be valid for other types of company (see **17.13**). The chairman should seek clarification before the meeting as to whether there are any circumstances in which he may exercise any such power.

■ 20.9 Subsidiary chairman

Where a meeting is held at more than one location, it will be necessary from a practical perspective for someone to be appointed to facilitate or chair the proceedings at any of the subsidiary locations. It would also be advantageous if that person was able to be given certain powers that assist in the conduct of the proceedings and the maintenance of order at those subsidiary proceedings. It is probably within the chairman's power to delegate some aspects of his authority for these purposes without any specific provision being made in the company's articles. In the case of the model articles, the directors are given power to make whatever arrangements they consider appropriate to enable those attending a general meeting to exercise their rights. However, some companies have decided to make specific provision with regard to the powers of subsidiary chairmen (see example at **Precedent 20.9**).

■ 20.10 Chairman's scripts and rehearsal

It is sensible for the chairman to follow a basic script at a general meeting, which should be drafted on the assumption that everything will run smoothly. The chairman should also have several other scripts to hand for dealing with other situations that may arise. These could include scripts for:

■ dealing with a demand for a poll from the floor;
■ the conduct of a poll;
■ proposing an adjournment or dealing with such a proposal from the floor;
■ dealing with disorder;
■ dealing with amendments; and
■ procedural resolutions for the management of the proceedings.

Examples of various chairman's scripts (including a script for an annual general meeting) can be found in **Appendix 3**.

If possible, the chairman should be given the opportunity to rehearse the script and should be thoroughly briefed on the actions he should take if anything unusual happens. Many companies also try to anticipate questions which share-holders may ask and prepare answers to these hypothetical questions.

20.10.1 Other things that the chairman needs to know

It is obviously helpful if the chairman knows how meetings should be run. However, even the most experienced chairman will need a bit of help occasion-ally, and it is normally the company secretary who will sit next to the chairman at the meeting ready to offer that help if it is required. It is not necessarily as easy as it looks to chair a meeting, particularly where things are not going to plan. The secretary should not sit idly by if the chairman takes a wrong turn. However, the chairman will not normally welcome constant interruptions from the secretary. This can be avoided to a certain extent by preparing a good script. However, it also helps if the chairman has been briefed on a range of other matters before the meeting.

Such a briefing should cover the basic concepts of the law of meetings and, in particular, the specific requirements of the company's articles. In preparing such a briefing, it is a good idea to produce a marked-up copy of the articles, which highlights any provisions that may no longer apply because of subsequent statu-tory modifications.

The briefing should probably cover, but not necessarily be limited to, matters such as:

■ The chairman's duties.
■ The chairman's powers under the general law and under the articles.
■ What quorum is required for the meeting to proceed to business, and who can be counted for the purposes of calculating whether that quorum has been obtained?

- What should the chairman do if a quorum is not obtained at the time specified in the notice for the start of the meeting?
- What should the chairman do if a quorum was present at the start of the meeting but is subsequently lost?
- Who has a right to attend and what measures have been put in place to ensure that only those who have that right or have been invited to attend are allowed to gain admittance?
- Who has a right to speak?
- What method of voting will be used for substantive and procedural resolutions?
- Who has a right to vote on a show of hands?
- Who can make a valid demand for a poll?
- Who has a right to vote on a poll?
- Have any members appointed the chairman of the meeting as their proxy and, if so, for each resolution what are the total number of votes that they have instructed him or her to cast in favour, against or withhold and the total number for which they have given him or her discretion as to how to vote?
- What procedures should be followed if someone proposes an amendment to a substantive or procedural resolution?

21

Right to attend and speak

■ 21.1 Summary

- The right to attend general meetings usually goes hand-in-hand with the right to vote. However, the Act gives various people a statutory right to attend and the articles may allow others to attend or give the chairman discretion in this regard (see **21.2**).
- A record should be kept of the names of the members, proxies and corporate representatives who attend any general meeting (see **21.3**).
- It may not be necessary for all the participants in a general meeting to attend the meeting at the same place (see **21.4**).
- Members entitled to attend and vote at general meetings also have a common law right to speak at the meeting. The Companies Act 2006 appears to give proxies and corporate representatives the same rights as the member who appointed them in this regard. Auditors have a statutory right to speak on matters which concern them as auditors. The articles usually give the directors a right to speak even if they are not members (see **21.5**).
- The chairman has a duty to ensure that all shades of opinion are given a fair hearing. However, this does not mean that every member must be allowed to speak on a resolution or that they should be allowed to speak for as long as they want (see **21.6**).
- Members may ask questions at general meetings, but have no general right to have their questions answered (see **21.7**).
- However, traded companies have certain limited obligations to answer questions (see **21.8**).

■ 21.2 Right to attend

Company meetings are private meetings and, as such, the company is bound to admit only those who are legally entitled to attend. The right to attend usually goes hand in hand with the right to vote.

21.2.1 Members and corporate representatives

Voting at general meetings is usually conducted by a show of hands or a poll. Both methods require the presence of the person voting (or their proxy). It follows that in order to exercise their right to vote, the members must also have a right to attend the meeting. However, a member who does not have a right to vote may still have a right to attend to attend the meeting, unless the articles provide otherwise.

Companies whose shares have been admitted to CREST may specify in the notice a time, not more than 48 hours before the time fixed for the meeting, by which a person must be entered on the relevant register of securities in order to have the right to attend and vote at the meeting (see **17.2**).

A member who persistently disrupts the meeting may be ejected (see **22.4**). However, a member who is wrongfully excluded from a meeting, and thereby prevented from voting, may be able to challenge the validity of the proceedings. For example, it would be wrong to exclude a person without the backing of some sort of court order merely because they have disrupted previous meetings.

Care should be taken to ensure that a member's right to attend is not prejudiced by the terms and conditions imposed under the licence to use the venue where the meeting is to be held. For example, it would be unwise to choose a venue which imposes a dress code. Some companies have taken powers in their articles that allow them to exclude members who refuse to comply with conditions imposed for the purposes of security, e.g. electronic screening and prohibitions on taking hand baggage into the meeting (see **22.2**).

If the meeting room is not big enough to accommodate all the members who wish to attend, the meeting should be adjourned, unless overflow facilities have been provided (see **19.4**).

21.2.2 Joint holders

Where shares are registered in the names of joint holders, each of the joint holders is a member of the company and therefore entitled to attend the meeting, unless the articles provide otherwise. Articles commonly make special provision to enable the company to determine which vote should be accepted if more than one of the joint holders tenders a vote (e.g. reg. 55 of Table A). In the absence of anything in a company's articles on voting by joint holders, s. 286 of the Act applies, which makes the same provision as Table A. The rules do not restrict the right of each of the joint holders to vote at the meeting. So any one of them could turn up and vote. Even if more than one of the joint holders attends, the company cannot predict which, if any of them, will tender a vote. All the company knows is that if more than one of them tenders a vote, only one of those votes can be accepted. Accordingly, the Act or the company's own articles provide the method of determining which vote should be accepted. This normally depends on the order in which their names appear in the register of members with the votes of the senior taking priority.

21.2.3 Death or bankruptcy

Articles commonly provide that a person who becomes entitled to a share in consequence of the death or bankruptcy of a member shall not be entitled to attend or vote at any meeting of the company or of the holders of any class of shares until he has been registered as the holder of the share (e.g. reg. 31 of Table A, pcls 27 and plc 66).

21.2.4 Corporate representatives
Corporate representatives are deemed to have the same rights as individual members by virtue of s. 323. Accordingly, they have the same right to attend as an individual member. However, they should be required to provide evidence of their appointment before being admitted (see **16.4**).

21.2.5 Proxies
Proxies have a statutory right to attend on behalf of those who appointed them (s. 324). If the person who appointed the proxy is not entitled to attend, their proxy will not be entitled to attend. Any proxy appointed by a member may attend even if the member who appointed them attends the meeting. If the member does not vote, the proxy may do so.

21.2.6 Indirect investors
Investors who hold shares through an intermediary or nominee do not have a right to attend unless the registered shareholder appoints them as a proxy or corporate representative. A company's articles may allow members to identify another person or persons to enjoy or exercise all or any specified rights of a member, which could include the right to vote (s. 145). In order to exercise the right to vote it would normally be necessary to confer rights of attendance as well, unless the right to vote was restricted to voting in advance. Companies sometimes allow indirect investors to attend general meetings as guests without conferring upon them any rights, although there would seem to be no reason why the chairman should not also allow them to speak at the meeting in these circumstances.

21.2.7 Auditors
A company's auditors have a statutory right to receive notice of any general meeting of the company and to attend and speak at any such meeting on any part of the business which concerns them as auditors (s. 502(2)). The rights conferred by s. 502(2) are also extended to:

(a) an auditor who has been removed from office in relation to any general meeting at which his term of office would otherwise have expired or at which it is proposed to fill the vacancy caused by his removal (s. 513); and
(b) to a resigning auditor in relation to a meeting convened on his requisition or at any general meeting at which his term of office would otherwise have expired or at which it is proposed to fill the vacancy caused by his resignation (s. 518(10)).

21.2.8 Directors

Directors do not have a statutory right to attend general meetings, except where a resolution to remove them is to be proposed under s. 168 (s. 169(2)). However, directors who are members (or a representative or proxy of a member) will have a right to attend in that capacity.

It is highly likely that a director who is not a member has a common law right to attend, although that right may be subject to the will of the meeting. It would be odd if a director who was not a member but who had, for example, been appointed as the chairman of the board of directors (and therefore, under the company's articles, as the chairman of the general meeting) did not have a right to attend.

In order to remove any doubt on the matter, articles usually state that directors who are not members shall be entitled to attend and speak at meetings of the company (e.g. reg. 44 of Table A, pcls 40, clg 26 and plc 32). There is some doubt as to whether a director who is not a member could enforce such a right as he is not a party to the contract which is deemed to exist between the members and the company by virtue of the articles. His exclusion from the meeting would be unlikely to invalidate the proceedings except in the case of a resolution to remove him as a director. Any right which a director has to attend a meeting must presumably be subject to the usual rules on ejection on the grounds of disorderly conduct.

The 1948 Act Table A makes no such provision, presumably because directors were usually required to hold some shares in the company which would give them the right to attend general meetings. A company which proposes to delete an article which imposes a share qualification, should perhaps ensure that it also adopts a provision similar to reg. 44 of the 1985 Table A.

21.2.9 Company secretary

The company secretary has no statutory right to attend general meetings. Articles rarely address the subject. However, in view of the role, it would be unusual for the secretary to be excluded from the meeting.

21.2.10 Other classes of member

All members have the right to attend general meetings unless the articles provide otherwise. Where a company has more than one class of shares, it is usual for the articles to specify the voting rights of each class. For example, preference shareholders are not usually entitled to vote at general meetings unless their dividends are in arrears. If they are not entitled to vote, they would not normally be entitled to attend. Members of a class will, of course, be entitled to attend meetings of their own class.

21.2.11 Attendance by invitation

It is normal for a public company to invite its lawyers, specialist advisers, brokers, analysts, press representatives, etc. These invitations are usually issued by the secretary on behalf of the company. The presence at a meeting of persons not entitled to be present or to vote does not invalidate the meeting (*Re Quinn and the National Society's Arbitration* [1921] 2 Ch. 318).

Under the model articles, the chairman of the meeting is given specific power to permit any person who is not a member of the company or otherwise entitled to attend and speak, to attend and speak at a general meeting (pcls 40(2), clg 26(2), plc 32(2)). Where the articles make no such provision, the chairman can undoubtedly allow other people to attend. However, his power to do so might be subject to the will of the meeting, which could decide otherwise. The inclusion of a power in the articles means that the decision as to who can and cannot attend lies solely with the chairman of the meeting, who may obviously revoke any permission previously given and who will undoubtedly take into account the views of the members in deciding whether or not to do so. If a person who is an invited guest refuses to leave upon being asked to do so, reasonable force may be used to eject them.

Companies should employ some method of ensuring that people attending by invitation cannot vote on any resolution (e.g. by issuing voting cards to the members) or are not counted when a vote is taken (e.g. by placing them in a separate area).

■ 21.3 Record of attendance

A record should be kept of the names of the members, proxies and corporate representatives who attend any general meeting (see **Precedent 21.3A**). The record is used primarily to ensure that a quorum is present throughout the proceedings. Totals of the members, corporate representatives and proxies present should be calculated and shown in the minutes. The record of attendance can also be useful in helping to reconcile the votes cast on a poll. In theory, no-one should vote on a poll unless they are present in person or represented by a proxy or corporate representative or, in the case of a company whose articles allow voting in advance, they have voted in advance.

Listed companies usually send each shareholder an attendance card with a unique bar-coding and request members to produce it on arrival at the meeting (see **Precedent 21.3B**). The information on the attendance card is scanned and fed into a computer which holds details of the register of members. The computer is then able to calculate the number of members present in person or by proxy and to print out a list of attendees. This also enables the company to identify whether certain shareholders are present, e.g. institutional investors or members who represent pressure groups.

Regulation 100 of Table A requires the minutes to show the names of the directors present at general meetings.

■ 21.4 Attendance

Traditionally, the right to attend a meeting and to participate in it could only be exercised by turning up in person at the designated venue. However, modern articles allow the use of multiple locations which need not necessarily be in the same country. For example, the model articles (but not Table A) provide that, in determining attendance at a general meeting, it is immaterial whether any two or more members attending it are in the same place as each other, and that two or more persons who are not in the same place as each other attend a general meeting if their circumstances are such that if they have (or were to have) rights to speak and vote at that meeting, they are (or would be) able to exercise them (pcls 37, clg 23 and plc 29). This provision is also reflected in the provisions of the model articles on the quorum at general meetings, which provide that no business other than the appointment of the chairman of the meeting is to be transacted at a general meeting if the *persons attending it* do not constitute a quorum (pcls 38, clg 24 and plc 30). This means that even where the quorum is two, the two people who must attend the meeting in order for it to transact any business do not have to be in the same place.

Under the model articles, the directors may make whatever arrangements they consider appropriate to enable those attending the meeting to exercise their rights to speak and vote at it. However those arrangements must enable a person who has the right to speak at the meeting to communicate to all those attending the meeting, during the meeting, any information or opinions which he has on the business of the meeting. The arrangements must also ensure that a person who has the right to vote is able to do so during the meeting on resolutions put to the vote at the meeting, and ensure that their vote can be taken into account in determining whether or not such resolutions are passed at the same time as the votes of all the other persons attending the meeting.

Section 311 requires the notice of any general meeting to state the place of the meeting. Accordingly, where attendance at different locations is allowed, it must be necessary for the notice to state each of those locations. This would seem to preclude the use of certain types of electronic communications which might enable people to attend from unpredictable locations. However, s. 360A(1) provides that nothing in Part 13 of the Act shall be taken to preclude the holding and conducting of a meeting in such a way that persons who are not present together at the same place may by electronic means attend and speak and vote at it.

In the case of a traded company (see definition at **8.5.1**), the use of electronic means for the purpose of enabling members to participate in a general meeting may be made subject only to such requirements and restrictions as are:

(a) necessary to ensure the identification of those taking part and the security of the electronic communication; and
(b) proportionate to the achievement of those objectives.

■ 21.5 Right to speak

The primary purpose of holding general meetings is to enable the members to make decisions by a majority or special majority after listening to, or participating in, a debate on each proposal. Where voting is allowed to be conducted without holding a meeting (e.g. by a written resolution of a private company), the members are given no formal opportunity to judge or question the arguments of those proposing the resolution and or listen to the arguments of those who may oppose the proposals. The minority is to a certain extent deprived of their opportunity to persuade the majority of the merits of its arguments. In practice, by allowing members of private companies to take majority decisions by written resolution, the Act assumes that members of private companies are able to communicate with each other outside the confines of a general meeting. This is likely to be the case in private companies with relatively few members. The rights of the minority are protected to a certain extent by having the ability to circulate their own written resolutions (accompanied by a statement) and to demand that a general meeting be held. However, although they are entitled to have a statement circulated in connection with any business proposed at a general meeting, they are not entitled to do so in connection with a written resolution proposed by the directors or another member.

A general meeting is an opportunity for both sides to put their case to the floating voter. Where all or most of the members attend, the debate may have an influence on the final outcome. In practice, the outcome is often determined in advance by the votes given by proxy before the meeting. In the case of listed companies, it is not uncommon for the proxy votes in favour of resolutions proposed by the board to exceed the total number of votes held by all the members actually present at the meeting and the proxy votes cast against the resolution. In other words, even if a speaker persuaded everyone at the meeting to oppose a resolution, it would still be carried on a poll called by the chairman. Nevertheless, this does not mean that the chairman would be justified in curtailing debate on the issues. A member who has appointed a proxy could attend and vote at the meeting in person, and in so doing would override any voting instructions give to his proxy. It is also possible for a member to issue new voting instructions any time before the vote is taken. These two factors mean that the outcome will not always be a foregone conclusion.

Members entitled to attend and vote at general meetings have a common law right to speak at the meeting. Whether a member who is entitled to attend but not to vote is entitled to speak is a moot point. This will be relevant where the articles provide that the vote of the senior joint holder shall be accepted to the exclusion of all others but do not restrict the other joint holders' right to attend meetings of the company. The question may also be relevant for a member who has been disenfranchised for some reason (typically, in the case of listed companies, for failing to respond to a s. 793 notice). In practice, most companies allow members who are entitled to attend to speak even though they are not entitled to vote, and this is undoubtedly the safest course of action.

A corporate representative is deemed to have the same rights that the corporate member who appointed him would have if it were an individual member by virtue of s. 323. Accordingly a corporate representative will have the right to speak if the corporate member would have been so entitled.

Potentially, all proxies have the right to speak at a meeting. A member has a right to appoint another person as his proxy to exercise all or any of his rights to attend and to speak and vote at a meeting of a company (s. 324(1)). Assuming that the member does actually appoint the proxy to speak on his behalf, the proxy will have a right to speak. However, it may be possible for a member to appoint a proxy to exercise his right to attend or vote without giving him the right to speak. Indeed, it may be possible for a member to appoint a proxy to attend and speak on his behalf, but not to vote. If a member has appointed a proxy to speak on his behalf, the proxy will undoubtedly have a right to do so. Even if a proxy has not been appointed to speak on behalf of the member, he will have a statutory right to demand or join in a demand for a poll if he was authorised under the terms of his appointment to vote on that matter (s. 329).

Although it would be unusual to do so, there is nothing to prevent the articles restricting the rights of members who are entitled to attend and vote from speaking at the meeting. A member's right to speak is a common law right and, as such, is capable of modification by the articles. The Act would not prevent this provided that the restrictions were applied to members rather than being directed at proxies or corporate representatives. Under the Act, proxies only have the same rights as the member who appointed them, and corporate representatives the same rights as the corporation would have if it were an individual member. Accordingly, if the rights of the member were restricted, then the rights of their proxies or corporate representatives would be similarly restricted.

Directors are given a statutory right to speak on a resolution to remove them as directors (s. 169(2)). Apart from this, directors who are not members or a corporate representative or proxy of a member do not have a statutory right to speak at meetings. However, articles usually give directors who are not members the right to speak (e.g. reg. 44 of Table A, pcls 40, clg 26 and plc 32). Where they are silent on the matter, it is possible that the meeting could refuse to allow directors to speak if they are not otherwise qualified to do so. Clearly, this is not something which the members would normally wish to do. In practice, directors will normally be invited by the chairman to speak as and when necessary, and it should be assumed that they may do so unless the meeting objects.

The model articles provide that the chairman of the meeting may permit any other person who is not a member of the company or otherwise entitled to attend and speak, to attend and speak at a general meeting (pcls 40(2), clg 26, plc 32). This is a sensible provision and one which companies with older articles might sensibly adopt. Where the articles make no such provision, the chairman undoubtedly can invite other people to attend and speak. However, his power to do so might be subject to the will of the meeting, which could decide otherwise. The inclusion of a power in the articles means that the decision as to who can and cannot attend and speak lies solely with the chairman of the meeting, who clearly may revoke any permission previously given and who will undoubtedly take into account the views of the members in deciding whether or not to do so.

Auditors have a statutory right to speak on matters which concern them as auditors (s. 502(2)). This right is preserved in certain respects in the case of auditors who have been removed before the expiry of their period of office (s. 513) and resigning auditors (s. 518(10)) (see **21.2.7**).

■ 21.6 Common law restrictions on the right to speak

The members' right to speak will always be subject to any reasonable limitations imposed by the chairman or the meeting itself. Under the common law, the chairman has a duty to ensure that all shades of opinion on a resolution before the meeting are given a fair hearing. In particular, the chairman should seek to ensure that the minority has had a reasonable opportunity to put its views (*Wall v. London & Northern Assets Corporation Ltd.* [1898] 2 Ch. 469). This does not mean that all those who hold those views must be allowed to speak. It will suffice if members representing the range of views on a resolution have been allowed to do so.

The chairman also has a duty to ensure that all the business before the meeting is conducted. In order to facilitate the conduct of the meeting, the chairman may, if the meeting does not object, apply various rules of debate. The most commonly applied is that speakers must confine themselves to the subject of the resolution before the meeting. This is particularly appropriate where a member is speaking on a matter which will be the subject of a subsequent resolution put to the meeting. From a practical point of view, it is normal for the chairman to inform speakers that they will be given an opportunity to raise these matters at the appropriate time and to ask them to keep to the subject of the resolution. It is not so easy to apply this rule where a member wishes to raise a matter which, strictly speaking, is not on the agenda. Here the chairman ought, perhaps, to allow slightly more leeway, particularly if other members want to speak on the same subject. In reality, it is often difficult for the chairman to rule that an issue raised by a member has no connection with the resolution before the meeting. Experienced speakers will normally be able to manufacture a reason why the point they wish to make is relevant and the chairman cannot really decide whether their contribution is relevant without giving them an opportunity to state their case. In such circumstances, it might be advisable for the chairman to allocate time at the end of the meeting to discuss the issues raised.

Another rule of debate which is sometimes applied is that no person other than the proposer of the resolution may speak more than once in connection with it. In the context of general meetings, this may not always be appropriate. For example, members who exercise their right to speak by asking a question probably ought to be given an opportunity to comment on any answer given. Ordinarily, there is no reason why a member who has spoken previously should not be allowed to respond to comments made by other speakers, particularly if that member is in the minority. It may, however, be appropriate to apply this rule where there is only limited time available for debate and there are still several members who wish to speak. In addition, there will always come a point where a member has had a reasonable opportunity to make his or her point. The chairman need not allow a member to make the same points over and over again or to speak for an inordinate length of time.

The amount of time which should be made available for debate will vary depending on the nature of the business and the number of people wishing to speak on it. This does not mean that the discussion should be allowed to go on forever or that everyone who wishes to speak must be allowed to do so. Shortly before closing the debate, the chairman should ask members to refrain from speaking unless they have a different point to make. Although it is not an easy thing to do without causing offence, the chairman should at this point cut short any speaker who is repeating a point made earlier in the debate in order to ensure that those with different views are given a fair hearing. When the chairman considers that a full range of views have been expressed, he may seek to curtail the discussion and put the resolution to a vote. If several members object, the chairman could seek the consent of the meeting by proposing a formal 'closure motion', i.e. that the question before the meeting be now put to the vote (see further **23.14** and the example of a chairman's script at **Appendix 3**). If the resolution is defeated on a show of hands, the chairman could, if the articles so provide, demand a poll on the question and would be justified in casting votes given to him as proxy in favour of the substantive resolution in favour of the formal closure motion.

■ 21.7 Shareholder questions

In exercising their right to speak, members may ask questions that are relevant to the business in hand. Whether or not the company has a legal obligation to respond (see **21.8** regarding the obligations of traded companies), it is usual for the chairman and the directors to do so in order to explain their point of view and to persuade the members to support the resolution before the meeting. It is reasonable on this basis for the chairman to refuse to answer questions that are not pertinent to the business in hand. It is also reasonable for the directors to refuse to divulge commercially sensitive information and for listed companies to be cautious about disclosing potentially price-sensitive information in any answer without taking steps to release the information to the market by way of an announcement. Within these constraints, one might expect the directors to do their best to answer questions. However, they may simply not know the answer.

On occasion, their lack of knowledge or refusal to disclose information may be sufficient to turn the meeting against them. The members could, for example, decide that they cannot be expected to make a decision on the resolution without certain information and may use one of the procedural resolutions to defer consideration of the matter until a later date. All these factors mitigate towards a tendency on the part of the directors to be co-operative and to strive to answer relevant questions to the satisfaction of the members present. However, the fact that the chairman may be certain of the outcome of the meeting by virtue of proxies lodged in favour of a resolution before the meeting can breed complacency in this regard, particularly at meetings of listed companies.

Public companies are required to 'lay' their accounts before the company in general meeting (s. 437). Private companies are no longer required to do so by the Act but may be required to do so under their articles. The requirement to 'lay' accounts is nothing more than an obligation to make them an item of business at the meeting. This is traditionally done by making the accounts the subject of a resolution; the company lays the accounts before the members so the members are asked to vote to 'receive' them. It does not really matter how the resolution is framed or whether it is defeated. The accounts will still have been laid before the meeting and will still be the company's statutory accounts. On this basis, it can be seen that sole purpose of the requirement to lay the accounts is to make them an item of business upon which discussion, debate and questions may ensue. In practice, it affords the members an opportunity to question the directors on their stewardship of the company. No other purpose is served by laying the accounts except, where a resolution is put to the members in connection with them, for the fact that it enables the members to signify a vote of no confidence in the directors.

In practice, when the meeting moves to the business of the report and accounts, the chairman will normally invite questions and comments from the floor. Questions and debate are usually allowed on a broad range of issues because it is difficult to define the scope of the meeting at that point. Almost any subject raised by a member could have an impact on the financial performance of the company. The chairman would, however, be justified in refusing to allow questions or discussion on a matter which has already been dealt with in a previous item of business or that will be the subject of subsequent item of business at the meeting.

Although slightly overtaken by recent developments for traded companies (see **21.8**), ICSA's *Guide to Best Practice for Annual General Meetings* makes the following recommendations on the subject of shareholder questions and debate:

- Boards should provide adequate time for shareholder questions at AGMs.
- When moving the adoption or receipt of the accounts, the chairman should allow shareholders to raise questions on any item concerning the company's past performance, its results and its intended future performance. However, the directors need not answer questions which are irrelevant to the company

or its business or which could result in the release of commercially sensitive information. Nor should they disclose price-sensitive information unless it can be done in compliance with the Listing Rules and guidance regarding the release of price-sensitive information.

■ Before each resolution is put to the vote, the chairman should explain again its purpose and effect. If necessary, he should elaborate on the information previously provided in the explanatory circular which accompanied the notice of the meeting. He should also invite shareholders to speak.

■ Where concerns are raised by a shareholder at the AGM and the chairman undertakes to consider them, the shareholder should subsequently be sent a full report of the action taken.

The *Guide* also suggests that when a particular issue has been raised by a shareholder, the chairman may assist the flow of the meeting by inviting other shareholders who wish to speak on the same subject to do so at that time.

Some companies include in the documents sent to shareholders prior to the annual general meeting an invitation to submit questions in advance of the meeting. This enables them to select the most common questions and provide an answer for each one at the meeting. Answers can be given orally by the chairman or the relevant director, or they can be distributed to shareholders in the form of a printed question and answer sheet. The latter allows more detailed information to be provided in numerical or graphical form and enables the chairman to refer questioners who raise similar issues at the meeting to the relevant written answer. Although ICSA urged more companies to invite shareholders to submit questions in advance in its *Guide to Best Practice for Annual General Meetings*, it did not include it as one of its 24 best practice points. It said:

> Of course giving shareholders the opportunity to raise questions in advance of the AGM may not always assuage all their concerns. Questions on broadly the same subject may arrive in 40 or 50 different forms for the company to co-ordinate into a single response. Such a reply may satisfactorily answer most points, but is unlikely to address them all.
>
> We recommend that companies invite shareholders to submit questions in advance, as this makes structuring the AGM more manageable. We leave it to companies to decide how best to convey the invitation. We stress that inviting questions in advance is not to be deployed by companies as a method of manipulating the AGM by requiring written notice of questions; nor is it intended to replace spontaneity at the AGM, which we regard as one of its greatest attributes.

■ 21.8 Traded companies: questions at meetings

Section 319A(1) provides that at a general meeting of a traded company (see definition at **8.5.1**), the company must answer any question relating to the business being dealt with at the meeting put by a member attending the meeting. However, no such answer need be given:

- if to do so would interfere unduly with the preparation for the meeting, or involve the disclosure of confidential information;
- if the answer has already been given on a website in the form of an answer to a question; or
- if it is undesirable in the interests of the company or the good order of the meeting that the question be answered.

It should be noted that s. 319A is framed so as to impose duties on the traded company and makes no provision to enable members to enforce any consequent rights they may have. Members may presumably do so by some sort of injunctive relief. However, there is absolutely no suggestion that any failure on the part of a company to answer questions will have any effect on the validity of the business transacted at the meeting.

Any rights which shareholders have under s. 319A(1) are severely limited by subsection (2) and it is doubtful whether the requirements do anything other than codify what companies already do. A possible cause for concern could be where the company does not know the answer to the question and cannot refuse to answer it on any of the grounds in subsection (2). In such circumstances, the company could presumably give a holding answer (e.g. 'We don't know, but we'll get back to you on that one if you provide us with your details [and/or publish the answer on our website]').

Another concern could be that s. 319A may make it difficult for the chairman to curtail the debate until all the members who want to ask a question have done so. It is not difficult for a speaker to frame his speech in the form of a question. General meetings in Germany have been known to go on through the night because German company law gives members an unrestricted right to speak. In the UK, it is very likely that the courts would support any company which sought to curtail the debate after giving members a reasonable opportunity to speak and ask questions, and would not look kindly on behaviour by the members which could be interpreted as filibustering. The curtailment of questions and debate in these circumstances would presumably fall within the exception provided in s. 319A regarding the 'good order of the meeting'.

22

Security and disorder

22.1 Summary

- Security is not normally a problem for private companies. However, for companies which are in the public eye, it is becoming an increasingly important issue. Pressure groups frequently disrupt meetings of listed companies in order to gain publicity for their cause. In the current political and social environment, companies can no longer discount the possibility of terrorist attack or the possibility that a member or customer with a grudge against the company will behave in a violent manner at the meeting. Many companies now invest a considerable amount of time and money on security measures to counter these threats.
- The company's main line of defence is the registration process. Some listed companies still allow members of the public to attend their annual general meetings without an invitation. However, more and more are restricting entry for the purposes of security and require people wishing to gain entry to prove their identity (see **22.2**).
- Companies that face disruption need to be prepared to tackle it. A security checklist is included at **22.3**.
- Disruption at general meetings is nothing new, and the common law has developed various rules that enable the chairman to deal with it. A skilful chairman can sometimes avoid undue disruption by dealing with dissident members firmly, politely and fairly and with good humour. Even if this has no effect on the dissident members, it will probably ensure that the chairman retains the support of the meeting should further action need to be taken. If the dissident members persist in their disorderly conduct to such an extent that the meeting is no longer able to transact the business before it, the chairman may either order the ejection of those who are causing the disorder or adjourn the meeting in an attempt to restore order (see **22.4**).

22.2 Security

22.2.1 Proof of identity

A company may refuse to admit members who cannot provide satisfactory evidence of their identity. If it were otherwise, the company would be forced to admit two people claiming to be the same member. The same can be said with regard to proxies and corporate representatives. Most members will have no difficulty satisfying any reasonable request made by the company. This might include the production of a driving licence or some other document showing their name and address. A company should, perhaps, also accept the confirmation of an individual's identity by someone else who is known to the company. It is also arguable that anyone who is able to furnish accurate information about their holding (e.g. full name, address, size of holding, date of purchase of shares, mandate details, etc) should also be admitted. In cases of doubt, it is probably wise to err on the side of caution as the exclusion of a person entitled to attend and vote could render the meeting liable to challenge. However, admitting people who are not entitled to attend, and allowing them to vote, could be considered just as dangerous as unjustly excluding people who are entitled to attend.

If proof of identity is required, security and registration staff should be properly briefed. The procedures which should be followed before refusing entry to a person who would be entitled to attend if able to prove their identity should be approved by the chairman. Indeed, it may be preferable to refer difficult cases to the chairman. In cases of doubt, the person could be admitted but asked to sit in a specially allocated area. If that person's vote would have affected the outcome on a show of hands, the chairman may need to make a ruling on the validity of their vote, which under most articles will be deemed to be conclusive. Alternatively, the chairman could demand a poll (if the articles so allow) in the hope that this will resolve the difficulty. This would also enable the company to take further steps to establish the identity of the person claiming to be a member, etc. If the result of the poll is affected by the disputed votes, the chairman will have to make a ruling on their validity. The courts have endorsed the use by the chairman of a 'conditional' casting vote where the validity of some votes had been in doubt and it was not clear whether or not the vote was tied (see **17.14**).

22.2.2 Attendance cards

Some companies send shareholders attendance cards and request that they produce them on arrival in order to gain entry to the meeting (see **Precedent 21.3B**). The main advantage of this system is that it helps to speed up the registration process. It does, however, have a number of weaknesses. The first of these is that attendance cards actually facilitate impersonation where no other identity checks are made. In addition, a company cannot refuse to admit members merely because they are unable to produce an attendance card, unless the articles specify this as a condition of entry or the chairman is able to do so under powers conferred by the articles. Even then, it would probably be unreasonable not to allow members who cannot produce their attendance cards to prove their identity in some other way However, it would not be unreasonable to impose more exacting standards on members who do not bring their attendance cards than those that do.

Companies sometimes request proxies and corporate representatives to bring the member's attendance card with them. If the member has appointed more than one proxy or corporate representative, it will be impossible for them all to do so. They should therefore be allowed to prove their identity in some other way. In the case of corporate representatives, they should also be required to produce evidence of their authority at the meeting (see **16.3**).

22.2.3 Security checks

Some companies have taken specific powers in their articles to refuse entry to members who fail to comply with certain conditions of entry (see **Precedent 22.2**). Neither Table A nor the model articles make specific provision in this regard, although the model articles do provide that the directors may make whatever arrangements they consider appropriate to enable those attending a general meeting to exercise their rights to speak or vote at it (pcls 37(3), clg 23(3) and plc 29(3)). However, it is submitted that even if the articles do not make specific provision with regard to security, the company can (and perhaps should) take reasonable security measures, particularly where it has reason to believe that the meeting might be disrupted or that the safety of those attending might be at risk.

The chairman has a duty to preserve order at meetings and to ensure the business of the meeting is properly conducted. Security procedures such as screening devices and baggage searches are, it is suggested, a legitimate method of ensuring that the meeting is not disrupted and that it is able to complete its business. Many listed companies deliberately hold their meetings at venues which have built-in security screening at the point of entry. Anyone wishing to attend must pass through an electronic screening device and have their baggage inspected. It is submitted that a company can exclude a person who refuses to be screened if the purpose of that screening is to ensure the safety of other members present and to prevent disorder at the meeting. If a person refuses on medical grounds to be screened electronically, they should still be prepared to submit to some sort of manual screening. Clearly, it would be irresponsible to admit anyone found in possession of explosives. They should be arrested and handed over to the police. On the other hand, it might be considered unreasonable to exclude a person found in possession of a klaxon or whistle. A more reasonable course of action in these circumstances would be to ask the person to surrender these items for the duration of the meeting.

Companies sometimes seek to prevent members taking cameras and recording equipment into the meeting. It is sometimes difficult to see how this can be justified on the grounds of security. However, it could be argued that continual flash photography could disrupt the meeting and that recording equipment could be used to play back some sort of previously recorded protest. It is, of course, increasingly difficult for companies to impose these rules because most members will come to the meeting armed with mobile phones capable of taking photographs, video and sound recordings and playing them back.

■ 22.3 Security checklist for annual general meeting

The following checklist is based on material produced by company secretaries of companies whose meetings have been disrupted by protesters and demonstrations.

Planning the meeting

■ Make someone responsible for security.
■ Identify issues which are likely to be controversial, e.g.:
  – any company issues likely to lead to demonstrations;
  – any staff issues likely to lead to demonstrations;
  – any shareholder issues likely to lead to demonstrations;
  – any active shareholder protest groups;
  – any known agitators likely to attend; and
  – any historical issues which have arisen at company meetings.
■ Consider issuing a statement concerning any controversial or difficult issues prior to the meeting to diffuse potential protests.
■ Notify the local police of security concerns and request their availability.
■ Persuade the chairman to rehearse any complications.
■ If cameras and tape recorders are not to be allowed in, the notice to shareholders should include this information.
■ Be aware of the possibilities for various forms of protest and take appropriate precautions, e.g.:
  – irrelevant questioning;
  – mass sit-in;
  – storming the platform;
  – handcuffing to immovable objects;
  – protests outside the venue; and
  – abseiling from the roof.

The AGM venue

■ Ensure that the company's security staff are involved in selecting the venue.
■ Can entry to the venue can be controlled with limited access points?
■ Consider which access routes to the meeting hall are to be used.
■ Is there a clear route for the directors to the meeting hall from the venue of any pre-meeting get-together? Can they enter and leave the room by a separate exit which is easily accessible from the stage?
■ Is physical security satisfactory?
■ Are there any areas which are always open to the public?
■ Who else has booked conference facilities on the same day?
■ Does the venue have adequate security procedures, e.g. to deal with bomb alerts?
■ Does it have a security manager or other in-house security staff?
■ Has the venue hosted company meetings before?

- What are the normal arrangements for dealing with disturbances?
- Where does the venue boundary meet the public highway?
- Is there a tannoy system?
- Does it have a controlled car parking area?
- Is it possible to erect barriers at the venue entrance and reception areas to control the flow of attendees?
- Is the reception area large enough to accommodate all attendees before entering the meeting hall?
- Are the toilets inside the secure area or will attendees need to go through security checks each time they enter the hall?
- Check availability of discrete exits to remove demonstrators.
- Are the seats fixed?
- Are the hand rails or other fittings removable?
- Are there any balconies or other public areas from which items could be thrown, banners displayed or photographers planted?

Precautions

- Prevent demonstrators erecting banners on the stage by using floral arrangements or guards.
- Thoroughly search the meeting area before commencement of meeting for suspicious objects and then secure until access is opened for the meeting.
- Conduct regular security patrols.
- Consider personal searches, including metal detectors. If detectors or scans are to be used, ensure that trained staff are employed to operate them.
- Consider inspection of baggage and/or barring of baggage from the meeting hall. If baggage is not allowed in, consider providing clear plastic folder for documents.
- Establish a policy on:
  - cameras and videos;
  - recording equipment;
  - mobile telephones; and
  - access for TV/radio crews.
- Display clear notices detailing the items not allowed in the meeting.
- Arrange for secure storage of items not allowed into the meeting.
- Alert venue staff to any person who may be carrying anything unusual.
- Send out invitation cards which must be presented to gain access to the meeting. In the event of failure to produce invitation, entry to meeting should only be permitted on production of identification, personal verification by a known third party or, for shareholders, identification on the share register.
- Organise a system of security passes for all attendees and staff.
- Rotate the colour of passes each year.
- Prepare a script for the chairman to follow in the event of disruptions, covering ejection of protesters by stewards and/or adjournment of the meeting.
- Use radio mikes to prevent attachment or damage to cables.

- Ensure that radio microphones do not interfere with security radio network and vice versa.
- Use hands-free radios for security guards.
- Have the following equipment available:
  - large bolt cutters;
  - solvent for superglue;
  - smother blankets for smoke bombs; and
  - tools to remove handrails.
- Bring spare clothes for chairman in case missiles thrown.
- Consider videoing the proceedings.
- Have paramedics (e.g. St John's Ambulance) standing by.

Demonstrators

- Identify known activists.
- Review recent purchases of small number of shares, paying particular attention to purchases of one share. Obtain details of purchaser (and, if off-market, the transferor) and obtain background information on them if possible (some registrars have compiled a database of shareholders who are known to be connected with certain groups).
- Alert staff on the registration desk of suspects' names.
- Obtain copies of questions if possible.
- Be positive with demonstrators – they will attempt to intimidate or antagonise.
- Consider delaying opening doors to meeting hall until, say, half an hour before the start of the meeting. This may prevent potential agitators obtaining pole positions.
- Consider refusing entry to any press not authorised by the company's PR department.
- Protest groups often pre-warn the press. The company's PR department may be able to find out whether this has happened from its press contacts.

Staffing

- If necessary, engage additional security staff and ensure that the security staff includes a number of women. Use well-trained staff.
- Arrange protection for chairman, directors and senior executives especially during period of mingling with shareholders.
- If there is risk of violence to the chairman or other speakers, access to the rostrum should be restricted by security staff facing the audience.
- Consider the need to have extra security staff available but hidden in the immediate vicinity of the meeting hall.
- Stewards and security staff should be briefed and given a checklist on the arrangements for, and their powers for dealing with, disturbances.
- Place staff on every door leading to the meeting hall and only allow persons with the requisite pass to enter the hall.

- Arrange for venue's own security staff to be present to help in fire or bomb emergencies.
- Consider how security staff (company's own staff, external staff and venue staff) are to be dressed – high or low profile.
- Clearly identify the role of all staff involved.
- Establish with the venue's management that they will deal with the removal if necessary of demonstrators from their property to the public highway boundary.
- If staff demonstrations are anticipated, arrange for an industrial relations manager to be available to meet with staff representatives.
- Use staff as fillers to occupy areas of seating and/or form barriers.

■ 22.4 Preservation of order

The chairman's primary responsibility is to ensure that all the business before the meeting is properly and fairly transacted. This is unlikely to be achieved if the meeting is constantly disrupted by dissident members. The chairman is therefore responsible for the preservation of order at the meeting and should seek to ensure that the meeting is conducted without undue disruption.

A skilful chairman can sometimes avoid undue disruption by dealing with dissident members firmly, politely and fairly and with good humour. Even if this has no effect on the dissident members, it will probably ensure that the chairman retains the support of the meeting should further action need to be taken.

Where it is known that a group of shareholders is likely to attempt to disrupt the meeting, the chairman may take preventative action before the meeting, e.g. to prevent members entering the hall with klaxons, tape recorders, banners, and any other objects which could be used to disrupt the meeting.

22.4.1 Adjournment to restore order

If there is persistent and violent disorder, the chairman has a right and may even have a duty to adjourn the meeting in order to restore order. In *John v. Rees* [1969] 2 W.L.R. 1294, Megarry J explained this principle as follows:

> The first duty of the chairman of a meeting is to keep order if he can. If there is disorder, his duty, I think, is to make earnest and sustained efforts to restore order, and for this purpose to summon to his aid any officers or others whose assistance is available. If all his efforts are in vain, he should endeavour to put into operation whatever provisions for adjournment there are in the rules, as by obtaining a resolution to adjourn. If this proves impossible, he should exercise his inherent power to adjourn the meeting for a short while, such as 15 minutes, taking due steps to ensure as far as possible that all persons know of this adjournment. If instead of mere disorder there is violence, I think that he should take similar steps, save that the greater the violence the less prolonged

should be his efforts to restore order before adjourning. In my judgment, he has not merely a power but a duty to adjourn in this way, in the interests of those who fear for their safety. I am not suggesting that there is a power and a duty to adjourn if the violence consists of no more than a few technical assaults and batteries. Mere pushing and jostling is one thing; it is another when people are put in fear, where there is heavy punching, or the knives are out, so that blood may flow, and there are prospects, or more, of grievous bodily harm. In the latter case the sooner the chairman adjourns the meeting the better. At meetings, as elsewhere, the Queen's Peace must be kept.

If then, the chairman has this inherent power and duty, what limitations, if any, are there upon its exercise? First, I think that the power and duty must be exercised bona fide for the purpose of forwarding and facilitating the meeting, and not for the purpose of interruption or procrastination. Second I think that the adjournment must be for no longer than the necessities appear to dictate. If the adjournment is merely for such period as the chairman considers to be reasonably necessary for the restoration of order, it would be within his power and his duty; a long adjournment would not. One must remember that to attend a meeting may for some mean travelling far and giving up much leisure. An adjournment to another day when a mere 15 minutes might suffice to restore order may well impose an unjustifiable burden on many; for they must either once more travel far and give up their leisure, or else remain away and lose their chance to speak and vote at the meeting.

22.4.2 Powers of ejection

Members may be expelled from a meeting if they seriously interfere with the business of the meeting. 'The power . . . of suspending a member guilty of obstruction or disorderly conduct during the continuance of [a meeting] is . . . reasonably necessary for the proper exercise of the functions of any . . . assembly' (*Barton v. Taylor* (1886) 11 App. Cas. 197, *per* Lord Selborne at p. 204).

If possible, the chairman should seek the consent of the meeting before ordering that a person be expelled. In practice, it will rarely be possible to take a vote on the matter and the chairman must rely on his innate authority to take action to preserve order at the meeting. Expulsion should only be used as a last resort or in cases of severe disorder. Members should, if possible, be warned of the consequences of their actions. If they continue to disrupt the meeting, they should be given an opportunity to leave the meeting voluntarily. If they refuse to do so, they can be forcibly ejected, although only reasonable force should be used (*Collins v. Renison* (1754) 1 Sayer 138). If unnecessary force is used, the person removed will have a cause of action for assault against the persons responsible (*Doyle v. Falconer* (1866) L.R. 1 P.C. 328.). This may include the chairman as the person who authorised their removal.

See **Appendix 3** for example of chairman's scripts dealing with disorder.

23

Adjournment and other procedural motions

■ 23.1 Summary

- This chapter deals with procedural motions. It deals with the rules on adjournment first (**23.3** to **23.11**) and then addresses various other types of procedural motions that may be proposed at a meeting (see **23.12** to **23.15**). A resolution to adjourn is just one of the many procedural motions that may be proposed at a meeting. Although amendments are technically procedural motions, they are dealt with separately in **Chapter 24**.

- Procedural motions concern the conduct of the proceedings rather than the business of the meeting itself. Resolutions regarding the business of the meeting are usually referred to as substantive resolutions. It is not normally necessary to give any notice of a procedural motion. Procedural questions normally have to be dealt with as and when they arise. Some have to be dealt with formally as a procedural motion. However, some procedural matters may fall within the inherent powers of the chairman (see **23.2**).

- An adjournment is a temporary halt to the proceedings, usually initiated with a view to reconvening at some other time or place to complete the unfinished business. The Companies Act has very little to say on the subject of adjournment. Thus the common law rule that the power to adjourn is vested in the meeting itself normally applies (see **23.3**).

- Articles usually provide that a meeting will be adjourned automatically if a quorum is not obtained within a certain period after the time designated in the notice for the meeting to start (see **23.4**).

- The chairman will usually have no power to adjourn of his own volition unless the articles provide otherwise (see **23.5**).

- The only exceptions to this rule are that the chairman has the power to adjourn to conduct a poll, to restore order, or to facilitate the business of the meeting (see **23.6**).

- A resolution to adjourn must specify when the adjourned meeting is to be held or who is to decide when the meeting is to be held. The articles may specify that a poll may not be demanded on a resolution to adjourn or that a poll on such a resolution must be taken immediately (see **23.7**).

- The company may need to give notice of an adjourned meeting in certain circumstances (see **23.8**).

- The adjourned meeting cannot normally be used to transact any business other than the unfinished business of the original meeting (see **23.9**).
- A proxy submitted for the original meeting will normally be valid at any adjournment of that meeting. Articles usually make special provision to allow for the submission of proxies between the original meeting and the adjourned meeting (see **23.10**).
- It is not possible for the directors to postpone a meeting once it has been called, unless the articles allow (see **23.11**).

23.2 Procedural motions

- Meetings are called to deal with items of business. The resolutions that are proposed in connection with each item of business (e.g. a resolution to appoint a director) are known as substantive resolutions because they concern the substance of the meeting, the reason why it was called. By contrast, procedural motions or resolutions (sometimes referred to as 'formal motions') are used to regulate or facilitate the conduct of the meeting, i.e. matters of procedure. Nobody would call a meeting just to debate matters of procedure, or at least one would hope not.
- The distinction between procedural motions and substantive resolutions can sometimes feel a bit hazy, mainly because the outcome of the meeting can be affected by procedural motions. For example, a proposal to amend a substantive resolution can be characterised as a procedural motion. The fact that it can alter the substance of the original resolution and thereby affect the outcome of the meeting does not mean that it cannot be properly viewed as a procedural motion. Indeed, it is better to view things the other way. The reason why certain things have to be done by way of a procedural resolution is precisely because they are capable of affecting the outcome of the meeting. A decision to adjourn is capable of affecting the outcome of the proceedings. That is why it must normally be proposed as a formal resolution.
- The terminology used to describe procedural motions is often old-fashioned and obscure. There is no magic or mystery in the use of this terminology. Provided that the intention of the motion is clear, there is little to be gained from insisting that it be used. Indeed, it is probably more likely to cause confusion.

As procedural motions relate to the conduct, rather than the substance, of the meeting, no prior notice is normally required or, indeed, could normally be given. Although the chairman is the person who is most likely to propose a procedural resolution, any member, representative or proxy entitled to vote and speak at the meeting may do so.

One common exception to this rule, is that a company's articles may require members to notify the company in advance of any amendments they wish to propose (see **24.3**). The purpose of such a rule is to give the company enough time to work out whether the amendment can be properly proposed. Articles do not normally require the company to notify members of any amendments that it has decided to accept or that it intends to propose itself, and neither does the common law.

Decisions on procedural resolutions are usually taken, at least initially, on a show of hands at the meeting. A poll can be demanded unless the articles provide otherwise, which they occasionally do for certain types of procedural resolution. Even if the articles do not prohibit a poll on a procedural resolution, they may require any poll that is demanded on certain procedural matters to be taken immediately (such as the election of the chairman). Articles that may appear to require all resolutions to be taken on a poll typically only apply to substantive resolutions. It is possible that they may also apply to procedural motions. However, this will probably not be by design but as a consequence of bad drafting.

23.2.1 Formal motions, implied consent or a ruling by the chairman

It is not necessary for all matters of procedure at general meetings to be decided by a procedural motion (or 'formal motion'). No decision is required at all if the procedure that is being followed is in line with the fundamental expectations as to how a meeting should be run under the company's articles and any applicable common law rules. However, some sort of decision will be required if the chairman or anybody else wants to depart from those fundamental rules or principles, assuming that it is possible to do so.

Examples of these fundamental rules and principles would include (but not necessarily be limited to) the expectation that:

(a) the meeting will start at the appointed time;
(b) the meeting will deal with all the business on the agenda in the order that it appears on the agenda;
(c) resolutions included in the notice will be put to the meeting in the form that they appear in the notice;
(d) that members have the right to speak; and
(e) the meeting will continue until all the business has been completed.

Although these can be described as fundamental expectations, some are not as critical in terms of the outcome of the meeting as others. As we will see, the chairman can usually make informal rulings on minor matters of procedure himself. However, decisions on matters of procedure which could potentially affect the outcome of the meeting usually have to be dealt with as a formal motion. For example, the chairman clearly cannot propose a resolution that is materially different from the one that was included in the notice without proposing a formal amendment. To do so would fly in the face of one of the fundamental expectations as to how a meeting should be run and could materially affect the outcome of proceedings. Amendments that materially affect the substance of a resolution always have to be proposed as a formal motion. It may not be necessary to do so to correct a minor clerical error or spelling mistake. However, it is always better to do so because it is difficult to say for certain that a formal motion is not required unless it is a patent error.

A resolution to adjourn usually has to be proposed as a formal resolution because it involves a change to one of the fundamental expectations and could affect the outcome of the meeting. The same would also be true of any decision not to propose a resolution. These are not minor matters of procedure that fall within the chairman's powers. They can materially affect the outcome of the meeting. Accordingly they should be proposed as a formal motion.

The mere fact that some procedural matters have to be dealt with by proposing a procedural motion helps to explains why people sometimes refer to them as 'formal motions'.

It is inevitable that there will be some grey areas where it is difficult to decide whether a formal motion is actually required. After all, we are dealing with the common law. For example, one could argue that the order in which the items on the agenda are taken will not normally affect the outcome as long as all the items are dealt with eventually. However, the fact is that the order in which the items are taken can affect the outcome, and the normal expectation is that if you issue an agenda, you will follow it. Accordingly if you want to change the order of the items, it is sensible to obtain the consent of the meeting before doing so. The right and proper way of doing this is to propose and pass an appropriate procedural resolution. However, where the matter is not as critical to the outcome of the proceedings, it may be sufficient for the chairman to draw attention to the action he is proposing to take, and to ask whether there are any objections. It would definitely be wrong for the chairman to change the order of the agenda without at least having obtained the implied consent of the meeting in this way. If there is a good reason to change the order, it is highly unlikely that anybody would object. However, if the reason for changing the order was to try to prevent a particular item from being dealt with, or to ensure that it can be dealt with while certain people are not there, you might reasonably expect some members to object. If anybody does object, the chairman would be well-advised to put the matter to a formal vote, from both a political and legal perspective.

Chairmen also tend to use this technique when dealing with minor matters of procedure that will not necessarily affect the outcome of the meeting. It is accepted under the common law that the chairman may make rulings on minor matters of procedure and points of order. However, it is important to understand that the courts view the chairman's authority in this regard as a form of delegated authority that is vested in him by the meeting but, critically, not to the exclusion of its own powers in this regard. In other words, unless the chairman has an inherent or specific power to make a ruling on a matter of procedure, his rulings can be overturned by the meeting (see **20.5**). On this basis it is arguable that the chairman should inform members of any rulings that he proposes to make on matters of procedure that depart from the norm, and offer them the opportunity to object where it is within their power to overrule his decision. In practice, it will not necessarily be fatal if the chairman does not do so on minor matters of procedure. The acid test for the chairman is whether the thing that he is proposing to do could affect the validity of the proceedings. If so, it should not really be treated as a minor matter. At the very least, the chairman should offer members the opportunity to object and ensure that the minutes record the fact that he did so. Although this is far better than doing nothing, it would be much safer for the chairman to propose a formal motion where the matter is potentially critical, and for the fact that he did so to be recorded in the minutes together with the fact that it was passed. Even though this is the safest course of action, companies often seem to be reluctant to do it. Where this is the case, it is normally because they are seeking to avoid the possibility of a poll being demanded on the matter, which could raise some very difficult issues for the chairman regarding the proper use any proxy votes he may have.

It is fairly obvious that the chairman need not worry as much about minor matters of procedures that will not affect the outcome of the meeting or the validity of the proceedings. Almost by definition, it will not make much difference whether or not the chairman asks members whether they have any objections to any rulings he makes in this regard. To take an example, it is highly unlikely that the validity of the proceedings will ever be affected by the fact that somebody has been allowed to speak who did not have the right to speak. Accordingly, it would not normally make any difference whether the chairman had or had not sought permission from the members before inviting such a person to speak. If the chairman had bussed in thousands of non-members and invited them to speak in order to prevent the members from speaking, things might be different.

Although it may not always be necessary for the chairman to ask whether there are any objections to his rulings on minor matters of procedure, it is normally considered polite to do so. If the chairman did so on every trivial matter he might appear obsequious. If he were to do so for matters on which he cannot be overruled, there is a danger that he might appear both foolish and obsequious.

■ 23.3 Adjournment

Under the common law the right to adjourn any meeting (including a general meeting of a company) is vested in the meeting itself (*Kerr v. Wilkie* (1860) 1 L.T. 501). If the chairman, contrary to the wishes of the majority, purports to halt the proceedings before the business of the meeting has been completed, the meeting may elect a new chairman and continue to transact the unfinished business (*Stoughton v. Reynolds* (1736) 2 Strange 1044). These basic common law rules are subject to a number of exceptions and are subject to modification by the articles. Articles usually contain detailed provisions setting out when, how and by whom general meetings can be adjourned (see below).

The purpose of an adjournment is to enable the meeting to be reconstituted at some time in the future. When a meeting has been adjourned it has not been permanently dissolved or closed. The proceedings have merely been suspended. A meeting may be adjourned:

(a) for a fixed interval of time (e.g. for 15 minutes) or until a specified time (e.g. 3.30 pm) on the same day;
(b) to another place (maybe with a brief interval to allow everyone to get there);
(c) to a fixed time on a specified date and at a named place;
(d) for an unspecified period not exceeding a given maximum;
(e) until a time and place to be specified by a person or body; and
(f) indefinitely (in which case the meeting is said to be adjourned *sine die*).

Legally, there is not much difference between an adjournment to a time and place to be specified and an indefinite adjournment. In both cases, the adjourned meeting could be reconvened by the relevant convening body. However, the former tends to be used where it is intended to reconvene the meeting whereas meetings tend to be adjourned *sine die* where there is no such intention. However, there is no reason why the convening authority should not change its mind and proceed to reconvene a meeting that has been adjourned *sine die*.

■ 23.4 Adjournment where no quorum

Articles usually make provision as to what happens (or should happen) where a quorum is never obtained or a quorum ceases to exist at some point during a meeting. Under Table A, meetings are liable to be adjourned automatically in these circumstances. Under the model articles, the meeting probably enters into a state of paralysis and should be adjourned by the chairman. It is worth noting when considering this area that it is possible (although admittedly unusual) for a general meeting to be quorate for certain items of business but not others even though the same number of members are present throughout (see **15.7**).

Regulation 40 of Table A sets out the quorum requirements at general meetings (normally two persons entitled to attend and vote). However, reg. 41 of Table A provides:

> **41.** If such a quorum is not present within half an hour from the time appointed for the meeting, or if during a meeting such a quorum ceases to be present, *the meeting shall stand adjourned to the same day in the next week at the same time and place or to such time and place as the directors may determine.*

By contrast, the model articles provide (at pcls 41(1), clg 27(1) and plc 35(1)) that:

> (1) If the persons attending a general meeting within half an hour of the time at which the meeting was due to start do not constitute a quorum, or if during a meeting a quorum ceases to be present, *the chairman of the meeting must adjourn it.*

The above provision found in the model articles is preferable in some respects to reg. 41 of Table A, but maybe not in others. A meeting will be adjourned automatically under Table A to the same time and same place even if nobody turns up, and will be automatically adjourned again if nobody turns up at the designated time in the following week, and again in the next following week, and so forth. In fact, under Table A, a meeting can never die of neglect in these circumstances. Instead, it clutches on to life in a state of suspended animation in the vain hope that at some point in the future (at the same time and place and on the same day of the week) somebody will care enough to turn up and take advantage of its facilities. Indeed, it is intriguing to imagine just how many adjourned meetings must be taking place each and every day on this basis. If only somebody would provide some tea and biscuits, these adjourned meetings might be put out of their misery.

The automatic nature of an adjournment under Table A can be seen as an advantage in that it enables the meeting to be held the following week if so desired without any action on the part of the chairman or the directors. However, this could also be viewed as a disadvantage because members who are able to form a quorum might be able to turn up at the same time and place on the same day in any future week, elect their own chairman and proceed to transact the business of the meeting.

Another thing that is tricky about reg. 41 of Table A is that the meeting is adjourned automatically unless it is adjourned to some other time or place by 'the directors'. Normally, when articles use the word 'directors', it is interpreted as meaning the board of directors and not an individual director. This may mean that a valid decision of the directors is required to prevent a meeting being automatically adjourned under reg. 41 of Table A. This is not particularly a problem where a quorum is never obtained because the meeting will automatically stand adjourned to the same time and place in the following week and the directors will have time to decide otherwise if they wish to adjourn it to another time or place before the adjourned meeting takes place. However, it can cause a problem if a quorum ceases to exist in the middle of the meeting. In these circumstances it may be desirable to be able to declare a temporary adjournment, particularly where the absence of a quorum is only expected to be temporary. It is possible that the word 'directors' might be capable of being interpreted more flexibly for the purposes of reg. 41 of Table A. The directors could, for example, be deemed to have delegated their authority to determine such matters to the chairman. Alternatively, the term 'directors' could be interpreted as meaning the 'directors present at the general meeting' in these circumstances or to include the chairman acting individually. The courts could decide that the chairman has inherent power to adjourn the meeting. In any case, any decision made at the general meeting could be ratified by the board at a later date and could, in the absence of any such ratification be saved by the principle of unanimous consent. One thing that reg. 41 of Table A definitely does not allow, however, is for a member who is not a director, but who has been elected as chairman of the meeting, to adjourn the meeting to some other time and place where a quorum ceases to exist unless this is viewed as something that the chairman has an inherent power to do. It should also be noted that the meeting itself, being inquorate, cannot resolve to adjourn in these circumstances, unless it does so immediately prior to the event giving rise to the lack of a quorum.

23.4.1 Model articles

Under the model articles, general meetings are not automatically adjourned and resurrected on a weekly basis where a quorum is not obtained or not maintained. Instead, they provide that the chairman of the meeting 'must' adjourn the meeting in these circumstances (pcls 41(1), clg 27(1) and plc 35(1)). This begs a number of questions that are so difficult to answer that it might have been better if the model articles had said that the chairman of the meeting 'can and should adjourn the meeting in these circumstances if he wants to avoid having to take expensive legal advice as a result of his oversight'. The author does not particularly recommend that readers try to make sense of the following analysis of the questions raised by a failure on the part of the chairman to adjourn a meeting in these circumstances, unless absolutely necessary, but does recommend that they should read it at least once, if only to underline the importance of getting the chairman to turn up and to adjourn the meeting.

The first question we will try to address is what happens if the person who was meant to chair the meeting does not turn up but somebody else does? The answer here is that under the model articles the meeting can still appoint a chairman even though it is not quorate (see pcls 38, clg 24 and plc 30) and that any person eligible to be elected as the chairman of the meeting and who is so elected could then proceed to adjourn the meeting to a date, time and place of their choosing.

The next question is what happens if nobody turns up at all or if nobody who has power to do so actually adjourns the meeting? The position under the common law is not clear in this area, which is one of the reasons why Table A provides for an automatic adjournment regime. It has been suggested by an eminent authority that:

> . . . until a quorum is present no meeting technically exists . . . Strictly speaking, if a quorum has not assembled at the precise time fixed for the commencement of the meeting, the meeting fails and those present are not competent to resolve upon its adjournment. Fresh notices will, therefore, have to be sent out if it is desired to proceed with the business for which the meeting was convened. (*The Law of Meetings*, Sir Sebag Shaw and Judge Dennis Smith, Macdonald & Evans, 1967, p. 90.)

This position makes sense on the basis that it would be unreasonable for a member who turned up at the designated time and then left after discovering that there was nobody else there, to subsequently discover that the other people did eventually turn up after the appointed time and that they purported to transact the business of the meeting in his absence. However, it also makes sense to say that this does not necessarily mean that the meeting cannot be commenced slightly later if all the members who attend remain in attendance and are not therefore prejudiced by the delay. Article provisions generally recognise that it is not appropriate to delay the meeting for any longer than 30 minutes for these purposes, and it is possible that the courts would rule that even in the absence of any provision in the articles, a member might reasonably be expected to wait that long before leaving the meeting.

On this basis, it is perhaps reasonable to assume that under the common law, a meeting would be deemed to have been dissolved if a quorum was still not present after about 30 minutes. However, the model articles say that if a quorum is not present within 30 minutes, the chairman must adjourn it. So, if our imaginary member attends a meeting called under the model articles which turns out to be inquorate, he will probably be expected to attend for at least 30 minutes and to wait and see what ruling the chairman may make regarding the adjournment of the meeting. If our imaginary member is aware that there is nobody at the meeting in a position as chairman of it to make the necessary adjournment declaration, he would presumably be quite justified in deciding to leave on the assumption that the meeting has failed and that there will be no adjournment. It may well be therefore that if nobody adjourns the meeting in accordance with the articles, the meeting will be deemed to have been dissolved, i.e. no longer be capable of being held. This would mean that a new meeting would have to be convened in order to transact any of the business.

Or at least that is the theory. Other interpretations are possible, including one where the meeting continues in existence but in a state of paralysis which can be cured by a decision of the chairman that it be adjourned and subsequently reconvened, or by the subsequent attendance of a quorum. If it can be cured by a decision to adjourn made after the event by the person who would have been entitled to chair the meeting (i.e. the chairman of the board of directors), fresh notice would have to be given of the meeting if it were to be held more than 14 days after the original meeting. If the paralysis can be cured by the attendance of a quorum, this would mean that a quorum of members could turn up at the venue for the meeting at any time in the future and proceed to elect a chairman and transact the business of the meeting. It is not even certain whether the rule regarding notice of any continuation of an adjourned meeting would apply in these circumstances, because the meeting will never have been properly adjourned, although it is possible that it might be deemed to have been adjourned out of neglect.

This solution does not seem very satisfactory when applied to a meeting at which a quorum was never obtained but might be more so where a meeting starts out with a quorum but that quorum is not maintained. Say this only happens on a temporary basis during a meeting and the chairman does not notice it. It would be far more sensible to assume that the business transacted in the absence of a quorum was invalid because the meeting was in a state of paralysis, but that any business transacted if and when the quorum was restored was valid. For this to work, it can be seen that the temporary state of paralysis has to be capable of being cured by the re-establishment of a quorum and not depend upon the fact that the chairman has adjourned the meeting properly. In the absence of an adjournment declared by the chairman, a dissolution in these circumstances would invalidate all of the business of the meeting transacted after a quorum ceased to exist. It is possible that the principles that apply where a quorum is never obtained are different from those that apply to situations where a quorum has ceased to exist. In the latter case, it is suggested that in the absence of any action to adjourn by the chairman of the meeting, the meeting continues but enters into a state of paralysis which can be converted into an adjournment at any time by the chairman of the meeting but which can also be cured by the re-establishment of a quorum. This sits more kindly with the notion that it is possible for the quorum requirements to be satisfied for certain items of business at a general meeting but not for others because a member might be disqualified from voting on certain resolutions. This never arises by virtue of any statutory prohibition but could arise by virtue of some additional provision in a company's articles.

In view of the difficulties that can arise in these circumstances where a general meeting is not properly adjourned, it is understandable why the model articles say that the chairman of the meeting *must* adjourn it.

■ 23.5 General power to adjourn in articles

Articles usually contain detailed provisions setting out when, how and by whom general meetings can be adjourned. Regulation 45 of Table A states:

> **45.** The chairman may, with the consent of a meeting at which a quorum is present (and shall if so directed by the meeting), adjourn the meeting from time to time and from place to place, but no business shall be transacted at an adjourned meeting other than that business which might properly have been transacted at the meeting had the adjournment not taken place. When a meeting is adjourned for fourteen days or more, at least seven days' notice shall be given specifying the time and place of the adjourned meeting and the general nature of the business to be transacted. Otherwise it shall not be necessary to give any such notice.

This type of article leaves the matter of adjournment in the hands of the meeting. The chairman must adjourn the meeting if a resolution to adjourn is duly passed.

If, however, a company's articles provide that the chairman may adjourn with the consent of the meeting, and omit the words 'and shall if so directed by the meeting', the chairman can refuse to adjourn despite the fact that a resolution to adjourn has been passed by the meeting (*Salisbury Gold Mining Co. v. Hathorn* [1897] A.C. 268).

Some articles give the chairman power to adjourn without the consent of the meeting. The model articles follow the same formula as Table A, but also provide that the chairman may adjourn a general meeting at which a quorum is present if it appears to him that an adjournment is necessary to protect the safety of any person attending the meeting or ensure that the business of the meeting is conducted in an orderly manner (at pcls 41, clg 27 and plc 35). This modification can be said to summarise the chairman's inherent power to adjourn under the common law (see below).

■ 23.6 Chairman's inherent power to adjourn

The chairman has inherent power to adjourn to facilitate the conduct of the meeting. The leading authority on this matter is *R. v. D'Oyly* (1840) 12 Ad. & El. 139, and the following extract from this case sets out the position:

> Setting aside the inconvenience that might arise if a majority of the parishioners could determine the point of adjournment, we think that the person who presides at the meeting is the proper individual to decide this. It is on him that it devolves, both to preserve order in the meeting, and to regulate the proceedings so as to give all persons entitled a reasonable opportunity of voting. He is to do the acts necessary for those purposes on his own responsibility, and subject to being called upon to answer for his conduct if he has done anything improperly.

23.6.1 To conduct a poll

In *Jackson v. Hamlyn* [1953] Ch. 577 it was held that the chairman's inherent power to adjourn to enable a poll to be conducted survived even though the company's articles stated that the chairman could only adjourn with the consent of the meeting. In this case the chairman adjourned the meeting in order to take a poll on a resolution to adjourn the meeting. Quite naturally, those seeking to oppose the resolution to adjourn objected. However, it was held that the chairman had power to stand over the proceedings to another time, since some such power had to exist in order to give effect to the provisions as to polls in the articles. Upjohn J stated that although this standing over was not an adjournment within the meaning of the articles, the chairman had a residual power to take such steps as would in the ordinary usage of the word amount to an adjournment.

Most articles which allow a poll on a resolution to adjourn state that the poll must be taken immediately (see below).

23.6.2 Room too small

The concept of the chairman's inherent or residual power to adjourn in order to facilitate the conduct of the meeting was taken a step further in *Byng v. London Life Association Ltd.* [1989] 1 All E.R. 560. The articles of London Life provided that the chairman may, with the consent of any meeting at which a quorum is present (and shall if so directed by the meeting), adjourn the meeting from time to time and from place to place. The venue for an extraordinary general meeting of the company was not large enough to accommodate the members wishing to attend and communications between the main meeting room and overflow facilities proved to be inadequate. As it was impossible to take a proper vote, the chairman purported to adjourn the meeting himself to an alternative venue later on the same day. The Court of Appeal held that the company's articles did not exclude the chairman's inherent power to adjourn the meeting where it proved to be impossible to ascertain the wishes of the meeting. However, the chairman's inherent power was only exercisable for the purpose of giving members a proper opportunity to debate and vote on the resolutions before the meeting. On the facts of this case the chairman's decision to adjourn the meeting to the Café Royal later in the day was held to be unreasonable and declared invalid because it did not achieve this purpose. The chairman did not properly take into account the fact that a significant proportion of the members who had attended the original meeting would not be able to attend the adjourned meeting and would therefore be unable to vote because the company's articles required proxies to be delivered 48 hours before the meeting. Browne-Wilkinson V-C suggested that the correct course of action in this case would have been either to abandon the meeting or to adjourn it *sine die* and to give 21 days' notice of a fresh meeting to be held, say, a month later. He added:

> The chairman's decision will not be declared invalid unless on the facts which he knew or ought to have known he failed to take into account all the relevant factors, took into account irrelevant factors or reached a conclusion which no reasonable chairman, properly directing himself as to his duties, could have reached, i.e. the test is the same as that applicable on judicial review in accordance with the principles of *Associated Provincial Picture Houses Ltd. v. Wednesbury Corp* [1947] 2 All E.R. 680.

As a result of this case, some companies modified their articles to give the chairman complete discretion to adjourn to another time or place without the consent of the meeting where it appears to him that it is likely to be impracticable to hold or continue to hold the meeting because of the number of members or their proxies present or wishing to attend (see example at **Precedent 23.6**). The model articles potentially give the chairman power to adjourn for these purposes, although it is debateable whether any such articles would prevent the courts from interfering if the nature of the adjournment did not actually facilitate the conduct of the meeting, as was found to be the case in the *Bing* case.

23.6.3 Adjournment to restore order

The chairman has inherent power to adjourn if there is persistent and violent disorder, but for no longer than is necessary to restore order (*John v. Rees* [1969] 2 W.L.R. 1294) (see **22.4**).

■ 23.7 Resolution to adjourn

Except where the chairman exercises an inherent power to adjourn, or a power given to him under the articles, a formal resolution to adjourn the meeting must be proposed and passed by the meeting. The resolution can be proposed by the chairman or a member from the floor. For example scripts, see **Appendix 3**.

A meeting may be adjourned for as long as necessary, although it may be necessary under the articles to give notice if it is adjourned for longer than a certain number of days. A meeting may also be adjourned to another place. If the purpose of the adjournment is to restore order, an adjournment of 15 minutes may suffice. It is not necessary to state specifically that it will be reconvened at the same place in these circumstances. In the absence of anything to the contrary in a resolution to adjourn, it can be assumed that the adjourned meeting will take place at the same place as the original meeting. An indefinite adjournment may be appropriate where it is not known when the unfinished business can be dealt with, in which case the meeting is said to have been adjourned *sine die*. If an adjournment is not planned or expected, the company is not likely to have made arrangements to reserve a venue for the adjourned meeting. In these circumstances the original meeting may have to be adjourned to a time and place to be determined by the directors. The range of options on a resolution to adjourn are summarised at **23.3**.

23.7.1 Poll on a resolution to adjourn

Section 321 provides members with a statutory right to demand a poll. However, s. 321(1) specifically allows a company's articles to exclude that right on a resolution to adjourn. Most articles (including Table A and the model articles) do not do so. However, both Table A and the model articles for public companies require a poll on a resolution to adjourn to be taken forthwith/immediately (see reg. 51 of Table A and plc 37(4)). The model articles for private companies require all polls to be taken immediately (pcls 44 and clg 30). If the right to demand a poll on a resolution to adjourn is excluded, a dissident minority may be able to obstruct the will of the majority by packing the meeting and proposing a long adjournment to prevent a poll being conducted on a resolution to which they are opposed. Under Table A and the model articles, the chairman would be entitled to demand a poll on the question of adjournment which would be taken forthwith (reg. 51, pcls 44(2), clg 30(2) and plc 36(2)). The chairman would normally cast those proxies which he holds in favour of the substantive resolution against the resolution to adjourn.

■ 23.8 Notice of adjourned meeting

Under the common law, there is no need to give notice of an adjourned meeting if the resolution to adjourn specifies the time and place at which the meeting is to be held (*Kerr v. Wilkie* (1860) 6 Jur. (N.S.) 383). Articles usually modify this rule by requiring notice to be given of any meeting which is adjourned for longer than a specified period. For example reg. 45 of Table A states:

45. . . . When a meeting is adjourned for fourteen days or more, at least seven days' notice shall be given specifying the time and place of the adjourned meeting and the general nature of the business to be transacted. Otherwise it shall not be necessary to give any such notice.

Under this rule and the equivalent provision in the model articles, notice must be given where the adjournment is for 14 days or more. Notice must also be given in both cases where a meeting has been adjourned indefinitely (*sine die*) or to a time and place to be specified by the chairman or the directors.

The rule in reg. 45 of Table A could restrict the ability of members to transact business at a meeting that is being adjourned automatically on a weekly basis under reg. 41 because of a failure to obtain or maintain a quorum. Whether or not it does so depends on whether one starts counting from the date of the original meeting or on the date of each automatic adjournment.

The model articles provide (at pcls 41(5), clg 27(5) and plc 33(5)) that:

(5) If the continuation of an adjourned meeting is to take place more than 14 days after it was adjourned, the company must give at least 7 clear days' notice of it (that is, excluding the day of the adjourned meeting and the day on which the notice is given) –
(a) to the same persons to whom notice of the company's general meetings is required to be given, and
(b) containing the same information which such notice is required to contain.

■ 23.9 Business of an adjourned meeting

Where a resolution is passed at an adjourned meeting, it is treated for all purposes as having been passed on the date on which it is in fact passed, and not on any earlier date (s. 332).

Articles normally provide that no business may be transacted at an adjourned general meeting which could not properly have been transacted at the meeting if the adjournment had not taken place (e.g. reg. 45 of Table A, pcls 41(5), clg 27(5) and plc 33(5)). The position under the common law is that although it is not always necessary to give notice of an adjourned meeting (*Kerr v. Wilkie*, see above), nothing can be transacted without notice at an adjourned meeting except the unfinished business of the original meeting (*R. v Grimshaw* (1847) 10 Q.B. 747).

■ 23.10 Attendance, voting and proxies at adjourned meetings

A member who was not present at the original meeting may attend and vote at the adjourned meeting (*R. v. D'Oyly* (1840) 12 Ad. & El. 139). An instrument of proxy deposited in time for the original meeting is also valid for any adjournment of that meeting on the basis that the adjourned meeting is merely a continuation of the original meeting (*Scadding v. Lorrant* (1851) 3 H.L.C. 418).

Proxies submitted after the deadline for the original meeting are not valid for the adjourned meeting unless the articles make provision to that effect (*McLaren v. Thomson* [1917] 2 Ch. 261). Most articles (e.g. reg. 62 of Table A) provide that a proxy lodged at least 48 hours before an adjourned meeting will be valid for that meeting. Proxy forms usually state that the appointment is made in respect of the original meeting 'and any adjournment thereof'. A proxy appointment made in this form submitted the appropriate number of hours before the adjourned meeting would be valid even though it was not submitted in time for the original meeting.

■ 23.11 Postponement

Once a meeting has been duly called, it is not possible to postpone it unless the articles so provide. Thus the meeting should be held at the appointed time and place. If the chairman and the directors fail to attend, the members present can elect their own chairman and proceed to transact the business of the meeting (*Smith v. Paringa Mines Ltd.* [1906] 2 Ch. 193). If nobody attends or there is no quorum, the meeting may be adjourned automatically under the articles (see **23.4**). The correct procedure is therefore to open the meeting in the normal way and, if appropriate, to adjourn it to another time or place or, if the purpose of the meeting is redundant, to close it after passing a resolution not to put any of the business to a vote.

The immediate adjournment procedure was used by two major listed companies in the 1990s after their AGM venues were destroyed by a terrorist bomb in London. Both companies advertised the change of venue in national newspapers prior to the meeting and posted staff at access points to the original venue to direct members to the new venue. The chairman and sufficient members to form a quorum held a meeting as close as possible to the original venue at the appointed hour and immediately adjourned to the new venue. Had there been any contentious business at either meeting, the safest course of action might have been to adjourn the meeting for longer and to give notice to the members in accordance with the articles. To prevent any problems in this regard, some companies now include articles which allow the directors to postpone and change the place of the meeting (see example article at **Precedent 23.11**).

■ 23.12 Other procedural motions

The remaining paragraphs of this chapter deal with a variety of other procedural motions that may need to be proposed at a general meeting. It is not necessary to use old-fashioned language and terminology when proposing procedural motions. Indeed, it is almost certainly better not to. It is necessary for procedural motions to be drafted carefully to ensure that they achieve their intended purpose. It is also important for the chairman to ensure that members understand the consequences of any procedural motion before it is voted upon. If the motion is proposed from the floor, the chairman may need to invite the proposer to explain the intended consequences, and may need to help the member draft a motion that achieves those consequences.

■ 23.13 Motion to appoint or remove the chairman

Any motion to appoint or remove a chairman of the meeting is a procedural motion. The ability of the members to propose such motions will depend on the procedures in the articles on the appointment of the chairman (see **20.2** and **20.3**). If it is allowed at all, a proposal to remove the chairman is traditionally framed as a motion of no confidence in the chair. One of the possible reasons for this is to avoid confusion with a motion 'that the chairman leave the chair', which is apparently similar to a motion to adjourn *sine die* (until further notice). It would be easy for such a motion to be confused with a motion to remove the chairman. Plainly, it would be sensible to clarify the intention of any such proposal from the floor. Procedural motions proposed do not need be seconded. Despite the fact that a proposal from the floor would be unlikely to be carried if a seconder could not be found, it would be wrong to insist that it be seconded unless, unusually, the articles impose such a requirement.

■ 23.14 Closure motion

A closure motion is a simple way of curtailing the debate on the question that is currently before the meeting. The chairman or any member may simply propose 'that the question before the meeting should now be put to a vote' or words to that effect. In practice, the chairman will only tend to propose a formal motion if he has attempted to wind up the debate and in doing so has encountered objections from the floor. It is certainly not necessary for the chairman to propose a formal closure motion at the end of every debate. If a closure motion is proposed from the floor, it is suggested that the chairman may refuse to put the motion to the vote on the ground that it is an infringement of the rights of the minority. However, if, acting in good faith, the chairman allows it to be put, the court will not intervene (*Wall v. London & Northern Assets Corporation* [1898] 2 Ch. 469). No debate need be allowed on a closure motion, although it might be difficult to prevent objections from those who still wish to speak on the question before the meeting. If a closure motion is carried, the question before the meeting must be put to a vote immediately. If it is not carried, the debate should be allowed to continue. See **Appendix 3** for a chairman's script for a closure motion.

▣ 23.15 Dealing with the business

As mentioned previously, there is a fundamental expectation that:

(a) the meeting will deal with all the business on the agenda in the order that it appears on the agenda;
(b) resolutions included in the notice will be put to the meeting in the form that they appear in the notice; and
(c) the meeting will continue until all the business has been dealt with.

The normal way to deal with business, is to propose and vote on a resolution. It is possible for more than one resolution to be proposed in connection with a single item of business. However, it is also possible to include items of business on the agenda merely to enable discussion, and for no resolution to be proposed in connection with it.

Ordinarily, the chairman would work his or her way through the agenda dealing with each item of business in the order that it appears and propose any resolutions connected with each item. Certain resolutions may also be the subject of proposed amendments, which would have to be dealt with before any vote on the substantive resolution (see **Chapter 24**). Any proposal to depart from these normal procedures ought to be agreed by the meeting (whether the proposal emanates from the chair or the floor). The normal way to obtain the consent of the meeting is to propose a procedural motion and to take a vote on it, although for certain less important matters the chairman could obtain members' consent informally (see **23.2**).

Departures from the norm would include proposals:

(a) to adjourn the meeting, thereby deferring consideration of the unfinished business but not preventing it from being dealt with if the meeting is reconvened (see **23.3** to **23.11**);
(b) not to deal with an item of business in the order that it appears in the agenda, but to deal with it later (i.e. to change the order of the business);
(c) that a matter lie on the table with a possibility of being restored;
(d) not to deal with an item of business at all (i.e. to remove the item from the agenda completely with no prospect of it being restored);
(e) not to put a substantive resolution to a vote; and
(f) not to put a question that is before the meeting to a vote, which could include an amendment.

23.15.1 Changing the order of the business

Generally speaking the chairman would not need to propose a formal resolution to change the order of the business. Typically, all the chairman would need to do is explain why he is proposing to change the order and to ask whether there are any objections. If the reasons for the change of order make sense, there would not normally be any objections. However, if there are then the chairman may need to propose a procedural resolution that would achieve the desired effect. In the author's view it is best to do so using plain English rather any traditional jargon. For example, the chairman could propose that:

(a) 'consideration of item [x] should be deferred until after item [y] has been dealt with';
(b) 'item [y] should be dealt with before item [x]'; and
(c) 'the items of business on the agenda should be taken in the following order, namely [c], [b], [a] and [d]'.

23.15.2 Allowing a matter to lie on the table

A proposal that 'a matter should lie on the table' enables that matter to be put aside for the time being without specifying when it will be dealt with or, indeed, how or whether it will be dealt with. Matter that are lying on the table at a meeting still potentially form part of the business of the meeting. However, it may take an active decision for it to be restored to the agenda. Any member (or the chairman) can propose at any time that it be restored. However, such a proposal may, in itself, end up being the subject of debate and, possibly, a procedural motion.

It is arguable that the chairman should not close the meeting without determining how to deal with matters that are still lying on the table or without offering members the opportunity to decide for themselves how to deal with them. Although the business has been removed from the agenda, the decision whether or not to restore it to the agenda remains open. In other words, there is potentially unfinished business. Accordingly, it is advisable for the chairman to dispose of it in some way before closing the meeting. One way of doing this would be for the chairman to inform the members that unless there are any objections, he is minded to close the meeting without dealing with a matter that is still lying on the table and to explain why. If nobody does object, the chairman could safely declare the meeting closed. However, if a member does object, it will presumably be on the basis that they want to deal with the unfinished business that is lying on the table in a different way. Effectively, by objecting, they are proposing that the business that is lying on the table be restored to the agenda. Accordingly, the chairman should allow that matter to be decided conclusively before closing the meeting, otherwise there is a danger that the members could continue to deal with the unfinished business without him (see the discussion of *National Dwelling Society v. Sykes* at **20.5**).

Having said this, it is highly unlikely that the validity of the other proceedings would be affected if the chairman failed to offer members the opportunity to decide how to deal with matters that are left lying on the table. Failure to deal with those matters properly will not affect the validity of resolutions and decisions that were made properly. The only real issue is whether the business of the meeting has been completed and whether the chairman can properly declare the meeting closed.

It is, of course, possible that a member may suggest that a matter should be allowed to 'lie on the table' without understanding the full implications of what they are saying. It is also possible that the other members may not understand the implications if such a proposal is put to a vote. Bearing this in mind, the chairman probably ought to explain how such matters would normally be dealt with and seek confirmation from the member who made the proposal that this is what they intended, before putting any such proposal to a vote.

23.15.3 Removing items of business from the agenda completely

It may, of course, be desirable to remove an item of business from the agenda completely so as to preclude it from being raised or dealt with at the meeting at all. The traditional method of doing this is to propose a formal motion when that item of business is reached to move on to the next item of business. In truth, if that is all that is proposed, the members may not be very clear as to whether it is intended to return to the original item or whether this would be possible. Accordingly, some sort of clarification would be required, preferably in the wording of the formal motion itself, or at the very least in the explanation given by the chairman. For example it would be preferable to propose that the item of business be removed from the agenda to preclude any further discussion of it or decisions being made in connection with it at the meeting and that, if so agreed, the meeting should accordingly move on to the next item of business.

It is possible to propose such a motion at any time during discussion of an item of business, including during the discussion of an amendment. If the motion is carried, no further discussion or decision on the item of business (including any substantive resolutions included in the notice and any amendments proposed in connection with them) should be allowed at the meeting (or any adjournment thereof) as its effect is to remove the question from the scope of the meeting. The question can only be considered again if it is proposed at a subsequent meeting. If it is rejected, discussion on the main issue may continue.

More often than not each item of business in the notice will be connected with only one substantive resolution. However, it is possible for a single item of business on the agenda to embrace the possibility of more than one resolution. In such circumstances, if the item of business is removed from the agenda, none of the resolutions can be proposed. If this is not what is desired, then some way has to be found to prevent any decision being made on some but not all of the resolutions. One way of doing this is to clarify that for the purposes of the proposal, each resolution is treated as a separate item of business and that the proposal only relates to one of those resolutions, which would then need to be clearly identified. Another way of dealing with it could be to propose at the appropriate juncture that the question before the meeting should not be put to a vote (see below).

23.15.4 Not putting a question to a vote

A proposal not to put a substantive resolution to a vote can be dealt with simply by proposing that it should not be. The motion should clarify the resolution to which it refers. If that resolution is an item of business in itself, a decision not to put it to the vote effectively removes the whole item from the agenda. In other words, the effect is similar to a proposal to move on to the next item of business. However, if an item of business embraces the possibility of more than substantive resolution, then a decision not to put one of those resolutions does not preclude the others from still being put.

If somebody were to propose that 'the question before the meeting should not be put', the chairman would have to be careful to clarify what they meant, because it is possible that the substantive resolution is not actually the question that is before the meeting. The question that actually is before the meeting could be an amendment or some other type of procedural motion. Equally, if somebody were to propose that a question 'be not now put' or 'be not put now', the chairman would need to seek clarification as to whether they are proposing that it should not be put at all or that it should be put later, possibly after something else has been decided. Indeed, the chairman could justifiably request that they frame their proposal in plain English and avoid using jargon that they may have read in textbooks like this. In previous editions of this book, we attempted to explain the jargon that is traditionally used in this area, some of which derives from Parliamentary procedures. However, we have tried to avoid doing so in this edition so as not to give the impression that it is necessary or sufficient to use these words or phrases in a formal motion, or that they necessarily have a consistent and reliable meaning.

23.15.5 That the matter be referred back to . . .

One of the ways in which a meeting could decide to dispose of an item of business is to refer the matter back to some other person or body. This will not tend to be something that is proposed as a formal motion at a general meeting, although it will commonly happen at board meetings. The normal course of events at general meetings is for the meeting to vote on the resolution, and if it is rejected, for the people who proposed it (typically the directors) to consider coming back with a revised proposal at a separate meeting called for that purpose. However, it is not beyond the realms of possibility that somebody (possibly the chairman) may propose that a matter be referred back to another body (e.g. the directors) before a vote has actually been taken. The effect of such a proposal would be similar to a proposal not to put the matter to a vote. At a board meeting, a decision to refer a matter back to another person or body would typically be couched with certain conditions and reservations. A proposal couched in similar terms and passed by the members as a formal resolution would not be binding on the directors because the members can only issue instructions to the directors by special resolution, and it is impossible to pass a special resolution without giving prior notice of it (see **13.4**).

24
Amendments

■ 24.1 Summary

- Dealing with amendments is one of the most difficult duties of the chairman. Unless the articles require prior notice of amendments to be given, the chairman will have to decide at the meeting whether to allow an amendment to be put to the meeting. If the chairman wrongly refuses to admit an amendment, the resolution is liable to be declared invalid unless the articles provide some protection in this regard (see **24.2**).

- The model articles include a provision dealing with amendments which requires members to give prior notice and protects the validity of resolutions where the chairman has ruled an amendment out of order in good faith. The articles of most listed companies make similar provision (see **24.3**).

- The question as to whether amendments should be allowed to ordinary resolutions depends on a variety of factors (see **24.3** and **24.4**).

- Special problems can arise with regard to amendments on proposals to appoint directors (see **24.5**).

- Amendments are only allowed to special resolutions in very restricted circumstances (see **24.6**).

- The position is not clear with regard to ordinary resolutions that require special notice (see **24.7**).

- Special procedural rules must be followed where amendments are proposed, particularly where a series of amendments to the same resolution, or amendments to amendments, are proposed (see **24.8**).

■ 24.2 Consequences of wrongly refusing to submit

If the chairman wrongly refuses to submit an amendment to a general meeting and the original resolution is passed, it will be invalid. It makes no difference whether the mover of the amendment contested the chairman's ruling or left the meeting (*Henderson v. Bank of Australasia* (1890) 45 Ch.D. 330). Modern articles often provide that a resolution shall not be invalidated by any error in good faith on the part of the chairman in ruling an amendment out of order (e.g. pcls 47(3), clg 33(3) and plc 40(3)) (see **24.3**). This type of provision can be viewed as a sensible precaution on the part of the company in view of the difficulties that can arise in this area. However, where the chairman is found to have made a mistake, the courts are likely to apply a fairly restrictive interpretation of 'good faith'. The chairman will, for example, be expected to have acted with scrupulous fairness and, if possible, taken any necessary advice.

Articles sometimes provide that no amendment shall be considered (except at the discretion of the chairman) unless prior notice in writing of the proposed amendment has been given to the company (see **24.3** re the model articles and, for further example, **Precedents 24.2A** and **B**). This type of article enables the chairman to take considered legal advice before the meeting as to whether the amendment should be accepted.

Companies often find that they need to make amendments to resolutions themselves in order to correct clerical errors. Accordingly, it is not normally sensible for the articles to prohibit amendments altogether.

The model articles prescribed under the 2006 Act all include a provision which enables the chairman to accept/propose amendments to resolutions proposed at a general meeting, but which requires members to give prior notice of amendments to ordinary resolutions and prohibits them from proposing amendments to special resolutions.

No such provision can be found in any version of Table A. Accordingly, the chairman will be expected to make rulings on the validity of amendments proposed from the floor of which he has no prior notice.

■ 24.3 Amendments to ordinary resolutions under the model articles

The model articles allow amendments to be made to ordinary resolutions proposed at a general meeting by ordinary resolution provided that the following conditions are satisfied:

(a) notice of the proposed amendment is given to the company in writing by a person entitled to vote at the general meeting at which it is to be proposed not less than 48 hours before the meeting is to take place (or such later time as the chairman of the meeting may determine); and

(b) the proposed amendment does not, in the reasonable opinion of the chairman of the meeting, materially alter the scope of the resolution.

The requirements as to notice in (a) above apply to amendments proposed by the directors or by the members. Under the model articles, notice 'in writing' can be given in hard copy or electronic form (see the definition of writing in pcls, clg and plc 1). The requirement to give not less than 48 hours notice will be satisfied even though some of those hours were part of a non-working day, e.g. for a meeting held on a Monday, the notice need only be given on the Saturday. The chairman of the meeting is given discretion to accept amendments at shorter notice. However, written notice would still be required and an amendment could not therefore be proposed unless and until it is reduced to writing.

The model articles provide that an amendment may only be made if it does not, in the reasonable opinion of the chairman of the meeting, materially alter the scope of the resolution. An amendment is made by being put to the meeting and passed by the meeting. In normal circumstances, one would imagine that the only way the chairman can prevent an amendment being made would be to refuse to allow it to be put to the vote at the meeting.

The question as to whether an amendment would materially alter the scope of a resolution will presumably fall to be decided by the usual common law rules. It should be noted that that the wording used in the model articles does not necessarily reflect the position under the common law unless the 'scope of the resolution' is taken to be dependent on the scope of the notice given for that item of business in the notice of meeting. This question is discussed further in **24.4.1**.

It should also be noted amendments can be rejected on other grounds under the common law and that the model articles do not necessarily restrict the chairman from doing so on these other grounds (see **24.4**).

The model articles provide that if the chairman of the meeting, acting in good faith, wrongly decides that an amendment to a resolution is out of order, the chairman's error does not invalidate the vote on that resolution (pcls 47(3), clg 33(3) and plc 40(3)). This saving would presumably apply to amendments which the chairman has rejected on any grounds and not just those rejected on the grounds that they would have materially altered the scope of the resolution. However, it is worth pointing out that this saving does not apply to amendments which the chairman wrongly allowed to be made which will therefore still be liable to challenge notwithstanding the fact the chairman acted in good faith.

Separate rules apply under the model articles to amendments to special resolutions (see **24.6**).

■ 24.4 Amendment of ordinary resolutions

An amendment to an ordinary resolution must be put to the vote unless it is:

■ outside the scope of the notice of the meeting;
■ irrelevant in so far as it bears no relation to the original motion or subject matter;
■ redundant because its effect is simply to negative the resolution or to propose something which has already been resolved by the meeting;
■ incompatible with a decision previously made by the meeting;
■ vexatious, i.e. its sole purpose is to obstruct the transaction of business; or
■ rejected by the chairman under a discretion granted by the articles.

Such an amendment may be passed by an ordinary resolution of the meeting.

24.4.1 Outside the scope of the notice

Under the common law, amendments must be within the scope of the notice given for that item of business in the notice of meeting. The meeting may transact any business which is within the 'general nature' of the business set out in the notice. In deciding what the 'general nature' of the business in the notice is, the test is what a reasonable shareholder reading the notice would consider the business to be. The courts normally adopt a practical approach and, where there is any ambiguity, apply a restrictive interpretation, so as to protect the absent shareholder. A guide endorsed by the courts is that an amendment should not be allowed if it would have affected a member's decision to attend. For example, a resolution authorising the directors to allot shares could be amended to reduce the number they may allot, but not necessarily to increase it.

In *Betts & Co. Ltd. v MacNaghten* [1910] 1 Ch. 430, it was held that the notice of meeting, which set out the names of the proposed directors, was sufficient to enable unnamed directors to be elected in place of or in addition to the named directors, because on reading the notice a reasonable shareholder would realise that those nominated might not be elected and therefore that others could be put up in their place. In this case the notice stated that the meeting was to consider resolutions 'with such amendments and alterations as shall be determined upon at such meeting'. However, these words could be considered redundant as it can be assumed that resolutions might be amended at the meeting.

In *Choppington Collieries Ltd. v. Johnson* [1944] 1 All E.R. 762, the Court of Appeal held that a notice which referred to the election of directors but which also stated that only one director was retiring and offering himself for re-election was wide enough to permit the election of directors, up to the maximum allowed by the articles. The court's decision was based on the general nature of the phrase in the notice 'to elect directors' which a shareholder might reasonably interpret as contemplating the appointment of more than one director. In this and other cases, the courts have emphasised that the question of the scope of the notice of meeting will turn on the construction of the notice in any given case.

24.4.2 Ordinary and special business

Articles sometimes distinguish between 'ordinary' and 'special' business (e.g. reg. 52 of the 1948 Table A and the articles of many listed companies). Matters specified in the articles as 'ordinary' business may be considered at an annual general meeting without prior notice having been given. These usually include:

- declaration of a dividend;
- consideration of the report and accounts;
- election of directors in the place of those retiring; and
- appointment and remuneration of the auditors.

In effect, notice is deemed to have been given of any of these matters even if it is not included in the AGM notice. Thus any resolution on these matters will be within the scope of the notice of the annual general meeting. This also makes it more likely that an amendment to any such resolution will be within the scope of the notice, although this may be limited where the notice sets out the general nature of the resolutions to be proposed under these headings or sets out the resolutions in full. By default, under articles like reg. 52 of the 1948 Table A, any other business proposed at an annual general meeting and all business proposed at a general meeting will be deemed to be 'special' business and, as such, the notice must specify the general nature of that business for it to be within the scope of the notice. Where articles adopt this formula it is usual for the AGM notice to distinguish between items which are proposed as ordinary business and those which are proposed as special business, and usual to dispose of the ordinary business before the special business.

The 1985 version of Table A requires the notice of a general meeting to specify 'the general nature of the business to be transacted' (reg. 38). The model articles rely on the statutory provision in this regard which provides that, in the absence of any other provision in a company's articles, the notice must state the general nature of the business (s. 311). In other words, under both the model articles and the 1985 Table A, all business is treated in the same way as special business.

24.4.3 Other reasons for rejecting amendments

An amendment need not be allowed if its effect is to negate the original resolution. The chairman should refuse to put such an amendment and point out that those who support it can achieve the same result by voting against the original resolution. For example, an amendment may be proposed to a resolution authorising the board to fix the remuneration of the auditors which imposes a maximum sum. But if the amendment proposes a limit of 1p, it effectively negates the resolution to authorise the board to fix the remuneration.

The chairman can reject amendments if they seek to re-open business already settled at the meeting or they are incompatible with a previous decision of the meeting. The chairman may sometimes do so where the proposed amendment is either obstructive, vexatious, dilatory or irrelevant. For example, where the proposer is merely attempting to obstruct the conduct of the business by proposing a series of amendments.

■ 24.5 Amending a resolution to appoint directors

Amendments to resolutions to appoint directors are probably the most common as shareholders often seek to propose a new person as a director, whether in place of or in addition to a nominated director. Unfortunately, this area is beset with difficulties. The principles outlined above in respect of ordinary resolutions apply and the basic question which must be considered is whether the amendment is within the scope of the notice. Before addressing this point, the chairman should, however, check the following points which may prevent the amendment being put.

(a) The articles may fix (or determine the method of fixing) the maximum number of directors that may be appointed. If that maximum would be exceeded by passing the amendment, it can be rejected.

(b) The articles may require notice to be given to the company of the intention to propose someone as a director who is not recommended by the board, e.g. reg. 76 of Table A which requires notice to be given by a member not less than 14 nor more than 35 clear days before the date appointed for the meeting together with the particulars which would, if that person was appointed, be required to be included in the company's register of directors together with notice executed by that person of his willingness to be appointed. Assuming that the company receives no such notice from a member entitled to vote 14 clear days before the meeting, no-one other than a director retiring at the meeting or a person recommended by the board would be eligible for election as a director at the meeting.

(c) The articles may require prior notice to be given to the company of any amendments to be proposed at the meeting. If no such notice has been given, the chairman may reject the amendment.

■ 24.6 Amendment of special resolutions

Special resolutions may only be amended in very limited circumstances. Under the Act, a resolution passed at a meeting will not be a special resolution unless the notice of the meeting included the text of the resolution and specified the intention to propose it as a special resolution (s. 283(6)). Accordingly, if a special resolution is to be validly passed, the resolution as passed must be the same resolution as that identified in the preceding notice. Inclusion in the notice of such words as 'with such amendments and alterations as shall be determined on at such meeting' would make no difference in this regard. However, based on the ruling of Slade J. in *Re Moorgate Mercantile Holdings Ltd.* [1980] 1 All E.R. 40 (a case decided under the equivalent provisions of the 1948 Act), a resolution as passed can properly be regarded as 'the resolution' identified in a preceding notice, even though:

■ it departs in some respects from the text of a resolution set out in such notice (for example by correcting those grammatical or clerical errors which can be corrected as a matter of construction, or by reducing the words to more formal language); or

■ it is reduced into the form of a new text, which was not included in the notice, provided only that in either case there is no departure from the substance.

In deciding whether there is complete identity between the substance of a resolution passed and the substance of an intended resolution as notified, Slade J. suggested that there was no room for the court to apply the de minimis principle or a 'limit of tolerance'. The substance must be identical. Otherwise the condition precedent to the validity of a special resolution as passed, imposed by s. 283, namely that notice has been given 'specifying the intention to propose the resolution as a special resolution' is not satisfied.

It follows from the above propositions that an amendment to a previously circulated text of a special resolution can be properly be put to and voted on at a meeting if, but only if, the amendment involves no departure from the substance of the circulated text, in the sense indicated above, with questions as to the notice given of the resolution being determined by reference the notice and any circulars which accompany it.

It should be noted, however, that the above propositions may be subject to modification where all the members or a class of members, of a company unanimously agree to waive their rights to notice under s. 283, see *Re Pearce, Duff & Co Ltd*. and *Re Duomatic Ltd*. [1969] 1 All E.R. 161.

The 1985 Act makes similar provision with regard to the notice required to be given to members of extraordinary resolutions, which are preserved for certain purposes. Accordingly, the same principles will apply to amendments of such resolutions.

In *Re Willaire Systems* [1987] B.C.L.C. 67, it was held that where a special resolution for the reduction of a company's capital contained an error (the number of shares was said to be 14,926,580 instead of 14,926,583), the court could confirm the reduction on terms which corrected the error provided that it was so insignificant that no-one could be thought to be prejudiced by its correction and the way in which it was to be corrected was clear. This case is probably an example of an amendment which could have been made at the meeting in order to rectify a minor clerical error (see also *Re European Home Products plc* [1988] 4 B.C.C. 779).

To eliminate any uncertainty with regard to amendments, companies sometimes adopt an article which disallows any amendment of extraordinary and special resolutions.

24.6.1 Amendment of special resolutions under the model articles

The model articles only allow an amendment to be proposed to a special resolution by the chairman of the meeting at which the resolution is to be proposed. Any such amendment may be made by ordinary resolution, but may not go beyond what is necessary to correct a grammatical or other non-substantive error in the resolution (pcls 47(2), clg 33(2) and plc 40(2)).

■ 24.7 Amendment of resolutions requiring special notice

It is arguable that the common law rules on amending special resolutions may also apply to resolutions requiring special notice. Section 312 provides that where by any provision of the Companies Acts special notice is required of a resolution, the resolution is not effective unless notice of the intention to move it has been given to the company at least 28 days before the meeting at which it is moved (s. 312(1)). The company is then required under s. 312(2) to give notice to the members of 'any such resolution in the same manner and at the same time as it gives notice of the meeting'. If a resolution to which these rules apply is amended, there is a danger that it is no longer the resolution of which special notice was given, and that it would accordingly be ineffective. For example, an amendment to a resolution to remove Mr Y as a director plainly cannot be amended to read to remove Mr X as a director, despite the fact that the removal of directors is within the scope of the notice. It is also arguable that the resolution should not be amended to propose the appointment of Mr Z as a replacement if it is agreed to remove Mr Y. That is not to say that a separate resolution to that effect could not be proposed if Mr Y is actually removed. However, the question as to whether this would be allowed would depend on the scope of the notice and any restrictions in the articles regarding the process for appointing directors.

It is submitted however that although the substance of an ordinary resolution for which special notice is required should not be amended, amendments can be made to rectify a clerical error (see above).

■ 24.8 Procedure on an amendment

Under the common law, an amendment may be moved at any time after discussion on the original motion has been invited by the chairman and before the motion has been put to the vote. Where articles require prior notice of a proposed amendment, it will still be up to the person who notified it to propose the amendment at the meeting, although the chairman of the meeting will have discretion to do so on their behalf. For an example of a chairman's script dealing with an amendment proposed from the floor, see **Appendix 3**. It is not necessary for an amendment to be seconded (*Re Horbury Bridge Coal, Iron & Waggon Co.* (1879) 11 Ch.D. 109).

An amendment may alter the original motion by making deletions, additions or insertions. The proposal must be carefully drafted and, if necessary, the chairman should assist the proposers in giving proper effect to their proposal.

For example, on a resolution 'to appoint ABC as auditors until the next annual general meeting at which accounts are laid and to authorise the directors to fix their remuneration' the following amendment might be proposed:

THAT the motion before the meeting be amended by deleting the word 'annual' and adding after the word 'remuneration' the words 'provided that the amount paid as remuneration shall not exceed £25,000'.

24.8.1 Order in which amendments taken

A properly moved amendment must be considered and put to the meeting before the original motion. There are no strict rules of debate that must be followed.

However, it is normal for discussion to be restricted to the amendment itself until it has been properly dealt with. If it is carried, the chairman should read out the amended motion and may invite discussion on it again before putting it to the vote. However, it may not be necessary to do so if, during the discussion of the amendment, all the relevant issues have already been discussed. If more than one amendment is proposed to the same motion, each amendment should be considered in the order in which it affects the motion. Where there are a series of amendments to a resolution, it is probably sensible for the chairman to require a more structured debate which follows the amendments before the meeting and defers discussion of any other matters until the amendments have all been dealt with. Where the chairman has refused to allow any debate on the main subject while an amendment is being considered, he clearly needs to afford members a subsequent opportunity to raise those matters, assuming that they are still germane to the resolution.

An amendment to an amendment may be proposed before the principal amendment is put to the vote. In these circumstances, the secondary amendment must be taken first. If it is carried, it must be embodied in the principal amendment which should then be read to the meeting before discussion is invited.

For example, on a motion 'to appoint ABC as auditors until the next general meeting at which accounts are laid and to authorise the directors to fix their remuneration' the following amendments might be proposed:

(a) to delete 'ABC' and to insert 'BCD';
(b) to delete 'ABC' and insert 'BCD and XYZ';
(c) to add after the word 'remuneration' the words 'provided that the amount paid as remuneration shall not exceed £25,000'.

In the above scenario amendment (b) should be redrafted and proposed as an amendment to amendment (a) and dealt with first. If it is passed, amendment (a) (which would now read 'to delete "ABC" and to insert "BCD and XYZ"') should be put to the meeting, followed by amendment (c) which may no longer be appropriate if two different firms of auditors are to be appointed. It is feasible at this point that somebody may propose an amendment to amendment (c). If so, this should be considered first.

25

Dealing with common items of business

25.1 Summary

This chapter outlines the procedures for dealing with some of the more common items of business at general meetings as follows:

- Laying of the report and accounts (see **25.2**).
- Approval of the directors' remuneration report of a quoted company (see **25.3**).
- Audit concerns raised by members of a quoted company (see **25.4**).
- Appointment and reappointment of auditors (see **25.5**).
- Auditors' remuneration (see **25.6**).
- Change of auditors (see **25.7**).
- Auditors' liability limitation agreements (see **25.8**).
- Resignation of auditors (see **25.9** and **25.10**).
- Removal of auditors (see **25.11**).
- Dividends (see **25.12**).
- Appointment of directors (see **25.13**).
- Retirement by rotation (see **25.14**).
- Removal of directors (see **25.15**).
- Annual authority required to enable a listed company to call general meetings at 14 days' notice (see **25.16**).
- Directors' authority to allot shares (see **25.17**).
- Disapplication of pre-emption rights (see **25.18**).
- Market purchases of own shares (see **25.19**).

25.2 Report and accounts

The directors of a public company must lay its accounts and reports before the company in general meeting (s. 437). The meeting at which the accounts and reports are laid is referred to in the Act as the 'accounts meeting'.

The directors of a private company are not required to lay the accounts and reports before the company in general meeting unless the articles of the company so require. Where this is the case, it cannot be assumed that any of the requirements of the Act relating to public companies apply in default and it is possible, as a consequence, that the exact procedures that must be followed by a private company will not be totally clear. For example, unless the articles say anything to the contrary, it would not be necessary for a private company to send members copies of the accounts at least 21 days before the meeting. The accounts would need to be sent before the meeting, probably at the same time as the notice or earlier. In addition, unless the articles make specific provision in this regard, there would probably be no fixed period within which the accounts should be laid.

25.2.1 Time for laying and delivering – public companies

The accounts of a public company must be laid before the company in general meeting before the end of the period for filing the accounts and reports in question, which for a public company is normally six months after the relevant year-end (s. 442). It should be noted that the period allowed for filing is subject to modification in certain circumstances (see below) and that where it is modified, it also directly affects the period allowed for laying the accounts.

Section 443 defines how to calculate the periods allowed for filing accounts and reports. In general this is the same date the relevant number of months later. So, for example, if the end of the accounting reference period is 5 June, six months from then is 5 December. However, as months are of unequal length, there can be confusion as to whether six months from, say, 30 June is 30 December (exactly six months later) or 31 December (the end of the sixth month). Under the rule laid down in s. 443, six months from 30 June will be 31 December. This reverses the 'corresponding date rule' laid down by the House of Lords in *Dodds v. Walker* [1981] 1 W.L.R. 1027.

It is no longer possible for a company with overseas interests to claim an automatic three-month extension of the period allowed for laying and delivering reports and accounts. However, it is still possible to make an application to the Secretary of State for a discretionary extension to the period for laying and delivery under s. 442(5). This procedure is intended to be used in situations where there has, for example, been an unforeseen event, which was outside the control of the company and its auditors. It is highly unlikely that an extension would be granted under this procedure on the sole ground that the company has overseas interests. Applications must be made in writing, contain a full explanation of the reasons for the extension and the length of the extension needed.

If the first accounts of a newly-incorporated public company cover more than 12 months, the period allowed for filing is six months from the first anniversary of incorporation of the company or three months from the end of the first accounting reference period, whichever is later (s. 442(3)). For instance, in the case of a public company incorporated on 1 March 2009 whose first accounting reference period ends on 30 June 2010, the filing deadline will be 30 September 2010 (i.e. three months after the end of the accounting reference period) and not 1 September 2010 (i.e. six months after the first anniversary of incorporation) and not 31 December 2010 (the normal filing deadline under s. 442(2)).

The Act also includes a provision to ensure that a company does not immediately fall foul of the filing deadlines when it files a change of accounting reference date which has the effect of shortening the relevant accounting reference period. If in any year a company has shortened the relevant accounting reference period by filing a change of accounting reference date, the period allowed for filing is either the period applicable under the normal rules or three months from the date of the notice given to the Registrar under s. 392, whichever is the later (s. 442(4)).

Listed companies must publish their accounts as soon as possible after the period end and, in any event, within four months of the period end (Disclosure and Transparency Rule 6.3). Publication is not the same as laying or delivering for which the usual time limits apply. Publication is the act of issuing, publishing or sending out copies of the accounts. If a listed company is unable to publish its accounts within the four-month time limit, it will need to obtain an extension from the UK Listing Authority.

25.2.2 Persons entitled to receive copies of the accounts and reports

Every company must send a copy of its report and accounts (or summary financial statement) to every member and debenture holder and any person entitled to receive notice of general meetings (s. 423(1)). In the case of a company without a share capital, copies of the accounts do not need to be sent to anyone who is not entitled to receive notices of general meetings (s. 423(4)).

The accounts of a private company must be sent out not later than the end of the period for filing accounts with the Registrar or, if earlier, the date on which it actually files its accounts with the Registrar (s. 424(2)).

A public company must comply with the requirement in s. 423 to send a copy of the accounts to those entitled to receive one at least 21 days before the date of the relevant accounts meeting (i.e. the general meeting at which the accounts are to be laid) (s. 424(3)). Where copies of the accounts are sent out over a period of days (perhaps because of the sheer scale of the operation) they are deemed to have been sent out on the last of those days (s. 423(5)). It can be seen from this provision that the requirement to send the accounts at least 21 days before the meeting is not like the requirement to give notice. The accounts will be sent when they are actually sent by the company. This is reinforced by the fact that there is no hint that the clear days rule in s. 360 applies.

If copies of the accounts and reports are not sent out in accordance with the above requirements, the company and every officer in default are liable to a fine (s. 425). However, if copies of the accounts and reports of a public company are sent out less than 21 days before the date of the accounts meeting, they will be deemed to have been duly sent if it is so agreed by all the members entitled to attend and vote at the meeting (s. 424(4)) (see **Precedent 25.2A**). In practice, it will be possible to obtain such agreement only in the case of public companies with relatively few members (e.g. public companies which are established as wholly-owned subsidiaries) and not where the company is publicly traded.

It is arguable whether a public company can lay its accounts before the company in general meeting unless it has sent out the accounts at least 21 days before the meeting or obtained the consent of members for them to be treated as duly sent under s. 424(4). There is no direct link between s. 437 (public companies: laying of accounts) and ss. 423 and 424 (circulation of accounts and reports). It is possible that the only consequence of failure to send out the accounts 21 days before the accounts meeting is that it renders the company and its officers liable to a fine if consent has not been obtained under s. 424(4).

This does not seem logical, as it seems to imply that it is possible for a company to lay its accounts even though the members have not actually seen them. In point of fact, this may actually be possible if all members consent in accordance with s. 424(4), which would seem to be highly unlikely. A company could, for example, have given notice of its accounts meeting to members without enclosing a copy of the accounts and may not have been able to send out copies of the accounts until the day before or even until just before the meeting actually starts. Even though none of the members will probably have seen a copy of the accounts, it would still be possible technically for them to agree to a resolution under s. 424(4) that the accounts have been duly sent, although any company secretary who manages to pull that one off without providing members who attend the meeting with a copy of the accounts and a very good lunch deserves to be named company secretary of the year.

The safest assumption to make in this area is that a public company will not have complied with its obligation to lay accounts if the accounts have not been sent out at least 21 days before the meeting or the members entitled to attend and vote at the accounts meeting have not consented to treat the accounts as duly sent. If the company has not obtained the necessary consent and has not complied with its obligation to lay the accounts, it will be guilty of an offence under s. 438 for failing to lay its accounts and may also be guilty of an offence under s. 425, although it is not clear whether the meeting before which the failure occurred would still be its accounts meeting if the accounts were not laid at it. According to s. 437(3), the accounts meeting is the general meeting of the company at which the company's accounts are (or *are to be*) laid. Assuming that the company does not have time to hold another meeting to lay the accounts properly, the meeting at which they 'are to be laid' presumably includes the meeting where the company tried, but failed, to lay them.

A company need not send a copy of the accounts to a person for whom it does not have a current address. A company has a current address if an address has been notified to it by the person and the company has no reason to believe that documents sent to that address will not reach him (s. 423(2) and (3)).

Copies of the accounts must be sent in accordance with the company communications provisions of the Act (see **2.2**). These rules require all documents or information to be supplied by the company in hard copy unless the member has agreed to some other form of delivery (e.g. by e-mail or by the company making the accounts available on a website and notifying the member to that effect). Part 6 of Sch. 5 to the Act includes rules about the provision of copies of documents to joint holders and people who are entitled to shares as a consequence of the death or bankruptcy of the member, which apply in the absence of anything to the contrary in a company's articles.

Any member who elects to receive the accounts in electronic form may demand that the company provide him with a hard copy version free of charge (s. 1145). In addition, any member or debenture holder is entitled to be given a copy of the accounts without charge on demand, regardless of whether he is entitled to notice or not (ss. 421 and 432). It does not matter that he has already had a copy. Failure to comply with such a demand within seven days renders the company and every officer liable to penalty.

25.2.3 Summary financial statements

A company may send a summary financial statement instead of the full report and accounts to any person entitled to a copy of the accounts under s. 423, if that person agrees (s. 426). Copies of any summary financial statement must be sent to any such person in accordance with the provisions of ss. 423 and 424.

Copies of any summary financial statement must be sent in accordance with the company communications provisions of the Act (see **2.2**).

The information required to be included in summary financial statements and the acceptable methods of ascertaining shareholders' wishes regarding receipt of full accounts or the summary are contained in ss. 427–429 and the Companies (Summary Financial Statement) Regulations 2008 (SI 2008/374).

A summary financial statement must include a summary auditors' report, and for quoted companies, a summary directors' remuneration report. It does not need to include a summary directors' report (although companies may voluntarily provide such a summary). However, it must include information on dividends paid and proposed as a note to the summary profit and loss account.

Summary financial statements should be approved by the board of directors and be signed on behalf of the board by a director (copies sent to holders must state the name of the person who signed on behalf of the board). Summary financial statements are not required to be filed with the Registrar or laid before the members, but in the case of listed companies two copies should be sent to the UK Listing Authority (as they are communications with shareholders). Earnings per share must be stated in any summary financial statement (LR, para. 9.8.13).

25.2.4 Notice

The notice of the general meeting must refer to the laying of the report and accounts unless they are to be laid at an annual general meeting and the articles specify this as ordinary business (see, for example, reg. 52 of the 1948 Act Table A). There is little to commend this practice and it is only likely to confuse shareholders. In practice, most companies set out the nature of the business in the normal manner (see **Precedent 25.2B**).

The UK Corporate Governance Code recommends that at any general meeting, the company should propose a separate resolution on each substantially separate issue and should, in particular, propose a resolution at the AGM relating to the report and accounts (Code provision E.2.1). ICSA's *Guide to Best Practice for Annual General Meetings* recommends that the resolution to receive or adopt the accounts should be separate from any resolution to approve the payment of the final dividend recommended by the directors.

25.2.5 Procedure at the meeting

Although s. 437 does not require a resolution to receive the report and accounts to be put to the meeting, it is normal to do so as this is the standard way of putting business before the meeting. The requirement to lay the accounts is merely a device to ensure that the shareholders are given an opportunity to question the directors about the company's performance and their own performance as managers of the company. The wording of the resolution should not give the impression that the accounts and reports can be rejected or that they will not be laid if the members vote against the resolution. If a resolution on the accounts is lost, it does not alter the fact that they are the company's report and accounts or that they have been laid in accordance with s. 437. Such a resolution would normally be interpreted as a vote of no confidence in the directors although they would not be under any obligation to resign. Thus words such as 'to approve the accounts and reports . . .' and 'to lay the accounts and reports . . .' should be avoided.

ICSA's *Guide to Best Practice for Annual General Meetings* recommends that when moving the adoption or receipt of the accounts, the chairman should allow shareholders to raise questions on any item concerning the company's past performance, its results and its intended future performance (see further **20.7** and **20.8**).

■ 25.3 Approval of a directors' remuneration report

Quoted companies (see definition at **8.5.2**) are required to make detailed disclosures regarding directors' remuneration in a separate remuneration report and to put that report to a vote by shareholders (ss. 420–422).

The remuneration report must be approved by the board of directors and signed on its behalf by a director or secretary (s. 422), sent to members (s. 423) and filed at Companies House (s. 447).

Under s. 439, quoted companies must give members notice of the intention to move an ordinary resolution at the meeting at which its accounts and reports are to be laid 'approving the directors' remuneration report for the financial year' (see **Precedent 25.3**). The existing directors (i.e. anyone who was a director immediately before the meeting) have a duty to ensure that the resolution is put to a vote at that meeting (s. 439(4)). However, s. 439(5) specifies that no entitlement to remuneration is made conditional on the resolution being passed.

■ 25.4 Audit concerns raised by members of quoted companies

Members of a quoted company (see definition at **8.5.2**) satisfying the requirements of s. 527 may require the company to publish on a website a statement by them relating to the audit of the company's accounts which are to be laid before the next accounts meeting (including the auditor's report and the conduct of the audit) or, where applicable, any circumstances connected with an auditor of the company ceasing to hold office since the previous accounts meeting at which accounts were laid. Should a valid request for the publication of such a statement be received, the company must within three working days of receipt publish the statement on a website and forward a copy of it to its auditors. Any statement published on a website under these rules forms part of the business which may be dealt with at the next accounts meeting.

Under s. 529, a quoted company must in the notice it gives of the accounts meeting draw attention to the possibility of a statement being placed on a website in pursuance of members' requests under s. 527 and the fact that it may not require members making such a statement to pay its expenses in doing so, and state that a copy of any such statement will be forwarded to its auditors and that any published statement will form part of the business which may be dealt with at the meeting (see notes to the AGM notice at **Precedent 10.3**).

■ 25.5 Appointment of auditors

A company must appoint auditors unless it is:

- exempt from audit as a dormant company under s. 480;
- exempt from audit as a small company under s. 480; or
- exempt from the requirements of Part 16 of the Act under s. 482 (non-profit-making companies subject to public sector audit).

25.5.1 Appointment of auditors by a private company

Auditors (or an auditor) of a private company must be appointed for each financial year of the company, unless the directors reasonably resolve otherwise on the ground that audited accounts are unlikely to be required (s. 485). For each financial year for which auditors are to be appointed (other than the company's first financial year), the appointment must be made before the end of the period of 28 days beginning with:

(a) the end of the period allowed for filing accounts for the previous financial year with the Registrar; or

(b) (if earlier) the day on which copies of the company's accounts for the previous financial year are sent out to members under s. 423 of the 2006 Act.

The directors may appoint auditors (see **Precedent 25.5A**):

(a) at any time before the company's first period for appointing auditors;
(b) following a period during which the company (being exempt from audit) did not have any auditor, at any time before the company's next period for appointing auditors; or
(c) to fill a casual vacancy in the office of auditor.

The members may appoint an auditor or auditors by ordinary resolution (see **Precedents 25.5B to 25.5D**):

(a) during a period for appointing auditors;
(b) if the company should have appointed an auditor or auditors during a period for appointing auditors but failed to do so; or
(c) where the directors had power to appoint but have failed to make an appointment.

If a private company fails to appoint auditors in accordance with s. 485, the Secretary of State has default powers to appoint (s. 486). Where company fails to make an appointment before the end of the period for appointing auditors, the company must within one week of the end of that period give notice to the Secretary of State of that power having become exercisable.

Auditors of a private company hold office in accordance with the terms of their appointment, but do not take office until any previous auditor or auditors cease to hold office, and cease to hold office at the end of the next period for appointing auditors unless reappointed (s. 487).

Subject to the provisions of the Act concerning the removal and resignation of auditors, where no auditor has been appointed by the end of the next period for appointing auditors, any auditor in office immediately before that time is deemed to be reappointed, unless:

(a) he was appointed by the board; or
(b) the company's articles require actual reappointment; or
(c) the deemed reappointment is prevented by the members under s. 488; or
(d) the members have resolved that he should not be reappointed; or
(e) the directors have resolved that no auditors should be appointed for the financial year.

An auditor of a private company is not deemed to be reappointed under the above provisions, if the company has received notices under s. 488 from members representing at least 5% of the total voting rights of all members who would be entitled to vote on a resolution that the auditor should not be reappointed (or any lower percentage specified in the company's articles). The notice must be received by the company before the end of the accounting reference period immediately preceding the time when the deemed reappointment would have effect.

25.5.2 Appointment auditors – public companies

Unless exempt from audit, a public company is required to appoint auditors. A public company may be exempt from audit as a dormant company. The first auditors may be appointed by the directors. However, auditors so appointed must be reappointed at each general meeting at which accounts are laid (i.e. at the meeting known as the accounts meeting). They hold office until the end of the next general meeting at which accounts are laid (s. 489).

The directors may appoint the first auditors at any time before the first general meeting at which accounts are laid (see **Precedent 25.5A**) (s. 489(3)). Auditors so appointed hold office until the conclusion of the first accounts meeting (i.e. the general meeting at which accounts are laid). If the directors fail to appoint the first auditors, the company in general meeting may do so (see **Precedent 25.5B**) (s. 489(4)).

Thereafter, auditors must be appointed or reappointed at each general meeting at which accounts are laid (s. 489(2) and (4)). The resolution to appoint auditors is usually passed after the accounts have been laid. The resolution should be worded so that the auditors are appointed until the conclusion of the next accounts meeting or the next general meeting at which accounts are laid rather than for a year or until the conclusion of the next annual general meeting (see **Precedent 25.5C**). Special procedures apply where an auditor other than the retiring auditor is being appointed (see **25.9**).

If no auditors are appointed in accordance with s. 489 before the end of the period for appointing auditors, the company must notify the Secretary of State who may appoint one or more persons to fill the vacancy (s. 490) and fix their remuneration (s. 492(3)).

A casual vacancy can be caused by the resignation or death of the existing auditor. The directors may fill any such vacancy in the office of auditor (s. 489(3)). Where they have not done so, the members may fill a casual vacancy (s. 489(4)).

■ 25.6 Remuneration of auditors

Generally speaking, the remuneration of auditors must be fixed by those who appoint them. If appointed by the directors, their remuneration must be fixed by the directors (s. 492(2)). If appointed by the Secretary of State, their remuneration must be fixed by the Secretary of State (s. 492(3)).

However, the remuneration of auditors appointed (or reappointed) by the members must be fixed by the members by ordinary resolution or in such manner as the members by ordinary resolution may determine (s. 492(1)). This is usually done at the same time as the appointment by authorising the directors to fix their remuneration (see **Precedent 25.5C**). In the case of a private company, the initial resolution confirming the appointment of the auditors will probably need to authorise the directors to fix their remuneration not just for the current financial year but for all financial years where they are deemed to have been reappointed (see **Precedent 25.5D**). Although s. 492 envisages that the members themselves can fix the auditors' remuneration, this is not normally a practicable solution for either public or private companies. It will normally be difficult to predict the precise audit costs for the forthcoming year, not least because remuneration is deemed to include any of the auditors' expenses paid by the company (s. 492(4)). The members may only be able to fix the remuneration after the audit is complete. This is unlikely to be acceptable to the auditors as the members may not approve payment of the full amount. A resolution to approve the remuneration of auditors could, however, place some cap on the fees to be paid to them.

■ 25.7 Change of auditors

Where a company wishes to change its auditors, it is normal to approach the existing auditors to see whether they would be prepared to resign voluntarily or agree not to seek reappointment. If they agree to resign, the procedures outlined in **25.9** would apply and the directors could then appoint new auditors to fill the resulting vacancy. Where the directors have filled a casual vacancy in this manner the appointment of the new auditors must be confirmed by the members before the end of the next period for appointing auditors under the special procedures set out in **25.7.1**. These procedures must also be followed where the auditors have agreed not to seek reappointment at the end of their period of office. However, if the matter is urgent, perhaps because relations have irretrievably broken down, a general meeting could be held to remove the auditors by ordinary resolution before the end of their term of office (s. 510) (see **25.11**).

25.7.1 Special notice and procedural requirements for certain appointments

Certain special procedural requirements must be followed by both public and private companies for certain appointments. If these procedures are not followed, any appointment will be ineffective. Generally speaking, the circumstances in which these special procedures must be followed can be characterised as being where the members are asked to approve the appointment of new auditors in place of any auditors previously appointed by them. If that is not what the relevant sections of the 2006 Act provide, which is a distinct possibility in view of the obscure language used, it is probably what they were meant to provide as that was the position under the 1985 Act which they were intended to replicate. It is submitted that these circumstances can arise where it is proposed to appoint a person as auditor in place of a person whose office has expired (e.g. because of the resignation or removal of the previous auditors), or whose office is about to expire (e.g. because the auditors are not seeking reappointment). These circumstances will arise even where an appointment has been made by the directors to fill a casual vacancy in mid year (perhaps as a result of the resignation or removal of the previous auditors). In the case of both public and private companies, any such appointment must be approved by the members for the following financial year, and in the case of private companies, they are not deemed to be reappointed for these purposes.

In all of the above circumstances where the resolution is to be proposed at a general meeting of a company, special notice must be given of intention to propose the resolution at least 28 days before the meeting and a copy of it must be sent to the outgoing auditors forthwith (s. 515). If the resolution is to be proposed as a written resolution of a private company, a copy of the proposed resolution must also be sent to the outgoing auditors (s. 514). In both cases the outgoing auditor may make written representations (not exceeding a reasonable length) and request that they be circulated to members of the company.

In the case of a written resolution of a private company, the outgoing auditor must make these representations within 14 days after receiving the notice of the resolution. If the auditor does so, the company must circulate the representations together with the copy or copies of the written resolution circulated in accordance with s. 291 (written resolution proposed by the directors) or s. 293 (written resolution proposed by the members). Where a private company has circulated representations by an outgoing auditor on such a resolution, the period allowed under s. 293(3) for service of copies of the proposed resolution is 28 days instead of 21 days.

In the case of a resolution to be proposed at a general meeting of either a public or private company (see **Precedent 25.7B**), the company must (unless the representations made by the outgoing auditor are received too late for it do so):

(a) in any notice of the resolution given to members, state the fact that representations have been made; and

(b) send a copy of the representations to every member of the company to whom notice of the meeting is or has been sent.

If a copy of the outgoing auditor's representations are not sent to members for any reason, he may insist that they be read out at the meeting. The outgoing auditor also has a right to be heard on the resolution whether or not his representations are read out at the meeting.

Under both the written resolution procedure and the special notice procedure any person claiming to be aggrieved can apply to the court to prevent the representations being sent to members or, where applicable, read out at the meeting on the grounds that the auditor is abusing his rights in order to secure needless publicity for defamatory matter.

The above rules also apply where it is proposed to fill a vacancy caused by the resignation of an auditor (see **25.9**). Special notice of a resolution to remove the auditors before the end of their period of office is also required.

■ 25.8 Approval of an auditor's limitation of liability agreement

A company is prohibited from indemnifying its auditor (whether in its articles or by an agreement) against claims by the company in the case of negligence or other default (s. 532). However, ss. 534–538 of the Act permit auditors to limit their liability by agreement with the company. Such agreements are effective only to the extent that they are fair and reasonable. The court is empowered to substitute its own limitation if the agreement purports to limit liability to an amount that is not fair and reasonable in all the circumstances. Such a 'liability limitation agreement' can cover liability for negligence, default, breach of duty or breach of trust by the auditor. To be within the exception the agreement must:

(a) relate to the audit of one specified financial year; the limitation may be expressed in any terms, not necessarily as a fixed financial amount or a formula (s. 535 (2006)); and

(b) be approved by the members of the company (without which approval the agreement will not be effective).

The members of a private company can pass a resolution waiving the need for approval. The members of a private or public company can pass a resolution before an agreement is signed approving its principal terms, or can approve the agreement after it is signed. The resolution may be an ordinary resolution, unless a higher threshold is set in the company's articles. For this purpose the principal terms of a liability limitation agreement specify, or enable the determination of, the kinds of faults by the auditor that are covered, the financial year in relation to which those faults are covered and the limit on the auditor's liability. The members may, by passing an ordinary resolution, withdraw their approval of a liability limitation agreement at any time before the agreement is entered into. If the company has already entered into the agreement, approval can be withdrawn, by ordinary resolution, only before the start of the financial year to which the agreement relates (s. 536).

A company is required to disclose any liability limitation agreement made with its auditor in accordance with any regulations made by the Secretary of State (s. 538). The Companies (Disclosure of Auditor Remuneration and Liability Limitation Agreements) Regulations 2008 (SI 2008/489) set out the detailed disclosure requirements. A company which has entered into a liability limitation agreement must disclose the principal terms of the agreement in a note to the company's annual accounts for the financial year to which the agreement relates, unless the agreement was entered into too late for it to be reasonably practicable for the disclosure to be made in those accounts, in which case it must be disclosed in the next annual accounts.

In July 2008, the Financial Reporting Council (FRC) published guidance on auditor liability limitation agreements. The FRC guidance:

(a) explains what is and is not allowed under the Companies Act 2006;
(b) sets out some of the factors that will be relevant when assessing the case for an agreement;
(c) explains what matters should be covered in an agreement, and provides specimen clauses for inclusion in agreements; and
(d) explains the process to be followed for obtaining shareholder approval, and provides specimen wording for inclusion in resolutions and the notice of the general meeting.

25.9 Resignation of auditors

Auditors may resign by depositing a notice in writing to that effect at the registered office of the company (s. 516(1)). However, the notice of resignation is not effective unless it is accompanied by a statement regarding the circumstances of the resignation prepared in accordance with s. 519 (s. 516(2)) (see **25.10**). On receipt of a valid resignation, the company must file a copy of the notice (but not the accompanying statement) at Companies House within 14 days (s. 517).

25.9.1 Rights of resigning auditors

Where the auditor's notice of resignation is accompanied by a statement of the circumstances connected with his resignation under s. 519 which must be circulated to the members by the company in accordance with s. 520, the resigning auditor also has a right to deposit with his notice of resignation a requisition calling on the directors to convene a general meeting of the company to consider such explanation of the circumstances connected with his resignation as he may wish to place before the meeting (s. 518(1) and (2)).

Notwithstanding the fact that his statement of circumstances made under s. 519 must be circulated by the company to its members, the resigning auditor is also given the right to require the company to circulate an additional statement (not exceeding a reasonable length) of the circumstances connected with his resignation before any meeting requisitioned by him or before any general meeting at which his term of office would have expired or at which it is proposed to fill the vacancy caused by his resignation (s. 518(3)). A resigning auditor is entitled to receive notice of these meetings under s. 518(10)).

The company must comply with any such request to call a meeting within 21 days from the date of deposit and convene the meeting for a date not more than 28 days after the date on which the notice of meeting is given. Where the auditor has requested that a statement be circulated before a general meeting, the company must (unless the statement is received too late for it to comply) state in the notice of meeting that a statement has been made by the auditor and send a copy of that statement to every member of the company to whom notice of the meeting has been sent (s. 518(4)). The resigning auditors have a right to receive notice of and to attend and speak at any such meetings.

If the auditor's statement is received too late for circulation, the auditor may require it to be read out at the relevant meeting (s. 518(8)). The court may relieve the company of these obligations if it is satisfied that the auditors are using the provisions to secure needless publicity for defamatory matter (s. 518(9)).

◼ 25.10 Statement by auditor on ceasing to hold office

Where an auditor of a company ceases to hold office for any reason, he must deposit at the company's registered office a statement in accordance with s. 519, which:

(a) in the case of an unquoted company, sets out the circumstances connected with his ceasing to hold office which he believes should be drawn to the attention of the members (in which case the company must circulate them to members in accordance with s. 520) or states that there are no circumstances in connection with his ceasing to hold office that need to be brought to the attention of members (in which case the statement does not need to be circulated by the company to its members); and

(b) in the case of a quoted company (see **8.5.2**), sets out the circumstances connected with his ceasing to hold office, which the company must always circulate to members in accordance with s. 520.

An auditor must deposit such a statement with his notice of resignation or, where he is not seeking reappointment, not less than 14 days after the time allowed for next appointing an auditor or, where he has ceased to hold office for any other reason (e.g. removal), 14 days after ceasing to hold office.

If the auditor's statement is one which must be drawn to the attention of members:

(a) the company must within 14 days of deposit of the statement either apply to the court for an order restraining publication or send a copy to every person entitled under s. 423 to be sent copies of the statutory accounts (s. 520);

(b) the auditor must file a copy of his statement at Companies House. However he is required to wait 21 days before doing so in order to ensure that anybody who wishes to do so has time to apply for a court order restraining publication of his statement. If at the end of that 21-day period no such order has been served on him, he has a further seven days in which to file the statement at Companies House (s. 521);

(c) both the auditor and the company may have a duty under ss. 522 and 523 respectively to notify an appropriate audit authority.

◼ 25.11 Removal of auditors

A company's auditor may be removed before the end of his period of office by an ordinary resolution passed at a general meeting of the company (s. 510). It is not possible for a private company to pass such a resolution by written resolution (s. 288(2)).

Special notice (see **13.14**) must be given to the company at least 28 days before the meeting of the intention to propose a resolution to remove an auditor under s. 510 (s. 511). On receipt of notice of the intended resolution, the company must immediately send a copy of it to the auditor proposed to be removed (s. 511(2)).

The auditor proposed to be removed may make written representations (not exceeding a reasonable length) to the company on the proposed resolution and demand that they be circulated to the members (s. 511(3)). Unless the representations are received too late for it to do so, the company must comply with such a demand and state in the notice of the resolution given to members that representations have been made (s. 511(4)). If the representations are not circulated to the members for any reason, the auditor may require them to be read out at the meeting (s. 511(5)). The court may relieve the company of these obligations if it is satisfied that the auditors are using the provisions to secure needless publicity for defamatory matter (s. 511(6)).

The auditor proposed to be removed will have the right under s. 502(2) to receive notice of the meeting at which it is proposed to remove him and the right to attend and speak at that meeting on matters which concern him as the company's auditor (which will include his proposed removal). An auditor who is removed retains the rights conferred by s. 502(2) in relation to any general meeting of the company at which his term of office would otherwise have expired or at which it is proposed to fill the vacancy caused by his removal (s. 513) and may attend and speak on matters that concern him as a former auditor.

An auditor who is removed from office must make a statement as to the circumstances connected with his removal at least 14 days after his removal (s. 519), which the company may in addition be required to circulate to the members (see **25.10**).

25.12 Dividends

25.12.1 Final dividend

Most articles provide that dividends may be declared by an ordinary resolution of the company in general meeting and that no dividend may exceed the amount recommended by the directors (e.g. reg. 102 of Table A, pcls 30 and plc 70). Dividends can only be paid out of profits available for distribution (ss. 829 to 853). In recommending the final dividend, the directors must ensure that there are sufficient funds available for distribution. It is therefore usual for the resolution to declare a dividend to be proposed at the general meeting at which the accounts have been laid. The wording of the notice with regard to dividends is usually very simple (see **Precedents 25.12A** to **25.12C**).

The UK Corporate Governance Code recommends that at any general meeting, the company should propose a separate resolution on each substantially separate issue, and should in particular propose a resolution at the AGM relating to the report and accounts (Code provision E.2.1). ICSA's *Guide to Best Practice for Annual General Meetings* recommends that the resolution to receive or adopt the accounts should be separate from any resolution to approve the payment of the final dividend recommended by the directors.

25.12.2 Interim dividend

Articles usually also provide that the directors may pay interim dividends without reference to the members (e.g. reg. 103) (see **Precedent 25.12D**). The directors should not pay a dividend unless it is clear that sufficient funds are available for distribution as dividends.

■ 25.13 Appointment of directors

Articles usually contain detailed procedures on the appointment of directors. Any natural or legal person may be appointed as a director. However, at least one director of a company must be an individual person (s. 155) and no director may be appointed who is under the age of 16 (s. 157). Subject to these rules, a company may be appointed as a director of another company. The method of appointment and the persons or body authorised to make the appointment may differ according to the type of appointment being made. The position under the model articles is simple. They provide that any person who is willing to act as a director, and is permitted by law to do so, may be appointed to be a director either by an ordinary resolution of the members or by a decision of the directors (pcls 17, clg 17 and plc 20). The position is not quite so simple under Table A (see Table 25.1).

Table 25.1 Methods of appointing directors under the 1985 Table A

Type of appointment	Appointed by	Source
First directors	Subscribers to the memorandum	CA 2006, ss. 9, 12 & 16
Additional directors	Board of directors	reg. 79
	Members	regs. 76 to 78
Appointments to fill a casual vacancy	Board of directors	reg. 79
	Members	regs. 76 to 78
Reappointment following retirement by rotation	Members	regs. 72 to 75 and 78
Reappointment following retirement at first AGM after appointment	Members	regs. 72, 78 and 79
Alternate directors	Directors	regs. 65 to 69

25.13.1 Procedure for appointment of directors

(a) Check articles for the method of appointment.

(b) If additional appointment, check that it will not cause the number of directors to exceed any maximum prescribed by the articles.

(c) Check compliance with any age requirements.

(d) Check articles for any share qualifications.

(e) Obtain approval for the appointment at a board meeting or, as the case may be, at a general meeting (if a private company, members' approval may be obtained by written resolution).

(f) Notify appointment to Companies House within 14 days of appointment ensuring that the new director consented to act.

(g) Enter details of the new director in the register of directors.

(h) Remind director of any share qualification required by the articles.

(i) Request director to give general notice of any interest in contracts or proposed contracts with the company.

(j) Notify the company's bankers as appropriate.

(k) Obtain details of the director's PAYE coding and NI number and instructions as to method of payment of remuneration.

(l) If appropriate, settle terms of service agreement (not to exceed two years without shareholder approval) and issue terms of reference or letter of appointment.

(m) Provide new director with any documentation (such as the company's articles, governance policies) and any necessary induction training.

25.13.2 Minimum and maximum number

The Companies Act 2006 provides that every private company (whether limited by shares, limited by guarantee or unlimited) must have at least one director and that every public company must have at least two (s. 154). Articles may require a higher number than the statutory minimum but not a lower number.

Articles may also specify the maximum number of directors who may be appointed or provide a mechanism for determining such a limit. Any appointment which would cause the number of directors to exceed that maximum will be invalid.

The model articles do not impose any maximum. Regulation 64 of Table A provides that the number of directors shall not be subject to any maximum unless the members determine otherwise by ordinary resolution. This is a rather ungainly provision. It is easy to imagine circumstances where the existence of a limit imposed by ordinary resolution might be forgotten as such a resolution does not operate to amend the articles and can only be proved by reference to the minutes of the general meeting at which it was passed (or the record of any relevant written resolution). It is better to fix a maximum by amending the relevant article. If, however, a maximum is imposed or changed by ordinary resolution under reg. 64, it is advisable to make a note referring to that resolution on the master copy of the articles. It may also be a good idea to make a note that no such resolution has ever been passed if, indeed, that is the case. Regulation 64 can also cause problems if the members vote to impose a maximum which is less than the number of directors currently holding office. It is doubtful whether such a resolution would have the effect of removing any of the directors unless special notice was given of a resolution to remove one or more of those directors in accordance with s. 168. Such a resolution would, however, be effective in preventing any future appointments or reappointments in breach of the maximum.

25.13.3 First directors

Before a company can be registered, the subscribers to the memorandum (i.e. the people who will become the company's first members) must provide the registrar of companies with the name(s) and details of the first director(s). On incorporation, the people named as directors in the incorporation documents are deemed to have been appointed and no further action is required (s. 16). It is, however, standard practice to note in the minutes of the first board meeting the method by which they were appointed (see **Precedents 4.6B** and **4.6C**). There is nothing to prevent the subscribers nominating themselves as the first directors.

If the articles require the directors to hold shares in the company, they may provide that they will cease to be directors if they do not satisfy that requirement within a certain period. The articles may also require the directors to satisfy other qualifications or provide for their removal from office on the happening of certain events.

25.13.4 Subsequent appointments

Subsequent appointments must be made in accordance with the procedures laid down in the company's articles of association and the requirements of the Companies Act 2006. The Act only interferes by providing:

- at least one of the directors must be an individual person (s. 155);
- a director must be at least 16 years of age (s. 157);
- that a motion for the appointment of two or more persons as directors of a public company by a single resolution at a general meeting shall not be valid unless the meeting agrees unanimously to a proposal that the resolution be proposed in that manner (s. 160); and
- that details of appointments of directors must be entered in a register by the company and notified to Companies House, although failure to do so does not invalidate the appointment (ss. 162 to 167).

All other questions relating to the appointment of directors must be resolved by reference to the articles. This is one of the areas where articles are likely to differ from the norm and a careful examination of the relevant company's articles will be necessary to ensure that the correct procedures are followed. If the articles make no provision for the appointment of directors, appointments must be made by the members.

25.13.5 Appointment by the directors

Under the model articles, the directors may appoint new directors (pcls 17, clg 17 and plc 20). Under Table A the directors may appoint new directors either to fill vacancies or as additional directors (subject to any maximum fixed in accordance with the articles) (reg. 79). A vacancy arises where an existing director has died, resigned or become disqualified. Such appointments should be made in accordance with the decision-making procedures for directors provided for in the company's articles. See **Precedents 25.13A** and **25.13B** for examples of board resolutions appointing directors.

The model articles for private companies do not make any provision for retirement of directors whether by rotation or otherwise. Accordingly, a person appointed as a director of a private company will remain a director until they resign, are removed, or cease to hold office for any other reason.

The model articles for public companies require all the directors to retire at the company's first annual general meeting and for the following directors to retire at every subsequent annual general meeting (plc 21):

(a) all directors who have been appointed by the directors since the last annual general meeting; and
(b) any directors who were not appointed or reappointed at one of the preceding two annual general meetings.

Under Table A, directors appointed by the board must retire at the annual general meeting following their appointment and offer themselves for election by the members (reg. 79). Not less than seven nor more than 28 days before the meeting the company must give notice of any person retiring in this manner who is recommended by the directors for appointment or reappointment. The notice must include the details which would be required to be included in the register of directors if that person was appointed or reappointed (reg. 77). The purpose of this provision is to ensure that the directors cannot propose a person for appointment or reappointment without giving the members prior notice of his details, e.g. by including in the notice of the meeting an item of business to elect directors without naming them. If the company fails to give notice in accordance with reg. 77 the appointment will be invalid. If the members resolve not to reappoint a director, the director ceases to hold office at the conclusion of the annual general meeting. Directors retiring in this manner are not taken into account in determining the directors who are to retire by rotation at the meeting (see **25.14**).

A person appointed as a director of a private company to fill a casual vacancy may never be required to retire under this type of provision if the company never holds an annual general meeting. If for any reason an annual general meeting is subsequently held, directors appointed under reg. 79 should retire at that meeting and offer themselves for re-election.

Regulation 79 applies in respect of vacancies and appointments of additional directors. However, articles sometimes allow the directors to make appointments to fill casual vacancies only. In these circumstances, the directors may only appoint a person to replace a director who has died, resigned or been disqualified from acting as a director. They may not fill any vacancy which arises by virtue of the procedures on rotation of directors or any vacancy which arises because an appointment made for a fixed period has ceased, e.g. an appointment for fixed term of one year or an appointment which ceases at the conclusion of the next annual general meeting (*York Tramways Co. v. Willows* (1882) 8 Q.B.D. 685).

Where the articles restrict the powers of the directors to filling casual vacancies, the members retain the power to appoint additional directors.

25.13.6 Appointment by the members

If the articles give the directors power to fill casual vacancies and appoint additional directors, the members will have no power to do so unless the articles make specific provision to that effect. The model articles allow the members of both public and private companies to appoint directors by ordinary resolution, whether as additional directors or to fill casual vacancies, or otherwise.

Under Table A, the members can also appoint directors to fill casual vacancies or as additional directors by ordinary resolution at a general meeting (subject to any maximum) (reg. 78). However, under Table A, the members proposing the appointment must give the company prior notice of their intention to propose a person as a director who is not recommended by the board, not less than 14 days nor more than 35 days before the date of the meeting. The notice given to the company must include the details which would be required to be included in the register of directors if that person was appointed and notice signed by the person nominated of his willingness to act as a director (reg. 76). The purpose of reg. 76 is to prevent the members from relying on the inclusion in the notice of the meeting of an item of business to elect or re-elect directors in order to propose a person not recommended by the directors. It should be noted, however, that the fact that a member has given notice in accordance with reg. 76 does not guarantee that the proposal will be within the scope of the notice of the meeting (see **24.4**).

Not less than seven nor more than 28 days before the meeting, the company must give notice to every person who is entitled to receive notice of the meeting of any person in respect of whom notice has been given to the company of the intention to propose him at the meeting for appointment or reappointment as a director in accordance with reg. 76. The notice given by the company must include the details which would be required to be included in the register of directors (reg. 77).

Listed companies used to be required to adopt an article similar to reg. 76 (requiring members to give prior notice) but were not (and still are not) required to adopt an article similar to reg. 77 (requiring the company to give notice of any such proposals to members). Articles similar to reg. 76 are still commonly found in the articles of listed companies but very few still have anything like reg. 77.

Under reg. 76, the members may notify the company of their intention to propose a person as a director as little as 14 days before the meeting, i.e. after the notice calling the meeting has been sent. In order to comply with the requirements of reg. 77 in these circumstances, the company would have to do a second mailing to its members. The purpose of reg. 77 is to ensure that the members have advance warning that a person not recommended by the board is to be proposed as a director at the meeting and act accordingly, e.g. by attending the meeting or by appointing proxies to vote for or against the resolution. Giving notice in this manner enables the board to mobilise opposition to the appointment. In practice, listed companies tend to rely on the fact that the chairman controls sufficient proxy votes to defeat any such resolution.

Although it is clear that a resolution of the members in general meeting to appoint a person as a director not recommended by the board will be invalid if the members have not complied with the requirement to give the company prior notice in accordance with reg. 76, it is not clear whether such an appointment would be invalid if the company fails to give notice to the members in accordance with reg. 77. Also, it is not clear whether the company, by giving notice in accordance with reg. 77, automatically brings the resolution to be proposed by the members within the scope of the notice of the meeting, e.g. where the reg. 77 notice was not sent within the normal period of notice and the resolution is not within the scope of the notice of the meeting already sent to members. With these difficulties in mind, it is hardly surprising that reg. 77 is rarely adopted by listed companies.

A number of points should be noted with regard to the above regulations:

- although they do not apply to the reappointment of a director retiring by rotation, they do to a director appointed by the directors to fill a casual vacancy or as an additional director who is required to retire at the annual general meeting next following his or her appointment;
- notice must be given to the members in accordance with reg. 77 in respect of any person recommended by the directors;
- a valid resolution of the board of directors will be required for a person to qualify as being recommended by the directors;
- two conditions must be satisfied for a person to be proposed who is not recommended by the directors, namely notice must be given to the company in accordance with reg. 76 (see **Precedent 25.13D**) and the company must give notice to the members in accordance with reg. 77 (see **Precedent 25.13E**).

25.13.7 1948 Act Table A

The 1948 Act Table A provisions are much simpler and are commonly adopted by public companies in preference to the 1985 Table A provisions. Regulation 93 of the 1948 Table A provides:

93. No person other than a director retiring at the meeting shall unless recommended by the directors be eligible for election to the office of director at any general meeting unless not less than three nor more than twenty-one days before the date appointed for the meeting there shall have been left at the registered office of the company notice in writing, signed by a member duly qualified to attend and vote at the meeting for which such notice is given, of his intention to propose such person for election, and also notice in writing signed by that person of his willingness to be elected.

Regulation 93 does not apply to any director retiring at the meeting whether by rotation or otherwise. Although a member is still required to give notice to the company, there is no corresponding requirement for the company to give notice to the members.

Under reg. 97 of the 1948 Act Table A, the members may by ordinary resolution appoint another person in place in place of a director who has been removed from office and, without prejudice to the powers of the directors (essentially the same as under the 1985 Table A), appoint any person to be a director either to fill a casual vacancy or as an additional director. There is no corresponding requirement for the members to give notice of their intention to propose such a resolution.

25.13.8 Other methods of appointment

A company's articles may provide for different methods of appointment. For example, the articles could provide that directors may be appointed or removed from office by notice in writing signed by members holding a majority of the voting shares. This method is most likely to be used by subsidiary companies as it enables the parent company to make appointments without having to hold a meeting of the subsidiary.

A variation on this theme can be useful for joint venture companies where each of the partners in the joint venture is given the right to appoint a fixed number of directors (and replace them with others) by giving notice in writing. This can be achieved by having different classes of shares with each class having separate rights to appoint a fixed number of directors.

The articles of small owner-managed companies are frequently modified to ensure that the founders retain the right to participate in their management. Some amendment may be necessary even where all the company's shares are held equally by two people who are both appointed as directors. This is because under the original version of the 1985 Table A (and previous versions), the chairman of the general meeting has a casting vote and could therefore appoint and remove directors against the wishes of the other member to gain management control. The simplest solution in these circumstances is to amend the articles to exclude the application of any article which gives the chairman a casting vote. For a person holding less than 50% of the company's shares more elaborate protection is necessary. The articles could be amended so that a special resolution is required (i.e. a majority of 75%) to appoint new directors. The major problem for a minority shareholder, however, is the fact that the members in general meeting have a statutory right to remove a director from office by ordinary resolution (s. 168). There are a number of ways in which this problem can be overcome (see further **25.15** on the removal of directors).

■ 25.14 Retirement by rotation of directors

25.14.1 Retirement provisions in the model articles

The model articles for private companies make no provision for retirement by rotation. The model articles for public companies require all the directors to retire at the company's first annual general meeting and for the following directors to retire at every subsequent annual general meeting (plc 21):

(a) all directors who have been appointed by the directors since the last annual general meeting; and

(b) any directors who were not appointed or reappointed at one of the preceding two annual general meetings.

Directors who retire under this provision must retire from office and may (but need not) offer themselves for reappointment by the members.

The UK Corporate Governance Code recommends that all directors of listed companies should retire and offer themselves for re-election at least once every three years or, in the case of FTSE 350 companies, annually (see below). Although the Code does not have the force of law, most listed companies now comply with this recommendation in respect of both executive and non-executive directors.

25.14.2 1985 Table A

Table A also makes provision for directors to retire by rotation, although the standard Table A provisions are often excluded for owner-managed private companies, subsidiaries and joint venture companies. Particular attention should be paid to the articles of any company bought 'off-the-shelf' from a company registration agent. These often contain non-standard provisions on retirement which may, for example, require the board to determine when an appointment is made whether the director is to be subject to the retirement provisions. If no decision is taken at the time of the appointment, the assumption will often be that the director will be subject to the retirement provisions.

The basic provisions on rotation in Table A are as follows:

73. At the first annual general meeting all the directors shall retire from office, and at every subsequent annual general meeting one-third of the directors who are subject to retirement by rotation or, if their number is not three or a multiple of three, the number nearest to one third shall retire from office;

but, if there is only one director who is subject to retirement by rotation, he shall retire.

74. Subject to the provisions of the Act, the directors to retire by rotation shall be those who have served longest in office since their last appointment or reappointment, but as between persons who became or were last reappointed directors on the same day those to retire shall (unless they otherwise agree among themselves) be determined by lot.

75. If the company, at the meeting at which a director retires by rotation, does not fill the vacancy the retiring director shall, if willing to act, be deemed to have been reappointed unless at the meeting it is resolved not to fill the vacancy or unless a resolution for the reappointment of the director is put to the meeting and lost.

25.14.3 Number to retire

In order to determine who must retire each year, it is necessary to determine which directors are subject to retirement by rotation. Under reg. 84 of Table A, the executive directors are not subject to retirement by rotation. If all the directors hold some executive office, the rotation provisions will not apply.

Articles based on Table A normally provide that the number nearest to one-third of the directors subject to retirement by rotation shall retire. The normal rounding up and rounding down rules should be applied when calculating the number of directors who must retire unless the articles state that the number nearest to, but not exceeding, one-third shall retire, in which case the figure must always be rounded down.

Table 25.2 Retirement of directors

Number of directors subject to retirement by rotation	Number to retire at each AGM	
	1948 and 1985 Table A	'Nearest to, but not exceeding one third'
One	1	0
Two	1	0
Three	1	1
Four	1	1
Five	2	1
Six	2	2

Under reg. 73 of the 1985 Table A, it is clear that even where only one director is subject to retirement by rotation, that person must retire at each annual general meeting. The same is true where the articles follow reg. 89 of 1948 Table

A by providing that the 'number nearest one-third' shall retire (*Re New Cedos Engineering Co Ltd.* [1994] 1 B.C.L.C. 797, 810). In both cases, one person must retire at each annual general meeting if two directors are subject to retirement by rotation. However, if the articles provide that 'the number nearest to, but not exceeding, one-third' shall retire and the number of directors subject to retirement by rotation is two or less, then no directors need to retire (*Re Moseley & Sons Ltd.* [1939] Ch. 719).

25.14.4 Who is to retire?

The directors to retire by rotation will normally be those who have served longest since their last appointment or reappointment. Articles normally provide that, where the number who must retire is less than the number who are eligible under this rule because they were appointed or last reappointed on the same day, the selection of those to retire is to be determined by lot, unless they otherwise agree among themselves (in which case their unanimous agreement is required with respect to the decision or the method of reaching that decision). A lot may be performed by the drawing of straws or some other similar method of chance. It has been held that where the articles state that the matter is to be settled by ballot, this also means by lot rather than by any method of voting (*Eyre v. Milton Proprietary* [1936] Ch. 244). This case is also authority for the fact that temporary directors (e.g. those appointed by the directors under reg. 79 and who must therefore automatically retire at the next following AGM) should not be included when calculating how many directors should retire under the rotation provisions.

Table 25.3 Example of retirement by rotation under 1985 Table A (all directors subject to rotation)

Event	AGM	Directors to retire
A, B, C & D appointed as first directors on formation	First AGM	A, B, C, & D (under reg. 73)
	Second AGM	C (drawn by lot between A, B, C & D)
	Third AGM	B (drawn by lot between A, B & D)
Board appoints E as additional director	Fourth AGM	A & D (under reg. 73 & 74) & E (under reg. 79)
	Fifth AGM	B & C (under reg. 73 & 74)
	Sixth AGM	A & E (by lot between A, D & E)

25.14.5 UK Corporate Governance Code recommendations

The UK Corporate Governance Code recommends that all directors should be subject to election by shareholders at the first annual general meeting after their appointment and to re-election thereafter at intervals of no more than three years or, in the case of FTSE 350 companies, annually. It also provides that the names of directors submitted for election or re-election should be accompanied by sufficient biographical details and any other relevant information to enable shareholders to take an informed decision on their election (Code provision B.7.1). The board should set out to shareholders in the papers accompanying a resolution to elect a non-executive director why they believe an individual should be elected. The chairman should confirm to shareholders when proposing re-election that, following formal performance evaluation, the individual's performance continues to be effective and to demonstrate commitment to the role (Code provision B.7.2).

Listed companies normally adopt special articles to ensure compliance with the provisions of the Code (see example article at **Precedent 25.14**).

25.14.6 Notice and proxy forms

Unless the articles specify that the re-election of directors retiring by rotation at the annual general meeting is part of the ordinary business of that meeting, it will normally be necessary for a company to indicate the general nature of the business in the notice. This can be done simply by stating as an item of business 'to re-elect directors retiring by rotation'. However, it is standard practice for the notice to name the directors who will be retiring and seeking re-election at the meeting. ICSA's *Guide to Best Practice for Annual General Meetings* recommends that directors standing for re-election to the board should be named in the notice and form of proxy. The UK Corporate Governance Code recommends that the names of directors submitted for election or re-election should be accompanied by sufficient biographical details to enable shareholders to take an informed decision on their election (Code provision B.7.1). ICSA's *Guide to Best Practice for Annual General Meetings* expands upon this by recommending that a brief description of the relevant directors should be given, including their ages; their relevant experience (not merely a list of other directorships they hold); the dates that they were first appointed to the board; and details of any board committees to which they belong. This could be done in any circular which accompanies the notice or in the directors' report if the accounts are sent to the members with the notice.

Listed companies must send proxy cards to members which allow them to indicate how their proxy should vote on every resolution (other than procedural resolutions) which will be put to the meeting (Listing Rule 9.3.6). If the resolutions to be proposed include the re-election of retiring directors and the number of retiring directors standing for re-election exceeds five, the proxy form may give shareholders the opportunity to vote for or against (or abstain from voting on) the re-election of the retiring directors as a whole but must also allow votes to be cast for or against (or for shareholders to abstain from voting on) the re-election of the retiring directors individually (Listing Rule 9.3.7).

The Act provides that a motion for the appointment of two or more persons as directors by a single resolution at a general meeting of a public company shall not be valid unless the meeting agrees unanimously to a proposal that the resolution be proposed in that manner (s. 160).

25.14.7 Failure to hold an AGM

If a company which is required to hold an annual general meeting fails to do so, the directors who were due to retire at that meeting may be deemed to have retired at the end of the period during which the annual general meeting was meant to be held. In *Re Consolidated Nickel Mines Ltd.* [1914] 1 Ch. 883, the company's articles of association provided that an annual general meeting should be held once in every year and that at the first such meeting of the company (due in 1906), all the directors should retire from office. No such meeting was held or called. It was held that the directors vacated office on 31 December 1906, i.e. the last day on which the meeting for that year could have been held. This decision was followed in *Re Zinotty Properties Ltd.* [1984] 3 All E.R. 754 in a case concerning an article based on reg. 89 of the 1948 Table A.

Re Consolidated Nickel Mines and *Re Zinotty Properties* were, however, both decided at a time when all companies were required by law to hold annual general meetings. As private companies are no longer required to hold annual general meetings, it is unlikely that these cases would apply, unless the company's articles required the company to hold annual general meetings.

Articles may contain provisions which save the situation where no meeting is held or the wrong directors retire (see, for example, reg. 75 of Table A). In addition, s. 161 ensures that the acts of a person acting as a director are valid notwithstanding that it is afterwards discovered that he had ceased to hold office (perhaps as a result of a failure on the part of the company to comply with the retirement by rotation provisions in its articles).

◼ 25.15 Removal of directors from office

The statutory rules on removal of directors apply to public and private companies alike and cannot be excluded by the articles. The articles may, however, provide an additional method of removal. If so, the members may use the statutory procedures or the additional method provided by the articles to remove a director.

The statutory procedures on removal are designed primarily to ensure that a simple majority of the members have the power to remove a director. This is a crucial safeguard for the members who might otherwise have little or no control over the directors. The statutory procedures also ensure that directors are given a fair chance to defend themselves against any proposal to remove them as directors. Directors are not normally afforded similar rights where an additional procedure is provided for by the articles.

Section 168 provides that the members in general meeting may by ordinary resolution remove a director provided that special notice of that resolution has been given in accordance with s. 312 (see **Precedents 25.15A** to **25.15C**). This statutory power applies notwithstanding anything in the company's articles or in any agreement between the company and the director. Special notice is also required with respect to any resolution to appoint at the same meeting another person instead of a director removed under these statutory powers (s. 168(2)).

A vacancy caused by the removal of a director may, if not filled at the meeting at which he is removed, be filled as a casual vacancy (s. 168(3)).

A person appointed in place of a director removed under s. 168 is treated, for the purpose of determining the time at which he or any other director is to retire, as if he had become a director on the same day on which the director who he has replaced was last appointed (s. 168(4)).

25.15.1 Director's right to protest removal

Under the special notice rules, a resolution to remove a director under s. 168 will not be effective unless notice of the intention to move it has been given to the company at least 28 days before the meeting at which it is moved (s. 312(1)). On receipt of a valid notice from a member, the company must immediately send a copy of it to the director concerned (see **Precedent 24.15C**) (s. 169(1)).

The director is entitled to be heard on the resolution at the meeting whether or not he or she is a member of the company (s. 169(2)), but is also allowed to make written representations (not exceeding a reasonable length). If the director makes written representations to the company in connection with the resolution and requests their notification to the members, the company must, unless the representations are received too late for it to do so:

(a) state in any notice of the resolution given to members that representations have been made; and
(b) send a copy of the director's representations to every member to whom notice of the meeting is sent (whether before or after receipt of the representations by the company) (s. 169(3)).

Special notice may be served on the company up to 28 days before the meeting. The company may not have time to wait for the director to make representations if it is to meet the deadline for giving notice of the meeting to the members. If notice of the meeting has already been given or if there is not sufficient time to have the notice reprinted, the company need not comply with subparagraph (a) above. However, even if the notice has already been sent, the company must still send a copy of the director's representations to each member (and bear the cost of doing so) unless it is impossible to deliver them to the members before the meeting.

If, for any reason, a copy of the director's representations is not sent to the members, the director may require them to be read out at the meeting. In these circumstances, the director still has a right to be heard on the resolution at the meeting (s. 169(4)).

The company or any other person who claims to be aggrieved may apply to the court for an order that the director's representations should not be sent to members or read out at the meeting on the grounds that the director is abusing the rights conferred by s. 169 (s. 169(5)). The type of abuse envisaged here would include, but not necessarily be restricted to, matters such as securing needless publicity for defamatory matter.

It is possible to avoid the effect of s. 168. In *Bushell v. Faith* [1970] A.C. 1099, the articles of a company with three equal shareholders provided that in the event of a resolution being proposed at any general meeting of the company for the removal from office of any director, any shares held by that director shall on a poll in respect of such resolution carry the right to three votes per share. When two of the shareholders tried to remove Faith as a director he was therefore able to outvote them by demanding a poll on the resolution. It was held by the House of Lords that the article was valid and did not infringe the statutory rules regarding removal of directors.

■ 25.16 Resolution to enable a traded company to call meetings at less than 21 days' notice

The Companies Act 2006 originally enabled all public companies to call a general meeting (other than an annual general meeting) on 14 clear days' notice. However, as a consequence of the EU Shareholders' Rights Directive, the Act was amended to require traded companies (see definition at **8.5.1**) to call such general meetings on at least 21 clear days' notice unless certain conditions are complied with, in which case the company can hold general meetings (other than the annual general meeting) with as little as 14 days' clear notice. One of those conditions is that the company must offer the facility for shareholders to vote by electronic means accessible to all shareholders. The other is that it must have obtained prior shareholder approval for the holding of general meetings at not less than 14 clear days' notice (s. 307A).

The resolution reducing the period of notice to not less than 14 days (see **Precedent 25.16**) must be passed as a special resolution either at the immediately preceding annual general meeting or at a general meeting held since that annual general meeting (s. 307A(4)). However, in the case of a company which has not yet held an annual general meeting, the resolution must be passed at a general meeting (s. 307A(5)).

Any such resolution is only valid up to the next annual general meeting of the company and will need to be renewed at annual general meeting in each succeeding year.

■ 25.17 Directors' authority to allot shares

The directors of listed companies routinely request shareholders to renew their authority to allot shares at the annual general meeting. Authority may be given to the directors to allot some or all of the unissued share capital by ordinary resolution in accordance (s. 551). Institutional investors, impose certain conditions on the amount of shares over which they are willing to give authority to allot and generally insist that new issues of shares above a certain threshold be conducted on a pre-emptive basis (e.g. as a right issue). Where shares are issued on this basis existing holders are offered the opportunity to subscribe for the shares. If they decide not to take up their entitlements, the shares are subsequently sold to the highest bidder through the market and the original shareholder is paid the difference between the subscription price and the price obtained in the market.

Institutional investors also impose a limit on the amount of shares which may be issued under a routine s. 551 allotment authority as a rights issue. The maximum limit is two-thirds of issued share capital. However, if the directors proceed to issue any more than one-third of the company's existing share capital in the following year, they are all expected to offer themselves for re-election at the next annual general meeting. For an example of a s. 551 resolution of a listed company, see the notice of annual general meeting at **Precedent 10.3**.

◼ 25.18 Disapplication of pre-emption rights

Listed companies routinely request shareholders to approve a resolution to disapply the statutory pre-emption rights over some or all of the shares covered by the directors' authority to allot shares. This resolution must be passed as a special resolution in accordance with either ss. 570 or 571.

Institutional investors impose limits on the amount of shares which may be issued on a non pre-emptive basis but are prepared to disapply the statutory pre-emption rights over the whole of any allotment authority provided that any issue above that threshold is carried out on a pre-emptive basis in accordance with the requirements of the Listing Rules. For an example of a resolution of a listed company to disapply pre-emption rights, see the notice of annual general meeting at **Precedent 10.3**.

◼ 25.19 Market purchases of own shares

Many listed companies routinely request authority from shareholders at the annual general meeting to enable them to make market purchases of their own shares. Under the Act, authority for such market purchases may be given by ordinary resolution. However, institutional investors expect listed companies to put forward any such proposal as a special resolution. Resolutions authorising the directors to make market purchases must comply with the requirements of s. 701 and the Listing Rules. The directors do not have to exercise their authority to make market purchases and may only do so in accordance with the terms of the resolution approved by shareholders.

PART 5

Minutes

The Act requires minutes to be kept of general meetings and meetings of directors and records to be kept of members' written resolutions and any informal decisions of sole members. Although this may, at times, seem a burdensome requirement, it is the company that stands to benefit if it is done properly. This is because minutes signed by the chairman are deemed to be evidence of the proceedings. In other words, if the company produces a set of minutes signed by the chairman, those minutes are taken as evidence that the meeting actually took place properly and as evidence of the decisions taken at that meeting. Unless other evidence to the contrary is submitted during legal proceedings, the company will not need to tender any other evidence in support of the minutes.

Because the primary purpose of the minutes and records is to provide evidence of the decisions taken, it is essential that they accurately record those decisions. As a rule of thumb, this means they should contain sufficient information to enable a person who did not attend to ascertain what decisions were taken.

26

Minutes

26.1 Summary

- Companies have a duty to keep minutes of meetings and records of certain decisions taken without holding a meeting (see **26.2**).
- A company must keep minutes of meetings of directors (see **26.3**).
- A company must keep minutes of general meetings (see **26.4**).
- A company must keep a record of any written resolution of the members (see **26.5**).
- A company must keep a record of any informal decisions taken by the sole member of the company (see **26.6**).
- A company must keep minutes of any class meeting, and a record of any written resolutions passed by a class of members and any informal decisions taken by the sole member of a class (see **26.7**).
- Minutes and related records form part of the company's statutory records and must be retained permanently if they relate to decisions made before 1 October 2007 and for at least ten years if they relate to decisions taken on or after that date (see **26.8**).
- Minutes and related records are normally kept in a minute book. However, they can be kept in other forms, including electronic form (see **26.9**).
- Minutes of general meetings, members' written resolutions and other related records must be made available for inspection by the members. Members do not have a right to inspect the minutes of board meetings. Auditors have a right to inspect all of the company's books and records (see **26.10**).
- Minutes signed by the chairman are given special evidential status (see **26.11** and **26.15.1**).
- Once the minutes have been signed they should not be amended (see **26.12**).
- The task of writing minutes normally falls to the company secretary (see **26.13**).
- Minutes should contain certain basic information and provide an accurate record of the proceedings. There are many ways of doing this and the style adopted will depend on the use to which they are put and the preferences of the directors and secretary (see **26.14**).

■ 26.2 General duty to prepare and keep

Every company must keep the following records:

- minutes of all proceedings at meetings of directors (s. 248);
- minutes of general meetings;
- copies of any written resolutions of the members;
- a record of any decisions taken by the sole member of a company (s. 355);
- minutes of any class meetings;
- copies of any written resolutions of a class of members; and
- a record of any decisions taken by the sole member of a class (s. 359).

The main purpose of these requirements could be said to be to ensure that a proper record is kept of the decisions made by and on behalf of the company by its members or directors as proof of those decisions and the fact that they were properly made. For this purpose, the records are given special evidential status. However, a subsidiary purpose in all cases is that certain people are given the right to inspect the records the company is required to keep.

■ 26.3 Minutes of directors' meetings

Every company must keep minutes of all proceedings at meetings of directors (s. 248(1)). Minutes of meetings of directors held on or after 1 October 2007 must be kept for at least ten years from the date of the meeting (s. 248(2)). Minutes of directors' meetings held before that date should be kept in accordance with the requirements of s. 382 of the Companies Act 1985 (see Sch. 3, para. 19 to the Companies Act 2006 (Commencement No. 3, Consequential Amendments, Transitional Provisions and Savings) Order 2007 (SI 2007/2194)). This means that they should be kept permanently.

The company secretary (if any) and the directors can be fined for any default by the company of the provisions of the Act relating to the maintenance of these minutes and records under s. 248(3) (or s. 382 of the 1985 Act).

26.3.1 Evidential status of minutes of meetings of directors

Minutes of meetings of directors recorded in accordance with s. 248 are evidence (in Scotland, sufficient evidence) of the proceedings at the meeting, if purporting to be authenticated by the chairman of the meeting or the chairman of the next directors' meeting (s. 249(1)). Where minutes have been made of the proceedings of a meeting of directors in accordance with the Act, then, until the contrary is proved:

(a) the meeting is deemed duly held and convened;
(b) all proceedings at the meeting are deemed to have duly taken place; and
(c) all appointments at the meeting are deemed valid (s. 249(2)).

26.3.2 Minutes of board committees

It is logical to assume that the phrase 'meetings of directors' in s. 248 includes committees of directors and, therefore, that a company has a statutory duty to keep minutes of such committee meetings. However, in *Guinness plc v. Saunders* [1988] 2 All E.R. 940, a case concerning the duty of a director under s. 317 of the 1985 Act to disclose at a meeting of directors his interest in a proposed transaction, the Court of Appeal held that the phrase 'meeting of directors' did not include a committee of the board. Quite apart from the different context in which the words appear in the two sections, the slight difference in their wording might be sufficient to enable any court to distinguish the interpretation of the Court of Appeal; the phrase used in s. 248 of the 2006 Act regarding the duty to keep minutes is 'meetings of directors' whereas the phrase used in s. 317 of the 1985 Act was 'a meeting of directors'.

This is not merely an academic question. Unless s. 248 requires companies to keep minutes of proceedings of committees of directors, minutes of those proceedings will not be afforded special evidential status under s. 249. Nor would it be an offence not to keep minutes of such committees. Nor would the auditors necessarily have a statutory right to inspect those minutes as they may not form part of the company's books. All these factors would probably lead the courts to decide that the meaning of the words 'meetings of directors' is not the same in relation to the requirement under s. 248 of the 2006 Act to keep minutes of meetings of directors as it was in relation to a directors' duty to disclose his interests at a meeting of directors under s. 371 of the 1985 Act.

Articles sometimes state explicitly that the directors must keep minutes of committees of directors (e.g. reg. 100 of Table A). However, this is not the case in any of the model articles prescribed under the 2006 Act. The model articles for private companies do, however, require the directors to ensure that the company keeps a record in writing, for at least ten years from the date of the decision recorded, of every unanimous or majority decision taken by the directors (pcls 15 and clg 15). They also require majority decisions to be taken at meetings (pcls 7 and clg 7) and state that committees must follow procedures which are based as far as they are applicable on the provisions of the articles which govern the taking of decisions by directors (pcls 6(1) and clg 6(1)). Assuming that the directors do not override the rule regarding minutes and records of decisions in respect of a committee (which it seems they may do under pcls 6(2) and clg 6(2)), it would appear therefore that the model articles for private companies require minutes of committee meetings to be kept.

The model articles for public companies do not specifically require minutes to be kept of board meetings but do specifically require records of written resolutions to be kept (plc 18(4)). Accordingly, when the article regarding procedures at committee meetings (plc 6(1)) is strictly applied, it would appear that committees are required to keep records of any written resolutions but not minutes of their meetings. It is doubtful whether this is intentional and it would, of course, be open to the directors to require committees to keep minutes of their proceedings.

In practice, where power to bind the company has been delegated by the board to a committee, it will be necessary to keep minutes of the proceedings of board committees as evidence that transactions have been duly authorised. Even if the Act does not confer special evidential status on the minutes of board committees, it is possible that the common law would do so.

26.3.3 Directors' written resolutions and unanimous decisions

It would be stretching credulity to suggest that the requirement in s. 248 to keep minutes of proceedings at meetings of directors also includes a requirement to keep records of decisions made by directors as written resolutions or unanimous decisions under procedures provided for by a company's articles or of decisions made informally under the principle of unanimous consent. None of these decisions would normally be made at a meeting of directors and it would appear that, unlike minutes of meetings, even if records of these decisions are kept, they may not be afforded any special evidential status under s. 249. This may seem slightly strange because the parallel requirements relating to members do require records to be kept of written resolutions, which are then afforded special evidential status (see below). The fact that the Act does not do so in relation to directors' decisions taken outside of meetings cannot be viewed as an oversight because the model articles prescribed under the Act require the directors to keep a record of any such decisions for at least ten years. The reason why the Act makes no provision in this regard but does in relation to members' written resolutions is probably because it makes direct provision on the procedures to be followed for members' written resolutions but does not do so with regard to directors' written resolutions and informal decisions. The procedures to be followed in the case of directors' decision-making are generally governed by the articles and the common law rather than the Act.

This suggests that, even now, there may be some advantage to be gained from using the traditional decision-making method of holding a directors' meeting and preparing a set of minutes rather than using any other decision-making procedures because the minutes of such meetings are afforded special evidential status by the Act. It should be noted, however, that the records of written resolutions and unanimous decisions may still be given special evidential status by the courts under the common law.

The model articles for private companies require the directors to ensure that the company keeps a record, for at least ten years from the date of the decision recorded, of every unanimous or majority decision taken by the directors (pcls 15 and clg 15). The model articles for public companies require the company secretary to ensure that the company keeps a record in writing of all directors' written resolutions for at least ten years from the date of their adoption (plc 18(4)). The relevant records are required to be kept 'in writing'. However under all three versions of the model articles, this means in hard copy or electronic form. Unlike the model articles for private companies, the model articles for public companies do not specifically require minutes of directors' meetings to be kept, and presumably rely on the statutory requirement in this regard.

Notwithstanding the fact that the articles may require records of directors' written resolutions and unanimous decisions to be kept, no offence will be committed if they fail to do so.

■ 26.4 Minutes of general meetings

Every company must keep minutes of all general meetings held (including annual general meetings) (s. 355(1)(b)).

In relation to resolutions passed, meetings held or decisions made on or after 1 October 2007, the above records must be kept for at least ten years from the date of the resolution, meeting or decision (as appropriate) (s. 355(2)).

Records of resolutions passed, meetings held and decisions made before that date must be kept in accordance with the requirements of s. 382 of the Companies Act 1985 (see Sch. 3, para. 40 to the Companies Act 2006 (Commencement No. 3, Consequential Amendments, Transitional Provisions and Savings) Order 2007 (SI 2007/2194)). This means permanently as s. 382 of the 1985 Act made no provision allowing the records or minutes to be disposed of.

The company secretary (if any) and the directors can be fined for any default regarding compliance with the requirements of s. 355 of the 2006 Act and s. 382 of the 1985 Act relating to the maintenance of minutes.

26.4.1 Evidential status of general meeting minutes

Section 356 confers special evidential status on minutes kept in accordance with s. 355. The minutes of proceedings of a general meeting, if purporting to be signed by the chairman of that meeting or by the chairman of the next general meeting, are evidence (in Scotland, sufficient evidence) of the proceedings at the meeting (s. 356(4)). Where there is a record of proceedings of a general meeting of a company, then, until the contrary is proved:

(a) the meeting is deemed duly held and convened;
(b) all proceedings at the meeting are deemed to have duly taken place; and
(c) all appointments at the meeting are deemed valid (s. 356(5)).

Section 382(4) of the 1985 Act makes similar provision regarding minutes of meetings kept in accordance with the requirements of that Act.

■ 26.5 Written resolutions

Every company must keep copies of all resolutions of members passed otherwise than at general meetings (e.g. resolutions passed as written resolutions) (s. 355(1)(a)).

In relation to resolutions passed on or after 1 October 2007, the copies must be kept for at least ten years from the date of the resolution (s. 355(2)).

Copies of resolutions passed before that date must be kept permanently because they are still required to be kept in accordance with the requirements of s. 382A of the Companies Act 1985 (see Sch. 3, para. 40 to the Companies Act 2006 (Commencement No. 3, Consequential Amendments, Transitional Provisions and Savings) Order 2007 (SI 2007/2194)). Section 382B of the 1985 Act requires copies of written resolutions to be entered in the company's minute books and makes no provision allowing for the copies to be disposed of.

The company secretary (if any) and the directors can be fined for any default regarding compliance with the requirements of s. 355 of the 2006 Act and s. 382A of the 1985 Act relating to the maintenance of these records.

26.5.1 Evidential status of copies of written resolutions

Section 356 confers special evidential status on copies of resolutions kept in accordance with s. 355. A record of a resolution passed otherwise than at a general meeting, if purporting to be signed by a director of the company or by the company secretary, is evidence (in Scotland, sufficient evidence) of the passing of the resolution (s. 356(2)). Where there is a record of a written resolution of a private company, the requirements of the Act with respect to the passing of the resolution are deemed to be complied with unless the contrary is proved (s. 356(3)).

Section 382A(2) of the 1985 Act makes similar provision regarding records kept in accordance with the requirements of that Act.

■ 26.6 Informal decisions by a sole member

Where a company limited by shares or guarantee has only one member and that member takes any decision which may be taken by the company in general meeting and which has effect as if agreed by the company in general meeting, he shall (unless that decision is taken by way of a written resolution) provide the company with details of that decision (s. 357) (see **Precedent 9.6**). Failure to do so renders the sole member liable to a fine (s. 357(3) and (4)) but does not invalidate the decision (s. 357(5)).

A company must keep a record containing details of decisions taken by a sole member provided to the company by the sole member in accordance with s. 357 (s. 355(1)(c)).

In relation to decisions of a sole member made on or after 1 October 2007, the records must be kept for at least ten years from the date of the decision (s. 355(2)).

Records of decisions made by a sole member before that date must be kept in accordance with the requirements of the Companies Act 1985 (see Sch. 3, para. 40 to the Companies Act 2006 (Commencement No. 3, Consequential Amendments, Transitional Provisions and Savings) Order 2007 (SI 2007/2194)). Section 382B of the 1985 Act imposed a duty on the part of the sole member to provide a written record of any such decision but did not (and still does not) make any provision regarding what the company should do with the record. However, it is normally assumed that the correct course of action would have been to enter the record in the minute books in the same way as was required for written resolutions. In any case, s. 382B of the 1985 Act makes no provision allowing any of the records given to the company by a sole member under that section to be disposed of.

The company secretary (if any) and the directors can be fined for any default regarding compliance with the requirements of s. 355 of the 2006 Act relating to the maintenance of these records. There is no equivalent penalty under the 1985 Act.

The above rules might be thought not to apply where a company has two or more members, one of whom holds the whole of the ordinary shares giving the right to vote with the other (or others) holding another class (or classes) of non-voting shares. However, they do apply with suitable modification to decisions relating to a class of members by virtue of s. 359. It is not easy to say what sort of modification ought to be made to s. 357 in relation to class decisions. Section 357(1) states that the rules apply to a company limited by shares or by guarantee that has only one member. Unless this is modified in some way, the requirements in that section will only apply to class decisions in a company limited by shares if the same person holds all the shares of each class. With some modification, the rule in s. 357 could apply to a company limited by shares or guarantee where there is only one person who is a member of a class or only one person who holds a particular class of shares. This is probably the safest interpretation and the one which makes the most sense. However, it does throw up some interesting questions. For example, would the requirement on the part of the sole member of a class to provide details to the company of any informal decisions he has made apply to the sole member of a class in a public company? It should be noted that the application of s. 357 is not restricted to private companies, so the answer to this question is probably yes. In addition, would an informal decision made by the only holder of ordinary voting shares in a private company fall to be notified if the company had other members who were not entitled to participate in that decision because the class of shares which they hold did not confer the right to vote? The answer to this question must also be yes if the sole ordinary shareholder can be deemed to be the holder of a class of shares. Fortunately, the validity of such decisions is not affected by any failure on the part of a member to comply with s. 357 and the only reason why this would ever be tested in the courts would be if a member was being prosecuted for failure to disclose such a decision to the company. In view of the tortuous nature of the relevant sections, it is unlikely that the courts would have much sympathy with the case for the prosecution in this regard. However, it is probably good practice to assume that this is what s. 357 requires in the absence of any clarification.

■ 26.7 Minutes of class meetings and records of class resolutions

Section 359 provides that the provisions on records of resolutions and minutes of general meetings in Part 13, Chapter 6 of the Act apply (with necessary modifications) in relation to resolutions and meetings of:

(a) holders of a class of shares; and
(b) in the case of a company without a share capital, a class of members.

Accordingly, the following rules can be said to apply:

(a) a company must keep:
　(i)　copies of all resolutions of a class of members or shareholders passed otherwise than at a class meeting (e.g. as written resolutions) (applying s. 355(1)(a));
　(ii)　minutes of all class meetings (applying s. 355(1)(b));
　(iii)　details of decisions taken by a sole (class) member provided to the company by the sole class member in accordance with s. 357 (applying s. 355(1)(c)) (but see **26.6**);
(b) any failure to do so is an offence for which any officer in default may be fined (applying s. 355(3) and (4));
(c) records kept in accordance with s. 355 will be afforded special evidential status (applying s. 356) (see **26.4.1**);
(d) a sole member of a class may have to notify the company in writing of any decision he makes which could be taken at a class meeting and has effect as if agreed to at a class meeting (applying s. 357), although it has to be said that this section could be applied in a number of different ways (see **26.6**);
(e) any records kept under these rules must be made available for inspection (applying s. 358) (see **26.10**).

■ 26.8 Retention of minutes and related records

The 2006 Act imposes a minimum retention period of ten years in relation to minutes and other records to which s. 248 and 355 apply. This retention period only applies to records relating to meetings held, resolutions passed or decisions made on or after 1 October 2007. Any records relating to earlier meetings, resolutions or decisions must be kept in accordance with the requirements of the Companies Act 1985. Minutes and related records kept under the provisions of the 1985 Act should be retained permanently, i.e. for at least the life of the company and possibly beyond in view of the provisions of ss. 1024 to 1034 (restoration to the register) and reg. 3A of the Insolvency Regulations 1994.

Notwithstanding the fact that records kept under the provisions of the 2006 Act can now be kept for as little as ten years, it is still strongly recommended that they be kept for considerably longer, if not permanently. The reduction of the retention period in the 2006 Act seems to have been made in anticipation of reform to the law governing limitation of actions. The law generally restricts the time in which it is possible to commence civil legal proceedings. The relevant time limit in each case is known as the limitation period. The government has promised to implement reforms based on the recommendations of the Law Commission in this regard, which would give rise to maximum limitation period of ten years in most cases. At the time of writing in the first half of 2009, the government has yet to table any such legislation. Accordingly, the old limitation periods still apply, some of which last for considerably longer than ten years. Accordingly a company which disposes of minutes and other related records after ten years may find that it has disposed of the evidence which may have helped it to defend or prosecute a civil action. In any case, even under the proposed regime for limitation periods, certain civil actions will be capable of being brought beyond the proposed ten-year long-stop limitation period (e.g. any action relating to personal injury or any action where the defendant has dishonestly concealed the facts), and there will be no time limit on criminal prosecutions.

Irrespective of the legal issues involved, it is hard to imagine any company wishing to dispose of records such as minutes, which will often form an invaluable historical record and contain potentially useful business information. As far as company secretaries are concerned, the minutes could be invaluable if it ever proved to be necessary to re-construct the company's registers and records.

It is arguable whether it is necessary to keep the original signed copies of minutes if they have been scanned into a document imaging system (see **26.9**). However, most companies still do so on the basis that the validity of the signature might be an important component in establishing the special evidential status of the minutes. If copies of signed minutes are scanned into a computerised document imaging system, the company should, at the very least, comply with the recommendations of the British Standards Institute for retaining documents in that form. However, if minutes are still manually signed, it may still be advisable to keep the original copies for at least the minimum ten-year period required for records held in accordance with the 2006 Act.

■ 26.9 Form in which minutes and records should be kept

26.9.1 Minutes and records kept under the 1985 Act

The requirements of ss. 382 to 383 of the Companies Act 1985 still apply in relation to minutes of general meetings held, members' resolutions passed, and decisions of sole members made before 1 October 2007 and to the inspection and copying of those records.

Section 382 of the 1985 Act requires minutes of general meetings to be entered in books kept for that purpose and this rule must still be assumed to apply for minutes required to be kept under that section of the 1985 Act. Section 382A of the 1985 Act requires a record of any members' written resolution passed before 1 October 2007 (and of the signatures) to be entered in a book in the same way as minutes of general meetings.

Section 382B required the sole member of a private company limited by shares or guarantee to provide the company with a written record of any informal decision made by him before 1 October 2007 which could have been taken by the company in general meeting and had effect as if agreed at such a meeting. Although there is nothing in the 1985 Act that specifically states what the company should do with such a record, it was normally assumed that it should be entered in the minute book.

Section 722 of the 1985 Act (which has now been repealed without any saving provisions) provided that any minute book required to be kept by the company under the 1985 Act could be kept either by making entries in bound books or 'by recording the entries in any other manner', provided in the latter case that adequate precautions were taken to guard against falsification and for facilitating its discovery. Section 723 of the 1985 Act (which has also now been repealed without any saving provisions), provided that the words 'in any other manner' in s. 722(1) included computer records provided those records were capable of being reproduced in a legible form. As these sections have now been repealed, it is assumed that ss. 1134 to 1138 of the 2006 Act and any regulations made under those sections must apply. Books and records required to be kept under the Companies Act 1985 are presumably included in the description of company records in s. 1134 of the 2006 Act, which embraces minutes and other records required to be kept under the Companies Acts. This must include any provision of the Companies Act 1985 which continues to have effect.

26.9.2 Minutes and records kept under the 2006 Act

Records required to be kept under the 2006 Act in relation to meetings held, resolutions passed or decisions made on or after 1 October 2007 must be kept in the form and manner prescribed by the provisions of the 2006 Act on company records in ss. 1134 to 1138. Section 1134 states that for the purposes of these requirements company records means 'any register, index, accounting records, agreement, memorandum, minutes or other document required by the Companies Acts to be kept by a company' and 'any register kept by the company of its debenture holders'. These provisions will also apply to records that still have to be retained under the Companies Act 1985 (see above).

Section 1135 states that the company records may be kept in hard copy or electronic form and may be arranged in such manner as the directors of the company think fit, provided that the information is adequately recorded for future reference (s. 1135(1)). Where the records are kept in electronic form, they must be capable of being reproduced in hard copy form (s. 1135(2)). Failure to comply with these requirements is an offence for which any officer in default may be fined (s. 1135 (3) and (4)).

Where a company's records are kept otherwise than in bound books, adequate precautions should be taken to guard against falsification and to facilitate the discovery of falsification (s. 1138(1)). Failure to comply with this requirement is also an offence for which any officer in default may be fined (s. 1138(2) and (3)).

26.9.3 Minute books

Minutes were traditionally handwritten in bound books kept for that purpose. Although it is still perfectly acceptable to record minutes in this manner, it is far more likely that minutes will be produced as a print-out of a word-processor file (or less commonly these days, typed on sheets of paper). Where bound books are still used, the print-out or typed-up copy of the minutes can then be pasted in the serially numbered pages of the bound minute book. Copies of other resolutions or records can also be produced in the same manner and pasted into the bound minute book.

Minute books specifically designed for purpose often include pages that allow an index to be created. Many company secretaries use these to index the minutes by subject and names mentioned. Although there is no legal requirement to do this, it is considered good practice and will be particularly helpful when it is necessary to refer, for example, to decisions of the directors which have the effect of modifying the company's articles (e.g. by setting the quorum for directors' meetings).

Many companies now use loose-leaf minute books. Although this is allowed under the Act, additional precautions must be taken to guard against falsification as they are not bound books. If a loose-leaf minute book is used, it is preferable (but not essential) to use one which has a locking device either in the spine or between the covers. Strict control should be exercised over access to the keys to the minute book and any duplicates should be lodged in a secure place such as a safe or safety deposit box. When a loose-leaf folder is used, the pages should be serially numbered at the time of insertion in the binder, normally under the control of the secretary or the person acting as the secretary to the relevant body. The items minuted are also usually numbered consecutively from one meeting to the next so as to prevent the insertion of a false set of minutes.

All minute books, whether bound books or loose-leaf folders, should be kept in a secure place. Ideally this should be a robust, lockable and fireproof filing cabinet or safe to which access is restricted. This is of even greater importance if minutes are kept in an ordinary unlockable, loose-leaf folder.

Separate minute books would normally be used to keep minutes of general meetings and meetings of directors, with subsidiary minute books being used for each board committee. The items minuted at meetings would normally be numbered consecutively from No. 1 upwards throughout each minute book (see further below). One would normally expect the minutes of meetings to be entered in the minute books in date order, and the appearance of any minutes out of order could give rise to questions as to their veracity should the minute book ever need to be tendered as evidence in legal proceedings.

If for any genuine reason, including oversight, it is necessary to insert a set of minutes or a record in a minute book out of date order, it would be advisable for some sort of reference to be included in a subsequent set of minutes of that body confirming that the minutes are genuine and explaining the reason for the insertion. This might also be necessary if two sets of minutes have used the same serial numbers. In either case, the very least that should be done is for a note to be included in the minute book by the chairman or the secretary explaining the reason for the discrepancy.

26.9.4 Guarding against falsification

Minutes may not be acceptable as evidence unless adequate precautions have been taken to guard against falsification and to facilitate its discovery. In a judgment prior to the current legislation, a loose-leaf minute book was rejected on the basis that: 'anyone wishing to do so . . . can take a number of leaves out and substitute any number of other leaves. It is a thing with which anyone disposed to be dishonest can easily tamper' (*Heart of Oaks Assurance Co. Ltd. v. James Flower & Sons* [1936] 1 Ch. 76). Although the law allows companies to use loose-leaf minute books, their content could easily be challenged if it could be proved that the security measures taken to guard against falsification were inadequate. In a more recent case, purported minutes of a directors' meeting were rejected as evidence of the proceedings because it was impossible to tell from the document who had chaired the meeting or who had signed them and because the document had never been kept in a minute book (*POW Services v. Clare* [1995] 2 B.C.L.C. 435).

Some or all of the following safeguards should be adopted where minutes are kept in minute books:

- sequential numbering of the minutes of each type of meeting, e.g. if the last minute of the first meeting of company's board of directors is numbered minute 20, the first minute of the second meeting of the board of directors should be numbered minute 21 and so on;
- the chairman should initial every page;
- pages should be numbered sequentially on specially printed paper;
- when pasted into bound books or onto number sheets, the chairman's signature and initials should start on the printed sheet and run on to the bound page;
- the minute book should be kept in a safe (preferably fireproof) with restricted access;
- a lockable binder should be used, particularly for minutes kept in a loose-leaf folder; and
- minutes of general meetings and board meetings should be kept in separate books or folders to prevent members (who are entitled to inspect the minutes of general meetings) from gaining access to the minutes of meetings of directors and managers.

It should be noted that serially numbering minutes does not of itself prevent falsification, particularly where the series is started again each year or the minutes are kept in a loose-leaf folder. Where a loose-leaf folder is used, the original pages can simply be removed and new ones inserted with false minutes or records which utilise the same serial numbers. Where the numerical series is started again at the beginning of each year (e.g. by using a system such as 2009/0001 for the first minute in the year 2009 and 2010/0001 for the first minute in the year 2010), it would in theory be possible for somebody to insert a false set of minutes at the end of each year unless some system is used to record the fact that a particular minute or record is the last entry for that year. It would be even worse if the numbering system was based on the month in which the meeting was held (e.g. 2009/03/0001 for the first minute of a meeting held in March 2009). Using a numbering based on years, months or dates will undoubtedly make cross-referencing and indexing of the minutes easier, but it may also make it easier for a person to falsify minutes. Accordingly, if any such system is used, even greater precautions should be taken to guard against falsification, such as the use of bound books, lockable folders, and the initialling of each page by the chairman.

26.9.5 Electronic minutes and records

If minutes are kept in electronic form they must still be authenticated by the chairman to be treated as evidence of the proceedings under s. 249 (minutes of directors' meetings) or s. 356 (minutes of general meetings and records of resolutions). Any doubts over the admissibility of electronic signatures in legal proceedings for these purposes have been removed by the Electronic Communications Act 2000. Accordingly, the chairman could apply an electronic signature to a file containing the minutes which could then be stored on a computer. As the security of the technique used to apply the electronic signature could have a bearing on the weight the courts give to the minutes, it would be preferable for the chairman to use the most modern cryptographic techniques to do this (see **2.13**).

Different considerations arise where it is proposed, for example, to scan manually signed minutes for retention in computerised form and to destroy the original paper copies. Where this is done, the electronic image may ultimately need to be tendered in evidence in court, as secondary evidence of the signature of the minutes and of their contents. To ensure that it is acceptable as evidence in this regard, it will be essential to follow the British Standards Institute's *Code of Practice for Legal Admissibility of Information Stored Electronically*.

If minutes are kept in computerised form, they must still be capable of being reproduced in hard copy form (s. 1135(2)). This probably sounds simpler than it is in reality. The minutes must still be capable of being reproduced in hard copy form not just today but for at least ten years (or indefinitely if they are 1985 Act records). Ideally, whenever a new computer system or new software is adopted, checks should be carried out to ensure that the files containing the minutes can still be read. If not, it may be possible to convert them into a suitable format.

However, if this is not possible (e.g. because doing so would compromise the electronic signature), it may be necessary to retain the old hardware and software forever. These considerations will obviously be less of a problem for minutes and records kept under the 2006 Act regarding meetings and decisions made on or after 1 October 2007 as these only have to be kept for ten years. Nevertheless, many companies will probably wish to keep these records for longer than the ten-year minimum prescribed by the Act.

■ 26.10 Inspection of minutes and other records

26.10.1 Minutes of general meetings and related records kept under the 1985 Act

The requirements of ss. 382 to 383 of the 1985 Act still apply in relation to the records which must be kept of minutes of general meetings held, members' resolutions passed and decisions taken before 1 October 2007 and to the inspection and copying of those records.

Section 383 of the 1985 Act requires the books containing the minutes of proceedings of general meetings of the company (which should also include records of members' written resolutions) to be kept at the company's registered office and to be open to the inspection of any member without charge (s. 383(1), 1985 Act). It should be noted that s. 383(1) does not allow the inspection place to be anywhere other than the company's registered office, although the provisions of the 2006 Act and the Companies (Company Records) Regulations 2008 (SI 2008/3006) may prevail in this regard and enable the records to be made available either at the registered office or some other place notified to the registrar (see below).

Under s. 383(3) of the 1985 Act, members are entitled on payment of a prescribed fee to be furnished with a copy of any minutes of general meetings (and presumably any written resolutions included in the minute book) within seven days of making a request. The relevant fee for these purposes is 10p per 100 words or part thereof. This is different to the prescribed fee under the Companies Act 2006, which is 10p per 500 words (plus expenses). The fee for the purposes of 1985 Act records is prescribed in para. 3(b) of Sch. 2 to the Companies (Inspection and Copying of Registers, Indices and Documents) Regulations 1991, which continues to apply in respect of requests relating to minutes of general meetings which are subject to s. 383 of the Companies Act 1985 by virtue of para. 40(2) of Sch. 3 to the Companies Act 2006 (Commencement No. 3, Consequential Amendments, Transitional Provisions and Savings) Order 2007 (see reg. 5(3) of the Companies (Fees for Inspection and Copying of Company Records) Regulations 2007 (SI 2007/2612).

26.10.2 Minutes of general meetings and related records kept under the 2006 Act

The records required to be kept under s. 355 of the 2006 Act (i.e. minutes of general meetings held, records of members' resolutions passed and decisions of sole members made on or after 1 October 2007) must be made available for inspection in accordance with s. 358 of the 2006 Act. Section 358 only requires records relating to the previous ten years to be made available for inspection. No company will have ten years' worth of records that have to be made available for inspection under this rule until October 2017. All minutes of general meetings held, records of resolutions passed and decision of sole members made before 1 October 2007 must be made available for inspection and copying under the rules set out in s. 383 of the Companies Act 1985 (i.e. permanently).

2006 Act records relating to the previous ten years must be made available for inspection to members without charge:

(a) at the company's registered office; or
(b) at a place specified in regulations under s. 1136 (known as the single alternative inspection location or SAIL) (s. 358).

A company must give notice to the registrar of the place at which the records are kept available for inspection, and of any change in that place, unless they have at all times been kept at the company's registered office (s. 358(2)). The regulations made under s. 1136 allow a company to make its company records available for inspection at a single location other than its registered office (see the Companies (Company Records) Regulations 2008 (SI 2008/3006)). That location must have been notified to the registrar of companies and must be situated in the same part of the United Kingdom as the company is registered (reg. 3 of SI 2008/3006).

Any member may require a copy of any of these 2006 Act records on payment of a prescribed fee (s. 358(4)). The prescribed fee is 10 pence per 500 words or part thereof copied plus any reasonable costs incurred by the company in delivering the copy of the company record (reg. 4 of the Companies (Fees for Inspection and Copying of Company Records) Regulations 2007 (SI 2007/2612)).

Members are entitled to be provided with copies of minutes of general meetings within 14 days of making a request. If the company wrongly refuses to allow an inspection or fails to provide copies of the minutes within the proper time, any officer in default can be fined (s. 358(5) and (6)). In such circumstances, the court may order an immediate inspection or direct that the desired copies be sent (s. 358(7)).

Members are entitled to be accompanied by an adviser when they inspect the minutes of general meetings (*McCrusker v. McRae*, 1966 S.C. 253).

26.10.3 Common inspection and copying rules

The Companies (Company Records) Regulations 2008 (SI 2008/3006) ('the Records Regulations 2008') set out the obligations of companies in relation to company records (including minutes of general meetings and records of resolutions, etc) in respect of which there is a right of inspection. The following rules apply to inspection and copying under s. 358 of the 2006 Act and s. 383 of the 1985 Act.

A private company is required to make its company records available for inspection for at least two hours between 9 am and 5 pm on a working day. A person wishing to inspect the records of a private company is required to give the company at least ten working days' notice of the working day on which they wish to carry out their inspection. However, they only need to give two days' notice if they wish to inspect the records during the notice period of a general meeting or a class meeting or during a period for agreeing a written resolution under s. 297(1) of the Act, provided that the two-day notice period given for their inspection request both begins and ends during the relevant period. The person wishing to inspect is also required to specify in both cases the time at which he wants to start his inspection on the relevant day, which must be between the hours of 9 am and 3 pm. The company is then required to make its records available for inspection for at least two hours from the time specified (reg. 4 of the Records Regulations 2008).

A public company is required to make its company records available for inspection between 9 am and 5 pm on every working day (reg. 5 of the Records Regulations 2008).

A 'working day' is defined for these purposes in s. 1173(1) of the 2006 Act as a day that is not a Saturday or Sunday, Christmas Day, Good Friday or any day that is a bank holiday under the Banking and Financial Dealings Act 1971 in the part of the United Kingdom where the company is registered.

A company is not required to present a company record in a different order, structure or form to the one set out in that record (reg. 6(1) of the Records Regulations 2008). A person may make a copy of a company record but a company is not required to assist that person in making that copy (reg. 6(2) of the Records Regulations 2008). However, nothing in the regulations prevents a company from providing more extensive facilities than those provided for in the regulations (see s. 1137(5)(a)).

The regulations also expand upon the obligations of companies in relation to the provision of copies of company records. The terms 'hard copy form', 'electronic copy form' and related expressions are defined in s. 1168 of the Act. Company records may be kept in hard copy or electronic form provided that the information is adequately recorded (see s. 1135(1)) but if kept in electronic form, they must be capable of being reproduced in hard copy form (see s. 1135(2)).

A person who requests a hard copy of a company record must be supplied with a hard copy (reg. 7 of the Records Regulations 2008). A person who requests an electronic copy of a record must be supplied with an electronic copy unless the record is only kept in hard copy (reg. 8(1) and (2) of the Records Regulations 2008). The company can decide the electronic form in which it will supply the record (reg. 8(1) of the Records Regulations 2008) (subject to s. 1168(5) and (6) which imposes conditions relating to the form and legibility of the copy).

Where a company provides a copy of a company record in electronic form to a company member or debenture holder, it is not then obliged to send a hard copy of that record to such a person free of charge (reg. 8(3) of the Records Regulations 2008). Regulation 8(3), in conjunction with s. 1143, disapplies s. 1145 of the Act.

A company is not required to present information in a copy of a company record in a different order, structure or form to the one set out in that record (reg. 9 of the Records Regulations 2008).

26.10.4 Meetings of directors

It is standard practice to distribute copies of the minutes to the directors before the next meeting or with the papers for the next succeeding meeting. In addition, however, directors have a common law right to inspect the minutes and to be accompanied by an adviser when they do so (*McCrusker v. McRae*, 1966 S.C. 253).

Members, creditors and members of the public are not entitled to inspect nor to take copies of the minutes of meetings of directors or managers.

26.10.5 Inspection by auditors

A company's auditors have a right of access at all times to the company's books, accounts and vouchers (in whatever form they are held) and such information and explanations necessary for the performance of their duties as auditors (s. 499). The company's books presumably include all of the company's statutory books and records, including any minutes and records the company is required to keep under ss. 248 or 355. The auditors' letter of engagement will normally make some reference to the obligation of the company to make these and other records available for inspection.

■ 26.11 Approval and signature by chairman

Minutes are evidence of the proceedings of the relevant meeting once they have been signed by the chairman of that meeting or by the chairman of the next succeeding meeting (s. 249 and s. 356). However, they are only *prima facie* (on their face) evidence of the proceedings (*Re Indian Zoedone Co.* (1884) 26 Ch.D. 70). Other evidence is admissible to show that the they are not an accurate record (*Re Llanharry Hematite Iron Ore Co., Roney's Case* (1864) 4 De G.J. & Sm. 426) even if the articles state that they are to be taken as conclusive evidence without further proof (*Kerr v. Mottram* [1940] Ch. 657 and *Re Caratal (New) Mines Ltd.* [1902] 2 Ch. 498).

Companies are given considerable leeway in the methods which they can adopt for approving the minutes and the ICSA's *Code on Good Boardroom Practice* recommends that boards should establish written procedures with regard to minutes of board meetings. Although minutes which have not been signed by the chairman may be admissible as evidence of the proceedings, they will certainly not be accorded the same weight.

26.11.1 General meetings

It is standard practice for the minutes of general meetings to be signed shortly after the meeting by the person who acted as the chairman of the meeting. This is often done at the first available board meeting so as to allow the other directors to make any comments, but also so that an entry may be made in the board minutes to the effect that they were duly signed. If this procedure is followed, it is not necessary to seek the approval of the members at the next general meeting nor, indeed, to refer to the minutes of the previous meeting at all.

If the person who acted as the chairman of the meeting is unable or unwilling to sign the minutes, they should be signed by the chairman of the next general meeting.

If it is not possible to adopt this procedure, then the minutes may need to be read at the next general meeting (they cannot be taken as read unless all the members have received a copy) and a resolution put to the meeting that they be approved.

26.11.2 Meetings of directors

Board minutes are usually distributed in draft form to the directors for comment and signed by the chairman of the next succeeding board meeting. They are often included in the agenda papers for the meeting at which they are to be approved, particularly if any changes have been made to the first draft as a consequence of comments by directors. At the meeting, the minutes are usually taken as read and a motion is put recommending their adoption as a true and accurate record of the proceedings of the meeting to which they refer. If approved, they should be signed immediately by the chairman who need not have been present at the original meeting.

The chairman may, however, sign the minutes before the next succeeding meeting of the board and need not necessarily give the other directors an opportunity to comment on them before doing so. This will rarely be necessary and any chairman who follows this procedure should be prepared to explain to his fellow directors why he departed from the usual practice and expect to have the minutes scrutinised more closely than might normally be the case. If this procedure is followed and the directors disagree with the chairman's interpretation of the proceedings, they could pass a resolution to that effect which would be recorded in the minutes of that meeting. The minutes which were the subject of the disagreement should not be altered although it might be sensible for the secretary to make a marginal note in the original minutes cross-referring to the subsequent decision.

In the unlikely event that the chairman refuses to sign the minutes, it should be recorded in the minutes of the next meeting that they were approved as a true record by the other directors who were present at the original meeting, if that was the case.

■ 26.12 Amendment

Alterations can be made to the minutes before they have been signed as an accurate record by the chairman. The directors may wish to amend the company secretary's original draft and may request the chairman to amend the draft that is put before them at the next board meeting. Once the minutes have been included in the papers for a board meeting, best practice dictates that they should be amended by longhand or typed entries on the original copy and each amendment should be initialled by the chairman before signing the minutes themselves. It may not be practical to follow precisely the same procedures where the minutes are to be kept on a computer and signed by the chairman electronically.

Alterations should not be made after the minutes have been signed by the chairman. If the directors present at a subsequent meeting disagree with a decision taken at a previous meeting that is properly recorded in signed minutes, they should pass a further resolution rescinding or amending their previous decision which should be recorded in the minutes of that meeting. Similarly, if it is discovered after the minutes have been signed that they are inaccurate, a further resolution should be passed and recorded in the minutes of the meeting at which the inaccuracy was raised.

Details which were not available at the meeting should not be inserted in the minutes, e.g. the date of a call (*Re Cawley & Co.* (1889) 42 Ch.D. 209). However, resolutions can be framed so that they allow a director or the secretary to action a matter which is contingent upon further details being available.

■ 26.13 Who should take the minutes?

Preparing minutes of company meetings is one of the company secretary's core duties. If the company secretary is not available, it normally falls to the deputy or assistant secretary to undertake the task. Although not good practice, there is nothing to prevent someone else performing these functions. The report of the Cadbury Committee states at para. 4.25: 'It should be standard practice for the company secretary to administer, attend and prepare minutes of board proceedings.' ICSA's *Code on Good Boardroom Practice* also states:

> 9. The company secretary should be responsible to the chairman for the proper administration of meetings of the company, the board and any committees thereof. To carry out this responsibility the company secretary should be entitled to be present at (or represented at) and prepare (or arrange for the preparation of) minutes of the proceedings of all such meetings.

The company secretary and the directors can be fined for any default by the company of the provisions of the Act relating to the maintenance of minutes (s. 248(3) and 4 and s. 355(3) and (4)). Although the directors share responsibility with the company secretary (if any) for ensuring that minutes are kept, it is difficult for anyone to contribute effectively to the business of the meeting if they are also required to record the proceedings. It could also be argued that they lack the impartiality which the secretary can provide when drafting the minutes.

It is quite common for company secretaries to use an assistant to help take notes of the proceedings. This allows them to concentrate more on their advisory role during the meeting. It is also increasingly common for a recording or transcript of the meeting to be made to assist in the preparation of the minutes. This can be particularly helpful at AGMs where it is often difficult for the secretary to record all the names of speakers from the floor and, sometimes, difficult to understand the meaning of their questions or statements. It should also be noted that transcripts and recordings of meetings can be tendered as evidence during legal proceedings to rebut the evidence of the minutes, and would have to be disclosed during the discovery process prior to those proceedings.

■ 26.14 Content and style

Different people often have different views about what took place at a meeting. These views tend to become even more polarised as those present become blessed with the benefit of hindsight. There is little point holding formal meetings if no-one can remember what was decided at the meeting. The decisions taken must be recorded and those present should confirm that the record properly reflects what was decided. Preparing minutes is therefore an essential part of the decision-making process. It is also something of an art.

The secretary is expected to be psychic. Matters are decided without being expressed verbally. Individuals signal their agreement by gestures that would tax the most experienced auctioneer. Issues are discussed which no-one expects to be included in the minutes. The chairman does not follow the order of the agenda. The meeting will spend hours on trivial matters which are expected to be minuted in great detail and then gallop through the most important items. Despite all this, the secretary is expected to make sense of the meeting and produce in a timely manner (i.e. by tomorrow morning) an accurate and clear set of minutes. To cap it all, although everyone expects the minutes to record what they said in great detail, they also expect them to be concise.

The art of preparing minutes is not simply doing so concisely, accurately and clearly in the shortest possible time, although achieving these objectives requires a degree of aptitude. It is knowing when to sacrifice or adapt these principles. Egos must be smoothed. Detailed explanations may sometimes be required. On other occasions, brevity will be the only way to avoid opening old wounds.

Thus, although certain conventions are normally followed, the presentational style can be tailored. The preferences of the chairman will usually be the most influential. What can never be compromised, however, is the principle that the minutes should contain an accurate record of the decisions taken.

Although the minutes should represent a true and accurate record of the proceedings of the meeting, it is neither necessary, nor is it desirable, to include a transcript of the proceedings. According to ICSA's *Code of Good Boardroom Practice* (1991), the minutes should record the decisions taken and provide sufficient background to those decisions. Many different styles of presentation may be adopted provided that the minutes include the following basic elements:

- name of the company;
- type of meeting, e.g. annual general meeting or audit committee;
- place where the meeting was held;
- day of the meeting (optional);
- date of the meeting;
- time of the meeting (optional, but see below);
- names and/or numbers present (see *Record of attendance* below);
- record of the proceedings; and
- chairman's signature.

26.14.1 Time of the meeting

Although it may not be strictly necessary to include the time of the meeting, there may be good reason to do so. If the time of the meeting is included in the heading of the minutes, it ought to state the actual time that the meeting started, rather than the time the meeting was meant to start. It may be necessary to record the time a meeting started as evidence that one meeting took place before another where, for example, the business at the second meeting was conditional upon approval being obtained at the first. It may also be necessary to record the time certain decisions were made (e.g. for tax purposes).

26.14.2 Record of attendance

There is no need to keep a separate record of attendance at either general or board meetings unless the articles so provide (see, for example, reg. 86 of the 1948 Act Table A). However, it is important to include sufficient details in the minutes to show that a quorum was present for each item of business or, where relevant, that a disinterested quorum was present. It should also be clear from the minutes who chaired the meeting. This is normally done by adding the words 'chairman' or 'chairperson' or 'chair' next to the name of the relevant person. If someone other than a director chairs a general meeting, this should also be apparent from the minute referring to the election of the chairman.

Regulation 100 of Table A requires the names of the directors present at meetings (including general meetings) to be included in the minutes of that meeting. If a director attends for only part of a meeting, this should be recorded in the minutes, normally by annotating the list of directors present with the words such as 'for minutes 23 to 34 only'. By doing so, it should be clear whether or not a disinterested quorum was present throughout the meeting. It should be assumed that the director who was present when a decision was made was present for that item unless he absents himself from participating in that decision, which he may sometimes do on the basis that he has not participated in the discussion.

Although it is not necessary to record in the minutes of general meetings the names of the members present at the meeting, it is essential to record the numbers present or represented so that the minutes prove that a quorum was present for each item of business. As reg. 100 of Table A requires the names of the directors present at general meetings to be recorded in the minutes (whether or not they are also members), care should be taken not to include the directors who are also members in the number of other members present.

26.14.3 Record of proceedings

The record of the proceedings should include the text of any resolutions put to the meeting and the result of any vote. It should also include a record of any amendments and procedural resolutions proposed at the meeting and the results of any vote on them. Any rulings made by the chairman should also be recorded, e.g. on a demand for a poll. If a resolution is passed on a show of hands it is only necessary to state that the chairman declared the resolution carried. If a poll is called and taken, the number of votes for and against should be included in the minutes together with a statement as to whether the resolution was or was not carried (see **Precedent 26.14A**).

All papers presented at the meeting should be clearly identified in the minutes (see minute 77 of **Precedent 26.14B**) and retained for reference. In the interests of brevity, it is possible to refer in the minutes to papers presented at the meeting which contain the detailed proposals, rather than reproduce the proposals in full. Any such document should be initialled by the chairman for the purpose of identification and the minutes should record that fact. However, it should be noted that minutes are not user-friendly at the best of times and it will not help matters if readers have to make continuous reference to other documents in order to discern what decisions were taken. In addition, documents which are essential in order to understand the record of decisions taken in the minutes should be retained in the same way and for as long as the minutes themselves.

26.14.4 Registers which may form a subset of the minutes

It is relatively common for certain matters that would otherwise need to be recorded in the minutes of directors' meetings to be included in registers specifically kept for that purpose. Examples include:

(a) registers of documents sealed;
(b) registers of transfers;
(c) registers of allotments; and
(d) registers of disclosures by directors of interests in transactions or arrangements.

For example, where the articles require the board to authorise the use of the company seal, approval may be obtained and recorded in the minutes by making reference to entries in the sealing register. Where such registers are used, they should be treated as a subset of the minutes, accorded the same sort of security and retained for at least as long as the original minutes which refer to them.

■ 26.15 Matters which must be recorded in board minutes

26.15.1 Contract with sole member who is also a director

Where a limited company having only one member enters into a contract with the sole member who is also a director of the company and the contract is not entered into in the ordinary course of the company's business, the company must, unless the contract is in writing, ensure that the terms of the contract are either:

(a) set out in a written memorandum; or
(b) recorded in the minutes of the first meeting of the directors of the company following the making of the contract (s. 231).

If a company fails to comply with this section an offence is committed by every officer of the company who is in default, who may be fined (s. 231(3) and (4)). However, failure to comply with this requirement in relation to a contract does not affect the validity of the contract (s. 231(6)), and nothing in s. 231 should be read as excluding the operation of any other enactment or rule of law applying to contracts between a company and a director of the company (s. 231(7)).

26.15.2 Declarations of interest

If a director makes a declaration of interest at a meeting of directors under s. 177 (proposed transactions or arrangements) or s. 182 (existing transactions or arrangements), the declaration must be recorded in the minutes as part of the proceedings.

In addition, if a director makes a declaration of interest:

(a) by giving notice in writing in accordance with s. 184 he must send the notice to the other directors. In addition, the making of the declaration is deemed to form part of the proceedings at the next meeting of the directors after the notice is given, and the provisions of s. 248 (minutes of meetings of directors) apply as if the declaration had been made at that meeting (s. 184(5));
(b) by general notice in accordance with s. 185, the notice is not effective unless it is given at a meeting of the directors or the director takes reasonable steps to secure that it is brought up and read at the next meeting of the directors after it is given (in either case, one would expect the minutes to record the fact that the director had given general notice of an interest) (s. 185(4));
(c) under s. 182 (duty to declare interest in existing transaction or arrangement) and the director is the sole director of a company that is required to have more than one director, the declaration must be recorded in writing and the making of the declaration is deemed to form part of the proceedings at the next meeting of the directors after the notice is given, and the provisions of s. 248 (minutes of meetings of directors) apply as if the declaration had been made at that meeting (s. 186(1)).

PART 6
Precedents

The precedents are numbered according to the main paragraph in the text to which they relate.

CHAPTER 26: MINUTES

CHAPTER 2: ELECTRONIC COMMUNICATIONS

P. 2.9A Form of election to receive documents in electronic form or via a website

You may elect to receive documents and information from us (such as AGM notices and the company's annual report and accounts) in electronic form instead of receiving them through the post. The options available to you are set out below. If you would like us to use one of these methods, please complete the attached form and return it using the envelope provided. [You may also register your choice via our website at [address]. You will need the identification number printed at the top of this form in order to do so.]

If you would like to continue receiving company documents in paper form through the post, you need take no further action. [However, you may request the company to continue sending documents by post and notify you by e-mail when documents such as the AGM notice have been published on the company's website.]

Documents that we may send using your chosen option

You may [may not] elect to receive documents and information from us in different ways, although you may elect to receive notifications regarding publication on our website and continue to receive the documents in paper form through the post.

If you make an election using this form, we may use electronic communications to send you any document or information we are required or authorised to send to you in your capacity as a shareholder, including:

- notices of meetings (including the AGM) and associated documents;
- the company's annual report and accounts and any documents, reports, notices that are required to be contained in it or sent with it under applicable rules and regulations;
- any summary financial statement;
- any other document or information that we are required or authorised to send to you under the company's articles of association or any applicable law, rule or regulation; and
- general shareholder correspondence and literature.

The available options

- Via e-mail
  If you choose this option, we will send you the documents in full in an e-mail or as an e-mail attachment to the e-mail address notified by you for these purposes.
- Notification of availability on our website
  If you choose this method, we will send you an e-mail (or, if you choose, a notification by post) informing you when the documents have been published on our web site. The notification will also tell you the address of the web site and how to find the information on the website. Unless you opt to continue to receive the relevant documents in paper form through the post, it will then be up to you whether to access the website and view the documents. The documents on the website will be made available in commonly used formats. You will, however, need to an internet connection in order to access them. If you choose to be notified by e-mail, we will send the e-mail to the address notified by you for these purposes.

Please read the following notes before making your election.

If you choose an option which requires the company to use an electronic address such as an e-mail address, you will need to inform us of the address you wish us to use and notify us whenever that address changes. You may inform us of such changes by [ ]. If you choose an option which requires the company to send any document or notification through the post, we will use the address that we currently use for these purposes which is normally your registered address.

If we are aware that an electronic transmission has failed, we will make at least one more attempt to send it. If that attempt fails, we will notify you by post that we have tried without apparent success to send you a document via your chosen method. If possible, we will also send you a copy of that document by post. However, this may not always be possible and the company will be deemed under the articles to have fulfilled its obligations to serve the document or notice on you at the first attempt, even though it failed.

The election that you make and any address that you provide will be used by us until you give us different instructions.

We may decide to send you certain documents through the post even though you have elected to receive them electronically. You should therefore continue to inform us of any change to your postal address.

We will take all reasonable precautions to ensure that no viruses are present in any communications sent electronically. However, we cannot accept any liability for any loss or damage arising from the opening or use of any e-mail or attachments.

I agree to accept, in the manner indicated below, and until such time as I notify the company otherwise, service of any document or information which the company may be required or authorised to send me in my capacity as a shareholder.

PLEASE TICK ONLY ONE OF OPTIONS A OR B

☐ *Option A: Notification of publication on our website*
If you select this option we will send you a notification when the relevant documents are published on our website. We will send the notification in the manner which you select and to the address you provide.

Please tick one of the following to indicate the method you would like us to use to send the notification and provide an e-mail address or fax number as appropriate.

☐ Notification sent by e-mail to _____

☐ Notification sent by post to my/our registered address

☐ *Option B: By sending the documents in full to the following e-mail address*

_____

DATA PROTECTION STATEMENT

A. The identity of the Data Controller

The company is a Data Controller for the purposes of the Data Protection Act 1998. This means that it is responsible for making decisions about how your personal data will be processed and how it may be used.

B. Use of your personal data

The company will record any election you make on this form and any information which you provide that is necessary for the company to give effect to that election. The data will be used to determine what methods the company may use to serve documents and notices on you and the address that should be used for that purpose. The company will use any e-mail address you supply only to send company documents connected with your election.

The company will disclose to [its registrars], some or all of the data you provide. The registrars will use that data solely for the purposes of distributing documents connected with your election. In addition, the company will receive certain administrative data from its registrars, which it has created for the purposes of carrying out its function as registrar and which relates to your shareholding.

C. Security of your personal data

The company has put in place appropriate technical and organisational measures to prevent the unauthorised or unlawful processing of your personal data. These include restricted access to databases that contain personal data, access restricted by password authentication and training of personnel on the rules of data protection and obligations of confidentiality.

D. Updating your personal data

Under the Data Protection Act you have the right to be told what personal data the company holds about you and to request that it be updated. This may be done by contacting: [name and address].

P. 2.9B Ordinary resolution to authorise the use of electronic communications

THAT the company be and is hereby generally and unconditionally authorised to use electronic communications with its shareholders and in particular authorised to send or supply documents or information to its shareholders by making them available on a website.

P. 2.9C Form of election – Deemed website communications consultation

Dear Shareholder,

One of the resolutions passed at the Annual General Meeting on [date] allows the company to send or supply documents and information to shareholders by making them available on a website. This method of communicating with shareholders will enable us to communicate with you in the most convenient way for you and will offer significant cost savings for the company, as well as reducing our impact on the environment.

Enclosed with this letter you will find a registration form for paper communications. Please read the information contained in this letter before making your decision. If you want to continue to receive paper communications from us, please return the form to our Registrar in the pre-paid envelope provided by [date]. Alternatively, you may register your choice at [website address].

If you do nothing you will be deemed to have agreed to access documents and information via the company's website at [website address]. You will not automatically receive paper documents from the company. If you do not provide us with an email address we will notify you by post when documents such as the annual report and accounts are published on our website.

Further information on electronic communications

The Companies Act 2006 contains provisions facilitating communications between companies and their shareholders in electronic form. As a result, companies can now change their principal method of communication from sending paper documents to making them available on a website.

There are a number of benefits associated with communicating electronically, some of which are detailed below. Given the benefits that electronic communications would have for the company and its shareholders, the directors proposed to change the company's principal method of communication to communication via website. The resolution approving this change was passed at the company's Annual General Meeting on [date].

We are now therefore giving you the opportunity to choose how we communicate with you in the future. You can elect to be part of the electronic communications initiative and access all documents via the company's website at [website address]. Alternatively, you can opt to continue to receive paper documents.

The benefits of electronic communications

The advantages of electronic communications are numerous both for shareholders and the company:

- Cost effective – Reduced printing and postage costs will save the company, and therefore you as its shareholders, money.

- Faster access – You will be able to access documents the day they are published on our website.
- Secure access – Your documents cannot be lost in the post.
- Environmentally friendly – Reducing the amount of paper used and the amount of harmful greenhouse gases produced during the printing and delivery of paper documents will help to protect the environment.

Questions and answers

I don't have an email address – how will you let me know that something is available on the website?

Shareholders who do not have an email address will be notified by post when new documents become available on our website at [website address]. Any notification, whether by email or by post, will provide the following information:

- the address of the website on which the document is available (this might not always be the company's website);
- the place on the website where the document may be accessed;
- how the document or information may be accessed.

I am already signed up to receive electronic communications from the company. How do these changes affect me?

If you have already elected to receive electronic communications and you wish to continue receiving electronic communications in the future, you do not need to return the registration form. If however you would like to revert to receiving paper documents, please complete the registration form.

How do I register my email address?

You can change the email address we have for you at [website address]. If you have not already provided us with an email address, you can register your email address at the same website.

What do I need in order to access the company's website?

You will need:

- A computer which has access to the internet; and
- Adobe Acrobat Reader (in order to view Adobe Acrobat documents) which you can download free of charge from www.adobe.com.

What happens if I opt for electronic communications and then decide that I want to receive paper documents again?

You can change the method by which the company communicates with you at any time via the company's website at [website address]. In addition you may request a paper copy of any document without changing your election by [method].

What documents will be available on the website?

Documents such as the annual report and accounts and notices of shareholder meetings will be available on our website. We may also use this method of communication for any documents or information required or authorised to be sent or supplied by us to you under the Companies Act and for other regulatory purposes.

Yours sincerely

Secretary

REGISTRATION FORM

[Shareholder details]   [Shareholder Reference Number]

Please use a black pen
to mark an X inside
the box.

I would like to receive paper communications by post	

To continue to receive documents and information from us in printed form please mark a cross in the box above and return this form in the pre-paid envelope provided. If you hold shares jointly with someone else, you should obtain the consent of all the joint holders before returning this form.

If you do not return this completed form to us by [date], you will be deemed to have agreed to access information and documentation via our website at [website address] and you will no longer automatically receive paper copies of documents and information from us.

If you wish to access documents and information via our website and to be notified by email when they become available, please register your details at [website address].

[See the *Notes* to **Precedent 2.9D**.]

P. 2.9D Form of election – Alternative form for website communications

REGISTRATION FORM

Please complete your name and details (in block capitals) in the relevant section below and sign this reply slip before returning it to [the company/our registrars] in the pre-paid envelope provided.

I would like to continue to receive paper communications by post

Full name of shareholder(s) . . . .
Full address of shareholder . . . .
[Investor code . . . .]
Signature of shareholder(s) . . . .

I wish to receive notification by email that copies of documents and information from the company have been placed on a website

Full name of shareholder(s) . . . .
Full email address of shareholder . . . .
[Investor code . . . .]
Signature of shareholder(s) . . . .

[*Note:* In this example, shareholders are expected to sign the form. One of the reasons why is because the form can also be used to notify an email address for the purposes of notifications regarding website communications. The requirement to sign the form could make it more difficult to complete for joint shareholders and corporate shareholders. In the above example, the shareholder could be required to enter a unique investor code, which could serve as some sort of proof of their identity and may enable a more relaxed approach to be taken with regard to signatures of joint holders and execution by corporate shareholders. The Registration Form in **Precedent 2.9C** does not require any signature. This is partly because the form includes sufficient details to enable the shareholder to be identified (by virtue of the inclusion by the company of the shareholder's unique reference number) and partly because the making of the mark in the box is intended to serve as an indication of shareholder's agreement to the statement. The person making the mark is assumed to have authority and to have obtained the necessary agreement of any joint holders. The form in **Precedent 2.9C** is not designed to enable shareholders to provide an email address for the purposes of website communications notifications. It is arguable that if it was, a signature ought to be required, and that if a signature was required to do one thing (i.e. notify an email address), it might look strange if it was not also required for the other (i.e. elect to receive paper communications).]

CHAPTER 3: DIRECTORS

P. 3.3A Board minute of resolution to appoint managing director

There was produced a draft of a service contract between the company and [name] appointing [name] as managing director of the company with effect from [date], on the terms and conditions set out in the service contract.

It was resolved:

THAT [name] be appointed managing director of the company with effect from [date] on the terms set out in the service contract produced at the meeting and that the chairman be authorised to sign the service agreement on behalf of the company.

P. 3.3B Extract from directors' service agreement

The director shall exercise such powers and functions and perform such duties in relation to the company or any of its subsidiaries and associates as may from time to time be vested in or assigned to him by the board and shall comply with all directions from time to time given to him by the Board (or anyone authorised by the board) and with all rules and regulations from time to time laid down by the company concerning employees.

CHAPTER 4: BOARD MEETINGS

P. 4.5 Notice of board meeting

XYZ LIMITED

[Address]
[Date]

To the directors of XYZ Limited

Notice of board meeting
A meeting of the directors of the company will be held at [place] on [date] at [time].

[Signature]
Secretary
By order of the chairman

P. 4.6A Agenda for board meeting of public company

XYZ PLC

Agenda for board meeting to be held at [place] on [date] at [time].

Item		Agenda paper
1.	*Minutes of previous meeting*	
	To approve the minutes of the board meeting held on [date].	2013/04-01
2.	*Management accounts* To consider:	
	(a) a list of bank balances as at [date];	2013/04-02a
	(b) cash flow statements for the period to [date];	2013/04-02b
	(c) financial statement as at [date].	2013/04-02c
3.	*Audit committee* To note the minutes of the [audit] committee meeting held on [date], and the committee's recommendations regarding the financial statements.	2013/04-03
4.	*Annual report and accounts* To approve the directors' report, [directors' remuneration report], chairman's statement, corporate governance reports, statement of directors' responsibility, and annual accounts for the financial year ended [date].	2013/04-04

Item		Agenda paper
5.	*Dividend* To recommend a final dividend of [ ]p per share recommended therein (making a total dividend of [ ]p per share for the year) be approved and that, subject to approval by the company in general meeting, such dividend be paid on [date] to shareholders registered at the close of business on [date].	2013/04-5
6.	*Preliminary announcement* To authorised the release of the preliminary announcement of the results for the year ended [date].	2013/04-6
7.	*Sealing* To authorise the affixing of the common seal of the company to the documents set out against items Nos. . . . to . . . inclusive in the sealing register.	2013/04-7 briefly explains each transaction
8.	*Future meetings* To confirm the dates (and general themes) of future board meetings.	2013/04-8

[Date]

[Secretary]

By order of the Chairman

P. 4.6B Agenda for first board meeting (private company)

XYZ LIMITED

Agenda for board meeting to be held at [place] on [date] at [time]

1. To produce the certificate of incorporation and a copy of the memorandum and articles of association as registered.
2. To note that the first directors of the company named by the subscribers in the documents delivered to the Registrar of Companies with the memorandum of association are: [names].
3. To consider and, if thought fit, resolve that [name of director] be appointed chairman of the board.
4. To note that [name] was named by the subscribers as secretary in the documents delivered to the Registrar of Companies and to consider and, if thought fit, resolve:
   THAT the appointment of [name] as secretary be confirmed at a salary payable from [date] at the rate of [amount] per annum, such appointment being terminable by [period] notice in writing given by either party to the other at any time.

5. To consider and, if thought fit, resolve:
   THAT the situation of the company's registered office shown in the documents delivered with the memorandum to the Registrar of Companies (namely, [address]) be confirmed.
6. To consider and, if thought fit, resolve:
   THAT the seal, of which an impression is affixed in the margin hereof, be adopted as the common seal of the company.
7. To consider opening a bank account with [name of bank] and, if thought fit, resolve:
   [Resolutions in accordance with bank's printed form for opening an account.]
8. To consider and, if thought fit, resolve:
   THAT [name] be appointed auditors of the company.
9. To produce and read to the meeting declarations made by the directors of interests in transactions or arrangements pursuant to sections 177 and 182 of the Companies Act 2006.
10. To produce forms of application for 98 shares of £1 each in the capital of the company, together with cheques for a total of £100, being payment in full for the said shares and the two shares taken by the subscribers to the memorandum of association.
    To consider and, if thought fit, resolve:
    (a) THAT 49 shares of £1 each, fully paid and numbered 3 to 51 inclusive, be allotted to [applicant 1];
    (b) THAT 49 shares of £1 each, fully paid and numbered 52 to 100 inclusive, be allotted to [applicant 2];
    (c) THAT all the shares of the company shall henceforth cease to bear distinguishing numbers;
    (c) THAT the undermentioned share certificates drawn in respect of subscribers' shares and the allotments made by resolutions (a) and (b) above be approved and that the common seal be affixed thereto:
    No. 1   [applicant 1]   50 shares
    No. 2   [applicant 2]   50 shares
11. To consider fixing dates for future board meetings.

P. 4.6C Minutes of first board meeting (private company)

XYZ LIMITED

Minutes of a board meeting held at [place] on [date] at [time]
Present: [name] (chairman)
                  [name]
In attendance: [name] (secretary)

1. There were produced the certificate of incorporation and a copy of the memorandum and articles of association as registered.

2. It was noted that the first directors of the company named by the subscribers in the documents delivered to the Registrar of Companies with the memorandum of association are: [names].

3. It was resolved:

   THAT [name of director] be appointed chairman of the board.

4. It was noted that [name] was named by the subscribers as secretary in the documents delivered to the Registrar of Companies and resolved:

   THAT the appointment of [name] as secretary be confirmed at a salary payable from [date] at the rate of [amount] per annum, such appointment being terminable by [period] notice in writing given by either party to the other at any time.

5. It was resolved:

   THAT the situation of the company's registered office shown in the documents delivered with the memorandum to the Registrar of Companies (namely, [address]) be confirmed.

6. It was resolved:

   THAT the seal, of which an impression is affixed in the margin hereof, be adopted as the common seal of the company.

7. It was resolved:

   THAT a bank account be opened with [name of bank] and . . . [Resolutions in accordance with bank's printed form for opening an account.]

8. It was resolved:

   THAT [name] be appointed auditors of the company to hold office until the conclusion of the first general meeting at which accounts are laid before the company.

9. There were produced and read to the meeting notices given by [names of directors] pursuant to sections 177 and 182 of the Companies Act 2006. The secretary was instructed to enter details of the declarations in a register that is to be kept for this purpose.

10. There were produced forms of application for 98 shares of £1 each in the capital of the company, together with cheques for a total of £100, being payment in full for the said shares and the two shares taken by the subscribers to the memorandum of association.

    It was resolved:

    (a) THAT 49 shares of £1 each, fully paid and numbered 3 to 51 inclusive, be alloted to [applicant 1];

    (b) THAT 49 shares of £1 each, fully paid and numbered 52 to 100 inclusive, be alloted to [applicant 2];

    (c) THAT all the shares of the company shall henceforth cease to bear distinguishing numbers.

    (d) THAT the undermentioned share certificates drawn in respect of subscribers' shares and the allotments made by resolutions (a) and (b) above be approved and that the common seal be affixed thereto:

No. 1   [applicant 1]   50 shares
No. 2   [applicant 2]   50 shares

11. It was resolved that the next meeting of the board of directors would be held at [place] on [date] at [time].

[Signed]

[Chairman]

P. 4.8A Quorum – Board resolution to fix quorum for meetings of directors

THAT pursuant to article [no.] of the articles of association of the company the quorum necessary for the transaction of the business of the directors be fixed at three.

P. 4.8B Quorum – Article allowing interested directors to vote and be counted in quorum

A director may vote at a meeting of directors or any committee of directors on any contract or arrangement in which he is interested and on any incidental matter, and a director who is so interested shall be counted in calculating whether a quorum exists for that item of business[; and Regulation 94 of Table A shall be modified accordingly].

P. 4.8C Quorum – Article allowing sole director to act

The quorum for the transaction of business of the directors may be fixed by the directors and unless so fixed at any other number shall be two; but if and so long as there is a sole director, he may exercise all the powers and authorities vested in the directors by these Articles [and Table A; and Regulation 89 of Table A shall be modified accordingly]. A person who holds office only as an alternate director shall, if his appointor is not present, be counted in the quorum.

P. 4.10 Quorum – Article allowing directors to attending meetings by telephone to be counted in the quorum

The quorum necessary for the transaction of business of the Board may be fixed from time to time by the Board and unless so fixed at any other number shall be three. For the purposes of these Articles any Director who is able (directly or by telephonic communication) to speak and be heard by each of the other Directors present or deemed to be present at any meeting of the Board, shall be deemed to be present in person at such meeting and shall be entitled to vote or be counted in the quorum accordingly. Such meeting shall be deemed to take place where the largest group of those participating is assembled, or, if there is no such group, where the chairman of the meeting then is, and the word "meeting" shall be construed accordingly.

P. 4.11A Alternate director – Form of appointment

Pursuant to article [no.] of the articles of association of [name of company] and subject to the approval of the board of [name of company], I [name of director making appointment] being a director of [name of company] hereby appoint [name of person to be appointed as alternate] to be my alternate director.

P. 4.11B Alternate director – Board resolution approving appointment of

There was produced a form of appointment dated [date] by which [name of director] appoints [name of alternate] to be his alternate director.

It was resolved THAT the appointment by [name of director] of [name of alternate] to be his alternate director be approved.

P. 4.11C Alternate director – Form of revocation of appointment

Pursuant to article [no.] of the articles of association of [name of company], I hereby revoke the appointment dated [date] of [name of alternate appointed] as my alternate director.

P. 4.11D Alternate director – Board minute noting revocation of appointment

A form of revocation dated [date] by which [name of director] revokes the appointment of [name of alternate] as his alternate was produced and noted.

P. 4.12A Director's interests – General notice of interests in transactions or arrangements

The Directors

.... Limited/p.l.c.

Pursuant to section 185, Companies Act 2006, I give notice that I have the interest in each of the companies or firms listed below which is shown against its name below and that I am to be regarded as interested in any transaction or arrangement which may, after the date hereof, be made with any of the those companies and firms.

Name of company or firm	Nature and extent of interest

I also give notice under that section that I am connected with each of the person(s) listed below and am to be regarded as interested in any transaction or arrangement which may, after the date hereof, be made with any of the under-mentioned persons.

Name of person	Nature of connection with that person
(Date)	*(Signature)*

P. 4.12B Director's interests – Board minute relating to general notice

There was produced and read to the meeting a notice dated [date] given by [name of director] pursuant to section 185 of the Companies Act 2006 [which has been entered in the Company's register of directors interests as entry no [x]].

[*Note:* Such notices would normally be kept in a separate register, which effectively forms a subset of the minutes. The reference in the minutes may also refer to the serial number of the entry in this register. If the company does not keep a separate register, details of the interests notified should be minuted.]

CHAPTER 5: COMMITTEES OF DIRECTORS

P. 5.2A   Board resolution to appoint committee

THAT, pursuant to article [no.] of the company's articles of association, A, B, and C (any two of whom shall be a quorum) be appointed a committee with power to . . .

P. 5.4 Board resolution to appoint committee of any two directors

THAT, pursuant to article [no.] of the company's articles of association, any two directors be appointed a committee to take such action and to complete all documents necessary for [reason].

P. 5.11 Written resolution of committee of one director

XYZ LIMITED

Pursuant to the authority given by article [no.] of the company's articles of association, I, the undersigned, being the sole member of a committee established by the board of directors on [date] to [short description of purpose], hereby resolve;

THAT . . . . .

[Date]

[Signature]

P. 5.15 Nomination committee – ICSA's model terms of reference

[Updated October 2010]

1. *Membership*
   1.1 The committee shall comprise at least [three] directors. A majority of the members of the committee shall be independent non-executive directors.
   1.2 Only members of the committee have the right to attend committee meetings. However, other individuals such as the chief executive, the head of human resources and external advisers may be invited to attend for all or part of any meeting, as and when appropriate and necessary.
   1.3 Appointments to the committee are made by the board and shall be for a period of up to three years, which may be extended for further periods of up to three-years, provided the director still meets the criteria for membership of the committee.
   1.4 The board shall appoint the committee chairman who should be either the chairman of the board or an independent non-executive director. In the absence of the committee chairman and/or an appointed deputy, the remaining members present shall elect one of themselves to chair the meeting from those who would qualify under these terms of reference to be appointed to that position by the board. The chairman of the board shall not chair the committee when it is dealing with the matter of succession to the chairmanship.

2. *Secretary*
   The company secretary or his or her nominee shall act as the secretary of the committee.

3. *Quorum*
   The quorum necessary for the transaction of business shall be [two] [both of whom must be independent non-executive directors]. A duly convened meeting of the committee at which a quorum is present shall be competent to exercise all or any of the authorities, powers and discretions vested in or exercisable by the committee.

4. *Frequency of meetings*
   The committee shall meet at least [twice] a year[1] and otherwise as required.[2]

5. *Notice of meetings*
   5.1 Meetings of the committee shall be called by the secretary of the committee at the request of the committee chairman.

5.2 Unless otherwise agreed, notice of each meeting confirming the venue, time and date, together with an agenda of items to be discussed, shall be forwarded to each member of the committee, any other person required to attend and all other non-executive directors, no later than [five] working days before the date of the meeting. Supporting papers shall be sent to committee members and to other attendees as appropriate, at the same time.

6. *Minutes of meetings*
   6.1 The secretary shall minute the proceedings and resolutions of all meetings of the committee, including the names of those present and in attendance.
   6.2 Draft minutes of committee meetings shall be circulated promptly to all members of the committee. Once approved, minutes should be circulated to all other members of the board unless it would be inappropriate to do so.

7. *Annual General Meeting*
   The committee chairman should attend the annual general meeting to answer any shareholder questions on the committee's activities.

8. *Duties*
   The committee should carry out the duties below for the parent company, major subsidiary undertakings and the group as a whole, as appropriate.
   The committee shall:
   8.1 regularly review the structure, size and composition (including the skills, knowledge, experience and diversity) of the board and make recommendations to the board with regard to any changes;
   8.2 give full consideration to succession planning for directors and other senior executives in the course of its work, taking into account the challenges and opportunities facing the company, and the skills and expertise needed on the board in the future;
   8.3 keep under review the leadership needs of the organisation, both executive and non-executive, with a view to ensuring the continued ability of the organisation to compete effectively in the marketplace;
   8.4 keep up to date and fully informed about strategic issues and commercial changes affecting the company and the market in which it operates;
   8.5 be responsible for identifying and nominating for the approval of the board, candidates to fill board vacancies as and when they arise;
   8.6 before any appointment is made by the board, evaluate the balance of skills, knowledge, experience and diversity on the board, and, in the light of this evaluation prepare a description of the role and capabilities required for a particular appointment. In identifying suitable candidates the committee shall:

8.6.1 use open advertising or the services of external advisers to facilitate the search,

8.6.2 consider candidates from a wide range of backgrounds,

8.6.3 consider candidates on merit and against objective criteria and with due regard for the benefits of diversity on the board, including gender, taking care that appointees have enough time available to devote to the position[3]

8.7 for the appointment of a chairman, the committee should prepare a job specification, including the time commitment expected. A proposed chairman's other significant commitments should be disclosed to the board before appointment and any changes to the chairman's commitments should be reported to the board as they arise[4];

8.8 prior to the appointment of a director, the proposed appointee should be required to disclose any other business interests that may result in a conflict of interest and be required to report any future business interests that could result in a conflict of interest[5];

8.9 ensure that on appointment to the board, non-executive directors receive a formal letter of appointment setting out clearly what is expected of them in terms of time commitment, committee service and involvement outside board meetings;

8.10 review the results of the board performance evaluation process that relate to the composition of the board;

8.11 review annually the time required from non-executive directors. Performance evaluation should be used to assess whether the non-executive directors are spending enough time to fulfil their duties.

The committee shall also make recommendations to the board concerning:

8.12 formulating plans for succession for both executive and non-executive directors and in particular for the key roles of chairman and chief executive;

8.13 suitable candidates for the role of senior independent director;

8.14 membership of the audit and remuneration committees, and any other board committees as appropriate, in consultation with the chairmen of those committees;

8.15 the re-appointment of any non-executive director at the conclusion of their specified term of office having given due regard to their performance and ability to continue to contribute to the board in the light of the knowledge, skills and experience required;

8.16 the re-election by shareholders of directors under the annual re-election provisions of the Code[6] or the retirement by rotation provisions in the company's articles of association, having due regard to their performance and ability to continue to contribute to the board in the light of the knowledge, skills and experience required and the need for progressive refreshing of the board (particularly in relation to directors being re-elected for a term beyond six years);

8.17 any matters relating to the continuation in office of any director at any time including the suspension or termination of service of an executive director as an employee of the company subject to the provisions of the law and their service contract;

8.18 the appointment of any director to executive or other office.

9. *Reporting responsibilities*

9.1 The committee chairman shall report to the board on its proceedings after each meeting on all matters within its duties and responsibilities.

9.2 The committee shall make whatever recommendations to the board it deems appropriate on any area within its remit where action or improvement is needed.

9.3 The committee shall produce a report to be included in the company's annual report about its activities, the process used to make appointments and explain if external advice or open advertising has not been used.

10. *Other matters*

The committee shall

10.1 have access to sufficient resources in order to carry out its duties, including access to the company secretariat for assistance as required;

10.2 be provided with appropriate and timely training, both in the form of an induction programme for new members and on an ongoing basis for all members;

10.3 give due consideration to laws and regulations, the provisions of the Code and the requirements of the UK Listing Authority's Listing, Prospectus and Disclosure and Transparency Rules and any other applicable Rules, as appropriate;

10.4 arrange for periodic reviews of its own performance and, at least annually, review its constitution and terms of reference to ensure it is operating at maximum effectiveness and recommend any changes it considers necessary to the board for approval.

11. *Authority*

The committee is authorised by the board to obtain, at the company's expense, outside legal or other professional advice on any matters within its terms of reference.

Notes

1. Some small companies and investment trusts may not need more than one scheduled meeting of the nomination committee each year.

2. The frequency and timing of meetings will differ according to the needs of the company. Meetings should be organised so that attendance is maximised (for example by timetabling them to coincide with board meetings).

3. When considering a new appointment the proposed new non-executive director's other commitments should be taken into account to ensure he or she
has sufficient time to devote to the company. For an appointment to an FSA
regulated company, FSA policy statement 10/15 page 26 states the FSA will
consider the candidate's existing commitments when assessing their suitability for the role.
4. UK Corporate Governance Code, provision B.3.1. This information should
also be disclosed in the next annual report.
5. Companies Act 2006, s. 175
6. UK Corporate Governance Code, provision B.7.1

CHAPTER 6: DIRECTORS' WRITTEN RESOLUTIONS AND INFORMAL CONSENT

P. 6.2A Written resolution of the directors

XYZ LIMITED

Pursuant to the authority given by article [no.] of the company's articles of association, we, the undersigned, being all the directors of XYZ Limited [entitled to
receive notice of a meeting of directors (option under Table A)] [eligible to vote
on the following resolution had it been proposed at a directors' meeting (option
under the model articles)], hereby resolve;

THAT . . . . .

[Date]

[Signatures]

P. 6.2B Article allowing written resolutions approved by a percentage of directors

A resolution in writing signed or approved [by fax or by any electronic system
or by telephone and subsequently confirmed in writing or by fax or by electronic
systems] by not less than [90%] of the directors [for the time being in the United
Kingdom and] entitled to vote thereon shall be as valid and effectual as a resolution duly passed at a meeting of the directors and may consist of several documents or other such forms of approval in the like form each signed or so approved
by one or more directors.

CHAPTER 8:   MEMBERS' DECISIONS

P. 8.7 Form for the nomination of indirect investors

ICSA **INFORMATION RIGHTS NOMINATION FORM**
REGISTRARS GROUP

This form is to be completed by a registered holder of shares for the purposes of nominating a beneficial owner to receive shareholder documents in accordance with sections 146 – 151 of the Companies Act 2006 and for updating or terminating previously lodged nominations.

Full name of company in which shares are held

Section A: Registered Shareholder Details

Full name of registered shareholder

Account Designation (If any)

CREST member account ID
(only applicable for holders in CREST)

Participant ID

Address of registered shareholder

Security Description

ISIN – if known

Section B: Adding or Deleting Nominated Persons Details

Custodian Reference – to be used in all future communications with relation to this holder

Please tick one of the following: Add ☐   Delete ☐

Full name of nominated person

Address of nominated person

Email address / new email address of nomination person (leave blank if terminating a nomination)

Communication preference – please tick as appropriate:
Hard Copy ☐   Email ☐

Website communication will be adopted as a default position where an email address is supplied.

PLEASE RETURN THIS FORM TO THE APPROPRIATE REGISTRAR FOR PROCESSING

ICSA INFORMATION RIGHTS NOMINATION FORM
REGISTRARS GROUP

Section C: Editing Nominated Persons details

Previous Full name of nominated person

Previous Address of nominated person

Custodian Reference – used on all previous communications with relation to this holder

Previous email address of nominated person

New Full name of nominated person

New Address of nominated person

New email address of nomination person

Communication preference – please tick as appropriate:

Hard Copy ☐   Email ☐

Website communication will be adopted as a default position where an email address is supplied.

PLEASE RETURN THIS FORM TO THE APPROPRIATE REGISTRAR FOR PROCESSING

CHAPTER 9: MEMBERS' WRITTEN RESOLUTIONS AND UNANIMOUS CONSENT

P. 9.2A Written resolution (members)

.... LIMITED

[Address]

Circulation Date: [Date].

We, the undersigned, being members of the Company eligible to vote on the proposals at the time and date of circulation, hereby pass the following resolution(s) pursuant to sections 288 to 300 of the Companies Act 2006:

As a Special Resolution
THAT ....

As an Ordinary Resolution
THAT ....

(Signatures)   (Date of signature)

Notes:
1. Members may signify their agreement to the resolution by returning a hard copy of the resolution signed by them (or on their behalf) to the company at the address shown above. Agreement may also be signified by e-mail as follows: ....
2. The proposed resolution(s) will lapse if not passed within the period of 28 days beginning with the circulation date shown above.

P. 9.2B   Written resolution (class of members)
.... LIMITED

[Address]

Circulation Date: [Date].

We, the undersigned, being members of the Company eligible to vote on the proposals at the time and date of circulation, hereby pass the following resolution(s) as a written resolution in accordance with Chapter 2 of Part 13 of the Companies Act 2006:

As a Special Resolution
THAT ....

(Signatures)   (Date of signature)

Notes:
1. Members may signify their agreement to the resolution by returning a hard copy of the resolution signed by them (or on their behalf) to the company at the address shown above. Agreement may also be signified by e-mail as follows: ....
2. The proposed resolution(s) will lapse if not passed within the period of [28 days] beginning with the circulation date shown above.

[*Note:* The date of the resolution is the date when it was signed by the last member required to sign in order to pass the resolution by the requisite majority. Special care will need to be taken if the same written resolution is used to propose both a special resolution and an ordinary resolution. In those circumstances, it may be preferable to make the resolutions the subject of separate written resolutions.]

P. 9.2C.............................LIMITED

Letter to auditors to accompany copy of statutory written resolution

[On the company's headed stationery]

To: the Auditors

Proposed written resolution

We enclose a copy of a resolution which it is proposed to be agreed as a written resolution of the above-named company in accordance with Chapter 2 of Part 13 of the Companies Act 2006 ("the Act") [together with the documents which are required by the Act to be circulated with it to members of the company]. This copy is being sent to you for your information in accordance with the requirements of section 502(1) of the Act. No action on your part is required. However, if you would like to discuss any matter regarding the proposed resolution that concerns you as the company's auditors, please do not hesitate to contact me.

Yours faithfully,

Secretary

On behalf of XYZ Limited

P. 9.2D   Record of a written resolution

Record of a written resolution of XYZ LIMITED

The following resolution(s) was/were passed as a written resolution on [date], being the date on which the written resolution was signed by the last member required to do so in order to pass the resolutions:

A copy of the resolution was delivered to the auditors on [date].

The signatories to the resolution were:
[Names of directors]

Signature
[Director/Secretary]
[Date]

P. 9.6 Record of decision by sole member of a company

XYZ LIMITED

Written record of a decision made by the sole member of the Company which could have been taken by the company in general meeting and has effect as if it were so taken.

The following resolution, having effect as an [ordinary/special] resolution, was approved on [date] by a decision of the undersigned sole member of the Company:

THAT ....

[Signature]
[Date]

CHAPTER 10: ANNUAL GENERAL MEETINGS

P. 10.3 Notice of annual general meeting of listed company

NOTICE OF XYZ ANNUAL GENERAL MEETING 2010

This document is important and requires your immediate attention. If you are in any doubt about the action you should take, you should consult an appropriate independent financial adviser. If you have recently sold or transferred your shares in XYZ plc you should forward this document to your bank, stockbroker or other agent through whom the sale or transfer was effected for transmission to the purchaser or transferee.

[Chairman's letter – will normally include directors' recommendations on how to vote on the business]

Notice of XYZ Annual General Meeting [year]

Notice is hereby given that an Annual General Meeting of XYZ PLC (the Company) will be held at [place] on [date] at [time] for the following purposes:

[Ordinary business]

Resolution 1 – Report and accounts
Ordinary Resolution: To receive the report of the directors and the accounts for the year ended [date]. *See notes on page [x].*

Resolution 2 – Dividend
Ordinary Resolution: To approve the final dividend recommended by the directors. *See notes on page [x].*

Resolution 3 – Directors' remuneration report
Ordinary Resolution: To approve the directors' remuneration report for the year ended [date]. *See notes on page [x].*

Resolution 4 – Re-election of director
Ordinary Resolution: To re-elect [director A] as a director. *See biography on page [x].*

Resolution 5 – Re-election of director
Ordinary Resolution: To re-elect [director B] as a director. *See biography on page [x].*

Resolution 6 – Re-election of director

Ordinary Resolution: To re-elect [director C] as a director. *See biography on page [x].*

Resolution 7 – Reappointment of auditors

Ordinary Resolution: To reappoint [name of auditors] as auditors from the conclusion of this meeting until the conclusion of the next general meeting before which accounts are laid and to authorise the directors to fix the auditors' remuneration. *See notes on page [x].*

[Special business]

Resolution 8 – Share buyback

Special Resolution: To authorise the company generally and unconditionally to make market purchases (as defined in section 693(2) of the Companies Act 2006) of ordinary shares with nominal value of [nominal value] each in the company, provided that:

(a) the company does not purchase under this authority more than [number] ordinary shares;

(b) the company does not pay less than [amount] for each share; and

(c) the company does not pay more for each share than 5% over the average of the middle market price of the ordinary shares for the five business days immediately preceding the date on which the company agrees to buy the shares concerned, based on share prices and currency exchange rates published in the Daily Official List of the London Stock Exchange.

This authority shall continue for the period ending on the date of the annual general meeting in 2011 or 15 [date], whichever is the earlier, provided that, if the company has agreed before this date to purchase ordinary shares where these purchases will or may be executed after the authority terminates (either wholly or in part), the company may complete such purchases.

See notes on page [x].

Resolution 9 – Directors' authority to allot shares (Section 551)

Ordinary Resolution:

(A) THAT the board be and it is hereby generally and unconditionally authorised to exercise all powers of the company to allot relevant securities (within the meaning of section 551 of the Companies Act 2006) up to an aggregate nominal amount of £... A... provided that this authority shall expire on ....*...... save that the company may before such expiry make an offer or agreement which would or might require relevant securities to be allotted after such expiry and the board may allot relevant securities in pursuance of such an offer or agreement as if the authority conferred hereby had not expired, and further,

(B) THAT the board be and it is hereby generally and unconditionally authorised to exercise all powers of the company to allot equity securities (within the meaning of section 560 of the said Act) in connection with a rights issue in favour of ordinary shareholders where the equity securities respectively attributable to the interests of all ordinary shareholders are proportionate (as nearly as may be) to the respective numbers of ordinary shares held by them up to an aggregate nominal amount of £... A... provided that this authority shall expire on the date of the next annual general meeting of the company after the passing of this resolution save that the company may before such expiry make an offer or agreement which would or might require relevant securities to be allotted after such expiry and the board may allot relevant securities in pursuance of such an offer or agreement as if the authority conferred hereby had not expired.

Resolution 10 – Disapplication of pre-emption rights
Special Resolution:
Subject to the passing of the previous resolution, to authorise the board pursuant to section 570 of the Companies Act 2006 to allot equity securities (within the meaning of section 560 of the said Act) for cash pursuant to the authority conferred by the previous resolution as if sub-section (1) of section 561 of the said Act did not apply to any such allotment provided that this power shall be limited

(i) to the allotment of equity securities in connection with a rights issue in favour of ordinary shareholders where the equity securities respectively attributable to the interests of all Ordinary shareholders are proportionate (as nearly as may be) to the respective numbers of Ordinary shares held by them and,
(ii) to the allotment (otherwise than pursuant to sub-paragraph (i) above) of equity securities up to an aggregate nominal value of £... B...

and shall expire (on the date of the next annual general meeting of the company after the passing of this resolution) save that the company may before such expiry make an offer or agreement which would or might require equity securities to be allotted after such expiry and the board may allot equity securities in pursuance of such an offer or agreement as if the power conferred hereby had not expired.
See notes on page [x].

Resolution 11 – Notice of general meetings
Special Resolution: To authorise the calling of general meetings of the company (not being an annual general meeting) by notice of at least 14 clear days. *See notes on page [x].*

By order of the board
[name]
Company Secretary
[date]

NOTES:
Members' right to appoint a proxy
1. A member entitled to attend and vote at the meeting is entitled to appoint one or more proxies to attend and vote on his or her behalf. A proxy need not also be a member. A member may appoint more than one proxy in relation to the meeting provided that each proxy is appointed to exercise the rights to a different share or shares held by the member.
2. To be effective the proxy appointment must be completed in accordance with the instructions and received by the company's registrars no later than 48 hours before the time for which the meeting is convened.
[Further instructions on how to appoint proxies]

CREST
3. CREST members who wish to appoint a proxy or proxies through the CREST electronic proxy appointment service may do so for the AGM and any adjournment by using the procedures described in the CREST Manual. CREST personal members or other CREST sponsored members and those CREST members who have appointed a voting service provider should refer to their CREST sponsor or voting service provider, who will be able to take the appropriate action on their behalf. In order for a proxy appointment or instruction made using the CREST service to be valid, the appropriate CREST message (a CREST Proxy Instruction) must be properly authenticated in accordance with Euroclear's specifications and must contain the information required for such instructions, as described in the CREST Manual. All messages relating to the appointment of a proxy or an instruction to a previously appointed proxy must be transmitted so as to be received by our Registrar [CREST ID] by [time and date]. It is the responsibility of the CREST member concerned to take such action as shall be necessary to ensure that a message is transmitted by means of the CREST system by any particular time. In this connection, CREST members and, where applicable, their CREST sponsors or voting service providers are referred, in particular, to those sections of the CREST Manual concerning practical limitations of the CREST system and timings. The company may treat a CREST Proxy Instruction as invalid in the circumstances set out in Regulation 35(5)(a) of the Uncertificated Securities Regulations 2001.

Indirect investors
4. Any person to whom this notice of general meeting has been sent, whose shares are held on their behalf by another person and who has been nominated to receive communications from the company in accordance with section 146 of the Companies Act 2006 (a 'nominated person') may have a right under an agreement with the registered shareholder who holds the shares on their behalf to be appointed (or to have someone else appointed) as a proxy. If a nominated person has no such right, or does not wish to exercise it, they

may have a right under such an agreement to give instructions to the person holding the shares as to the exercise of voting rights.

5. The statement of the rights of shareholders in relation to the appointment of proxies in notes 1 to 3 above do not apply to nominated persons. The rights described in these notes can only be exercised by shareholders.

Record date for attendance and voting

6. To be entitled to attend and vote at the meeting (and for the purpose of the determination by the company of the number of votes they may cast), members must be entered on the company's register of members at [time and date not more than 48 hours before the time fixed for the meeting] ('the specified time'). If the meeting is adjourned to a time not more than 48 hours after the specified time applicable to the original meeting, that time will also apply for the purpose of determining the entitlement of members to attend and vote (and for the purpose of determining the number of votes they may cast) at the adjourned meeting. If, however, the meeting is adjourned for a longer period then, to be so entitled, members must be entered on the company's register of members at the time which is [number of hours, e.g. 48] before the time fixed for the adjourned meeting or, if the Company gives notice of the adjourned meeting, at the time specified in that notice.

Shares in issue at [date]

7. As at [date] (being the latest practicable date prior to the printing of this notice) the issued share capital of the company conferring the right to vote at the meeting consisted of. . . . . .. Therefore the total number of voting rights in the company as at that date was . . . .

Audit concerns

8. Members satisfying the requirements of section 527 of the Companies Act 2006 may require the company to publish on a website a statement by them (at the company's cost) relating to the audit of the company's accounts which are being laid before this meeting (including the auditor's report and the conduct of the audit) or, where applicable, any circumstances connected with an auditor of the company ceasing to hold since the previous general meeting at which accounts were laid. As at [date], no such statement has been received by the company. Should such a statement be received, it will be published on the company's website at www.......... In those circumstances the company would be under an obligation to forward a copy of the statement to the auditors forthwith and the statement would form part of the business which may be dealt with at this meeting.

Holders of [class of shares]

9. This notice is sent for information only to holders of [class of shares], who are not entitled to attend and vote at the meeting.

[Corporate representatives

10. In order to facilitate voting by corporate representatives at the meeting, arrangements will be put in place at the meeting so that:

(i) if a corporate shareholder has appointed the Chairman of the meeting as its corporate representative with instructions to vote on a poll in accordance with the directions of all of the other corporate representatives for that shareholder at the meeting, then on a poll those corporate representatives will give voting directions to the Chairman and the Chairman will vote (or withhold a vote) as corporate representative in accordance with those directions; and

(ii) if more than one corporate representative for the same corporate shareholder attends the meeting but the corporate shareholder has not appointed the Chairman of the meeting as its corporate representative, a designated corporate representative will be nominated, from those corporate representatives who attend, who will vote on a poll and the other corporate representatives will give voting directions to that designated corporate representative. Corporate shareholders are referred to the guidance issued by the Institute of Chartered Secretaries and Administrators on proxies and corporate representatives — www.icsa.org.uk — for further details of this procedure. The guidance includes a sample form of representation letter if the Chairman is being appointed as described in (i) above.]

[Notes 3–8 would not be required if the company was not publicly traded. Note 9 is included for the purposes of clarification if the notice is sent to other holders (e.g. because it is included in the annual report and accounts). It may no longer be necessary to include Note 10 (see further **16.5**).]

The AGM notice would normally include further detailed instructions for shareholders about the venue (including a map and travel details), security measures and registration, how to ask questions at the meeting (or in advance), how voting will be conducted (particularly if all votes will be taken on a poll), and specify the rights of any employee share plan participants and ADS holders.]

P. 10.4A Requisition of AGM resolution [and supporting statement]

The Directors
XYZ plc
[Registered office address]

We the undersigned being [members of the Company representing not less than five per cent of the total voting rights of all the members having at the date hereof a right to vote at the next annual general meeting of the company][1], hereby require you pursuant to section 338 of the Companies Act 2006 to give to the members entitled to receive notice of the next annual general meeting notice of the following resolution, which it is intended to move thereat as an [ordinary resolution/special resolution] [, and pursuant to section 314 of the Companies

Act 2006 to circulate to the members entitled to have notice of the meeting sent to them the annexed statement with respect to the matter referred to in the pro- posed resolution]:

[ORDINARY/SPECIAL] RESOLUTION
[Text of resolution]

[STATEMENT IN SUPPORT]
[Text of statement of not more than 1,000 words]

[A cheque for £ .... is enclosed to meet the company's expenses in giving effect to this requisition.][3]

[Signed]   [Address]
[Date]

Notes:
1. The precise form of words will depend on the condition the members satisfy.
2. Listed companies cannot charge members for circulating an AGM resolution.

P. 10.4B Requisitioned resolution in notice of annual general meeting

To consider the following resolution intended to be moved at the meeting as a special resolution, notice of which is given by the company pursuant to section 338 of the Companies Act 2006 at the request of certain members:

SPECIAL RESOLUTION
[Text of resolution]

CHAPTER 11: CLASS MEETINGS

P. 11.4 Notice of class meeting

XYZ Limited

Notice is hereby given that a separate meeting of the holders of the six per cent £1 preference shares in the capital of the company will be held on [date] at [place] at [time] to propose the following resolution as an special resolution:

THAT this separate class meeting of the holders of the six per cent £1 preference shares in the capital of the company hereby sanctions [resolution being sanc- tioned] and hereby sanctions any variation, modification or abrogation of the rights and privileges attached or belonging to the six per cent £1 preference shares effected thereby or necessary to give effect thereto.

By order of the Board
[Signature]
Secretary
[registered office address]
[date]

Notes:

1. Holders of 6% preference shares entitled to attend and vote at the meeting are entitled to appoint one or more proxies to attend and vote on their behalf. A proxy need not also be a member or a holder of six per cent preference shares. Holders of six per cent preference shares may appoint more than one proxy in relation to the meeting provided that each proxy is appointed to exercise the rights to a different six per cent preference share or shares held by the member.
2. To be effective the form of proxy must be completed in accordance with the instructions and received by the company no later than 48 hours before the time for which the meeting is convened.

CHAPTER 12: CALLING GENERAL MEETINGS

P. 12.2A Board resolution convening annual general meeting

It was resolved:

THAT an Annual General Meeting of the Company be convened and held at [place] on [date] at [time] for the following purposes:

1. To receive the accounts and the reports of the directors and auditors for the financial year ending [date].
2. To re-appoint ABC as auditors until the conclusion of the next meeting at which accounts are laid and to authorise the directors to fix their remuneration.
3. To authorise the Directors to allot shares pursuant to section 551 of the Companies Act 2006.

THAT the secretary be authorised to sign the notice on behalf of the Board and to issue notices accordingly, together with a form of proxy in accordance with the proof print submitted to and approved by this meeting.

P. 12.2B Board resolution convening general meeting

It was resolved:

THAT [an Extraordinary/a] General Meeting of the Company be convened and held at [place] on [date] at [time] for the following purposes:

1. To . . . . . .
2. To . . . . . .

THAT the Secretary be authorised to sign the notice on behalf of the Board and to issue notices accordingly, together with a form of proxy in accordance with the proof print submitted to and approved by this meeting.

P. 12.5A Members' requisition for general meeting

The Directors
XYZ p.l.c.

We the undersigned, being members of XYZ p.l.c. holding in the aggregate [number] ordinary shares of £1 each out of the issued and paid-up capital of [number] ordinary shares of £1 each, require you, pursuant to section 303 of the Companies Act 2006, to convene a general meeting of the company for the purpose of considering the following resolutions, which will be proposed as ordinary resolutions:

1. THAT [name A] be appointed a director of the company.
2. THAT [name B] be appointed a director of the company.

[Signatures]   [Addresses]
[Date]

[Note: If (unusually) the company's articles provide a more relaxed regime for a members requisition and the members are unable to meet the statutory requirements, the wording of the requisition should refer to the relevant article.]

P. 12.5B Notice of requisitioned meeting given by requisitionists

XYZ P.l.c.

NOTICE IS HEREBY GIVEN that, pursuant to a requisition dated [date] made in accordance with the provisions of section 303 of the Companies Act 2006, and deposited at the registered office of the company on [date of deposit], a General Meeting of the company will be held at [place] on [date], at [time] for the purpose of considering the following resolutions, which will be proposed as ordinary resolutions:

RESOLUTIONS
1. THAT [name A] be appointed a director of the company.
2. THAT [name B] be appointed a director of the company.

[Signatures and names]   [Addresses]
[Date]

Notes
1. A member entitled to attend and vote at the meeting is entitled to appoint one or more proxies to attend and vote on his or her behalf. A proxy need not also be a member. A member may appoint more than one proxy in relation to the meeting provided that each proxy is appointed to exercise the rights to a different share or shares held by the member.

2. To be effective the form of proxy must be completed in accordance with the instructions and received by the company no later than 48 hours before the time for which the meeting is convened.

[The notice would normally be accompanied by an explanatory letter from the requisitionists and a form of proxy in their favour.]

CHAPTER 13: NOTICE OF GENERAL MEETINGS

P. 13.6A Consent to short notice of an annual general meeting

We, the undersigned, being all the members for the time being of XYZ plc, and [in attendance/having a right to attend and vote] at the annual general meeting of the company to be held on [date], hereby agree:

(a) to accept shorter notice of the said meeting than the period of notice prescribed by section 307(2)(a) of the Companies Act 2006; and
(b) to accept copies of the company's accounts less than 21 days before the date of the said meeting as required by section 424(3) of the Companies Act 2006.

Dated this .... day of .... 20......
[Signatures]

[*Note:* The above document incorporates agreement to late acceptance of the accounts as well as short notice of the meeting. If all the signatures cannot be obtained on one document, several documents in similar form may be prepared and the reference to being in attendance at the meeting should be omitted. A separate attendance sheet would then be signed by those present at the meeting.]

P. 13.6B Consent to short notice of a general meeting

We, the undersigned, being a majority in number of the members together holding not less than [90 per cent/95 per cent] of the share capital of XYZ [Limited/plc] having a right to attend and vote at the meeting referred to below, hereby agree to a general meeting of the company being held on [date], notwithstanding that shorter notice has been given of the said meeting than the period of notice prescribed by section 307 of the Companies Act 2006.

Dated this .... day of .... 20......

[Signatures]

[*Note:* The relevant percentage is 90 per cent for a private company and 95 per cent for a public company.]

P. 13.8   Notice of general meeting

XYZ Limited

Notice is hereby given that an extraordinary general meeting of XYZ Limited will be held at [place] on [date] at [time] for the purpose of considering and, if thought fit, passing the following resolution as a special resolution:

SPECIAL RESOLUTION
THAT the name of the company be changed to "[name] Limited".
By order of the Board

[Name]
Secretary

[Registered office address]
[Date]

Note:
A member entitled to attend and vote at the meeting is entitled to appoint a proxy to attend and vote instead of him. A proxy need not be a member.

P. 13.11 Regulations 50 and 52 of the 1948 Act Table A regarding ordinary business

50. An Annual General Meeting and a Meeting called for the passing of a Special Resolution shall be called by twenty-one days' notice in writing at the least, and a Meeting of the Company other than an Annual General Meeting or a Meeting for the passing of a Special Resolution shall be called by fourteen days' notice in writing at the least. The notice shall be exclusive of the day on which it is served or deemed to be served and of the day for which it is given, and shall specify the place, the day and the hour of meeting and, in case of special business, the general nature of that business, and shall be given, in manner hereinafter mentioned or in such other manner, if any, as may be prescribed by the Company in General Meeting, to such persons as are, under the regulations of the Company, entitled to receive such notices from the Company:

Provided that a Meeting of the Company shall, notwithstanding that it is called by shorter notice than that specified in this regulation, be deemed to have been duly called if it is so agreed—

(a) in the case of a Meeting called as the Annual General Meeting, by all the Members entitled to attend and vote thereat; and
(b) in the case of any other Meeting, by a majority in number of the Members having a right to attend and vote at the Meeting, being a majority together holding not less than 95 per cent. in nominal value of the Shares giving that right.

52 All business shall be deemed special that is transacted at an Extraordinary General Meeting, and also all that is transacted at an Annual General Meeting, with the exception of declaring a dividend, the consideration of the accounts, balance sheets, and the reports of the Directors and Auditors, the election of Directors in the place of those retiring and the appointment of, and the fixing of the remuneration of, the Auditors.

P. 13.14A Special notice from member to company

To: The directors,
XYZ plc
[Registered Office]

I hereby give notice, pursuant to section 312 of the Companies Act 2006, of my intention to propose the following resolution as an ordinary resolution at the next [annual] general meeting of the company:

ORDINARY RESOLUTION
[Text of resolution]

[Signed]   [Address]
[Date]

P. 13.14B Notice of resolution requiring special notice

To consider and, if thought fit, to pass as an ordinary resolution the following resolution for which special notice has been given in accordance with section 312 of the Companies Act 2006:

THAT ....

P. 13.15A Members' request for circulation of statement under section 314 of the Companies Act 2006

The Directors
XYZ plc
[Registered office address]

We the undersigned being [members of XYZ plc representing not less than five per cent of the total voting rights of all the members having at the date hereof a right to vote at the [annual] general meeting of the company convened for [insert date of meeting], hereby require you pursuant to section 314 of the Companies Act 2006 to circulate to the members entitled to have notice of the meeting sent to them the following statement with respect of the resolution set out in the notice of the said meeting:

STATEMENT
[Text of statement of not more than 1,000 words]

A cheque for £ .... is enclosed to meet the company's expenses in giving effect to this requisition.

[Signed]   [Address]
[Date]

P. 13.15B   Statement circulated at request of members

XYZ plc
STATEMENT BY CERTAIN MEMBERS

The [following/attached] statement in connection with [the business to be transacted at] the [annual] general meeting of the Company to be held on [date] is being circulated to members by the Company at the request of certain members in accordance with ss. 314 of the Companies Act 2006:

[Signed]
Secretary

[Text of statement]

CHAPTER 14: RESOLUTIONS

See also **P. 9.2D** for a certified copy of a members' written resolution.

P. 14.8A Copy resolution for filing at Companies House

[Company Number]
RESOLUTION OF
[NAME OF COMPANY]

At [an annual general/ a general] meeting of the members of the above-named company held on [date] the following resolutions were duly passed:

As a special resolution
[Text of resolution]
As an ordinary resolution
[Text of resolution]

[Signature]
[Secretary/Director]
[Date]

P. 14.8B Copy of members' written resolution for filing at Companies House

[Company Number]

RESOLUTION OF
XYZ LIMITED

On the ……….. day of ………….. 20…, the following resolution(s) were duly passed by a written resolution of the members of the Company pursuant to sections 288 to 300 of the Companies Act 2006:

As a special resolution
[Text of resolution]

As an ordinary resolution
[Text of resolution]

[Signed]
[Secretary/Director]
[Date]

P. 14.8C Copy of decision by sole member for filing at Companies House

[Company Number]

RESOLUTION OF
XYZ LIMITED

The following resolution(s), having effect as shown below, was/were duly passed on [date] by a decision of the sole member of the Company:

As a special resolution
[Text of resolution]

As an ordinary resolution
[Text of resolution]

[Signature]
[Secretary/Director]
[Date]

CHAPTER 15: QUORUM

P. 15.4 Article on failure to obtain a quorum at a general meeting

(A) This article applies if a quorum is not present within five minutes of the time fixed for a general meeting to start or within any longer period not exceeding one hour which the chairman of the meeting can decide or if a quorum ceases to be present during a general meeting.

(B) If the meeting was called by shareholders it will be cancelled. Any other meeting will be adjourned to any day (being not less than three nor more than 28 days later), time and place stated in the notice of meeting. If the notice does not provide for this, the meeting shall be adjourned to a day (being not less than ten nor more than 28 days later), time and place decided on by the chairman of the meeting and in this case the company will give not less than seven clear days' written notice of the adjourned meeting.

(C) One shareholder present in person or by proxy and entitled to vote will constitute a quorum at any adjourned meeting and any notice of an adjourned meeting will say this.

CHAPTER 16: PROXIES AND CORPORATE REPRESENTATIVES

P. 16.3A Article on authority of corporate representatives

Any corporation which is a member of the company may by resolution of its directors or other governing body authorise such person as it thinks fit to act as its representative at any meeting of the company, and any person so authorised shall be entitled to exercise the same powers on behalf of the corporation which he represents as that corporation could exercise if it were an individual member of the company, but such representative may be required to produce evidence of such authorisation on admission or at any time during the meeting or in connection with the exercise of any right in respect of such meeting, including without limitation participation in a poll on any resolution. Any such authorisation in writing purporting to be signed by an officer of or other person duly authorised for the purpose by the said corporation shall be conclusive evidence of the authority of the representative to act on behalf of the corporation.

P. 16.3B Corporate representative – Board minute appointing

It was resolved:

THAT [name A] or, failing him, [name B] or, failing her, [name C] be appointed, pursuant to section 323 of the Companies Act 2006, to act as the company's representative at any meeting of the members or creditors of other companies in which the company is or may become interested as a member or creditor.

or

It was resolved:

THAT the following persons be appointed, pursuant to section 323 of the Companies Act 2006, to act as the company's representative at the general meeting of [name of company] to be held on [date] (or any adjournment thereof) in respect of the number of shares shown next to their respective names:

[name A], or failing him, [name B]   12,000 shares
[name C]   24,000 shares

[name D] and [name E] jointly   30,000 shares
[name F]   over the balance of the company's holding.

P. 16.3C Corporate representative – Letter certifying the appointment of

[Headed notepaper of company making the appointment]
[Date]

To the Directors of [name of company]
Confirmation of appointment of corporate representative

It is hereby certified that the person or persons named below were appointed by a board resolution of the above-named company dated [date] pursuant to section 323 of the Companies Act 2006 to act as the company's corporate representative(s) at the [annual] general meeting of [name of company] to be held on [date] in respect of the number of shares shown next to their respective names.

Names	Number of shares
[corporate representative A]	23,090
[corporate representative B]	the balance of our holding

It is hereby certified that the authority of any person appointed to act as the company's corporate representative other than those named above, and any evidence of that person's authority, is [hereby revoked/shall continue to have effect] in respect of the abovementioned meeting.

Signed
[Director/Secretary/Authorised Officer]

[The above letter must be an original, on the registered member's stationery and signed by an authorised signatory.]

P. 16.5A Corporate representative – Wording for a letter of representation where the chairman is to be appointed as the designated corporate representative

ABC Registrars or XYZ plc

Dear Sir,

Letter of representation
Pursuant to section 323 of the Companies Act 2006 the persons named below have been authorised by a Board Resolution passed on [date] to act as the representatives of [nominee name as it appears on the Register, including any account designation] in relation to the AGM/GM [specify] of [company name] to be held on the [date] at [time] or any adjournment thereof:

1. The Chairman of the meeting is authorised and instructed to act as representative to vote (or withhold a vote) on a poll as the designated corporate

representative in accordance with the voting directions of any other corporate representatives for [nominee name excluding any account designation] at the meeting (whether given in a directions card or via an electronic handset).

2. [Name of corporate representative] is authorised and instructed to act as representative to speak, demand a poll and, on a poll, to give directions (whether in a directions card or via an electronic handset) to vote (or withhold a vote) to the Chairman of the meeting appointed pursuant to this letter. For administrative purposes, any directions to vote given by this representative (or any other powers exercised) shall be treated as relating to the number of shares in account [insert designation details] at the relevant time [or insert number of shares].

[This appointment does not revoke or replace any other appointment of a corporate representative.]*

Yours faithfully

Note: The letter must be on the company's letterhead and bear the original signature of an authorised signatory.

* If a corporate shareholder wishes to appoint or may be appointing more than one corporate representative, it is essential that it be made very clear in the letter of representation whether the appointment is additional to, or in place of, any other appointments in respect of that holding (or any part of it).

P. 16.5B Corporate representative – Wording to be added to a poll card for designated corporate representatives

By submitting this poll card, a corporate representative who is the designated corporate representative for a shareholder casts (or withholds) the total number of votes he is directed to cast (or withhold) by any other corporate representatives for that shareholder as shown in, and in accordance with, the directions cards submitted (or via the electronic handsets used) by them before the close of the poll, in addition to casting (or withholding) any votes specified in this poll card.

[*Note:* The above wording is designed to be added to all poll cards to be used at the meeting, so that just one poll card format is necessary for all those voting on the poll.]

P. 16.5C Corporate representative – Wording for use on a directions card where the designated corporate representative method is used

I hereby give directions to cast (or withhold) votes on a poll as specified in this card to the person who is the designated corporate representative of the shareholder who has also appointed me as corporate representative.

[*Note:* The directions card should include the above wording, but should otherwise be completed in the same way as a poll card and have the same system (e.g.

by use of identification numbers) for identifying who has completed it and how many shares it relates to.]

P16.5D Corporate representative – Explanatory note for multiple corporate representatives

This note is to explain the procedures at this meeting if more than one representative for the same corporate shareholder attends the meeting.

Section 323 of the Companies Act 2006 (Representation of corporations at meetings) provides that:

(1) If a corporation (whether or not a company within the meaning of this Act) is a member of a company, it may by resolution of its directors or other governing body authorise a person or persons to act as its representative or representatives at any meeting of the company.

(2) Where the corporation authorises only one person, he is entitled to exercise the same powers on behalf of the corporation as the corporation could exercise if it were an individual member of the company.

(3) Where the corporation authorises more than one person, any one of them is entitled to exercise the same powers on behalf of the corporation as the corporation could exercise if it were an individual member of the company.

(4) Where the corporation authorises more than one person and more than one of them purport to exercise a power under subsection (3):

(a) if they purport to exercise the power in the same way, the power is treated as exercised in that way;

(b) if they do not purport to exercise the power in the same way, the power is treated as not exercised.

In the light of this provision, and in particular section 323(4), procedures have been put in place at the meeting to ensure that the voting intentions of all of the corporate representatives who attend the meeting can be taken into account. This involves one of the corporate representatives acting as the designated corporate representative (DCR).

When the DCR submits his poll card (or inputs his electronic instructions if an electronic voting system is being used), the voting instructions of all of the other corporate representatives are given effect on the poll in accordance with directions cards submitted by them (or in accordance with their electronic instructions). There are two ways of determining who should be the DCR:

1. Chairman appointed as DCR

If the corporate shareholder has appointed the Chairman as the DCR, then all of the other corporate representatives for that shareholder receive a directions card rather than a poll card and submit the directions card on the poll (or in the case of an electronic voting system, it is noted on the electronic entry on registration that they are giving directions when using the electronic handsets). The Chairman of the meeting will sign and submit a poll card and by doing so he votes shares for and against (or withholds votes) on the poll in accordance with the directions (whether submitted on a directions card or via an electronic handset) from all representatives who have submitted them before the close of the poll.

2. DCR determined in another way

For cases where the corporate shareholder has not appointed the Chairman as the DCR, then the DCR is chosen from the representatives who attend the meeting. The DCR will normally be the first to register his attendance at the meeting (unless some other method of determining the DCR for that shareholder is decided at the meeting). The DCR receives a poll card (or, if the electronic voting system is being used to process his votes, is noted as being the voting representative and receives an electronic voting handset). He will also be asked on registration to sign and deposit a reserve poll card (covering all of the resolutions and matters which may be the subject of a poll). By depositing the reserve poll card when he registers at the meeting, that representative is giving instructions to the Chairman to submit the reserve poll card on his behalf if he does not himself submit a poll card in relation to any of the polls held at the meeting (so as to give effect to the directions of the other representatives, but without casting any votes himself other than those he is directed to cast by the other representatives). Any other corporate representatives for that shareholder receive directions cards instead of poll cards (or are noted on the electronic voting system as giving directions). By submitting a poll card (or using the electronic handset) the DCR also casts votes in accordance with the voting directions given by the other corporate representatives (whether on directions cards or via electronic handsets). If for whatever reason the DCR does not submit a poll card (or use the electronic handset) on any particular poll then the chairman will submit the reserve poll card, so that the directions of the other representatives can still be taken into account.

P. 16.11 Example of article allowing electronic proxies

An appointment of a proxy shall be in any usual or common form or in any other form which the directors may prescribe or accept and, in the case of an instrument in writing:

(a) in the case of an individual shall be signed by the appointor or by his attorney; and

(b) in the case of a corporation shall be either given under its common seal or executed in any manner prescribed by the Statutes to have the same effect as if given under the common seal of the corporation or signed on its behalf by an attorney or duly authorised officer of the corporation.

The directors may, but shall not be bound to, require evidence of the authority of any such attorney or officer. The signature on such instrument need not be witnessed.

An appointment of a proxy may be contained in an electronic communication in accordance with these articles, authenticated or executed in such manner as is specified by the directors.

P. 16.13 Three-way proxy which complies with the Listing Rules

XYZ plc

FORM OF PROXY FOR USE AT [ANNUAL] GENERAL MEETING

I/We (Block Capitals, please), ...
.... being a member/members
of the above-named Company, hereby appoint the chairman of the meeting* ...
.... as my/
our proxy to vote for me/us on my/our behalf at the Annual General Meeting
of the Company to be held at 12 noon on .... day, the .... day of
.... 20........., and at any adjournment thereof.

I/We hereby authorise and instruct the proxy to vote on the resolutions to be proposed at such meeting as indicated in the boxes below. Unless otherwise directed,
the proxy will vote or abstain from voting as he or she thinks fit. Should any
resolutions, other than those specified, be proposed at the meeting, the proxy may
vote thereon as he or she thinks fit.

Signature ....
Dated .... 20........

[* Delete if it is desired to appoint any other person and insert his or her name
and address in the space provided.]

Please indicate with an X in the spaces below how you wish your votes to be cast.

		For	Against	Votes withheld
Resolution 1	To receive the report and accounts			
Resolution 2	To approve the directors' remuneration report			
Resolution 3	To declare a final dividend			
Resolution 4	To re-elect [name A] as a director			
Resolution 5	To re-elect [name B] a director			
Resolution 6	To re-elect [name C] a director			
Resolution 7	Reappointment of auditors			
Resolution 8	Share buyback			

		For	Against	Votes withheld
Resolution 9	Directors' authority to allot shares (Section 551)			
Resolution 10	Disapplication of pre-emption rights			
Resolution 11	Notice of general meetings			

Date

Signature

NOTES

1. A member may appoint a proxy of his own choice. If such an appointment is made, delete the words 'the chairman of the meeting' and insert the name of the person appointed proxy in the space provided.
2. Appointing a proxy does not prevent a member from attending the meeting in person if he so wishes.
3. If the appointer is a corporation, this form must be under its common seal or under the hand of some officer or attorney duly authorised in that behalf.
4. In the case of joint holders, the signature of any one holder will be sufficient, but the names of all the joint holders should be stated.
5. If you wish your proxy to cast your votes for or against a resolution you may insert an 'X' in the appropriate box. If you do not want your proxy to vote on any particular resolution, you may insert an 'X' in the 'Vote withheld' box. A 'Vote withheld' is not a vote in law and will not be counted in the calculation of votes 'For' and 'Against' a resolution. If you do not indicate how your proxy is to vote, you will be deemed to have authorised your proxy to vote or to withhold your vote as your proxy thinks fit. Your proxy will also be entitled to vote at his or her discretion on any other resolution properly put before the meeting.
6. Particulars of the directors standing for re-election are set out on pages x to x of [circular/annual report].
7. To be valid, this form must be completed and deposited at the registered office of the Company not less than 48 hours before the time fixed for holding the meeting or adjourned meeting.

P. 16.17 Article on non-revocation of proxies

A vote given in accordance with the terms of an instrument of proxy shall be valid, notwithstanding the previous death or insanity of the principal or revocation of the proxy, or of the authority under which the proxy was executed, or the transfer of the share in respect of which the proxy is given, provided that no intimation in writing of such death, insanity, revocation or transfer shall have been received by the Company at the Office (or other place in the United Kingdom specified pursuant to Article [No.]) before the commencement of the meetings or adjourned meeting at which the proxy is used.

P. 16.21 Article limiting liabilities in connection with proxies
To the extent permitted by law, each of the directors, the secretary and each person employed or, directly or indirectly, retained or used by the Company in the processes of receiving and validating the appointment and revocation of proxies shall not be liable to any persons other than the Company in respect of any acts or omissions (including negligence) occurring in the execution or purported execution of his tasks relating to such processes, provided that he shall have no such immunity in respect of any act done or omitted to be done in bad faith.

P. 16.22A Article on the maximum validity of a proxy
A proxy form will cease to be valid 12 months from the date of its receipt. But it will be valid, unless the proxy form itself states otherwise, if it is used at an adjourned meeting or on a poll after a meeting or an adjourned meeting even after 12 months, if it was valid for the original meeting.

P. 16.22B Article extract on the retention of records
(A) The Company shall be entitled to destroy:
. . . .
(v) all proxy appointments which have been used for the purpose of a poll at any time after the expiration of one year from the date of use; and
(vi) all proxy appointments which have not been used for the purpose of a poll at any time after one month from the end of the meeting to which the proxy appointment relates and at which no poll was demanded.
(B) It shall conclusively be presumed in favour of the Company that:
. . . .
(iv) every other document destroyed in accordance with paragraph (A) above was a valid and effective document in accordance with its recorded particulars in the books or records of the Company, but:
(a) the provisions of this Article apply only to the destruction of a document in good faith and without notice of any claim (regardless of the parties) to which the document might be relevant;
(b) nothing in this Article shall be construed as imposing on the Company any liability in respect of the destruction of any document earlier than the time specified in paragraph (A) above or in any other circumstances which would not attach to the Company in the absence of this Article; and
(c) any reference in this Article to the destruction of any document includes a reference to its disposal in any manner or deletion.
[Note: See also article 82 of the model articles for public companies at Annex C4.]

CHAPTER 17: VOTING

P 17.2 Article on bearer shares

(A) A Bearer may at any time deposit the Share Warrant together with a written declaration specifying his name and postal address at such place as the Directors may from time to time appoint (or, in default of such appointment, at the Transfer Office), and, so long as the Share Warrant remains so deposited, the depositor shall have the same right of signing a requisition for calling a meeting of the Company, of giving notice of intention to submit a resolution to a meeting, of attending and voting, giving a proxy and exercising the other rights and privileges of a member at any meeting held after the expiration of forty-eight hours from the time of deposit, as if from the time of deposit his name were inserted in the Register as the holder of the shares specified in the deposited Share Warrant. Not more than one person shall be recognised as depositor of any Share Warrant. Every Share Warrant which shall have been so deposited as aforesaid shall remain so deposited until after the conclusion of the meeting (including any adjournment) at which the depositor desires to attend or to be represented. Save as otherwise expressly provided, no person shall, as bearer of a Share Warrant, be entitled to sign a requisition for calling a general meeting;

(B) In the case of any notice or document or other communication with members or any class of members, it shall be sufficient, so far as any Bearer is concerned, to advertise the notice, document or other communication once in a leading London daily newspaper, and such other newspapers (if any) as the Directors may from time to time determine, and to give a postal address (and, if the Directors see fit, the address of a website) where copies of the notice, document or other communication may be obtained by any Bearer.

P. 17.4A Article on voting rights where a call is unpaid

No member shall, unless the Board otherwise determines be entitled to vote at a General Meeting either personally or by proxy, or to exercise any privilege as a member unless all calls or other sums presently payable by him in respect of shares in the Company have been paid.

P. 17.4B Article of public company removing voting rights for failure to respond to a s. 793 notice

(A) If any member, or any other person appearing to be interested in shares held by such member, has been duly served with a notice under Section 793 of the Companies Act 2006 and is in default for the Designated Period in supplying to the Company the information thereby required, then the Directors may in their absolute discretion at any time thereafter by notice (a 'Direction Notice') to such member direct that in respect of the shares in relation to which the default occurred (the 'Default Shares') (which expression shall include any further shares which are issued in respect of such shares) the member shall not (for so long as the default continues) nor shall any transferee to whom any of such shares are transferred (other than pursuant to an approved transfer or pursuant to (C) below) be entitled to vote either personally or by proxy at a general meeting of the Company or a meeting of the holders of any class of shares of the Company or to exercise any other right to attend or vote at general meetings of the Company or meetings of the holders of any class of shares of the Company.

(B) The Company shall send to each other person appearing to be interested in the shares the subject of any Direction Notice a copy of the said notice, but the failure or omission by the Company to do so shall not invalidate such Direction Notice.

(C) Where the Default Shares represent at least 0.25% of the issued shares of that class then the Direction Notice may additionally direct:

(i) that any cash dividend or other such money, or shares issued in lieu of a dividend, which would otherwise be due in respect of each of the Default Shares shall (in whole or any part thereof) be retained (or, as the case may be, not issued) by the Company without any liability to pay interest thereon when such dividend or other money or shares is finally paid or issued to the member; and/or

(ii) that no transfer of any of the shares held by such member shall be registered unless:

(a) the member is not himself in default as regards supplying the information required and the transfer is of part only of the member's holding and when presented for registration is accompanied by a certificate by the member in a form satisfactory to the Directors to the effect that after due and careful enquiry the member is satisfied that no person in default as regards supplying such information is interested in any of the shares the subject of the transfer; or

(b) the transfer is an Approved Transfer.

(D) Any Direction Notice shall have effect in accordance with its terms for so long as the default in respect of which the Direction Notice was issued continues and (unless the Directors otherwise determine) for a period of one week thereafter but shall cease to have effect in relation to any Default Shares which are transferred by such member by means of an Approved Transfer. The Directors may at any time give notice cancelling a Direction Notice.

(E) For the purpose of this Article:

(i) a person shall be treated as appearing to be interested in any shares if the member holding such shares has given to the Company a notification under the said Section 793 which either (a) names such person as being so interested or (b) fails to establish the identities of those interested in the shares and (after taking into account the said notification and any other relevant Section 793 notification) the Company knows or has reasonable cause to believe or suspects on reasonable grounds that the person in question is or may be interested in the shares;

(ii) the Designated Period is twenty-eight days from the date of service of the notice under the said Section 793 except that if the Default Shares represent at least 0.25% of the issued shares of that class, the Designated Period is fourteen days from such date; and

(iii) a transfer of shares is an Approved Transfer if but only if:

(a) it is a transfer of shares to an offeror by way or in pursuance of acceptance of a take-over offer for a company (as defined in Section 974 of the Companies Act 2006); or

(b) the Directors are satisfied that the transfer is made pursuant to a sale of the whole of the beneficial ownership of the shares to a party unconnected with the member and with other persons appearing to be interested in such shares; or

(c) the transfer results from a sale made through a Recognised Investment Exchange.

(H) Nothing contained in this Article shall limit the power of the Directors under the Companies Act 2006.

P. 17.5   Article giving enhanced voting rights

(a) Subject to sub-paragraphs (b) and (c) below, on a show of hands every member who (being an individual) is present in person or (being a corporation) is present by a duly authorised representative, not being himself a member, shall have one vote and on a poll every member shall have one vote for every share of which he is the holder.

(b) If at any general meeting a poll is duly demanded on a resolution to remove a director from office, the director named in the resolution shall be entitled to [number] votes for each share of which he is the holder.

(c) If at any general meeting a poll is duly demanded on a resolution to delete or amend the provisions of this article, every director shall have [number] votes for each share of which he is the holder if voting against such a resolution.

P. 17.9A Voting card for use by members and corporate representatives on a poll

VOTING CARD

For the [Annual] General Meeting of

XYZ PLC

held on [date]

(To be used as instructed by the chairman)

Name of shareholder (in Block Capitals)

....

Signature ....

Number of shares voted (see note 1) ....

		For	Against	Votes withheld
Resolution 1	To receive the report and accounts			
Resolution 2	To approve the directors' remuneration report			
Resolution 3	To declare a final dividend			
Resolution 4	To re-elect [name A] as a director			
Resolution 5	To re-elect [name B] a director			
Resolution 6	To re-elect [name C] a director			
Resolution 7	Reappointment of auditors			
Resolution 8	Share buyback			
Resolution 9	Directors' authority to allot shares (Section 551)			
Resolution 10	Disapplication of pre-emption rights			
Resolution 11	Notice of general meetings			

Notes
1. It is not necessary to complete the number of shares voted, provided that your vote is being given in respect of the entire holding of the member.
2. If you wish to cast all the votes covered by this voting form in the same way, you may do so by placing an X in the appropriate column above. If you place an X in more than one column for any resolution, your vote(s) on that resolution will not be counted.
3. If you wish to cast your votes in different ways, you may do so by indicating the number of votes cast 'for' or 'against' or the number of votes withheld in the appropriate columns.
4. A 'vote withheld' on any resolution is not a vote in law and will not be counted for the purposes of determining whether or not that resolution has been passed by a particular majority.

P. 17.9B Voting card for use by proxies on a poll

VOTING CARD
For the [Annual] General Meeting of
XYZ PLC
held on [date]

(To be used as instructed by the chairman)

Name of proxy ....

(In Block Capitals)

Signature of proxy ....

Name of shareholder represented ....

(In Block Capitals)

Number of shares represented by proxy ....

[The rest of the voting card will be the same as for shareholders above.]

P. 17.9C Voting card for use by chairman on a poll

CHAIRMAN'S VOTING CARD
For the [Annual/Extraordinary] General Meeting of
XYZ PLC
held on [date]

Signature of chairman of meeting . . . .

See attached sheet for names and holdings of shareholders represented.

Number of votes

		For	Against	Votes withheld
Resolution 1	To receive the report and accounts			
Resolution 2	To approve the directors' remuneration report			
Resolution 3	To declare a final dividend			
Resolution 4	To re-elect [name A] as a director			
Resolution 5	To re-elect [name B] a director			
Resolution 6	To re-elect [name C] a director			
Resolution 7	Reappointment of auditors			
Resolution 8	Share buyback			
Resolution 9	Directors' authority to allot shares (Section 551)			
Resolution 10	Disapplication of pre-emption rights			
Resolution 11	Notice of general meetings			

P. 17.14 Articles on votes counted in error
Alternative A
If:

(i) any objection to the right of any person to vote is made;
(ii) any votes have been counted which ought not to have been counted or which might have been rejected; or
(iii) any votes are not counted which ought to have been counted, the objection or error must be raised or pointed out at the meeting (or the adjourned meeting) or poll at which the vote objected to is cast or at which the error occurs. Any objection or error must be raised with or pointed out to the chairman of the meeting. His decision is final. If a vote is allowed at a meeting or poll, it is valid for all purposes and if a vote is not counted at a meeting or poll, this will not affect the decision of the meeting or poll.

Alternative B
No person other than the Company or some person acting on its behalf may raise an objection to the admissibility of any vote except at the meeting or adjourned meeting or subsequent poll at which that vote may be, or is, given or tendered. Any such objection shall be referred to the person presiding when the objection is raised. The person presiding, or some person appointed by him, shall rule on the objection, and such ruling shall be final and conclusive. If a vote is ruled in order it shall then be valid for all purposes unless previously or subsequently disallowed by the Company.

CHAPTER 19: ORGANISING GENERAL MEETINGS

P. 19.4 Article dealing with overflow arrangements at general meetings
(A) The Board may make arrangements for simultaneous attendance and participation in General Meetings by members and proxies entitled to attend such meetings at places other than the place specified in the Notice convening the meeting ('the specified place').
(B) Any arrangements for simultaneous attendance at other places shall operate so that any members and proxies excluded from attendance at the specified place are able to attend at one or more of the other places. For the purposes of all other provisions of these Articles any such meeting shall be treated as being held and taking place at the specified place.
(C) The right of any member or proxy otherwise entitled to attend a General Meeting at the specified place shall be subject to any arrangements that the Board may at its discretion make from time to time (whether before or after the date of the Notice convening the meeting) for facilitating the organisation and administration of any General Meeting by requiring any such person (selected on such basis as the Board may at its discretion decide) to attend the meeting at one or more of the other places.

CHAPTER 20: CHAIRMAN

P. 20.9 Article giving subsidiary chairman power to promote order at meetings

Every Subsidiary Chairman shall keep good order at the location where he is presiding, and he shall have all powers necessary or desirable for that purpose. Every Subsidiary Chairman shall also carry out all requests made of him by or on behalf of the chairman of the meeting in which he is participating, and he shall have all powers necessary or desirable for that purpose.

[*Note:* A Subsidiary Chairman is a person appointed by the chairman of the meeting to chair those parts of the meeting which may be taking place at another location.]

CHAPTER 21: RIGHT TO ATTEND AND SPEAK

P. 21.3A Attendance sheet (members)

XYZ PLC

Members present at the annual general meeting held on [date]

NAME (IN BLOCK CAPITALS)   SIGNATURE

[Names]   [Signatures]

P. 21.3B Attendance card

XYZ PLC
Annual General Meeting 2010
Admission Card

If you intend to come to the Annual General Meeting, please bring this card with you to ensure that you gain admission as quickly as possible. Please present this card at a Registration Desk where it will be exchanged for a Voting Card. The Meeting will start at [time] and is being held on [date] at [place]. You may register from [time]. [A map of the venue and instructions on how to get there can be found on the reverse of this card.] Detailed instructions are also contained in the accompanying Notice of Meeting.

Name of shareholder
[Shareholder's address]

[Event Reference Number or Barcode]
Unique Shareholder Reference Number or Barcode

[*Note:* Some companies require shareholders to sign and date the attendance card. As the company is unlikely to have time to check signatures at the Registration Desk or have anything to check them against, this is presumably intended to deter people from trying to impersonate a shareholder.]

CHAPTER 22: SECURITY AND DISORDER

P. 22.2 Article allowing security checks at general meetings

The chairman of a meeting, or the company secretary, can take any action they consider appropriate for:

(a) the safety of people attending a general meeting;
(b) proper and orderly conduct at a general meeting; or
(c) the meeting to reflect the wishes of the majority.

For example, they can require any people to prove who they are, they can carry out security searches, and stop certain things being taken into the meeting. They can refuse to allow any person into a meeting, or can arrange for any person who refuses to comply with any requirements imposed under this Article to be removed from a meeting.

   [*Note:* this article was written in plain English!]

CHAPTER 23: ADJOURNMENT AND OTHER PROCEDURAL MOTIONS

P. 23.6 Article giving the chairman power to adjourn

The Chairman of a General Meeting may, with the consent of any meeting at which a quorum is present (and shall if so directed by the meeting) adjourn the meeting from time to time (or sine die) and from place to place, but no business shall be transacted at any adjourned meeting except business left unfinished at the meeting from which the adjournment took place. If it appears to the Chairman of the meeting that it is likely to be impracticable to hold or continue the meeting because of the number of members or their proxies present or wishing to attend or that an adjournment is otherwise necessary so that the business of the meeting may be properly conducted, he may without the need for such consent adjourn the meeting to such other time and place as he may determine (or sine die). When a meeting is adjourned sine die the time and place of the adjourned meeting shall be fixed by the Board. When a meeting is adjourned for thirty days or more or sine die, notice of the adjourned meeting shall be given as in the case of the original meeting. Save as expressly provided by these Articles it shall not be necessary to give any notice of an adjournment or of the business to be transacted at an adjourned meeting.

P. 23.11 Article giving the directors power to postpone or change the place of a meeting

If the directors consider that it is impracticable or undesirable to hold a general meeting on the date or at the time or place stated in the notice calling the meeting, they can move or postpone the meeting (or do both). If the directors do this, an announcement of the date, time and place of the rearranged meeting will, if practicable, be published in at least two national newspapers in the United Kingdom. Notice of the business of the meeting does not need to be given again. The directors must take reasonable steps to ensure that any shareholder trying to attend the meeting at the original time and place is informed of the new arrangements. If a meeting is rearranged in this way, proxy forms are valid if they are received as required by these articles not less than 48 hours before the time of the rearranged meeting. The directors can also move or postpone the rearranged meeting (or do both) under this article.

CHAPTER 24: AMENDMENTS

P. 24.2A Article requiring prior notice of amendments

Amendments can be proposed to any type of resolution if the amendments are only clerical amendments to correct an obvious error. No other amendments to any special resolution can be proposed or voted on. In the case of an ordinary resolution any amendments to the resolution can be proposed and voted on (even if they are more than clerical amendments made to correct an obvious error), but such amendments can only be proposed and voted on if written notice of the proposed amendment and the intention to propose the amendment is delivered to the Registered Office at least 48 hours before the time fixed for the meeting or adjourned meeting.

P. 24.2B Article on validity of amendments

If an amendment shall be proposed to any resolution under consideration but shall in good faith be ruled out of order by the Chairman of the meeting the proceedings on the substantive resolution shall not be invalidated by any error in such ruling. In the case of a resolution duly proposed as a special resolution no amendment thereto (other than a mere clerical amendment to correct a manifest error) may in any event be considered or voted upon.

CHAPTER 25: DEALING WITH COMMON ITEMS OF BUSINESS

P. 25.2A Accounts – Agreement to accept accounts less than 21 days before general meeting

We, the undersigned, being all the members of [name of company] entitled to attend and vote at the [annual] general meeting, convened for [date of meeting], hereby agree that copies of the documents required to be sent to us pursuant to section 423 of the Companies Act 2006 shall be deemed to have been duly sent for the purposes of sections 423 and 424 of that Act notwithstanding that they were sent less than twenty-one days before the date of the meeting.

[Date]
[Signatures]

P. 25.2B Accounts – Notice of AGM re laying of accounts

To receive the accounts and reports of the directors [and the auditors] for the year ended [date].

P. 25.3 Directors' remuneration report – Ordinary resolution to approve

To approve the directors' remuneration report for the year ended [date].

P. 25.5A Auditors – Board resolution to appoint first auditors of a private company or to fill a casual vacancy

THAT [name of auditors], of [address of auditors] be and are hereby appointed as the auditors of the company with effect from [date], at a fee to be agreed by the board [on the recommendation of the Audit Committee].

[*Note:* The directors may appoint the first auditors of the company or appoint auditors to fill a casual vacancy. Auditors appointed by the directors hold office (a) in the case of a public company until the next general meeting at which accounts are laid whereupon the members must either reappointed them or appoint new auditors and (b) in the case of a private company until the end of the first period for appointing auditors whereupon their reappointment will need to be approved by the members either at a general meeting or by written resolution.]

P. 25.5B Auditors – Board resolution to appoint first auditors of a public company or to fill a casual vacancy

THAT [name of auditors] be appointed auditors of the company to hold office until the conclusion of the next general meeting at which accounts are laid before the company[and that their remuneration be fixed by the directors].

P. 25.5C Auditors – Resolution to reappoint auditors at general meeting

THAT [name of auditors] be and are hereby reappointed as auditors of the company from the conclusion of this meeting until the conclusion of the next general meeting before which accounts are laid [and that the directors be and are hereby authorised to fix their remuneration].

P. 25.5D Auditors – Resolution of a private company to appoint auditors and fix their remuneration

THAT [name of auditors] be and are hereby appointed auditors of the company [and that for so long as they hold office as the company's auditors the directors be and are hereby authorised to fix their remuneration].

[*Note:* It is not necessary to say how long the appointment of the auditors shall last. If no term of office is specified, reappointment will normally be deemed under s. 487. However the resolution should authorise the directors to fix the remuneration of the auditors not just for the current financial year but also for any future years in which they are deemed to have been reappointed.]

P. 25.7B Auditors – Resolution of general meeting for appointment of auditors other than retiring auditors

THAT [name of auditors] be appointed auditors of the company in place of the retiring auditors [to hold office from the conclusion of this meeting until the conclusion of the next general meeting before which accounts are laid] [and that the directors be and are hereby authorised to fix their remuneration].

P. 25.8 Auditors – Ordinary resolution to approve an auditors' liability limitation agreement

THAT the principal terms (as defined in section 536(4) of the Companies Act 2006), produced to the meeting and initialled by the chairman for the purposes of identification, of a liability limitation agreement (as defined in section 534 of the Companies Act 2006) for the financial year ending [date] proposed to be entered into by the company and [name of auditor] be and are hereby approved.

P. 25.11 Auditors' removal – Resolution of general meeting for

THAT [name of auditors] be removed from office as auditors of the company with immediate effect [and that [name of anew auditors] be appointed auditors of the company in their place to hold office until the conclusion of the next general meeting a which accounts are laid and that their remuneration be fixed by the directors].

P. 25.12A Dividends – Statement in directors' report

An interim dividend of 5p per share has been paid and the directors recommend a final dividend of 9p per share in respect of the year ended [date], making a total for the year of 14p per share. The proposed dividend will, if approved at the annual general meeting, be paid on [date] to shareholders on the register at the close of business on [date].

P. 25.12B Dividends – Notice of resolution to declare a dividend

To declare a dividend.

P. 25.12C Dividends – Minute of resolution declaring a dividend

It was resolved:

THAT a final dividend of 9p per 25p ordinary share in respect of the year ended [date] be declared payable on [date] to shareholders registered at the close of business on [date].

P. 25.12D Dividends – Board resolution to pay an interim dividend

It was resolved:

THAT an interim dividend for the year ended [date] of 7p per share on the ordinary shares of 25p each be paid on [date] to shareholders registered at the close of business on [date].

P. 25.13A Directors – Board resolution to fill a casual vacancy

THAT [name of new director] be appointed a director of the company in the place of [name of former director] with effect from [date] [and shall hold office until the next annual general meeting].

P. 25.13B Directors – Board resolution to appoint an additional director

THAT [name of new director] be appointed a director of the company with effect from [date] [and shall hold office until the next annual general meeting].

P. 25.13C Directors – Appointment of additional director by sole continuing director

XYZ LIMITED

Pursuant to the authority given by regulation 90 of Table A in The Companies (Tables A to F) Regulations 1985 (which regulation is incorporated in the company's articles of association), I, [name], the sole continuing director of the company, hereby appoint [name of person to be appointed] to be a director of the company to fill the vacancy caused by [circumstances, e.g. death or resignation] of [name].

[Date]

[Signature]

P. 25.13D Directors – Notice given by member to the company of intention to propose person (not recommended by the directors) for appointment or reappointment as a director

To the Directors
XYZ Ltd

Pursuant to reg. 76 of Table A, I hereby give notice of my intention to propose [name] for election as a director at the annual general meeting of the company to be held on [date]. The particulars regarding [name] which would, if he were so appointed or reappointed, be required to be included in the company's register of directors are set out below.

[Particulars]
[Signature]
[Date]

I, [name], hereby give notice that I am willing, if elected, to act as a director of XYZ Ltd.

[Signature]
[Date]

P. 25.13E Directors – Notice given by company to members in accordance with reg. 77 of resolution to appoint director not retiring by rotation

To elect [name] as a director (see Note 1).

Note 1: [Particulars which would be required to be included in the register of directors.]

P. 25.14 Directors – Retirement by rotation article to comply with Combined Code

(A) At each annual general meeting:

(a) any director who was elected or last re-elected a director at or before the annual general meeting held in the third calendar year before the current year shall retire by rotation; and

(b) such further directors (other than any directors who, pursuant to article [No.], are not then subject to retirement by rotation) shall retire by rotation as would bring the number retiring by rotation up to one-third of the number of directors in office at the date of the notice of the meeting (or, if their number is not a multiple of three, the number nearest to but not greater than one-third).

(B) The directors to retire by rotation at any general meeting shall exclude any directors who, pursuant to article [No.], are not then subject to retirement by rotation, but shall include (so far as necessary to obtain the number required) any director who is due to retire at the meeting by reason of age or who wishes to retire and not to offer himself for re-election. Any further directors so to retire shall be those of the other directors who have been longest in office since their election or last re-election and so that as between persons who were last elected or re-elected directors on the same day those to retire shall in the absence of agreement be selected by lot. A retiring director shall be eligible for re-election.

(C) The company at the meeting at which a director retires under any provision of these articles may by ordinary resolution fill the office being vacated by electing thereto the retiring director or some other person eligible for election.

(D) The retirement shall not have effect until the conclusion of the meeting except where a resolution is passed to elect some other person in place of the retiring director or a resolution is put to the meeting and lost. Accordingly a retiring director whi is re-elected or deemed to have been re-elected will continue in office without a break.

P. 25.15A Director's removal – Special notice to company to remove director

The Directors
XYZ Limited

I hereby give notice pursuant to sections 303 and 379 of the Companies Act 1985 of my intention to propose the following resolution as an ordinary resolution at the next annual general meeting of the company:

THAT Mrs S Brown be removed from office as a director of the company.

[Signature]
[Address]   [Date]

P. 25.15B Director's removal – Notice given by company to members or resolution to remove director

Special notice has been given to the company in accordance with sections 303 and 379 of the Companies Act 1985 of the intention to propose the following resolution as an ordinary resolution:

THAT Mrs S Brown be removed from office as a director of the company.

P. 25.15C Director's removal – Letter from company accompanying copy of notice sent to the director concerned

Dear Mrs Brown,
Please find enclosed a copy of a notice received by the company from Mr Brown (a member of the company) stating that he intends at the next general meeting of the company to propose a resolution to remove you as a director of the company.
Yours sincerely,

[Secretary]
[Copy of notice enclosed]

P. 25.16 Special resolution to allow 14 days' notice of general meetings of a listed company

To authorise the calling of general meetings of the company (not being an annual general meeting) by notice of at least 14 clear days.

[*Note:* Unless this resolution is passed at every annual general meeting of a listed company, the company will be required under s. 307 to give 21 days' notice of all general meetings. The company must also offer the facility for shareholders to vote by electronic means accessible to all shareholders in order to call general meetings at less than 21 days' notice.]

CHAPTER 26: MINUTES

See also **Precedents for Chapter 4**

P. 26.14A Minutes of Annual General Meeting of Public Limited Company

Minutes of the annual general meeting of XYZ PLC held on [date] at [place]

Present: [Name of director], Chairman
[Names of other directors]
[Number] members
[Number] proxies representing [number] members

In attendance Secretary

1. The chairman opened the meeting at 11.00 a.m.
2. The chairman proposed and the meeting agreed to take the notice of the meeting as read.
3. [Name] representing [name of auditors] read the report of the auditors to the members.

RESOLUTION 1: LAYING OF ACCOUNTS

4. The chairman proposed THAT the report of the Directors and the audited accounts for the year ended [date], now laid before the meeting, be received. After dealing with questions, the chairman put the resolution to the meeting and declared it carried.

RESOLUTION 2: RE-ELECTION OF DIRECTOR

5. The chairman proposed THAT [name 1], a director retiring by rotation, be re-elected a director of the company.
The resolution was put to the meeting and the chairman declared it carried.

RESOLUTION 3: RE-ELECTION OF DIRECTOR

6. The chairman proposed THAT [name 2], a director retiring by rotation, be re-elected a director of the company.
During the discussion of this proposal, [name], a proxy for a member of the company opposed to the reappointment of [Name 2], attempted to make a speech in breach of article [No.] of the company's articles of association. Despite repeated warnings from the chairman, the proxy refused to be quiet. To general acclamation, the chairman warned him that if he did not comply he would be asked to leave the meeting. The proxy continued speak in a highly aggressive manner. Accordingly, the chairman ordered him to leave the meeting. The proxy ignored the chairman's order and advanced towards the stage in a threatening manner. The chairman ordered the stewards to remove him from the meeting and he was removed following a brief struggle.
After dealing with further questions, the chairman put the resolution to the meeting and declared it carried.

RESOLUTION 4: RE-APPOINTMENT OF AUDITORS

7. The chairman proposed THAT [name of auditors] be reappointed as auditors to hold office until the conclusion of the next general meeting at which accounts are laid before the company and that their remuneration be determined by the directors.

   The resolution was put to the meeting and the chairman declared it carried.

   [Name], a member of the company holding [number] shares, demanded a poll. The chairman ruled that the member was not able satisfy the requirements of article [No.] of the company's articles of association and that the demand was therefore invalid, and confirmed that the resolution had been carried.

RESOLUTION 5: AUTHORITY TO ALLOT

8. The chairman proposed as a special resolution:

   THAT the authority and power conferred on the Directors by Article [No.] (Authority to allot securities) of the Articles of Association of the Company be renewed for the period expiring on the date of the annual general meeting of the Company to be held in [year + 1] and that:

   a   for the purposes of Article [No.], the prescribed amount for the above period shall be [amount 1] and

   b   for the purposes of the proviso to Article [No.], the aggregate nominal amount of equity securities allotted wholly for cash during such period, otherwise than as mentioned in such proviso, shall not exceed [amount 2].

   [Name], a member of the company, proposed an amendment the effect of which would have been to substitute [amount 3] as the prescribed amount for the purposes of Article [No.]. The chairman ruled the amendment out of order and explained that it was not possible to amend the substance of a special resolution.

   After further discussion, the chairman put the resolution to the meeting and declared it carried.

   [Name], a member of the company, and [name], a proxy representing a member of the company, demanded a poll on the resolution. The chairman informed the meeting that the demand was valid and that a poll would be held immediately at which representatives of the company's auditors would act as scrutineers. After the chairman informed the meeting of the poll procedures, voting papers were issued and collected by the company's registrars.

The results of the poll were as follows:

For:	13,567,342
Against:	1,003,231
Votes withheld:	4,006

42. The chairman closed the meeting.

[Signed]
Chairman

P. 26.14B Minutes of board meeting of a public company

EXAMPLE PLC

Minutes of a meeting of the BOARD OF DIRECTORS held on [date] at 27 Fitzwilliam Place, London W1.

Present:	Graham Ware	Director (in the chair)
	Susan Silver	Director
	Richard Wood	Director
	Keith Forbes	Director (for minutes 74 to 79 only)
	Alan Jones	Director
	Fiona Cockburn	Director
In attendance:	A Scribe	Secretary

72. The chairman signed the minutes of the board meeting held on [date], copies having been circulated to the directors.

73. Subsequent to a recommendation by the Nomination Committee it was resolved:

    THAT Mr Andrew de Chancery be and is hereby appointed a director of the company and shall hold office until the next annual general meeting.

74. Mr Keith Forbes joined the meeting.

75. It was resolved:

    THAT pursuant to article [No.] of the company's articles of association, any two directors be appointed a committee to take any actions and to complete all documents necessary to purchase the freehold on 27 Fitzwilliam Place, London W1.

76. There were produced and considered:

    (a) group management accounts made up to 30th September 1994 (Board paper 94/10);

    (b) predicted cash flow statement for the six months to 30th April 1995 (Board paper 94/11).

    It was resolved:

    THAT the company's bankers be approached by Richard Wood to negotiate an increase in the company's overdraft facilities to £2,000,000 to cover the cash shortfall predicted to arise between [date] and [date].

77. There was produced and discussed a paper a document prepared by Susan Silver entitled `Going greener' (Board paper 94/12), on the company's environmental policy. It was resolved:

    THAT no decision could be made to implement the proposals in the paper without detailed costings. The chairman requested Susan Silver to resubmit the proposals at the next board meeting together with a schedule of the projected costs of implementing each of the recommendations for each of the company's subsidiaries.

78. The chairman stated that the next meeting of the board of directors would be held on [date] at Fitzwilliam Place.

79. There being no further business the meeting was closed.

[Signature]
Chairman

P. 26.14C Minutes of a general meeting of a single member company

XYZ LIMITED

Minutes of an extraordinary general meeting held at [place] on [date]
Present: [name] (Chairman)
In attendance: [name] (Company Secretary)

The chairman proposed as a [special] resolution:
THAT ....

After declaring an interest in the resolution to the extent that [nature of interest] this was passed by the sole member of the company as a [special] resolution of the company.

[Signature]
Chairman

PART 7

Appendices, Guidance and Scripts

APPENDIX 1
ICSA's Guidance on Electronic Communications with Shareholders 2007

[Extract from the February 2007 edition of the ICSA Guidance on Electronic Communications with Shareholders 2007]

B6 Failed delivery or non-receipt of information

When the electronic communications provisions were inserted into the Companies Act 1985 by the 2000 Order, Regulation 115 of Table A was amended to refer to the ICSA best practice guide on Electronic Communications with Shareholders. It was provided that 'proof that a notice contained in an electronic communication was sent in accordance with guidance issued by the Institute of Chartered Secretaries & Administrators shall be conclusive evidence that the notice was given'. For those companies which have adopted Regulation 115 in their articles this guidance reproduces here the relevant provisions of the original ICSA best practice guide. It is important that such companies follow the best practice recommended in this section.

With material sent by post the company has only to provide proof of posting. Given the large mailings that are normally involved, this is usually a matter of routine. With information delivered electronically, however, this may not be quite so simple. It will be necessary for the company to set up systems to provide evidence that information has been properly sent by each of the methods being used.

Although the use of the telephone for delivering notices is expected to be a rarity and used only by small companies with few shareholders, it is recommended best practice that when notices are delivered by telephone the company should compile and retain a suitable evidential record of all those contacted with the date and time of the call. A copy of an itemised telephone account showing the numbers called would provide additional evidence of the call but not, of course, of the subject matter.

It is recommended best practice that, when information or notifications of availability are sent by fax, a comprehensive transaction report or log generated by the fax machine should be suitably certified and retained by or on behalf of the company as 'proof of sending'.

It is recommended best practice that, when information or notifications of availability are sent by e-mail, the company should ensure that it uses a system which produces either confirmation of the total number of recipients e-mailed or, preferably, a record of each recipient to whom the message has been sent. A copy of such record and any notices of any failed transmissions and subsequent re-sending, suitably certified, should be retained by or on behalf of the company as 'proof of sending'.

It is recommended best practice that the company should alert those shareholders electing to receive communications electronically that the company's obligation is satisfied when it transmits an electronic message and that it cannot be held responsible for a failure in transmission beyond its control.

However, where the sender of a fax or an e-mail receives a fairly prompt message back to say that delivery was unsuccessful, the company is put on almost immediate notice that the information has not got through to the recipient. It is recommended best practice that the company should, where it is aware of the failure in delivery of an electronic communication (and subsequent attempts do not remedy the situation), revert to sending a hard copy of the communication by mail to the recipient's last known postal address. This should be done within 48 hours of the original attempt. The company should include a standard notice advising the shareholder why he/she is being sent a copy by post and should take the opportunity of asking him/her to confirm his contact details.

It should be noted that it is only a hard copy of the actual document which is being sent electronically which needs to be posted in the event of a communications failure. If that document is merely a notification of availability to say that certain information will be accessible on the website from a specified date, it is not suggested that hard copies of the report and accounts or whatever other information is being made available on the website should also be posted. If, on the other hand, it has been agreed that the shareholder will be sent a full copy of the notice of meeting, the report and accounts etc by fax and it is that transmission which fails then it must be a copy of that same material that is sent by post.

Another point which has been raised regarding the use of e-mail is the ability for some systems to trigger an 'out of office' response to incoming messages. An 'out of office' response cannot be considered to be a failed delivery of the e-mail as to have generated the response the message must have reached its destination. This would be analogous to post piling up on the doormat of a shareholder who has gone on holiday.

The ICSA Guide, *Electronic Communications with Shareholders*, can be obtained from the Policy Unit, ICSA, 16 Park Crescent, London W1N 4AH (see www.icsa.org.uk or call 020 7580 4741 for details).

APPENDIX 2

Matters requiring members' approval

Description of resolution	Type	CA 2006
Articles		
Alteration of articles of association (Note 1)	Special	21(1)
Alteration of an entrenched article (Note 1)	Higher majority than a special	22
Company name		
Change of company name (Note 1) May also be altered by other means provided for by the company's articles (see s. 79).	Special	77
Resolution of a Welsh company that its registered office is to be situated in Wales (Note 1)	Special	88(2)
Resolution of a Welsh company that its registered office is to be situated in England and Wales (Note 1)	Special	88(3)
Re-registration		
Re-registration of private company as public (Note 1)	Special	90(1)
Re-registration of public company as private (Note 1)	Special	97(1)
Re-registration of private company as unlimited	Unanimous	102
Re-registration of unlimited company as limited (Note 1)	Special	105(1)
Re-registration of public company as private unlimited	Unanimous	109
Directors		
Removal of a director (Notes 4 & 5)	Ordinary	168(1)
Approval of a directors' long-term service contract	Ordinary	188(2)

Description of resolution	Type	CA 2006
Approval of substantial property transaction involving director	Ordinary	190(1) and (2)
Approval of a loan to a director	Ordinary	197(1) and (2)
Approval of a quasi-loan to a director	Ordinary	198(2) and (3)
Approval of loans or quasi-loans to persons connected with directors	Ordinary	200(2) and (3)
Approval of credit transaction in favour of director	Ordinary	201(2) and (3)
Approval of related loan, quasi-loan and credit transaction arrangements	Ordinary	203(1) and (2)
Affirmation of a transaction or arrangement entered into by a company in contravention of sections 197, 198, 200, 201 or 203	Ordinary	214
Approval of payment for loss of office to director	Ordinary	217(1) and (2)
Approval of payment for loss of office to a director in connection with the transfer of an undertaking	Ordinary	218(1) and (2)
Approval of payment for loss of office to a director in connection with a transfer of shares in the company, or a subsidiary, resulting from a takeover bid	Ordinary	219(1) and (2)
Ratification by a company of conduct by a director amounting to negligence, default, breach of duty or breach of trust in relation to the company (Note 6)	Ordinary	239(2)
Making provision for employees on cessation or transfer of business	Ordinary	247
Election of a proxy as the chairman of a general meeting	Ordinary	328
Political donations		
Authorisation of political donations or expenditure	Ordinary	366
Accounts		
Public company required to lay its accounts before the company in general meeting (Note 2)	[Ordinary]	437

Description of resolution	Type	CA 2006
Approval of directors' remuneration report of a quoted company	Ordinary	439(1)
Auditors		
Appointment of auditors by the members of a private company	Ordinary	485(4)
Appointment of auditors by the members of a public company	Ordinary	489(4)
Resolution to fix remuneration of auditors	Ordinary	492(1)
Removal of auditors (Note 4)	Ordinary	510(2)
Authorisation by private company of liability limitation agreement with auditors	Ordinary	536(2)
Authorisation by public company of liability limitation agreement with auditors	Ordinary	536(3)
Withdrawal of authorisation of liability limitation agreement with auditors	Ordinary	536(5)
Share capital		
Authority for directors to allot shares (Note 1)	Ordinary	551
Disapplication of pre-emption rights by a private company with only one class of shares (Note 1)	Special	569(1)
Disapplication of pre-emption rights: directors acting under general authorisation (Note 1)	Special	570(1)
Disapplication of pre-emption rights (Note 1)	Special	571(1)
Disapplication of pre-emption rights: sale of treasury shares (Note 1)	Special	573(2) and (4)
Transfer to public company of non-cash asset in initial period (Note 1)	Ordinary	601
Sub-division or consolidation of shares	Ordinary	618(3)
Reconversion of stock into shares	Ordinary	620
Redenomination of share capital (Note 1)	Ordinary	622
Reduction of capital in connection with redenomination (Note 1)	Special	626(2)
Variation of class rights: companies having a share capital (Note 1)	Special	630(4)

Description of resolution	Type	CA 2006
Variation of class rights: companies without a share capital (Note 1)	Special	631(4)
Reduction of capital with solvency statement (Note 1)	Special	641(1) and 642
Reduction of capital (court procedure) (Note 1)	Special	641(1) and 645
Authorisation of the directors of a limited company to determine the terms, conditions and manner of redemption of shares (Note 7)	Ordinary	685(1) and (2)
Authority for off-market purchase of own shares (Notes 1 & 6)	Special	694(2)
Variation of contract for off-market purchase (Notes 1 & 6)	Special	697
Release of company's rights under contract for off-market purchase (Notes 1 and 6)	Special	700
Authority for market purchase of own shares (Notes 1 & 3)	Ordinary / special	701(1) and (4)
Payment out of capital for the redemption or purchase of own shares (Notes 1 & 6)	Special	713 and 716
Debentures		
Power to re-issue redeemed debentures	Ordinary	752(1)
Schemes of arrangement, mergers and divisions		
Scheme of arrangement	75% majority by value of each class	899
Approval of a merger of a public company	75% majority by value of each class	907
Approval of articles of new transferee company (merger)	Ordinary	912
Approval of a division of a public company	75% majority by value of each class	922
Approval of articles of new transferee company (division)	Ordinary	928

Description of resolution	Type	CA 2006
Takeovers		
Opting in and opting out resolutions by listed companies in relation to impediments to takeovers (Note 1)	Special	966(1) and (5)
Electronic communications		
Approval required for deemed agreement of members of company etc to use of website (Note 1)	Ordinary	Sch. 5, para. 10

Insolvency	Type	IA 1986
Resolution to wind up voluntarily (Note 1)	Special	s. 84(1)
Authorise liquidator to transfer assets of company to new company in exchange for securities in the new company (Note 1)	Special	s. 110(3)
Resolution to be wound up by court (Note 1)	Special	s. 122(1)
Members' voluntary winding up, to sanction liquidator's proposals for a compromise with the company's creditors (Note 1)	Special	s. 165(2)

Requirements found in articles	Type	Model Articles
Directions to directors (Note 1)	Special	pcls 4, clg 4 and plc 4
Resolution to disapply article provision which would otherwise prevent a director from being counted as participating in, or voting at, a directors' meeting	Ordinary	pcls 14, clg 14 and plc 17
Appointment of director (Note 8)	Ordinary	pcls 17, clg 17 and plc 20
Issue of a new class of shares	Ordinary	pcls 22 / plc 43
Final dividend	Ordinary	pcls 30 and plc 70
Capitalisation issue	Ordinary	pcls 36 / plc 78
Adjournment of general meeting (Note 9)	Ordinary	pcls 41, clg 27 and plc 33

Common law	Type	
Procedural resolutions at general meetings	Ordinary	

Listed companies	Type	Listing Rules
Cancellation of primary listing (Note 1)	Special	LR 5.2
Employee share schemes and long-term incentive plans	Ordinary	LR 9.4
Class 1 transactions	Ordinary	LR 10.5
Reverse takeover	Ordinary	LR 5.6
Related-party transactions	Ordinary	LR 11.1
Class approval for purchase of own shares (Note 1)	Special	LR 12.4.7

Notes

1 Resolution must be filed at Companies House and embodied in the articles.
2 The Act does not specifically require the company to put a resolution to the members regarding the accounts. However, this is the standard way of dealing with the requirement to lay accounts. Laying means to make them an item of business.
3 The Pre-emption Group Guidelines require listed companies to pass a special resolution.
4 A resolution which requires special notice to be given in accordance with s. 312.
5 Articles cannot exclude the members' right to remove a director by ordinary resolution.
6 Special voting rules apply to these resolutions (see the relevant section of the Act).
7 Although this resolution is not required by the Act to be embodied in the articles, it is suggested that the company does so (particularly where the resolution has the effect of amending the articles).
8 Articles also usually allow appointments of directors to be made by the board.
9 The chairman of the meeting is also given power to adjourn in certain circumstances

APPENDIX 3
Chairman's scripts

This appendix includes specimen scripts for use by the chairman at general meetings. The examples given include scripts for:

- an annual general meeting (this is merely provided as an example and will need to be modified to reflect the resolutions to be proposed) (see **Script 1**);
- delaying the meeting to allow members to register (see **Script 2**);
- dealing with overcrowding in the meeting room (see **Script 3**);
- a poll called by the chairman or one demanded by a member (see **Script 4**);
- a resolution to adjourn (see **Script 5**);
- dealing with amendments (see **Script 6**);
- dealing with disruption (see **Script 7**);
- proposing a formal closure motion to put the question to the vote (see **Script 8**).

1. Chairman's script for annual general meeting

Chairman:	Ladies and gentlemen, I am pleased to welcome you to the annual general meeting of [Company] and declare the meeting open. I propose to take the notice of the meeting as read.
	SHORT PAUSE TO SEE WHETHER ANYONE OBJECTS
Chairman:	Thank you. Before we start the business of the meeting, I would like to take this opportunity to explain how voting will be conducted on the matters before the meeting today, the procedures we will be following to afford as many people as possible with the opportunity to speak and ask questions and various other matters concerning the conduct of the meeting. (*See notes 1 to 5*)
	EXPLAIN VOTING SYSTEM AND PROCEDURES FOR SPEAKING AND ASKING QUESTIONS, ETC
Chairman:	If you have any questions about any of these procedures, please ask a member of the company's staff for assistance. [If you have any questions about your shareholding, please speak to a

member of the registration team on the registration desk either during or after the meeting.] [If you have any questions about any other matter not connected with the business of the meeting, please speak to [person or persons]].

Chairman: I now turn to the business of the meeting.

Chairman: And I call upon [name of auditor] to read the report of the auditors to the financial statements.

AUDITOR TO READ REPORT

Resolution 1:   **Report and accounts**

Chairman: Thank you. I now propose resolution 1 in the notice of meeting [and on your voting cards], namely:

THAT the report of the directors and the audited accounts for the year ended [date], now laid before the meeting, be received.

A copy of the report and accounts was sent to members with the notice of this meeting [and published on our website]. But before putting the resolution to the vote, I would like to draw your attention to certain matters in the report and accounts and update you on the company's performance since the end of the financial year. I will then invite questions and comments from the floor.

CHAIRMAN TO MAKE STATEMENT

Chairman: I now invite questions and comments from the floor on the report and accounts. I will also take questions on my statement. If you wish, you may direct your questions to [Mr Z], the chairman of the Company's Audit Committee, who is seated to my [left/right].

INIVITE [MR Z] TO STAND SO THAT MEMBERS CAN IDENTIFY HIM

Chairman: If you have a question or a point to make, I would be grateful if you [could make yourself known to the staff at the question point nearest to you][raise your hand and wait until a member of staff has supplied you with a microphone]. Before asking your question, you should state your name and whether you are a shareholder or a proxy or corporate representative of a shareholder. If you are a proxy or representative, please state both your name and the name of the shareholder you represent. (*See note 5*)

INVITE QUESTION AND COMMENTS FROM THE FLOOR

Chairman: If nobody has any further questions or points to make on the report and accounts (*slight pause*), I would now ask you to vote on the resolution before the meeting, namely:

THAT the report of the directors and the audited accounts for the year ended [date], now laid before the meeting, be received.

[Those in favour (*pause to count votes*) – those against (*pause to count votes*).

I declare the resolution carried.] (*see note 1*)

Chairman: [The proxy votes submitted before the meeting are shown on the screen and were as follows: [proxy votes]] (*see note 3*)

Resolution 2: Directors' remuneration report

Chairman: I now propose resolution 2 in the notice of meeting [and on your voting cards], namely:

THAT the Directors' Remuneration Report for the year ended [date] be approved.

Before inviting question and comments from the floor, I would like to invite [Mr Y], the chairman of the Company's Remuneration Committee to explain briefly how the committee works.

CHAIRMAN OF REMUNERATION COMMITTEE TO MAKE REPORT

Chairman: I now invite questions and comments on the Directors' Remuneration Report. You may direct any questions you have on the Report either to me or [Mr Z].

AFTER DEALING WITH QUESTIONS, IF ANY

Chairman: I now put the resolution THAT the Directors' Remuneration Report for the year ended [date] be approved.

[Those in favour (*pause to count votes*) – those against (*pause to count votes*)

I declare the resolution carried.] (*see note 1*)

Chairman: [The proxy votes submitted before the meeting are shown on the screen and were as follows: [proxy votes]] (*see note 3*)

Resolution 3: Dividends

Chairman: I now propose resolution 3 in the notice of meeting [and on your voting cards], namely:

THAT the final dividend of [5.8p] per share recommended by the directors of the Company be declared payable on [date] to the holders of ordinary shares registered at the close of business on [date].

Does anyone have any questions or points to make on this resolution?

AFTER DEALING WITH QUESTIONS, IF ANY

Chairman: I now put the resolution THAT the final dividend of [5.8p] per share recommended by the directors of the Company be declared payable on [date] to the holders of ordinary shares registered at the close of business on [date].

[Those in favour *(pause to count votes)* – those against *(pause to count votes)*

I declare the resolution carried.] *(see note 1)*

Chairman: [The proxy votes submitted before the meeting are shown on the screen and were as follows: [proxy votes]] *(see note 3)*

Resolutions 4: Re-election of director

Chairman: I now turn to the re-election of directors retiring by rotation (resolutions 4 and 5 in the notice of meeting [and on your voting cards]). As you may be aware, under the company's articles of association one third of the directors (including the executive directors) must retire each year and offer themselves for re-election [and that any director who has not been re-elected at either of the last two annual general meetings must retire and offer themselves for re-election]. This year the directors to retire by rotation are [name] and me. As I am one of the directors seeking reappointment, it would not be right for me to propose that resolution. I will therefore ask my colleague [name] to do so when we come to that item. However, before doing so I have pleasure in proposing:

THAT [name], a director retiring by rotation, be re-elected a director of the company.

Chairman: [Name] has been a director of the company since [year]. [Other statement regarding [name]. Brief biographical details regarding [name] can be found on page [x] of the notice of meeting.

INVITE QUESTIONS & COMMENTS

Chairman: I now put the resolution to the meeting. Those in favour [pause to count votes] – those against [pause to count votes].

I declare the resolution carried.

Chairman: Thank you. [The proxy votes submitted before the meeting are shown on the screen and were as follows: [proxy votes]] *(see note 3)*

Resolutions 5: Re-election of chairman as a director

Chairman: I now call upon [name] to propose the next resolution (resolution 5 in the notice of meeting [and on your voting cards].

[Name]:   Thank you, I propose:

THAT [name of chairman], a director retiring by rotation, be re-elected a director of the company.

INVITE QUESTIONS & COMMENTS

Chairman: If there are no [further] questions, I now put the resolution to the meeting.

[Those in favour (*pause to count votes*) – those against (*pause to count votes*)

I declare the resolution carried.] (*see note 1*)

Chairman: Thank you. [The proxy votes submitted before the meeting are shown on the screen and were as follows: [proxy votes]] (*see note 3*)

Resolution 6: Reappointment of auditors

Chairman: The next resolution (resolution 6 in the notice) is:

THAT [name of auditors] be reappointed auditors of the company to hold office to the conclusion of the next general meeting at which accounts are laid and that their remuneration be fixed by the directors

and I ask [name of shareholder], a shareholder, to propose this resolution.

[Shareholder]:   I propose the resolution.

Chairman: Thank you. The reappointment of the auditors has been recommended by the Company's Audit Committee. If you wish, you may direct your questions to [Mr Z], the Chairman of the Audit Committee, or to me. I can confirm that the Company is not proposing to adopt an auditors' liability limitation agreement as we do not feel it would be in the best interests of shareholders to do so.

INVITE QUESTIONS & COMMENTS

Chairman: If there are no further questions or comments, I now put the resolution to the meeting, namely THAT [name of auditors] be reappointed auditors of the company to hold office to the conclusion of the next general meeting at which accounts are laid and that their remuneration be fixed by the directors.

[Those in favour (*pause to count votes*) – those against (*pause to count votes*)

I declare the resolution carried.] (*see note 1*)

Chairman: [The proxy votes submitted before the meeting are shown on the screen and were as follows: [proxy votes]] (*see note 3*)

Resolution 7:   Adoption of new Articles of Association

Chairman: I now turn to the last item of business on the agenda for today's meeting, namely resolution 7. I therefore propose as a special resolution:

THAT the regulations in the document produced at the meeting, and signed by me so as to identify it, be adopted as the company's articles of association in substitution for and to the exclusion of all existing articles of association of the Company.

The reasons for recommending these alterations and their effect is explained on page [No.] of the notice of this meeting. In view of the number of changes it was decided that it would be easier to adopt new articles incorporating all of the changes to the existing articles. As the adoption of new articles is proposed, a separate resolution to renew the directors' authority to allot unissued shares in the capital of the Company will not be put to the annual general meeting. Instead, new allotment authority amounts have been inserted in the new articles of association and will become effective if the resolution to adopt the new articles is passed. The relevant amounts are set out on page [No.] of the notice.

I am happy to take questions on this item of business but may ask [name from the company's solicitors or the Company Secretary] to deal with any technical or legal points which arise.

INVITE QUESTIONS & COMMENTS

If there are no further questions, I now put the resolution to the meeting.

[Those in favour (*pause to count votes*) – those against (*pause to count votes*)

I declare the resolution carried.] (*see note 1*)

Chairman: [The proxy votes submitted before the meeting are shown on the screen and were as follows: [proxy votes]] (*see note 3*)

Close the meeting

Chairman: That concludes the business of the meeting and I thank you for your patience. Refreshments will now be served in [place]. All the directors will be available to answer any additional questions which you may have. We will be wearing [red badges/a buttonhole] so that you can identify us. Thank you. We look forward to seeing you next year.

Notes

1. *Voting* – Some companies now take all votes on substantive resolutions at general meetings on poll rather than on a show of hands. Other companies take a show of hands but automatically proceed to a poll on every substantive resolution. Where this is the case, the script will need to be modified accordingly. In some cases companies ask shareholders to complete the voting card on each resolution at the same time that it is put to the meeting (for example, the chairman may say 'I now invite members to vote on resolution number [x] on their voting cards, namely that ...'). In other cases, the chairman puts all the resolutions to the meeting at or near the beginning of the meeting and then invites question or comments on each item in turn. Some companies prefer to do this because it allows members to vote on all the resolutions immediately, enabling those who want to do so to enter their votes on the voting card and hand them in at any stage during the proceedings. Where this is done the chairman will need to explain the voting procedures at the start of the meeting.

2. *Electronic voting* – The chairman may also need to explain how any electronic voting gadgets should be used, which are now relatively commonplace at meetings of listed companies.

3. *Disclosure of proxy votes* – In the case of a listed company, the chairman may also need to disclose details of proxy votes submitted in advance by way of voting instructions on each resolution after any vote on a show of hands in accordance with the requirements of the Combined Code. The chairman may need to explain at the start of the meeting how these proxy votes will be disclosed, particularly if no votes are to be taken on a show of hands.

4. *Conduct of the meeting* – If the meeting is being held in more than one location, the chairman may need to explain how the proceedings will be managed. It may be preferable for a person at each subsidiary location to give a separate explanation simultaneously while the chairman is doing so at the main meeting location.

5. *Questions* – Shareholders of listed companies have something akin to a right to ask questions. Accordingly, the chairman should be careful to give adequate opportunity for them to do so (see **Chapter 21**).

2. Registration incomplete

Chairman: Despite our best efforts to speed up registration there are still people who are waiting to register. I am told that registration is likely to be completed in about [15 minutes] and I therefore propose, with your consent, to delay the start of the meeting until [time].

IF ANYONE OBJECTS

Chairman: There is room to accommodate everyone now waiting outside and I believe it would be courteous to them to wait [15] minutes so that they can be admitted.

> *Note: If necessary, temporary registration cards should be used so that those affected can be admitted. If a vote is required the votes of those with temporary cards could be taken by requiring them to register.*

3. Room too small

Chairman: Despite booking a room which we expected to be large enough, it is clear that not everyone can be accommodated in this room.

There are approximately [ ] people waiting to get in. People other than members present in person, by corporate representative or by proxy are reminded that they have no absolute right to be present at the meeting. In order to enable members who are outside to be accommodated in this hall, which is where the meeting is being held, it would be most helpful if about [ ] persons present who are not members or proxy holders or corporate representatives of members could volunteer to go to [another specified room]. [There is a one-way audio link so that those in the [specified room] will be able to hear the debate.]

IF ANNOUNCEMENT IS MADE AFTER TIME SET FOR THE MEETING

Chairman: I propose, with your consent, to delay the start of the meeting until [ ] to enable everyone to get settled.

IF ANYONE OBJECTS

Chairman: There is room to accommodate all members in this room and all non-members who cannot get into this room in the [ ] room. It would be courteous to those outside to wait [half an hour] to enable everyone to be accommodated.

> *Note: If after [fifteen minutes] non-members have left but registration is still not complete, temporary registration cards should be used so that those affected can be admitted. If a vote is required the votes of those with temporary cards should be taken by requiring them to register.*

IF PEOPLE REFUSE TO MOVE OR THE ARRANGEMENTS FOR USING THE ROOM DO NOT WORK FOR ANY REASON

Chairman: It is clear that not everyone can be accommodated in this room. Unfortunately, if this meeting is to proceed to business it will be necessary for at least [ ] non-members to leave the meeting to enable members and proxy holders outside this room to get in. Will these people please leave [and go to the [ ] room].

IF INSUFFICIENT NON-MEMBERS LEAVE

Chairman: As non-members are unwilling to leave I propose to adjourn this meeting for [15] minutes while the stewards assist in accommodating them in the [ ] room. If insufficient non-members leave then this meeting cannot continue. If we have to reconvene this meeting further delay and additional expense will be incurred. This can be avoided if non-members (and that includes members of the press who are not themselves members) who have no entitlement to attend this meeting, now leave [and go to the [ ] room].

IF RESISTANCE IS ENCOUNTERED

Chairman: In the circumstances I have no alternative other than to propose the adjournment of this meeting to an alternative venue [which we have arranged at [ ] on [ ] at [ ]]. In order to ensure a valid vote on the question of adjournment I ask again if non-members will please leave now. They should not miss anything as they will have the opportunity to attend the adjourned meeting if the vote to adjourn the meeting is passed.

IF NON-MEMBERS DO THEN LEAVE AND MEMBERS GET IN – PUT MOTION TO ADJOURN TO A VOTE. IF NECESSARY CALL A POLL IF EVERYBODY IS STILL NOT ACCOMMODATED

Chairman: There are still some members outside but I am going to put to the vote my proposal to adjourn to [ ] on [ ] at [ ] anyway. The stewards will attempt to count the votes of those outside.

IF THE VOTE IS LOST ON A SHOW OF HANDS, AN ATTEMPT SHOULD BE MADE TO PUT IT TO A POLL

Chairman: I also adjourn the meeting on my own authority pursuant to the inherent power vested in me as Chairman of this meeting. A further registration form will be posted to you to enable you to attend the adjourned meeting. [If you are uncertain whether you will be able to attend this meeting, proxy cards can be collected on the way out.] Proxies should be returned by [not less than 48 hours before the time of the adjourned meeting].

4. Poll procedures

Subject to the articles, the chairman has power to suspend the proceedings for the purposes of taking a poll on a resolution. If the demand for a poll is valid, the poll is normally taken either immediately or at the end of the meeting after any other business has been concluded. A poll may need to be taken immediately because the nature of the business requires it (e.g. a poll on resolution to adjourn) or because the articles require all polls to be taken immediately. A poll called on an amendment will need to be taken before the vote on the substantive resolution. See further Chapter 16 on voting, Chapter 22 on adjournments and Chapter 23 on amendments.

4.A Poll called by chairman

Chairman: In the circumstances, I exercise my right [under the articles] as Chairman of the meeting to call a poll on the resolution. The poll will be conducted [immediately] [at the end of the meeting and in the meantime I will proceed with the remaining business of the meeting] [on [date], at [time] and [place] and in the meantime I will proceed with the remaining business of the meeting].

WHEN TIME FOR POLL, GO TO POLL PROCEDURE AT 4.C

4.B Demand by a member

Member(s): [Demand(s) a poll.]

Chairman: [I should point out that proxies representing [number] of votes have instructed me to vote in favour of the resolution and that proxies have given me discretion as to how to vote in respect of [number] of shares, which I also intend to vote in favour of the resolution, giving a total of [number] of votes in favour. This represents [percent] of all of the proxy votes lodged when the [number] votes which proxies have instructed me to vote against the resolution are included. In view of the [considerable] level of support in favour of the resolution, it seems highly likely that it will be carried [by a significant majority/by the required majority of 75%]. As the conduct of a poll is a lengthy process, do those calling for a poll still feel that this is a worthwhile exercise?]

IF MEMBER STANDS DOWN

Chairman: Thank you. I will proceed with the business of the meeting.

IF MEMBER PERSISTS

Chairman: Under the Company's Articles of Association, a poll can only be demanded by the Chairman or by [state relevant conditions].
       Do you satisfy any of these conditions?

IF NO, RULE OUT OF ORDER AND:
(A) IF THE POLL WAS DEMANDED BEFORE A SHOW OF HANDS, PROCEED WITH THE VOTE ON A SHOW OF HANDS.
(B) IF THE POLL WAS DEMANDED AFTER A SHOW OF HANDS, STATE THAT THE RESULT OF THE VOTE ON THE SHOW OF HANDS STILL STANDS AND DECLARE THE RESOLUTION CARRIED [OR NOT CARRIED], WHETHER OR NOT THIS DECLARATION WAS PREVIOUSLY MADE

IF YES:

Chairman: So that we can verify that the request is properly made, will you please make yourselves provide your name(s) and details to the Company's Registrar.

IF VALID DEMAND FOR POLL ON RESOLUTION TO ADJOURN, GO TO # OTHERWISE

Chairman: If the poll has been validly demanded, it will be conducted [immediately. Accordingly I would ask members to be patient while we check whether the demand is valid.] [at the end of the meeting and I will explain the procedures when the time comes. In the meantime, I propose to proceed with the other business of the meeting] [on a later date which I will announce before the close of the meeting.]

IF NOT TO BE TAKEN IMMEDIATELY, RETURN TO MAIN SCRIPT WHEN REMAINING BUSINESS COMPLETE, GO TO POLL PROCEDURE AT 4.C

4.C Conduct of poll

Chairman: A poll on resolution [No.] [text of resolution] will now be conducted [by our Registrars] and I would ask the Secretary to describe the procedure for taking the poll.

Secretary: Please remain in your seats while the poll is being conducted. Polling cards will now be distributed.
       On a poll each member present in person, by corporate representative or proxy has one vote for every share held. If you have

already lodged a form of proxy you do not have to vote again now unless you wish to change the way you originally voted. If you do not wish to change your mind it will speed up the poll procedure if you do not vote again now.

A separate poll card should be used for each separate holding. If you are representing more than one holding, please ask for additional cards as necessary. If you are not authorised or do not want to vote all the shares owned by a member, you should indicate the number of shares to be voted in the appropriate box on the voting card. If you do not, all the shares registered in your name or in the name of the person you are representing will be included in the count. If two or more persons are jointly registered as shareholders, any one of them may vote either in person or by proxy. If more than one of the joint holders votes then only the vote of the joint holder whose name appears first on the register of members will be counted.

Proxies and corporate representatives should complete a separate voting card and should provide their own details and the name of the member they represent. If requested to do so corporate representatives must be prepared to provide the registrars with some form of identification and their written authority to exercise the votes.

Note. Articles rarely require presentation of authority and it should only be insisted upon if a reasonable suspicion exists of wrongdoing.

Completed cards should be placed in one of the boxes at the exits from the hall. If you are unsure about how to complete the voting card or have any other questions about the poll procedures our staff will be pleased to answer your queries.

IN ADDITION TO CASTING HIS OWN VOTE (IF ANY), CHAIRMAN SHOULD COMPLETE VOTING CARDS FOR AND AGAINST THE RESOLUTION IN ACCORDANCE WITH THE PROXIES HELD BY HIM.

AFTER A SUITABLE INTERVAL THE CHAIRMAN SHOULD GIVE NOTICE OF HIS INTENTION TO CLOSE THE POLL

Chairman: I intend to declare the poll closed in five minutes. Please ensure that your completed card has been handed in.

WHEN THE CARDS HAVE ALL BEEN HANDED IN EITHER:

Chairman: Thank you ladies and gentlemen, the poll is now closed. The voting cards will be processed by the scrutineers who will calculate the results of the poll as soon as possible. The results of the poll will be announced in this room but this will probably take about [ ] hours. I therefore adjourn the meeting pending the declaration of the result of the poll.

OR:

Chairman: Thank you ladies and gentlemen. The poll is now closed. As the results of the poll will need to be checked, it will not be possible to know the result for some time. We expect that the result of the poll(s) will [be published on our website and in an announcement via our regulatory information service]. This concludes the business of the meeting and I now declare the meeting closed pending the calculation of the results. Thank you very much for attending.

5. Adjournment

5.A Proposal by chairman

The motion for adjournment should include the day, time and place of the adjourned meeting or authorise the Board or the Chairman to determine such matters. The Chairman should give his views on or reasons for the proposal and invite debate from the floor.

The Chairman has an inherent power, in limited circumstances, to adjourn the meeting if it is necessary to enable members to debate and vote on the business of the meeting (e.g. if the room is too small to accommodate those entitled to attend or to deal with a disturbance).

If the meeting is adjourned, further proxies may become valid as the articles may allow proxies to be lodged up to 48/24 hours before the time of the adjourned meeting.

Chairman: In accordance with Article [ ] of the Company's Articles of Association I propose that this meeting be adjourned:
- [for [x] minutes]
- [to [another place]]
- [until date, time and place]
- [indefinitely]
- [to a time, date and place to be fixed by the directors and notified to members].

AFTER DEBATE ENDS

I now propose to put the proposal to adjourn to the vote. Ladies and gentlemen the proposal is that the meeting be adjourned:

- [for [x] minutes]
- [to [another place]]
- [until date, time and place]
- [indefinitely]
- [to a time, date and place to be fixed by the directors and notified to members].

Will those in favour of the proposal to adjourn please raise their hands / [colour] voting cards.
Thank you.
Those against. Thank you.

IF VOTE CARRIED EITHER:

Chairman: The proposal to adjourn the meeting has been carried.
This meeting stands adjourned:
- [for [x] minutes]
- [to [another place]]
- [until date, time and place]
- [indefinitely]
- [to a time, date and place to be fixed by the directors and notified to members].

IF VOTE NOT CARRIED:

Chairman: I declare the resolution not passed on a show of hands and in accordance with article [No.] of the Company's Articles of Association I therefore exercise my right to demand a poll on the proposal to adjourn the meeting.

Note: The Chairman should state how he intends to vote the proxies that he holds. When deciding how to cast the votes of proxies the Chairman should consider the intentions of the shareholders who have appointed him as their proxy and act accordingly. Therefore how the Chairman votes will depend on the circumstances. If in doubt the Chairman should seek advice on the matter.

THE POLL MAY NEED TO BE TAKEN IMMEDIATELY
GO TO POLL PROCEDURES AT 4.C.

5.B Proposal for adjournment from the floor

Member: I propose that the meeting be adjourned.
Chairman: Are you a member, proxy or corporate representative?

IF NO:

Chairman: Rule out of order.

IF YES:

Chairman: I will ask the Registrars to verify your status. Will shareholders please bear with me while this exercise is completed.
Note: This must be done immediately – no other business can be carried out if a valid proposal to adjourn is outstanding.

IF STATUS IS NOT CORRECT:

Chairman: The Registrars advise me that you do not have the required status to propose an adjournment. I therefore rule the proposed adjournment out of order. (Return to main script.)

IF STATUS IS CORRECT:

Chairman: What exactly is your proposal? How long do you propose the adjournment should be for?
Member: [At least [No of days] – give reasons].
Chairman: Would your proposal then be [for example, to adjourn for a minimum of [No of days] to a place, date and time to be fixed by the Board]?
Note: The Chairman may have to assist the shareholders in formulating a suitable proposal.
Member: [Yes]
Note: The Chairman should allow the Member to explain his point of view and allow debate on the motion generally.
Chairman: I now propose to put the proposal to adjourn to the vote. Ladies and gentlemen, the proposal is that the meeting be adjourned [in accordance with the proposal agreed with the member]. Will those in favour of the proposal place please raise their hands/ [colour] voting cards.
Thank you.

PAUSE TO ESTIMATE VOTES.

Those against. Thank you.

IF PROPOSAL IS CARRIED, CHAIRMAN COULD CALL FOR A POLL:

Note: When deciding how to cast the votes of proxies, the Chairman must consider the intentions of the shareholders who have appointed him as their proxy and act accordingly. Therefore how the Chairman votes will depend on the circumstances. For instance, if the intention of the adjournment is to defeat the resolution, the Chairman should cast the votes of those proxies who voted against the resolution in favour of the proposal to adjourn. If in doubt the Chairman should seek advice on the matter.

Chairman: In accordance with Article [No] of the Company's Articles of Association, I call for a poll on the proposal to adjourn the meeting. On this poll on the proposal to adjourn I am assuming that those members who have appointed me with a direction that I vote in favour of [resolution [ ]] [the resolutions proposed in the notice of meeting] approve of the conduct of the business before the meeting at this time.

Accordingly, I intend to cast those votes against the proposal to adjourn. I also propose to cast against the proposal those votes where I have been given a discretion how to vote. These amount in total to [ ] votes. [I intend to abstain] in relation to those members who have appointed me with a direction that I vote against [resolution [ ]] [the resolutions proposed in the notice of meeting].

GO TO POLL PROCEDURE AT 4.C.

IF PROPOSAL NOT CARRIED, PROCEED WITH BUSINESS OF MEETING

IF PROPOSAL IS NOT CARRIED BUT THERE IS A CALL FOR A POLL FROM THE FLOOR:

Chairman: A proposal to adjourn the meeting has been called for. Before I explain the procedure I think the meeting should be aware that on the poll I am assuming that those members who have appointed me with a direction that I vote in favour of [resolution [ ]] [the resolutions proposed in the notice of meeting] approve of the conduct of the business before the meeting at this time. Accordingly, I intend to cast those votes against the proposal to adjourn. I also propose to cast against the proposal those votes where I have been given a discretion how to vote. These amount in total to [ ] votes. I intend to abstain in relation to those members who have appointed me with a discretion that I vote against [resolution [ ]] [the resolutions proposed in the notice of meeting]. In view of the substantial majority of votes against the proposal to adjourn and as the conducting of a poll is a lengthy process, do those calling for a poll feel that this is a worthwhile exercise?

IF PROPOSAL IS WITHDRAWN PROCEED WITH BUSINESS OF MEETING IF MEMBER PERSISTS, GO TO POLL PROCEDURE AT 4.B.

6. Demand for an amendment to a resolution

An amendment to an ordinary resolution must be relevant to the resolution and with the scope of the notice convening the meeting. Otherwise, it should be ruled out of order. In addition, the amendment must not be so fundamental as to destroy the intent of the original resolution. If it does, it should be ruled out of order. A special resolution may only be passed in the form set out in the notice, so any amendment (other than typographical or grammatical corrections) should be ruled out of order.

Chairman:	Can you tell me whether you are a member, proxy or a corporate representative of a member.
	IF NOT, PROPOSED AMENDMENT SHOULD BE RULED OUT OF ORDER.
Chairman:	What is your full name and in what name is the shareholding registered? I will ask the Registrars to verify your status. Will shareholders please bear with me while this exercise is completed.
	IF STATUS IS NOT CORRECT:
Chairman:	The Registrar advises me that you do not have the required status to call for an amendment so I must rule the proposed amendment out of order.
	RETURN TO THE MAIN SCRIPT.
	IF STATUS IS CORRECT:
Chairman:	The Registrar advises me that your status has been verified. Would you now please state precisely what your proposed amendment is.
Member:	[...............................]
	Note: The Chairman and the Secretary may need to assist the member in framing the amendment.
Chairman:	The proposal is that we amend Resolution [ ] to read as follows [...............................]
	Note: Chairman gives his views on the amendment (taking advice as necessary) and invites debate from the floor, taking comments/questions in turn. After debate ends, the Chairman assesses the mood of the meeting and (if appropriate) asks

whether in the light of the debate the person wishes to withdraw the proposed amendment. If the member does withdraw, return to the main script. If person does not withdraw, or there appears to be support for the amendment, the Chairman should propose a vote.

Chairman: I now put the proposal to amend the Resolution to the vote. The proposal is [repeat proposed amendment].

Those in favour of the proposal to amend the resolution please raise your hands/voting cards.

Thank you.

Those against?

IF AMENDMENT IS CARRIED, CHAIRMAN MAY DEMAND A POLL.

Chairman: In accordance with article [No.] of the Company's Articles of Association I exercise my right to demand a poll on the proposal to amend resolution [ ].

On this poll on the proposal to amend resolution [ ], I am assuming that those members who have appointed me with a direction that I vote in favour of the resolution which it is proposed to amend approve of the resolution in its existing form. Accordingly, I intend to cast those votes against the proposal to amend the resolution. I also propose to cast against the proposal those votes where I have been given a discretion how to vote. These amount in total to [ ] votes. I intend to abstain in relation to those members who have appointed me with a discretion that I vote against the resolution which it is proposed to amend.

GO TO POLL PROCEDURE AT 4.C

IF AMENDMENT NOT CARRIED, PROCEED TO A VOTE ON THE SUBSTANTIVE RESOLUTION UNLESS A POLL IS DEMANDED FROM THE FLOOR, IN WHICH CASE, PROCEED AS FOLLOWS.

Chairman: A poll on the proposed amendment to resolution [No.] has been called for. Before I explain the procedure I think that the meeting should be aware that on the poll I am assuming that those members who have appointed me with a direction that I vote in favour of the resolution which it is proposed to amend approve of the resolution in its existing form. Accordingly, I intend to cast those votes against the proposal to amend the resolution. I also propose to cast against the proposal those votes where I have been given a discretion how to vote. These amount in total to [ ] votes. I intend to abstain in relation to those members who have appointed me with a direction that I vote against the resolution which it is proposed to amend. In view of the substantial majority of votes against the proposal to amend the resolution, and as the conducting of a poll is a lengthy process, do those calling for a poll feel that this is a worthwhile exercise?

Note: As regards proxy votes against the resolution, it is difficult to decide whether the Chairman should vote them for or against the amendment. Accordingly, the safest course is to abstain. The proxy form should be drafted so as to give the Chairman the discretion to vote as he thinks fit on other business at the meeting (including adjournments and amendments validly coming before the meeting). The Chairman may wish to adopt the proposed amendment.

IF MEMBER WITHDRAWS:

Chairman: As you have now decided not to call for a poll, I will proceed with the business of the meeting. I therefore intend to propose the resolution in its original format. Are there any more questions or comments on the main resolution?

RETURN TO MAIN SCRIPT

IF MEMBER PERSISTS, GO TO POLL PROCEDURE AT 4.B

7. Disruption

Chairman: Would you please be quiet so that other members can be heard and the meeting can proceed.

Member: No [or equivalent].

Chairman: If you do not stop I will have to ask you to leave the meeting.

Member: No [or equivalent].

Chairman: This behaviour is intolerable. With the consent of the meeting I propose to expel you from this meeting [pause to assess dissension]. [Mr X] would you please arrange for the stewards to escort this gentleman/lady from the meeting.

IF DISRUPTION IS SUCH AS TO REQUIRE A BRIEF ADJOURNMENT

Chairman: It is quite impossible for this meeting to continue while this disruption is going on. In order to allow tempers to cool and to enable order to be restored I declare this meeting adjourned for 15 minutes or, if necessary, until order has been restored.

Note: In the event that disruption comes from an external source – e.g. a fire alarm is set off – consult advisers. It may be possible to have a short interruption and avoid a full adjournment.

8. Vote on closure of the debate

Chairman: We have now debated this proposal for [time] and I believe that despite the opposition of a small minority, most members would like now to vote on the resolution.

IF NO OPPOSITION, ANNOUNCE A VOTE ON THE RESOLUTION

IF THERE IS STILL OPPOSITION TO THIS

Chairman: In the circumstances I formally propose the following procedural motion, namely:

'THAT the debate be closed and a vote be now taken on the resolution before the meeting.'

No debate is allowed on such a motion. Accordingly, I will shortly be asking you to vote on the motion by a show of hands. If the motion is defeated, the debate on the main resolution will be allowed to continue. If the motion is carried, we will then proceed immediately with a vote on the main resolution before the meeting.

PROCEED TO VOTE ON A SHOW OF HANDS

Chairman: I declare the motion carried. Accordingly we will now vote on the original resolution before the meeting.

IF CLOSURE MOTION IS NOT CARRIED, DISCUSSION ON THE RESOLUTION MUST BE ALLOWED TO CONTINUE

APPENDIX 4
Specimen briefing document for AGM

1. Location

The company's AGM will take place at [Venue], [Address]

The areas being used are as follows:

Registration	Foyer, ground floor
Cloakroom	Foyer, ground floor
Shareholders' catering	[Room 1], third floor
Customer enquiries	[Room 1], third floor
Shareholder enquiries	[Room 1], third floor
Exhibition	[Room 2], third floor
Board members' lounge	[Room 3], third floor
Registrars' room	[Room 4], third floor
Organisers' office	[Room 5], third floor
Press office	[Room 6], third floor
Investor relations office	[Room 7], third floor
Researchers' room	[Room 8], third floor
AGM	[Room 9 and Room 2], third floor
Lunch	[Room 10], second floor

2. Car Parking

Chauffeurs bringing directors and their guests to the AGM may drive onto the forecourt of the [Venue]. If chauffeurs remain with their vehicles, they may wait on the forecourt but otherwise they must leave the area for the duration of the AGM.

There are no car parking facilities for company staff or shareholders on site, but there are car parks within walking distance at [locations].

3. Timetable

[Day before AGM]
Delivery and installation of stage set, display stands, question and answer system and exhibition panels throughout the morning.

1400	Company staff arrive for familiarisation tours and briefing
1430	Registrars' equipment delivery and installation
1600	Lighting check
1630	Company researchers arrive for briefing with Q & A personnel in [Room 8]
1700	Directors arrive for rehearsals

Friday 5 August 1994

0800	Chairman's rehearsal
0830	Company staff arrive
0845	Security and fire safety briefing
0930	All staff at their posts
0945	All public areas to be ready
1000	Doors open
1055	Board escorted onto stage
1100	AGM commences
1300–1330	AGM ends
1330	Lunch commences
1400	Displays dismantled and removed according to agreed delivery schedule
1800	All company equipment to be removed from the building

4. Security and Fire Safety Procedures

In the event of an emergency, the security personnel at [Venue] will take all necessary action. If a suspicious object is discovered or if there is any other security or safety problem, please contact the organisers' office in [Room 5] immediately. The organisers can then take steps to contact all the relevant authorities.

Company personnel will be briefed by Venue staff on the fire alarm and safety procedures at the Security and Fire Safety Briefing on the morning of the AGM. The Venue has confirmed that there will be no fire alarm tests on the day of the AGM.

In the event of a fire alarm or security alert, the chairman will immediately adjourn the meeting [for a short period] in order to establish whether the Venue needs to be evacuated. If on the advice of Venue staff, it is recommended that the venue be evacuated, the chairman will adjourn the meeting for [one hour] but also inform them that if it proves to be impossible to reconvene in [one hour] that the meeting will be adjourned until further notice. He will then request members and guests to leave the venue by the designated exits. Company personnel should assist and guide members and guests (particularly those who are disabled) to the exits.

If it proves to be possible to re-enter the Venue and to reconvene the meeting within [one hour], Registration Personnel should only admit those who have the correct badges or who can prove their identity in some other way.

5. First Aid Procedures

First aid staff from St John's Ambulance Brigade will be in attendance at the Meeting and there is a fully equipped first aid room on site. In the event of an emergency, please contact the St John's Ambulance Brigade representative in [Room 2] direct or contact the organisers' office in [Room 5].

6. Guidelines for [Company] Registration Personnel

Registration is the point at which it is established whether people have the right to attend the meeting and also the means whereby shareholder attendance numbers are obtained. Company personnel are to follow the procedures set out below:

(a) Shareholders should bring with them their admission card sent to them with the Company's annual report. (Samples will be provided to Company personnel involved.)

(b) Shareholders producing such cards should be asked to hand you the card in return for which you should give them a yellow shareholder (voting) card and a folder containing the Chairman's welcome letter and notice for the meeting. Shareholders are also to be provided with a badge. It is imperative that you obtain their admission card before handing them a shareholder badge card and folder. Thereafter shareholders are free to make their way to the lifts for the exhibition and catering area and meeting room which are all on the third floor.

(c) Shareholders who wish to bring a guest into the meeting with them can do so but the guest is to be given a shareholder guest badge together with a pink guest card (which is non-voting), and a folder.

(d) Where two people are joint shareholders and both wish to attend, only the first named may have a yellow voting card, the second must be given a pink guest card and folder. Although the second shareholder is not technically a guest, this is the only practical way of preventing a double vote against a single holding.

(e) Staff shareholders who only hold free and matching shares are not entitled to attend the meeting and any staff producing any blue card should be referred to [Registrars] personnel.

(f) Institutional shareholders or corporate bodies are entitled to appoint a corporate representative to attend the meeting and vote on their behalf. Such corporate representatives should produce a letter of authorisation on their company letter heading to this effect. Such letters should be signed by their company secretary or director and strictly speaking should also bear their company's seal, but the latter is not always applied. If you consider this letter to be authentic hand the representative a shareholder badge, a yellow shareholder voting card and folder. If you are in any doubt refer the individual to [Registrars] personnel.

(g) Shareholders without admission cards or anyone who says they are a proxy, should be referred to the desks staffed by [Registrars] personnel.

(h) Likewise, there are separate registration procedures for the press and guests of the company who should be referred to the appropriate desk.

(i) Under no circumstances should anyone who does not have any means of identification be admitted. If in any doubt, refer to [Name] of [Registrars] who will contact security if necessary.

(j) Please retain all admission cards as the barcodes on these cards will be scanned by [Registrars] personnel during the meeting to enable an accurate count of shareholders attending.

7. Guidelines for [Registrars] Verification Personnel

Verification is the area which handles shareholders who cannot be admitted to the meeting directly through registration. Most of these will be shareholders who have forgotten their admission cards but there may also be proxies.

The clerical procedures are as follows:

(a) A person claiming to be a shareholder who has forgotten his voting card should be asked his name, address and number of shares. These details should be compared to the details on the computer and if the details agree the shareholder should be asked to sign the attendance record and is given a yellow shareholder voting card.

(b) A person claiming to be a proxy should be asked his name and that of the shareholder he represents. These details should be compared to the list of proxies provided and if the details agree the proxy should be asked to sign the attendance record and given a blue proxy card. Any proxy who is not on the list may not be admitted, except as a guest under certain circumstances.

(c) There will be separate registration procedures for people who are guests of the company or members of the press, and these people should be referred to the appropriate desk staffed by Company personnel.

(d) Employees who hold free and matching shares or share options are not shareholders and may only be admitted to the meeting if they have stock as well. If such staff are insisting on admission it is suggested that you contact [Name] and the Company's security adviser, who collectively will determine the appropriate course of action.

(e) At the end of the meeting the admission cards and signatures can be counted to establish how many people attended the meeting.

8. Guidelines for Press Registration

The Company's press officer will brief the staff on the press desk as to the procedures to be adopted.

9. Guidelines for Visitors' Registration

Staff on this desk will be provided with guest lists before the meeting. These lists will provide the names of the guests and their status, that is shareholder or guest, so that these staff may issue the appropriate cards, that is yellow or pink and folders.

10. Displays

There will be a series of small displays at the back of the main auditorium for shareholders' general interest before and after the AGM. The displays cover the main businesses such as [. . . .].

Company personnel acting as stewards are to encourage shareholders to visit the display stands and models in the main auditorium. The doors to the main auditorium will be open at 1000 and a P.A. announcement will inform shareholders that the exhibition area is open.

11. Customer and Shareholder Enquiries

There will be a customer enquiry desk situated in [Room 1] staffed by company personnel who will be pleased to answer queries on [. . .].

Shareholders with enquiries relating to their shareholding should be directed to the shareholder enquiry desk situated [. . .]. This desk will be staffed by [Registrars] personnel and company personnel. Any documents on display at the meeting will be available for inspection by shareholders at this desk.

12. Question Points

There will be four question points, two in [Room 1] and two in the auditorium, for any shareholder wishing to raise a question. Question should be registered in advance of the meeting as far as possible – details of this will be given to shareholders on their arrival. Included in the shareholders' folders will be a shareholder question card. The question card is for those shareholders who would prefer to receive a written answer – or if there is insufficient time for their question to be asked at the Meeting.

A number of questions that shareholders may have can be answered either at the customer enquiry desk or the shareholder enquiry desk and personnel at the question points should direct them as necessary.

13. Question and Answer Management System

The system consists of purpose-designed software running on a network of IBM compatible PCs. The configuration of the system consists of four question registration points, each with a computer and printer, two PCs and printers processing the answers to the questions and two further PCs outputting the next question (preview) or the 'on air' question (current). The system is split into four parts:

- front of house question registration points, two in [Room 1] and two in the auditorium;
- the research area behind the scenes;
- outputting information to the platform; and
- on stage equipment.

At each registration point there is a computer and printer. There will be two personnel, a computer operator and a member of Company staff. The company employee is the first to meet the questioner. They make sure that he/she is entitled to ask a question (i.e. is a shareholder holding a yellow voting card). They should have sufficient procedural knowledge to be able to allocate the question to the correct resolution by reference to the Notice of Meeting.

Shareholders may need assistance to compose their questions and therefore company staff may wish to encourage questioners to draft questions on the pads provided at each point.

The question is then dictated to the computer operator. It is allocated a unique number which relates to the resolution to which it applies. Once the question has been entered, a print-out of the question is provided for the questioner to keep. A badge is also generated with all the essential information on it (i.e. question number, resolution number and the question point in the auditorium from which it is to be asked).

The badge is marked with a colour sticker and worn by the questioner to aid his or her identification as the questioner by company personnel and [Event Organisers] staff marshalling questioners within the auditorium.

As the question is printed out for the questioner it is simultaneously networked to the research area, stored on the file server, and printed out on two part paper. In the research area there would be a number of senior company representatives with their own co-ordinator. One copy of the question goes to the co-ordinator who will then decide which researcher will answer it and pass it on. The other copy is filed as a control by the question controller backstage in [Room 8].

Once the question has been answered, hopefully with bullet points provided by the researchers, it is collected by either of two computer operators who add the answers to the questions. Once the answer has been added the page is re-stored on the fileserver and printed out again, locally, on two part paper. One copy is given to the question controller and the other held as a paper back-up.

The PCs and operators output to the stage. They will output the questions in the order called by the question controller. One PC is dedicated to previewing the next question, the other outputs the current question. At any time additional information can be added to the displayed page to cope with supplementary or non pre-registered questions. Any alterations made on the screen will be reflected instantly on the on-stage monitors.

On the platform the Chairman will have one monitor dedicated to the current question and one dedicated to the next question, or preview. Executive directors will have one monitor each with a switch to select 'next' or 'on-air' and non-executive directors will have one switchable monitor between two.

14. Entrance to the Auditorium

Company personnel acting as stewards will monitor the admission of people entering the auditorium. Shareholders and their guests should have badges and have yellow or pink cards. Proxies should have a badge and blue card. Other personnel entering the auditorium should be wearing badges: either Company personnel, or [Registrars] personnel or representatives from the press or organisers.

15. Seating Arrangements

Seating for guests will be in the front row of the two seating blocks. Seating for questioners is in the back row of the two seating blocks, adjacent to the question points. Shareholders with pre-registered questions will be identified with badges and staff marshalling this area should seat questioners next to question point A or B in the auditorium as per the instruction on the badge. The question points are identified by overhead signs.

An area of the right side of the auditorium has been reserved for shareholders with wheelchairs and a signed area has been fitted with an induction loop system for the hard of hearing. Chairs will also be allocated for those accompanying the disabled.

Other shareholders may sit where they choose but if possible should be encouraged to sit near the front so that late arrivals sit towards the back. No special arrangements have been made for the press.

16. Annual General Meeting

The meeting will commence at 1100. Prior to this background music will be played in the auditorium from 1000. A short opening sequence of slides will be shown during this period. Once the meeting has commenced, company personnel may take their seats in the reserved area at the rear of the auditorium.

The finishing time of the meeting cannot be ascertained, but the anticipated time is between 1300 and 1330. At this time, **all** exhibition, registration and customer/shareholder enquiry personnel should resume their positions until the last shareholder leaves the building.

17. Counting of Votes by a Show of Hands

[Registrars] personnel will be responsible for recording and counting the show of hands (that is, by shareholders raising their yellow cards) if it is not clear whether the resolution has been carried or not. [Name] of [Registrars] will be positioned near one of the Question Points in the auditorium so as to communicate with the Chairman.

18. Poll

[Registrars] personnel are responsible for conducting a poll should the event occur. Again, [Name] of [Registrars] will be strategically placed near one of the question points so as to be able to communicate with the Chairman as to the validity of the poll request. The detailed procedure on the conduct of a poll will be dealt with by the Company Secretary at the Meeting. Ballot boxes and poll cards will be stored under lock and key in the registrars' office and only brought out by [Registrars] personnel in the event of a poll.

19. Organisers' Staff

The Company AGM is organised by the [Venue] and [Event Organisers]. As well as technical crew, stewards, caterers and security staff, the following people will be on duty throughout the day.

[Name]	event director	[Event Organisers]
[Name]	question controller	[Event Organisers]
[Name]	senior producer	[Venue]
[Name]	producer	[Venue]
[Name]	centre co-ordinator	[Venue]
[Name]	head of security	[Venue]

In the event of any queries or problems, please go to the organisers' office in room 3/10 on the third floor. They are both linked to the other members of the crew by walkie-talkie and can issue instructions as required.

20. Communications

The general telephone number for the [Venue] is [Tel. No.]. To contact representatives of the [Venue] or [Event Organisers], the direct lines to the Company AGM organisers' office are as follows:

[Tel. No.] telephone   [Tel. No.] facsimile

To contact [Company] staff, the direct lines to the investor relations office are as follows:

[Tel. No.] telephone   [Tel. No.] facsimile

21. Catering

Shareholders will be served tea, coffee, orange juice or mineral water in [Room 1] before and after the AGM. The catering service will operate from 1000 to 1100 and 1300 to 1400.

Light refreshments will be served for the board in [Room 3] before and after the AGM.

Lunch will be served to invited guests in [Room 10] from 1330 as a seated buffet.

Appendices

[Location Map of [Venue]]
[Plan of Registration Area (Room 1) and the Auditorium (Room 2 and Room 10)]

PART 8
Statutory Materials

ANNEX A
Companies Act 2006 provisions on meetings

Part 9: Exercise of Members' Rights (ss 145–153)

145   Effect of provisions of articles as to enjoyment or exercise of members' rights
146   Traded companies: nomination of persons to enjoy information rights
147   Information rights: form in which copies to be provided
148   Termination or suspension of nomination
149   Information as to possible rights in relation to voting
150   Information rights: status of rights
151   Information rights: power to amend
152   Exercise of rights where shares held on behalf of others: exercise in different ways
153   Exercise of rights where shares held on behalf of others: members' requests

Part 13: Resolutions and Meetings (ss 281–361)

Chapter 1: General provisions about resolutions
281   Resolutions
282   Ordinary resolutions
283   Special resolutions
284   Votes: general rules
285.   Voting by proxy
285A   Voting rights on poll or written resolution
286   Votes of joint holders of shares
287   Saving for provisions of articles as to determination of entitlement to vote

Chapter 2: Written resolutions
288   Written resolutions of private companies
289   Eligible members
290   Circulation date
291   Circulation of written resolutions proposed by directors
292   Members' power to require circulation of written resolution
293   Circulation of written resolution proposed by members

Chapter 3: Resolutions at meetings

Chapter 4: Public companies and traded companies: additional requirements for AGMs

Chapter 5: Additional requirements for quoted companies and traded companies

ANNEX B1
Companies Act 1985 Table A: Contents and table of destinations

This annex shows the content and layout of the 1985 Table A and the location of any equivalent provisions in the Companies Act 2006 model articles for private companies limited by shares.

1985 Table A	2006 Act model articles for private companies limited by shares
1. Interpretation	1. Defined terms
	2. Liability of members
	21. All shares to be fully paid up
2–3. Share capital	22. Powers to issue different classes of share
4. Power to pay commissions	N/A – see ss. 552 & 553
5. Company not bound by less than absolute interests	23. Company not bound by less than absolute interests
6. Share certificates	24. Share certificates
7. Replacement share certificates	25. Replacement share certificates
8–11. Lien 12–17. Calls on shares 18–22. Forfeiture	N/A
23–28. Share transfers	26. Share transfers
29–31. Transmission of shares	27. Transmission of shares 28. Exercise of transmittees' rights 29. Transmittees bound by prior notices
32–33. Alteration of share capital	N/A – see ss. 617 & 618
34. Power to reduce capital	N/A – see s. 641
35. Power to purchase own shares	N/A – see s. 690

1985 Table A	2006 Act model articles for private companies limited by shares
36. Extraordinary general meetings	N/A
37. Calling general meetings	N/A – see ss. 302–304
38. Notice of general meetings	N/A – see s. 307 (notice required), s. 311 (contents of notices of meetings) and s. 310 (persons entitled to receive notice of meetings)
39. Notice – accidental omission	N/A – see s. 313
40. Quorum – general meetings	37. Attendance and speaking at general meetings 38. Quorum for general meetings See also s. 318
41. Adjournment if no quorum present	41. Adjournment
42–43. Chairing general meetings	39. Chairing general meetings
44. Attendance and speaking by directors	40. Attendance and speaking by directors and non-shareholders
45. Adjournment	41. Adjournment
46. Voting: general 46. Demand for a poll 47. Declaration by the chairman of result on a show hands 48. Demand for poll may be withdrawn 49. Method of taking poll	42. Voting: general 44. Poll votes See also s. 320 (declaration by chairman on a show of hands), s. 321 (right to demand a poll), s. 322 (voting on a poll) and s. 329 (right of proxy to demand a poll)
50. Chairman's casting vote	N/A
51. Timing of certain polls 52. Notice of a poll	See Article 44(4) (Poll votes)
53. Members' written resolutions	N/A – see ss. 288–300
54. Votes of members	N/A – see ss. 284–287
55. Votes of joint holders	N/A – see s. 286
56. Voting by member subject to a mental health order	See Article 27(3) and Article 1 (definition of 'transmittee')
57. No votes on shares unless all moneys presently payable have been paid	N/A – all shares must be fully paid
58. Objection to qualification of any voter	43. Errors and disputes

1985 Table A	2006 Act model articles for private companies limited by shares
59. Voting by proxies on a poll	N/A – see ss. 284–287 & 322
60–62. Appointment of proxies 63. Determination of proxy	45. Content of proxy notices 46. Delivery of proxy notices
	47. Amendments to resolutions
64. Number of directors	N/A
65–69. Alternate directors	N/A
70. Powers of directors	3. Directors' general authority 4. Shareholders' reserve power
71. Power to appoint agents 72. Delegation of directors' powers	5. Directors may delegate 6. Committees
73–75. Retirement of directors	N/A
76–78. Appointment by members 79. Appointment by directors	17. Methods of appointing directors
80. Retiring director continues in office until end of meeting	N/A
81. Disqualification and removal of directors	18. Termination of director's appointment
82. Remuneration of directors	19. Directors' remuneration
83. Directors' expenses	20. Directors' expenses
84. Directors' appointments	19. Directors' remuneration
85–86. Directors' interests	N/A – see ss. 182 to 187
87. Director's gratuities and pensions	19. Directors' remuneration
88. Proceedings of directors	7. Directors to take decisions collectively 9. Calling a directors' meeting 13. Casting vote 16. Directors' discretion to make further rules
89. Quorum for directors' meetings 90. Continuing directors may act to fill vacancies or call a general meeting.	10. Participation in directors' meetings 11. Quorum for directors' meetings
91. Chairing of directors' meetings	12. Chairing of directors' meetings

1985 Table A	2006 Act model articles for private companies limited by shares
92. Directors' acts valid notwithstanding any defects	N/A – see s. 161
93. Written resolution of directors	8. Unanimous decisions
94. Conflicts of interest – voting 95. Director not counted in the quorum if not entitled to vote. 96. Company may suspend or relax rules prohibiting a director from voting	14. Conflicts of interest
97. Appointment of two or more directors to offices or employments with the company	N/A
98. Questions as to the right of a director to vote to be referred to the chairman of the meeting	See Article 14(7) (Conflicts of interest)
99. Secretary	N/A
100. Minutes	15. Records of [directors'] decisions to be kept See also s. 248 and ss. 355 to 359.
101. The seal	49. Company seals
102. Declaration of dividends 103. Interim dividends 104. Apportionment of dividends 105. Non-cash distributions 106. Payment of dividends 107. No interest on distributions 108. Unclaimed distributions	30. Procedure for declaring dividends 31. Payment of dividends and other distributions 32. No interest on distributions 33. Unclaimed distributions 34. Non-cash distributions 35. Waiver of distributions
109. No right to inspect accounts and other records	50. No right to inspect accounts and other records
110. Capitalisation of profits	36. Capitalisation of profits
111–116. Notices	48. Means of communication to be used 29. Transmittees bound by prior notices
117. Winding up – distribution of assets	N/A
	51. Provision for employees on cessation of business
118. Indemnity	52. Indemnity 53. Insurance

ANNEX B2
Companies Act 1985
Table A (as amended)

The default model articles for a company limited by shares incorporated under the Companies Act 1985 are known as the '1985 Table A' and are contained in the Companies (Tables A to F) Regulations 1985. Various amendments have been made to the 1985 Table A over time. If a company is subject to Table A, the applicable version is the one that was in force on the date the company was incorporated. Subsequent statutory modifications do not affect existing companies.

The version of Table A in this Annex is the version which applied to private companies limited by shares incorporated under the Companies Act 1985 between 1 October 2007 and 30 September 2009. Table A was amended:

(a) for companies incorporated on or after 22 December 2000 by the Companies Act 1985 (Electronic Communications) Order 2000 to make provision for the use by companies of electronic communications. Companies incorporated before this date whose articles are based on the unamended version of Table A can still take advantage of the statutory procedures allowing the use of electronic communications (see Chapter 2); and

(b) for companies incorporated on or after 1 October 2007 to reflect the provisions of Part 13 of the Companies Act 2006 on resolutions and meetings that were commenced on that date. These amendments were made by the Companies (Tables A to F) (Amendment) Regulations 2007 (SI 2007/2541) and the Companies (Tables A to F) (Amendment) (No. 2) Regulations 2007 (SI 2007/2826).

The amendments made by these statutory instruments have been incorporated in the following text and are highlighted in italics. Where necessary, the previous text is given by way of notes. Companies subject to Table A that were incorporated under the Companies Act 1985 prior to 22 December 2000 or between that date and 30 September 2007 will need to refer to these notes in order to work out the text that applies to them.

October 2007 changes

The changes made by SI 2007/2541 and SI 2007/2826 for companies incorporated on or after 1 October 2007 were designed to reflect the provisions of Part 13 of the Companies Act 2006 on resolutions and meetings that were commenced on that date. One of the consequences of those amendments was that the regulations made provision for separate versions of Table A for public and private companies to cater for the fact that private companies were no longer required to hold annual general meetings.

The principal changes made by the above regulations are as follows:

- Reg. 2 – Interpretation – The definition of 'the Act' was amended to include provisions of the 2006 Act already in force.
- Reg. 36 – Any meeting not an AGM to be called an extraordinary general meeting – This regulation was deleted for both public and private companies together with all references throughout Table A to 'extraordinary general meetings', which are now referred to as 'general meetings'.
- Reg. 37 – Directors' power/duty to call general meetings – References to the date by which a general meeting must be called deleted to reflect ss. 302–304 of 2006 Act and, in particular, s. 304(1).
- Reg. 38 – Notice of general meetings – For private companies, all references to notice of annual general meetings were deleted. For public companies, reg. 38 remains unchanged barring the deletion of references to extraordinary general meetings.
- Reg. 40 – Quorum – Amended to reflect the fact that, where there is only one member, s. 318 allows a quorum of one qualifying person.
- Reg. 50 – Chairman's casting vote – This regulation was deleted as it was said to conflict with sections 281 and 282 of the Companies Act 2006. The effect of these sections is that a resolution cannot be passed by use of a casting vote by a chairman, although this subject to certain transitional adaptations for private companies.
- Reg. 53 – Written resolutions – Deleted for both public and private companies because it was in conflict with section 281(1) of the 2006 Act for private companies and section 281(2) of the 2006 Act for public companies.
- Reg. 54 – Rights of proxies – This regulation was amended to reflect the new rights for proxies to vote on a show of hands provided by sections 284(2)(b) and 324(1) of the 2006 Act. This regulation now reads: '54. Subject to any rights or restrictions attached to any shares, on a show of hands every member who (being an individual) is present in person or by proxy or (being a corporation) is present by a duly authorised representative or by proxy, unless the proxy (in either case) or the representative is himself a member entitled to vote, shall have one vote and on a poll every member shall have one vote for every share of which he is the holder.'
- Regs. 60–62 – Appointment of a proxy – The forms of proxy provided in regs. 60 and 61 were amended to omit the words 'annual/extraordinary' for private companies and 'extraordinary' for public companies.
- Regs. 73–77, 79 and 80 – Appointment and retirement of directors – For private companies, regs. 73–75 and reg. 80 (retirement of directors) were deleted.

Regs. 76 and 77 have been retained other than references to the appointment and retirement of directors by rotation. The words 'Subject as aforesaid' have been deleted from Reg. 78 and last two sentences deleted from Reg. 79.

■ Reg. 117 – Winding up – A special resolution is now required to authorise a winding up rather than an extraordinary resolution.

TABLE A

(As applicable to private companies limited by shares incorporated between 1 October 2007 and 30 September 2009)

REGULATIONS FOR MANAGEMENT OF A PRIVATE COMPANY LIMITED BY SHARES

INTERPRETATION

1. In these regulations-

"the Act" means the Companies Act 1985 including any statutory modification or reenactment thereof for the time being in force and any provisions of the Companies Act 2006 for the time being in force;[1]

"the articles" means the articles of the company.

"clear days" in relation to the period of notice means that period excluding the day when the notice is given or deemed to be given and the day for which it is given or on which it is to take effect.

[*"communication" means the same as in the Electronic Communications Act 2000, "electronic communication" means the same as in the Electronic Communications Act 2000*][2]

"executed" includes any mode of execution.

"office" means the registered office of the company.

"the holder" in relation to shares means the member whose name is entered in the register of members as the holder of the shares.

"the seal" means the common seal of the company.

"secretary" means the secretary of the company or any person appointed to perform the duties of the secretary of the company, including a joint, assistant or deputy secretary.

"the United Kingdom" means Great Britain and Northern Ireland.

Unless the context otherwise requires, words or expressions contained in these regulations bear the same meaning as in the Act but excluding any statutory

---

1   The italicised words were modified by SI 2007/2541 for companies incorporated on or after 1 October 2007. Prior to that date the definition read: "the Act" means the Companies Act 1985 including any statutory modification or re-enactment thereof for the time being in force.

2   The italicised words were inserted by the Schedule 1 of the Companies Act 1985 (Electronic Communications) Order 2000 on 22 December 2000. Prior to that date Table A did not include a definition of an "electronic communication" or a "communication".

modification thereof not in force when these regulations become binding on the company.

SHARE CAPITAL

2. Subject to the provisions of the Act and without prejudice to the rights attached to any existing shares, any share may be issued with such rights or restrictions as the company may by ordinary resolution determine.

3. Subject to the provisions of the Act, shares may be issued which are to be redeemed or are to be held liable to be redeemed at the option of the company or the holder on such terms and in such manner as may be provided by the articles.

4. The company may exercise the powers of paying commissions conferred by the Act. Subject to the provisions of the Act, any such commissions may be satisfied by the payment of cash or by the allotment of fully or partly paid shares or partly in one way and partly in the other.

5. Except as required by law, no person shall be recognised by the company as holding a share upon any trust and (except as otherwise provided by the articles or by law) the company shall not be bound by or recognise any interest in any share except an absolute right to the entirety thereof in the holder.

SHARE CERTIFICATES

6. Every member, upon becoming the holder of any shares, shall be entitled without payment to one certificate for all the shares of each class held by him (and, upon transferring part of his holding of shares of any class, to a certificate for the balance of such holding) or several certificates each for one or more of his shares upon payment for every certificate after the first of such reasonable sum as the directors may determine. Every certificate shall be sealed with the seal and shall specify the number, class and respective amounts paid thereon. The company shall not be bound to issue more than one certificate for shares held jointly by several persons and delivery of a certificate to one joint holder shall be sufficient delivery to all of them.

7. If a share certificate is defaced, worn-out, lost or destroyed, it may be renewed on such terms (if any) as to evidence and indemnity and payment of the expenses reasonably incurred by the company in investigating evidence as the directors may determine but otherwise free of charge, and (in the case of defacement or wearing-out) on delivery up of the old certificate.

LIEN

8. The company shall have a first and paramount lien on every share (not being a fully paid share) for all moneys (whether presently payable or not) payable at a fixed time or called in respect of that share. The directors may at any time declare any share to be wholly or in part exempt from the provisions of this regulation. The company's lien on a share shall extend to any amount payable in respect of it.

9. The company may sell in such manner as the directors determine any shares on which the company has a lien if a sum in respect of which the lien exists is presently payable and is not paid within fourteen clear days after notice has been given to the holder of the share or to the person entitled to it in consequence of the death or bankruptcy of the holder, demanding payment and stating that if the notice is not complied with the shares may be sold.

10. To give effect to a sale the directors may authorise some person to execute an instrument of transfer of the shares sold to, or in accordance with the directions of, the purchaser. The title of the transferee to the shares shall not be affected by any irregularity in or invalidity of the proceedings in reference to the sale.

11. The net proceeds of the sale, after payment of the costs, shall be applied in payment of so much of the sum for which the lien exists as is presently payable, and any residue shall (upon surrender to the company for cancellation of the certificate for the shares sold and subject to a like lien for any moneys not presently payable as existed upon the shares before the sale) be paid to the person entitled to the shares at the date of the sale.

CALLS ON SHARES AND FORFEITURE

12. Subject to the terms of allotment, the directors may make calls upon the members in respect of any moneys unpaid on their shares (whether in respect of nominal value or premium) and each member shall (subject to receiving at least fourteen clear days' notice specifying when and where payment is to be made) pay to the company as required by the notice the amount called on his shares. A call may be required to be paid by instalments. A call may, before receipt by the company of any sum due thereunder, be revoked in whole or part and payment of a call may be postponed in whole or part. A person upon whom a call is made shall remain liable for calls made upon him notwithstanding the subsequent transfer of the shares in respect whereof the call was made.

13. A call shall be deemed to have been made at the time when the resolution of the directors authorising the call was passed.

14. The joint holders of a share shall be jointly and severally liable to pay all calls in respect thereof.

15. If a call remains unpaid after it has become due and payable the person from whom it is due and payable shall pay interest on the amount unpaid from the day it became due and payable until it is paid at the rate fixed by the terms of allotment of the share or in the notice of the call or, if no rate is fixed, at the appropriate rate (as defined by the Act) but the directors may waive payment of the interest wholly or in part.

16. An amount payable in respect of a share on allotment or at any fixed date, whether in respect of nominal value or premium or as an instalment of a call, shall be deemed to be a call and if it is not paid the provisions of the

articles shall apply as if the amount had become due and payable by virtue of a call.

17. Subject to the terms of allotment, the directors may make arrangements on the issue of shares for a difference between the holders in the amounts and times of payment of calls on their shares.

18. If a call remains unpaid after it has become due and payable the directors may give to the person from whom it is due not less than fourteen clear days' notice requiring payment of the amount unpaid together with any interest which may have accrued. The notice shall name the place where payment is to be made and shall state that if the notice is not complied with the shares in respect of which the call was made will be liable to be forfeited.

19. If the notice is not complied with any share in respect of which it was given may, before the payment required by the notice has been made, be forfeited by a resolution of the directors and the forfeiture shall include all dividends or other moneys payable in respect of the forfeited shares and not paid before the forfeiture.

20. Subject to the provisions of the Act, a forfeited share may be sold, re-allotted or otherwise disposed of on such terms and in such manner as the directors determine either to the person who was before the forfeiture the holder or to any other person and at any time before sale, re-allotment or other disposition, the forfeiture may be cancelled on such terms as the directors think fit. Where for the purposes of its disposal a forfeited share is to be transferred to any person the directors may authorise some person to execute an instrument of transfer of the shares to that person.

21. A person any of whose shares have been forfeited shall cease to be a member in respect of them and shall surrender to the company for cancellation the certificate for the shares forfeited but shall remain liable to the company for all moneys which at the date of forfeiture were presently payable by him to the company in respect of those shares with interest at the rate at which interest was payable on those moneys before the forfeiture or, if no interest was so payable, at the appropriate rate (as defined by the Act) from the date of forfeiture until payment but the directors may waive payment wholly or in part or enforce payment without any allowance for the value of the shares at the time of forfeiture or for any consideration received on their disposal.

22. A statutory declaration by a director or the secretary that a share has been forfeited on a specified date shall be conclusive evidence of the facts stated in it as against all persons claiming to be entitled to the share and the declaration shall (subject to the execution of an instrument of transfer if necessary) constitute a good title to the share and the person to whom the share is disposed of shall not be bound to see to the application of the consideration, if any, nor shall his title to the share be affected by any irregularity in or invalidity of the proceedings in reference to the forfeiture or disposal of the share.

TRANSFER OF SHARES

23. The instrument of transfer of a share may be in any usual form or in any other form which the directors may approve and shall be executed by or on behalf of the transferor and, unless the share is fully paid, by or on behalf of the transferee.

24. The directors may refuse to register the transfer of a share which is not fully paid to a person of whom they do not approve and they may refuse to register the transfer of a share on which the company has a lien. They may also refuse to register a transfer unless-

    (a) it is lodged at the office or at such other place as the directors may appoint and is accompanied by the certificate for the shares to which it relates and such other evidence as the directors may reasonably require to show the right of the transferor to make the transfer;

    (b) it is in respect of only one class of shares; and

    (c) it is in favour of not more than four transferees.

25. If the directors refuse to register a transfer of a share, they shall within two months after the date on which the transfer was lodged with the company send to the transferee notice of the refusal.

26. The registration of transfers of shares or of transfers of any class of shares may be suspended at such times and for such periods (not exceeding thirty days in any year) as the directors may determine.

27. No fee shall be charged for the registration of any instrument of transfer or other document relating to or affecting the title to any share.

28. The company shall be entitled to retain any instrument of transfer which is registered, but any instrument of transfer which the directors refuse to register shall be returned to the person lodging it when notice of the refusal is given.

TRANSMISSION OF SHARES

29. If a member dies the survivor or survivors where he was a joint holder, and his personal representatives where he was a sole holder or the only survivor of joint holders, shall be the persons recognised by the company as having any title to his interest; but nothing herein contained shall release the estate of a deceased member from any liability in respect of any share which had been jointly held by him.

30. A person becoming entitled to a share in consequence of the death or bankruptcy of a member may, upon such evidence being produced as the directors may properly require, elect either to become the holder of the share or to have some other person nominated by him registered as the transferee. If he elects to become the holder he shall give notice to the company to that effect. If he elects to have another person registered he shall execute an instrument of transfer of the share to that person. All the articles relating to the transfer of shares shall apply to the notice or instrument of transfer as if it were an

instrument of transfer executed by the member and the death or bankruptcy of the member had not occurred.

31. A person becoming entitled to a share in consequence of the death or bankruptcy of a member shall have the rights to which he would be entitled if he were the holder of the share, except that he shall not, before being registered as the holder of the share, be entitled in respect of it to attend or vote at any meeting of the company or at any separate meeting of the holders of any class of shares in the company.

ALTERATION OF SHARE CAPITAL

32. The company may by ordinary resolution
    (a) increase its share capital by new shares of such amount as the resolution prescribes;
    (b) consolidate and divide all or any of its share capital into shares of larger amount than its existing shares;
    (c) subject to the provisions of the Act, sub-divide its shares, or any of them, into shares of smaller amount and the resolution may determine that, as between the shares resulting from the sub-division, any of them may have any preference or advantage as compared with the others; and
    (d) cancel shares which, at the date of the passing of the resolution, have not been taken or agreed to be taken by any person and diminish the amount of its share capital by the amount of the shares so cancelled.

33. Whenever as a result of a consolidation of shares any members would become entitled to fractions of a share, the directors may, on behalf of those members, sell the shares representing the fractions for the best price reasonably obtainable to any person (including, subject to the provisions of the Act, the company) and distribute the net proceeds of sale in due proportion among those members, and the directors may authorise some person to execute an instrument of transfer of the shares to, or in accordance with the directions of, the purchaser. The transferee shall not be bound to see to the application of the purchase money nor shall his title to the shares be affected by any irregularity in or invalidity of the proceedings in reference to the sale.

34. Subject to the provisions of the Act, the company may by special resolution reduce its share capital, any capital redemption reserve and any share premium account in any way.

PURCHASE OF OWN SHARES

35. Subject to the provisions of the Act, the company may purchase its own shares (including any redeemable shares) and, if it is a private company, make a payment in respect of the redemption or purchase of its own shares otherwise than out of distributable profits of the company or the proceeds of a fresh issue of shares.

GENERAL MEETINGS

36. . . . .[3]

37. The directors may call general meetings and, on the requisition of members pursuant to the provisions of the Act, shall forthwith proceed to convene *a general meeting in accordance with the provisions of the Act*[4]. If there are not within the United Kingdom sufficient directors to call a general meeting, any director or any member of the company may call a general meeting.

NOTICE OF GENERAL MEETINGS

38. *General meetings shall be called by at least fourteen clear days' notice but a general meeting may be called by shorter notice if it is so agreed-*

(a) . . .

(b) by a majority in number of the members having a right to attend and vote being a majority together holding not less than ninety per cent in the nominal value of the shares giving that right.

The notice shall specify the time and place of the meeting and the general nature of the business to be transacted.

Subject to the provisions of the articles and to any restriction imposed on any shares, the notice shall be given to all members, to all person entitled to a share in consequence of the death or bankruptcy of a member and to the directors and auditors.[5]

---

3   Regulation 36 was deleted by SI 2007/2541 for companies incorporated on or after 1 October 2007. It read "All general meetings other than annual general meetings shall be called extraordinary general meetings."

4   The words in italics were substituted by SI 2007/2541 for the words "an extraordinary general meeting for a date not later than eight weeks after receipt of the requisition" for companies incorporated on or after 1 October 2007.

5   Reg. 38 was amended by SI 2007/2541 for companies incorporated on or after 1 October 2007 to delete all references to annual general meetings and to reduce the percentage required to consent to short notice. It previously read:

38. An annual general meeting and an extraordinary general meeting called for the passing of a special resolution or a resolution appointing a person as a director shall be called by at least twenty-one clear days' notice. All other extraordinary general meetings shall be called by at least fourteen clear days' notice but a general meeting may be called by shorter notice if it is so agreed-

(a) in the case of an annual general meeting, by all the members entitled to attend and vote thereat; and

(b) in the case of any other meeting by a majority in number of the members having a right to attend and vote being a majority together holding not less than ninety-five per cent in the nominal value of the shares giving that right.

The notice shall specify the time and place of the meeting and the general nature of the business to be transacted and, in the case of an annual general meeting, shall specify the meeting as such.

Subject to the provisions of the articles and to any restriction imposed on any shares, the notice shall be given to all members, to all person entitled to a share in consequence of the death or bankruptcy of a member and to the directors and auditors.

39. The accidental omission to give notice of a meeting to, or the non-receipt of notice of a meeting by, any person entitled to receive notice shall not invalidate the proceedings at that meeting.

PROCEEDINGS AT GENERAL MEETINGS

40. *Save in the case of a company with a single member*[6] no business shall be transacted at any meeting unless a quorum is present. Two persons entitled to vote upon the business to be transacted, each being a member or a proxy for a member or a duly authorised representative of a corporation, shall be a quorum.

41. If such a quorum is not present within half an hour from the time appointed for the meeting, or if during a meeting such a quorum ceases to be present, the meeting shall stand adjourned to the same day in the next week at the same time and place or to such time and place as the directors may determine.

42. The chairman, if any, of the board of directors or in his absence some other director nominated by the directors shall preside as chairman of the meeting, but if neither the chairman nor any such other director (if any) be present within fifteen minutes after the time appointed for holding the meeting and willing to act, the directors present shall elect one of their number to be chairman and, if there is only one director present and willing to act, he shall be chairman.

43. If no director is willing to act as chairman, or if no director is present within fifteen minutes after the time appointed for holding the meeting, the members present and entitled to vote shall choose one of their number to be chairman.

44. A director shall, notwithstanding that he is not a member, be entitled to attend and speak at any general meeting and at any separate meeting of the holders of any class of shares in the company.

45. The chairman may, with the consent of a meeting at which a quorum is present (and shall if so directed by the meeting), adjourn the meeting from time to time and from place to place, but no business shall be transacted at an adjourned meeting other than that business which might properly have been transacted at the meeting had the adjournment not taken place. When a meeting is adjourned for fourteen days or more, at least seven days' notice shall be given specifying the time and place of the adjourned meeting and the general nature of the business to be transacted. Otherwise it shall not be necessary to give any such notice.

46. A resolution put to the vote of a meeting shall be decided on a show of hands unless before, or on the declaration of the result of, the show of hands a

6   The words in italics were inserted by SI 2007/2541 for companies incorporated on or after 1 October 2007.

poll is duly demanded. Subject to the provisions of the Act, a poll may be demanded-

(a) by the chairman; or

(b) by at least two members having the right to vote at the meeting; or

(c) by a member or members representing not less than one-tenth of the total voting rights of all the members having the right to vote at the meeting; or

(d) by a member or members holding shares conferring a right to vote at the meeting being shares on which an aggregate sum has been paid up equal to not less than one-tenth of the total sum paid up on all the shares conferring that right;

and a demand by a person as proxy for a member shall be the same as a demand by the member.

47. Unless a poll is duly demanded a declaration by the chairman that a resolution has been carried unanimously, or by a particular majority, or lost, or not carried by a particular majority and an entry to that effect in the minutes of the meeting shall be conclusive evidence of the fact without proof of the number or proportion of the votes recorded in favour or against the resolution.

48. The demand for a poll may, before the poll is taken, be withdrawn but only with the consent of the chairman and a demand so withdrawn shall not be taken to have invalidated the result of a show of hands declared before the demand was made.

49. A poll shall be taken as the chairman directs and he may appoint scrutineers (who need not be members) and fix a time and place for declaring the result of the poll. The result of the poll shall be deemed to be the resolution of the meeting at which the poll was demanded.

50. . . . .[7]

51. A poll demanded on the election of a chairman or on a question of adjournment shall be taken forthwith. A poll demanded on any other question shall be taken either forthwith or at such time and place as the chairman directs not being more than thirty days after the poll is demanded. The demand for a poll shall not prevent the continuance of a meeting for the transaction of any business other than the question on which the poll was demanded. If a poll is demanded before the declaration of the result of a show of hands and the demand is duly withdrawn, the meeting shall continue as if the demand had not been made.

---

7 Reg. 50 (chairman's casting vote) ceased to have effect for companies incorporated on or after 1 October 2007 by virtue of SI 2007/2826. It previously provided: "50. In the case of an equality of votes, whether on a show of hands or on a poll, the chairman shall be entitled to a casting vote in addition to any other vote he may have."

52. No notice need be given of a poll not taken forthwith if the time and place at which it is to be taken are announced at the meeting at which it is demanded. In any other case at least seven clear days' notice shall be given specifying the time and place at which the poll is to be taken.

53. . . .[8]

VOTES OF MEMBERS

54. Subject to any rights or restrictions attached to any shares, on a show of hands every member who (being an individual) is present in person *or by proxy or (being a corporation) present by a duly authorised representative or by proxy, unless the proxy (in either case) or the representative is*[9] himself a member entitled to vote, shall have one vote and on a poll every member shall have one vote for every share of which he is the holder.

55. In the case of joint holders the vote of the senior who tenders a vote, whether in person or by proxy, shall be accepted to the exclusion of the votes of the other joint holders; and seniority shall be determined by the order in which the names of the holders stand in the register of members.

56. A member in respect of whom an order has been made by any court having jurisdiction (whether in the UK or elsewhere) in matters concerning mental disorder may vote, whether on a show of hands or on a poll, by his receiver, curator bonis or other person authorised in that behalf appointed by that court, and any such receiver, curator bonis or other person may, on a poll, vote by proxy. Evidence to the satisfaction of the directors of the authority of the person claiming to exercise the right to vote shall be deposited at the office, or at such other place as is specified in accordance with the articles for the deposit of instruments of proxy, not less than 48 hours before the time appointed for holding the meeting or adjourned meeting at which the right to vote is to be exercised and in default the right to vote shall not be exercisable.

57. No member shall vote at any general meeting or at any separate meeting of the holders of any class of shares in the company, either in person or by proxy, in respect of any share held by him unless all moneys presently payable by him in respect of that share have been paid.

---

8   Regulation 53 ceased to have effect for companies incorporated on or after 1 October 2007 by virtue of SI 2007/2541. It provided: "53. A resolution in writing executed by or on behalf of each member who would have been entitled to vote upon it if it had been proposed at a general meeting at which he was present shall be as effectual as if it had been passed at a general meeting duly convened and held and may consist of several instruments in the like form executed by or on behalf of one or more members."

9   Reg. 54 was amended by SI 2007/2826 for companies incorporated on or after 1 October 2007. It formerly read: "54. Subject to any rights or restrictions attached to any shares, on a show of hands every member who (being an individual) is present in person or (being a corporation) present by a duly authorised representative, not being himself a member entitled to vote, shall have one vote and on a poll every member shall have one vote for every share of which he is the holder."

58. No objection shall be raised to the qualification of any voter except at the meeting or adjourned meeting at which the vote objected to is tendered, and every vote not disallowed at the meeting shall be valid. Any objection made in due time shall be referred to the chairman whose decision shall be final and conclusive.

59. On a poll votes may be given either personally or by proxy. A member may appoint more than one proxy to attend on the same occasion.

60. *The appointment of a proxy shall be executed by or on behalf of the appointor and shall be in the following form (or in a form as near thereto as circumstances allow or in any other form which is usual or which the directors may approve)-*[10]

   " .... PLC/Limited
   I/We, ..., of ...., being a member/members of the above-named company, hereby appoint ....
   .... of, or failing him, ... of...............
   .... , as my/our proxy to vote in my/our name[s] and on my/our behalf at the *general meeting* [11] of the company to be held on ....
   .... 19........, and at any adjournment thereof.
   Signed on .... 19........"

61. Where it is desired to afford members an opportunity of instructing the proxy how he shall act the *appointment of*[12] a proxy shall be in the following form (or in a form as near thereto as circumstances allow or in any other form which is usual or which the directors may approve)-

   " .... PLC/Limited
   I/We, ..., of ...., being a member/members of the above-named company, hereby appoint ....
   .... of, or failing him, ... of.............
   ...., as my/our proxy to vote in my/our name[s] and on my/our

---

10 Regulation 60 was amended by Schedule 1 of the Companies Act 1985 (Electronic Communications) Order 2000 on 22 December 2000. Prior to that date it read as follows: "An instrument appointing a proxy shall be in writing, executed by or on behalf of the appointor and shall be in the following form . . .".

11 The forms of proxy in regs. 60 and 61 were amended by SI 2007/2541 for companies incorporated on or after 1 October 2007 to delete the words annual/extraordinary before the words "general meeting".

12 The words "appointment of" were inserted in reg. 61 by Schedule 1 of the Companies Act 1985 (Electronic Communications) Order 2000 on 22 December 2000. Prior to that date it read as follows: "Where it is desired to afford members an opportunity of instructing the proxy how he shall act the instrument appointing a proxy . . ."

behalf at the general meeting[13] of the company to be held on ....
.... 19........, and at any adjournment thereof.
This form is to be used in respect of the resolutions mentioned below as follows:
Resolution No 1 *for *against
Resolution No 2 *for *against.
*Strike out whichever is not desired.
Unless otherwise instructed, the proxy may vote as he thinks fit or abstain from voting.
Signed this .... day of .... 19........."

[**62.** *The appointment of a proxy and any authority under which it is executed or a copy of such authority certified notarially or in some other way approved by the directors may-*

(a) in the case of an instrument in writing, be deposited at the office or such other place within the United Kingdom as is specified in the notice convening the meeting or in any instrument of proxy sent out by the company in relation to the meeting not less than 48 hours before the time for holding the meeting or adjourned meeting at which the person named in the instrument proposes to vote; or

(aa) in the case of an appointment contained in an electronic communication, where an address has been specified for the purpose of receiving electronic communications-

(i) in the notice convening the meeting, or

(ii) in any instrument of proxy sent out by the company in relation to the meeting, or

(iii) in any invitation contained in an electronic communication to appoint a proxy issued by the company in relation to the meeting,

be received at such address not less than 48 hours before the time for holding the meeting or adjourned meeting at which the person named in the appointment proposes to vote;

(b) in the case of a poll taken more than 48 hours after it is demanded, be deposited or received as aforesaid after the poll has been demanded and not less than 24 hours before the time appointed for the taking of the poll; or

(c) where the poll is not taken forthwith but is taken not more than 48 hours after it was demanded, be delivered at the meeting at which the poll was demanded to the chairman or to the secretary or to any director; *and an appointment of proxy which is not deposited, delivered or received in a manner so permitted shall be invalid. In this regulation and the*

---

13 See Note 9 above.

next, "address", in relation to electronic communications, includes any number or address used for the purposes of such communications.][14]

63. A vote given or poll demanded by proxy or by the duly authorised representative of a corporation shall be valid notwithstanding the previous determination of the authority of the person voting or demanding a poll unless notice of the determination was received by the company at the office or at such other place at which the instrument of proxy was duly deposited *or, where the appointment of the proxy was contained in an electronic communication, at the address at which the appointment was duly received* before the commencement of the meeting or adjourned meeting at which the vote is given or the poll demanded or (in the case of a poll taken otherwise than on the same day as the meeting or adjourned meeting) the time appointed for taking the poll.[15]

NUMBER OF DIRECTORS

64. Unless otherwise determined by ordinary resolution, the number of directors (other than alternate directors) shall not be subject to any maximum but shall be not less than two.

ALTERNATE DIRECTORS

65. Any director (other than an alternate director) may appoint any other director, or any other person approved by resolution of the directors and willing to act, to be an alternate director and may remove from office an alternate director so appointed by him.

66. An alternate director shall be entitled to receive notice of all meetings of directors and of all meetings of committees of directors of which his appointor

---

14 Regulation 62 was amended by Schedule 1 of the Companies Act 1985 (Electronic Communications) Order 2000 on 22 December 2000. Prior to that date it read as follows: "The instrument appointing a proxy and any authority under which it is executed or a copy of such authority certified notarially or in some other way approved by the directors may-

(a) be deposited at the office or such other place within the United Kingdom as is specified in the notice convening the meeting or in any instrument of proxy sent out by the company in relation to the meeting not less than 48 hours before the time for holding the meeting or adjourned meeting at which the person named in the instrument proposes to vote; or

(b) in the case of a poll taken more than 48 hours after it is demanded, be deposited as aforesaid after the poll has been demanded and not less than 24 hours before the time appointed for the taking of the poll; or

(c) where the poll is not taken forthwith but is taken not more than 48 hours after it was demanded, be delivered at the meeting at which the poll was demanded to the chairman or to the secretary or to any director;

and an instrument of proxy which is not deposited or delivered in a manner so permitted shall be invalid."

15 The words in italics in reg. 63 were inserted by Schedule 1 of the Companies Act 1985 (Electronic Communications) Order 2000 on 22 December 2000.

is a member, to attend and vote at any such meeting at which the director appointing him is not personally present, and generally to perform all the functions of his appointor as a director in his absence but shall not be entitled to receive any remuneration from the company for his services as an alternate director. But it shall not be necessary to give notice of such a meeting to alternate director who is absent from the United Kingdom.

67. An alternate director shall cease to be an alternate director if his appointor ceases to be a director; but if a director retires by rotation or otherwise but is reappointed or deemed to have been reappointed at the meeting at which he retires, any appointment of an alternate director made by him which was in force immediately prior to his retirement shall continue after his reappointment.

68. Any appointment or removal of an alternate director shall be by notice to the company signed by the director making or revoking the appointment or in any other manner approved by the directors.

69. Save as otherwise provided in the articles, an alternate director shall be deemed for all purposes to be a director and shall alone be responsible for his own acts and defaults and he shall not be deemed to be the agent of the director appointing him.

POWERS OF DIRECTORS

70. Subject to the provisions of the Act, the memorandum and the articles and to any directions given by special resolution, the business of the company shall be managed by the directors who may exercise all the powers of the company. No alteration of the memorandum or articles and no such direction shall invalidate any prior act of the directors which would have been valid if that alteration had not been made or that direction had not been given. The powers given by this regulation shall not be limited by any special power given to the directors by the articles and a meeting of directors at which a quorum is present may exercise all powers exercisable by the directors.

71. The directors may, by power of attorney or otherwise, appoint any person to be the agent of the company for such purposes and on such conditions as they determine, including authority for the agent to delegate all or any of his powers.

DELEGATION OF DIRECTORS' POWERS

72. The directors may delegate any of their powers to any committee consisting of one or more directors. They may also delegate to any managing director or any director holding any other executive office such of their powers as they consider desirable to be exercised by him. Any such delegation may be made subject to any conditions the directors may impose, and either collaterally with or to the exclusion of their own powers and may be revoked or altered. Subject to any such conditions, the proceedings of a committee with two or

more members shall be governed by the articles regulating the proceedings of directors so far as they are capable of applying.

APPOINTMENT AND RETIREMENT OF DIRECTORS

73–75 . . . . [16]

76. No person[17] shall be appointed or reappointed a director at any general meeting unless-

(a) he is recommended by the directors; or

(b) not less than fourteen nor more than thirty-five clear days before the date appointed for the meeting, notice executed by a member qualified to vote at the meeting has been given to the company of the intention to propose that person for appointment or reappointment stating the particulars which would, if he were so appointed or reappointed, be required to be included in the company's register of directors together with notice executed by that person of his willingness to be appointed or reappointed.

77. Not less than seven nor more than twenty-eight clear days before the date appointed for holding a general meeting notice shall be given to all who are entitled to receive notice of the meeting of any person[18] who is recommended by the directors for appointment or reappointment as a director at the meeting or in respect of whom notice has been duly given to the company of the intention to propose him at the meeting for appointment or reappointment as a director. The notice shall give particulars of that person which would, if he were so appointed or reappointed, be required to be included in the company's register of directors.

16 Regulations 73–75 were deleted by SI 2007/2541 for companies incorporated on or after 1 October 2007. They read:

73. At the first annual general meeting all the directors shall retire from office, and at every subsequent annual general meeting one-third of the directors who are subject to retirement by rotation or, if their number is not three or a multiple of three, the number nearest to one third shall retire from office; but, if there is only one director who is subject to retirement by rotation, he shall retire.

74. Subject to the provisions of the Act, the directors to retire by rotation shall be those who have served longest in office since their last appointment or reappointment, but as between persons who became or were last reappointed directors on the same day those to retire shall (unless they otherwise agree among themselves) be determined by lot.

75. If the company, at the meeting at which a director retires by rotation, does not fill the vacancy the retiring director shall, if willing to act, be deemed to have been reappointed unless at the meeting it is resolved not to fill the vacancy or unless a resolution for the reappointment of the director is put to the meeting and lost.

17 For companies incorporated on or after 1 October 2007, SI 2007/2541 deleted the words "other than a director retiring by rotation".

18 For companies incorporated on or after 1 October 2007, SI 2007/2541 deleted the words "(other than a director retiring by rotation at the meeting)".

78. The[19] company may by ordinary resolution appoint a person who is willing to act to be a director either to fill a vacancy or as an additional director and may also determine the rotation in which any additional directors are to retire.

79. The directors may appoint a person who is willing to act to be director, either to fill a vacancy or as an additional director, provided that the appointment does not cause the number of directors to exceed the number fixed by or in accordance with the articles as the maximum number of directors.[20]

80. Subject as aforesaid, a director who retires at an annual general meeting may, if willing to act, be reappointed. If he is not reappointed, he shall retain office until the meeting appoints someone in his place, or if it does not do so, until the end of the meeting.

DISQUALIFICATION AND REMOVAL OF DIRECTORS

81. The office of director shall be vacated if-

(a) he ceases to be a director by virtue of any provision of the Act or becomes prohibited by law from being a director; or

(b) he becomes bankrupt or makes any arrangement or composition with his creditors generally; or

(c) he is, or may be, suffering from mental disorder and either-

    (i) he is admitted to hospital in pursuance of an application for treatment under the Mental Health Act 1983 or, in Scotland, an application for admission under the Mental Health (Scotland) Act 1960, or

    (ii) an order is made by a court having jurisdiction (whether in the United Kingdom or elsewhere) in matters concerning mental disorder for his detention or for the appointment of a receiver, curator bonis or other person to exercise powers with respect to his property or affairs; or

(d) he resigns his office by notice to the company; or

(e) he shall for more than six consecutive months have been absent without permission of the directors from meetings of the directors held during that period and the directors resolve that his office be vacated.

---

19 For companies incorporated on or after 1 October 2007, SI 2007/2541 deleted the words "Subject as aforesaid".

20 For companies incorporated on or after 1 October 2007, SI 2007/2541 deleted the words "A director so appointed shall hold office only until the next following annual general meeting and shall not be taken into account in determining the directors who are to retire by rotation at the meeting. If not reappointed at such annual general meeting, he shall vacate office at the conclusion thereof."

REMUNERATION OF DIRECTORS

82. The directors shall be entitled to such remuneration as the company may by ordinary resolution determine and, unless the resolution provides otherwise, the remuneration shall be deemed to accrue from day to day.

DIRECTORS' EXPENSES

83. The directors may be paid all travelling, hotel, and other expenses properly incurred by them in connection with their attendance at meetings of directors or committees of directors or general meetings or separate meetings of the holders of any class of shares or of debentures of the company or otherwise connection with the discharge of their duties.

DIRECTORS' APPOINTMENTS AND INTERESTS

84. Subject to the provisions of the Act, the directors may appoint one or more of their number to the office of managing director or to any other executive office under the company and may enter into an agreement or arrangement with any director for his employment by the company or for the provision by him of any services outside the scope of the ordinary duties of a director. Any such appointment, agreement or arrangement may be made on such terms as the directors determine and they may remunerate any such director for his services as they think fit. Any appointment of a director to an executive office shall terminate if he ceases to be a director but without prejudice to any claim for damages for breach of the contract of service between the director and the company. A managing director and a director holding any other executive office shall not be subject to retirement by rotation.

85. Subject to the provisions of the Act, and provided that he has disclosed to the directors the nature and extent of any material interest of his, a director notwithstanding his office-

(a) may be a party to, or otherwise interested in, any transaction or arrangement with the company or in which the company is otherwise interested;

(b) may be a director or other officer of, or employed by, or party to any transaction or arrangement with, or otherwise interested in, any body corporate promoted by the company or in which the company is otherwise interested; and

(c) shall not, by reason of his office, be accountable to the company for any benefit which he derives from any such office or employment or from any such transaction or arrangement or from any interest in any such body corporate and no such transaction or arrangement shall be liable to be avoided on the ground of any such interest or benefit.

86. For the purposes of regulation 85-

(a) a general notice given to the directors that a director is to be regarded as having an interest of the nature and extent specified in the notice in any transactions or arrangement in which a specified person or class of

persons is interested shall be deemed to be a disclosure that the director has an interest in any such transaction of the nature and extent so
specified; and

(b) an interest of which a director has no knowledge and of which it is
unreasonable to expect him to have knowledge shall not be treated as
an interest of his.

DIRECTOR'S GRATUITIES AND PENSIONS

87. The directors may provide benefits, whether by payment of gratuities or pen-
sions or by insurance or otherwise, for any director who has held but no
longer holds any executive office or employment with the company or with
any body corporate which is or has been a subsidiary of the company or a
predecessor in business of the company or of any such subsidiary, and for any
member of his family (including a spouse and a former spouse) or any person
who is or was dependent upon him, and may (as well before as after he ceases
to hold such office or employment) contribute to any fund and pay premiums
for the purchase of any such benefit.

PROCEEDINGS OF DIRECTORS

88. Subject to the provisions of the articles, the directors may regulate their proceedings as they think fit. A director may, and the secretary at the request of a
director shall, call a meeting of the directors. It shall not be necessary to give
notice of a meeting to a director who is absent from the United Kingdom.
Questions arising at a meeting shall be decided by a majority of votes. In the
case of an equality of votes, the chairman shall have a second or casting vote.
A director who is also an alternate director shall be entitled in the absence of
his appointor to a separate vote on behalf of his appointor in addition to his
own vote.

89. The quorum for the transaction of business of the directors may be fixed by
the directors and unless so fixed at any other number shall be two. A person
who holds office only as an alternate director shall, if his appointor is not
present, be counted in the quorum.

90. The continuing directors or a sole continuing director may act notwithstanding any vacancies in their number, but, if the number of directors is less than
the number fixed as the quorum, the continuing directors or director may act
only for the purpose of filling vacancies or of calling a general meeting.

91. The directors may appoint one of their number to be the chairman of the
board of directors and may at any time remove him from that office. Unless
he is unwilling to do so, the director so appointed shall preside at every meeting of directors at which he is present. But if there is no director holding that
office, or if the director holding it is unwilling to preside or is nor present
within five minutes after the time appointed for the meeting, the directors
present may appoint one of their number to be chairman of the meeting.

92. All acts done by a meeting of directors, or of a committee of directors, or by a person acting as a director shall, notwithstanding that it be afterwards discovered that there was a defect in the appointment of any director or that any of them were disqualified from holding office, or had vacated office, or were not entitled to vote, be as valid as if every such person had been duly appointed and was qualified and had continued to be a director and had been entitled to vote.

93. A resolution signed in writing by all the directors entitled to receive notice of a meeting of directors or of a committee of directors shall be as valid and effectual as if it had been passed at a meeting of directors or (as the case may be) a committee of directors duly convened and held and may consist of several documents in the like form each signed by one or more directors; but a resolution signed by an alternate director need not also be signed by his appointor and, if it is signed by a director who has appointed an alternate director, it need not be signed by the alternate in that capacity.

94. Save as otherwise provided by the articles, a director shall not vote at a meeting of directors or a committee of directors on any resolution concerning a matter in which he has, directly or indirectly, an interest or duty which is material and which conflicts or may conflict with the interests of the company unless his interest or duty arises only because the case falls within one or more of the following paragraphs-

    (a) the resolution relates to the giving to him of a guarantee, security, or indemnity in respect of money lent to, or an obligation incurred by him for the benefit of, the company or any of its subsidiaries;

    (b) the resolution relates to the giving to a third party of a guarantee, security, or indemnity in respect of an obligation the company or any of its subsidiaries for which the director has assumed responsibility in whole or in part and whether alone or jointly with others under a guarantee or indemnity or by the giving of security;

    (c) his interest arises by virtue of his subscribing or agreeing to subscribe for any shares, debentures or other securities of the company or any of its subsidiaries, or by virtue of his being, or intending to become, a participant in the underwriting or sub-underwriting of an offer of any such shares, debentures or other securities by the company or any of its subsidiaries for subscription, purchase or exchange;

    (d) the resolution relates in any way to a retirement benefits scheme which has been approved, or is conditional upon approval, by the Board of Inland Revenue for taxation purposes.

For the purposes of this regulation, an interest of a person who is, for any purpose of the Act (excluding any statutory modification thereof not in force when this regulation becomes binding on the company), connected with a director shall be treated as an interest of the director and, in relation to an alternate director, an interest of his appointor shall be treated as an interest of the alternate director without prejudice to any interest which the alternate director has otherwise.

95. A director shall not be counted in the quorum present at a meeting in relation to a resolution on which he is not entitled to vote.

96. The company may by ordinary resolution suspend or relax to any extent, either generally or in respect of any particular matter, any provision of the articles prohibiting a director from voting at a meeting of directors or of a committee of directors.

97. Where proposals are under consideration concerning the appointment of two or more directors to offices or employments with the company or any body corporate in which the company is interested the proposals may be divided and considered in relation to each director separately and (provided he is not for another reason precluded from voting) each of the directors concerned shall be entitled to vote and be counted in the quorum in respect of each resolution except that concerning his own appointment.

98. If a question arises at a meeting of directors or of a committee of directors as to the right of a director to vote, the question may, before the conclusion of the meeting, be referred to the chairman of the meeting and his ruling in relation to any director other than himself shall be final and conclusive.

SECRETARY

99. Subject to the provisions of the Act, the secretary shall be appointed by the directors for such term, at such remuneration and upon such conditions as they may think fit; and any secretary so appointed may be removed by them.

MINUTES

100. The directors shall cause minutes to be made in books kept for the purpose-
    (a) of all appointments of officers made by the directors; and
    (b) of all proceedings at meetings of the company, of the holders of any class of shares in the company, and of the directors, and of committees of directors, including the names of the directors present at each such meeting.

THE SEAL

101. The seal shall only be used by the authority of the directors or of a committee of directors authorised by the directors. The directors may determine who shall sign any instrument to which the seal is affixed and unless otherwise so determined it shall be signed by a director and by the secretary or by a second director.

DIVIDENDS

102. Subject to the provisions of the Act, the company may by ordinary resolution declare dividends in accordance with the respective rights of members, but no dividend shall exceed the amount recommended by the directors.

103. Subject to the provisions of the Act, the directors may pay interim dividends if it appears to them that they are justified by the profits of the company available for distribution. If the share capital is divided into different classes, the directors may pay interim dividends on shares which confer deferred or non-preferred rights with regard to dividend as well as on shares which confer preferential rights with regard to dividend, but no interim dividend shall be paid on shares carrying deferred or non-preferred rights if, at the time of payment, any preferential dividend is in arrear. The directors may also pay at intervals settled by them any dividend payable at a fixed rate if it appears to them that the profits available for distribution justify the payment. Provided the directors act in good faith they shall not incur any liability to the holders of shares conferring preferred rights for any loss they may suffer by the lawful payment of an interim dividend on any shares having deferred or non-preferred rights.

104. Except as otherwise provided by the rights attached to shares, all dividends shall be declared and paid according to the amounts paid up on the shares on which the dividend is paid. All dividends shall be apportioned and paid proportionately to the amounts paid up on the shares during any portion or portions of the period in respect of which the dividend is paid; but, if any share is issued on terms providing that it shall rank for dividend from a particular date, that share shall rank for dividend accordingly.

105. A general meeting declaring a dividend may, upon the recommendation of the directors, direct that it shall be satisfied wholly or partly by the distribution of assets and, where any difficulty arises in regard to the distribution, the directors may settle the same and in particular may issue fractional certificates and fix the value for distribution of any assets and may determine that cash shall be paid to any member upon the footing of the value so fixed in order to adjust the rights of members and may vest assets in trustees.

106. Any dividend or other moneys payable in respect of a share may be paid by cheque sent by post to the registered address of the person entitled or, if two or more persons are the holders of the share or are jointly entitled to it by reason of the death or bankruptcy of the holder, to the registered address of that one of those persons who is first named on the register of members or to such person and to such address as the person or person entitled may in writing direct. Every cheque shall be made payable to the order of the person or persons entitled or to such other person as the person or persons entitled may in writing direct and payment of the cheque shall be a good discharge to the company. Any joint holder or other person jointly entitled to a share as aforesaid may give receipts for any dividend or other moneys payable in respect of the share.

107. No dividend or other moneys payable in respect of a share shall bear interest against the company unless otherwise provided by the rights attached to the share.

108. Any dividend which has remained unclaimed for twelve years from the date when it became due for payment shall, if the directors so resolve, be forfeited and cease to remain owing by the company.

ACCOUNTS

109. No member shall (as such) have any right of inspecting any accounting records or other book or document of the company except as conferred by statute or authorised by the directors or by ordinary resolution of the company.

CAPITALISATION OF PROFITS

110. The directors may with the authority of an ordinary resolution of the company-

(a) subject as hereinafter provided, resolve to capitalise any undivided profits of the company not required for paying any preferential dividend (whether or not they are available for distribution) or any sum standing to the credit of the company's share premium account or capital redemption reserve;

(b) appropriate the sum resolved to be capitalised to the members who would have been entitled to it if it were distributed by way of dividend and in the same proportion and apply such sum on their behalf either in or towards paying up the amounts, if any, for the time being unpaid on any shares held by them respectively, or in paying up in full unissued shares or debentures of the company of a nominal amount equal to that sum, and allot the shares or debentures credited as fully paid to those members, or as they may direct, in those proportions, or partly in one way and partly in the other: but the share premium account, the capital redemption reserve, and any profits which are not available for distribution may, for the purposes of this regulation, only be applied in paying up unissued shares to be allotted members credited as fully paid;

(c) make such provision by the issue of fractional certificates or by payment in cash or otherwise as they determine in the case of shares or debentures becoming distributable under this regulation in fractions; and

(d) authorise any person to enter on behalf of all members concerned into an agreement with the company providing for the allotment to them respectively, credited as fully paid, of any shares or debentures to which they are entitled upon such capitalisation, any agreement made under such authority being binding on all such members.

NOTICES

111. Any notice to be given to or by any person pursuant to the articles (other than a notice calling a meeting of the directors) shall be in writing or shall be given using electronic communications to an address for the time being notified for that purpose to the person giving the notice.

In this regulation, "address", in relation to electronic communications, includes any number or address used for the purposes of such communications.[21]

112. The company may give any notice to a member either personally or by sending it by post in a prepaid envelope addressed to the member at his registered address *or by leaving it at that address or by giving it using electronic communications to an address for the time being notified to the company by the member.* In the case of joint holders of a share, all notices shall be given to the joint holder whose name stands first in the register of members in respect of the joint holding and notice so given shall be sufficient notice to all the joint holders. A member whose registered address is not within the United Kingdom and who gives to the company an address within the United Kingdom at which notices may be given to him, *or an address to which notices may be sent by electronic communications*, shall be entitled to have notices given to him at that address, but otherwise no such member shall be entitled to receive any notice from the company. *In this regulation and the next, "address", in relation to electronic communications, includes any number or address used for the purposes of such communications.*[22]

113. A member present, either in person or by proxy, at any meeting of the company or of holders of any class of shares in the company shall be deemed to have received notice of the meeting and, where requisite, of the purposes for which it was called.

114. Every person who becomes entitled to a share shall be bound by any notice in respect of that share which, before his name is entered in the register of members, has been duly given to a person from whom he derives his title.

115. Proof that an envelope containing a notice was properly addressed, prepaid and posted shall be conclusive evidence that the notice was given. *Proof that notice contained in an electronic communication was sent in accordance with guidance issued by the Institute of Chartered Secretaries and Administrators shall be conclusive evidence that the notice was given.* A notice shall be deemed to be given at the expiration of 48 hours after the

---

21 Regulation 111 was amended by Schedule 1 of the Companies Act 1985 (Electronic Communications) Order 2000 on 22 December 2000. Prior to that date it read as follows: "Any notice to be given to or by any person pursuant to the articles shall be in writing except that notice calling a meeting of directors need not be in writing."

22 The words in italics in reg. 112 were inserted by Schedule 1 of the Companies Act 1985 (Electronic Communications) Order 2000 on 22 December 2000.

envelope containing it was posted *or, in the case of a notice contained in an electronic communication, at the expiration of 48 hours after the time it was sent.*[23]

116. A notice may be given by the company to the persons entitled to a share in consequence of death or bankruptcy of a member by sending or delivering it, in any manner authorised by the articles for the giving of notice to a member, addressed to them by name, or by the title of representatives of the deceased, or trustee of the bankrupt or by any description at the address, if any, within the United Kingdom supplied for that purpose by the persons claiming to be so entitled. Until such an address has been supplied, a notice may be given in any manner in which it might have been given if the death or bankruptcy had not occurred.

WINDING UP

117. If the company is wound up, the liquidator may, with the sanction of a special[24] resolution of the company and any other sanction required by the Act, divide among the members in specie the whole or any part of the assets of the company and may, for that purpose, value any assets and determine how the division shall be carried out as between members or different classes of members. The liquidator may, with the like sanction, vest the whole or any part of the assets in trustees upon such trusts for the benefit of the members as he with the like sanction determines, but no member shall be compelled to accept any assets upon which there is a liability.

INDEMNITY

118. Subject to the provisions of the Act, but without prejudice to any indemnity to which a director may otherwise be entitled, every director or other officer or auditor of the company shall be indemnified out of the assets of the company against any liability incurred by him in defending any proceedings, whether civil or criminal, in which judgment is given in his favour or in which he is acquitted or in connection with any application in which relief is granted to him by the court from liability for negligence, default, breach of duty or breach of trust in relation to the affairs of the company.

23 The words in italics in reg. 115 were inserted by Schedule 1 of the Companies Act 1985 (Electronic Communications) Order 2000 on 22 December 2000.

24 Regulation 117 was amended by SI 2007/2541 for companies incorporated on or after 1st October 2007 to require a special resolution. Previous versions of Table A provide for "an extraordinary resolution".

Index to 1985 Table A

ANNEX C1

Companies Act 2006 Model Articles: Contents and comparative location of provisions

Key to Table
* indicates that the relevant model articles shown in the same row are identical.
*¹ indicates that the relevant model articles shown in the same row are the same other than for the use of the word 'shareholder' in the model articles for private companies limited by shares where the word 'member' is used in the model articles for guarantee companies and the model articles for public companies.

Schedule 1 of SI 2008/3229 MODEL ARTICLES FOR PRIVATE COMPANIES LIMITED BY SHARES	Schedule 2 of SI 2008/3229 MODEL ARTICLES FOR PRIVATE COMPANIES LIMITED BY GUARANTEE	Schedule 3 of SI 2008/3229 MODEL ARTICLES FOR PUBLIC COMPANIES
See Annex C2	See AnnexC3 for articles not marked with a '*' or '*¹'	See Annex C4 for articles not marked with a '*' or '*¹'
PART 1: INTERPRETATION AND LIMITATION OF LIABILITY 1. Defined terms 2. Liability of members	PART 1: INTERPRETATION AND LIMITATION OF LIABILITY 1. Defined terms 2. Liability of members	PART 1: INTERPRETATION AND LIMITATION OF LIABILITY 1. Defined terms 2. Liability of members
PART 2: DIRECTORS *Directors' powers and responsibilities* 3. Directors' general authority * 4. Members' reserve power *¹ 5. Directors may delegate * 6. Committees *	PART 2: DIRECTORS *Directors' powers and responsibilities* 3. Directors' general authority * 4. Members' reserve power *¹ 5. Directors may delegate * 6. Committees *	PART 2: DIRECTORS *Directors' powers and responsibilities* 3. Directors' general authority * 4. Members' reserve power *¹ 5. Directors may delegate * 6. Committees *

Schedule 1 of SI 2008/3229 MODEL ARTICLES FOR PRIVATE COMPANIES LIMITED BY SHARES	Schedule 2 of SI 2008/3229 MODEL ARTICLES FOR PRIVATE COMPANIES LIMITED BY GUARANTEE	Schedule 3 of SI 2008/3229 MODEL ARTICLES FOR PUBLIC COMPANIES
Decision-making by directors 7. Directors to take decisions collectively * 8. Unanimous decisions * 9. Calling a directors' meeting * 10. Participation in directors' meetings * 11. Quorum for directors' meetings *	*Decision-making by directors* 7. Directors to take decisions collectively * 8. Unanimous decisions * 9. Calling a directors' meeting * 10. Participation in directors' meetings * 11. Quorum for directors' meetings *	*Decision-making by directors* 7. Directors to take decisions collectively 8. Calling a directors' meeting 9. Participation in directors' meetings * 10. Quorum for directors' meetings 11. Meetings where total number of directors less than quorum
12. Chairing of directors' meetings *	12. Chairing of directors' meetings *	12. Chairing of directors' meetings 13. Voting at directors' meetings: general rules
13. Chairman's casting vote *	13. Chairman's casting vote *	14. Chairman's casting vote * 15. Alternates voting at directors' meetings
14. Conflicts of interest * 15. Records of decisions to be kept *	14. Conflicts of interest * 15. Records of decisions to be kept *	16. Conflicts of interest
		17. Proposing directors' written resolutions 18. Adoption of directors' written resolutions
16. Directors' discretion to make further rules *	16. Directors' discretion to make further rules *	19. Directors' discretion to make further rules *
Appointment of directors 17. Methods of appointing directors *¹	*Appointment of directors* 17. Methods of appointing directors *¹	*Appointment of directors* 20. Methods of appointing directors 21. Retirement of directors by rotation
18. Termination of director's appointment * 19. Directors' remuneration * 20. Directors' expenses *	18. Termination of director's appointment * 19. Directors' remuneration * 20. Directors' expenses	22. Termination of director's appointment * 23. Directors' remuneration * 24. Directors' expenses *

Schedule 1 of SI 2008/3229 MODEL ARTICLES FOR PRIVATE COMPANIES LIMITED BY SHARES	Schedule 2 of SI 2008/3229 MODEL ARTICLES FOR PRIVATE COMPANIES LIMITED BY GUARANTEE	Schedule 3 of SI 2008/3229 MODEL ARTICLES FOR PUBLIC COMPANIES
		Alternate directors 25. Appointment and removal of alternates 26. Rights and responsibilities of alternate directors 27. Termination of alternate directorship
	PART 3: MEMBERS BECOMING AND CEASING TO BE A MEMBER 21. Applications for membership 22. Termination of membership	
PART 3: SHARES AND DISTRIBUTIONS *Shares* 21. All shares to be fully paid up 22. Powers to issue different classes of share *		PART 4: SHARES AND DISTRIBUTIONS *Issue of shares* 43. Powers to issue different classes of share * 44. Payment of commissions on subscription for shares
23. Company not bound by less than absolute interests *		*Interests in shares* 45. Company not bound by less than absolute interests *
24. Share certificates		*Share certificates* 46. Certificates to be issued except in certain cases 47. Contents and execution of share certificates 48. Consolidated share certificates
25. Replacement share certificates		49. Replacement share certificates

Schedule 1 of SI 2008/3229 MODEL ARTICLES FOR PRIVATE COMPANIES LIMITED BY SHARES	Schedule 2 of SI 2008/3229 MODEL ARTICLES FOR PRIVATE COMPANIES LIMITED BY GUARANTEE	Schedule 3 of SI 2008/3229 MODEL ARTICLES FOR PUBLIC COMPANIES
		Shares not held in certificated form 50. Uncertificated shares 51. Share warrants
		Partly paid shares 52. Company's lien over partly paid shares 53. Enforcement of the company's lien 54. Call notices 55. Liability to pay calls 56. When call notice need not be issued 57. Failure to comply with call notice: automatic consequences 58. Notice of intended forfeiture 59. Directors' power to forfeit shares 60. Effect of forfeiture 61. Procedure following forfeiture 62. Surrender of shares
26. Share transfers 27. Transmission of shares 28. Exercise of transmittees' rights 29. Transmittees bound by prior notices		*Transfer and transmission of shares* 63. Transfers of certificated shares 64. Transfer of uncertificated shares 65. Transmission of shares 66. Transmittees' rights 67. Exercise of transmittees' rights 68. Transmittees bound by prior notices
		Consolidation of shares 69. Procedure for disposing of fractions of shares

Schedule 1 of SI 2008/3229 MODEL ARTICLES FOR PRIVATE COMPANIES LIMITED BY SHARES	Schedule 2 of SI 2008/3229 MODEL ARTICLES FOR PRIVATE COMPANIES LIMITED BY GUARANTEE	Schedule 3 of SI 2008/3229 MODEL ARTICLES FOR PUBLIC COMPANIES
Dividends and other distributions 30. Procedure for declaring dividends 31. Payment of dividends and other distributions * 32. No interest on distributions * 33. Unclaimed distributions * 34. Non-cash distributions 35. Waiver of distributions *		*Distributions* 70. Procedure for declaring dividends 71. Calculation of dividends 72. Payment of dividends and other distributions * 73. Deductions from distributions in respect of sums owed to the company 74. No interest on distributions * 75. Unclaimed distributions * 76. Non-cash distributions 77. Waiver of distributions *
Capitalisation of profits 36. Authority to capitalise and appropriation of capitalised sums		*Capitalisation of profits* 78. Authority to capitalise and appropriation of capitalised sums
PART 4: DECISION-MAKING BY SHAREHOLDERS *Organisation of general meetings* 37. Attendance and speaking at general meetings * 38. Quorum for general meetings * 39. Chairing general meetings *[1] 40. Attendance and speaking by directors and non-members *[1] 41. Adjournment *	*Organisation of general meetings* 23. Attendance and speaking at general meetings * 24. Quorum for general meetings * 25. Chairing general meetings *[1] 26. Attendance and speaking by directors and non-members 27. Adjournment *	PART 3: DECISION-MAKING BY MEMBERS *Organisation of general meetings* 28. Members can call general meeting if not enough directors 29. Attendance and speaking at general meetings * 30. Quorum for general meetings * 31. Chairing general meetings *[1] 32. Attendance and speaking by directors and non-members *[1] 33. Adjournment *

Schedule 1 of SI 2008/3229 MODEL ARTICLES FOR PRIVATE COMPANIES LIMITED BY SHARES	Schedule 2 of SI 2008/3229 MODEL ARTICLES FOR PRIVATE COMPANIES LIMITED BY GUARANTEE	Schedule 3 of SI 2008/3229 MODEL ARTICLES FOR PUBLIC COMPANIES
Voting at general meetings 42. Voting: general * 43. Errors and disputes * 44. Poll votes *[1]	*Voting at general meetings* 28. Voting: general * 29. Errors and disputes * 30. Poll votes *[1]	*Voting at general meetings* 34. Voting: general * 35. Errors and disputes * 36. Demanding a poll 37. Procedure on a poll
45. Content of proxy notices *[1] 46. Delivery of proxy notices * 47. Amendments to resolutions *	31. Content of proxy notices *[1] 32. Delivery of proxy notices * 33. Amendments to resolutions *	38. Content of proxy notices *[1] 39. Delivery of proxy notices 40. Amendments to resolutions
		Restrictions on members' rights 41. No voting of shares on which money owed to company
		Application of rules to class meetings 42. Class meetings
PART 5: ADMINISTRATIVE ARRANGEMENTS 48. Means of communication to be used *	PART 4: ADMINISTRATIVE ARRANGEMENTS 34. Means of communication to be used *	PART 5: MISCELLANEOUS PROVISIONS *Communications* 79. Means of communication to be used * 80. Failure to notify contact details *Administrative arrangements*
49. Company seals *	35. Company seals *	81. Company seals 82. Destruction of documents
50. No right to inspect accounts and other records *[1] 51. Provision for employees on cessation of business *	36. No right to inspect accounts and other records *[1] 37. Provision for employees on cessation of business *	83. No right to inspect accounts and other records *[1] 84. Provision for employees on cessation of business *

Schedule 1 of SI 2008/3229 MODEL ARTICLES FOR PRIVATE COMPANIES LIMITED BY SHARES	Schedule 2 of SI 2008/3229 MODEL ARTICLES FOR PRIVATE COMPANIES LIMITED BY GUARANTEE	Schedule 3 of SI 2008/3229 MODEL ARTICLES FOR PUBLIC COMPANIES
Directors' indemnity and insurance 52. Indemnity * 53. Insurance *	*Directors' indemnity and insurance* 38. Indemnity * 39. Insurance *	*Directors' indemnity and insurance* 85. Indemnity * 86. Insurance *

ANNEX C2

Companies Act 2006 Model Articles for Private Companies Limited by Shares

Schedule 1 of the Companies (Model Articles) Regulations 2008 (SI 2008/3229)

INDEX TO ARTICLES

[See Annex C1]

PART 1 INTERPRETATION AND LIMITATION OF LIABILITY

Defined terms

1. In the articles, unless the context requires otherwise—

   "articles" means the company's articles of association;

   "bankruptcy" includes individual insolvency proceedings in a jurisdiction other than England and Wales or Northern Ireland which have an effect similar to that of bankruptcy;

   "chairman" has the meaning given in article 12;

   "chairman of the meeting" has the meaning given in article 39;

   "Companies Acts" means the Companies Acts (as defined in section 2 of the Companies Act 2006), in so far as they apply to the company;

   "director" means a director of the company, and includes any person occupying the position of director, by whatever name called;

   "distribution recipient" has the meaning given in article 31;

   "document" includes, unless otherwise specified, any document sent or supplied in electronic form;

   "electronic form" has the meaning given in section 1168 of the Companies Act 2006;

   "fully paid" in relation to a share, means that the nominal value and any premium to be paid to the company in respect of that share have been paid to the company;

   "hard copy form" has the meaning given in section 1168 of the Companies Act 2006;

   "holder" in relation to shares means the person whose name is entered in the register of members as the holder of the shares;

   "instrument" means a document in hard copy form;

"ordinary resolution" has the meaning given in section 282 of the Companies Act 2006;

"paid" means paid or credited as paid;

"participate", in relation to a directors' meeting, has the meaning given in article 10;

"proxy notice" has the meaning given in article 45;

"shareholder" means a person who is the holder of a share;

"shares" means shares in the company;

"special resolution" has the meaning given in section 283 of the Companies Act 2006;

"subsidiary" has the meaning given in section 1159 of the Companies Act 2006;

"transmittee" means a person entitled to a share by reason of the death or bankruptcy of a shareholder or otherwise by operation of law; and

"writing" means the representation or reproduction of words, symbols or other information in a visible form by any method or combination of methods, whether sent or supplied in electronic form or otherwise.

Unless the context otherwise requires, other words or expressions contained in these articles bear the same meaning as in the Companies Act 2006 as in force on the date when these articles become binding on the company.

Liability of members

2. The liability of the members is limited to the amount, if any, unpaid on the shares held by them.

PART 2 DIRECTORS

DIRECTORS' POWERS AND RESPONSIBILITIES

Directors' general authority

[Same as clg 3 and plc 3]

3. Subject to the articles, the directors are responsible for the management of the company's business, for which purpose they may exercise all the powers of the company.

Shareholders' reserve power

[Same as clg 4 and plc 4 except that those articles use the word 'members' instead of 'shareholders']

4. —(1) The shareholders may, by special resolution, direct the directors to take, or refrain from taking, specified action.

(2) No such special resolution invalidates anything which the directors have done before the passing of the resolution.

Directors may delegate

[Same as clg 5 and plc 5]

5 —(1) Subject to the articles, the directors may delegate any of the powers which are conferred on them under the articles—

(a) to such person or committee;

(b) by such means (including by power of attorney);

(c) to such an extent;

(d) in relation to such matters or territories; and

(e) on such terms and conditions;

as they think fit.

(2) If the directors so specify, any such delegation may authorise further delegation of the directors' powers by any person to whom they are delegated.

(3) The directors may revoke any delegation in whole or part, or alter its terms and conditions.

Committees

[Same as clg 6 and plc 6]

6. —(1) Committees to which the directors delegate any of their powers must follow procedures which are based as far as they are applicable on those provisions of the articles which govern the taking of decisions by directors.

(2) The directors may make rules of procedure for all or any committees, which prevail over rules derived from the articles if they are not consistent with them.

DECISION-MAKING BY DIRECTORS

Directors to take decisions collectively

[Same as clg 7]

7. —(1) The general rule about decision-making by directors is that any decision of the directors must be either a majority decision at a meeting or a decision taken in accordance with article 8.

(2) If—

(a) the company only has one director, and

(b) no provision of the articles requires it to have more than one director, the general rule does not apply, and the director may take decisions without regard to any of the provisions of the articles relating to directors' decision-making.

Unanimous decisions

[Same as clg 8]

8. —(1) A decision of the directors is taken in accordance with this article when all eligible directors indicate to each other by any means that they share a common view on a matter.

(2) Such a decision may take the form of a resolution in writing, copies of which have been signed by each eligible director or to which each eligible director has otherwise indicated agreement in writing.

(3) References in this article to eligible directors are to directors who would have been entitled to vote on the matter had it been proposed as a resolution at a directors' meeting.

(4) A decision may not be taken in accordance with this article if the eligible directors would not have formed a quorum at such a meeting.

Calling a directors' meeting
[Same as clg 9]

9. —(1) Any director may call a directors' meeting by giving notice of the meeting to the directors or by authorising the company secretary (if any) to give such notice.

(2) Notice of any directors' meeting must indicate—

(a) its proposed date and time;

(b) where it is to take place; and

(c) if it is anticipated that directors participating in the meeting will not be in the same place, how it is proposed that they should communicate with each other during the meeting.

(3) Notice of a directors' meeting must be given to each director, but need not be in writing.

(4) Notice of a directors' meeting need not be given to directors who waive their entitlement to notice of that meeting, by giving notice to that effect to the company not more than 7 days after the date on which the meeting is held. Where such notice is given after the meeting has been held, that does not affect the validity of the meeting, or of any business conducted at it.

Participation in directors' meetings
[Same as clg 10 and plc 9]

10. —(1) Subject to the articles, directors participate in a directors' meeting, or part of a directors' meeting, when—

(a) the meeting has been called and takes place in accordance with the articles, and

(b) they can each communicate to the others any information or opinions they have on any particular item of the business of the meeting.

(2) In determining whether directors are participating in a directors' meeting, it is irrelevant where any director is or how they communicate with each other.

(3) If all the directors participating in a meeting are not in the same place, they may decide that the meeting is to be treated as taking place wherever any of them is.

Quorum for directors' meetings
[Same as clg 11]

11.—(1) At a directors' meeting, unless a quorum is participating, no proposal is to be voted on, except a proposal to call another meeting.

(2) The quorum for directors' meetings may be fixed from time to time by a decision of the directors, but it must never be less than two, and unless otherwise fixed it is two.

(3) If the total number of directors for the time being is less than the quorum required, the directors must not take any decision other than a decision—

   (a) to appoint further directors, or

   (b) to call a general meeting so as to enable the shareholders to appoint further directors.

Chairing of directors' meetings
[Same as clg 12]

12.—(1) The directors may appoint a director to chair their meetings.

(2) The person so appointed for the time being is known as the chairman.

(3) The directors may terminate the chairman's appointment at any time.

(4) If the chairman is not participating in a directors' meeting within ten minutes of the time at which it was to start, the participating directors must appoint one of themselves to chair it.

Casting vote
[Same as clg 13 and plc 14]

13.—(1) If the numbers of votes for and against a proposal are equal, the chairman or other director chairing the meeting has a casting vote.

(2) But this does not apply if, in accordance with the articles, the chairman or other director is not to be counted as participating in the decision-making process for quorum or voting purposes.

Conflicts of interest
[Same as clg 14]

14.—(1) If a proposed decision of the directors is concerned with an actual or proposed transaction or arrangement with the company in which a director is interested, that director is not to be counted as participating in the decision-making process for quorum or voting purposes.

(2) But if paragraph (3) applies, a director who is interested in an actual or proposed transaction or arrangement with the company is to be counted as participating in the decision-making process for quorum and voting purposes.

(3) This paragraph applies when—

   (a) the company by ordinary resolution disapplies the provision of the articles which would otherwise prevent a director from being counted as participating in the decision-making process;

(b) the director's interest cannot reasonably be regarded as likely to give rise to a conflict of interest; or

(c) the director's conflict of interest arises from a permitted cause.

(4) For the purposes of this article, the following are permitted causes—

(a) a guarantee given, or to be given, by or to a director in respect of an obligation incurred by or on behalf of the company or any of its subsidiaries;

(b) subscription, or an agreement to subscribe, for shares or other securities of the company or any of its subsidiaries, or to underwrite, sub-underwrite, or guarantee subscription for any such shares or securities; and

(c) arrangements pursuant to which benefits are made available to employees and directors or former employees and directors of the company or any of its subsidiaries which do not provide special benefits for directors or former directors.

(5) For the purposes of this article, references to proposed decisions and decision-making processes include any directors' meeting or part of a directors' meeting.

(6) Subject to paragraph (7), if a question arises at a meeting of directors or of a committee of directors as to the right of a director to participate in the meeting (or part of the meeting) for voting or quorum purposes, the question may, before the conclusion of the meeting, be referred to the chairman whose ruling in relation to any director other than the chairman is to be final and conclusive.

(7) If any question as to the right to participate in the meeting (or part of the meeting) should arise in respect of the chairman, the question is to be decided by a decision of the directors at that meeting, for which purpose the chairman is not to be counted as participating in the meeting (or that part of the meeting) for voting or quorum purposes.

Records of decisions to be kept

[Same as clg 15]

15. The directors must ensure that the company keeps a record, in writing, for at least 10 years from the date of the decision recorded, of every unanimous or majority decision taken by the directors.

Directors' discretion to make further rules

[Same as clg16 and plc 19]

16. Subject to the articles, the directors may make any rule which they think fit about how they take decisions, and about how such rules are to be recorded or communicated to directors.

APPOINTMENT OF DIRECTORS

Methods of appointing directors
[Same as clg 17 except that clg 17 uses the words 'member' and 'members' instead of 'shareholder' and 'shareholders' respectively]

17.—(1) Any person who is willing to act as a director, and is permitted by law to do so, may be appointed to be a director—

  (a) by ordinary resolution, or
  (b) by a decision of the directors.

(2) In any case where, as a result of death, the company has no shareholders and no directors, the personal representatives of the last shareholder to have died have the right, by notice in writing, to appoint a person to be a director.

(3) For the purposes of paragraph (2), where 2 or more shareholders die in circumstances rendering it uncertain who was the last to die, a younger shareholder is deemed to have survived an older shareholder.

Termination of director's appointment
[Same as clg 18 and plc 22]

18. A person ceases to be a director as soon as—

  (a) that person ceases to be a director by virtue of any provision of the Companies Act 2006 or is prohibited from being a director by law;
  (b) a bankruptcy order is made against that person;
  (c) a composition is made with that person's creditors generally in satisfaction of that person's debts;
  (d) a registered medical practitioner who is treating that person gives a written opinion to the company stating that that person has become physically or mentally incapable of acting as a director and may remain so for more than three months;
  (e) by reason of that person's mental health, a court makes an order which wholly or partly prevents that person from personally exercising any powers or rights which that person would otherwise have;
  (f) notification is received by the company from the director that the director is resigning from office, and such resignation has taken effect in accordance with its terms.

Directors' remuneration
[Same as clg 19 and plc 23]

19.—(1) Directors may undertake any services for the company that the directors decide.

(2) Directors are entitled to such remuneration as the directors determine—

  (a) for their services to the company as directors, and
  (b) for any other service which they undertake for the company.

(3) Subject to the articles, a director's remuneration may—
  (a) take any form, and
  (b) include any arrangements in connection with the payment of a pension, allowance or gratuity, or any death, sickness or disability benefits, to or in respect of that director.
(4) Unless the directors decide otherwise, directors' remuneration accrues from day to day.
(5) Unless the directors decide otherwise, directors are not accountable to the company for any remuneration which they receive as directors or other officers or employees of the company's subsidiaries or of any other body corporate in which the company is interested.

Directors' expenses
[Same as plc 24]
20. The company may pay any reasonable expenses which the directors properly incur in connection with their attendance at—
  (a) meetings of directors or committees of directors,
  (b) general meetings, or
  (c) separate meetings of the holders of any class of shares or of debentures of the company,
or otherwise in connection with the exercise of their powers and the discharge of their responsibilities in relation to the company.

PART 3 SHARES AND DISTRIBUTIONS

SHARES

All shares to be fully paid up
21.—(1) No share is to be issued for less than the aggregate of its nominal value and any premium to be paid to the company in consideration for its issue.
(2) This does not apply to shares taken on the formation of the company by the subscribers to the company's memorandum.

Powers to issue different classes of share
[Same as plc 43]
22.—(1) Subject to the articles, but without prejudice to the rights attached to any existing share, the company may issue shares with such rights or restrictions as may be determined by ordinary resolution.
(2) The company may issue shares which are to be redeemed, or are liable to be redeemed at the option of the company or the holder, and the directors may determine the terms, conditions and manner of redemption of any such shares.

Company not bound by less than absolute interests

[Same as plc 45]

23. Except as required by law, no person is to be recognised by the company as holding any share upon any trust, and except as otherwise required by law or the articles, the company is not in any way to be bound by or recognise any interest in a share other than the holder's absolute ownership of it and all the rights attaching to it.

Share certificates

24.—(1) The company must issue each shareholder, free of charge, with one or more certificates in respect of the shares which that shareholder holds.

(2) Every certificate must specify—

(a) in respect of how many shares, of what class, it is issued;

(b) the nominal value of those shares;

(c) that the shares are fully paid; and

(d any distinguishing numbers assigned to them.

(3) No certificate may be issued in respect of shares of more than one class.

(4) If more than one person holds a share, only one certificate may be issued in respect of it.

(5) Certificates must—

(a) have affixed to them the company's common seal, or

(b) be otherwise executed in accordance with the Companies Acts.

Replacement share certificates

25.—(1) If a certificate issued in respect of a shareholder's shares is—

(a) damaged or defaced, or

(b) said to be lost, stolen or destroyed,

that shareholder is entitled to be issued with a replacement certificate in respect of the same shares.

(2) A shareholder exercising the right to be issued with such a replacement certificate—

(a) may at the same time exercise the right to be issued with a single certificate or separate certificates;

(b) must return the certificate which is to be replaced to the company if it is damaged or defaced; and

(c) must comply with such conditions as to evidence, indemnity and the payment of a reasonable fee as the directors decide.

Share transfers

26.—(1) Shares may be transferred by means of an instrument of transfer in any usual form or any other form approved by the directors, which is executed by or on behalf of the transferor.

(2) No fee may be charged for registering any instrument of transfer or other document relating to or affecting the title to any share.

(3) The company may retain any instrument of transfer which is registered.

(4) The transferor remains the holder of a share until the transferee's name is entered in the register of members as holder of it.

(5) The directors may refuse to register the transfer of a share, and if they do so, the instrument of transfer must be returned to the transferee with the notice of refusal unless they suspect that the proposed transfer may be fraudulent.

Transmission of shares

27.—(1) If title to a share passes to a transmittee, the company may only recognise the transmittee as having any title to that share.

(2) A transmittee who produces such evidence of entitlement to shares as the directors may properly require—

(a) may, subject to the articles, choose either to become the holder of those shares or to have them transferred to another person, and

(b) subject to the articles, and pending any transfer of the shares to another person, has the same rights as the holder had.

(3) But transmittees do not have the right to attend or vote at a general meeting, or agree to a proposed written resolution, in respect of shares to which they are entitled, by reason of the holder's death or bankruptcy or otherwise, unless they become the holders of those shares.

Exercise of transmittees' rights

28.—(1) Transmittees who wish to become the holders of shares to which they have become entitled must notify the company in writing of that wish.

(2) If the transmittee wishes to have a share transferred to another person, the transmittee must execute an instrument of transfer in respect of it.

(3) Any transfer made or executed under this article is to be treated as if it were made or executed by the person from whom the transmittee has derived rights in respect of the share, and as if the event which gave rise to the transmission had not occurred.

Transmittees bound by prior notices

29. If a notice is given to a shareholder in respect of shares and a transmittee is entitled to those shares, the transmittee is bound by the notice if it was given to the shareholder before the transmittee's name has been entered in the register of members.

DIVIDENDS AND OTHER DISTRIBUTIONS

Procedure for declaring dividends

30.—(1) The company may by ordinary resolution declare dividends, and the directors may decide to pay interim dividends.

(2) A dividend must not be declared unless the directors have made a recommendation as to its amount. Such a dividend must not exceed the amount recommended by the directors.

(3) No dividend may be declared or paid unless it is in accordance with shareholders' respective rights.

(4) Unless the shareholders' resolution to declare or directors' decision to pay a dividend, or the terms on which shares are issued, specify otherwise, it must be paid by reference to each shareholder's holding of shares on the date of the resolution or decision to declare or pay it.

(5) If the company's share capital is divided into different classes, no interim dividend may be paid on shares carrying deferred or non-preferred rights if, at the time of payment, any preferential dividend is in arrear.

(6) The directors may pay at intervals any dividend payable at a fixed rate if it appears to them that the profits available for distribution justify the payment.

(7) If the directors act in good faith, they do not incur any liability to the holders of shares conferring preferred rights for any loss they may suffer by the lawful payment of an interim dividend on shares with deferred or non-preferred rights.

Payment of dividends and other distributions
[Same as plc 72]

31.—(1) Where a dividend or other sum which is a distribution is payable in respect of a share, it must be paid by one or more of the following means—

(a) transfer to a bank or building society account specified by the distribution recipient either in writing or as the directors may otherwise decide;

(b) sending a cheque made payable to the distribution recipient by post to the distribution recipient at the distribution recipient's registered address (if the distribution recipient is a holder of the share), or (in any other case) to an address specified by the distribution recipient either in writing or as the directors may otherwise decide;

(c) sending a cheque made payable to such person by post to such person at such address as the distribution recipient has specified either in writing or as the directors may otherwise decide; or

(d) any other means of payment as the directors agree with the distribution recipient either in writing or by such other means as the directors decide.

(2) In the articles, "the distribution recipient" means, in respect of a share in respect of which a dividend or other sum is payable—

(a) the holder of the share; or

(b) if the share has two or more joint holders, whichever of them is named first in the register of members; or

(c) if the holder is no longer entitled to the share by reason of death or bankruptcy, or otherwise by operation of law, the transmittee.

No interest on distributions

[Same as plc 74]

32. The company may not pay interest on any dividend or other sum payable in respect of a share unless otherwise provided by—

(a) the terms on which the share was issued, or

(b) the provisions of another agreement between the holder of that share and the company.

Unclaimed distributions

[Same as plc 75]

33.—(1) All dividends or other sums which are—

(a) payable in respect of shares, and

(b) unclaimed after having been declared or become payable, may be invested or otherwise made use of by the directors for the benefit of the company until claimed.

(2) The payment of any such dividend or other sum into a separate account does not make the company a trustee in respect of it.

(3) If—

(a) twelve years have passed from the date on which a dividend or other sum became due for payment, and

(b) the distribution recipient has not claimed it, the distribution recipient is no longer entitled to that dividend or other sum and it ceases to remain owing by the company.

Non-cash distributions

34.—(1) Subject to the terms of issue of the share in question, the company may, by ordinary resolution on the recommendation of the directors, decide to pay all or part of a dividend or other distribution payable in respect of a share by transferring non-cash assets of equivalent value (including, without limitation, shares or other securities in any company).

(2) For the purposes of paying a non-cash distribution, the directors may make whatever arrangements they think fit, including, where any difficulty arises regarding the distribution—

(a) fixing the value of any assets;

(b) paying cash to any distribution recipient on the basis of that value in order to adjust the rights of recipients; and

(c) vesting any assets in trustees.

Waiver of distributions

[Same as plc 77]

35. Distribution recipients may waive their entitlement to a dividend or other distribution payable in respect of a share by giving the company notice in writing to that effect, but if—

(a) the share has more than one holder, or

(b) more than one person is entitled to the share, whether by reason of the death or bankruptcy of one or more joint holders, or otherwise,

the notice is not effective unless it is expressed to be given, and signed, by all the holders or persons otherwise entitled to the share.

CAPITALISATION OF PROFITS

Authority to capitalise and appropriation of capitalised sums

36.—(1) Subject to the articles, the directors may, if they are so authorised by an ordinary resolution—

(a) decide to capitalise any profits of the company (whether or not they are available for distribution) which are not required for paying a preferential dividend, or any sum standing to the credit of the company's share premium account or capital redemption reserve; and

(b) appropriate any sum which they so decide to capitalise (a "capitalised sum") to the persons who would have been entitled to it if it were distributed by way of dividend (the "persons entitled") and in the same proportions.

(2) Capitalised sums must be applied—

(a) on behalf of the persons entitled, and

(b) in the same proportions as a dividend would have been distributed to them.

(3) Any capitalised sum may be applied in paying up new shares of a nominal amount equal to the capitalised sum which are then allotted credited as fully paid to the persons entitled or as they may direct.

(4) A capitalised sum which was appropriated from profits available for distribution may be applied in paying up new debentures of the company which are then allotted credited as fully paid to the persons entitled or as they may direct.

(5) Subject to the articles the directors may—

(a) apply capitalised sums in accordance with paragraphs (3) and (4) partly in one way and partly in another;

(b) make such arrangements as they think fit to deal with shares or debentures becoming distributable in fractions under this article (including the issuing of fractional certificates or the making of cash payments); and

(c) authorise any person to enter into an agreement with the company on behalf of all the persons entitled which is binding on them in respect of the allotment of shares and debentures to them under this article.

PART 4 DECISION-MAKING BY SHAREHOLDERS

ORGANISATION OF GENERAL MEETINGS

Attendance and speaking at general meetings
[Same as clg 23 and plc 29]

37.—(1) A person is able to exercise the right to speak at a general meeting when that person is in a position to communicate to all those attending the meeting, during the meeting, any information or opinions which that person has on the business of the meeting.

(2) A person is able to exercise the right to vote at a general meeting when—

(a) that person is able to vote, during the meeting, on resolutions put to the vote at the meeting, and

(b) that person's vote can be taken into account in determining whether or not such resolutions are passed at the same time as the votes of all the other persons attending the meeting.

(3) The directors may make whatever arrangements they consider appropriate to enable those attending a general meeting to exercise their rights to speak or vote at it.

(4) In determining attendance at a general meeting, it is immaterial whether any two or more members attending it are in the same place as each other.

(5) Two or more persons who are not in the same place as each other attend a general meeting if their circumstances are such that if they have (or were to have) rights to speak and vote at that meeting, they are (or would be) able to exercise them.

Quorum for general meetings
[Same as clg 24 and plc 30]

38. No business other than the appointment of the chairman of the meeting is to be transacted at a general meeting if the persons attending it do not constitute a quorum.

Chairing general meetings
[Same as clg 25 and plc 31 except that those articles use the word 'member' instead of 'shareholder']

39.—(1) If the directors have appointed a chairman, the chairman shall chair general meetings if present and willing to do so.

(2) If the directors have not appointed a chairman, or if the chairman is unwilling to chair the meeting or is not present within ten minutes of the time at which a meeting was due to start—

(a) the directors present, or

(b) (if no directors are present), the meeting,

must appoint a director or shareholder to chair the meeting, and the appointment of the chairman of the meeting must be the first business of the meeting.

(3) The person chairing a meeting in accordance with this article is referred to as "the chairman of the meeting".

Attendance and speaking by directors and non-shareholders
[Same as plc 32 except that plc 32 uses the word 'members' instead of 'shareholders']
40.—(1) Directors may attend and speak at general meetings, whether or not they are shareholders.
(2) The chairman of the meeting may permit other persons who are not—
  (a) shareholders of the company, or
  (b) otherwise entitled to exercise the rights of shareholders in relation to general meetings, to attend and speak at a general meeting.

Adjournment
[Same as clg 27 and plc 33]
41.—(1) If the persons attending a general meeting within half an hour of the time at which the meeting was due to start do not constitute a quorum, or if during a meeting a quorum ceases to be present, the chairman of the meeting must adjourn it.
(2) The chairman of the meeting may adjourn a general meeting at which a quorum is present if—
  (a) the meeting consents to an adjournment, or
  (b) it appears to the chairman of the meeting that an adjournment is necessary to protect the safety of any person attending the meeting or ensure that the business of the meeting is conducted in an orderly manner.
(3) The chairman of the meeting must adjourn a general meeting if directed to do so by the meeting.
(4) When adjourning a general meeting, the chairman of the meeting must—
  (a) either specify the time and place to which it is adjourned or state that it is to continue at a time and place to be fixed by the directors, and
  (b) have regard to any directions as to the time and place of any adjournment which have been given by the meeting.
(5) If the continuation of an adjourned meeting is to take place more than 14 days after it was adjourned, the company must give at least 7 clear days' notice of it (that is, excluding the day of the adjourned meeting and the day on which the notice is given)—
  (a) to the same persons to whom notice of the company's general meetings is required to be given, and
  (b) containing the same information which such notice is required to contain.
(6) No business may be transacted at an adjourned general meeting which could not properly have been transacted at the meeting if the adjournment had not taken place.

VOTING AT GENERAL MEETINGS

Voting: general
[Same as clg 28 and plc 34]

42. A resolution put to the vote of a general meeting must be decided on a show of hands unless a poll is duly demanded in accordance with the articles.

Errors and disputes
[Same as clg 29 and plc 35]

43.—(1) No objection may be raised to the qualification of any person voting at a general meeting except at the meeting or adjourned meeting at which the vote objected to is tendered, and every vote not disallowed at the meeting is valid.

(2) Any such objection must be referred to the chairman of the meeting, whose decision is final.

Poll votes
[Same as clg 30 except that clg 30 uses the word 'members' instead of 'shareholders']

44.—(1) A poll on a resolution may be demanded—

    (a) in advance of the general meeting where it is to be put to the vote, or

    (b) at a general meeting, either before a show of hands on that resolution or immediately after the result of a show of hands on that resolution is declared.

(2) A poll may be demanded by—

    (a) the chairman of the meeting;

    (b) the directors;

    (c) two or more persons having the right to vote on the resolution; or

    (d) a person or persons representing not less than one tenth of the total voting rights of all the shareholders having the right to vote on the resolution.

(3) A demand for a poll may be withdrawn if—

    (a) the poll has not yet been taken, and

    (b) the chairman of the meeting consents to the withdrawal.

(4) Polls must be taken immediately and in such manner as the chairman of the meeting directs.

Content of proxy notices
[Same as clg 31 and plc 38 except that those articles use the word 'member' instead of 'shareholder']

45.—(1) Proxies may only validly be appointed by a notice in writing (a "proxy notice") which—

    (a) states the name and address of the shareholder appointing the proxy;

    (b) identifies the person appointed to be that shareholder's proxy and the general meeting in relation to which that person is appointed;

(c) is signed by or on behalf of the shareholder appointing the proxy, or is authenticated in such manner as the directors may determine; and

(d) is delivered to the company in accordance with the articles and any instructions contained in the notice of the general meeting to which they relate.

(2) The company may require proxy notices to be delivered in a particular form, and may specify different forms for different purposes.

(3) Proxy notices may specify how the proxy appointed under them is to vote (or that the proxy is to abstain from voting) on one or more resolutions.

(4) Unless a proxy notice indicates otherwise, it must be treated as—

(a) allowing the person appointed under it as a proxy discretion as to how to vote on any ancillary or procedural resolutions put to the meeting, and

(b) appointing that person as a proxy in relation to any adjournment of the general meeting to which it relates as well as the meeting itself.

Delivery of proxy notices

[Same as clg 32]

46.—(1) A person who is entitled to attend, speak or vote (either on a show of hands or on a poll) at a general meeting remains so entitled in respect of that meeting or any adjournment of it, even though a valid proxy notice has been delivered to the company by or on behalf of that person.

(2) An appointment under a proxy notice may be revoked by delivering to the company a notice in writing given by or on behalf of the person by whom or on whose behalf the proxy notice was given.

(3) A notice revoking a proxy appointment only takes effect if it is delivered before the start of the meeting or adjourned meeting to which it relates.

(4) If a proxy notice is not executed by the person appointing the proxy, it must be accompanied by written evidence of the authority of the person who executed it to execute it on the appointor's behalf.

Amendments to resolutions

[Same as clg 33]

47.—(1) An ordinary resolution to be proposed at a general meeting may be amended by ordinary resolution if—

(a) notice of the proposed amendment is given to the company in writing by a person entitled to vote at the general meeting at which it is to be proposed not less than 48 hours before the meeting is to take place (or such later time as the chairman of the meeting may determine), and

(b) the proposed amendment does not, in the reasonable opinion of the chairman of the meeting, materially alter the scope of the resolution.

(2) A special resolution to be proposed at a general meeting may be amended by ordinary resolution, if—

(a) the chairman of the meeting proposes the amendment at the general meeting at which the resolution is to be proposed, and

(b) the amendment does not go beyond what is necessary to correct a grammatical or other non-substantive error in the resolution.

(3) If the chairman of the meeting, acting in good faith, wrongly decides that an amendment to a resolution is out of order, the chairman's error does not invalidate the vote on that resolution.

PART 5 ADMINISTRATIVE ARRANGEMENTS

Means of communication to be used

[Same as clg 33 and plc 79]

48.—(1) Subject to the articles, anything sent or supplied by or to the company under the articles may be sent or supplied in any way in which the Companies Act 2006 provides for documents or information which are authorised or required by any provision of that Act to be sent or supplied by or to the company.

(2) Subject to the articles, any notice or document to be sent or supplied to a director in connection with the taking of decisions by directors may also be sent or supplied by the means by which that director has asked to be sent or supplied with such notices or documents for the time being.

(3) A director may agree with the company that notices or documents sent to that director in a particular way are to be deemed to have been received within a specified time of their being sent, and for the specified time to be less than 48 hours.

Company seals

[Same as clg 35]

49.—(1) Any common seal may only be used by the authority of the directors.

(2) The directors may decide by what means and in what form any common seal is to be used.

(3) Unless otherwise decided by the directors, if the company has a common seal and it is affixed to a document, the document must also be signed by at least one authorised person in the presence of a witness who attests the signature.

(4) For the purposes of this article, an authorised person is—

(a) any director of the company;

(b) the company secretary (if any); or

(c) any person authorised by the directors for the purpose of signing documents to which the common seal is applied.

No right to inspect accounts and other records

[Same as clg 36 and plc 83 except that those articles use the word 'member' instead of 'shareholder']

50. Except as provided by law or authorised by the directors or an ordinary resolution of the company, no person is entitled to inspect any of the company's accounting or other records or documents merely by virtue of being a shareholder.

Provision for employees on cessation of business
[Same as clg 37 and plc 84]
51. The directors may decide to make provision for the benefit of persons employed or formerly employed by the company or any of its subsidiaries (other than a director or former director or shadow director) in connection with the cessation or transfer to any person of the whole or part of the undertaking of the company or that subsidiary.

DIRECTORS' INDEMNITY AND INSURANCE

Indemnity
[Same as clg 38 and plc 85]
52.—(1) Subject to paragraph (2), a relevant director of the company or an associated company may be indemnified out of the company's assets against—
- (a) any liability incurred by that director in connection with any negligence, default, breach of duty or breach of trust in relation to the company or an associated company,
- (b) any liability incurred by that director in connection with the activities of the company or an associated company in its capacity as a trustee of an occupational pension scheme (as defined in section 235(6) of the Companies Act 2006),
- (c) any other liability incurred by that director as an officer of the company or an associated company.
- (2) This article does not authorise any indemnity which would be prohibited or rendered void by any provision of the Companies Acts or by any other provision of law.
- (3) In this article—
  - (a) companies are associated if one is a subsidiary of the other or both are subsidiaries of the same body corporate, and
  - (b) a "relevant director" means any director or former director of the company or an associated company.

Insurance
[Same as clg 39 and plc 86]
53.—(1) The directors may decide to purchase and maintain insurance, at the expense of the company, for the benefit of any relevant director in respect of any relevant loss.

(2) In this article—

(a) a "relevant director" means any director or former director of the company or an associated company,

(b) a "relevant loss" means any loss or liability which has been or may be incurred by a relevant director in connection with that director's duties or powers in relation to the company, any associated company or any pension fund or employees' share scheme of the company or associated company, and

(c) companies are associated if one is a subsidiary of the other or both are subsidiaries of the same body corporate.

ANNEX C3

Companies Act 2006 Model Articles for Private Companies Limited by Guarantee

Schedule 2 of the Companies (Model Articles) Regulations 2008 (SI 2008/3229)

INDEX TO THE ARTICLES

[See Annex C1]

PART 1 INTERPRETATION AND LIMITATION OF LIABILITY

Defined terms

1. In the articles, unless the context requires otherwise—

    "articles" means the company's articles of association;

    "bankruptcy" includes individual insolvency proceedings in a jurisdiction other than England and Wales or Northern Ireland which have an effect similar to that of bankruptcy;

    "chairman" has the meaning given in article 12;

    "chairman of the meeting" has the meaning given in article 25;

    "Companies Acts" means the Companies Acts (as defined in section 2 of the Companies Act 2006), in so far as they apply to the company;

    "director" means a director of the company, and includes any person occupying the position of director, by whatever name called;

    "document" includes, unless otherwise specified, any document sent or supplied in electronic form;

    "electronic form" has the meaning given in section 1168 of the Companies Act 2006;

    "member" has the meaning given in section 112 of the Companies Act 2006;

    "ordinary resolution" has the meaning given in section 282 of the Companies Act 2006;

    "participate", in relation to a directors' meeting, has the meaning given in article 10;

    "proxy notice" has the meaning given in article 31;

    "special resolution" has the meaning given in section 283 of the Companies Act 2006;

"subsidiary" has the meaning given in section 1159 of the Companies Act 2006; and

"writing" means the representation or reproduction of words, symbols or other information in a visible form by any method or combination of methods, whether sent or supplied in electronic form or otherwise.

Unless the context otherwise requires, other words or expressions contained in these articles bear the same meaning as in the Companies Act 2006 as in force on the date when these articles become binding on the company.

Liability of members

2. The liability of each member is limited to £1, being the amount that each member undertakes to contribute to the assets of the company in the event of its being wound up while he is a member or within one year after he ceases to be a member, for—

(a) payment of the company's debts and liabilities contracted before he ceases to be a member,

(b) payment of the costs, charges and expenses of winding up, and

(c) adjustment of the rights of the contributories among themselves.

PART 2 DIRECTORS

DIRECTORS' POWERS AND RESPONSIBILITIES

Directors' general authority

3. [Same as pcls 3 (see Annex C2)]

Members' reserve power

4. [Same as pcls 4 (see Annex C2) except clg 4 uses the word 'members' where pcls 4 uses the word 'shareholders]

Directors may delegate

5. [Same as pcls 5 (see Annex C2)]

Committees

6. [Same as pcls 6 (see Annex C2)]

DECISION-MAKING BY DIRECTORS

Directors to take decisions collectively

7. [Same as pcls 7 (see Annex C2)]

Unanimous decisions

8. [Same as pcls 8 (see Annex C2)]

Calling a directors' meeting
9. [Same as pcls 9 (see Annex C2)]

Participation in directors' meetings
10. [Same as pcls 10 (see Annex C2)]

Quorum for directors' meetings
11. [Same as pcls 11 (see Annex C2)]

Chairing of directors' meetings
12. [Same as pcls 12 (see Annex C2)]

Casting vote
13. [Same as pcls 13 (see Annex C2)]

Conflicts of interest
14. [Same as pcls 14 (see Annex C2)]

Records of decisions to be kept
15. [Same as pcls 15 (see Annex C2)]

Directors' discretion to make further rules
16. [Same as pcls 16 (see Annex C2)]

APPOINTMENT OF DIRECTORS

Methods of appointing directors
17. [Same as pcls 17 (see Annex C2) except clg 17 uses the word 'member' where pcls 17 uses the word 'shareholder']

Termination of director's appointment
18. [Same as pcls 18 (see Annex C2)]

Directors' remuneration
19. [Same as pcls 19 (see Annex C2)]

Directors' expenses
20. The company may pay any reasonable expenses which the directors properly incur in connection with their attendance at—
- (a) meetings of directors or committees of directors,
- (b) general meetings, or
- (c) separate meetings of the holders of debentures of the company, or otherwise in connection with the exercise of their powers and the discharge of their responsibilities in relation to the company.

PART 3 MEMBERS

BECOMING AND CEASING TO BE A MEMBER

Applications for membership
21. No person shall become a member of the company unless—
- (a) that person has completed an application for membership in a form approved by the directors, and
- (b) the directors have approved the application.

Termination of membership
22.—(1) A member may withdraw from membership of the company by giving 7 days' notice to the company in writing.

(2) Membership is not transferable.

(3) A person's membership terminates when that person dies or ceases to exist.

ORGANISATION OF GENERAL MEETINGS

Attendance and speaking at general meetings
23. [Same as pcls 37 (see Annex C2)]

Quorum for general meetings
24. [Same as pcls 38 (see Annex C2)].

Chairing general meetings
25. [Same as pcls 39 (see Annex C2) except clg 25 uses the word 'member' where pcls 39 uses the word 'shareholder']

Attendance and speaking by directors and non-members
26.—(1) Directors may attend and speak at general meetings, whether or not they are members.

(2) The chairman of the meeting may permit other persons who are not members of the company to attend and speak at a general meeting.

Adjournment
27. [Same as pcls 41 (see Annex C2)]

VOTING AT GENERAL MEETINGS

Voting: general
28. [Same as pcls 42 (see Annex C2)]

Errors and disputes
29. [Same as pcls 43 (see Annex C2)]

Poll votes
30. [Same as pcls 44 (see Annex C2) except clg 30 uses the word 'member' where pcls 44 uses the word 'shareholder']

Content of proxy notices
31. [Same as pcls 45 (see Annex C2) except clg 31 uses the word 'member' where pcls 45 uses the word 'shareholder']

Delivery of proxy notices
32. [Same as pcls 46 (see Annex C2)]

Amendments to resolutions
33. [Same as pcls 47 (see Annex C2)]

PART 4 ADMINISTRATIVE ARRANGEMENTS

Means of communication to be used
34. [Same as pcls 48 (see Annex C2)]

Company seals
35. [Same as pcls 49 (see Annex C2)]

No right to inspect accounts and other records
36. [Same as pcls 50 (see Annex C2) except clg 36 uses the word 'member' where pcls 50 uses the word 'shareholder']

Provision for employees on cessation of business
37. [Same as pcls 51 (see Annex C2)]

DIRECTORS' INDEMNITY AND INSURANCE

Indemnity
38. [Same as pcls 52 (see Annex C2)]

Insurance
39. [Same as pcls 53 (see Annex C2)]

ANNEX C4

Companies Act 2006 Model Articles for Public Companies

Schedule 3 of the Companies (Model Articles) Regulations 2008 (SI 2008/3229)

INDEX TO THE ARTICLES

[See Annex C1]

PART 1 INTERPRETATION AND LIMITATION OF LIABILITY

Defined terms

1. In the articles , unless the context requires otherwise—

"alternate" or "alternate director" has the meaning given in article 25;

"appointor" has the meaning given in article 25;

"articles" means the company's articles of association;

"bankruptcy" includes individual insolvency proceedings in a jurisdiction other than England and Wales or Northern Ireland which have an effect similar to that of bankruptcy;

"call" has the meaning given in article 54;

"call notice" has the meaning given in article 54;

"certificate" means a paper certificate (other than a share warrant) evidencing a person's title to specified shares or other securities;

"certificated" in relation to a share, means that it is not an uncertificated share or a share in respect of which a share warrant has been issued and is current;

"chairman" has the meaning given in article 12;

"chairman of the meeting" has the meaning given in article 31;

"Companies Acts" means the Companies Acts (as defined in section 2 of the Companies Act 2006), in so far as they apply to the company;

"company's lien" has the meaning given in article 52;

"director" means a director of the company, and includes any person occupying the position of director, by whatever name called;

"distribution recipient" has the meaning given in article 72;

"document" includes, unless otherwise specified, any document sent or supplied in electronic form;

"electronic form" has the meaning given in section 1168 of the Companies Act 2006;

"fully paid" in relation to a share, means that the nominal value and any premium to be paid to the company in respect of that share have been paid to the company;

"hard copy form" has the meaning given in section 1168 of the Companies Act 2006;

"holder" in relation to shares means the person whose name is entered in the register of members as the holder of the shares, or, in the case of a share in respect of which a share warrant has been issued (and not cancelled), the person in possession of that warrant;

"instrument" means a document in hard copy form;

"lien enforcement notice" has the meaning given in article 53;

"member" has the meaning given in section 112 of the Companies Act 2006;

"ordinary resolution" has the meaning given in section 282 of the Companies Act 2006;

"paid" means paid or credited as paid;

"participate", in relation to a directors' meeting, has the meaning given in article 9;

"partly paid" in relation to a share means that part of that share's nominal value or any premium at which it was issued has not been paid to the company;

"proxy notice" has the meaning given in article 38;

"securities seal" has the meaning given in article 47;

"shares" means shares in the company;

"special resolution" has the meaning given in section 283 of the Companies Act 2006;

"subsidiary" has the meaning given in section 1159 of the Companies Act 2006;

"transmittee" means a person entitled to a share by reason of the death or bankruptcy of a shareholder or otherwise by operation of law;

"uncertificated" in relation to a share means that, by virtue of legislation (other than section 778 of the Companies Act 2006) permitting title to shares to be evidenced and transferred without a certificate, title to that share is evidenced and may be transferred without a certificate; and

"writing" means the representation or reproduction of words, symbols or other information in a visible form by any method or combination of methods, whether sent or supplied in electronic form or otherwise.

Unless the context otherwise requires, other words or expressions contained in these articles bear the same meaning as in the Companies Act 2006 as in force on the date when these articles become binding on the company.

Liability of members

2. The liability of the members is limited to the amount, if any, unpaid on the shares held by them.

PART 2 DIRECTORS

DIRECTORS' POWERS AND RESPONSIBILITIES

Directors' general authority

3. [Same as pcls 3 (see Annex C2)]

Members' reserve power

4. [Same as pcls 4 (see Annex C2) except plc 4 uses the word 'members' where pcls 4 uses the word 'shareholders']

Directors may delegate

5. [Same as pcls 5 (see Annex C2)]

Committees

6. [Same as pcls 6 (see Annex C2)]

DECISION-MAKING BY DIRECTORS

Directors to take decisions collectively

7. Decisions of the directors may be taken—
    (a) at a directors' meeting, or
    (b) in the form of a directors' written resolution.

Calling a directors' meeting

8.—(1) Any director may call a directors' meeting.
(2) The company secretary must call a directors' meeting if a director so requests.
(3) A directors' meeting is called by giving notice of the meeting to the directors.
(4) Notice of any directors' meeting must indicate—
    (a) its proposed date and time;
    (b) where it is to take place; and
    (c) if it is anticipated that directors participating in the meeting will not be in the same place, how it is proposed that they should communicate with each other during the meeting.
(5) Notice of a directors' meeting must be given to each director, but need not be in writing.
(6) Notice of a directors' meeting need not be given to directors who waive their entitlement to notice of that meeting, by giving notice to that effect to the company not more than 7 days after the date on which the meeting is held.

Where such notice is given after the meeting has been held, that does not affect the validity of the meeting, or of any business conducted at it.

Participation in directors' meetings

9. [Same as pcls 10 (see Annex C2)]

Quorum for directors' meetings

10.—(1) At a directors' meeting, unless a quorum is participating, no proposal is to be voted on, except a proposal to call another meeting.

(2) The quorum for directors' meetings may be fixed from time to time by a decision of the directors, but it must never be less than two, and unless otherwise fixed it is two.

Meetings where total number of directors less than quorum

11.—(1) This article applies where the total number of directors for the time being is less than the quorum for directors' meetings.

(2) If there is only one director, that director may appoint sufficient directors to make up a quorum or call a general meeting to do so.

(3) If there is more than one director—

(a) a directors' meeting may take place, if it is called in accordance with the articles and at least two directors participate in it, with a view to appointing sufficient directors to make up a quorum or calling a general meeting to do so, and

(b) if a directors' meeting is called but only one director attends at the appointed date and time to participate in it, that director may appoint sufficient directors to make up a quorum or call a general meeting to do so.

Chairing directors' meetings

12.—(1) The directors may appoint a director to chair their meetings.

(2) The person so appointed for the time being is known as the chairman.

(3) The directors may appoint other directors as deputy or assistant chairmen to chair directors' meetings in the chairman's absence.

(4) The directors may terminate the appointment of the chairman, deputy or assistant chairman at any time.

(5) If neither the chairman nor any director appointed generally to chair directors' meetings in the chairman's absence is participating in a meeting within ten minutes of the time at which it was to start, the participating directors must appoint one of themselves to chair it.

Voting at directors' meetings: general rules

13.—(1) Subject to the articles, a decision is taken at a directors' meeting by a majority of the votes of the participating directors.

(2) Subject to the articles, each director participating in a directors' meeting has one vote.

(3) Subject to the articles, if a director has an interest in an actual or proposed transaction or arrangement with the company—

(a) that director and that director's alternate may not vote on any proposal relating to it, but

(b) this does not preclude the alternate from voting in relation to that transaction or arrangement on behalf of another appointor who does not have such an interest.

Chairman's casting vote at directors' meetings

14. [Same as pcls 13 (see Annex C2)]

Alternates voting at directors' meetings

15. A director who is also an alternate director has an additional vote on behalf of each appointor who is—

(a) not participating in a directors' meeting, and

(b) would have been entitled to vote if they were participating in it.

Conflicts of interest

16.—(1) If a directors' meeting, or part of a directors' meeting, is concerned with an actual or proposed transaction or arrangement with the company in which a director is interested, that director is not to be counted as participating in that meeting, or part of a meeting, for quorum or voting purposes.

(2) But if paragraph (3) applies, a director who is interested in an actual or proposed transaction or arrangement with the company is to be counted as participating in a decision at a directors' meeting, or part of a directors' meeting, relating to it for quorum and voting purposes.

(3) This paragraph applies when—

(a) the company by ordinary resolution disapplies the provision of the articles which would otherwise prevent a director from being counted as participating in, or voting at, a directors' meeting;

(b) the director's interest cannot reasonably be regarded as likely to give rise to a conflict of interest; or

(c) the director's conflict of interest arises from a permitted cause.

(4) For the purposes of this article, the following are permitted causes—

(a) a guarantee given, or to be given, by or to a director in respect of an obligation incurred by or on behalf of the company or any of its subsidiaries;

(b) subscription, or an agreement to subscribe, for shares or other securities of the company or any of its subsidiaries, or to underwrite, sub-underwrite, or guarantee subscription for any such shares or securities; and

(c) arrangements pursuant to which benefits are made available to employees and directors or former employees and directors of the company or any of its subsidiaries which do not provide special benefits for directors or former directors.

(5) Subject to paragraph (6), if a question arises at a meeting of directors or of a committee of directors as to the right of a director to participate in the meeting (or part of the meeting) for voting or quorum purposes, the question may, before the conclusion of the meeting, be referred to the chairman whose ruling in relation to any director other than the chairman is to be final and conclusive.

(6) If any question as to the right to participate in the meeting (or part of the meeting) should arise in respect of the chairman, the question is to be decided by a decision of the directors at that meeting, for which purpose the chairman is not to be counted as participating in the meeting (or that part of the meeting) for voting or quorum purposes.

Proposing directors' written resolutions

17.—(1) Any director may propose a directors' written resolution.

(2) The company secretary must propose a directors' written resolution if a director so requests.

(3) A directors' written resolution is proposed by giving notice of the proposed resolution to the directors.

(4) Notice of a proposed directors' written resolution must indicate—
   (a) the proposed resolution, and
   (b) the time by which it is proposed that the directors should adopt it.

(5) Notice of a proposed directors' written resolution must be given in writing to each director.

(6) Any decision which a person giving notice of a proposed directors' written resolution takes regarding the process of adopting that resolution must be taken reasonably in good faith.

Adoption of directors' written resolutions

18.—(1) A proposed directors' written resolution is adopted when all the directors who would have been entitled to vote on the resolution at a directors' meeting have signed one or more copies of it, provided that those directors would have formed a quorum at such a meeting.

(2) It is immaterial whether any director signs the resolution before or after the time by which the notice proposed that it should be adopted.

(3) Once a directors' written resolution has been adopted, it must be treated as if it had been a decision taken at a directors' meeting in accordance with the articles.

(4) The company secretary must ensure that the company keeps a record, in writing, of all directors' written resolutions for at least ten years from the date of their adoption.

Directors' discretion to make further rules
19. [Same as pcls 16 (see Annex C2)]

APPOINTMENT OF DIRECTORS

Methods of appointing directors
20. Any person who is willing to act as a director, and is permitted by law to do so, may be appointed to be a director—
- (a) by ordinary resolution, or
- (b) by a decision of the directors.

Retirement of directors by rotation
21.—(1) At the first annual general meeting all the directors must retire from office.

(2) At every subsequent annual general meeting any directors—
- (a) who have been appointed by the directors since the last annual general meeting, or
- (b) who were not appointed or reappointed at one of the preceding two annual general meetings,

must retire from office and may offer themselves for reappointment by the members.

Termination of director's appointment
22. [Same as pcls 18 (see Annex C2)]

Directors' remuneration
23. [Same as pcls 19 (see Annex C2)]

Directors' expenses
24. [Same as pcls 20 (see Annex C2)]

ALTERNATE DIRECTORS

Appointment and removal of alternates
25.—(1) Any director (the "appointor") may appoint as an alternate any other director, or any other person approved by resolution of the directors, to—
- (a) exercise that director's powers, and
- (b) carry out that director's responsibilities,

in relation to the taking of decisions by the directors in the absence of the alternate's appointor.

(2) Any appointment or removal of an alternate must be effected by notice in writing to the company signed by the appointor, or in any other manner approved by the directors.

(3) The notice must—
- (a) identify the proposed alternate, and
- (b) in the case of a notice of appointment, contain a statement signed by the proposed alternate that the proposed alternate is willing to act as the alternate of the director giving the notice.

Rights and responsibilities of alternate directors

26.—(1) An alternate director has the same rights, in relation to any directors' meeting or directors' written resolution, as the alternate's appointor.

(2) Except as the articles specify otherwise, alternate directors—
- (a) are deemed for all purposes to be directors;
- (b) are liable for their own acts and omissions;
- (c) are subject to the same restrictions as their appointors; and
- (d) are not deemed to be agents of or for their appointors.

(3) A person who is an alternate director but not a director—
- (a) may be counted as participating for the purposes of determining whether a quorum is participating (but only if that person's appointor is not participating), and
- (b) may sign a written resolution (but only if it is not signed or to be signed by that person's appointor).

No alternate may be counted as more than one director for such purposes.

(4) An alternate director is not entitled to receive any remuneration from the company for serving as an alternate director except such part of the alternate's appointor's remuneration as the appointor may direct by notice in writing made to the company.

Termination of alternate directorship

27. An alternate director's appointment as an alternate terminates—
- (a) when the alternate's appointor revokes the appointment by notice to the company in writing specifying when it is to terminate;
- (b) on the occurrence in relation to the alternate of any event which, if it occurred in relation to the alternate's appointor, would result in the termination of the appointor's appointment as a director;
- (c) on the death of the alternate's appointor; or
- (d) when the alternate's appointor's appointment as a director terminates, except that an alternate's appointment as an alternate does not terminate when the appointor retires by rotation at a general meeting and is then re-appointed as a director at the same general meeting.

PART 3 DECISION-MAKING BY MEMBERS

ORGANISATION OF GENERAL MEETINGS

Members can call general meeting if not enough directors

28. If—

(a) the company has fewer than two directors, and

(b) the director (if any) is unable or unwilling to appoint sufficient directors to make up a quorum or to call a general meeting to do so,

then two or more members may call a general meeting (or instruct the company secretary to do so) for the purpose of appointing one or more directors.

Attendance and speaking at general meetings

29. [Same as pcls 37 (see Annex C2)]

Quorum for general meetings

30. [Same as pcls 38 (see Annex C2)]

Chairing general meetings

31. [Same as pcls 39 (see Annex C2)]

Attendance and speaking by directors and non-members

32. [Same as pcls 40 (see Annex C2) except plc 32 uses the word 'members' where pcls 40 uses the word 'shareholders]

Adjournment

33. [Same as pcls 41 (see Annex C2)]

VOTING AT GENERAL MEETINGS

Voting: general

34. [Same as pcls 42 (see Annex C2)]

Errors and disputes

35. [Same as pcls 43 (see Annex C2)]

Demanding a poll

36.—(1) A poll on a resolution may be demanded—

(a) in advance of the general meeting where it is to be put to the vote, or

(b) at a general meeting, either before a show of hands on that resolution or immediately after the result of a show of hands on that resolution is declared.

(2) A poll may be demanded by—

(a) the chairman of the meeting;

(b) the directors;

(c) two or more persons having the right to vote on the resolution; or

(d) a person or persons representing not less than one tenth of the total voting rights of all the members having the right to vote on the resolution.

(3) A demand for a poll may be withdrawn if—

(a) the poll has not yet been taken, and

(b) the chairman of the meeting consents to the withdrawal.

Procedure on a poll

37.—(1) Subject to the articles, polls at general meetings must be taken when, where and in such manner as the chairman of the meeting directs.

(2) The chairman of the meeting may appoint scrutineers (who need not be members) and decide how and when the result of the poll is to be declared.

(3) The result of a poll shall be the decision of the meeting in respect of the resolution on which the poll was demanded.

(4) A poll on—

(a) the election of the chairman of the meeting, or

(b) a question of adjournment,

must be taken immediately.

(5) Other polls must be taken within 30 days of their being demanded.

(6) A demand for a poll does not prevent a general meeting from continuing, except as regards the question on which the poll was demanded.

(7) No notice need be given of a poll not taken immediately if the time and place at which it is to be taken are announced at the meeting at which it is demanded.

(8) In any other case, at least 7 days' notice must be given specifying the time and place at which the poll is to be taken.

Content of proxy notices

38. [Same as pcls 45 (see Annex C2) except plc 38 uses the word 'member' where pcls 45 uses the word 'shareholder']

Delivery of proxy notices

39.—(1) Any notice of a general meeting must specify the address or addresses ("proxy notification address") at which the company or its agents will receive proxy notices relating to that meeting, or any adjournment of it, delivered in hard copy or electronic form.

(2) A person who is entitled to attend, speak or vote (either on a show of hands or on a poll) at a general meeting remains so entitled in respect of that meeting or any adjournment of it, even though a valid proxy notice has been delivered to the company by or on behalf of that person.

(3) Subject to paragraphs (4) and (5), a proxy notice must be delivered to a proxy notification address not less than 48 hours before the general meeting or adjourned meeting to which it relates.

(4) In the case of a poll taken more than 48 hours after it is demanded, the notice must be delivered to a proxy notification address not less than 24 hours before the time appointed for the taking of the poll.

(5) In the case of a poll not taken during the meeting but taken not more than 48 hours after it was demanded, the proxy notice must be delivered—
   (a) in accordance with paragraph (3), or
   (b) at the meeting at which the poll was demanded to the chairman, secretary or any director.

(6) An appointment under a proxy notice may be revoked by delivering a notice in writing given by or on behalf of the person by whom or on whose behalf the proxy notice was given to a proxy notification address.

(7) A notice revoking a proxy appointment only takes effect if it is delivered before—
   (a) the start of the meeting or adjourned meeting to which it relates, or
   (b) (in the case of a poll not taken on the same day as the meeting or adjourned meeting) the time appointed for taking the poll to which it relates.

(8) If a proxy notice is not signed by the person appointing the proxy, it must be accompanied by written evidence of the authority of the person who executed it to execute it on the appointor's behalf.

Amendments to resolutions

40.—(1) An ordinary resolution to be proposed at a general meeting may be amended by ordinary resolution if—
   (a) notice of the proposed amendment is given to the company secretary in writing by a person entitled to vote at the general meeting at which it is to be proposed not less than 48 hours before the meeting is to take place (or such later time as the chairman of the meeting may determine), and
   (b) the proposed amendment does not, in the reasonable opinion of the chairman of the meeting, materially alter the scope of the resolution.

(2) A special resolution to be proposed at a general meeting may be amended by ordinary resolution, if—
   (a) the chairman of the meeting proposes the amendment at the general meeting at which the resolution is to be proposed, and
   (b) the amendment does not go beyond what is necessary to correct a grammatical or other non-substantive error in the resolution.

(3) If the chairman of the meeting, acting in good faith, wrongly decides that an amendment to a resolution is out of order, the chairman's error does not invalidate the vote on that resolution.

RESTRICTIONS ON MEMBERS' RIGHTS

No voting of shares on which money owed to company

41. No voting rights attached to a share may be exercised at any general meeting, at any adjournment of it, or on any poll called at or in relation to it, unless all amounts payable to the company in respect of that share have been paid.

APPLICATION OF RULES TO CLASS MEETINGS

Class meetings

42. The provisions of the articles relating to general meetings apply, with any necessary modifications, to meetings of the holders of any class of shares.

PART 4 SHARES AND DISTRIBUTIONS

ISSUE OF SHARES

Powers to issue different classes of share

43. [Same as pcls 22 (see Annex C2)]

Payment of commissions on subscription for shares

44.—(1) The company may pay any person a commission in consideration for that person—

  (a) subscribing, or agreeing to subscribe, for shares, or

  (b) procuring, or agreeing to procure, subscriptions for shares.

(2) Any such commission may be paid—

  (a) in cash, or in fully paid or partly paid shares or other securities, or partly in one way and partly in the other, and

  (b) in respect of a conditional or an absolute subscription.

INTERESTS IN SHARES

Company not bound by less than absolute interests

45. [Same as pcls 23 (see Annex C2)]

SHARE CERTIFICATES

Certificates to be issued except in certain cases

46.—(1) The company must issue each member with one or more certificates in respect of the shares which that member holds.

(2) This article does not apply to—

  (a) uncertificated shares;

  (b) shares in respect of which a share warrant has been issued; or

  (c) shares in respect of which the Companies Acts permit the company not to issue a certificate.

(3) Except as otherwise specified in the articles, all certificates must be issued free of charge.

(4 No certificate may be issued in respect of shares of more than one class.

(5) If more than one person holds a share, only one certificate may be issued in respect of it.

Contents and execution of share certificates

47.—(1) Every certificate must specify—
- (a)   in respect of how many shares, of what class, it is issued;
- (b)   the nominal value of those shares;
- (c)   the amount paid up on them; and
- (d)   any distinguishing numbers assigned to them.

(2) Certificates must—
- (a)   have affixed to them the company's common seal or an official seal which is a facsimile of the company's common seal with the addition on its face of the word "Securities" (a "securities seal"), or
- (b)   be otherwise executed in accordance with the Companies Acts.

Consolidated share certificates

48.—(1) When a member's holding of shares of a particular class increases, the company may issue that member with—
- (a)   a single, consolidated certificate in respect of all the shares of a particular class which that member holds, or
- (b)   a separate certificate in respect of only those shares by which that member's holding has increased.

(2) When a member's holding of shares of a particular class is reduced, the company must ensure that the member is issued with one or more certificates in respect of the number of shares held by the member after that reduction. But the company need not (in the absence of a request from the member) issue any new certificate if—
- (a)   all the shares which the member no longer holds as a result of the reduction, and
- (b)   none of the shares which the member retains following the reduction,

were, immediately before the reduction, represented by the same certificate.

(3) A member may request the company, in writing, to replace—
- (a)   the member's separate certificates with a consolidated certificate, or
- (b)   the member's consolidated certificate with two or more separate certificates representing such proportion of the shares as the member may specify.

(4) When the company complies with such a request it may charge such reasonable fee as the directors may decide for doing so.

(5) A consolidated certificate must not be issued unless any certificates which it is to replace have first been returned to the company for cancellation.

Replacement share certificates

49.—(1) If a certificate issued in respect of a member's shares is—

(a) damaged or defaced, or

(b) said to be lost, stolen or destroyed,

that member is entitled to be issued with a replacement certificate in respect of the same shares.

(2) A member exercising the right to be issued with such a replacement certificate—

(a) may at the same time exercise the right to be issued with a single certificate or separate certificates;

(b) must return the certificate which is to be replaced to the company if it is damaged or defaced; and

(c) must comply with such conditions as to evidence, indemnity and the payment of a reasonable fee as the directors decide.

SHARES NOT HELD IN CERTIFICATED FORM

Uncertificated shares

50.—(1) In this article, "the relevant rules" means—

(a) any applicable provision of the Companies Acts about the holding, evidencing of title to, or transfer of shares other than in certificated form, and

(b) any applicable legislation, rules or other arrangements made under or by virtue of such provision.

(2) The provisions of this article have effect subject to the relevant rules.

(3) Any provision of the articles which is inconsistent with the relevant rules must be disregarded, to the extent that it is inconsistent, whenever the relevant rules apply.

(4) Any share or class of shares of the company may be issued or held on such terms, or in such a way, that—

(a) title to it or them is not, or must not be, evidenced by a certificate, or

(b) it or they may or must be transferred wholly or partly without a certificate.

(5) The directors have power to take such steps as they think fit in relation to—

(a) the evidencing of and transfer of title to uncertificated shares (including in connection with the issue of such shares);

(b) any records relating to the holding of uncertificated shares;

(c) the conversion of certificated shares into uncertificated shares; or

(d) the conversion of uncertificated shares into certificated shares.

(6) The company may by notice to the holder of a share require that share—

(a) if it is uncertificated, to be converted into certificated form, and

(b) if it is certificated, to be converted into uncertificated form, to enable it to be dealt with in accordance with the articles.

(7) If—

(a) the articles give the directors power to take action, or require other persons to take action, in order to sell, transfer or otherwise dispose of shares, and

(b) uncertificated shares are subject to that power, but the power is expressed in terms which assume the use of a certificate or other written instrument, the directors may take such action as is necessary or expedient to achieve the same results when exercising that power in relation to uncertificated shares.

(8) In particular, the directors may take such action as they consider appropriate to achieve the sale, transfer, disposal, forfeiture, re-allotment or surrender of an uncertificated share or otherwise to enforce a lien in respect of it.

(9) Unless the directors otherwise determine, shares which a member holds in uncertificated form must be treated as separate holdings from any shares which that member holds in certificated form.

(10) A class of shares must not be treated as two classes simply because some shares of that class are held in certificated form and others are held in uncertificated form.

Share warrants

51.—(1) The directors may issue a share warrant in respect of any fully paid share.

(2) Share warrants must be—

(a) issued in such form, and

(b) executed in such manner, as the directors decide.

(3) A share represented by a share warrant may be transferred by delivery of the warrant representing it.

(4) The directors may make provision for the payment of dividends in respect of any share represented by a share warrant.

(5) Subject to the articles, the directors may decide the conditions on which any share warrant is issued. In particular, they may—

(a) decide the conditions on which new warrants are to be issued in place of warrants which are damaged or defaced, or said to have been lost, stolen or destroyed;

(b) decide the conditions on which bearers of warrants are entitled to attend and vote at general meetings;

(c) decide the conditions subject to which bearers of warrants may surrender their warrant so as to hold their shares in certificated or uncertificated form instead; and

(d) vary the conditions of issue of any warrant from time to time, and the bearer of a warrant is subject to the conditions and procedures in force in relation to it, whether or not they were decided or specified before the warrant was issued.

(6) Subject to the conditions on which the warrants are issued from time to time, bearers of share warrants have the same rights and privileges as they would if their names had been included in the register as holders of the shares represented by their warrants.

(7) The company must not in any way be bound by or recognise any interest in a share represented by a share warrant other than the absolute right of the bearer of that warrant to that warrant.

PARTLY PAID SHARES

Company's lien over partly paid shares

52.—(1) The company has a lien ("the company's lien") over every share which is partly paid for any part of—

(a) that share's nominal value, and

(b) any premium at which it was issued, which has not been paid to the company, and which is payable immediately or at some time in the future, whether or not a call notice has been sent in respect of it.

(2) The company's lien over a share—

(a) takes priority over any third party's interest in that share, and

(b) extends to any dividend or other money payable by the company in respect of that share and (if the lien is enforced and the share is sold by the company) the proceeds of sale of that share.

(3) The directors may at any time decide that a share which is or would otherwise be subject to the company's lien shall not be subject to it, either wholly or in part.

Enforcement of the company's lien

53.—(1) Subject to the provisions of this article, if—

(a) a lien enforcement notice has been given in respect of a share, and

(b) the person to whom the notice was given has failed to comply with it, the company may sell that share in such manner as the directors decide.

(2) A lien enforcement notice—

(a) may only be given in respect of a share which is subject to the company's lien, in respect of which a sum is payable and the due date for payment of that sum has passed;

(b) must specify the share concerned;

(c) must require payment of the sum payable within 14 days of the notice;

(d) must be addressed either to the holder of the share or to a person entitled to it by reason of the holder's death, bankruptcy or otherwise; and

(e) must state the company's intention to sell the share if the notice is not complied with.

(3) Where shares are sold under this article—

(a) the directors may authorise any person to execute an instrument of transfer of the shares to the purchaser or a person nominated by the purchaser, and

    (b) the transferee is not bound to see to the application of the consideration, and the transferee's title is not affected by any irregularity in or invalidity of the process leading to the sale.

(4) The net proceeds of any such sale (after payment of the costs of sale and any other costs of enforcing the lien) must be applied—

    (a) first, in payment of so much of the sum for which the lien exists as was payable at the date of the lien enforcement notice,

    (b) second, to the person entitled to the shares at the date of the sale, but only after the certificate for the shares sold has been surrendered to the company for cancellation or a suitable indemnity has been given for any lost certificates, and subject to a lien equivalent to the company's lien over the shares before the sale for any money payable in respect of the shares after the date of the lien enforcement notice.

(5) A statutory declaration by a director or the company secretary that the declarant is a director or the company secretary and that a share has been sold to satisfy the company's lien on a specified date—

    (a) is conclusive evidence of the facts stated in it as against all persons claiming to be entitled to the share, and

    (b) subject to compliance with any other formalities of transfer required by the articles or by law, constitutes a good title to the share.

Call notices

54.—(1) Subject to the articles and the terms on which shares are allotted, the directors may send a notice (a "call notice") to a member requiring the member to pay the company a specified sum of money (a "call") which is payable in respect of shares which that member holds at the date when the directors decide to send the call notice.

(2) A call notice—

    (a) may not require a member to pay a call which exceeds the total sum unpaid on that member's shares (whether as to the share's nominal value or any amount payable to the company by way of premium);

    (b) must state when and how any call to which it relates it is to be paid; and

    (c) may permit or require the call to be paid by instalments.

(3) A member must comply with the requirements of a call notice, but no member is obliged to pay any call before 14 days have passed since the notice was sent.

(4) Before the company has received any call due under a call notice the directors may—

    (a) revoke it wholly or in part, or

    (b) specify a later time for payment than is specified in the notice,

by a further notice in writing to the member in respect of whose shares the call is made.

Liability to pay calls

55.—(1) Liability to pay a call is not extinguished or transferred by transferring the shares in respect of which it is required to be paid.

(2) Joint holders of a share are jointly and severally liable to pay all calls in respect of that share.

(3) Subject to the terms on which shares are allotted, the directors may, when issuing shares, provide that call notices sent to the holders of those shares may require them—

(a) to pay calls which are not the same, or

(b) to pay calls at different times.

When call notice need not be issued

56.—(1) A call notice need not be issued in respect of sums which are specified, in the terms on which a share is issued, as being payable to the company in respect of that share (whether in respect of nominal value or premium)—

(a) on allotment;

(b) on the occurrence of a particular event; or

(c) on a date fixed by or in accordance with the terms of issue.

(2) But if the due date for payment of such a sum has passed and it has not been paid, the holder of the share concerned is treated in all respects as having failed to comply with a call notice in respect of that sum, and is liable to the same consequences as regards the payment of interest and forfeiture.

Failure to comply with call notice: automatic consequences

57.—(1) If a person is liable to pay a call and fails to do so by the call payment date—

(a) the directors may issue a notice of intended forfeiture to that person, and

(b) until the call is paid, that person must pay the company interest on the call from the call payment date at the relevant rate.

(2) For the purposes of this article—

(a) the "call payment date" is the time when the call notice states that a call is payable, unless the directors give a notice specifying a later date, in which case the "call payment date" is that later date;

(b) the "relevant rate" is—

(i) the rate fixed by the terms on which the share in respect of which the call is due was allotted;

(ii) such other rate as was fixed in the call notice which required payment of the call, or has otherwise been determined by the directors; or

(iii) if no rate is fixed in either of these ways, 5 per cent per annum.

(3) The relevant rate must not exceed by more than 5 percentage points the base lending rate most recently set by the Monetary Policy Committee of the Bank of England in connection with its responsibilities under Part 2 of the Bank of England Act 1998.

(4) The directors may waive any obligation to pay interest on a call wholly or in part.

Notice of intended forfeiture

58. A notice of intended forfeiture—

(a) may be sent in respect of any share in respect of which a call has not been paid as required by a call notice;

(b) must be sent to the holder of that share or to a person entitled to it by reason of the holder's death, bankruptcy or otherwise;

(c) must require payment of the call and any accrued interest by a date which is not less than 14 days after the date of the notice;

(d) must state how the payment is to be made; and

(e) must state that if the notice is not complied with, the shares in respect of which the call is payable will be liable to be forfeited.

Directors' power to forfeit shares

59. If a notice of intended forfeiture is not complied with before the date by which payment of the call is required in the notice of intended forfeiture, the directors may decide that any share in respect of which it was given is forfeited, and the forfeiture is to include all dividends or other moneys payable in respect of the forfeited shares and not paid before the forfeiture.

Effect of forfeiture

60.—(1) Subject to the articles, the forfeiture of a share extinguishes—

(a) all interests in that share, and all claims and demands against the company in respect of it, and

(b) all other rights and liabilities incidental to the share as between the person whose share it was prior to the forfeiture and the company.

(2) Any share which is forfeited in accordance with the articles—

(a) is deemed to have been forfeited when the directors decide that it is forfeited;

(b) is deemed to be the property of the company; and

(c) may be sold, re-allotted or otherwise disposed of as the directors think fit.

(3) If a person's shares have been forfeited—

(a) the company must send that person notice that forfeiture has occurred and record it in the register of members;

(b) that person ceases to be a member in respect of those shares;

(c) that person must surrender the certificate for the shares forfeited to the company for cancellation;

(d) that person remains liable to the company for all sums payable by that person under the articles at the date of forfeiture in respect of those shares, including any interest (whether accrued before or after the date of forfeiture); and

(e) the directors may waive payment of such sums wholly or in part or enforce payment without any allowance for the value of the shares at the time of forfeiture or for any consideration received on their disposal.

(4) At any time before the company disposes of a forfeited share, the directors may decide to cancel the forfeiture on payment of all calls and interest due in respect of it and on such other terms as they think fit.

Procedure following forfeiture

61.—(1) If a forfeited share is to be disposed of by being transferred, the company may receive the consideration for the transfer and the directors may authorise any person to execute the instrument of transfer.

(2) A statutory declaration by a director or the company secretary that the declarant is a director or the company secretary and that a share has been forfeited on a specified date—

(a) is conclusive evidence of the facts stated in it as against all persons claiming to be entitled to the share, and

(b) subject to compliance with any other formalities of transfer required by the articles or by law, constitutes a good title to the share.

(3) A person to whom a forfeited share is transferred is not bound to see to the application of the consideration (if any) nor is that person's title to the share affected by any irregularity in or invalidity of the process leading to the forfeiture or transfer of the share.

(4) If the company sells a forfeited share, the person who held it prior to its forfeiture is entitled to receive from the company the proceeds of such sale, net of any commission, and excluding any amount which—

(a) was, or would have become, payable, and

(b) had not, when that share was forfeited, been paid by that person in respect of that share,

but no interest is payable to such a person in respect of such proceeds and the company is not required to account for any money earned on them.

Surrender of shares

62.—(1) A member may surrender any share—

(a) in respect of which the directors may issue a notice of intended forfeiture;

(b) which the directors may forfeit; or

(c) which has been forfeited.

(2) The directors may accept the surrender of any such share.

(3) The effect of surrender on a share is the same as the effect of forfeiture on that share.

(4) A share which has been surrendered may be dealt with in the same way as a share which has been forfeited.

TRANSFER AND TRANSMISSION OF SHARES

Transfers of certificated shares

63.—(1) Certificated shares may be transferred by means of an instrument of transfer in any usual form or any other form approved by the directors, which is executed by or on behalf of—

(a) the transferor, and

(b) (if any of the shares is partly paid) the transferee.

(2) No fee may be charged for registering any instrument of transfer or other document relating to or affecting the title to any share.

(3) The company may retain any instrument of transfer which is registered.

(4) The transferor remains the holder of a certificated share until the transferee's name is entered in the register of members as holder of it.

(5) The directors may refuse to register the transfer of a certificated share if—

(a) the share is not fully paid;

(b) the transfer is not lodged at the company's registered office or such other place as the directors have appointed;

(c) the transfer is not accompanied by the certificate for the shares to which it relates, or such other evidence as the directors may reasonably require to show the transferor's right to make the transfer, or evidence of the right of someone other than the transferor to make the transfer on the transferor's behalf;

(d) the transfer is in respect of more than one class of share; or

(e) the transfer is in favour of more than four transferees.

(6) If the directors refuse to register the transfer of a share, the instrument of transfer must be returned to the transferee with the notice of refusal unless they suspect that the proposed transfer may be fraudulent.

Transfer of uncertificated shares

64. A transfer of an uncertificated share must not be registered if it is in favour of more than four transferees.

Transmission of shares

65.—(1) If title to a share passes to a transmittee, the company may only recognise the transmittee as having any title to that share.

(2) Nothing in these articles releases the estate of a deceased member from any liability in respect of a share solely or jointly held by that member.

Transmittees' rights

66.—(1) A transmittee who produces such evidence of entitlement to shares as the directors may properly require—

(a) may, subject to the articles, choose either to become the holder of those shares or to have them transferred to another person, and

(b) subject to the articles, and pending any transfer of the shares to another person, has the same rights as the holder had.

(2) But transmittees do not have the right to attend or vote at a general meeting in respect of shares to which they are entitled, by reason of the holder's death or bankruptcy or otherwise, unless they become the holders of those shares

Exercise of transmittees' rights

67.—(1) Transmittees who wish to become the holders of shares to which they have become entitled must notify the company in writing of that wish.

(2) If the share is a certificated share and a transmittee wishes to have it transferred to another person, the transmittee must execute an instrument of transfer in respect of it.

(3) If the share is an uncertificated share and the transmittee wishes to have it transferred to another person, the transmittee must—

(a) procure that all appropriate instructions are given to effect the transfer, or

(b) procure that the uncertificated share is changed into certificated form and then execute an instrument of transfer in respect of it.

(4) Any transfer made or executed under this article is to be treated as if it were made or executed by the person from whom the transmittee has derived rights in respect of the share, and as if the event which gave rise to the transmission had not occurred.

Transmittees bound by prior notices

68. If a notice is given to a member in respect of shares and a transmittee is entitled to those shares, the transmittee is bound by the notice if it was given to the member before the transmittee's name has been entered in the register of members.

CONSOLIDATION OF SHARES

Procedure for disposing of fractions of shares

69.—(1) This article applies where—

(a) there has been a consolidation or division of shares, and

(b) as a result, members are entitled to fractions of shares.

(2) The directors may—

(a) sell the shares representing the fractions to any person including the company for the best price reasonably obtainable;

(b) in the case of a certificated share, authorise any person to execute an instrument of transfer of the shares to the purchaser or a person nominated by the purchaser; and

(c) distribute the net proceeds of sale in due proportion among the holders of the shares.

(3) Where any holder's entitlement to a portion of the proceeds of sale amounts to less than a minimum figure determined by the directors, that member's portion may be distributed to an organisation which is a charity for the purposes of the law of England and Wales, Scotland or Northern Ireland.

(4) The person to whom the shares are transferred is not obliged to ensure that any purchase money is received by the person entitled to the relevant fractions.

(5) The transferee's title to the shares is not affected by any irregularity in or invalidity of the process leading to their sale.

DISTRIBUTIONS

Procedure for declaring dividends

70.—(1) The company may by ordinary resolution declare dividends, and the directors may decide to pay interim dividends.

(2) A dividend must not be declared unless the directors have made a recommendation as to its amount. Such a dividend must not exceed the amount recommended by the directors.

(3) No dividend may be declared or paid unless it is in accordance with members' respective rights.

(4) Unless the members' resolution to declare or directors' decision to pay a dividend, or the terms on which shares are issued, specify otherwise, it must be paid by reference to each member's holding of shares on the date of the resolution or decision to declare or pay it.

(5) If the company's share capital is divided into different classes, no interim dividend may be paid on shares carrying deferred or non-preferred rights if, at the time of payment, any preferential dividend is in arrear.

(6) The directors may pay at intervals any dividend payable at a fixed rate if it appears to them that the profits available for distribution justify the payment.

(7) If the directors act in good faith, they do not incur any liability to the holders of shares conferring preferred rights for any loss they may suffer by the lawful payment of an interim dividend on shares with deferred or non-preferred rights.

Calculation of dividends

71.—(1) Except as otherwise provided by the articles or the rights attached to shares, all dividends must be—

(a) declared and paid according to the amounts paid up on the shares on which the dividend is paid, and

(b) apportioned and paid proportionately to the amounts paid up on the shares during any portion or portions of the period in respect of which the dividend is paid.

(2) If any share is issued on terms providing that it ranks for dividend as from a particular date, that share ranks for dividend accordingly.

(3) For the purposes of calculating dividends, no account is to be taken of any amount which has been paid up on a share in advance of the due date for payment of that amount.

Payment of dividends and other distributions
72. [Same as pcls 31 (see Annex C2)]

Deductions from distributions in respect of sums owed to the company
73.—(1) If—
  (a)   a share is subject to the company's lien, and
  (b)   the directors are entitled to issue a lien enforcement notice in respect of it,
they may, instead of issuing a lien enforcement notice, deduct from any dividend or other sum payable in respect of the share any sum of money which is payable to the company in respect of that share to the extent that they are entitled to require payment under a lien enforcement notice.
(2) Money so deducted must be used to pay any of the sums payable in respect of that share.
(3) The company must notify the distribution recipient in writing of—
  (a)   the fact and amount of any such deduction;
  (b)   any non-payment of a dividend or other sum payable in respect of a share resulting from any such deduction; and
  (c)   how the money deducted has been applied.

No interest on distributions
74. [Same as pcls 32 (see Annex C2)]

Unclaimed distributions
75. [Same as pcls 33 (see Annex C2)]

Non-cash distributions
76.—(1) Subject to the terms of issue of the share in question, the company may, by ordinary resolution on the recommendation of the directors, decide to pay all or part of a dividend or other distribution payable in respect of a share by transferring non-cash assets of equivalent value (including, without limitation, shares or other securities in any company).
(2) If the shares in respect of which such a non-cash distribution is paid are uncertificated, any shares in the company which are issued as a non-cash distribution in respect of them must be uncertificated.
(3) For the purposes of paying a non-cash distribution, the directors may make whatever arrangements they think fit, including, where any difficulty arises regarding the distribution—
  (a)   fixing the value of any assets;

(b) paying cash to any distribution recipient on the basis of that value in order to adjust the rights of recipients; and

(c) vesting any assets in trustees.

Waiver of distributions
77. [Same as pcls 35 (see Annex C2)]

CAPITALISATION OF PROFITS

Authority to capitalise and appropriation of capitalised sums
78.—(1) Subject to the articles, the directors may, if they are so authorised by an ordinary resolution—

(a) decide to capitalise any profits of the company (whether or not they are available for distribution) which are not required for paying a preferential dividend, or any sum standing to the credit of the company's share premium account or capital redemption reserve; and

(b) appropriate any sum which they so decide to capitalise (a "capitalised sum") to the persons who would have been entitled to it if it were distributed by way of dividend (the "persons entitled") and in the same proportions.

(2) Capitalised sums must be applied—

(a) on behalf of the persons entitled, and

(b) in the same proportions as a dividend would have been distributed to them.

(3) Any capitalised sum may be applied in paying up new shares of a nominal amount equal to the capitalised sum which are then allotted credited as fully paid to the persons entitled or as they may direct.

(4) A capitalised sum which was appropriated from profits available for distribution may be applied—

(a) in or towards paying up any amounts unpaid on existing shares held by the persons entitled, or

(b) in paying up new debentures of the company which are then allotted credited as fully paid to the persons entitled or as they may direct.

(5) Subject to the articles the directors may—

(a) apply capitalised sums in accordance with paragraphs (3) and (4) partly in one way and partly in another;

(b) make such arrangements as they think fit to deal with shares or debentures becoming distributable in fractions under this article (including the issuing of fractional certificates or the making of cash payments); and

(c) authorise any person to enter into an agreement with the company on behalf of all the persons entitled which is binding on them in respect of the allotment of shares and debentures to them under this article.

PART 5 MISCELLANEOUS PROVISIONS

COMMUNICATIONS

Means of communication to be used
79. [Same as pcls 48 (see Annex C2)]

Failure to notify contact details
80.—(1) If—
  (a) the company sends two consecutive documents to a member over a period of at least 12 months, and
  (b) each of those documents is returned undelivered, or the company receives notification that it has not been delivered,
that member ceases to be entitled to receive notices from the company.
(2) A member who has ceased to be entitled to receive notices from the company becomes entitled to receive such notices again by sending the company—
  (a) a new address to be recorded in the register of members, or
  (b) if the member has agreed that the company should use a means of communication other than sending things to such an address, the information that the company needs to use that means of communication effectively.

ADMINISTRATIVE ARRANGEMENTS

Company seals
81.—(1) Any common seal may only be used by the authority of the directors.
(2) The directors may decide by what means and in what form any common seal or securities seal is to be used.
(3) Unless otherwise decided by the directors, if the company has a common seal and it is affixed to a document, the document must also be signed by at least one authorised person in the presence of a witness who attests the signature.
(4) For the purposes of this article, an authorised person is—
  (a) any director of the company;
  (b) the company secretary; or
  (c) any person authorised by the directors for the purpose of signing documents to which the common seal is applied.
(5) If the company has an official seal for use abroad, it may only be affixed to a document if its use on that document, or documents of a class to which it belongs, has been authorised by a decision of the directors.
(6) If the company has a securities seal, it may only be affixed to securities by the company secretary or a person authorised to apply it to securities by the company secretary.
(7) For the purposes of the articles, references to the securities seal being affixed to any document include the reproduction of the image of that seal on or in a document by any mechanical or electronic means which has been approved by

the directors in relation to that document or documents of a class to which it belongs.

Destruction of documents

82.—(1) The company is entitled to destroy—

(a) all instruments of transfer of shares which have been registered, and all other documents on the basis of which any entries are made in the register of members, from six years after the date of registration;

(b) all dividend mandates, variations or cancellations of dividend mandates, and notifications of change of address, from two years after they have been recorded;

(c) all share certificates which have been cancelled from one year after the date of the cancellation;

(d) all paid dividend warrants and cheques from one year after the date of actual payment; and

(e) all proxy notices from one year after the end of the meeting to which the proxy notice relates.

(2) If the company destroys a document in good faith, in accordance with the articles, and without notice of any claim to which that document may be relevant, it is conclusively presumed in favour of the company that—

(a) entries in the register purporting to have been made on the basis of an instrument of transfer or other document so destroyed were duly and properly made;

(b) any instrument of transfer so destroyed was a valid and effective instrument duly and properly registered;

(c) any share certificate so destroyed was a valid and effective certificate duly and properly cancelled; and

(d) any other document so destroyed was a valid and effective document in accordance with its recorded particulars in the books or records of the company.

(3) This article does not impose on the company any liability which it would not otherwise have if it destroys any document before the time at which this article permits it to do so.

(4) In this article, references to the destruction of any document include a reference to its being disposed of in any manner.

No right to inspect accounts and other records

83. [Same as pcls 50 (see Annex C2) except plc 83 uses the word 'member' where pcls 50 uses the word 'shareholder']

Provision for employees on cessation of business

84. [Same as pcls 51 (see Annex C2)]

DIRECTORS' INDEMNITY AND INSURANCE

Indemnity

85. [Same as pcls 52 (see Annex C2)]

Insurance

86. [Same as pcls 53 (see Annex C2)]

ANNEX D
Uncertificated Securities Regulations 1995, reg. 34

Notices of meetings

34 – (1) For the purposes of determining which persons are entitled to attend or vote at a meeting, and how many votes such persons may cast, the participating issuer may specify in the notice of the meeting a time, not more than 48 hours before the time fixed for the meeting, by which a person must be entered on the relevant register of securities in order to have the right to attend or vote at the meeting.

(2) Changes to entries on the relevant register of securities after the time specified by virtue of paragraph (1) shall be disregarded in determining the rights of any person to attend or vote at the meeting, notwithstanding any provisions in any enactment, articles of association or other instrument to the contrary.

(3) For the purposes of serving notices of meetings, whether under section 370(2) of the 1985 Act, any other enactment, a provision in the articles of association or any other instrument, a participating issuer may determine that persons entitled to receive such notices are those persons entered on the relevant register of securities at the close of business on a day determined by him.

(4) The day determined by a participating issuer under paragraph (3) may not be more than 21 days before the day that the notices of the meeting are sent.

INDEX